Razeena

D0461612

MODERN ESSENTIALS

A CONTEMPORARY GUIDE TO THE THERAPEUTIC USE OF ESSENTIAL OILS

THIRD EDITION

Published and Distributed by:

Abundant Health
222 W. 3560 N.
Spanish Fork, UT 84660

Phone: 1-866-728-0070 • 801-798-7921

Internet: www.AromaTools.com

E-mail: Webmaster@AromaTools.com

Copyright:

© **2012 Abundant Health, LLC.** 3rd Edition, 2nd Printing, April 2012. All rights reserved. No part of this book may be reproduced or transmitted in any form or by any means, electronic or mechanical, including photocopying, recording, or by any other information storage or retrieval system, without written permission from Abundant Health, LLC.

ISBN Number:

978-0-9842658-8-6

Disclaimer:

This book has been designed to provide information to help educate the reader in regard to the subject matter covered. It is sold with the understanding that the publisher and the authors are not liable for the misconception and misuse of the information provided. It is not provided in order to diagnose, proscribe, or treat any disease, illness, or injured condition of the body. The authors and publisher shall have neither liability nor responsibility to any person or entity with respect to any loss, damage, or injury caused, or alleged to be caused, directly or indirectly by the information contained in this book. The information presented herein is in no way intended as a substitute for medical counseling. Anyone suffering from any disease, illness, or injury should consult a qualified health care professional.

Printed and Bound in the U.S.A.

TABLE OF CONTENTS

THE SCIENCE AND APPLICATION OF ESSENTIAL OILS

AN INTRODUCTION TO ESSENTIAL OILS

WHAT ARE ESSENTIAL OILS?

Essential oils are the volatile liquids that are distilled from plants (including their respective parts such as seeds, bark, leaves, stems, roots, flowers, fruit, etc.). One of the factors that determines the purity and therapeutic value of an oil is its chemical constituents. These constituents can be affected by a vast number of variables: the part(s) of the plant from which the oil was produced, soil condition, fertilizer (organic or chemical), geographic region, climate, altitude, harvest season and method, and distillation process. For example, common thyme, or thyme vulgaris, produces several different chemotypes (biochemical specifics or simple species) depending on the conditions of its growth, climate, and altitude. High levels of thymol depend on the time of year in which it is distilled. If distilled during mid-summer or late fall, there can be higher levels of carvacrol, which can cause the oil to be more caustic or irritating to the skin. Low pressure and low temperature are key to maintaining the purity, the ultimate fragrance, and the therapeutic value of the oil.

As we begin to understand the power of essential oils in the realm of personal holistic health care, we comprehend the absolute necessity of obtaining certified pure therapeutic-grade essential oils. No matter how costly certified pure therapeutic-grade essential oils may be, there can be no substitute. Chemists can replicate some of the known individual constituents, but they have yet to successfully recreate complete essential oils in the laboratory.

The information in this book is based on the use of certified pure therapeutic-grade essential oils. Those who are beginning their journey into the realm of aromatherapy and essential oils must actively seek for the purest quality and highest therapeutic-grade oils available. Anything less than certified pure therapeutic-grade essential oil may not produce the desired results and can, in some cases, be extremely toxic.

WHY IS IT SO DIFFICULT TO FIND CERTIFIED PURE THERAPEUTIC-GRADE ESSENTIAL OILS?

Producing the purest of oils can be very costly because it may require several hundred pounds, or even several thousand pounds, of plant material to extract 1 pound of pure essential oil. For example, 1 pound of pure melissa oil sells for $9,000–$15,000. Although this sounds quite expensive, one must realize that 3 tons of plant material are required to produce that single pound of oil. Because the vast majority of all the oils produced in the world today are used by the perfume industry, the oils are being purchased for their aromatic qualities only. High pressure, high temperatures, rapid processing, and the use of chemical solvents are often employed during the distillation process so that a greater quantity of oil can be produced at a faster rate. These oils may smell just as good and cost much less, but they will lack most, if not all, of the chemical constituents necessary to produce the expected therapeutic results.

WHAT BENEFITS DO CERTIFIED PURE, THERAPEUTIC-GRADE ESSENTIAL OILS PROVIDE?

Essential oils embody the regenerating, oxygenating, and immune-strengthening properties of plants.

Essential oils are so small in molecular size that they can quickly penetrate the skin.

Essential oils are lipid soluble and are capable of penetrating cell walls, even if they have hardened because of an oxygen deficiency. In fact, essential oils can affect every cell of the body within 20 minutes and then be metabolized like other nutrients.

Essential oils contain oxygen molecules that help to transport nutrients to the starving human cells. Because a nutritional deficiency is an oxygen deficiency, disease begins when the cells lack the oxygen for proper nutrient assimilation. By providing the needed oxygen, essential oils also work to stimulate the immune system.

Essential oils are very powerful antioxidants. Antioxidants create an unfriendly environment for free radicals. They prevent all mutations, work as free radical scavengers, prevent fungus, and prevent oxidation in the cells.

Essential oils are antibacterial, anticancer, antifungal, anti-infectious, antimicrobial, antitumor, antiparasitic, antiviral, and antiseptic. Essential oils have been shown to destroy all tested bacteria and viruses while simultaneously restoring balance to the body.

Essential oils may detoxify the cells and blood in the body.

Essential oils containing sesquiterpenes have the ability to pass the blood-brain barrier, enabling them to be effective in the treatment of Alzheimer's disease, Lou Gehrig's disease, Parkinson's disease, and multiple sclerosis.

Essential oils are aromatic. When diffused, they provide air purification by

- Removing metallic particles and toxins from the air;
- Increasing atmospheric oxygen;
- Increasing ozone and negative ions in the area, which inhibits bacterial growth;
- Destroying odors from mold, cigarettes, and animals; and
- Filling the air with a fresh, aromatic scent.

Essential oils help promote emotional, physical, and spiritual healing.

HOW LONG HAVE ESSENTIAL OILS BEEN AROUND?

Essential oils were mankind's first medicine. From Egyptian hieroglyphics and Chinese manuscripts, we know that priests and physicians have been using essential oils for thousands of years. In Egypt, essential oils were used in the embalming process, and well preserved oils were found in alabaster jars in King Tut's tomb. Egyptian temples were dedicated to the production and blending of the oils, and recipes were recorded on the walls in hieroglyphics. Additionally, there are 188 references to essential oils (such as frankincense, myrrh, rosemary, etc.) in the Bible.

HOW DO ESSENTIAL OILS AFFECT THE BRAIN?

The blood-brain barrier is the barrier membrane between the circulating blood and the brain that prevents certain damaging substances from reaching brain tissue and cerebrospinal fluid. The American Medical Association (AMA) deter-

mined that if they could find an agent that would pass the blood-brain barrier, they would be able to cure Alzheimer's disease, Lou Gehrig's disease, multiple sclerosis, and Parkinson's disease. Chemical constituents known as sesquiterpenes—commonly found in essential oils such as frankincense and sandalwood—are known to be able to go beyond the blood-brain barrier.

High levels of these sesquiterpenes help increase the amount of oxygen in the limbic system of the brain, particularly around the pineal and pituitary glands. This leads to an increase in secretions of antibodies, endorphins, and neurotransmitters.

Also present in the limbic system of the brain is a gland called the amygdala. In 1989, it was discovered that the amygdala plays a major role in the storing and releasing of emotional trauma. The only way to stimulate this gland is with fragrance or the sense of smell. Therefore, essential oils can be a powerful key to help unlock and release emotional trauma.

WHAT ENABLES ESSENTIAL OILS TO PROVIDE SUCH INCREDIBLE BENEFITS?

The heterogenetic benefits of an essential oil depend greatly on its diversity of chemical constituents—and not only on the existence of specific constituents but also on their amounts in proportion to other constituents present in the same oil. Some individual oils may have anywhere from 200 to 800 different chemical constituents. However, of the possible 800 different constituents, only about 200 of those have so far been identified. Although not everything is known about all the different constituents, most of them can be grouped into a few distinct families, each with some dominant characteristics. The following section provides greater insights into these constituent families.

ESSENTIAL OIL CONSTITUENTS

In general, pure essential oil constituents can be subdivided into two distinct groups: the hydrocarbons, which are made up almost exclusively of terpenes (monoterpenes, sesquiterpenes, and diterpenes), and the oxygenated compounds, which are mainly esters, aldehydes, ketones, alcohols, phenols, and oxides.

TERPENES

Terpenes are the largest family of natural products and are found throughout nature. High concentrations of terpenes are found directly after flowering[1]. The basic molecular structure of a terpene is an isoprene unit (which has a C_5H_8 molecular formula):

ISOPRENE UNIT (C_5H_8)

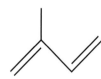

Figures such as the one shown at left represent the bonds between carbon (C) atoms in a molecule. Single lines represent a single bond, while double lines represent a double bond. Each intersecting point and the end of each line represents a carbon molecule along with any hydrogen molecules it is bonded to. Since each carbon molecule can have up to four bonds with other atoms, the number of hydrogen atoms can be determined by subtracting the number of bonds (lines) coming to each carbon atom from four. Thus the shorthand figure at top represents the same molecule shown below it.

ISOPRENE UNIT (C_5H_8)

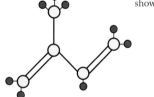

○ = CARBON

● = HYDROGEN

Classes of terpenes are named according to how many isoprene units are present.

- Monoterpenes (C10)   = two isoprene units
- Sesquiterpenes (C15) = three isoprene units
- Triterpenes (C30)   = six isoprene units
- Tetraterpenes (C40)   = eight isoprene units

Terpenes may also have oxygen-containing functional groups. Terpenes with these oxygen-

containing functional groups are referred to as terpenoids[2].

—MONOTERPENES

Monoterpenes occur in practically all essential oils and have many different activities. Most tend to inhibit the accumulation of toxins and help discharge existing toxins from the liver and kidneys. Some are antiseptic, antibacterial, stimulating, analgesic (weak), and expectorant; while other specific terpenes have antifungal, antiviral, antihistaminic, antirheumatic, antitumor (antiblastic, anticarcinogenic), hypotensive, insecticidal, purgative, and pheromonal properties. Monoterpenes, in general, have a stimulating effect and can be very soothing to irritated tissues as well. Most citrus oils (not bergamot) and conifer oils contain a high proportion of terpenes.

Found as a Significant Constituent in ALL Essential Oils Except: Basil, birch, cassia, cinnamon, clary sage, clove, geranium, sandalwood, vetiver, wintergreen, and ylang ylang.

Examples of Monoterpenes:

– PINENES (α- & β-)

α- and β- pinene are isomers (meaning

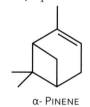

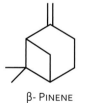

α- PINENE   β- PINENE

they have the same chemical formula but differing structures). They get their name because they are major constituents in pine resin or pine oil. They give off a resiny, piney smell. Pinenes have strong antiseptic, antibacterial, antifungal, and expectorant properties.

Bone Resorption Inhibition: α- and β-pinene (found in pine oil) were

---

1 Paduch et al., 2007.

2 McGarvey et al., 1995.

found in animal studies to inhibit bone resorption. Bone resorption is the process by which osteoclasts—macrophage cells that reside in the bones—break down bone and release the minerals, which can lead to the loss of bone, such as in osteoporosis. Further studies have indicated that while α- and β-pinene may not directly influence osteoclast activity and bone resorption rates, a metabolite (a product created by the body from the original molecule when taken internally) of the pinenes, cis-verbenol, did directly inhibit bone resorption and the formation of osteoclasts[3,4].

Mosquito Larvicide: α-pinenes found in *Alpinia speciosa* and *Rosmarinus officinalis* (ginger and rosemary) demonstrated effective larvicidal activity against the mosquito *Aedes aegypti L.* The *A. aegypti* is a carrier of the dengue virus that causes dengue fever in tropical areas of the world[5].

Antibacterial: It has been observed that the larvae of the Douglas fir tussock moth have digestive systems that are relatively clear of bacterial flora. These larvae feed on terpenes found in the bark of Douglas fir trees, of which α-pinene is a major constituent. α-pinene inhibits the growth of *Bacillus* species (gram-positive bacteria). The concentration needed for maximum inhibition is well below the concentrations of α-pinene found in Douglas fir pine trees. Bacterial inhibition occurs because α-pinene disrupts the cytoplasmic membranes of the bacterial species. α-pinene seems to perform more effectively against gram-positive bacteria than gram-negative bacteria due to the extra outer membrane found in the cell walls of gram-negative bacteria[6,7].

Anti-inflammatory: NF_KB is an important transcription factor in the body that regulates proinflammatory responses (signals proteins, specifically cytokines, to cause inflammation). When NF_KB is activated, it goes to the nucleus of the cells, binds to DNA, and activates transcription needed to produce cytokines, chemokines, and cell adhesion molecules. These molecules all help in producing inflammation in the body.

α-pinene has been shown to inhibit/block NF_KB from going to the nucleus. LPS (lipopolysaccharide, an endotoxin produced by gram-negative bacteria that causes inflammation in the body) was introduced to the cell culture of THP-1 cells to induce the activation of NF_KB. However, when α-pinene was present, activation was markedly reduced.

α-pinene inhibits NF_KB by blocking the degradation of $I_KBα$. $I_KBα$ is a protein that binds to NF_KB to prevent it from constantly transcribing proinflammatory genes. If LPS, a virus, or some stimulant of the immune system is recognized, $I_KBα$ will degrade and release/activate NF_KB. NF_KB will then transcribe genes to make proteins that cause inflammation at the site of "invasion," such as a cut, scrape, or burn.

Even in the presence of an immune system stimulant (LPS), α-pinene blocks $I_KBα$. During experimentation, it was also noted that the THP-1 cells received no cytotoxicity from the addition of α-pinene[8,9].

— CAMPHENE

CAMPHENE

Camphene is found in many oils, such as cypress, citronella, neroli, ginger, and others. It is an insect repellent. According to

---

3 Eriksson et al., 1996.
4 Muhlbauer et al., 2003.
5 Freitas et al., 2010.
6 Andrews et al., 1980.
7 Uribe et al., 1985.

8 Zhou et al., 2004.
9 Weaver, 2008.

the *Phytochemical Dictionary*, it is "used to reduce cholesterol saturation index in the treatment of gallstones."

– **β-MYRCENE**

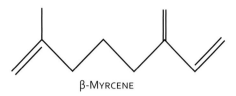

β-MYRCENE

β-Myrcene is found in oils such as lemongrass, verbena, and bay. It has cancer–preventative properties.

Antioxidant: Studies have elucidated that β-myrcene can reverse and prevent the damaging effects of TCDD (2,3,7,8-Tetrachloro-p-dibenzodioxin) to the liver of rats by increasing GSH (glutathione), SOD (superoxide dismutase), and catalase activation[1,2].

– **d-LIMONENE**

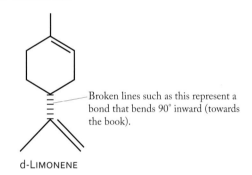

Broken lines such as this represent a bond that bends 90° inward (towards the book).

d-LIMONENE

d-Limonene is found in 90% of the citrus peel oils and in caraway seeds and dill. It is anticancer, antibacterial, antifungal, antiseptic (5x phenol), and highly antiviral.

Cancer Cell Inhibition: d-limonene has been found to be cancer-preventive in vitro and in human mammary cells. It acts as a selective isoprenylation inhibitor. d-Limonene specifically inhibits small g-proteins known as Ras p21 (or p21ras). p21ras is a critical protein for oncogenesis (formation of cancer cells) in the body. In order for oncogenesis to commence, the p21ras protein must be transferred within the cell to the plasma membrane. Once

p21ras is able to interact with the plasma membrane of the cell, it causes abnormal cell growth, intracellular localization, and transformations.

d-limonene inhibits the transferral of p21ras within the cell, blocking its access to the plasma membrane.

Researchers also found that d-limonene is selectively inhibitive. It targets only the transferral of Ras proteins and leaves all other ordinary cell functions alone. This makes d-Limonene a potentially effective chemopreventive agent because it targets areas of high oncogenic susceptibility and has no harmful side effects against critical cell components (low toxicity)[3,4,5].

Researchers have also observed that a continuous dose of limonene in the diets of rats with chemical-induced cancer helps inhibit the formation of secondary tumors and reduces the size of primary tumors. However, when limonene was removed from the rat's daily diet, tumors were more likely to return. This gives evidence that limonene works as a cytostatic agent (an agent that stops the tumor cells from creating new tumor cells) rather than a cytotoxic agent (an agent that kills the tumor cells). These researchers also observed that little toxicity occurred to the rats from the high doses of d-limonene[6].

Cholesterol Suppression: Researchers have discovered that when d-limonene is included in the daily diet of rats treated with a chemical (7,12-dimetylbenzantracene) that induced high cholesterol, there was a 45% decrease in hepatic HMG-CoA reductase activity. HMG-CoA reductase is an enzyme that converts HMG-CoA (93-hydroxy-3-methyl-glutaryl coenzyme A) to mevalonic acid, which acts as a precursor to the production of cholesterol. Inhibiting

1 Ciftci et al., 2011.
2 Gaetani et al., 1996.
3 Kato et al., 1992.
4 Crowell et al., 1991.
5 Morse et al., 1993.
6 Haag et al., 1992.

HMG-CoA reductase halts this process and, in effect, lowers cholesterol rates[7,8].

—Sesquiterpenes

Sesquiterpenes are found in great abundance in essential oils. They are antibacterial, strongly anti-inflammatory, slightly antiseptic and hypotensive, and sedative. Some have analgesic properties, while others are highly antispasmodic. They are soothing to irritated skin and tissue and are calming. They also work as liver and gland stimulants. Research from the universities of Berlin and Vienna shows that sesquiterpenes increase oxygenation around the pineal and pituitary glands. Further research has shown that sesquiterpenes have the ability to surpass the blood-brain barrier and enter the brain tissue. They are larger molecules than monoterpenes and have a strong aroma.

Found as a Major Constituent In: Ginger, myrrh, sandalwood, vetiver, and ylang ylang.

Found as a Minor Constituent In: Bergamot, cinnamon, clary sage, clove, cypress, white fir, frankincense, geranium, helichrysum, lavender, lemongrass, melaleuca, and peppermint.

Examples of Sesquiterpenes:

—β-Caryophyllene

β-Caryophyllene

β-caryophyllene is found in clove and cinnamon essential oils and is found in high proportions in plants from the Labiatae family. It is antiedema, anti-inflammatory, antispasmodic, and an insect and termite repellent.

Anesthetic: β-caryophyllene has been shown to act as a local anesthetic in vitro and in vivo. In an in vitro experiment, β-caryophyllene reduced the number of contractions electrically invoked in rat phrenic nerve-hemidiaphragms. Phrenic nerves are found in the spine, specifically at the 3rd, 4th, and 5th cervical vertebrae. These nerves provide sole motor control to the diaphragm. In this experiment, electrical impulses through the phrenic nerves induced diaphragm contractions, but the addition of β-caryophyllene reduced the number of contractions[9].

In an in vivo (real life) experiment, researchers performed a conjunctival reflex test on rabbits in which the conjunctival sac, found in the eye, was stimulated with a cat whisker to promote palpebral closure (or blinking). β-caryophyllene acted as a local anesthetic: when it was applied to the eye, more stimulation with the cat whisker was required in order to promote blinking in the rabbit[10].

—Chamazulene

Chamazulene

Chamazulene is found in chamomile oil and is very high in anti-inflammatory and antibacterial activity.

—Farnesene

α-Farnesene   β-Farnesene

Farnesene refers to several isomers with the chemical formula $C_{15}H_{24}$. Farnesene is

---

7 Sorentino et al., 2005.
8 Qureshi et al., 1988.

9 Bulbring, 1946.
10 Ghelardini et al., 2001.

11

found in ylang ylang, valerian, and German chamomile oil and is antiviral in action.

ALCOHOLS

Alcohols are any organic molecule with a carbon atom bound to a hydroxyl group. A hydroxyl group is an oxygen and hydrogen molecule (-OH).

METHANOL (CH$_3$OH)
— OH

METHANOL (CH$_3$OH)

Shorthand model of methanol, the simplest alcohol, and the molecular model it represents, below.

○ = CARBON

● = HYDROGEN

● = OXYGEN

Alcohols are commonly recognized for their antibacterial, anti-infectious, and antiviral activities. They are somewhat stimulating and help to increase blood circulation. Because of their high resistance to oxidation and their low toxicity levels, they have been shown in animal studies to revert cells to normal function and activity. They create an uplifting quality and are regarded as safe and effective for young and old alike.

Found as a Significant Constituent in ALL Essential Oils Except: Birch, cassia, clove, white fir, grapefruit, myrrh, oregano, and wintergreen.

—MONOTERPENE ALCOHOLS (OR MONOTERPENOLS)

Like monoterpenes, monoterpene alcohols are comprised of two isoprene units but have a hydroxyl group bound to one of the carbons instead of a hydrogen. Monoterpene alcohols are known for their ability to stimulate the immune system and to work as a diuretic and a general tonic. They are antibacterial and mildly antiseptic as well.

Examples of Monoterpene Alcohols:

—LINALOOL

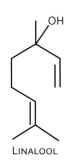

LINALOOL

Linalool is found in rosewood, bergamot, coriander, rose, jasmine, and lavender essential oils. It has a flowery aroma and is used to scent soaps, shampoos, and perfumes. Linalool can help relieve discomfort. It has antibacterial, antifungal, antiseptic (5x phenol), antispasmodic, antiviral, and sedative properties.

Anti-inflammatory: Linalool has been used to reduce paw swelling induced by carrageenan in mice. The effects of linalool work against swelling in a dose-dependent manner[1,2]. Linalool also mediates pain caused by inflammation. In a particular study, acetic acid was administered to mice via intraperitoneal (gut) injections. Mice that received a dose of linalool following administration of acetic acid exhibited less writhing (due to pain) than mice that acted as controls[3].

Antifungal: *Candida albicans* is the primary fungus responsible for yeast infections. Yeast infections are commonly exhibited as vulvovaginal candidiasis and thrush (oropharyngeal candidiasis, in the mouth). Thrush is commonly expressed in newborns and AIDS patients.

Candida albicans is also becoming a concern due to its emergence as a nosocomial infection (an infection contracted in a hospital) and its increasing resistance to fluconazole—an antifungal drug. *C. albicans* can form biofilms (aggregated colonies) on medical devices such as catheters and

---

1 Peana et al., 2002.
2 Skold et al., 2002.
3 Peana et al., 2003.

dentures[4,5].

Topical application of linalool to colonies of the polymorphic fungus *Candida albicans* results in growth inhibition and fungal death. Linalool affects growth by blocking passage beyond the G1 (cell growth) phase of the cell cycle[6].

Sedative: Linalool is a common sedative used in Brazilian folk medicine. According to studies using mice, inhaled linalool induces sleep or sedation[7,8].

Antiepileptic/Anticonvulsant: Epilepsy is characterized by seemingly spontaneous spasms of electrical activity in the brain. These spasms can cause seizures and convulsions. One hypothesis for the cause of epilepsy is excessive glutamate levels in neurons (nerve cells)[9,10,11,12]. Glutamates are a common form of neurotransmitter that are stored in special vesicles (storage containers) near nerve synapses (locations where nerve cells come close to each other in order to pass along electrical impulses and signals). Impulses along the nerve cause one nerve cell to release glutamate across the synapse where it is received by receptors on the second nerve cell, opening channels in that cell to allow it to pass ions through the cell membrane, changing the electrical potential of that cell[13].

Studies have shown that the release of large concentrations of glutamate will lead to too many open channels, which will cause high, intense depolarization sequences of the action potential. Disproportionate depolarizations are the basis for seizures and convulsions in epilepsy[14,15,16].

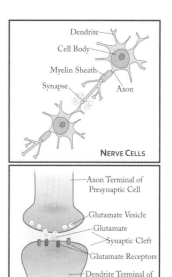

NERVE CELLS

SYNAPSE

Using mouse models, researchers have found that applications of linalool on cortical synaptosomes (isolated nerve terminals, or synapses) significantly inhibited glutamate uptake. Inhibition of glutamate is a method to reduce occurrences of epileptic seizures. These observations provide significant evidence for linalool acting as a possible antiepileptic agent[17,18].

−Citronellol

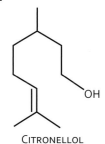

CITRONELLOL

Citronellol is found in citronella, rose, melissa, and eucalyptus essential oils. It has antibacterial, antifungal, antiseptic (3.8x phenol), and sedative properties.

Anticonvulsant Activity: Administered doses of citronellol given via the intraperitoneal cavity (gut) to rodents have been observed to reduce the convulsive effects in induced epileptic attacks. Epilepsy is studied in animal models by inducing convulsions with compounds such as pentylenetetrazol

4 Mukherjee et al., 2003.
5 Microbiology. 9th ed, 2007.
6 Zore et al., 2011.
7 Linck et al., 2009.
8 de Almeida et al., 2009.
9 Chapman et al., 2000.
10 Meldrum et al., 1999.
11 Meldrum, 1994.
12 Chapman, 1998.
13 Medical Physiology. 10th ed, 2000.
14 Chapman et al., 2000.
15 Meldrum et al., 1994.
16 Paolette et al., 2007.

17 Silva Brum et al., 2001a.
18 Silva Brum et al., 2001b.

(PTZ) and picrotoxin. Citronellol, over time, reduces the amplitude of the compound action potential (CAP) in neurons. This decreases the effect and intensity of convulsions[1].

Blood Pressure: Injections of citronellol into the blood were found by researchers to reduce blood pressure in animal models. Citronellol is theorized to decrease the flux of Ca^{2+} ions into smooth vascular muscle cells by deactivating VOCCs (voltage-operated calcium channels). Calcium is the principle regulator of tension in vascular smooth muscle (blood vessels). When the transport of Ca^{2+} into the cell is blocked, smooth muscle relaxation occurs. This leads to increased vasodilation (an increase in the diameter of the blood vessels, allowing a higher volume of blood flow) and, thus, lowered blood pressure[2,3,4].

–Geraniol

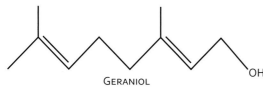

GERANIOL

Geraniol is found in rose, citronella, and lemon essential oils. It has antifungal, antiseptic (7x phenol), cancer preventative, and sedative properties.

–Other Monoterpene Alcohols:

Borneol, menthol, nerol, terpineol (which Dr. Gattefossé considered to be a decongestant), vetiverol, and cedrol.

—Sesquiterpene Alcohols (Sesquiterpenols)

Like sesquiterpenes, sesquiterpene alcohols are comprised of three isoprene units but have a hydroxyl group bound to one of the carbons instead of a hydrogen. Sesquiterpene alcohols are known to be antiallergic, antibacterial, anti-inflammatory, ulcer-protective (preventative), and liver and glandular stimulant.

Examples of Sesquiterpene Alcohols:

1   de Sousa et al., 2006.
2   Bastos et al., 2009.
3   Gurney, 1994.
4   Munzel et al., 2003.

–Farnesol

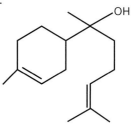

FARNESOL

Farnesol is found in rose, neroli, ylang ylang, and Roman chamomile essential oils. It is known to be good for the mucous membranes and to help prevent bacterial growth from perspiration.

–Bisabolol

BISABOLOL

Bisabolol is found in German chamomile essential oil. It is one of the strongest sesquiterpene alcohols.

–Other Sesquiterpene Alcohols:

Others include nerolidol and zingiberol.

Esters

Esters are the compounds resulting from the reaction of an alcohol with an acid (known as esterification). Esters consist of a carboxyl group (a carbon atom double bonded to an oxygen atom) bound to a hydrocarbon group on one side and bound to an oxygen and a hydrocarbon group on the opposite side.

Methyl Acetate (CH_3OOCH_3)

Methyl acetate (shown here) is a simple organic ester molecule.

Methyl Acetate (CH_3OOCH_3)

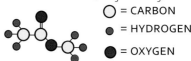

○ = CARBON
● = HYDROGEN
● = OXYGEN

Esters are very common and are found in the mildest essential oils. Mostly free of toxicity and irritants, they tend to be the most calming, relaxing, and balancing of all the essential oil constituents. They are also antifungal and antispasmodic. They have a balancing or regulatory effect, especially on the nervous system. Some examples are linalyl acetate, geranyl acetate (with strong anti-fungal properties), and bornyl acetate (effective on bronchial candida). Other esters include eugenyl acetate, lavendulyl acetate, and methyl salicylate.

Found as a Major Constituent In: Birch, bergamot, clary sage, geranium, helichrysum, lavender, wintergreen, and ylang ylang.

Found as a Minor Constituent In: Cassia, clove, cypress, white fir, lemon, lemongrass, marjoram, and orange.

ALDEHYDES

Aldehydes are often responsible for the fragrance of an oil. They exert powerful aromas and are often calming to the emotions. They are highly reactive and are characterized by a carboxyl group (a carbon atom double bonded to an oxygen atom) with a hydrogen atom on one side and a hydrocarbon group on the opposite side.

ACETALDEHYDE (CH$_3$CHO)

Acetaldehyde (shown here) is a simple organic aldehyde molecule.

ACETALDEHYDE (CH$_3$CHO)

○ = CARBON
• = HYDROGEN
● = OXYGEN

In general, they are anti-infectious, anti-inflammatory, calming to the central nervous system, fever-reducing, hypotensive, and tonic. Some are antiseptic, antimicrobial, and antifungal, while others act as vasodilators. They can be quite irritating when applied topically (citrals being an example). However, it has been shown that adding an essential oil with an equal amount of d-Limonene can negate the irritant properties of a high citral oil.

Found as a Major Constituent In: Cassia, cinnamon, and lemongrass.

Found as a Minor Constituent In: *Eucalyptus radiata*, grapefruit, lemon, myrrh, and orange.

Examples of Aldehydes:

—CITRALS

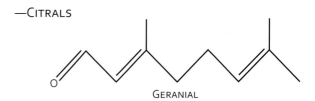

GERANIAL

Citrals (like neral, geranial, and citronellal) are very common and have a distinct antiseptic action. They also show antiviral properties (as is the case with melissa oil) when applied topically on herpes simplex.

—OTHER ALDEHYDES

Benzaldehyde, cinnamic aldehyde, cuminic aldehyde, and perillaldehyde.

KETONES

Ketones are organic compounds characterized by a carboxyl group (a carbon atom double bonded to an oxygen atom) with a hydrocarbon on both sides.

ACETONE (CH$_3$COCH$_3$)

Acetone (shown here) is a simple ketone molecule.

ACETONE (CH$_3$COCH$_3$)

○ = CARBON
• = HYDROGEN
● = OXYGEN

Ketones are sometimes mucolytic and neurotoxic when isolated from other constituents. However, all recorded toxic effects come from laboratory testing on guinea pigs and rats. No documented cases exist where oils with a high concentration of ketones (such as mugwort, tansy, sage, and wormwood) have ever caused a toxic effect on a human being. Also, large amounts of these oils would have to be consumed for them to result in a toxic neurological effect. Ketones stimulate cell regeneration, promote the formation of tissue, and liquefy mucous. They are helpful with conditions such as dry asthma, colds, flu, and dry cough and are largely found in oils used for the upper respiratory system, such as hyssop, rosemary, and sage.

Found as a Major Constituent In: rosemary (CT verbenon).

Found as a Minor (but significant) Constituent In: Fennel, geranium, helichrysum, lemongrass, myrrh, peppermint, and vetiver.

Examples of Ketones:

—THUJONE

α-THUJONE

Thujone is one of the most toxic members of the ketone family. It can be an irritant and upsetting to the central nervous system and may be neurotoxic when taken internally, such as in the banned drink absinthe. Although oils containing thujone may be inhaled to relieve respiratory distress and may stimulate the immune system, they should usually be used in dilution (1–2%) and/or for only short periods of time.

—JASMONE

JASMONE

Jasmone is found in jasmine essential oil and is nontoxic.

—FENCHONE

FENCHONE

Fenchone is found in fennel essential oil and is nontoxic.

—OTHER KETONES:

Camphor, carvone, menthone, methyl nonyl ketone, and pinocamphone.

PHENOLS

Phenols are a diverse group of compounds derived from a phenol group, which is comprised of a benzene ring (six carbon atoms bound in a circle) and a hydroxyl group (oxygen and hydrogen).

PHENOL (C_6H_6OH)
OH

Phenol (shown here) is a simple phenol molecule.

PHENOL (C_6H_6OH)

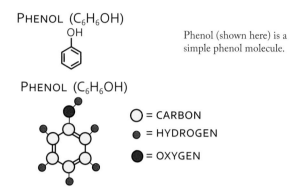

◯ = CARBON
◉ = HYDROGEN
⬤ = OXYGEN

Phenols comprise some of the most powerful antibacterial, anti-infectious, and antiseptic constituents in the plant world. They are also very stimulating to both the nervous and immune systems. They contain high levels of oxygenating molecules and have antioxidant properties. However, they can be quite caustic to the skin, and they present some concerns regarding liver toxicity. Essential oils that contain a high proportion of phenols should be diluted and/or used only for short periods of time.

Found as a Major Constituent In: Basil, birch, cinnamon, clove, fennel, melaleuca, oregano, peppermint, thyme, and wintergreen.

Found as a Minor Constituent In: Cassia, marjoram, and ylang ylang.

Examples of Phenols:

—EUGENOL

EUGENOL

Eugenol is found in clove, nutmeg, cinnamon, bay, and basil essential oils. It has analgesic, anesthetic (in dentistry), anticonvulsant, antifungal, anti-inflammatory, antioxidant, antiseptic, cancer-preventative, and sedative properties.

Vasodilator: Eugenol was found to increase vasodilation (increase the diameter of the opening through the blood vessels) in animal models. When blood vessels expand, the result is larger amounts of blood flow and, thus, a decrease in heart rate. In these particular studies, it was observed that heart rate decreased in conjunction with increased vasodilation, as compared to controls[1,2].

Eugenol is thought to increase vasodilation by inhibiting the action of calcium (Ca^{2+}) in voltage-operated calcium channels (VOCCs). Ca^{2+} is the main regulator of vascular smooth muscle (blood vessel) tension. When Ca^{2+} is blocked, blood vessels relax and widen, allowing for an increase in blood flow[3,4].

—THYMOL

THYMOL

Thymol is found in thyme and oregano essential oils. It may not be as caustic as other phenols. It has antibacterial, antifungal, anti-inflammatory, antioxidant, antiplaque, antirheumatic, antiseptic (20x phenol), antispasmodic, deodorizing, and expectorant properties.

Antibacterial: Thymol has been shown to inhibit the growth of microorganisms such as *Escherichia coli*, *Campylobacter jejuni*, *Porphyromonas gingivalis*, *Staphylococcus aureus*, and *Pseudomonas aeruginosa*. Thymol is thought to disrupt (or impair) the cytoplasmic membranes of microbes, causing cell leakage. Without the protective barrier of the cytoplasmic membrane, viability of these microorganisms significantly decreases[5,6,7,8].

1 Lahlou et al., 2004.
2 Damiani et al., 2003.
3 Gurney, 1994.
4 Munzel et al., 2003.
5 Shapiro et al., 1995.
6 Xu et al., 2008.
7 Lambert et al., 2001.
8 Evans et al., 2000.

—CARVACROL

CARVACROL

Carvacrol is a product of auto-oxidation of d-Limonene. It is antibacterial, antifungal, anti-inflammatory, antiseptic (1.5x phenol), antispasmodic, and expectorant. Researchers believe it may possibly have some anticancer properties as well.

—OTHER PHENOLS

Methyl eugenol, methyl chavicol, anethole, and safrole.

OXIDES

An organic oxide typically refers to an organic molecule (one that contains carbon and hydrogen) that has been oxidized, meaning an oxygen atom has become bound between two carbon atoms. According to the *American Heritage® Dictionary of the English Language*, an oxide is "a binary compound of an element or a radical with oxygen." Oxides often act as expectorants and are mildly stimulating.

Found as a Major Constituent In: *Eucalyptus radiata* and rosemary.

Found as a Minor Constituent In: Basil, lemongrass, melaleuca, thyme, and ylang ylang.

Examples of Oxides:

—1,8-CINEOL (EUCALYPTOL)

1,8-CINEOL
(EUCALYPTOL)

1,8-cineol is, by far, the most prevalent member of the oxide family and virtually exists in a class of its own. It is anesthetic, antiseptic, and works as a strong mucolytic as it thins mucus in respiratory tract infections.

Science & Application

Anti-Inflammatory: Researchers found in an animal experiment that rats that were given oral doses of 1,8-cineole before injection with lambda carrageenan (a sweetener that causes inflammation) had markedly decreased swelling when compared to rats that were given the injection without a dosage of 1,8-cineole.

It has been suggested by scientists that 1,8-cineole inhibits cytokine production. Inhibiting cytokine production would decrease inflammation despite having a stimulant present (such a carrageenan)[1,2].

Asthma: Asthma is a chronic inflammatory disease that restricts air flow to the lungs (specifically in the bronchial tubes). A double-blind, placebo-controlled study was performed to test the ability of 1,8-cineole to alleviate asthmatic symptoms. All subjects in the study suffered from bronchial asthma and required daily administration of oral glucocorticosteroids in order to maintain stable conditions.

At the conclusion of the study, which lasted over a course of 12 weeks, patients who received daily doses of 1,8-cineole were able to maintain stable conditions despite significantly reduced oral doses of glucocorticosteroids, as compared to the placebo group. Proper lung function was also maintained four times longer in the test group than in the placebo group[3,4].

Pain: In one study, mice were injected in the hind paw with a dose of 1% formalin (a common substance used to model pain in experimental studies)/99% saline solution. A portion of mice were given 1,8-cineole. It was observed that these mice who received 1,8-cineole licked their paw substantially less (meaning they did not feel as much pain) than mice that did not receive the 1,8-cineole treatment. In this study, researchers found that 1,8-cineole treatment produced antinociceptive (pain-blocking) effects comparable to those observed for morphine[5,6].

—OTHER OXIDES

Linalool oxide, ascaridol, bisabolol oxide, 1,4-cineol, and bisabolone oxide.

1 Santos et al., 2000.
2 Juergens et al., 2003.
3 Juergens et al., 2003.
4 Goodwin et al., 1986.
5 Santos et al., 2000.
6 Shibata et al., 1989.

ESSENTIAL OIL APPLICATION METHODS: TOPICAL—

Science & Application

Topical application is the process of placing an essential oil on the skin, hair, mouth, teeth, nails, or mucus membranes of the body. Applying essential oils directly on the body without any kind of dilution is commonly referred to as applying the oil "neat." Since essential oils are so potent, and because some essential oils may irritate the skin or other areas of the body, they are often diluted with a pure vegetable oil (usually called a "carrier oil") such as fractionated coconut oil, almond oil, olive oil, jojoba oil, etc. Several topical application methods are outlined below.

DIRECT APPLICATION:

Direct application is applying the oils directly on the area of concern. Because essential oils are so potent, more is not necessarily better. To achieve the desired results, 1–3 drops of oil are usually adequate. A few guidelines for direct application of the oils are as follow:

– The feet are the second fastest area of the body to absorb oils because of the large pores. Other quick-absorbing areas include behind the ears and on the wrists.

– To produce a feeling of peace, relaxation, or energy, 3–6 drops per foot are adequate.

– When massaging a large area of the body, always dilute the oils by 15% to 30% with fractionated coconut oil.

– When applying oils to infants and small children, dilute with fractionated coconut oil. Use 1–3 drops of an essential oil to 1 tablespoon (Tbs) of fractionated coconut oil for infants and 1–3 drops of an essential oil to 1 teaspoon (tsp) fractionated coconut oil for children ages 2–5.

– Use caution when creating blends for topical therapeutic use. Commercially-available blends have been specially formulated by someone who understands the chemical constituents of each oil and which oils blend well. The chemical properties of the oils can be altered when mixed improperly, resulting in some undesirable reactions.

– Layering individual oils is preferred over mixing your own blends for topical use. Layering refers to the process of applying one oil, rubbing it in, and then applying another oil. There is no need to wait more than a couple of seconds between each oil, as absorption occurs quite rapidly. If dilution is necessary, fractionated coconut oil may be applied on top. The layering technique is not only useful in physical healing but also in emotional clearing.

MASSAGE:

Massage is the stimulation of muscle, skin, and connective tissues using various techniques to help promote healing, balance, and connection. Massages can be invigorating, relaxing, stimulating, or soothing, and essential oils applied using massage can help enhance these benefits. There are many different massage techniques currently in use, and to explore all of the various techniques would be beyond the scope of this book.

Unless you are a certified massage therapist and have a thorough understanding of anatomy, it is best to use only light to medium massage strokes for applying oils and to avoid the spine and other sensitive areas of the body. Extreme caution must also be used when massaging pregnant women and others with certain health conditions.

To create a simple massage oil that includes the benefits of essential oils, combine 3–10 drops of your desired essential oil or blend with 1 tablespoon (15 ml) of fractionated coconut oil or another carrier oil. Apply a small amount of this mixture on location, and massage it into the skin using light to medium-light strokes of the hand or fingers.

AROMATOUCH™ TECHNIQUE:

This is a simple—yet powerful—technique for applying certain oils along the entire length of the spine and on the feet. This application of 8 essential oils has been shown to help achieve feelings of stress reduction, immune enhancement, inflammatory response reduction, and homeostasis. See the pages on the AromaTouch™ Technique in this section of the book for more details.

REFLEXOLOGY/REFLEX THERAPY:

Reflex therapy is a simple method of applying oils to contact points (or nerve endings) in the feet or hands. A series of hand rotation movements at those control points create a vibrational healing energy that carries the oils along the neuroelectrical pathways. The oils either help remove any blockage along the pathways or travel the length of the pathway to benefit the particular organ. Refer to the reflex hand and foot charts on the following pages for more details.

AURICULAR THERAPY

Auricular therapy is a method of applying the oils to various points on the rim of the ears to effect changes on internal body parts. Small amounts of the oil are applied to the point, and then the point is stimulated with the fingers or with a glass probe. See the Auricular Body Points chart on the following page for more details.

COMPRESSES

1. Basin. Fill a wash basin with 2 quarts of hot or cold water, and add the desired essential oils. Stir the water vigorously; then lay a towel on top of the water. Since the oils will float to the top, the towel will absorb the oils with the water. After the towel is completely saturated, wring out the excess water (leaving much of the oils in the towel), and place the towel over the area needing the compress. For a hot compress, cover with a dry towel and a hot water bottle. For a cold compress, cover with a piece of plastic or plastic wrap. Finally, put another towel on top, and leave for as long as possible (1–2 hours is best).

2. Massage. Apply a hot, wet towel and then a dry towel on top of an already massaged area. The moist heat will force the oils deeper into the tissues of the body.

BATHS

1. Bathwater. Begin by adding 3–6 drops of oil to the bathwater while the tub is filling. Because the individual oils will separate as the water calms down, the skin will quickly draw the oils from the top of the water. Some people have commented that they were unable to endure more than 6 drops of oil. Such individuals may benefit from adding the oils to a bath and shower gel base first. Soak for 15 minutes.

2. Bath and Shower Gel. Begin by adding 3–6 drops of oil to ½ oz of a bath and shower gel base; add to the water while the tub is filling. Adding the oils to a bath and shower gel base first allows one to obtain the greatest benefit from the oils as they are more evenly dispersed throughout the water and not allowed to immediately separate.

3. Bath Salts. Combine 3–10 drops essential oil with ¼–½ cup of bath salts or Epsom salts. Dissolve the salt mixture in warm bathwater before bathing.

4. Washcloth. When showering, add 3–6 drops of oil to a bath and shower gel base before applying to a washcloth and using to wash the body.

5. Body Sprays. Fill a small spray bottle with distilled water, and add 10–15 drops of your favorite oil blend or single oils. Shake well, and spray onto the entire body just after taking a bath or shower.

AURICULAR INTERNAL BODY POINTS

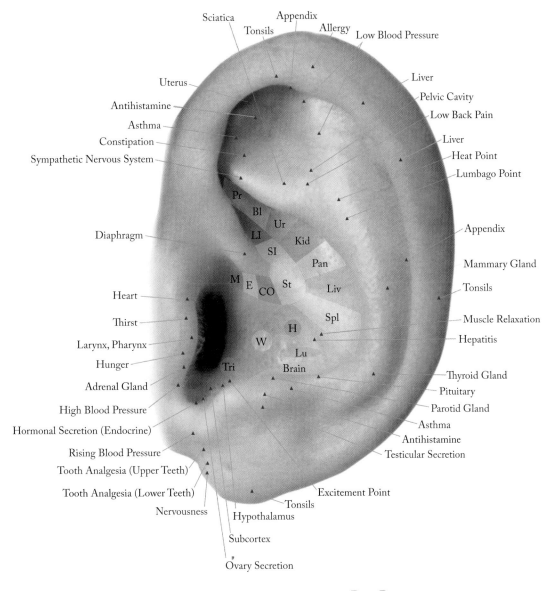

Sciatica
Appendix
Tonsils
Allergy
Low Blood Pressure
Uterus
Antihistamine
Asthma
Constipation
Sympathetic Nervous System
Diaphragm
Heart
Thirst
Larynx, Pharynx
Hunger
Adrenal Gland
High Blood Pressure
Hormonal Secretion (Endocrine)
Rising Blood Pressure
Tooth Analgesia (Upper Teeth)
Tooth Analgesia (Lower Teeth)
Nervousness
Hypothalamus
Subcortex
Ovary Secretion
Tonsils
Excitement Point
Testicular Secretion
Antihistamine
Asthma
Parotid Gland
Pituitary
Thyroid Gland
Hepatitis
Muscle Relaxation
Tonsils
Mammary Gland
Appendix
Lumbago Point
Heat Point
Liver
Low Back Pain
Pelvic Cavity
Liver

Pr
Bl
Ur
LI
Kid
SI
Pan
M
E
St
CO
Liv
H
Spl
W
Lu
Tri
Brain

Bl: Bladder

CO: Cardiac Orifice

E: Esophogus

H: Heart

Kid: Kidney

LI: Large Intestine

Liv: Liver

Lu: Lungs

M: Mouth

Pan: Pancreas

Pr: Prostate

SI: Small Intestine

Spl: Spleen

ST: Stomach

Tri: Triple Warmer

Ur: Ureter

W: Windpipe/Trachea

REFLEX THERAPY HAND CHART

Reflex points on this hand chart correspond to those on the feet. Occasionally the feet can be too sensitive for typical reflex therapy. Working with the hands will not only affect the specific body points but may also help to provide some pain relief to the corresponding points on the feet.

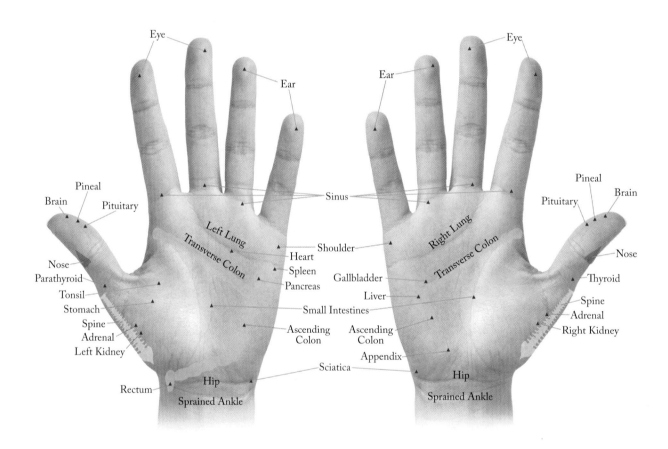

Eye

Eye

Ear

Ear

Pineal

Brain

Pituitary

Sinus

Pineal

Pituitary

Brain

Left Lung

Transverse Colon

Right Lung

Transverse Colon

Nose

Nose

Parathyroid

Shoulder

Heart

Spleen

Pancreas

Gallbladder

Liver

Thyroid

Tonsil

Stomach

Spine

Adrenal

Left Kidney

Small Intestines

Spine

Adrenal

Right Kidney

Ascending
Colon

Ascending
Colon

Appendix

Rectum

Hip

Sprained Ankle

Sciatica

Hip

Sprained Ankle

REFLEX THERAPY FEET CHARTS

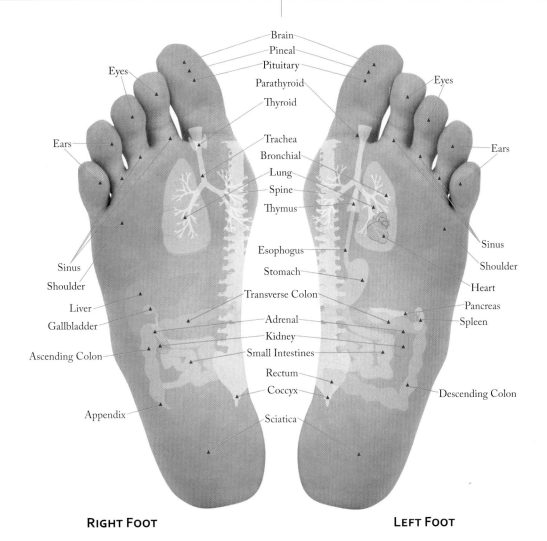

Brain
Pineal
Pituitary
Parathyroid
Thyroid

Eyes

Eyes

Trachea
Bronchial
Lung
Spine
Thymus

Ears

Ears

Sinus
Shoulder

Sinus

Esophogus
Stomach

Shoulder

Liver

Heart

Gallbladder

Transverse Colon

Pancreas

Adrenal
Kidney

Spleen

Ascending Colon

Small Intestines

Appendix

Rectum
Coccyx

Descending Colon

Sciatica

RIGHT FOOT

LEFT FOOT

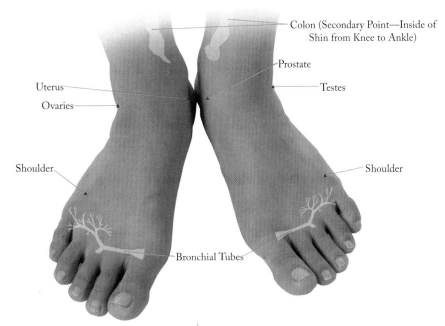

Colon (Secondary Point—Inside of
Shin from Knee to Ankle)

Prostate

Uterus

Testes

Ovaries

Shoulder

Shoulder

Bronchial Tubes

AromaTouch™ Technique

The AromaTouch™ Technique is an essential oil application technique that was developed by Dr. David K. Hill (an expert on the science and use of essential oils) in response to an increasing demand for a simple, yet effective, way that both beginners and experts alike could apply essential oils with meaningful results.

Drawing on his medical background and on his years of personal experience with essential oils, Dr. Hill selected eight individual essential oils and oil blends that have demonstrated profound effects on four conditions that constantly challenge the ability of the body's systems to function optimally: stress, increased toxin levels, inflammation, and autonomic nervous system imbalance.

Dr. Hill developed a system of simple application methods that would enable these powerful essential oils to reach the optimal areas within the body where they would be able to help combat stress, enhance immune function, decrease inflammation, and balance the autonomic nervous system within the recipient.

Stress:

Stress refers to the many systemic changes that take place within the body as it responds to challenging situations. Stress comes not only from difficult, new, and pressured circumstances but also from the body being challenged to cope with things such as abnormal physical exertion, a lack of proper nutrients in the diet, disease-causing microorganisms, and toxic chemicals that make their way into the body. While the systems within a healthy body can typically deal with most short-term challenges, having constant or chronic stress on these systems can overly fatigue them, limiting their abilities to respond to future challenges.

Toxic Insult:

The body is constantly working to cope with a vast array of toxins that continually bombard it. These toxins can come from many differ-ent sources, including chemical-laden foods, pollution in the air and water, and pathogenic microorganisms that invade the body. As the environment of the world becomes increasingly saturated with toxins and a rising number of resistant pathogens, the cells, tissues, and systems of the body are forced to work harder to process and eliminate these threats in order to maintain health.

Inflammation:

Inflammation is an immune system response that allows the body to contain and fight infection or to repair damaged tissue. This response dilates the blood vessels and increases vascular permeability to allow more blood to flow to an area with injured or infected tissue. It is characterized by redness, swelling, warmth, and pain. While a certain amount of inflammation can be beneficial in fighting disease and healing injuries, chronic inflammation can actually further injure surrounding tissues or cause debilitating levels of pain.

Autonomic Imbalance:

The autonomic nervous system is comprised of nerves that are connected to the muscles organs, tissues, and systems that don't require conscious effort to control. The autonomic system is divided into two main parts that each have separate, balancing functions: the sympathetic nervous system and the para-sympathetic nervous system. The sympathetic nervous system functions to accelerate heart rate, increase blood pressure, slow digestion, and constrict blood vessels. It activates the "fight or flight" response in order to deal with threatening or stressful situations. The para-sympathetic nervous system functions to slow heart rate, store energy, stimulate digestive activity, and relax specific muscles.

Maintaining a proper balance within the autonomic nervous system is important for optimal body function and maintenance.

OILS USED IN THE AROMATOUCH™ TECHNIQUE:

For additional information on the oils and blends used in this technique, see the Single Essential Oils and Essential Oil Blends sections of this book.

STRESS-REDUCING OILS:

Balance: is an oil blend formulated from oils that are known to bring a feeling of calmness, peace, and relaxation. It can aid in harmonizing the various physiological systems of the body and promote tranquility and a sense of balance.

Lavender: has been used for generations for its calming and sedative properties.

IMMUNE ENHANCEMENT OILS:

Melaleuca: has potent antifungal, antibacterial, and anti-inflammatory properties.

On Guard: is a blend of oils that have been studied for their strong abilities to kill harmful bacteria, mold, and viruses.

INFLAMMATORY RESPONSE–REDUCING OILS:

AromaTouch: is a blend of oils that were selected specifically for their ability to relax, calm, and relieve the tension of muscles, soothe irritated tissue, and increase circulation.

Deep Blue: is a blend containing oils that are well known and researched for their abilities to soothe inflammation, alleviate pain, and reduce soreness.

AUTONOMIC BALANCING OILS:

Peppermint: has invigorating and uplifting properties.

Wild Orange: has antidepressant properties and is often used to relieve feelings of anxiety and stress. Its aroma is uplifting to both the body and mind.

APPLYING THE OILS: STEP ONE—STRESS REDUCTION

BALANCE:

Apply Oil: Apply Balance oil blend from the base (top) of the sacrum to the base of the skull, distributing the oil evenly along the spine. Use the pads of your fingers to lightly distribute the oils over the length of the spine.

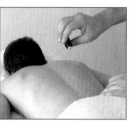

Palm Circles and Connection: With the hands palms down and fingers overlapping, make three clockwise circles over the heart area; hold the hands briefly in that area, and then slide one hand to the base of the sacrum and the other hand to the base of the skull.

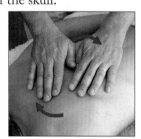

Hold as long as necessary to form a connection, balance, and feeling of trust.

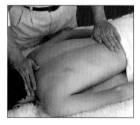

LAVENDER

Apply Oil: Apply lavender oil from the base of the sacrum to the base of the skull, distributing the oil evenly along the spine. Use the pads of your fingers to lightly distribute the oils over the length of the spine.

Alternating Palm Slide: Standing at the recipient's side, place both hands next to the spine on the opposite side of the back at the base of the sacrum, with the palms down and the fingers pointing away from you. Slide one hand away from the spine toward the side using a mild pressure; then repeat using alternating hands. Continue with this sliding motion as you slowly work your hands from the base of the sacrum to the base of the skull.

Repeat this step two more times on one side of the back; then move around the person to the opposite side, and repeat three times on that side.

5–Zone Activation: Standing at the head, place both hands together with the fingertips on either side of the spine at the base of the sacrum.

Using a medium downward pressure, pull the hands toward the head through zone 1; then continue through the neck and up to the top of the head.

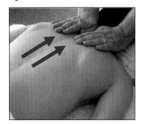

Return the hands to the base of the sacrum, and pull the hands in a similar manner through zone 2 to the shoulders.

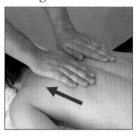

When the hands arrive at the shoulders, push the hands out to the points of the shoulders.

Rotate the hands around the points so that the fingers are on the underside of the shoulders.

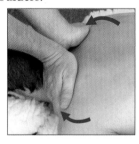

Pull the hands back to the neck, and continue up to the top of the head.

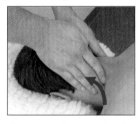

Repeat the steps for zone 2 through zones 3, 4, and 5, ending each pull at the top of the head.

Auricular Stress Reduction: Grip each earlobe between the thumb and forefinger; using gentle pressure, work your fingers in small circles along the ear to the top.

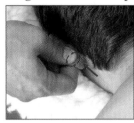

Slide your thumbs with gentle pressure along the backs of the ears returning to the lobes. Repeat this ear massage 3 times.

STEP TWO—IMMUNE ENHANCEMENT

MELALEUCA

Apply Oil: Apply melaleuca oil from the base of the sacrum to the base of the skull, distributing the oil evenly along the spine. Use the pads of your fingers to lightly distribute the oils over the length of the spine.

Alternating Palm Slide: Perform as outlined under Lavender above.

5–Zone Activation: Perform as outlined under Lavender above.

ON GUARD

Apply Oil: Apply On Guard oil blend from the base of the sacrum to the base of the skull, distributing the oil evenly along the spine. Use the pads of your fingers to lightly distribute the oils over the length of the spine.

Alternating Palm Slide: Perform as outlined under Lavender above.

5–Zone Activation: Perform as outlined under Lavender above.

Thumb Walk Tissue Pull: Place the hands with palms down on either side of the spine at the base of the sacrum, with the thumbs in the small depression between the spine and the muscle tissue. Using a medium pressure, move the pads of the thumbs in small semicircles, pulling the tissue up, away, and then down from the spine.

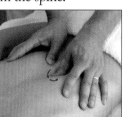

Gradually move each thumb up the spine in alternating fashion until you reach the base of the skull. Repeat this step two more times.

STEP THREE—INFLAMMATION REDUCTION

AROMATOUCH:

Apply Oil: Apply AromaTouch oil blend from the base of the sacrum to the base of the skull, distributing the oil evenly along the spine. Use the pads of your fingers to lightly distribute the oils over the length of the spine.

Alternating Palm Slide: Perform as outlined under Lavender above.

5–Zone Activation: Perform as outlined under Lavender above.

DEEP BLUE:

Apply Oil: Apply Deep Blue oil blend from the base of the sacrum to the base of the skull, distributing the oil evenly along the spine. Use the pads of your fingers to lightly distribute the oils over the length of the spine.

Alternating Palm Slide: Perform as outlined under Lavender above.

5–Zone Activation: Perform as outlined under Lavender above.

Thumb Walk Tissue Pull: Perform as outlined under On Guard above.

STEP FOUR—AUTONOMIC BALANCE

WILD ORANGE AND PEPPERMINT

Apply Oils to Feet: Place drops of wild orange oil on the palm of your hand, and apply this oil evenly over the entire bottom of the foot. Apply peppermint oil in the same manner.

Hold the foot with both hands. Beginning in region 1 at the point of the heel and using a medium pressure, massage the foot using first the pad of one thumb and then the pad of the other thumb. Continue this process, alternating thumbs, back and forth through region 1 to thoroughly relax all of the tissue in that region. Repeat through regions 2 and 3.

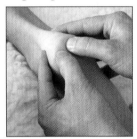

Beginning in zone 1 at the point of the heel, walk the pads of the thumbs through zone 1 using a medium pressure. Continue this process using alternating thumbs and working in a straight line through zone 1 to the tip of the big toe to thoroughly stimulate all of the tissue in that zone.

Repeat through zones 2–5.

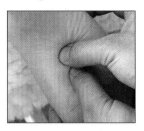

Using a medium pressure with the pad of your thumb, pull the tissue in zone 1—beginning at the point of the heel and ending at the toe. Repeat two additional times through zone 1, using alternate thumbs each time. Repeat this tissue pull process in zones 2–5 on the same foot.

Repeat this entire process, beginning with the application of wild orange oil, on the opposite foot.

Apply Oils to Back: Apply first wild orange and then peppermint oils from the base of the sacrum to the base of the skull, distributing the oils evenly along the spine. Use the pads of your fingers to lightly distribute the oils over the length of the spine.

Alternating Palm Slide: Perform as outlined under Lavender above.

LYMPHATIC STIMULATION:

Gentle Body Motion: Standing at the feet, grasp the feet so that the palms of your hands are against the soles of the recipient's feet and your arms are in a straight line with the recipient's legs. Use a repeated, gentle pressure on the feet that allows the recipient's body to translate (move) back and forth naturally on the table. Repeat this process for two or three 15–30 second intervals.

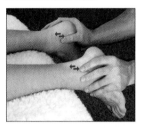

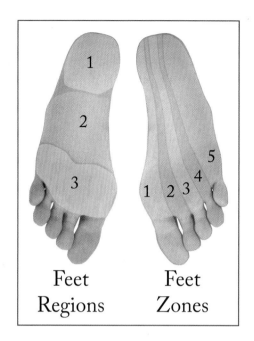

Feet Regions   Feet Zones

Zones of the Back and Head

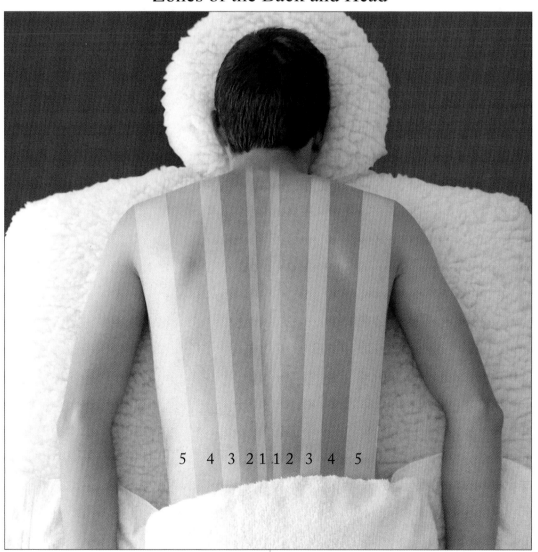

AUTONOMIC NERVOUS SYSTEM

SYMPATHETIC NERVOUS SYSTEM

- Dilates Pupils
- Inhibits Salivation
- Accelerates Heart Rate
- Dilates Bronchi
- Dilates Blood Vessels
- Inhibits Gastric Juice Production
- Stimulates Secretion of Epinephrine and Norepinephrine
- Inhibits Digestive Process
- Contracts Rectum
- Relaxes Bladder Muscles

PARASYMPATHETIC NERVOUS SYSTEM

- Constricts Pupils
- Stimulates Salivation
- Slows Heart Rate
- Constricts Bronchi
- Constricts Blood Vessels
- Stimulates Gastric Juice Production
- Stimulates Digestive Process
- Relaxes Rectum
- Contracts Bladder Muscles

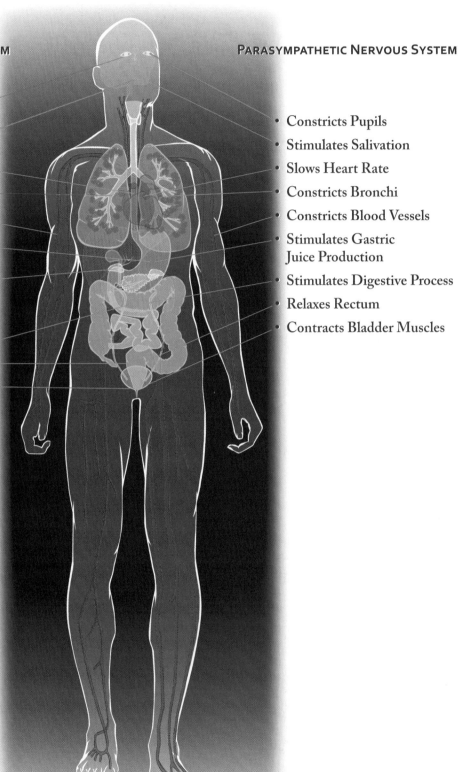

ESSENTIAL OIL APPLICATION METHODS: AROMATIC—

Aromatic application involves inhaling either a fine mist of the oil or a vapor of volatile aromatic components that have evaporated from the oil. Inhalation of the oil, or the aroma from the oil, can be a powerful way to affect memory, hormones, and emotions through the olfactory system (see the following page for further discussion on this topic). Inhalation of oils can also be a quick and effective way to affect the sinuses, larynx, bronchial tubes, and lungs.

DIFFUSION:

The easiest and simplest way of putting a fine mist of the whole oil into the air for inhalation is to use a nebulizing diffuser. A cool-air nebulizing diffuser uses room-temperature air to break the oils into a micro-fine mist that is then dispersed into the air, covering hundreds of square feet in seconds. An ultrasonic nebulizer uses ultrasonic vibrations to convert oil mixed with water into a fine water vapor. When diffused in this manner, the oils, with their oxygenating molecules, will then remain suspended for several hours to freshen and improve the quality of the air. The antiviral, antibacterial, and antiseptic properties of the oils kill bacteria and help to reduce fungus and mold.

Other diffusers may use either cool air blown through a pad containing the oil or a low level of heat to quickly evaporate the volatile oil molecules into the air. This type of diffusion is beneficial but may not be as effective for some therapeutic uses as nebulizing the whole oil can be.

Diffusers that use an intense heat source (such as a light bulb ring or candle) may alter the chemical makeup of the oil and its therapeutic qualities and are typically not recommended.

When diffused, essential oils have been found to reduce the amount of airborne chemicals and to help create greater physical and emotional harmony. The greatest therapeutic benefit is received by diffusing oils for only 15 minutes out of an hour so that the olfactory system has time to recover before receiving more oils. The easiest way to do this is by using a timer that can be set to turn the diffuser on in 15-minute increments over a 24-hour period.

DIRECT INHALATION:

Direct inhalation is the simplest way to inhale the aroma of an essential oil in order to affect moods and emotions. Simply hold an opened essential oil vial close to the face, and inhale. You may also apply 1–2 drops of oil on your hands, cup your hands over your mouth and nose, and inhale.

CLOTH OR TISSUE:

Put 1–3 drops of an essential oil on a paper towel, tissue, cotton ball, handkerchief, towel, or pillow case; hold it close to your face, and inhale.

HOT WATER VAPOR:

Put 1–3 drops of an essential oil into hot water, and inhale. Again, heat may reduce some of the benefits.

VAPORIZER OR HUMIDIFIER:

Put oil in a vaporizer or a humidifier. The cool mist types are best, since heat reduces some of the benefits. There are some commercially-available diffusers that utilize ultrasonic vibration to vaporize water into a cool mist. These work well with essential oils since they produce a very fine mist that helps suspend the oil particles in the air for extended periods of time.

FAN OR VENT:

Put oil on a cotton ball, and attach it to ceiling fans or air vents. This can also work well in a vehicle since the area is so small.

PERFUME OR COLOGNE:

Wearing the oils as a perfume or cologne can provide some wonderful emotional support and physical support as well—not just a beautiful fragrance. Apply 1–2 drops of oil to the wrists or neck, or create a simple perfume or cologne by dissolving 10–15 drops essential oil in 20 drops alcohol (such as vodka, or a perfumer's alcohol) and combining this mixture with 1 tsp distilled water. Apply or mist on wrists or neck.

NOSE AND OLFACTORY SYSTEM

When an odor molecule is inhaled into the nasal cavity, it is first sensed by the olfactory cells that are part of the olfactory epithelium. The olfactory epithelium is comprised of two small patches of olfactory nerves (each about 1 cm square) that lie on the roof of the nasal cavity. The olfactory cells within the olfactory epithelium are specialized nerve cells that extend cilia (small hair-like structures) from their dendrites into the nasal cavity. Each of these cilia have receptors that bind to a specific type of odor molecule. When an odor molecule binds to a receptor on the cilia of an olfactory cell, the olfactory cell passes the signal through the cribriform plate (the bone at the roof of the nasal cavity) to the olfactory bulb. The olfactory bulb, in turn, sends those impulses along the lateral olfactory tract to five different structures in the brain, including the amygdala (which is responsible for storing and releasing emotion-al trauma), the anterior olfactory nucleus (which helps process smells), the olfactory tubercle, the piriform cortex (which passes the signal on to other structures that create a conscious perception of the odor), and the entorhinal cortex (which processes stimuli before sending them on to the hippocampus, the long-term memory center of the brain). Anatomically, the olfactory system is closely connected to the limbic system of the brain. The limbic system includes structures such as the hippocampus (long-term memory), the amygdala (emotions), the hypothalamus (autonomic nervous system and hormones), and the cingulate gyrus (regulates blood pressure, heart rate, and attention). It is due to the fact that the olfactory system is so closely connected to the limbic system that essential oils have such profound physiological and psychological effects.

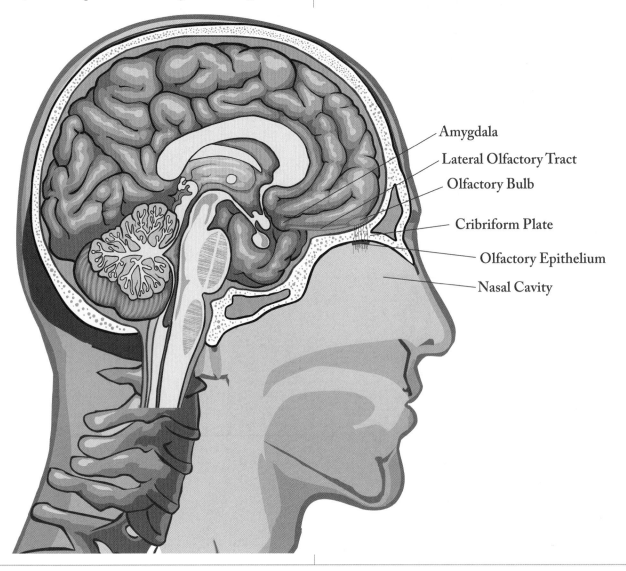

Amygdala
Lateral Olfactory Tract
Olfactory Bulb

Cribriform Plate

Olfactory Epithelium
Nasal Cavity

THE ART OF BLENDING

Blending essential oils is an art and usually requires a little bit of training and experimentation. If you choose to create your own blends, it is important to understand that the order in which the oils are blended is key to maintaining the desired therapeutic properties in a synergistic blend. An alteration in the sequence of adding selected oils to a blend may change the chemical properties, the fragrance, and, thus, the desired results. The "Blend Classification" and "Blends With" listings under each oil in the Single Oils section of this book should assist one in the blending process. In general, oils that are from the same botanical family usually blend well together. In addition, oils with similar constituents also mix well.

Another method utilizes four blending classifications. The following information explains the characteristics of each classification, the order in which they should be added to the blend (i.e. Personifiers first, Enhancers second, Equalizers third, and Modifiers fourth), and the amount of each type of oil as a percentage of the blend.

1st—The Personifier (1–5% of blend) oils have very sharp, strong, and long-lasting fragrances. They also have dominant properties with strong therapeutic action.

Oils in this classification may include birch, cinnamon, clary sage, clove, coriander, ginger, helichrysum, orange, peppermint, rose, wintergreen, and ylang ylang.

2nd—The Enhancer (50–80% of blend) oil should be the predominant oil as it serves to enhance the properties of the other oils in the blend. Its fragrance is not as sharp as the personifier's and is usually of a shorter duration.

Oils in this classification may include basil, bergamot, birch, eucalyptus, frankincense, geranium, grapefruit, lavender, lemon, lemongrass, marjoram, melaleuca, orange, oregano, rose, rosemary, thyme, and wintergreen.

3rd—The Equalizer (10–15% of blend) oils create balance and synergy among the oils contained in the blend. Their fragrance is also not as sharp as the personifier's and is of a shorter duration.

Oils in this classification may include basil, bergamot, cypress, fennel, white fir, frankincense, geranium, ginger, lavender, lemongrass, marjoram, melaleuca, myrrh, oregano, rose, sandalwood, and thyme.

4th—The Modifier (5–8% of blend) oils have a mild and short fragrance. These oils add harmony to the blend.

Oils in this classification may include bergamot, coriander, eucalyptus, fennel, grapefruit, lavender, lemon, myrrh, rose, sandalwood, and ylang ylang.

Depending upon the topical application of your blend, you will want to add some carrier/base oil. When creating a therapeutic essential oil blend, you may want to use about 28 drops of essential oil to ½ oz of fractionated coconut oil. When creating a body massage blend, you will want to use a total of about 50 drops of essential oils to 4 oz of fractionated coconut oil. Remember to store your fragrant creations in dark-colored glass bottles.

As essential oils can vary in thickness, the following are approximate measurements:

25–30 drops	= 1/4 tsp	= 1–2 ml	= 5/8 dram
45–50 drops	= 1/2 tsp	= 2–3 ml	= 1 dram
75–80 drops	= 3/4 tsp	= 3–4 ml	= 1/8 oz
100–120 drops	= 1 tsp	= 5 ml	= 1/6 oz
160 drops	= 1½ tsp	= 6–8 ml	= 1/4 oz
320–400 drops	= 3 tsp	= 13–15 ml	= 1/2 oz
600–650 drops	= 6 tsp	= 25–30 ml	= 1 oz

Learn to trust your nose, as it can help you decide which classification an oil should be in. More detailed information about these methods of blending is beyond the scope of this revision of the book. For additional information on using these classifications in your blending, we highly recommend Marcel Lavabre's *Aromatherapy Workbook*. Another very simple book about blending, with recipes and easy-to-follow guidelines, is Mindy Green's *Natural Perfumes*, which uses perfume notes (top, middle, base), odor, and odor intensity to help guide you in making your own fragrant blend creations (refer to the chart on the following page).

Essential Oil	Scent	Intensity
Top Notes	(5–20% of the blend)	
Orange	Fresh, citrusy, fruity, sweet, light	1
Bergamot	Sweet, lively, citrus, fruity	2
Grapefruit	Clean, fresh, bitter, citrusy	2
Lemon	Sweet, sharp, clear, citrusy	3
Lemongrass	Grassy, lemony, pungent, earthy	4
Top to Middle Notes	(20–80% of the blend)	
Basil	Spicy, anise-like, camphorous, lively	4
Fennel	Sweet, somewhat spicy, licorice-like	4
Middle Notes	(50–80% of the blend)	
Lavender	Floral, sweet, balsamic, slightly woody	2
Cypress	Fresh, herbaceous, slightly woody	3
Eucalyptus	Slightly camphorous, sweet, fruity	3
Fir	Fresh, woody, earthy, sweet	3
Geranium	Sweet, green, citrus-rosy, fresh	3
Helichrysum	Rich, sweet, fruity, slightly honey-like	3
Marjoram	Herbaceous, green, spicy	3

Essential Oil	Scent	Intensity
Middle Notes (continued)	(50–80% of the blend)	
Melaleuca	Medicinal, fresh, woody, earthy	3
Rosemary Cin.	Strong, camphorous, slightly woody	3
Ginger	Sweet, spicy-woody, warm, fresh, sharp	4
Thyme	Fresh, medicinal, herbaceous	4
Oregano	Herbaceous, sharp	5
Peppermint	Minty, sharp, intense	5
Middle to Base Notes	(20–80% of the blend)	
Clary Sage	Spicy, hay-like, sharp, fixative	3
Rose	Floral, spicy, rich, deep, sensual, green	3
Ylang Ylang	Sweet, heavy, narcotic, tropical, floral	5
Base Notes	(5–20% of the blend)	
Frankincense	Rich, deep, warm, balsamic, sweet	3
Sandalwood	Soft, woody, sweet, earthy, balsamic	3
Myrrh	Warm, earthy, woody, balsamic	4
Vanilla	Sweet, balsamic, heavy, warm	4
Vetiver	Heavy, earthy, balsamic, smoky	5

This chart was compiled from the book *Natural Perfumes* by Mindy Green and from various other sources. It lists essential oils by note types in order of odor intensity—1 being the lightest and 5 being the strongest. Please see the previous page for more information on this blending system.

ESSENTIAL OIL APPLICATION METHODS: INTERNAL—

Internal use is the process of consuming or otherwise internalizing the essential oil into the body. Only pure, therapeutic grade essential oils should be used for internal consumption, as other essential oils on the market may be diluted or processed using harmful chemicals.

The FDA has approved some essential oils for internal use and given them the designation of GRAS (Generally Recognized As Safe for human consumption). This designation is listed for each oil in the Single Essential Oils section of this book under Oral Use As Dietary Supplement. Oils without this designation should never be used internally without first consulting a certified health care professional.

CAPSULES

One of the most common ways to take essential oils internally is by placing 1–10 drops of essential oil inside an empty capsule, closing the capsule, and then swallowing it. It is also common to dilute the pure essential oil by filling the remainder of the capsule with olive oil before closing and swallowing.

BEVERAGE

An easy way to take essential oils internally is by adding them to a beverage. This is done by placing 1 drop of essential oil in 1–4 cups of rice milk, almond milk, or water, before drinking.

COOKING

Essential oils can easily be incorporated into your cooking, as long as you remember that they are very concentrated. Usually only 1 drop is necessary, and sometimes even less. Use a toothpick to help control the addition of smaller amounts of oil by dipping the toothpick into the oil (more oil on the toothpick = stronger flavor, etc.) and then stirring it into the food. Here are a couple examples of recipes where people have used the essential oils for flavoring.

Cream Cheese Icing

8 oz package of cream cheese
1½ cups of powdered sugar
1 stick of butter
3 drops wild orange essential oil

Cream together thoroughly the cream cheese, powdered sugar, and butter with an electric beater. Stir in the wild orange oil. Enjoy!

Lemon Tarragon Dressing

1 Tbs fresh tarragon diced, or 1 tsp dried tarragon
1 Tbs fresh or 1 tsp dried basil leaves
1 cup organic extra-virgin, cold-pressed olive oil
dash of pepper
dash of red pepper
6 drops lemon essential oil

Mix well, and drizzle on salad or fish or anything! Keep unused portion in the fridge.

VAGINAL INSERTION

There are three main ways to insert essential oils vaginally. First, the oils can be diluted in 2–3 tsp of a carrier oil, inserted using a vaginal syringe, and then held in place using a tampon. Alternately, the oils can be diluted in 1–2 tsp of carrier oil, and then a tampon can be used to soak up the mixture. This is then inserted and retained, typically all day or overnight. The third method is to add a few drops of oil to warm water and then to use a vaginal syringe to irrigate and rinse internally using the oil and water mixture.

RECTAL INSERTION

Rectal oil insertion is often recommended to aid various respiratory problems and other internal conditions. Two ways are often recommended for implanting the oils rectally. First, a rectal syringe can be used to deposit the oils into the rectum. Second, the oils can be placed in capsules and the capsules be inserted into the rectum. The oils are typically retained inside the rectum for several hours or overnight.

HOUSEHOLD APPLICATION METHODS

DISHWATER, CLOTHES WASHERS, AND CLOTHES DRYERS

The antibacterial properties of essential oils can effectively promote greater hygiene. Add a couple drops of lemon to dishwater for clean dishes and a great-smelling kitchen. Use lemon or Citrus Bliss to take gum out of clothes. A few drops of Purify in the wash water will kill bacteria and germs in clothes. Put Purify, Elevation, or another oil on a wet rag, and place it in the dryer with clothing; or mist oils from a spray bottle directly into the dryer.

CLEANING AND DISINFECTING

For polishing furniture and cleaning and disinfecting bathrooms and kitchens, put a few drops of lemon, Purify, or white fir oil on a dust cloth, or put 10 drops in water in a spray bottle.

PAINTING

To effectively remove paint fumes and after smell, add one 15 ml bottle of oil to any 5 gallon bucket of paint. The Purify blend and citrus single oils have been favorites, while Citrus Bliss and Elevation would work just as well. Either a paint sprayer or brush and roller may be used to apply the paint after mixing the oils into the paint by stirring vigorously. Oils may eventually rise to the top if using a water-based paint. Occasional stirring may be necessary to keep the oils mixed.

SINGLE ESSENTIAL OILS

SINGLE ESSENTIAL OILS

This section provides concise information about many of the pure essential oils that are available for use by the general public. The listings of possible uses are meant for external application unless otherwise directed. The included safety data is also based on the external use of the oils and may differ from other published information that is based on oral application.

Since pure essential oils are powerful healing agents, please remember to check the safety data before using an oil. Because there are several different oils that can help the same health condition, it should not be difficult to find one that will work for any particular situation.

BASIL ✆⚕❶

(Ocimum basilicum CT linalol)

Botanical Family: Lamiaceae or Labiatae (mint)

Extraction Method: Steam distillation of leaves, stems, and flowers

Chemical Constituents: Alcohols (up to 65%): linalol (>55%), fenchol (>10%), cis-3-hexenol; Phenolic Ethers: methyl chavicol (or estragole—up to 47%), methyl eugenol; Oxides (up to 6%): 1,8 cineol; Esters (<7%); Monoterpenes (<2%) α & β-pinenes.

Properties: Antibacterial[1], anti-infectious, anti-inflammatory, antioxidant[2], antispasmodic (powerful), antiviral, decongestant (veins, arteries of the lungs, prostate), diuretic, disinfectant (urinary/pulmonary), stimulant (nerves, adrenal cortex), and uplifting. Basil is also anticatarrhal, antidepressant, energizing, and restorative.

Common Primary Uses*: ✆Amenorrhea, ✆Autism, ✆Bee/Hornet Stings, ✆Bites/Stings, ✆⚕Bronchitis[3], ✆Bursitis, ✆Carpal Tunnel Syndrome, ✆⚕Chronic Fatigue, ✆⚕Cramps (Abdominal), ✆Cuts, ✆Earache, ✆Frozen Shoulder, ✆Greasy/Oily Hair, ✆Healing, ✆Hiatal Hernia, ✆Incisional Hernia, ✆Induce Sweating, ✆⚕Infertility, ✆Lactation (Increase Milk Production), ⚕✆Mental Fatigue, ✆⚕Migraines, ✆Mouth Ulcers, ✆Muscle Spasms, ✆Muscular Dystrophy, ⚕✆Olfactory Loss (Sense of Smell), ✆⚕Ovarian Cyst, ✆Schmidt's Syndrome, ✆Snake Bites, ✆Spider Bites, ✆Transition (Labor), ✆⚕Viral Hepatitis, ✆Wounds

Historical Uses: Basil was used anciently for respiratory problems, digestive and kidney ailments, epilepsy, poisonous insect or snake bites, fevers, epidemics, and malaria.

French Medicinal Uses: Migraines (especially from liver and gallbladder problems), mental fatigue, menstrual periods (scanty).

Other Possible Uses: This oil may be used for alertness, anxiety, chills, chronic colds, concentration, nervous depression, digestion, fainting, headaches, hiccups, insect bites (soothing), insect repellent[4], insomnia (from nervous tension), intestinal problems, poor memory, chronic mucus, prostate problems, rhinitis (inflammation of nasal mucus membranes), vomiting, wasp stings, and whooping cough.

Body System(s) Affected: Cardiovascular System, Muscles and Bones.

Aromatic Influence: Helps one maintain an open mind and increases clarity of thought.

Application: Can be applied neat (with no dilution) when used topically. Apply to temples, tip of nose, reflex points, and/or directly on area of concern; diffuse. May also be added to food or water as a dietary supplement.

Oral Use As Dietary Supplement: Generally recognized as safe (GRAS) for human consump-

---

1 Basil oil was found to strongly inhibit several multi-drug resistant bacteria (Opalchenova et al., 2003).

2 Basil and its component, linalol, were found to reduce spontaneous mutagenesis in bacteria cells (Berić et al., 2008).

3 In patients with chronic bronchitis, rosemary, basil, fir, and eucalyptus oils were found to demonstrate an antioxidant effect (Siurin, 1997).

4 Two basil oils (*Ocimum basilicum* and *O. gratissimum*) were found to be insecticidal against the cowpea weevil (an agricultural pest) beetle and eggs in both a diffused and aromatized powder form (Kéita et al., 2001).

---

*See Personal Usage Guide section for more details on these primary uses.   ✆=Neat, ✆=Dilute for Children/Sensitive Skin, ✆=Dilute

tion by the FDA (21CFR182.20). Dilute one drop oil in 1 tsp. honey or in 4 oz. of beverage (i.e. soy/rice milk). Not for children under 6-years-old; use with caution and in greater dilution for children 6-years-old and over.

Safety Data: Avoid during pregnancy. Not for use by people with epilepsy. It may also irritate sensitive skin (test a small area first).

Blend Classification: Enhancer and Equalizer.

Blends With: Bergamot, cypress, white fir, geranium, helichrysum, lavender, lemongrass, marjoram, peppermint, and wintergreen.

Odor: Type: Top to Middle Notes (20-80% of the blend); Scent: Herbaceous, spicy, anise-like, camphorous, lively; Intensity: 4.

BERGAMOT ⊤**ⒶⒾ
(Citrus bergamia)

Botanical Family: Rutaceae (citrus)

Extraction Method: Solvent extraction or vacuum distilled; pressed from rind or peel; rectified and void of terpenes

Chemical Constituents: Monoterpenes: d-Limonene (>30%), γ-terpinene, α & β-pinenes; Esters: linalyl acetate (usually around 20%); Alcohols: linalol, geraniol, nerol, α-terpineol; Sesquiterpenes: β-caryophyllene, β-bisabolene; Furanocoumarins; Aldehydes.

Properties: Analgesic, antibacterial (strep and staph infection), anti-infectious, anti-inflammatory, antiparasitic, antiseptic, antispasmodic, digestive, neuroprotective[5], sedative, and uplifting.

Common Primary Uses*: ⒶⓉAgitation (Calms), ⒶⓉBrain Injury, ⓉColic, ⒶⓉDepression, ⒶⓉEmotional Stress, ⒶⓉEnvironmental Stress, ⓉⒶInfection, ⒶⓉMental Stress, ⒶⓉPerformance Stress, ⒶPhysical Energy, ⒶⓉPhysi-

cal Stress, ⓉⒶPMS, ⓉRheumatoid Arthritis, ⒶⓉSedative, ⒶⓉStress

Historical Uses: Bergamot was used by the Italians to cool and relieve fevers, protect against malaria, and expel intestinal worms.

French Medicinal Uses: Agitation, appetite (loss of), colic, depression, indigestion, infection, inflammation, insect repellent, insomnia, intestinal parasites, rheumatism, stress, and vaginal candida.

Other Possible Uses: This oil may help acne, anxiety, appetite regulation, boils, bronchitis, carbuncles, cold sores, oily complexion, coughs, cystitis, digestion, eczema, emotions, endocrine system, fever, gallstones, gonorrhea, infectious disease, insect bites, soothe lungs, psoriasis, respiratory infection, scabies, sore throat, nervous tension, thrush, acute tonsillitis, ulcers, urinary tract infection, spot varicose veins, and wounds.

Body System(s) Affected: Digestive System, Emotional Balance, Skin.

Aromatic Influence: It may help to relieve anxiety, depression, stress, and tension. It is uplifting and refreshing.

Application: Can be applied neat (with no dilution) when used topically. Apply to forehead, temples, reflex points, and/or directly on area of concern; diffuse. May also be applied as a deodorant or added to food or water as a dietary supplement.

Oral Use As Dietary Supplement: Generally recognized as safe (GRAS) for human consumption by the FDA (21CFR182.20). Dilute one drop oil in 1 tsp. honey or in 4 oz. of beverage (i.e. soy/rice milk). Not for children under 6-years-old; use with caution and in greater dilution for children 6-years-old and over.

Safety Data: Repeated use can result in extreme contact sensitization. Avoid direct sunlight or ultraviolet light for up to 72 hours after use.

Blend Classification: Equalizer, Modifier, and Enhancer.

Blends With: Cypress, eucalyptus, geranium, lavender, lemon, and ylang ylang.

Odor: Type: Top Note (5-20% of the blend); Scent: Sweet, lively, citrusy, fruity; Intensity: 2.

---

5 Bergamot essential oil demonstrated neuroprotective effects against brain injury in rats with induced cerebral ischemia (Amantea et al., 2009).

⊤=Topical, Ⓐ=Aromatic, Ⓘ=Internal

Single Oils

BIRCH ⓣⒶ
(Betula lenta)

Botanical Family: Betulaceae

Extraction Method: Steam distillation from wood

Chemical Constituents: Esters (99%): methyl salicylate; betulene, betulinol.

Properties: Analgesic, anti-inflammatory, anti-rheumatic, antiseptic[1], antispasmodic, disinfectant, diuretic, stimulant (bone, liver), and warming.

Common Primary Uses*: ⓣCartilage Injury, ⓣMuscle Aches, ⓣMuscle Development, ⓣMuscle Tone, ⓣWhiplash

Historical Uses: Birch oil has a strong, penetrating aroma that most people recognize as wintergreen. Although birch (*Betula lenta*) is completely unrelated to wintergreen (*Gaultheria procumbens*), the two oils are almost identical in chemical constituents. The American Indians and early European settlers enjoyed a tea that was flavored with birch bark or wintergreen. According to Julia Lawless, "this has been translated into a preference for 'root beer' flavourings [*sic*]." A synthetic methyl salicylate is now widely used as a flavoring agent, especially in root beer, chewing gum, toothpaste, etc.

French Medicinal Uses: Rheumatism, muscular pain, cramps, arthritis, tendonitis, hypertension, inflammation.

Other Possible Uses: This oil may be beneficial for acne, bladder infection, cystitis, dropsy, eczema, edema, reducing fever, gallstones, gout, infection, reducing discomfort in joints, kidney stones, draining and cleansing the lymphatic system, obesity, osteoporosis, skin diseases, ulcers, and urinary tract disorders. It

is known for its ability to alleviate bone pain. It has a cortisone-like action due to the high content of methyl salicylate.

Body System(s) Affected: Muscles and Bones.

Aromatic Influence: It influences, elevates, opens, and increases awareness in the sensory system (senses or sensations).

Application: Can be applied neat (with no dilution), or dilute 1:1 (1 drop essential oil to 1 drop carrier oil) for children and for those with sensitive skin when using topically. Apply to reflex points and/or directly on area of concern. Apply topically on location, and use only small amounts (dilute with fractionated coconut oil for application on larger areas).

Oral Use as a Dietary Supplement: None.

Safety Data: Avoid during pregnancy. Not for use by people with epilepsy. Some people are very allergic to methyl salicylate. Test a small area of skin first.

Blend Classification: Personifier and Enhancer.

Blends With: Basil, bergamot, cypress, geranium, lavender, lemongrass, marjoram, and peppermint.

BLACK PEPPER ⓣⒶⓘ
(Piper nigrum)

Botanical Family: Piperaceae

Extraction Method: Steam distilled from berries

Chemical Constituents: Monoterpenes (up to 70%): l-limonene (<15%), δ-3-carene (<15%), β-pinene (<14%), sabinene (<10%), α-phellandrene (<9%), α-pinene (<9%), α-thujene (<4%), γ- & α-terpinene (<7%), p-cymene (<3%), myrcene (<3%), terpinolene (<2%); Sesquiterpenes (up to 60%): β-caryophyllene (up to 35%), β-selinene (<8%), β-bisabolene (<5%), α-, β-, & δ-elemenes, β-farnesene, humulene, α-copaene, α-guaiene, α- & β-cubebenes;

---

1   Subjects using a mouthwash containing thymol, menthol, methyl salicylate, and eucalyptol for 6 months were found to not have any oral bacteria that developed a resistance to the oils (Charles et al., 2000).

*See Personal Usage Guide section for more details on these primary uses.   ⓣ=Neat, ⓣ=Dilute for Children/Sensitive Skin, ⓣ=Dilute

Oxides: caryophyllene oxide (<8%); Ketones (<2%): acetophenone, hydrocarvone, piperitone; Aldehydes: piperonal; Carboxylic Acids: piperonylic acid; Furanocoumarin: α-bergamotene.

Properties: Analgesic, anticatarrhal, anti-inflammatory, antiseptic, antispasmodic, antitoxic, aphrodisiac, expectorant, laxative, rubefacient, and stimulant[2] (nervous, circulatory, digestive).

Common Primary Uses*: ♠Addictions (Tobacco)[3]

Historical Uses: Pepper has been used for thousands of years for malaria, cholera, and several digestive problems.

Other Possible Uses: This oil may increase cellular oxygenation[2], support digestive glands, stimulate the endocrine system, increase energy, and help rheumatoid arthritis. It may also help with loss of appetite, catarrh, chills, cholera, colds, colic, constipation, coughs, diarrhea, dysentery, dyspepsia, dysuria, flatulence (combine with fennel), flu, heartburn, influenza, nausea, neuralgia, poor circulation, poor muscle tone, quinsy, sprains, toothache, vertigo, viruses, and vomiting.

Body System(s) Affected: Digestive and Nervous Systems.

Aromatic Influence: Pepper is comforting and stimulating.

Application: Apply to reflex points and/or directly on area of concern; diffuse. Mix very sparingly with juniper and lavender in a bath to help with chills or to warm one up in the winter.

Oral Use As Dietary Supplement: Generally regarded as safe (GRAS) for human consumption by the FDA. Dilute one drop oil in 1 tsp. honey or in 4 oz. of beverage (i.e. soy/rice milk). Not for children under 6-years-old; use with caution and in greater dilution for children 6-years-old and over.

Safety Data: Can cause extreme skin irritation.

Odor: Type: Middle Note (50-80% of the blend); Scent: Spicy, peppery, musky, warm, with herbaceous undertones; Intensity: 3.

---

2 Inhalation of black pepper oil was found to increase cerebral blood flow and to improve the swallowing reflex in elderly patients who had suffered a stroke (Ebihara et al., 2006).
3 Inhaled vapor of black pepper oil was found to reduce cravings for cigarettes and symptoms of anxiety in smokers deprived from smoking, compared to a control (Rose et al., 1994).

CASSIA ⊤🅰①
(Cinnamomum cassia)

Botanical Family: Lauraceae (laurel)

Extraction Method: Steam distillation from bark

Chemical Constituents: Aldehydes: trans-cinnamaldehyde (up to 85%), benzaldehyde; Phenols (>7%): eugenol, chavicol, phenol, 2-vinylphenol; Esters: cinnamyl acetate, benzyl acetate.

Properties: Antibacterial, antifungal, and antiviral.

Historical Uses: Has been used extensively as a domestic spice. Medicinally, it has been used for colds, colic, flatulent dyspepsia, diarrhea, nausea, rheumatism, and kidney and reproductive complaints.

Other Possible Uses: This oil can be extremely sensitizing to the dermal tissues. Can provide some powerful support to blends when used in very small quantities.

Application: Dilute 1:4 (1 drop essential oil to 4 drops carrier oil) for topical use. Apply to forehead, muscles, reflex points, and/or directly on area of concern.

Oral Use As Dietary Supplement: Generally recognized as safe (GRAS) for human consumption by the FDA (21CFR182.20). Dilute one drop oil in 2 tsp. honey or in 8 oz. of beverage (i.e. soy/rice milk). May need to increase dilution even more due to this oil's potential for irritating mucus membranes. Not for children under 6-years-old; use with caution and in greater dilution for children 6-years-old and over.

Safety Data: Repeated use can result in extreme contact sensitization. Avoid during pregnancy. Can cause extreme skin irritation. Diffuse with caution; it will irritate the nasal membranes if it is inhaled directly from the diffuser.

Blend Classification: Personifier and Enhancer.

Odor: Type: Middle Note (50-80% of the blend); Scent: Spicy, warm, sweet; Intensity: 5.

⊤=Topical, 🅰=Aromatic, ①=Internal

CHAMOMILE, ROMAN (SEE ROMAN CHAMOMILE)

CILANTRO ⓉⒶⒾ
(Coriandrum sativum L.)

Botanical Family: Umbelliferae (parsley)

Extraction Method: Steam distillation from leaves (same plant as coriander oil, which is distilled from the seeds)

Chemical Constituents: Aldehydes (40-50%): tetradecanal, 2-dodecenal, 13-tetradecenal, dodecanal, decanal; Alcohols (up to 40%): cyclododecanol, 1-decanol, 1-dodecanol, 1-undecanol; Phenols: eugenol; Ketones: β-ionone.

Properties: Antibacterial.

Historical Uses: Cilantro leaves have been used since the times of ancient Greece as an herb for flavoring. Its aroma has also been used for anxiety and insomnia.

Other Possible Uses: Mainly used as a flavoring in cooking.

Application: Can be applied neat (with no dilution) when used topically. Apply to reflex points and directly on area of concern; diffuse.

Oral Use As Dietary Supplement: Generally recognized as safe (GRAS) for human consumption by the FDA (21CFR182.20). Dilute one drop oil in 1 tsp. honey or in 4 oz. of beverage (i.e. soy/rice milk). Not for children under 6-years-old; use with caution and in greater dilution for children 6-years-old and over.

Safety Data: May cause irritation on sensitive or damaged skin.

Odor: Scent: Herbaceous, citrusy, fresh.

CINNAMON ⓉⒶⒾ
(Cinnamomum zeylanicum)

Botanical Family: Lauraceae (laurel)

Extraction Method: Steam distillation from bark

Chemical Constituents: Aldehydes: trans-cinnamaldehyde (<50%), hydroxycinnamaldehyde, benzaldehyde, cuminal; Phenols (up to 30%): eugenol (<30%), phenol, 2-vinylphenol; Alcohols: linalol, cinnamic alcohol, benzyl alcohol, α-terpineol, borneol; Sesquiterpenes: β-caryophyllene; Carboxylic Acids: cinnamic acid.

Properties: Antibacterial[1,2,3,4], antidepressant, antifungal[5,6,7], anti-infectious (intestinal, urinary), anti-inflammatory, antimicrobial, antioxidant, antiparasitic, antiseptic, antispasmodic (light), antiviral, astringent, immune stimulant, purifier, sexual stimulant, and warming. It also enhances the action and activity of other oils.

Common Primary Uses*: ⒶAirborne Bacteria, ⓉⒶBacterial Infections, ⓉBites/Stings, ⒶⓉBreathing, ⓉⓉDiabetes[8,9], ⓉDiverticulitis, ⓉⒶFungal Infections, ⓉⒶGeneral Tonic, ⒶImmune System (Stimulates), ⓉⒶInfection, ⒶⓉLibido (Low), ⒶⓉMold, ⓉⒶPancreas Support, ⒶPhysical Fatigue, ⒶPneumonia, ⓉⒶTyphoid, ⓉVaginal Infection, ⓉVaginitis, ⓉViral Infections, ⓉWarming (Body)

1 Cinnamon, thyme, and clove essential oils demonstrated an antibacterial effect on several respiratory tract pathogens (Fabio et al., 2007).
2 Cinnamon oil exhibited strong antimicrobial activity against two detrimental oral bacteria. (Filoche et al., 2005).
3 Cinnamon bark, lemongrass, and thyme oils were found to have the highest level of activity against common respiratory pathogens among 14 essential oils tested (Inouye et al., 2001).
4 Bay, cinnamon, and clove oils reduced production of alpha-toxin and enterotoxin A by *Staphylococcus aureus* bacteria (Smith-Palmer et al., 2004).
5 In a test of nine oils, clove, followed by cinnamon, oregano, and mace oils, was found to be inhibitory to two toxin-producing fungi (Juglal et al., 2002).
6 Cinnamon, thyme, oregano, and cumin oils inhibited the production of aflatoxin by aspergillus fungus (Tantaoui-Elaraki et al., 1994).
7 Vapor of cinnamon bark oil and cinnamic aldehyde was found to be effective against fungi involved in respiratory tract mycoses (fungal infections) (Singh et al., 1995).
8 Cinnamaldehyde (found in cinnamon oil) was found to significantly reduce blood glucose levels in diabetic wistar rats (Subash et al., 2007).
9 Oral administration of cinnamon oil was found to significantly reduce blood glucose levels in diabetic KK-Ay mice (Ping et al., 2010).

*See Personal Usage Guide section for more details on these primary uses.   Ⓣ=Neat, Ⓣ=Dilute for Children/Sensitive Skin, Ⓣ=Dilute

Historical Uses: This most ancient of spices was included in just about every prescription issued in ancient China. It was regarded as a tranquilizer, tonic, and stomachic and as being good for depression and a weak heart.

French Medicinal Uses: Sexual stimulant, tropical infection, typhoid, vaginitis.

Other Possible Uses: This oil may be beneficial for circulation, colds, coughs, digestion, exhaustion, flu, infections, rheumatism, and warts. This oil fights viral and infectious diseases, and testing has yet to find a virus, bacteria, or fungus that can survive in its presence.

Body System(s) Affected: Immune System.

Application: Dilute 1:3 (1 drop essential oil to 3 drops carrier oil) before using topically. Apply to reflex points and directly on area of concern.

Oral Use As Dietary Supplement: Generally recognized as safe (GRAS) for human consumption by the FDA (21CFR182.20). Dilute one drop oil in 2 tsp. honey or in 8 oz. of beverage (i.e. soy/rice milk). May need to increase dilution even more due to this oil's potential for irritating mucus membranes. Not for children under 6-years-old; use with caution and in greater dilution for children 6-years-old and over.

Safety Data: Repeated use can result in extreme contact sensitization. Avoid during pregnancy. Can cause extreme skin irritation. Diffuse with caution; it will irritate the nasal membranes if it is inhaled directly from the diffuser. Use extreme caution when diffusing cinnamon bark because it may burn the nostrils if you put your nose directly next to the nebulizer of the diffuser.

Blend Classification: Personifier.

Blends With: All citrus oils, cypress, frankincense, geranium, lavender, rosemary, and all spice oils.

Odor: Type: Base Note (5-60% of the blend); Scent: Spicy, warm, sweet; Intensity: 5.

CLARY SAGE ⊤Ⓐ①
(Salvia sclarea)

Botanical Family: Labiatae (mint)

Extraction Method: Steam distillation from flowing plant

Chemical Constituents: Esters (up to 75%): linalyl acetate (20-75%); Alcohols (20%): linalol (10-20%), geraniol, α-terpineol; Sesquiterpenes (<14%): germacrene-D (up to 12%), β-caryophyllene; Diterpene alcohols: sclareol (1-7%); Monoterpenes: myrcene, α- and β-pinenes, l-limonene, ocimene, terpinolene; Oxides: 1,8 cineol, linalol oxide, sclareol oxide; Ketones: α- and β-thujone; Sesquiterpene alcohols; Aldehydes; Coumarins. (More than 250 constituents.)

Properties: Anticonvulsant, antifungal, antiseptic, antispasmodic, astringent, nerve tonic, sedative, soothing[10], tonic, and warming.

Common Primary Uses*: ⊤ⒶAneurysm, ⊤Breast Enlargement, ⊤Cholesterol, ⊤Convulsions, ⊤Cramps (Abdominal), ⊤Dysmenorrhea, Ⓐ⊤Emotional Stress, ⊤Endometriosis, ⊤Epilepsy, ⊤Estrogen Balance, Ⓐ⊤Frigidity, ⊤Hair (Fragile), ⊤ⒶHormonal Balance, ⊤Hot Flashes, ⊤ⒶImpotence, ⊤ⒶInfection, ⊤ⒶInfertility, Ⓐ⊤Insomnia (Older Children), ⊤Lactation (Start Milk Production), ⒶMood Swings, ⊤Muscle Fatigue, ⊤Parkinson's Disease, ⊤ⒶPMS, Ⓐ⊤Postpartum Depression, ⊤Premenopause, ⊤Seizure

Historical Uses: Nicknamed "clear eyes," it was famous during the Middle Ages for its ability to clear eye problems. During that same time, it was widely used for female complaints, kidney/digestive/skin disorders, inflammation, sore throats, and wounds.

---

10 Nurses working in an ICU setting demonstrated decreased perception of stress when receiving a topical application of *Lavandula angustifolia* and *Salvia sclarea* essential oils (Pemberton et al., 2008).

⊤=Topical, Ⓐ=Aromatic, ①=Internal

French Medicinal Uses: Bronchitis, cholesterol, frigidity, genitalia, hemorrhoids, hormonal imbalance, impotence, infections, intestinal cramps, menstrual cramps, PMS, premenopause, weak digestion.

Other Possible Uses: This oil may be used for amenorrhea, cell regulation, circulatory problems, depression, insect bites, kidney disorders, dry skin, throat infection, ulcers, and whooping cough.

Body System(s) Affected: Hormonal System.

Application: Can be applied neat (with no dilution) when used topically. Apply to reflex points and/or directly on area of concern; diffuse.

Oral Use As Dietary Supplement: Generally recognized as safe (GRAS) for human consumption by the FDA (21CFR182.20). Dilute one drop oil in 1 tsp. honey or in 4 oz. of beverage (i.e. soy/rice milk). Not for children under 6-years-old; use with caution and in greater dilution for children 6-years-old and over.

Safety Data: Use with caution during pregnancy. Not for babies. Avoid during and after consumption of alcohol.

Blend Classification: Personifier.

Blends With: Bergamot, citrus oils, cypress, geranium, and sandalwood.

Odor: Type: Middle to Base Notes (5-60% of the blend); Scent: Herbaceous, spicy, hay-like, sharp, fixative; Intensity: 3.

CLOVE ❶❷❸
(Eugenia caryophyllata)

Botanical Family: Myrtaceae (shrubs and trees)

Extraction Method: Steam distillation from bud and stem

Chemical Constituents: Phenols: eugenol (up to 85%), chavicol, 4-allylphenol; Esters: eugenyl acetate (up to 15%), styrallyl, benzyl, terpenyl,

ethyl phenyl acetates, methyl salicylate (tr.); Sesquiterpenes (up to 14%): β-caryophyllene (<12%), humulene, α-amorphene, α-muurolene, calamenene; Oxides (<3%): caryophyllene oxide, humulene oxide; Carboxylic Acids; Ketones.

Properties: Analgesic, antibacterial[1,2], antifungal[3,4], anti-infectious, anti-inflammatory[5], antiparasitic, strong antiseptic, antitumor, antiviral[6], disinfectant, antioxidant, and immune stimulant.

Common Primary Uses*: ❶Addictions (Tobacco), ❶Antioxidant, ❶❷Blood Clots[7], ❶❷Candida, ❶Cataracts, ❶Corns, ❷Disinfectant, ❶Fever, ❶❷Fungal Infections, ❶Herpes Simplex, ❶Hodgkin's Disease, ❷Hormonal Balance, ❶❷Hypothyroidism, ❶❷Liver Cleansing, ❶Lupus, ❶Macular Degeneration, ❷❶Memory, ❷Metabolism Balance, ❷❶Mold, ❶Muscle Aches, ❶Muscle Pain, ❶Osteoporosis, ❶❷Plague, ❶Rheumatoid Arthritis, ❷❶Termites, ❶❷Thyroid Dysfunction, ❶Toothache (Pain), ❶❷Tumor (Lipoma), ❶❷Viral Infections, ❶Warts, ❶Wounds

Historical Uses: Cloves were historically used for skin infections, digestive upsets, intestinal parasites, childbirth, and most notably for toothache. The Chinese also used cloves for diarrhea, hernia, bad breath, and bronchitis.

French Medicinal Uses: Impotence, intestinal parasites, memory deficiency, pain, plague, toothache, wounds (infected).

Other Possible Uses: Clove is valuable as a drawing salve—it helps pull infection from tissues. It may also help amebic dysentery, arthritis, bacterial colitis, bones, bronchitis, cholera, cystitis, dental infection, diarrhea, infectious acne, fatigue, flatulence (gas), flu, halitosis (bad breath), tension headaches, hypertension, infection (wounds and more), insect

1 Cinnamon, thyme, and clove essential oils demonstrated an antibacterial effect on several respiratory tract pathogens (Fabio et al., 2007).
2 Bay, cinnamon, and clove oils reduced production of alpha-toxin and enterotoxin A by *Staphylococcus aureus* bacteria (Smith-Palmer et al., 2004).
3 Clove oil was found to have very strong radical scavenging activity (antioxidant). It was also found to display an antifungal effect against tested *Candida* strains (Chaieb et al., 2007).
4 Eugenol from clove and thymol from thyme were found to inhibit the growth of *Aspergillus flavus* and *Aspergillus versicolor* at concentrations of .4mg/ml or less. (Hitokoto et al., 1980).
5 Eugenol (found in clove EO) was found to increase the anti-inflammatory activity of cod liver oil (lowered inflammation by 30%) (Reddy et al., 1994).
6 Eugenol was found to be virucidal to *Herpes simplex* and to delay the development of herpes-induced keratitis (inflammation of the cornea) in mice (Benencia et al., 2000).
7 Clove oil demonstrated an ability to prevent the aggregation of platelets that can lead to blood clots and thrombosis both in vivo and in vitro (Saeed et al., 1994).

See Personal Usage Guide section for more details on these primary uses.

❶=Neat, ❷=Dilute for Children/Sensitive Skin, ❶=Dilute

bites and stings, insect control (insecticidal)[8,9], nausea, neuritis, nettles and poison oak (takes out sting), rheumatism, sinusitis, skin cancer, chronic skin disease, smoking (removes desire), sores (speeds healing of mouth and skin sores), tuberculosis, leg ulcers, viral hepatitis, and vomiting.

Body System(s) Affected: Cardiovascular, Digestive, Immune, and Respiratory Systems.

Aromatic Influence: It may influence healing, improve memory (mental stimulant), and create a feeling of protection and courage.

Application: Dilute 1:1 (1 drop essential oil to 1 drop carrier oil) before topical use. Apply to reflex points and/or directly on area of concern. Rub directly on the gums surrounding an infected tooth. Place on tongue with finger to remove desire to smoke, or place on back of tongue to fight against tickling cough. Diffuse.

Oral Use As Dietary Supplement: Generally recognized as safe (GRAS) for human consumption by the FDA (21CFR182.20). Dilute one drop oil in 1 tsp. honey or in 4 oz. of beverage (i.e. soy/rice milk). Not for children under 6-years-old; use with caution and in greater dilution for children 6-years-old and over.

Safety Data: Repeated use can result in extreme contact sensitization. Use with caution during pregnancy. Can irritate sensitive skin.

Blend Classification: Personifier.

Blends With: Basil, bergamot, cinnamon, clary sage, grapefruit, lavender, lemon, orange, peppermint, rose, rosemary, and ylang ylang.

Odor: Type: Middle to Base Notes (20-80% of the blend); Scent: Spicy, warming, slightly bitter, woody, reminiscent of true clove buds but richer; Intensity: 5.

CORIANDER 🅣🅐🅘
(Coriandrum sativum L.)

Botanical Family: Umbelliferae (parsley)

Extraction Method: Steam distillation from seeds

Chemical Constituents: Alcohols (up to 80%): linalol (>30%), coriandrol (<30%), geraniol, terpinen-4-ol, borneol; Monoterpenes (up to 24%): α-pinene, γ-terpinene, l-limonene, p-cymene, myrcene, camphene; Esters: geranyl acetate, linalyl acetate; Ketones: camphor, carvone; Aldehydes: decanal.

Properties: Analgesic, antibacterial, antifungal, antioxidant, antirheumatic, antispasmodic[10], and stimulant (cardiac, circulatory, and nervous systems). It also has anti-inflammatory and sedative properties.

Common Primary Uses*: 🅣Cartilage Injury, 🅣Muscle Aches, 🅣Muscle Development, 🅣Muscle Tone, 🅣Whiplash

Historical Uses: The Chinese have used coriander for dysentery, piles, measles, nausea, toothache, and painful hernias.

Other Possible Uses: Coriander may help with anorexia, arthritis, colds, colic, diarrhea, digestive spasms, dyspepsia, flatulence, flu, gout, infections (general), measles, migraine, nausea, nervous exhaustion, neuralgia, piles, poor circulation, rheumatism, skin (oily skin, blackheads, and other impurities), and stiffness. It may also help during convalescence and after a difficult childbirth. It may regulate and help control pain related to menstruation.

Body System(s) Affected: Digestive and Hormonal Systems.

Aromatic Influence: Coriander is a gentle stimulant for those with low physical energy. It also helps one relax during times of stress, irritability, and nervousness. It may also provide

8 A blend of eugenol, alpha-terpineol, and cinnamic alcohol was found to be insecticidal against American cockroaches, carpenter ants, and German cockroaches (Enan, 2001).

9 Clove oil was found to be highly termiticidal (Zhu et al., 2001).

10 Linalol, found in several essential oils, was found to inhibit induced convulsions in rats by directly interacting with the NMDA receptor complex (Brum et al., 2001).

🅣=Topical, 🅐=Aromatic, 🅘=Internal

a calming influence to those suffering from shock or fear.

Application: Can be applied neat (with no dilution) when used topically. Apply to reflex points and directly on area of concern; diffuse.

Oral Use As Dietary Supplement: Generally recognized as safe (GRAS) for human consumption by the FDA (21CFR182.20). Dilute one drop oil in 1 tsp. honey or in 4 oz. of beverage (i.e. soy/rice milk). Not for children under 6-years-old; use with caution and in greater dilution for children 6-years-old and over.

Safety Data: Use sparingly, as coriander can be stupefying in large doses.

Blend Classification: Personifier and Modifier.

Blends With: Bergamot, cinnamon, clary sage, cypress, ginger, sandalwood, and other spice oils.

Odor: Type: Middle Note (50-80% of the blend); Scent: Woody, spicy, sweet; Intensity: 3.

CYPRESS ⓣⓐ
(Cupressus sempervirens)

Botanical Family: Cupressaceae (conifer: cypress)

Extraction Method: Steam distillation from branches

Chemical Constituents: Monoterpenes: α-pinene (>55%), δ-3-carene (<22%), l-limonene, terpinolene, sabinene, β-pinene; Sesquiterpene Alcohols: cedrol (up to 15%), cadinol; Alcohols: borneol (<9%), α-terpineol, terpinene-4-ol, linalol sabinol; Esters: α-terpinyl acetate (<5%), isovalerate, terpinen-4-yl acetate; Sesquiterpenes: δ-cadinene, α-cedrene; Diterpene Alcohols; labdanic alcohols, manool, sempervirol; Diterpene Acids; Oxides.

Properties: Antibacterial, anti-infectious, antimicrobial, mucolytic, antiseptic, astringent, deodorant, diuretic, lymphatic and prostate decongestant, refreshing, relaxing, and vasoconstricting.

Common Primary Uses*: ⓣⓐAneurysm, ⓣBone Spurs, ⓣBunions, ⓣBursitis, ⓣCarpal Tunnel Syndrome, ⓣⓐCatarrh, ⓣⓐCirculation, ⓣConcussion, ⓣDysmenorrhea, ⓣEdema, ⓣEndometriosis, ⓐⓣEnvironmental Stress, ⓣⓐFlu (Influenza), ⓣGreasy/Oily Hair, ⓣHemorrhoids, ⓣHernia (Hiatal), ⓣIncontinence, ⓣLou Gehrig's Disease, ⓐⓣLymphatic Decongestant, ⓣMenopause, ⓣMenorrhagia, ⓣMuscle Fatigue, ⓣMuscle Tone, ⓣPain (Chronic), ⓐⓣPleurisy, ⓣⓐPreeclampsia, ⓣProstatitis, ⓣⓐRaynaud's Disease, ⓣRetina (Strengthen), ⓣRheumatoid Arthritis, ⓣSkin (Revitalizing), ⓐⓣStroke, ⓣSwollen Eyes, ⓣⓐToxemia, ⓐⓣTuberculosis, ⓣVaricose Veins

Historical Uses: It was used anciently for its benefits on the urinary system and in instances where there is excessive loss of fluids, such as perspiration, diarrhea, and menstrual flow. The Chinese valued cypress for its benefits to the liver and to the respiratory system.

French Medicinal Uses: Arthritis, bronchitis, circulation, cramps, hemorrhoids, insomnia, intestinal parasites, lymphatic decongestant, menopausal problems, menstrual pain, pancreas insufficiencies, pleurisy, prostate decongestation, pulmonary tuberculosis, rheumatism, spasms, throat problems, varicose veins, water retention.

Other Possible Uses: This oil may be beneficial for asthma, strengthening blood capillary walls, reducing cellulite, improving the circulatory system, colds, strengthening connective tissue, spasmodic coughs, diarrhea, energy, fever, gallbladder, bleeding gums, hemorrhaging, influenza, laryngitis, liver disorders, lung circulation, muscular cramps, nervous tension, nose bleeds, ovarian cysts, increasing perspiration, skin care, scar tissue, whooping cough, and wounds.

Body System(s) Affected: Cardiovascular System, Muscles and Bones.

Aromatic Influence: It influences and strengthens and helps ease the feeling of loss. It creates a feeling of security and grounding.

Application: Can be applied neat (with no dilution) when used topically. Apply to reflex points and directly on area of concern; diffuse.

Oral Use As Dietary Supplement: None.

---

*See Personal Usage Guide section for more details on these primary uses.   ⓣ=Neat, ⓣ=Dilute for Children/Sensitive Skin, ⓣ=Dilute

Safety Data: Use with caution during pregnancy.

Blend Classification: Equalizer.

Blends With: Bergamot, clary sage, lavender, lemon, orange, and sandalwood.

Odor: Type: Middle Note (50-80% of the blend); Scent: Fresh, herbaceous, slightly woody with evergreen undertones; Intensity: 3.

EUCALYPTUS ⓣⒶ
(Eucalyptus radiata)

Botanical Family: Myrtaceae (Myrtle shrubs and trees)

Extraction Method: Steam distillation from leaves

Chemical Constituents: Oxides: 1,8 cineol (62-72%), caryophyllene oxide; Monoterpenes (up to 24%): α- & β-pinenes (<12%), l-limonene (<8%), myrcene, p-cymene; Alcohols (<19%): α-terpineol (14%), geraniol, borneol, linalol; Aldehydes (8%): myrtenal, citronellal, geranial, neral.

Properties: Analgesic[1,2], antibacterial[3], anticatarrhal, anti-infectious, anti-inflammatory[4,5], antiviral[6], insecticidal[7], and expectorant.

Common Primary Uses*: ⓣArterial Vasodilator, ⒶⓣAsthma, ⒶBrain Blood Flow, ⒶⓣBronchitis[8,9], ⓣⒶCongestion, ⓣⒶCooling (Body), ⒶⓣCoughs, ⓣⒶDiabetes, ⒶDisinfectant, ⓣDysentery, ⓣEar Inflammation, ⒶⓣEmphysema, ⒶⓣExpectorant, ⓣFever, ⒶⓣFlu (Influenza), ⓣHypoglycemia, ⓣInflammation, ⓣIris Inflammation, ⓣJet Lag, ⓣKidney Stones, ⓣLice, ⒶⓣMeasles, ⓣNeuralgia, ⓣNeuritis, ⓣOverexercised Muscles, ⓣPain, ⒶⓣPneumonia, ⒶRespiratory Viruses, ⒶⓣRhinitis, ⓣShingles, ⒶⓣSinusitis, ⓣTennis Elbow, ⒶⓣTuberculosis

Other Possible Uses: This oil, when combined with bergamot, has been used effectively on herpes simplex. It may also help with acne, endometriosis, hay fever, high blood pressure[10], nasal mucous membrane inflammation, and vaginitis.

Body System(s) Affected: Respiratory System, Skin.

Application: Can be applied neat (with no dilution), or dilute 1:1 (1 drop essential oil to 1 drop carrier oil) for children and for those with sensitive skin when using topically. Apply to reflex points and/or directly on area of concern; diffuse.

Odor: Type: Middle Note (50-80% of the blend); Scent: Slightly camphorous, sweet, fruity; Intensity: 3.

FENNEL (SWEET) ⓣⒶⒾ
(Foeniculum vulgare)

Botanical Family: Umbelliferae (parsley)

Extraction Method: Steam distillation from the crushed seeds

Chemical Constituents: Phenolic Ethers (up to 80%): trans-anethole (70%), methyl chavi-

1 1,8 cineole (eucalyptol) was found to have antinociceptive (pain-reducing) properties similar to morphine (Liapi et al., 2007).
2 1,8 cineole (eucalyptol) was found to display an anti-inflammatory effect on rats in several tests and was found to exhibit antinociceptive (pain-reducing) effects in mice, possibly by depressing the central nervous system (Santos et al., 2000).
3 Subjects using a mouthwash containing thymol, menthol, methyl salicylate, and eucalyptol for 6 months were found to not have developed oral bacteria that were resistant to the oils (Charles et al., 2000).
4 1,8 cineole (eucalyptol) was found to display an anti-inflammatory effect on rats in several tests and was found to exhibit antinociceptive (pain-reducing) effects in mice, possibly by depressing the central nervous system (Santos et al., 2000).
5 Eucalyptus oil was shown to ameliorate inflammatory processes by interacting with oxygen radicals and interfering with leukocyte activation (Grassmann et al., 2000).
6 Tea tree and eucalyptus oil demonstrated ability to inhibit the *Herpes simplex* virus (Schnitzler et al., 2001).
7 A blend of eugenol, alpha-terpineol, and cinnamic alcohol was found to be insecticidal against American cockroaches, carpenter ants, and German cockroaches (Enean, 2001).
8 Therapy with 1.8 cineole (eucalyptol) in both healthy and bronchitis-afflicted humans was shown to reduce production of LTB4 and PGE2 (both metabolites of arachidonic acid, a known chemical messenger involved in inflammation) in white blood cells (Juergens et al., 1998).
9 In patients with chronic bronchitis, rosemary, basil, fir, and eucalyptus oils were found to demonstrate an antioxidant effect. Lavender was found to promote normalization of lipid levels (Siurin et al., 1997).
10 Treatment of rats with 1,8-cineole (or eucalyptol, found in eucalyptus and rosemary) demonstrated an ability to lower mean aortic pressure (blood pressure), without decreasing heart rate, through vascular wall relaxation (Lahlou et al., 2002).

col (or estragole) (>3%); Monoterpenes (up to 50%): trans-ocimene (<12%), l-limonene (<12%), γ-terpinene (<11%), α- & β-pinenes (<10%), p-cymene, α- & β-phellandrenes, terpiolene, myrcene, sabinene; Alcohols (up to 16%): linalol (<12%), α-fenchol (<4%); Ketones (<15%): fenchone (12%), camphor; Oxides; Phenols.

Properties: Antiparasitic, antiseptic, antispasmodic[1], antitoxic, diuretic, and expectorant.

Common Primary Uses*: ❶Benign Prostatic Hyperplasia, ❶❶❹Blood Clots, ❶Bruises, ❶❶❹Digestive System Support, ❶❶Gastritis, ❶Kidney Stones, ❶Lactation (Increase Milk Production), ❶❶❹Pancreas Support, ❶❶Parasites, ❶Skin (Revitalizing), ❶Tissue (Toxin Cleansing), ❶Wrinkles

Historical Uses: The ancient Egyptians and Romans awarded garlands of fennel as praise to victorious warriors because fennel was believed to bestow strength, courage, and longevity. It has been used for thousands of years for snakebites, to stave off hunger pains, to tone the female reproductive system, for earaches, eye problems, insect bites, kidney complaints, lung infections, and to expel worms.

French Medicinal Uses: Cystitis, sluggish digestion, flatulence, gout, intestinal parasites, intestinal spasms, increase lactation, menopause problems, premenopause, urinary stones, vomiting.

Other Possible Uses: Fennel oil may be used for colic, stimulating the cardiovascular system, constipation, digestion (supports the liver), balancing hormones, nausea, obesity, PMS[2], and stimulating the sympathetic nervous system[3].

Body System(s) Affected: Digestive and Hormonal Systems.

Aromatic Influence: It increases and influences longevity, courage, and purification.

---

[1] Fennel oil was found to reduce contraction frequency and intensity in rat uterus induced to contract (Ostad et al., 2001).

[2] Fennel oil was found to reduce contraction frequency and intensity in rat uterus induced to contract (Ostad et al., 2001).

[3] Inhalation of essential oils such as pepper, estragon, fennel, and grapefruit was found to have a stimulating effect on sympathetic activity in healthy adults (Haze et al., 2002).

Application: Can be applied neat (with no dilution), or dilute 1:1 (1 drop essential oil to 1 drop carrier oil) for children and for those with sensitive skin when using topically. Apply to reflex points and directly on area of concern; diffuse.

Oral Use As Dietary Supplement: Generally recognized as safe (GRAS) for human consumption by the FDA (21CFR182.20). Dilute one drop oil in 1 tsp. honey or in 4 oz. of beverage (i.e. soy/rice milk). Not for children under 6-years-old; use with caution and in greater dilution for children 6-years-old and over.

Safety Data: Repeated use can possibly result in contact sensitization. Use with caution if susceptible to epilepsy. Use with caution during pregnancy.

Blend Classification: Equalizer and Modifier.

Blends With: Basil, geranium, lavender, lemon, rosemary, and sandalwood.

Odor: Type: Top to Middle Notes (20-80% of the blend); Scent: Sweet, somewhat spicy, licorice-like; Intensity: 4.

FIR, WHITE *(SEE WHITE FIR)*

FRANKINCENSE ❶❹❶
(Boswellia frereana)

Botanical Family: Burseraceae (resinous trees and shrubs)

Extraction Method: Steam distillation from gum/resin

Chemical Constituents: Monoterpenes (up to 90%): α- & β-pinenes (43%), α-thujene (<22%), l-limonene (<16%), myrcene (<12%), sabinene (<7%), p-cymene (<5%), α-terpinene, camphene, α-phellandrene; Sesquiterpenes (<10%): β-caryophyllene (<8%), α-gurjunene, α-guaiene; Alcohols (<5%): incensol, borneol, olibanol, trans-pinocarveol, farnesol.

---

*See Personal Usage Guide section for more details on these primary uses.   ❶=Neat, ❶=Dilute for Children/Sensitive Skin, ❶=Dilute

Properties: Anticatarrhal, anticancer[4,5,6,7,8,9,10], antidepressant[11], anti-infectious, anti-inflammatory[12,13,14], antiseptic, antitumor[15], expectorant, immune stimulant[16], and sedative.

Common Primary Uses*: ⓐⓣAlzheimer's Disease, ⓣⓐAneurysm, ⓣⓐArthritis, ⓐⓣAsthma, ⓣⓐBalance, ⓐⓣBrain (Aging), ⓐⓣBrain Injury, ⓐⓣBreathing, ⓐⓞⓣCancer, ⓣComa, ⓐⓣConcussion, ⓐConfusion, ⓐⓣCoughs, ⓐⓣDepression, ⓣFibroids, ⓣGenital Warts, ⓣⓐHepatitis, ⓣⓐImmune System Support, ⓣImprove Vision, ⓣⓐInfected Wounds, ⓣⓐInflammation, ⓣⓐLiver Cirrhosis, ⓣⓐLou Gehrig's Disease, ⓐⓣMemory, ⓐⓣMental Fatigue, ⓣMiscarriage (After), ⓣMoles, ⓣMRSA, ⓣⓐMultiple Sclerosis, ⓣⓐNasal Polyp, ⓐⓣParkinson's Disease, ⓣⓐPlague, ⓐⓣPostpartum Depression, ⓣScarring (Prevention), ⓣⓐTumor (Lipoma), ⓣⓐUlcers, ⓣUterus Tissue Regeneration, ⓣVirus of Nerves, ⓣWarts, ⓣWrinkles

Historical Uses: Frankincense is a holy oil in the Middle East. As an ingredient in the holy incense, it was used anciently during sacrificial ceremonies to help improve communication with the creator.

French Medicinal Uses: Asthma, depression, ulcers.

Other Possible Uses: This oil may help with aging, allergies, bites (insect and snake), bronchitis, carbuncles, catarrh, colds, diarrhea, diphtheria, gonorrhea, headaches, healing, hemorrhaging, herpes, high blood pressure, jaundice, laryngitis, meningitis, nervous conditions, prostate problems, pneumonia, respiratory problems, sciatic pain, sores, spiritual awareness, staph, strep, stress, syphilis, T.B., tension, tonsillitis, typhoid, and wounds. It contains sesquiterpenes, enabling it to go beyond the blood-brain barrier. It may also help oxygenate the pineal and pituitary glands. It increases the activity of leukocytes, defending the body against infection. Frankincense may also help a person have a better attitude, which may help to strengthen the immune system.

Body System(s) Affected: Emotional Balance, Immune and Nervous Systems, Skin.

Aromatic Influence: This oil helps to focus energy, minimize distractions, and improve concentration. It eases hyperactivity, impatience, irritability, and restlessness and can help enhance spiritual awareness and meditation.

Application: Can be applied neat (with no dilution) when used topically. Apply to reflex points and/or directly on area of concern; diffuse.

Oral Use As Dietary Supplement: Approved by the FDA (21CFR172.510) for use as a Food Additive (FA) and Flavoring Agent (FL). Dilute one drop oil in 1 tsp. honey or in 4 oz. of beverage (i.e. soy/rice milk). Not for children under 6-years-old; use with caution and in greater dilution for children 6-years-old and over.

Blend Classification: Enhancer and Equalizer.

Blends With: All oils.

Odor: Type: Base Note (5-20% of the blend); Scent: Rich, deep, warm, balsamic, sweet, with incense-like overtones; Intensity: 3.

4 An extract from frankincense was found to produce apoptosis in human leukemia cells (Bhushan et al., 2007).

5 Boswellic acid was found to cause differentiation in premyelocytic leukemia cells, while inhibiting growth of these cells in mice (Jing et al., 1992).

6 Boswellic acids demonstrated an antiproliferative and apoptotic effect on liver cancer cells (Liu et al., 2002).

7 Boswellic acids were found to have an antiproliferative and apoptotic effect on human colon cancer cells (Liu et al., 2002).

8 Boswellic acid induced apoptosis in prostate cancer cells (Lu et al., 2008).

9 Boswellic acids from frankincense were found to induce apoptosis (cell death) in human myeloid leukemia cell lines (Xia et al., 2005).

10 Boswellic acid was found to prevent and inhibit invasion and metastasis of melanoma (skin pigment) and fibrosarcoma (connective tissue cancer) cells (Zhao et al., 2003).

11 Incensole acetate (found in frankincense) was found to open TRPV receptors in mice brain, a possible channel for emotional regulation (Moussaieff et al., 2008).

12 Triterpene acids isolated from frankincense were found to exhibit marked anti-inflammatory activity in TPA-induced inflammation in mice (Banno et al., 2006).

13 Boswellic acid from frankincense was found in vitro to prevent expression and activity of several proteins involved in the inflammatory response. In vivo, boswellic acid was found to protect against experimental arthritis in rats (Roy et al., 2006).

14 Boswellic extract was found to affect genes related to the inflammatory response in human microvascular cells. Additionally, Boswellic extract was found to reduce inflammation in carrageenan-induced rat paw inflammation (Roy et al., 2005).

15 Boswellic acid reduced induced inflammation and tumors in mice and was found to inhibit DNA synthesis in human leukemia cells in culture (Huang et al., 2000).

16 Boswellic acids from frankincense were found to inhibit TH1 cytokines while potentiating TH2 cytokines when delivered with sesame seed oil, demonstrating their ability to modulate the immune response (Chevrier et al., 2005).

GERANIUM ⓣⓐⓘ
(Pelargonium graveolens)

Botanical Family: Geraniaceae

Extraction Method: Steam distillation from leaves

ⓣ=Topical, ⓐ=Aromatic, ⓘ=Internal

Chemical Constituents: Alcohols (up to 70%): citronellol (>32%), geraniol (<23%), linalol (<14%), nerol, γ-eudesmol, α-terpineol, menthol; Esters (up to 30%): citronellyl formate (14%), geranyl formate & acetate (<12%), other propionates, butyrates, & tiglates; Ketones: isomenthone (<8%), menthone, piperitone; Sesquiterpenes: 4-guaiadiene-6,9, α-copaene, δ- & γ-cadinenes, δ-guaiazulene, β-farnesene; Aldehydes: geranial (<6%), neral, citronellal; Monoterpenes (<5%): α- & β-pinenes, l-limonene, myrcene, ocimene; Sesquiterpene Alcohols: farnesol (<3%).

Properties: Antibacterial[1,2], anticonvulsant[3], antidepressant, anti-inflammatory[4], antiseptic, astringent, diuretic, insect repellent, refreshing, relaxing, sedative, and tonic.

Common Primary Uses*: ◐♈Agitation (Calms), ◐Airborne Bacteria, ♈Autism, ♈Bleeding, ♈Breasts (Soothes), ♈Bruises, ♈Calcified Spine, ♈◐Cancer, ♈Capillaries (Broken), ♈◐Diabetes, ♈Diarrhea, ♈Dysmenorrhea, ♈Endometriosis, ◐♈Environmental Stress, ♈Gallbladder Stones, ♈Hair (Dry), ♈Hernia (Incisional), ♈Impetigo, ◐♈Insomnia (Older Children), ♈◐Jaundice, ♈Jet Lag, ♈Libido (Low), ♈Menorrhagia, ♈Miscarriage (After), ♈MRSA, ♈Osteoarthritis, ♈Osteoporosis, ♈◐Pancreas Support, ♈◐Paralysis, ♈Pelvic Pain Syndrome, ◐♈Physical Stress, ♈◐PMS, ♈Post Labor, ♈Rheumatoid Arthritis, ♈Skin (Dry), ♈Skin (Sensitive), ◐♈Ulcer (Gastric), ♈Varicose Ulcer, ♈Vertigo, ♈Wrinkles

Historical Uses: Geranium oil has been used for dysentery, hemorrhoids, inflammations, heavy menstrual flow, and possibly even cancer (if the folktale is correct). It has also been said to be a remedy for bone fractures, tumors, and wounds.

French Medicinal Uses: Diabetes, diarrhea, gallbladder, gastric ulcer, jaundice, liver, sterility, urinary stones.

Other Possible Uses: This oil may be used for acne, bleeding (increases to eliminate toxins, then stops), burns, circulatory problems (improves blood flow), depression, digestion, eczema, hormonal imbalance, insomnia, kidney stones, dilating biliary ducts for liver detoxification, menstrual problems, neuralgia (severe pain along the nerve), regenerating tissue and nerves, pancreas (balances), ringworm, shingles, skin (may balance the sebum, which is the fatty secretion in the sebaceous glands of the skin that keeps the skin supple. It is good for expectant mothers. It works as a cleanser for oily skin and may even liven up pale skin), sores, sore throats, and wounds.

Body System(s) Affected: Emotional Balance, Skin.

Aromatic Influence: It may help to release negative memories and take a person back to peaceful, joyful moments. It may also help ease nervous tension and stress, balance the emotions, lift the spirit, and foster peace, well-being, and hope.

Application: Can be applied neat (with no dilution) when used topically. Apply to reflex points and directly on area of concern; diffuse.

Oral Use As Dietary Supplement: Generally recognized as safe (GRAS) for human consumption by the FDA (21CFR182.20). Dilute one drop oil in 1 tsp. honey or in 4 oz. of beverage (i.e. soy/rice milk). Not for children under 6-years-old; use with caution and in greater dilution for children 6-years-old and over.

Safety Data: Repeated use can possibly result in some contact sensitization.

Blend Classification: Enhancer and Equalizer.

Blends With: All oils.

Odor: Type: Middle Note (50-80% of the blend); Scent: Sweet, green, citrus-rosy, fresh; Intensity: 3.

---

1   A combination of Citricidal and geranium oil demonstrated strong antibacterial effects on MRSA. Geranium and tea tree demonstrated strong antibacterial effects on *Staphylococcus aureus* (Edwards-Jones et al., 2004).

2   A formulation of lemongrass and geranium oil was found to reduce airborne bacteria by 89% in an office environment after diffusion for 15 hours (Doran et al., 2009).

3   Linalol, found in several essential oils, was found to inhibit induced convulsions in rats by directly interacting with the NMDA receptor complex (Brum et al., 2001).

4   Topical application of geranium oil was found to reduce the inflammatory response of neutrophil (white blood cell) accumulation in mice (Maruyama et al., 2005).

See Personal Usage Guide section for more details on these primary uses.   ♈=Neat, ◐=Dilute for Children/Sensitive Skin, ♈=Dilute

GINGER —

GINGER ☥*ⓐⓘ
(Zingiber officinale)

Botanical Family: Zingiberaceae (ginger)

Extraction Method: Steam distillation from rhizomes

Chemical Constituents: Sesquiterpenes (up to 90%): zingiberene (up to 50%), α- & β-curcumene (<33%), β-farnesene (<20%), β-sesquiphellandrene (<9%), β- & γ-bisabolene (<7%), β-ylangene, β-elemene, α-selinene, germacrene-D; Monoterpenes: camphene (8%), β-phellandrene, l-limonene, p-cymene, α and β-pinenes, myrcene; Alcohols: nonanol (<8%), citronellol (<6%), linalol (<5%), borneol, butanol, heptanol; Sesquiterpene Alcohols: nerolidol (<9%), zingeberol, elemol; Ketones (<6%): heptanone, acetone, 2 hexanone; Aldehydes: butanal, citronellal, geranial; Sesquiterpene Ketones: gingerone.

Properties: Antiseptic, laxative, stimulant, tonic, and warming.

Common Primary Uses*: ☥ⓐAngina, ☥Club Foot, ☥☥Diarrhea, ☥☥Gas/Flatulence, ☥ⓐIndigestion, ⓐ☥Libido (Low), ☥☥ⓐMorning Sickness, ☥ⓐNausea[5,6,7], ☥Pelvic Pain Syndrome, ☥Rheumatic Fever (Pain), ☥Rheumatoid Arthritis, ☥☥Scurvy, ☥ⓐVertigo, ☥ⓐVomiting

Historical Uses: Anciently esteemed as a spice and recognized for its affinity for the digestive system, it has been used in gingerbread (up to 4,000 years ago in Greece), in Egyptian cuisine (to ward off epidemics), in Roman wine (for its aphrodisiac powers), in Indian tea (to soothe upset stomachs), and in Chinese tonics (to strengthen the heart and to relieve head congestion). It was also used in Hawaii to scent clothing, to cook with, and to cure indigestion. The Hawaiians also added it to their shampoos and massage oils.

French Medicinal Uses: Angina, prevention of contagious diseases, cooking, diarrhea, flatulence, impotence, rheumatic pain, scurvy, and tonsillitis.

Other Possible Uses: Ginger may be used for alcoholism, loss of appetite, arthritis[8,9], broken bones, catarrh (mucus), chills, colds, colic, congestion, coughs, cramps, digestive disorders, fevers, flu, impotence, indigestion, infectious diseases, memory, motion sickness, muscular aches/pains, rheumatism, sinusitis, sore throats, and sprains. Ginger may also be used in cooking.

Body System(s) Affected: Digestive and Nervous Systems.

Aromatic Influence: The aroma may help influence physical energy, love, money, and courage.

Application: Can be applied neat (with no dilution), or dilute 1:1 (1 drop essential oil to 1 drop carrier oil) for children and for those with sensitive skin when using topically. Apply to reflex points and directly on area of concern; diffuse.

Oral Use As Dietary Supplement: Generally recognized as safe (GRAS) for human consumption by the FDA (21CFR182.20). Dilute one drop oil in 1 tsp. honey or in 4 oz. of beverage (i.e. soy/rice milk). Not for children under 6-years-old; use with caution and in greater dilution for children 6-years-old and over.

Safety Data: Repeated use can possibly result in contact sensitization. Avoid direct sunlight for 3 to 6 hours after use.

Blend Classification: Personifier and Equalizer.

Blends With: All spice oils, all citrus oils, eucalyptus, frankincense, geranium, and rosemary.

Odor: Type: Middle Note (50-80% of the blend); Scent: Sweet, spicy-woody, warm, tenacious, fresh, sharp; Intensity: 4.

Single Oils

---

5   In a trial of women receiving gynecological surgery, women receiving ginger root had less incidences of nausea compared to a placebo. Ginger root demonstrates results similar to the antiemetic drug (a drug effective against vomiting and nausea) metoclopramide (Bone et al., 1990).

6   Ginger root given one hour before major gynecological surgery resulted in lower nausea and fewer incidences of vomiting compared to a control (Nanthakomon et al., 2006).

7   Ginger root given orally to pregnant women was found to decrease the severity of nausea and the frequency of vomiting compared to a control (Vutyavanich et al., 2001).

8   Powdered ginger supplementation was found to lower pain and swelling in arthritic patients and to relieve pain from muscle discomfort (Srivastava et al., 1992).

9   Eugenol and ginger oil taken orally were found to reduce paw and joint swelling in rats with induced severe arthritis (Sharma et al., 1994).

GRAPEFRUIT ⓉⒶⒾ
(Citrus x paradisi)

Botanical Family: Rutaceae (hybrid between *Citrus maxima* and *Citrus sinensis*)

Extraction Method: Cold-pressed from rind

Chemical Constituents: Monoterpenes (up to 95%): d-Limonene (<92%), myrcene, α-pinene, sabinene, β-phellandrene; Tetraterpenes: β-carotene, lycopene; Aldehydes (>2%): nonanal, decanal, citral, citronellal; Furanocoumarins: aesculetin, auraptene, bergaptol; Sesquiterpene Ketones (<2%): nootketone (used to determine harvest time); Alcohols: octanol.

Properties: Antidepressant, antiseptic, disinfectant, diuretic, stimulant, and tonic.

Common Primary Uses*: ⓉⒶAddictions (Drugs), ⒶAnorexia, ⒶAppetite Suppressant, ⒶBulimia, ⓉCellulite, ⓉⒶDry Throat, ⓉⒶEdema, ⓉGallbladder Stones, ⓉⒶHangovers, ⓉⒶLymphatic Decongestant, ⒶⓉMental Stress, ⓉMiscarriage (After), ⒶⒶObesity[1], ⒶOvereating, ⒶⓉPerformance Stress, ⓉⒶPMS, ⒶⓉSlimming/Toning, ⒶⓉStress, ⓉⒶWithdrawal

French Medicinal Uses: Cellulite, digestion, dyspepsia, lymphatic decongestant, water retention.

Other Possible Uses: Grapefruit oil may help with cancer[2,3], depression, eating disorders, fatigue, jet lag, liver disorders, migraine headaches, premenstrual tension, stress, and sympathetic nervous system stimulation[4]. It may also have

a cleansing effect on the kidneys, the lymphatic system, and the vascular system.

Body System(s) Affected: Cardiovascular System.

Aromatic Influence: It is balancing and uplifting to the mind and may help to relieve anxiety.

Application: Can be applied neat (with no dilution) when used topically. Apply to reflex points and/or directly on area of concern; diffuse. Because grapefruit oil has many of the same uses as other citrus oils, it can be used in their place when immediate exposure to the sun is unavoidable. This is because grapefruit oil does not cause as much photosensitivity as the other citrus oils.

Oral Use As Dietary Supplement: Generally recognized as safe (GRAS) for human consumption by the FDA (21CFR182.20). Dilute one drop oil in 1 tsp. honey or in 4 oz. of beverage (i.e. soy/rice milk). Not for children under 6-years-old; use with caution and in greater dilution for children 6-years-old and over.

Blend Classification: Modifier and Enhancer.

Blends With: Basil, bergamot, cypress, frankincense, geranium, lavender, peppermint, rosemary, and ylang ylang.

Odor: Type: Top Note (5-20% of the blend); Scent: Clean, fresh, bitter, citrusy; Intensity: 2.

HELICHRYSUM ⓉⒶⒾ
(Helichrysum italicum)

Botanical Family: Compositae

Extraction Method: Steam distilled from flowers

Chemical Constituents: Esters (up to 60%): neryl acetate (up to 50%), neryl propionate & butyrate (<10%); Ketones: italidione (<20%), β-diketone; Sesquiterpenes: γ-curcumene (<15%), β-caryophyllene (<5%); Monoterpenes: l-limonene (<13%), α-pinene; Alcohols:

---

1. The scent of grapefruit oil and its component, limonene, was found to affect the autonomic nerves and to reduce appetite and body weight in rats exposed to the oil for 15 minutes three times per week (Shen et al., 2005).
2. In a study of older individuals, it was found that there was a dose-dependent relationship between citrus peel consumption (which is high in d-Limonene) and a lower degree of squamous cell carcinoma (SCC) of the skin (Hakim et al., 2000).
3. In clinical trials, d-Limonene (found in most citrus oils) was found to elicit a response (kept patients stable) in some patients in advanced stages of cancer (1 breast and 3 colorectal carcinoma of 32 total patients). A secondary trial with just breast-cancer patients did not elicit any responses (Vigushin et al., 1998).
4. Inhalation of essential oils such as pepper, estragon, fennel, and grapefruit was found to have a stimulating effect on sympathetic activity in healthy adults (Haze et al., 2002).

See Personal Usage Guide section for more details on these primary uses.

Ⓣ=Neat, Ⓣ=Dilute for Children/Sensitive Skin, Ⓣ=Dilute

nerol (<5%), linalol (<4%), geraniol; Oxides: 1,8 cineol; Phenols: eugenol.

Properties: Antibacterial[5,6], anticatarrhal, anticoagulant, antioxidant[7], antispasmodic, antiviral[8,9], expectorant, and mucolytic.

Common Primary Uses*: 🅣Abscess (Tooth), 🅣🅐AIDS/HIV, 🅣🅐Aneurysm, 🅣🅐Bleeding, 🅣Bone Bruise, 🅣Broken Blood Vessels, 🅣Bruises, 🅣🅐Catarrh, 🅣Cholesterol, 🅣Cleansing, 🅣🅐Colitis, 🅣Cuts, 🅣Dermatitis/Eczema, 🅣Detoxification, 🅣🅐Earache, 🅣Fibroids, 🅣Gallbladder Infection, 🅣Hematoma, 🅣Hemorrhaging, 🅣Herpes Simplex, 🅣Incisional Hernia, 🅣🅐Liver Stimulant, 🅣Lymphatic Drainage, 🅣Nose Bleed, 🅣Pancreas Stimulant, 🅣🅐Phlebitis, 🅣Psoriasis, 🅣Sciatica, 🅣Shock, 🅣Staph Infection, 🅐🅣Stroke, 🅣Sunscreen, 🅣Swollen Eyes, 🅣Taste (Impaired), 🅣Tennis Elbow, 🅣Tinnitus, 🅣Tissue Pain, 🅣Tissue Repair, 🅣Vertigo, 🅣🅐Viral Infections, 🅣Wounds

Historical Uses: Helichrysum has been used for asthma, bronchitis, whooping cough, headaches, liver ailments, and skin disorders.

French Medicinal Uses: Blood cleansing, chelating agent for metallics, chemicals, and toxins, viral colitis, detoxification, gallbladder infection, hematoma, hypo-cholesterol, liver cell function stimulant, lymph drainage, pain reduction, pancreas stimulant, phlebitis, sciatica, sinus infection, skin conditions (eczema, dermatitis, psoriasis), stomach cramps, sunscreen.

Other Possible Uses: This oil may help with anger management, bleeding, circulatory functions, hearing, detoxifying and stimulating the liver cell function, pain (acute), relieve respiratory conditions, reduce scarring, scar tissue, regenerate tissue, and varicose veins.

Body System(s) Affected: Cardiovascular System, Muscles and Bones.

Aromatic Influence: It is uplifting to the subconscious and may help calm feelings of anger.

Application: Can be applied neat (with no dilution) when used topically. Apply to reflex points and directly on area of concern; diffuse.

Oral Use As Dietary Supplement: Generally recognized as safe (GRAS) for human consumption by the FDA (21CFR182.20). Dilute one drop oil in 1 tsp. honey or in 4 oz. of beverage (i.e. soy/rice milk). Not for children under 6-years-old; use with caution and in greater dilution for children 6-years-old and over.

Blend Classification: Personifier.

Blends With: Geranium, clary sage, rose, lavender, spice oils, and citrus oils.

Odor: Type: Middle Note (50-80% of the blend); Scent: Rich, sweet, fruity, with tea and honey undertones; Intensity: 3.

LAVENDER 🅣🅐🅘
(Lavandula angustifolia)

Botanical Family: Labiatae (mint)

Extraction Method: Steam distilled from flowering top

Chemical Constituents: Alcohols (up to 58%): linalol (>41%), α-terpineol, borneol, lavendulol, geraniol, nerol; Esters (approx. 50%): linalyl acetate (up to 45%), lavendulyl & geranyl acetates, α-terpenyl acetate; Monoterpenes (up to 24%): β-ocimene (<16%), d-Limonene (<5%), α- & β-pinenes, camphene, δ-3-carene; Sesquiterpenes: β-caryophyllene (<7%), χ-farnesene; Phenols: terpinen-4-ol (<6%); Aldehydes: benzaldehyde, cuminal, geranial, hexanal, myrtenal, neral; Oxides: 1,8 cineol, caryophyllene oxide, linalol oxide; Coumarins (<4%); Ketones: octanone (<3%), camphor; Lactones.

---

5 Helichrysum oil exhibited definite antibacterial activity against six tested Gram (+/-) bacteria (Chinou et al., 1996).

6 Helichrysum was found to inhibit both the growth and the formation of some enzymes of *Staphylococcus aureus* (staph) bacteria (Nostro et al., 2001).

7 Arzanol (extracted from helichrysum) at non-cytotoxic concentrations showed a strong inhibition of TBH-induced oxidative stress in VERO cells (Rosa et al., 2007).

8 Arzanol, extracted from helichrysum, inhibited HIV-1 replication in T-cells and also inhibited the release of pro-inflammatory cytokines (chemical messengers) in monocytes (Appendino et al., 2007).

9 Helichrysum showed significant antiviral activity against the herpes virus at non-cytotoxic concentrations (Nostro et al., 2003).

🅣=Topical, 🅐=Aromatic, 🅘=Internal

Properties: Analgesic[1], anticoagulant, anticonvulsant[2], antidepressant, antifungal[3], antihistamine, anti-infectious, anti-inflammatory[4,5], antimicrobial[6], antimutagenic[7], antiseptic, antispasmodic, antitoxic, antitumor[8,9,10], cardiotonic, regenerative, and sedative[11,12,13,14,15,16,17,18].

Common Primary Uses*: Abuse (Healing From), Agitation (Calms), Allergies, Anxiety[19], Appetite Loss, Arrhythmia, Atherosclerosis, Bites/Stings, Blisters, Boils, Breasts (Soothes), Burns, Calming, Cancer, Chicken Pox, Club Foot, Concentration, Convulsions, Crying, Cuts, Dandruff, Depression, Diabetic Sores, Diaper Rash, Diuretic, Dysmenorrhea, Exhaustion, Fever, Gangrene, Gas/Flatulence, Giardia, Gnats and Midges (Repellent), Grief/Sorrow, Hair (Dry), Hair (Fragile), Hair (Loss), Hay Fever, Hernia (Inguinal), Herpes Simplex, Hyperactivity, Impetigo, Inflammation, Insomnia, Itching, Jet Lag, Lips (Dry), Mastitis, Menopause, Mental Stress, Mood Swings, Mosquito Repellent, Muscular Paralysis, Pain, Parasympathetic Nervous System Stimulation, Parkinson's Disease, Phlebitis, Physical Stress, Poison Ivy/Oak, Post Labor, Postpartum Depression, Rashes, Relaxation, Rheumatoid Arthritis, Sedative, Seizure, Skin (Dry), Skin (Sensitive), Skin Ulcers, Sleep, Stress[20,21], Stretch Marks, Sunburn, Tachycardia, Teeth Grinding, Teething Pain, Tension, Thrush, Ticks, Ulcers (Leg), Varicose Ulcer, Vertigo, Withdrawal, Worms, Wounds, Wrinkles

Historical Uses: During Medieval times, people were obviously divided on the properties of lavender regarding love. Some would claim that it could keep the wearer chaste, while others claimed just the opposite—touting its aphrodisiac qualities. Its list of uses is long.

French Medicinal Uses: Acne, allergies[22], burns (cell renewal), cramps (leg), dandruff, diaper rash, flatulence, hair loss, herpes, indigestion, insomnia[23], lowering blood pressure[24], lymphatic system drainage, menopausal conditions, mouth abscess, nausea, phlebitis, premenstrual conditions, scarring (minimizes), stretch marks, tachycardia, thrush, water retention.

Other Possible Uses: Lavender is a universal oil that has traditionally been known to balance the body and to work wherever there is a need. If in doubt, use lavender. It may help anxiety, arthritis, asthma, body systems balance, bronchitis[25], bruises, carbuncles, cold sores,

---

1 Lavender oil was found to work as an anaesthetic (reducing pain) in rabbit reflex tests (Ghelardini et al., 1999).

2 Linalol, found in several essential oils, was shown to inhibit induced convulsions in rats by directly interacting with the NMDA receptor complex (Brum et al., 2001).

3 Lavender oil demonstrated both fungistatic (stopped growth) and fungicidal (killed) activity against *Candida albicans* (D'Auria et al., 2005).

4 Oil from *Lavandula angustifolia* was found to reduce writhing in induced writhing in rats and to reduce edema (swelling) in carrageenan-induced paw edema, indicating an anti-inflammatory effect (Hajhashemi et al., 2003).

5 Linalol and linalyl acetate (from lavender and other essential oils) were found to exhibit anti-inflammatory activity in rats subjected to carrageenin-induced edema (inflammation) (Peana et al., 2002).

6 Essential oil from *Lavandula angustifolia* demonstrated ability to eliminate protozoal pathogens *Giardia duodenalis*, *Thrichomonas vaginalis*, and *Hexamita inflata* at concentrations of 1% or less (Moon et al., 2006).

7 In tests for mutagenicity, both melaleuca (tea tree) and lavender oils were found to not be mutagenic. Lavender oil was also found to demonstrate a strong antimutagenic activity, reducing mutations of cells exposed to a known mutagen (Evandri et al., 2005).

8 Mice treated with perillyl alcohol (found in lavender and mint plants) had a 22% reduction in tumor incidence and a 58% reduction in tumor multiplicity during a mouse lung tumor bioassay (Lantry et al., 1997).

9 Rats with liver tumors that were treated with perillyl alcohol had smaller tumor sizes than untreated rats due to apoptosis in cancer cells in treated rats (Mills et al., 1995).

10 Rats fed diets containing perillyl alcohol (derived from lavender plants) were found to have less incidence of colon tumors and less multiplicity of tumors in the colon compared to a control. Colon tumors of animals fed perillyl alcohol were found to exhibit increased apoptosis of cells compared to control (Reddy et al., 1997).

11 Exposure to lavender odor was found to decrease anxiety in gerbils in the elevated plus maze. A further decrease in anxiety was found in females after prolonged (2 week) exposure (Bradley et al., 2007).

12 Exposure to lavender oil and to its constituents, linalol and linalyl acetate, was found to decrease normal movement in mice and was also found to return mice to normal movement rates after caffeine-induced hyperactivity (Buchbauer et al., 1991).

13 In patients admitted to an intensive care unit, those receiving lavender aromatherapy reported a greater improvement in mood and in perceived levels of anxiety compared to those receiving just massage or a period of rest (Dunn et al., 1995).

14 Swiss mice fed lavender oil diluted in olive oil were found to be more sedate in several common tests (Guillemain et al., 1989).

15 Patients being treated with chronic hemodialysis demonstrated less anxiety when exposed to lavender aroma (Itai et al., 2000).

16 Inhaling lavender oil was found to lower agitation in older adults suffering from dementia (Lin et al., 2007).

17 Lavender oil was found to inhibit sympathetic nerve activity in rats while exciting parasympathetic nerve activity. Linalol, a component of lavender, was shown to have similar effects (Shen et al., 2005).

18 Lavender oil demonstrated anticonflict effects in mice similar to the anxiolytic (anti-anxiety) drug diazepam (Umezu et al., 2000).

19 Patients waiting for dental treatment were found to be less anxious and have a better mood when exposed to the odor of lavender or orange oil compared to control (Lehrner et al., 2005).

20 Lavender odor was found to reduce mental stress while increasing arousal (Motomura et al., 2001).

21 Nurses working in an ICU setting demonstrated decreased perception of stress when receiving a topical application of *Lavandula angustifolia* and *Salvia sclarea* essential oils (Pemberton et al., 2008).

22 Lavender oil was found to inhibit immediate-type allergic reactions in mice and rats by inhibiting mast cell degranulation (Kim et al., 1999).

23 Female students suffering from insomnia were found to sleep better and to have lower levels of depression during weeks they used a lavender fragrance when compared to weeks they did not use a lavender fragrance (Lee et al., 2006).

24 Lavender oil scent was found to lower sympathetic nerve activity and blood pressure in rats while elevating parasympathetic nerve activity. It was further found that applying an anosmia-inducing agent (something that causes a loss of smell) eliminated the effects of the lavender oil scent (Tanida et al., 2006).

25 In patients with chronic bronchitis, lavender was found to promote normalization of

See Personal Usage Guide section for more details on these primary uses.

Ⓣ=Neat, Ⓣ=Dilute for Children/Sensitive Skin, Ⓣ=Dilute

earaches, fainting, gallstones, relieve head-aches, heart irregularity, reduce high blood pressure, hives (urticaria), hysteria, insect bites and bee stings, infection, influenza, injuries, repel insects[26,27], laryngitis, migraine headaches, mental clarity[28,29], mouth abscess, reduce mucus, nervous tension, pineal gland (activates), respiratory function, rheumatism, skin conditions (eczema, psoriasis, rashes), sprains, sunstroke, throat infections, tuberculosis, typhoid fever, and whooping cough.

Body System(s) Affected: Cardiovascular System, Emotional Balance, Nervous System, Skin.

Aromatic Influence: It promotes consciousness, health, love, peace, and a general sense of well-being. It also nurtures creativity.

Application: Can be applied neat (with no dilution) when used topically. Apply to reflex points and directly on area of concern; diffuse.

Oral Use As Dietary Supplement: Generally recognized as safe (GRAS) for human consumption by the FDA (21CFR182.20). Dilute one drop oil in 1 tsp. honey or in 4 oz. of beverage (i.e. soy/rice milk). Not for children under 6-years-old; use with caution and in greater dilution for children 6-years-old and over.

Blend Classification: Enhancer, Modifier, and Equalizer.

Blends With: Most oils (especially citrus oils), clary sage, and geranium.

Odor: Type: Middle Note (50-80% of the blend); Scent: Floral, sweet, herbaceous, balsamic, woody undertones; Intensity: 2.

LEMON ⊕*ⒶⒾ
(Citrus limon)

Botanical Family: Rutaceae (citrus)

Extraction Method: Cold-pressed from rind (requires 3,000 lemons to produce a kilo of oil)

Chemical Constituents: Monoterpenes (up to 90%): d-Limonene (up to 72%), α- & β-pinenes (<30%), α- & γ-terpinenes (7-14%), sabinene, p-cymene, terpinolene, α- & β-phellandrenes; Aldehydes (up to 12%): citral, citronellal, neral, geranial, heptanal, hexanal, nonanal, octanal, undecanal; Alcohols: hexanol, octanol, nonanol, decanol, linalol, α-terpineol; Esters (<5%): geranyl acetate, neryl acetate, methyl anthranilate; Sesquiterpenes (<5%): β-bisabolene, β-caryophyllene; Tetraterpenes (<4%): β-carotene, lycopene; Phenols: terpinen-4-ol; Coumarins and Furocoumarins (<3%): umberlliferone, bergaptene, α-bergamotene, limettine, psoralen, bergamottin, bergaptol, citroptene scopoletin.

Properties: Anticancer[30,31], antidepressant[32], antiseptic, antifungal[33], antioxidant[34], antiviral, astringent, invigorating, refreshing, and tonic.

Common Primary Uses*: ⒶAir Pollution, ⒶAnxiety[35], ⒶⓉAtherosclerosis, ⓉBites/Stings, ⓉBlood Pressure (Regulation), ⒶⓉBrain Injury, ⓉCold Sores, ⒶⓉColds (Common), ⒶConcentration,

---

lipid levels (Siurin et al., 1997).

26 Lavender oil was found to be comparable to DEET in its ability to repel ticks (*Hyalomma marginatum*) (Mkolo et al., 2007).

27 An infestation of the red bud borer pest was reduced by more than 95% in the grafted buds of apple trees by application of the essential oil of *Lavandula angustifolia* (van Tol et al., 2007).

28 Subjects exposed to 3 minutes of lavender aroma were more relaxed and were able to perform math computations faster and more accurately (Diego et al., 1998).

29 Subjects who smelled a cleansing gel with lavender aroma were more relaxed and were able to complete math computations faster (Field et al., 2005).

30 In a study of older individuals, it was found that there was a dose-dependent relationship between citrus peel consumption (which are high in d-Limonene) and a lower degree of squamous cell carcinoma (SCC) of the skin (Hakim et al., 2000).

31 In clinical trials, d-Limonene (found in most citrus oils and in dill, caraway, citronella, and nutmeg) was found to elicit a response (kept patients stable) in some patients in advanced stages of cancer (1 breast and 3 colorectal carcinoma of 32 total patients). A secondary trial with just breast cancer patients did not elicit any responses (Vigushin et al., 1998).

32 Lemon oil and its component, citral, were found to decrease depressed behavior in rats involved in several stress tests in a manner similar to antidepressant drugs (Komori et al., 1995).

33 Lemon oil was found to be an effective antifungal agent against two bread-mold species (Caccioni et al., 1998).

34 Lemon oil and one of its components, gamma-terpinene, were found to inhibit oxidation of low-density lipoprotein (LDL). Oxidation of LDL has been found to increase the risk of atherosclerosis and cardiac disease (Grassmann et al., 2001).

35 Rats exposed long-term to lemon essential oil were found to demonstrate different anxiety and pain threshold levels than untreated rats. It was also found that exposure to lemon oil induced chemical changes in the neuronal circuits involved in anxiety and pain (Ceccarelli et al., 2004).

⊕=Topical, Ⓐ=Aromatic, Ⓘ=Internal

❂Constipation, ❂❂❂Depression, ❂Digestion (Sluggish), ❂❂Disinfectant, ❂❂Dry Throat, ❂Dysentery, ❂Energizing, ❂Exhaustion, ❂❂Fever, ❂❂Flu (Influenza), ❂Furniture Polish, ❂❂Gout, ❂Greasy/Oily Hair, ❂❂Grief/Sorrow, ❂Gum/Grease Removal, ❂❂Hangovers, ❂Heartburn, ❂❂Intestinal Parasites, ❂Kidney Stones, ❂❂Lymphatic Cleansing, ❂MRSA, ❂Overeating, ❂❂Pancreatitis, ❂Physical Energy, ❂❂Postpartum Depression, ❂Purification, ❂Relaxation, ❂Skin (Tones), ❂❂Stress[1,2], ❂❂❂Throat Infection, ❂Tonsillitis, ❂Uplifting, ❂Varicose Veins, ❂❂Water Purification

Historical Uses: Lemon has been used to fight food poisoning, malaria and typhoid epidemics, and scurvy. (In fact, sources say that Christopher Columbus carried lemon seeds to America—probably just the leftovers from the fruit that was eaten during the trip.) Lemon has also been used to lower blood pressure and to help with liver problems, arthritis, and muscular aches and pains.

French Medicinal Uses: Air disinfectant, anemia, asthma, cold, fever (reduces), germicide, gout, heartburn, intestinal parasites, red blood cell formation, rheumatism, throat infection, ureter infections, varicose veins, water purification, white blood cell formation.

Other Possible Uses: This oil may be beneficial for soothing broken capillaries, dissolving cellulite, clarity of thought, debility, digestive problems[3], energy, gallstones, hair (cleansing), promoting leukocyte formation, liver deficiencies in children, memory improvement, nails (strengthening and hardening), nerves[4], nervous conditions, respiratory problems, cleaning children's skin, sore throats, and promoting a sense of well-being. It works extremely well in removing gum, wood stain, oil, and grease spots. It may also brighten a pale, dull complexion by removing dead skin cells.

---

1 Lemon odor was found to enhance the positive mood of volunteers exposed to a stressor (Kiecolt-Glaser et al., 2008).

2 Lemon oil vapor was found to have strong antistress and antidepressant effects on mice subjected to several common stress tests (Komiya et al., 2006).

3 The use of rosemary, lemon, and peppermint oils in massage demonstrated an ability to reduce constipation and to increase bowel movements in elderly subjects, compared to massage without the oils (Kime et al., 2005).

4 Pretreatment of human and rat astrocyte cells (cells found in the nerve and brain that support the blood-brain barrier and help repair the brain and spinal cord following injuries) with lemon oil was found to inhibit heat-shock induced apoptosis of these cells (Koo et al., 2002).

Body System(s) Affected: Digestive, Immune, and Respiratory Systems.

Aromatic Influence: It promotes health, healing, physical energy, and purification. Its fragrance is invigorating, enhancing, and warming.

Application: Can be applied neat (with no dilution) when used topically. Apply to reflex points and directly on area of concern; diffuse.

Oral Use As Dietary Supplement: Generally recognized as safe (GRAS) for human consumption by the FDA (21CFR182.20). Dilute one drop oil in 1 tsp. honey or in 4 oz. of beverage (i.e. soy/rice milk). Not for children under 6-years-old; use with caution and in greater dilution for children 6-years-old and over.

Safety Data: Avoid direct sunlight for up to 12 hours after use. Can cause extreme skin irritation.

Blend Classification: Modifier and Enhancer.

Blends With: Eucalyptus, fennel, frankincense, geranium, peppermint, sandalwood, and ylang ylang.

Odor: Type: Top Note (5-20% of the blend); Scent: Sweet, sharp, clear, citrusy; Intensity: 3.

LEMONGRASS ❂❂❂
(Cymbopogon flexuosus)

Botanical Family: Gramineae (grasses)

Extraction Method: Steam distilled from leaves

Chemical Constituents: Aldehydes (up to 80%): geranial (<42%), neral (<38%), farnesal (<3%), decanal; Alcohols (<15%): geraniol (<10%), α-terpineol (<3%), borneol (<2%), nerol, linalol, citronellol; Sesquiterpene Alcohols: farnesol (<13%); Esters (<11%): geranyl & linalyl acetates; Monoterpenes (<9%): myrcene (<5%), d-Limonene (<3%), β-ocimene; Sesquiterpenes: β-caryophyllene (<6%); Oxides: caryophyllene oxide (<4%); Ketones: methyl heptanone (<3%).

---

*See Personal Usage Guide section for more details on these primary uses.

❂=Neat, ❂=Dilute for Children/Sensitive Skin, ❂=Dilute

Properties: Analgesic, antibacterial[5,6,7], anticancer[8,9,10,11], anti-inflammatory, antiseptic, insect repellent, revitalizer, sedative, tonic, and vasodilator.

Common Primary Uses*: ⓐAir Pollution, ⓐAirborne Bacteria, ⓣCarpal Tunnel Syndrome, ⓘCholesterol[12], ⓣCramps/Charley Horses, ⓣCystitis/Bladder Infection, ⓣDiuretic, ⓣEdema, ⓣFleas, ⓣFrozen Shoulder, ⓘGastritis, ⓣⓐGrave's Disease, ⓣⓐHashimoto's Disease, ⓣHernia (Incisional), ⓣHernia (Inguinal), ⓣImprove Vision, ⓘⓣLactose Intolerance, ⓣⓐLymphatic Drainage, ⓐⓣMental Fatigue, ⓣMuscular Dystrophy, ⓣⓐParalysis, ⓐPurification, ⓣRetina (Strengthen), ⓣSprains, ⓣStrain (Muscle), ⓣTissue Repair, ⓣⓐUrinary Tract Infection, ⓣVaricose Veins, ⓣWhiplash (Ligaments), ⓣWounds

Historical Uses: Lemongrass has been used for infectious illnesses and fever, as an insecticide, and as a sedative to the central nervous system.

French Medicinal Uses: Bladder infection (cystitis), connective tissue (regenerates), digestive system, edema, fluid retention, kidney disorders, lymphatic drainage, parasympathetic nervous system (regulates), varicose veins, vascular walls (strengthens).

Other Possible Uses: This oil may help with circulation, improving digestion, improving eyesight, fevers, flatulence, headaches, clearing infections, repairing ligaments, waking up the lymphatic system, getting the oxygen flowing, respiratory problems[13], sore throats, tissue regeneration, and water retention.

---

5 A formulation of lemongrass and geranium oil was found to reduce airborne bacteria by 89% in an office environment after diffusion for 15 hours (Doran et al., 2009).

6 Lemongrass and lemon verbena oil were found to be bactericidal to *Helicobacter pylori* at very low concentrations. Additionally, it was found that this bacteria did not develop a resistance to lemongrass oil after 10 passages; while this bacteria did develop resistance to clarithromycin (an antibiotic) under the same conditions (Ohno et al., 2003).

7 Two components of lemongrass demonstrated antibacterial properties, while the addition of a third component, myrcene, enhanced the antibacterial activities (Onawunmi et al., 1984).

8 Geraniol, found in lemongrass oil (among others), was found to inhibit colon cancer cell growth while inhibiting DNA synthesis in these cells (Carnesecchi et al., 2001).

9 Lemongrass oil and its constituent, isointermedeol, were found to induce apoptosis in human leukemia cells (Kumar et al., 2008).

10 An extract from lemongrass was found to inhibit hepatocarcinogenesis (liver cancer genesis) in rats (Puatanachokchai et al., 2002).

11 Lemongrass oil was found to inhibit multiple cancer cell lines, both in vitro and in vivo in mice (Sharma et al., 2009).

12 Internal use of lemongrass capsules was found to reduce cholesterol in some subjects (Elson et al., 1989).

13 Cinnamon bark, lemongrass, and thyme oils were found to have the highest level of activity against common respiratory pathogens among 14 essential oils tested (Inouye

Body System(s) Affected: Immune System, Muscles and Bones.

Aromatic Influence: It promotes awareness and purification.

Application: Can be applied neat (with no dilution), or dilute 1:1 (1 drop essential oil to 1 drop carrier oil) for children and for those with sensitive skin when using topically. Apply to reflex points or directly on area of concern; diffuse.

Oral Use As Dietary Supplement: Generally recognized as safe (GRAS) for human consumption by the FDA (21CFR182.20). Dilute one drop oil in 1 tsp. honey or in 4 oz. of beverage (i.e. soy/rice milk). Not for children under 6-years-old; use with caution and in greater dilution for children 6-years-old and over.

Safety Data: Can cause extreme skin irritation.

Blend Classification: Enhancer and Equalizer.

Blends With: Basil, clary sage, eucalyptus, geranium, lavender, melaleuca, and rosemary.

Odor: Type: Top Note (5-20% of the blend); Scent: Grassy, lemony, pungent, earthy, slightly bitter; Intensity: 4.

LIME ⓣ*ⓐⓘ
(Citrus aurantifolia)

Botanical Family: Rutaceae (citrus)

Extraction Method: Cold expressed from peel

Chemical Constituents: Monoterpenes (up to 80%): d-Limonene (<65%), α- & β-pinenes (<17%), camphene, sabinene, p-cymene, myrcene, bisabolene, dipentene, phellandrene, cadinene; Oxides (<22%): 1,8 cineol (<20%), 1,4 cineol; Aldehydes (<20%): geranial (<8%), neral (<5%), citral, citronellal, octanal, nonanal, decanal, lauric aldehyde; Alcohols (4%): α-terpineol (<2%), borneol, α-fenchol, linalol;

et al., 2001).

Coumarins: limettine; Furanoids: furfural, garanoxycoumarin.

Properties: Antibacterial, antiseptic, antiviral, restorative, and tonic.

Common Primary Uses*: 🖐🖐Bacterial Infections, 🖐🖐🖐Fever, 🖐Gum/Grease Removal, 🖐Skin (Revitalizing)

Historical Uses: For some time, lime was used as a remedy for dyspepsia with glycerin of pepsin. It was often used in place of lemon for fevers, infections, sore throats, colds, etc.

Other Possible Uses: This oil may be beneficial for anxiety, blood pressure, soothing broken capillaries, dissolving cellulite, improving clarity of thought, debility, energy, gallstones, hair (cleansing), promoting leukocyte formation, liver deficiencies in children, lymphatic system cleansing, memory improvement, nails (strengthening), nervous conditions, cleaning children's skin, sore throats, water and air purification, and promoting a sense of well-being. It works extremely well in removing gum, wood stain, oil, and grease spots. It may also help brighten a pale, dull complexion by removing the dead skin cells. Lime oil is capable of tightening skin and connective tissue.

Body System(s) Affected: Digestive, Immune, and Respiratory Systems.

Aromatic Influence: Lime oil has a fresh, lively fragrance that is stimulating and refreshing. It helps one overcome exhaustion, depression, and listlessness. Although unverifiable, some sources claim that inhaling the oil may stimulate the muscles around the eyes.

Application: Apply to Vita Flex Points and/or directly on area of concern; diffuse. It makes an excellent addition to bath and shower gels, body lotions, and deodorants.

Oral Use As Dietary Supplement: Generally regarded as safe (GRAS) for human consumption by the FDA. Dilute one drop oil in 1 tsp. honey or in 4 oz. of beverage (i.e. soy/rice milk). Not for children under 6-years-old; use with caution and in greater dilution for children 6-years-old and over.

Safety Data: Avoid direct sunlight 12 hours after use.

Blend Classification: Enhancer and Equalizer.

Blends With: Citronella, clary sage, lavender, rosemary, other citrus oils.

Odor: Type: Top Note (5-20% of the blend); Scent: Sweet, tart, intense, lively; Intensity: 3

MARJORAM 🖐🔺ⓘ
(Origanum majorana)

Botanical Family: Labiatae (mint)

Extraction Method: Steam distilled from leaves

Chemical Constituents: Monoterpenes (up to 60%): α- & γ-terpinenes (<30%), sabinene (<8%), myrcene (<7%), terpinolene, ocimene, δ-3-carene, p-cymene, α- and β-pinenes, δ-cadinene, α- & β-phellandrenes, l-limonene; Alcohols (<30%): α-terpineol (<15%), cis- & trans-thujanol-4 (<12%), linalol (<8%); Phenols: terpinen-4-ol (>21%), terpinen-1-ol-3; Esters: geranyl acetate (<7%), linalyl acetate, α-terpenyl acetate; Aldehydes: citral (<6%); Sesquiterpenes (<5%): β-caryophyllene, humulene; Phenolic Ethers: trans-anethole.

Properties: Antibacterial, anti-infectious, antiseptic, antisexual, antispasmodic, arterial vasodilator, digestive stimulant, diuretic, expectorant, sedative, and tonic.

Common Primary Uses*: 🖐Arterial Vasodilator, 🖐🔺Arthritis, 🖐Bone Spurs, 🖐Carpal Tunnel Syndrome, 🖐Cartilage Injury, 🖐Colic, 🖐Constipation, 🖐Cramps/Charley Horses, 🔺🖐Croup, 🔺🖐Expectorant, 🖐🔺High Blood Pressure, 🖐Muscle Aches, 🖐Muscle Fatigue, 🖐Muscle Spasms, 🖐Muscle Tone, 🖐Muscular Dystrophy, 🖐Neuralgia, 🖐Osteoarthritis, 🖐🔺Pancreatitis, 🖐Parkinson's Disease, 🔺🖐Physical Stress, 🖐🔺Prolapsed Mitral Valve, 🖐Rheumatoid Arthritis, 🖐Sprains, 🖐Stiffness, 🖐Tendinitis, 🖐Tension (Muscle), 🖐Whiplash (Muscles)

Historical Uses: Marjoram was used to combat poisoning, fluid retention, muscle spasms,

---

*See Personal Usage Guide section for more details on these primary uses.　　🖐=Neat, 🖐=Dilute for Children/Sensitive Skin, 🖐=Dilute

58

rheumatism, sprains, stiff joints, bruises, obstructions of the liver and spleen, and respiratory congestions. According to Roberta Wilson, "Those curious about their futures anointed themselves with marjoram at bedtime so that they might dream of their future mates."

French Medicinal Uses: Aches, arthritis[1], asthma, bronchitis, colic, constipation, cramps, insomnia, intestinal peristalsis, migraine headaches, muscles, neuralgia, pains, parasympathetic nervous system (tones), blood pressure (regulates), rheumatism, sprains.

Other Possible Uses: It may be relaxing and calming to the muscles that constrict and sometimes contribute to headaches. It may help anxiety, boils, bruises, burns, carbuncles, celibacy (vow not to marry), colds, cold sores, cuts, fungus and viral infections, hysteria, menstrual problems, calm the respiratory system, ringworm, shingles, shock, sores, relieve spasms, sunburns, and water retention.

Body System(s) Affected: Cardiovascular System, Muscles and Bones.

Aromatic Influence: It promotes peace and sleep.

Application: Can be applied neat (with no dilution) when used topically. Apply to reflex points and directly on area of concern; diffuse.

Oral Use As Dietary Supplement: Generally recognized as safe (GRAS) for human consumption by the FDA (21CFR182.20). Dilute one drop oil in 1 tsp. honey or in 4 oz. of beverage (i.e. soy/rice milk). Not for children under 6-years-old; use with caution and in greater dilution for children 6-years-old and over.

Safety Data: Use with caution during pregnancy.

Blend Classification: Enhancer and Equalizer.

Blends With: Bergamot, cypress, lavender, orange, rosemary, and ylang ylang.

Odor: Type: Middle Note (50-80% of the blend); Scent: Herbaceous, green, spicy; Intensity: 3.

---

1 In patients suffering from arthritis, it was found that a blend of lavender, marjoram, eucalyptus, rosemary, and peppermint blended with carrier oils reduced perceived pain and depression compared to control (Kim et al., 2005).

MELALEUCA (TEA TREE) ⓉⒶⒾ
(Melaleuca alternifolia)

Botanical Family: Myrtaceae (Myrtle: shrubs and trees)

Extraction Method: Steam distilled from leaves

Chemical Constituents: Monoterpenes (up to 70%): α- & γ-terpinenes (<40%), p-cymene (<12%), α- and β-pinenes (<8%), terpinolene, l-limonene, sabinene, myrcene, α-thujene; Phenols: terpinen-4-ol (<40%); Sesquiterpenes (up to 20%): α- & δ-cadinenes (<8%), aromadendrene (<7%), viridiflorene (<5%), β-caryophyllene, α-phellandrene; Oxides: 1,8 cineol (<14%), 1,4 cineol (<3%), caryophyllene oxide; Alcohols: α- & β-terpineols (<8%); Sesquiterpene Alcohols (<5%): globulol, viridiflorol.

Properties: Analgesic, antibacterial[2,3,4,5,6,7,8,9], antifungal[10,11,12,13,14,15], anti-infectious,

---

2 MRSA (methicillin-resistant staph) and MSSA (methicillin-sensitive staph) in biofilms (plaque/microcolonies) were eradicated by a 5% solution of tea tree oil as well as 5 of 9 CoNS (coagulase-negative staph) (Brady et al., 2006).

3 66 isolates of *Staphylococcus aureus* (Staph), including 64 methicillin-resistant (MRSA) strains and 33 mupirocin-resistant strains, were inhibited by tea tree essential oil (Carson et al., 1995).

4 Tea tree oil was found to disrupt the cellular membrane and to inhibit respiration in *Candida albicans*, Gram-negative *E. coli*, and Gram-positive *Staphylococcus aureus* (Staph) (Cox et al., 2000).

5 Geranium and tea tree demonstrated strong antibacterial effects on *Staphylococcus aureus* (Edwards-Jones et al., 2004).

6 Tea tree oil and its component terpinen-4-ol demonstrated an effective antibacterial activity against *Staphylococcus aureus* (Staph) bacteria, superior to the activity of several antibiotic drugs—even against antibiotic-resistant strains (Ferrini et al., 2006).

7 Tea tree oil was found to kill transient skin flora at lower concentrations than it killed resident skin flora (Hammer et al., 1996).

8 Gram-positive strains of *Staphylococcus aureus* and *Enterococcus faecalis* were shown to have very low frequencies of resistance to tea tree oil (Hammer et al., 2008).

9 Tea tree oil demonstrated ability to kill *Staphylococcus aureus* (Staph) bacteria both within biofilms and in the stationary growth phase at concentrations below 1% (Kwieciński et al., 2009).

10 Tea tree oil was found to inhibit 301 different types of yeasts isolated from the mouths of cancer patients suffering from advanced cancer, including 41 strains that are known to be resistant to antifungal drugs (Bagg et al., 2006).

11 Eleven types of Candida were found to be highly inhibited by tea tree oil (Banes-Marshall et al., 2001).

12 Topical application of 100% tea tree oil was found to have results similar to topical application of 1% clotrimazole (antifungal drug) solution on onychomycosis (also known as tinea, or fungal nail infection) (Buck et al., 1994).

13 Tea Tree oil was found to alter the membrane properties and functions of *Candida albicans* cells, leading to cell inhibition or death (Hammer et al., 2004).

14 Terpinen-4-ol, a constituent of tea tree oil, and tea tree oil were found to be effective against several forms of vaginal candida infections in rats, including azole-resistant forms (Mondello et al., 2006).

15 Patients with tinea pedis (athlete's foot) were found to have a higher rate of cure and a higher clinical response when treated topically with 25% or 50% tea tree oil solution compared to control (Satchell et al., 2002).

Single Oils

anti-inflammatory[1,2,3,4,5], antioxidant, antiparasitic, a strong antiseptic, antiviral[6], decongestant, digestive, expectorant, immune stimulant, insecticidal, neurotonic, stimulant, and tissue regenerative.

Common Primary Uses*: ❂Acne[7,8,9], ❂Allergies, ❂❂Aneurysm, ❂Athlete's Foot, ❂Bacterial Infections, ❂Boils[10], ❂❂Bronchitis, ❂Candida, ❂Canker Sores, ❂Cavities, ❂❂Chicken Pox, ❂Cleansing, ❂Cold Sores, ❂❂Colds (Common), ❂❂Coughs, ❂Cuts, ❂Dermatitis/Eczema, ❂Dry/Itchy Eyes, ❂Ear Infection, ❂Earache, ❂❂Flu (Influenza), ❂Fungal Infections, ❂Gum Disease, ❂❂Hepatitis, ❂Herpes Simplex, ❂Hives, ❂❂Immune System (Stimulates), ❂❂Infected Wounds, ❂Infection, ❂❂Inflammation, ❂Jock Itch, ❂Lice, ❂MRSA, ❂❂Mumps, ❂Nail Infection, ❂❂Pink Eye, ❂Rashes, ❂Ringworm, ❂Rubella, ❂Scabies, ❂Shingles, ❂Shock, ❂❂Sore Throat, ❂Staph Infection, ❂Sunburn, ❂Thrush, ❂❂Tonsillitis, ❂Vaginal Infection, ❂Varicose Ulcer, ❂❂Viral Infections, ❂Warts, ❂Wounds

Historical Uses: The leaves of the melaleuca tree (or tea tree) have been used for centuries by the aborigines to heal cuts, wounds, and skin infections. With twelve times the antiseptic power of phenol, it has some strong immune-building properties.

French Medicinal Uses: Athlete's foot, bronchitis, colds, coughs, diarrhea, flu, periodontal (gum) disease, rash, skin healing, sore throat, sunburn, tonsillitis, vaginal thrush.

Other Possible Uses: This oil may help burns, digestion, hysteria, infectious diseases, mites[11,12], and ticks[13].

Body System(s) Affected: Immune and Respiratory Systems, Muscles and Bones, Skin.

Aromatic Influence: It promotes cleansing and purity.

Application: Can be applied neat (with no dilution) when used topically. Apply to reflex points and/or directly on area of concern; diffuse.

Oral Use As Dietary Supplement: Approved by the FDA (21CFR172.510) for use as a Food Additive (FA) or Flavoring Agent (FL). Dilute one drop oil in 1 tsp. honey or in 4 oz. of beverage (i.e. soy/rice milk). Not for children under 6-years-old; use with caution and in greater dilution for children 6-years-old and over.

Safety Data: Repeated use can possibly result in contact sensitization.

Blend Classification: Enhancer and Equalizer.

Blends With: All citrus oils, cypress, eucalyptus, lavender, rosemary, and thyme.

Odor: Type: Middle Note (50-80% of the blend); Scent: Medicinal, fresh, woody, earthy, herbaceous; Intensity: 3.

---

1 Tea tree oil was found to reduce swelling during a contact hypersensitivity response in the skin of mice sensitized to the chemical hapten (Brand et al., 2002).

2 *Melaleuca alternifolia* oil was found to reduce reactive oxygen species (ROS) production in neutrophils (a type of white blood cell), indicating an antioxidant effect and decreased Interleukin 2 (a chemical messenger that helps trigger an inflammatory response) secretion, while increasing the secretion of Interleukin 4 (a chemical messenger involved in turning off the inflammatory response) (Caldefie-Chézet et al., 2006).

3 Inhaled tea tree oil was found to have anti-inflammatory influences on male rats with induced peritoneal inflammation (Golab et al., 2007).

4 The water soluble terpinen-4-ol component of tea tree was found to suppress the production of pro-inflammatory mediators in human monocytes (a type of white blood cell that is part of the human immune system) (Hart et al., 2000).

5 Tea tree oil applied to histamine-induced weal and flare in human volunteers was found to decrease the mean weal volume when compared to a control (Koh et al., 2002).

6 Tea tree and eucalyptus oil demonstrated ability to inhibit the *Herpes simplex* virus (Schnitzler et al., 2001).

7 A gel with 5% tea tree oil was found to be as effective as a 5% benzoyl peroxide (a common chemical used to treat acne) lotion at treating acne, with fewer side effects (Bassett et al., 1990).

8 A topical gel containing 5% tea tree oil was found to be more effective than a placebo at preventing acne vulgaris lesions and at decreasing severity in patients suffering from acne vulgaris (Enshaieh et al., 2007).

9 Tea tree oil and several of its main components were found to be active against *Propionibacterium acnes*, a bacteria involved in the formation of acne. This oil was also found to be active against two types of *Staphylococcus* bacteria (Raman et al., 1995).

10 In a human trial, most patients receiving treatment with *Melaleuca alternifolia* oil placed topically on boils experienced healing or reduction of symptoms; while of those receiving no treatment (control), half required surgical intervention, and all still demonstrated signs of the infection (Feinblatt et al., 1960).

11 Tea tree oil scrub and shampoo were found to reduce demodex mite infestation on the eyelids of patients suffering from ocular irritation and inflammation who used this treatment daily for six weeks. It also dramatically decreased ocular irritation and inflammation (Kheirkhah et al., 2007).

12 Tea tree oil was found to be effective against both lice and dust mites in a mite chamber assay (Williamson et al., 2007).

13 Essential oil of *Melaleuca alternifolia* was found to be lethal for more than 80% of *Ixodes ricinus* tick nymphs (a carrier or Lyme disease) when they inhaled a 10 microl dose of the oil for 90 minutes or more (Iori et al., 2005).

---

*See Personal Usage Guide section for more details on these primary uses.   ❂=Neat, ❂=Dilute for Children/Sensitive Skin, ❂=Dilute

MELISSA (LEMON BALM) 🅣🅐🅘
(Melissa officinalis)

Botanical Family: Labiatae (mint)

Extraction Method: Steam distilled from leaves and flowers

Chemical Constituents: Aldehydes (up to 65%): geranial (<35%), neral (<28%), citronellal (<3%), α-cyclocitral; Sesquiterpenes (<35%): β-caryophyllene (<19%), α-copaene (<5%), germacrene-D (<4%), β-bourbonene, δ- & γ-cadinenes, humulene, β-elemene; Oxides (<11%): caryophyllene oxide (<7%), 1,8 cineol (<4%); Alcohols (<7%): linalol, octen-3ol, nerol, geraniol, citronellol, isopulegol, caryophyllenol, farnesol; Esters (<7%): methyl citronellate (<5%), citronellyl, geranyl, neryl, & linalyl acetates; Ketones (<7%): methyl heptanone (<5%), farnesylacetone, octanone; Monoterpenes (<3%): cis- & trans-ocimenes, l-limonene; Sesquiterpene Alcohols: elemol, α-cadinol; Furanocoumarins: aesculetin.

Properties: Antibacterial, antidepressant, antihistamine, antimicrobial, antispasmodic, antiviral[14], hypertensive, nervine, sedative[15,16], tonic, and uterine.

Common Primary Uses*: 🅐🅣Calming, 🅣Cold Sores, 🅣🅐Viral Infections

Historical Uses: Anciently, melissa was used for nervous disorders and many different ailments dealing with the heart or the emotions. It was also used to promote fertility. Melissa was the main ingredient in Carmelite water, distilled in France since 1611 by the Carmelite monks.

Other Possible Uses: Allergies, anxiety, asthma, bronchitis, chronic coughs, colds, cold-sore blisters[17] (apply directly three times per day), colic, depression, dysentery, eczema, erysipelas, fevers, heart conditions (where there is overstimulation or heat), hypertension, indigestion, insect bites, insomnia, menstrual problems, migraine, nausea, nervous tension, palpitations, shock, sterility (in women), throat infections, vertigo, and vomiting. Dr. Dietrich Wabner, a professor at the Technical University of Munich, reported that a onetime application of true melissa oil led to complete remission of herpes simplex lesions. According to Robert Tisserand, "Melissa is the nearest one can find to a rejuvenator—not something which will make us young again, but which helps to cushion the effect of our mind and the world outside on our body."

Body System(s) Affected: Emotional Balance, Skin.

Aromatic Influence: Melissa has a delicate, delightful, lemony scent that is unique among essential oils, providing a wonderful support to both body and mind. It is calming and uplifting and may help to balance the emotions.

Application: Can be applied neat (with no dilution) when used topically. Apply to reflex points and/or directly on area of concern.

Oral Use As Dietary Supplement: Generally recognized as safe (GRAS) for human consumption by the FDA (21CFR182.20). Dilute one drop oil in 1 tsp. honey or in 4 oz. of beverage (i.e. soy/rice milk). Not for children under 6-years-old; use with caution and in greater dilution for children 6-years-old and over.

Blend Classification: Enhancer, Equalizer, and Modifier.

Blends With: Geranium, lavender, and other floral and citrus oils.

Odor: Type: Middle Note (50-80% of the blend); Scent: Delicate, lemony; Intensity: 2.

Single Oils

14 Melissa oil demonstrated inhibition of *Herpes simplex* type 1 and 2 viruses. (Schnitzler et al., 2008).

15 Results of a clinical trial indicate that a combination of melissa and valerian oils may have anxiety-reducing properties at some doses (Kennedy et al., 2006).

16 Melissa (lemon balm) oil applied topically in a lotion was found to reduce agitation and to improve quality of life factors in patients suffering severe dementia compared to those receiving a placebo lotion (Ballard et al., 2002).

17 Melissa oil demonstrated inhibition of *Herpes simplex* type 1 and 2 viruses. (Schnitzler et al., 2008).

🅣=Topical, 🅐=Aromatic, 🅘=Internal

MYRRH ⓉⒶⓁ
(Commiphora myrrha)

Botanical Family: Burseraceae (resinous trees and shrubs)

Extraction Method: Steam distilled from gum/resin

Chemical Constituents: Sesquiterpenes (up to 75%): lindestrene (up to 30%), β-, γ-, & δ-elemenes (<40%), α-copaene (<12%), β-bourbonene (<5%), muurolene, δ-cadinene, humulene, curzerene; Furanoids (<27%): methoxyfurogermacrene (<9%), furoendesmadiene (<8%), α-bergamotene (<5%), methylisopropenylfurone (<5%), furfural (<3%), furanodione (<2%), rosefuran; Ketones: (<20%): curzenone (<11%), methylisobutyl ketone (<6%), germacrone (<4%); Triterpenes (<7%): α-amyrin (<4%), α-amyrenone (<3%); Monoterpenes (<6%): ocimene, p-cymene, α-thujene, l-limonene, myrcene; Aldehydes: methylbutynal (<3%), cinnamaldehyde, cuminal; Arenes: xylene; Carboxylic Acids: acetic acid, formic acid, palmitic acid; Phenols: eugenol, cresol.

Properties: Anti-infectious, anti-inflammatory[1], antiseptic, antitumor[2], astringent, and tonic.

Common Primary Uses*: ⒶⓉCancer, ⓉChapped/Cracked Skin, ⓉⒶCongestion, ⓉDysentery, ⓉGum Disease, ⓉⒶHashimoto's Disease, ⓉⒶHepatitis, ⓉⒶHyperthyroidism, ⓉⒶInfection, ⓉⒶLiver Cirrhosis, ⓉSkin Ulcers, ⓉStretch Marks, ⓉⓉUlcers (Duodenal), ⓉWeeping Wounds

Historical Uses: Myrrh was used as incense in religious rituals, in embalming, and as a cure for cancer, leprosy, and syphilis. Myrrh, mixed with coriander and honey, was used to treat herpes.

---

1 At subtoxic levels, myrrh oil was found to reduce interleukin (chemical signals believed to play a role in the inflammation response) by fibroblast cells in the gums (Tipton et al., 2003).

2 Treatment with elemene (found in myrrh oil) was found to increase survival time and to reduce tumor size in patients with malignant brain tumor, as compared to chemotherapy (Tan et al., 2000).

French Medicinal Uses: Bronchitis, diarrhea, dysentery, hyperthyroidism, stretch marks, thrush, ulcers, vaginal thrush, viral hepatitis.

Other Possible Uses: This oil may help with appetite (increase), asthma, athlete's foot, candida, catarrh (mucus), coughs, eczema, digestion, dyspepsia (impaired digestion), flatulence (gas), fungal infection, gingivitis, hemorrhoids, mouth ulcers, decongesting the prostate gland, ringworm, sore throats, skin conditions (chapped, cracked, and inflamed), wounds, and wrinkles.

Body System(s) Affected: Hormonal, Immune, and Nervous Systems; Skin.

Aromatic Influence: It promotes awareness and is uplifting.

Application: Can be applied neat (with no dilution) when used topically. Apply to reflex points and/or directly on area of concern.

Oral Use As Dietary Supplement: Approved by the FDA (21CFR172.510) for use as a Food Additive (FA) and Flavoring Agent (FL). Dilute one drop oil in 1 tsp. honey or in 4 oz. of beverage (i.e. soy/rice milk). Not for children under 6-years-old; use with caution and in greater dilution for children 6-years-old and over.

Safety Data: Use with caution during pregnancy.

Blend Classification: Modifier and Equalizer.

Blends With: Frankincense, lavender, sandalwood, and all spice oils.

Odor: Type: Base Note (5-20% of the blend); Scent: Warm, earthy, woody, balsamic; Intensity: 4.

ORANGE, WILD Ⓣ*ⒶⓁ
(Citrus sinensis)

Botanical Family: Rutaceae (citrus)

Extraction Method: Cold-pressed from rind

Chemical Constituents: Monoterpenes (up to 95%): d-Limonene (<90%), terpinolene,

---

**See Personal Usage Guide section for more details on these primary uses.*   Ⓣ=Neat, Ⓣ=Dilute for Children/Sensitive Skin, Ⓣ=Dilute

62

myrcene, α-pinene; Tetraterpenes (<8%): β-carotene (<6%), lycopene; Aldehydes (<8%): citral, decanal, citronellal, dodecanal, nonanal, octanal, α-sinensal; Alcohols (<6%): linalol, cis & trans-carveol, α-terpineol, geraniol; Ketones (<4%): l- & d-carvone (<3%), α-ionone; Esters (<3%): citronellyl acetate, geranyl acetate, linalyl acetate, methyl anthranilate; Furanoids: auraptene, bergaptol, imperatarine; Sesquiterpene Ketones: nootkatone.

Properties: Anticancer[3,4], antidepressant, antiseptic, antispasmodic, digestive, sedative[5,6], and tonic.

Common Primary Uses*: ⒶAnxiety, ⓉDigestion (Sluggish), ⒶFear, ⒶⓉHeart Palpitations, ⒶⓉInsomnia, ⓉMenopause, ⒶⓉNervousness, ⒶUplifting, ⓉⒶWithdrawal

Historical Uses: Oranges, particularly the bitter oranges, have been used for palpitation, scurvy, jaundice, bleeding, heartburn, relaxed throat, prolapse of the uterus and the anus, diarrhea, and blood in the feces.

French Medicinal Uses: Angina (false), cardiac spasm, constipation, diarrhea (chronic), dyspepsia (nervous), insomnia, menopause, palpitation.

Other Possible Uses: This oil may help appetite, bones (rickety), bronchitis, colds, colic (dilute for infants; helps them sleep), complexion (dull and oily), dermatitis, digestive system, fever, flu, lower high cholesterol, mouth ulcers, muscle soreness, obesity, sedation, tissue repair, water retention, and wrinkles.

Body System(s) Affected: Digestive and Immune Systems, Emotional Balance, Skin.

Aromatic Influence: Orange is calming and uplifting to the mind and body.

Application: Can be applied neat (with no dilution) when used topically. Apply to reflex points and directly on area of concern; diffuse.

Oral Use As Dietary Supplement: Generally recognized as safe (GRAS) for human consumption by the FDA (21CFR182.20). Dilute one drop oil in 1 tsp. honey or in 4 oz. of beverage (i.e. soy/rice milk). Not for children under 6-years-old; use with caution and in greater dilution for children 6-years-old and over.

Safety Data: Avoid direct sunlight for up to 12 hours after use.

Blend Classification: Enhancer and Personifier.

Blends With: Cinnamon, frankincense, geranium, and lavender.

Odor: Type: Top Note (5-20% of the blend); Scent: Fresh, citrusy, fruity, sweet; Intensity: 1.

OREGANO ⓉⒶⒾ
(Origanum vulgare)

Botanical Family: Labiatae

Extraction Method: Steam distilled from leaves

Chemical Constituents: Phenols (up to 80%): carvacrol (<75%), thymol (<5%), terpinen-4-ol; Monoterpenes (<25%): p-cymene (<10%), γ-terpinene (<9%), myrcene (<3%), α- and β-pinenes, camphene, l-limonene, α-terpinene; Sesquiterpenes (<6%): β-caryophyllene (<5%), β-bisabolene; Carboxylic Acids: rosmaric acid (<5%); Esters: linalyl acetate (<4%); Ketones: camphor, d-carvone; Alcohols: borneol, linalol, α-terpineol.

---

3 In a study of older individuals, it was found that there was a dose-dependent relationship between citrus peel consumption (which is high in d-Limonene) and a lower degree of squamous cell carcinoma (SCC) of the skin (Hakim et al., 2000).

4 In clinical trials, d-Limonene (found in most citrus oils, dill, caraway, citronella, and nutmeg) was found to elicit a response (kept patients stable) in some patients in advanced stages of cancer (1 breast and 3 colorectal carcinoma of 32 total patients). A secondary trial with just breast cancer patients did not elicit any responses (Vigushin et al., 1998).

5 Female patients waiting for dental treatment were found to be less anxious, more positive, and more calm when exposed to orange oil odor than patients who were not exposed to the orange oil odor (Lehrner et al., 2000).

6 Patients waiting for dental treatment were found to be less anxious and to have a better mood when exposed to the odor of lavender or orange oil compared to control (Lehrner et al., 2005).

Ⓣ=Topical, Ⓐ=Aromatic, Ⓘ=Internal

Properties: Antibacterial[1,2], antifungal[3,4,5,6], anti-parasitic[7], antiseptic to the respiratory system, antiviral, and immune stimulant[8].

Common Primary Uses*: ⓐⓣAthlete's Foot, ⓣCalluses, ⓣⓞCandida, ⓣCanker Sores, ⓣCarpal Tunnel Syndrome, ⓣEbola Virus, ⓣⓐⓞFungal Infections, ⓣⓐⓞImmune System (Stimulates), ⓣInflammation, ⓞⓣIntestinal Parasites, ⓣMRSA, ⓣMuscle Aches, ⓣⓐNasal Polyp, ⓞⓣParasites, ⓣⓐPlague, ⓐⓣPneumonia, ⓐⓣRingworm, ⓣⓞStaph Infection, ⓣⓞVaginal Candida, ⓣViral Infections, ⓣWarming (Body), ⓣWarts, ⓣWhooping Cough

French Medicinal Uses: Asthma, bronchitis (chronic), mental disease, pulmonary tuberculosis, and rheumatism (chronic).

Other Possible Uses: This oil may help colds, digestive problems, metabolic balance, viral and bacterial pneumonia, and strengthen vital centers.

Body System(s) Affected: Immune and Respiratory Systems, Muscles and Bones.

Aromatic Influence: Strengthens one's feeling of security.

Application: Dilute 1:3 (1 drop essential oil to 3 drops carrier oil) when used topically. Apply to reflex points and directly on area of concern; diffuse.

Oral Use As Dietary Supplement: Generally recognized as safe (GRAS) for human consumption by the FDA (21CFR182.20). Dilute one drop oil in 1 tsp. honey or in 4 oz. of beverage (i.e. soy/rice milk). Not for children under 6-years-old; use with caution and in greater dilution for children 6-years-old and over.

---

1 Oregano oil was found to inhibit MRSA (Nostro et al., 2004).
2 Oregano oil was found to kill antibiotic-resistant strains of *Staph, E. coli, Klebsiella pneumoniae, Helicobacter pylori,* and *Mycobacterium terrae* (Preuss et al., 2005).
3 The vapor of oregano oil was found to be fungicidal against the *Trichophyton mentagrophytes* fungi (a fungi that causes a skin infection known as Malabar itch) (Inouye et al., 2006).
4 In a test of nine oils, clove (followed by cinnamon, oregano, and mace oils) was found to be inhibitory to two toxin-producing fungi (Juglal et al., 2002).
5 Mice infected with *Candida albicans* who were fed origanum oil or carvacrol diluted in olive oil had an 80% survival rate after 30 days, while infected mice fed olive oil alone all died after 10 days (Manohar et al., 2001).
6 Cinnamon, thyme, oregano, and cumin oils inhibited the production of aflatoxin by aspergillus fungus (Tantaoui-Elaraki et al., 1994).
7 Oregano oil administered orally was found to improve gastrointestinal symptoms in 7 of 11 patients who had tested positive for the parasite *Blastocystis hominis* and caused the disappearance of this parasite in 8 cases (Force et al., 2000).
8 Growth-retarded pigs receiving a supplementation of oregano leaves and flowers enriched with cold-pressed oregano oil were found to have increased growth, decreased mortality, and higher numbers of immune-system cells and compounds when compared to control pigs who did not receive supplementation (Walter et al., 2004).

Safety Data: Can cause extreme skin irritation.

Blend Classification: Enhancer and Equalizer.

Blends With: Basil, fennel, geranium, lemongrass, thyme, and rosemary.

Odor: Type: Middle Note (50-80% of the blend); Scent: Herbaceous, sharp; Intensity: 5.

PATCHOULI (OR PATCHOULY) ⓣⓐ①
(Pogostemon cablin)

Botanical Family: Labiatae (mint)

Extraction Method: Steam-distilled from leaves and flowers

Chemical Constituents: Sesquiterpenes (up to 63%): α-bulnesene (<20%), β-bulnesene (<16%), aromadendrene (<15%), α-gaiene (>12%), seychellene (6%), α-, β- & γ-patchoulenes (<12%), β-caryophyllene (<4%), δ-cadinene (<3%), β-gaiene, β-elemene, humulene; Sesquiterpene Alcohols (<38%): patchoulol (up to 35%), pogostol, bulnesol, guaiol, patchoulenol; Oxides (<5%): bulnesene oxide, caryophyllene oxide, guaiene oxide; Ketones: patchoulenone (<3%); Monoterpenes: α- & β-pinenes, l-limonene.

Properties: Anti-infectious, anti-inflammatory, antifungal, antiseptic, antitoxic, astringent, decongestant, deodorant, diuretic, insecticidal[9,10,11], stimulant (digestive), and tonic.

Common Primary Uses*: ⓣDiuretic, ⓣⓞⓐFever, ⓣⓐMosquito Repellent, ⓣⓐTermite Repellent

Historical Uses: For centuries, the Asian people used patchouli to fight infection, cool fevers, tone the skin (and entire body), and to act as an antidote for insect and snake bites. It was also used to treat colds, headaches, nausea,

---

9 In a test of 34 different essential oils, patchouli (*Pogostemon cablin*) oil proved to be the most effective insecticide against the common house fly (Pavela, 2008).
10 Both patchouli oil and its constituent, patchouli alcohol (patchoulol), were found to be repellent and insecticidal to Formosan termites when applied topically (Zhu et al., 2003).
11 Clove, citronella, and patchouli oils were found to effectively repel 3 species of mosquitoes (Trongtokit et al., 2005).

---

*See Personal Usage Guide section for more details on these primary uses.   ⓣ=Neat, ⓣ=Dilute for Children/Sensitive Skin, ⓣ=Dilute

vomiting, diarrhea, abdominal pain, and halitosis (bad breath).

French Medicinal Uses: Allergies, dermatitis, eczema, hemorrhoids, tissue regeneration.

Other Possible Uses: This oil is a digester of toxic material in the body. It may also help acne, appetite (curbs), bites (insect and snake), cellulite, congestion, dandruff, depression, digestive system, relieve itching from hives, skin conditions (chapped and tightens loose skin), UV radiation (protects against), water retention, weeping wounds, weight reduction, and wrinkles prevention.

Body System(s) Affected: Skin.

Aromatic Influence: It is sedating, calming[12], and relaxing—allowing it to reduce anxiety. It may have some particular influence on sex, physical energy, and money.

Application: Apply to Vita Flex Points and directly on area of concern; diffuse.

Oral Use As Dietary Supplement: Approved by the FDA for use as a Food Additive (FA) and Flavoring Agent (FL). Dilute one drop oil in 1 tsp. honey or in 4 oz. of beverage (i.e. soy/rice milk). Not for children under 6-years-old; use with caution and in greater dilution for children 6-years-old and over.

Blend Classification: Enhancer

Blends With: Bergamot, clary sage, frankincense, geranium, ginger, lavender, lemongrass, myrrh, pine, rosewood, sandalwood.

Odor: Type: Base Note (5-20% of the blend); Scent: Earthy, herbaceous, sweet-balsamic, rich, with woody undertones; Intensity: 4

PEPPERMINT ⓉⒶⒾ
(Mentha piperita)

Botanical Family: Labiatae (mint)

Extraction Method: Steam distilled from leaves, stems, and flower buds

Chemical Constituents: Phenolic Alcohols (up to 44%): menthol (<44%), piperitols; Ketones (<25%): menthone (20-30% and up to 65% if distilled in September when flowering), pulegone (<5%), piperitone (<2%), carvone, jasmone; Monoterpenes (< 15%): α and β-pinenes (<6%), l-limonene (<6%), ocimene, myrcene, p-cymene, β-phellandrene, sabinene, α-terpinene, terpinolene, camphene; Sesquiterpenes (<10%): germacrene-D (<5%), β-bourbonene, ζ-bulgarene, γ-cadinene, β-caryophyllene, β-elemene, β-farnesene, muurolene; Esters (<9%): menthyl acetate (<9%), also menthyl butyrate & isovalerate; Oxides (<9%): 1,8 cineol (<5%), piperitone oxide, caryophyllene oxide; Furanoids: menthofuran (<8%); Phenols: terpinen-4-ol (<3%); Alcohols (<3%): α-terpineol, linalol; Sesquiterpene Alcohols: viridiflorol; Furanocoumarins: aesculetin; Sulphides: mint sulfide, dimenthyl sulfide.

Properties: Analgesic, antibacterial[13,14,15,16], anticarcinogenic, anti-inflammatory[17,18], antiseptic, antispasmodic[19], antiviral[20], and invigorating.

---

13 Subjects using a mouthwash containing thymol, menthol, methyl salicylate, and eucalyptol for 6 months were found to not have developed oral bacteria that were resistant to the oils (Charles et al., 2000).
14 Peppermint and spearmint oil inhibited resistant strains of *Staphylococcus, E. Coli, Salmonella,* and H*elicobacter pylori* (Imai et al., 2001).
15 Peppermint and rosemary oils were each found to be more effective at preventing dental biofilm (plaque) formation than chlorhexidine (an antiseptic) (Rasooli et al., 2008).
16 Peppermint oil blended with toothpaste was found to be more effective at lower concentrations in inhibiting the formation of dental plaque than chlorhexidine (an antiseptic) in human volunteers (Shayegh et al., 2008).
17 A combination of peppermint and caraway oil was found to reduce visceral hyperalgesia (pain hypersensitivity in the gastrointestinal tract) after induced inflammation in rats (Adam et al., 2006).
18 L-menthol was found to inhibit production of inflammation mediators in human monocytes (a type of white blood cell involved in the immune response) (Juergens et al., 1998).
19 Peppermint oil was found to be as effective as Buscopan (an antispasmodic drug) at preventing spasms during a barium enema (a type of enema used to place barium in the colon for X-ray imaging purposes) (Asao et al., 2003).
20 Peppermint oil demonstrated a direct virucidal activity against *Herpes* type 1 and 2

---

12 Inhalation of essential oils such as pepper, estragon, fennel, and grapefruit was found to have a stimulating effect on sympathetic activity, while inhalation of essential oils of rose or patchouli caused a decrease in sympathetic activity in healthy adults (Haze et al., 2002).

Ⓣ=Topical, Ⓐ=Aromatic, Ⓘ=Internal

Common Primary Uses*: ⏣⏦Alertness, ⏣⏦⏣Antioxidant, ⏣⏦Asthma, ⏦Autism, ⏦Bacterial Infections, ⏦⏣Bell's Palsy, ⏣⏦Brain Injury, ⏦⏣Chronic Fatigue, ⏦Cold Sores, ⏦⏦Colon Polyps, ⏦⏣Congestion, ⏦Constipation, ⏦⏣Cooling (Body), ⏦Cramps/Charley Horses, ⏦⏦Crohn's Disease, ⏦⏦Diarrhea, ⏦Dysmenorrhea, ⏣Endurance, ⏣Fainting, ⏦⏦⏣Fever, ⏣⏦⏦Flu (Influenza), ⏦⏦Gamma Radiation Exposure[1,2,3], ⏦⏦Gastritis, ⏦Halitosis, ⏦⏣Headaches[4], ⏦Heartburn, ⏦Heatstroke, ⏦Hernia (Hiatal), ⏦Herpes Simplex, ⏦Hives, ⏦Hot Flashes, ⏦⏣Huntington's Disease, ⏦⏦⏣Hypothyroidism, ⏦⏦⏣Indigestion, ⏦⏦Irritable Bowel Syndrome[5,6,7,8], ⏦Itching, ⏦Jet Lag, ⏦Lactation (Decrease Milk Production), ⏣⏦Memory[9], ⏦⏣Migraines, ⏣Motion Sickness, ⏦MRSA, ⏦⏣Multiple Sclerosis, ⏦Muscle Aches, ⏦Muscle Fatigue, ⏣⏦Myelin Sheath, ⏣Nausea, ⏣⏦Olfactory Loss (Sense of Smell), ⏦Osteoporosis, ⏦⏣Paralysis, ⏣⏦Rhinitis, ⏦Scabies, ⏦Sciatica, ⏦⏣Shock, ⏣⏦Sinusitis, ⏦Surgical Wounds, ⏦Swollen Eyes, ⏦Tennis Elbow, ⏦⏣⏦Throat Infection, ⏦⏣Typhoid, ⏦⏦Ulcer (Gastric), ⏦Varicose Veins, ⏦⏦Vomiting

Historical Uses: For centuries, peppermint has been used to soothe digestive difficulties, freshen breath, and to relieve colic, gas, headaches, heartburn, and indigestion.

French Medicinal Uses: Asthma, bronchitis, candida, diarrhea, digestion (aids)[10], fever (reduces), flu, halitosis, heartburn, hemorrhoids, hot flashes, indigestion[11,12], menstrual irregularity, migraine headache, motion sickness, nausea, respiratory function (aids), shock, skin (itchy), throat infection, varicose veins, vomiting.

Other Possible Uses: This oil may help anger, arthritis, colic, depression, fatigue, food poisoning, hysteria, inflammation, liver problems, nerves (regenerate and support)[13], rheumatism, elevate and open sensory system, soothe and cool skin (may help keep body cooler on hot days), toothaches, tuberculosis, and add flavor to water.

Body System(s) Affected: Digestive System, Muscles and Bones, Nervous and Respiratory Systems, Skin.

Aromatic Influence: It is purifying and stimulating to the conscious mind and may aid with memory and mental performance. It is cooling and may help reduce fevers.

Application: Can be applied neat (with no dilution), or dilute 1:1 (1 drop essential oil to 1 drop carrier oil) for children and for those with sensitive skin when using topically. Apply to reflex points and/or directly on area of concern.

Oral Use As Dietary Supplement: Generally recognized as safe (GRAS) for human consumption by the FDA (21CFR182.20). Dilute one drop oil in 1 tsp. honey or in 4 oz. of beverage (i.e. soy/rice milk). Not for children under 6-years-old; use with caution and in greater dilution for children 6-years-old and over.

Safety Data: Repeated use can possibly result in contact sensitization. Use with caution if dealing with high blood pressure. Use with caution during pregnancy.

Blend Classification: Personifier

---

viruses (Schuhmacher et al., 2003).

1 Mice pretreated with peppermint leaf extract demonstrated less bone marrow cell loss than mice not pretreated with peppermint when exposed to gamma radiation (Samarth et al., 2007).

2 In mice exposed to whole-body gamma irradiation, only 17% of mice who had been fed peppermint oil died, while 100% of mice who did not receive peppermint oil died. It was also found that mice pre-fed peppermint oil were able to return blood cell levels to normal after 30 days, while control mice were not (and consequently died), suggesting a protective or stimulating effect of the oil on blood stem cells (Samarth et al., 2004).

3 Peppermint extract fed orally to mice demonstrated the ability to protect the testis from gamma radiation damage (Samarth et al., 2009).

4 A combination of peppermint oil and ethanol was found to have a significant analgesic effect with a reduction in sensitivity to headache; while a combination of peppermint, eucalyptus, and ethanol was found to relax muscles and to increase cognitive performance in humans (Göbel et al., 1994).

5 In irritable bowel syndrome patients without bacterial overgrowth, lactose intolerance, or celiac disease, peppermint oil was found to reduce IBS symptoms significantly more than a placebo over 8 weeks (Cappello et al., 2007).

6 Children suffering from irritable bowel syndrome (IBS) who received peppermint oil in enteric-coated capsules (encapsulated so the capsules wouldn't open until they reached the intestines) reported a reduced severity of pain associated with IBS (Kline et al., 2001).

7 Patients with IBS symptoms who took a peppermint-oil formulation in an enteric-coated capsule were found to have a significantly higher reduction of symptoms compared to patients taking a placebo (Liu et al., 1997).

8 Peppermint oil in enteric-coated capsules was found to relieve symptoms of irritable bowel syndrome better than a placebo in patients suffering from IBS (Rees et al., 1979).

9 In human trials, the aroma of peppermint was found to enhance memory and to increase alertness (Moss et al., 2008).

10 The use of rosemary, lemon, and peppermint oils in massage demonstrated an ability to reduce constipation and to increase bowel movements in elderly subjects compared to massage without the oils (Kim et al., 2005).

11 In patients with dyspepsia (indigestion), treatments with capsules containing peppermint and caraway oil were found to decrease pain and pain frequency (Freise et al., 1999).

12 An enteric-coated capsule with peppermint and caraway oil was found to reduce pain and symptoms in patients with non-ulcer dyspepsia (indigestion) compared to a control (May et al., 1996).

13 Pretreatment of human and rat astrocyte cells (cells found in the nerve and brain that support the blood-brain barrier and help repair the brain and spinal cord following injuries) with peppermint oil was found to inhibit heat-shock-induced apoptosis of these cells (Koo et al., 2001).

*See Personal Usage Guide section for more details on these primary uses.   ⏦=Neat, ⏣=Dilute for Children/Sensitive Skin, ⏦=Dilute

Odor: Type: Middle Note (50-80% of the blend); Scent: Minty, sharp, intense; Intensity: 5.

ROMAN CHAMOMILE ⓉⒶⒾ
(Chamaemelum nobile or Anthemis nobilis)

Botanical Family: Compositae (daisy)

Extraction Method: Steam distillation from flowers

Chemical Constituents: Esters (up to 75%): isobutyl angelate (up to 25%), isoamyl methacylate (up to 25%), amyl butyrate (<15%), other angelate, butyrate, acetate, and tiglate esters; Monoterpenes (<35%): α- & β-pinenes (<20%), terpinenes, sabinene, camphene, d-Limonene, p-cymene, myrcene; Ketones: pinocarvone (14%); Sesquiterpenes (up to 12%): β-caryophyllene, chamazulene; Alcohols (>7%): trans-pinocarveol, farnesol, nerolidol.

Properties: Anti-infectious, anti-inflammatory[14], antiparasitic, antispasmodic, calming, and relaxing.

Common Primary Uses*: ⓉBee/Hornet Stings, ⒶⓉCalming, ⓉClub Foot, ⓉDysentery, ⒶⓉHyperactivity, ⒶⓉInsomnia, ⓉMenopause, ⓉMuscle Spasms, ⓉNeuralgia, ⓉNeuritis, ⒾⓉParasites, ⓉRashes, ⓉSciatica, ⓉShock, ⓉSkin (Dry), ⓉSore Nipples

Historical Uses: It was traditionally used by the ancient Romans to give them a clear mind and to empower them with courage for their battles. According to Roberta Wilson, "Chamomile was nicknamed the 'plant's physician' because it supposedly cured any ailing plant placed near it."

French Medicinal Uses: Intestinal parasites, neuritis, neuralgia, shock (nervous).

Other Possible Uses: Chamomile neutralizes allergies and increases the ability of the skin to regenerate. It is a cleanser of the blood and also helps the liver to reject poisons and to discharge them. This oil may help with allergies, bruises, cuts, depression, insomnia, muscle tension, nerves (calming and promoting nerve health), restless legs, and skin conditions such as acne, boils, dermatitis, eczema, rashes, and sensitive skin. Chamomile is mild enough to use on infants and children. For centuries, mothers have used chamomile to calm crying children, ease earaches, fight fevers, soothe stomachaches and colic, and relieve toothaches and teething pain. It can safely and effectively reduce irritability and minimize nervousness in children, especially hyperactive children.

Body System(s) Affected: Emotional Balance, Nervous System, Skin.

Aromatic Influence: Because it is calming and relaxing, it can combat depression, insomnia, and stress. It eliminates some of the emotional charge of anxiety, irritability, and nervousness. It may also be used to soothe and clear the mind, creating an atmosphere of peace and patience.

Application: Can be applied neat (with no dilution), or dilute 1:1 (1 drop essential oil to 1 drop carrier oil) for children and for those with sensitive skin when using topically. Apply to reflex points and/or directly on area of concern; diffuse.

Oral Use As Dietary Supplement: Generally recognized as safe (GRAS) for human consumption by the FDA (21CFR182.20). Dilute one drop oil in 1 tsp. honey or in 4 oz. of beverage (i.e. soy/rice milk). Not for children under 6-years-old; use with caution and in greater dilution for children 6-years-old and over.

Safety Data: Can irritate sensitive skin.

Blend Classification: Personifier

Blends With: Lavender, rose, geranium, and clary sage.

Odor: Type: Middle Note (50-80% of the blend); Scent: Fresh, sweet, fruity-herbaceous, apple-like, no tenacity; Intensity: 4.

---

14 Chamazulene, a chemical in chamomile oil, was found to block formation of leukotriene (a signaling chemical involved in the inflammation process) in neutrophilic (immune system) granulocytes (white blood cells containing granules). It also demonstrated an antioxidant effect (Safayhi et al., 1994).

Ⓣ=Topical, Ⓐ=Aromatic, Ⓘ=Internal

ROSE ⓣⒶⒾ
(Rosa damascena)

Botanical Family: Rosaceae

Extraction Method: Steam distilled from flowers (a two-part process)

Chemical Constituents: Alcohols (up to 70%): citronellol (up to 45%), geraniol (up to 28%), nerol (<9%), linalol, borneol, α-terpineol; Monoterpenes (<25%): stearoptene (<22%), α & β-pinenes, camphene, α-terpinene, l-limonene, myrcene, p-cymene, ocimene; Alkanes (<19%): nonadecane (<15%), octadecane, eicosane, and others; Esters (<5%): geranyl, neryl, and citronellyl acetates; Phenols (<4%): eugenol, phenylethanol; Sesquiterpene Alcohols: farnesol (<2%); Oxides: rose oxide; Ketones: α- & β-damascenone, β-ionone; Furanoids: rosefuran; Many other trace elements.

Properties: Antihemorrhagic, anti-infectious, aphrodisiac, and sedative[1].

Common Primary Uses*: ⒶⓣAphrodisiac, ⓣPoison Ivy/Oak, ⓣScarring (Prevention)

Historical Uses: The healing properties of the rose have been utilized in medicine throughout the ages and still play an important role in the East. Rose has been used for digestive and menstrual problems, headaches and nervous tension, liver congestion, poor circulation, fever (plague), eye infections, and skin complaints.

Other Possible Uses: This oil may help asthma, chronic bronchitis, frigidity, gingivitis, hemorrhaging, herpes simplex, impotence, infections, prevent scarring, sexual debilities, skin disease, sprains, thrush, tuberculosis, ulcers, wounds, and wrinkles.

Body System(s) Affected: Emotional Balance, Skin.

Aromatic Influence: It is stimulating and elevating to the mind, creating a sense of well-being. Its beautiful fragrance is almost intoxicating and aphrodisiac-like.

Application: Can be applied neat (with no dilution) when used topically. Apply to reflex points and/or directly on area of concern; diffuse.

Oral Use As Dietary Supplement: Generally recognized as safe (GRAS) for human consumption by the FDA (21CFR182.20). Dilute one drop oil in 1 tsp. honey or in 4 oz. of beverage (i.e. soy/rice milk). Not for children under 6-years-old; use with caution and in greater dilution for children 6-years-old and over.

Safety Data: Use with caution during pregnancy.

Blend Classification: Personifier, Enhancer, Equalizer, and Modifier

Odor: Type: Middle to Base Notes (20-80% of the blend); Scent: Floral, spicy, rich, deep, sensual, green, honey-like; Intensity: 3.

ROSEMARY ⓣⒶⒾ
(Rosmarinus officinalis CT 1,8 Cineol)

Botanical Family: Labiatae (mint)

Extraction Method: Steam distilled from flowering plant

Chemical Constituents: Oxides: 1,8 cineol (up to 55%), caryophyllene oxide, humulene oxide; Monoterpenes: α-pinene (<14%), β-pinene (<9%), camphene (<8%), l-limonene, myrcene, p-cymene, α- & β-phellandrenes, α- & γ-terpinenes; Ketones (<32%): camphor (<30%), β-thujone, verbenone, d-carvone, hexanone, heptanone; Alcohols (<20%): borneol (<12%), α-terpineol (<5%), linalol, verbenol; Sesquiterpenes (<3%): β-caryophyllene, humulene; Phenols: terpinen-4-ol; Esters: bornyl and fenchyl acetates; Acids: rosemaric acid.

---

1   Rose oil was found to have effects similar to the antianxiety drug diazepam (Valium) in mice but through a different cellular mechanism (Umezu, 1999).

---

*See Personal Usage Guide section for more details on these primary uses.

ⓣ=Neat, ⓣ=Dilute for Children/Sensitive Skin, ⓣ=Dilute

Properties: Analgesic[2], antibacterial[3], anticancer[4,5,6], anticatarrhal, antifungal[7], anti-infectious, anti-inflammatory[8], antioxidant[9,10,11], and expectorant.

Common Primary Uses*: ❶❸Addictions (Alcohol), ❶Adenitis, ❶❶❸Antioxidant, ❶Arterial Vasodilator, ❶❸Arthritis, ❶❸Bell's Palsy, ❶❸Cancer, ❶Cellulite, ❸❶Chemical Stress, ❶Cholera, ❶Club Foot, ❶Constipation, ❶Detoxification, ❶❸Diabetes, ❶Diuretic, ❸Fainting, ❶❸Fatigue, ❸❶Flu (Influenza), ❶Greasy/Oily Hair, ❶Hair (Loss), ❶❸Headaches, ❶Inflammation, ❶Kidney Infection, ❶Lice, ❸❶Low Blood Pressure, ❸❶Memory, ❶Muscular Dystrophy, ❶Osteoarthritis, ❶Schmidt's Syndrome, ❸❶Sinusitis, ❶Vaginal Infection, ❶Vaginitis, ❶❸Viral Hepatitis, ❶❶Worms

Historical Uses: The rosemary plant was regarded as sacred by many civilizations. It was used as a fumigant to help drive away evil spirits and to protect against plague and infectious illness.

French Medicinal Uses: Arthritis[12], blood pressure (low), bronchitis[13], cellulite, cholera, colds, dandruff, depression (nervous), diabetes, fatigue (nervous/mental), flu, fluid retention, hair loss[14], headache, hepatitis (viral), menstrual periods (irregular), sinusitis, tachycardia, vaginitis.

Other Possible Uses: This oil may help arteriosclerosis, bronchitis, chills, colds, colitis, cystitis, dyspepsia, nervous exhaustion, immune system (stimulate), otitis, palpitations, prevent respiratory infections, sour stomach, stress-related illness. Note: This chemotype is said to be best used for pulmonary congestion[15], slow elimination, candida, chronic fatigue, and infections (especially staph and strep).

Body System(s) Affected: Immune, Respiratory, and Nervous Systems.

Aromatic Influence: Stimulates memory[16,17] and opens the conscious mind.

Application: Can be applied neat (with no dilution) when used topically. Apply to reflex points and/or directly on area of concern; diffuse.

Oral Use As Dietary Supplement: Generally recognized as safe (GRAS) for human consumption by the FDA (21CFR182.20). Dilute one drop oil in 1 tsp. honey or in 4 oz. of beverage (i.e. soy/rice milk). Not for children under 6-years-old; use with caution and in greater dilution for children 6-years-old and over.

Safety Data: Avoid during pregnancy. Not for use by people with epilepsy. Avoid if dealing with high blood pressure.

Blend Classification: Enhancer

Blends With: Basil, frankincense, lavender, peppermint, eucalyptus, and marjoram.

Odor: Type: Middle Note (50-80% of the blend); Scent: Herbaceous, strong, camphorous, with woody-balsamic and evergreen undertones; Intensity: 3.

2 An ethanol extract of rosemary was found to demonstrate antinociceptive (pain-blocking) and anti-inflammatory activity in mice and rats (González-Trujano et al., 2007).

3 Peppermint and rosemary oils were each found to be more effective at preventing dental biofilm (plaque) formation than chlorhexidine (an antiseptic) (Rasooli et al., 2008).

4 An ethanol extract of rosemary was found to have an antiproliferative effect on human leukemia and breast carcinoma cells, as well as an antioxidant effect (Cheung et al., 2007).

5 Rosemary extract injected in rats was found to decrease mammary adenocarcinomas in rats (Singletary et al., 1996).

6 Carnosic acid (derived from rosemary) was found to inhibit the proliferation of human leukemia cells in vitro (Steiner et al., 2001).

7 Rosemary oil was found to inhibit aflatoxin production by aspergillus fungi (a highly toxic and carcinogenic substance produced by these fungi (Rasooli et al., 2008).

8 Rosemary oil was found to have anti-inflammatory and peripheral antinociceptive (pain-sensitivity-blocking) properties in mice (Takaki et al., 2008).

9 Extracts from rosemary were found to have high antioxidant properties. Rosmarinic acid and carnosic acid from rosemary were found to have the highest antioxidant activities of studied components of rosemary (Almela et al., 2006).

10 Extracts from rosemary were found to have high antioxidant levels (Moreno et al., 2006).

11 An ethanol extract of rosemary demonstrated a protective effect against the oxidative damage to DNA in cells exposed to H2O2 and light-excited methylene blue (Slamenova et al., 2002).

12 In patients suffering from arthritis, it was found that a blend of lavender, marjoram, eucalyptus, rosemary, peppermint, and carrier oils reduced perceived pain and depression compared to control (Kim et al., 2005).

13 In patients with chronic bronchitis, rosemary, basil, fir, and eucalyptus oils were found to demonstrate an antioxidant effect. Lavender was found to promote normalization of lipid levels (Siurin, 1997).

14 Patients with alopecia areata (hair loss) that massaged carrier oils containing a blend of thyme, rosemary, lavender, and cedarwood oils into their scalps were more likely to show improvement when compared to a control group that massaged carrier oils alone into their scalps (Hay et al., 1998).

15 Rosemary oil demonstrated a relaxant effect on smooth muscle from the trachea of rabbit and guinea pig (Aqel, 1991).

16 Subjects exposed to rosemary aroma were more alert and completed math computations faster than subjects not exposed to the aroma (Diego et al., 1998).

17 Volunteers completing a battery of tests were found to be more content when exposed to lavender and rosemary aromas. Rosemary aroma also was found to enhance quality of memory compared to control (Moss et al., 2003).

❶=Topical, ❸=Aromatic, ❶=Internal

SANDALWOOD ⓣⒶⓘ
(Santalum album)

Botanical Family: Santalaceae (sandalwood)

Extraction Method: Steam distilled from wood

Chemical Constituents: Sesquiterpene Alcohols: α- & β-santalols (<80%); Sesquiterpenes: α- & β-santalenes (<11%); Sesquiterpene Aldehydes: teresantalal (<3%); Carboxylic Acids: nortricycloekasantalic acid (<2%).

Properties: Antidepressant, antiseptic, antitumor[1,2,3], aphrodisiac, astringent, calming, sedative, and tonic.

Common Primary Uses*: ⒶⓉAlzheimer's Disease, ⒶⓉAphrodisiac, ⓉBack Pain, ⓉCancer, ⓉCartilage Repair, ⓉComa, ⒶConfusion, ⓉExhaustion, ⒶⓉFear, ⓉHair (Dry), ⒶⓉHiccups, ⒶⓉLaryngitis, ⒶⒶLou Gehrig's Disease, ⒶMeditation, ⓉMoles, ⓉⒶMultiple Sclerosis, ⓉRashes, ⓉSkin (Dry), ⓉUltraviolet Radiation, ⓉVitiligo, ⒶYoga

Historical Uses: Sandalwood was traditionally used as an incense during ritual work for enhancing meditation. The Egyptians also used sandalwood for embalming.

French Medicinal Uses: Bronchitis (chronic), diarrhea (obstinate), hemorrhoids, impotence.

Other Possible Uses: Sandalwood is very similar to frankincense in action. It may support the cardiovascular system and relieve symptoms associated with lumbago and the sciatic nerves. It may also be beneficial for acne, regenerating bone cartilage, catarrh, circulation (similar in action to frankincense), coughs, cystitis, depression, hiccups, lymphatic system, menstrual problems, nerves (similar in action to frankincense), nervous tension, increasing oxygen around the pineal and pituitary glands, skin infection and regeneration, and tuberculosis.

Body System(s) Affected: Emotional Balance, Muscles and Bones, Nervous System, Skin.

Aromatic Influence: Calms, harmonizes, and balances the emotions. It may help enhance meditation.

Application: Can be applied neat (with no dilution) when used topically. Apply to reflex points of the feet and/or directly on area of concern; diffuse.

Oral Use As Dietary Supplement: Approved by the FDA (21CFR172.510) for use as a Food Additive (FA) and Flavoring Agent (FL). Dilute one drop oil in 1 tsp. honey or in 4 oz. of beverage (i.e. soy/rice milk). Not for children under 6-years-old; use with caution and in greater dilution for children 6-years-old and over.

Blend Classification: Modifier and Equalizer

Blends With: Cypress, frankincense, lemon, myrrh, and ylang ylang.

Odor: Type: Base Note (5-20% of the blend); Scent: Soft, woody, sweet, earthy, balsamic, tenacious; Intensity: 3.

THYME ⓣⒶⓘ
(Thymus vulgaris CT Thymol)

Botanical Family: Labiatae (mint)

Extraction Method: Steam distilled from leaves, stems, and flowers

Chemical Constituents: Phenols (up to 60%): thymol (<55%), carvacrol (<10%); Monoterpenes (<54%): p-cymene (<28%), γ-terpinene (<11%), terpinolene (<6%), α-pinene (<6%), myrcene (<3%); Oxides: 1,8 cineol (<15%); Alcohols (<14%): linalol (<8%), borneol (<7%), thujanol, geraniol; Sesquiterpenes: β-caryophyllene (<8%); Carboxylic Acids: rosmaric acid (<2%), triterpenic acids (tr.);

---

1 Alpha-santalol, derived from sandalwood EO, was found to delay and decrease the incidence and multiplicity of skin tumor (papilloma) development in mice (Dwivedi et al., 2003).

2 Various concentrations of alpha-santalol (from sandalwood) were tested against skin cancer in mice. All concentrations were found to inhibit skin cancer development (Dwivedi et al., 2005).

3 Alpha-santalol was found to induce apoptosis in human skin cancer cells (Kaur et al., 2005).

---

*See Personal Usage Guide section for more details on these primary uses.

ⓣ=Neat, ⓣ=Dilute for Children/Sensitive Skin, ⓣ=Dilute

Ethers: methyl thymol (tr.), methyl carvacrol (tr.); Ketone: camphor (tr.); Also trace elements of menthone.

Properties: Highly antibacterial[4,5,6], antifungal[7,8], antimicrobial[9], antioxidant[10,11], antiviral, antiseptic.

Common Primary Uses*: ❶❶▲Antioxidant, ▲❶Asthma, ❶▲Bacterial Infections, ❶Bites/Stings, ❶❶▲Blood Clots, ❶❶Brain (Aging), ▲❶Bronchitis, ❶▲Colds (Common), ▲❶Croup, ❶Dermatitis/Eczema, ❶▲Fatigue, ❶Fungal Infections, ❶Greasy/Oily Hair, ❶Hair (Fragile), ❶Hair (Loss), ▲❶Mold, ❶MRSA, ❶❶Parasites, ▲❶Pleurisy, ▲❶Pneumonia, ❶Prostatitis, ❶Psoriasis, ❶Radiation Wounds, ❶Sciatica, ▲❶Tuberculosis

Historical Uses: It was used by the Egyptians for embalming and by the ancient Greeks to fight against infectious illnesses. It has also been used for respiratory problems, digestive complaints, the prevention and treatment of infection, dyspepsia, chronic gastritis, bronchitis, pertussis, asthma, laryngitis, tonsillitis, and enuresis in children.

French Medicinal Uses: Anthrax, asthma, bronchitis, colitis (infectious), cystitis, dermatitis, dyspepsia, fatigue (general), pleurisy, psoriasis, sciatica, tuberculosis, vaginal candida.

Other Possible Uses: This oil is a general tonic for the nerves and stomach. It may also help with circulation, depression, digestion, physical weakness after illness, flu, headaches, immunological functions, insomnia, rheumatism, urinary infections, viruses along the spine, and wounds.

---

4 Subjects using a mouthwash containing thymol, menthol, methyl salicylate, and eucalyptol for 6 months did not have oral bacteria that had developed a resistance to the oils (Charles et al., 2000).
5 Cinnamon, thyme, and clove essential oils demonstrated an antibacterial effect on several respiratory tract pathogens (Fabio et al., 2007).
6 Thyme oil demonstrated a strong antibacterial effect against *Staph* and *E. Coli* bacteria (Mohsenzadeh et al., 2007).
7 Thyme oil was found to inhibit Candida species by causing lesions in the cell membrane and inhibiting germ tube (an outgrowth that develops when the fungi is preparing to replicate) formation (Pina-Vaz et al., 2004).
8 Cinnamon, thyme, oregano, and cumin oils inhibited the production of aflatoxin by aspergillus fungus (Tantaoui-Elaraki et al., 1994).
9 Cinnamon bark, lemongrass, and thyme oils were found to have the highest level of activity against common respiratory pathogens among 14 essential oils tested (Inouye et al., 2001).
10 Older rats whose diets were supplemented with thyme oil were found have higher levels of the antioxidant enzymes superoxide dismutase and glutathione peroxidase in the heart, liver, and kidneys than did older rats without this supplementation (Youdim et al., 1999).
11 Aging rats fed thyme oil or the constituent thymol were found to have higher levels of the antioxidant enzymes superoxide dismutase and glutathione peroxidase in the brain than did aging rats not fed the oil or constituent (Youdim et al., 2000).

Body System(s) Affected: Immune System, Muscles and Bones.

Aromatic Influence: It helps energize in times of physical weakness and stress. It has also been thought to aid concentration. It is uplifting and helps to relieve depression.

Application: Dilute 1:4 (1 drop essential oil to 4 drops carrier oil) when used topically. Apply to reflex points and/or directly on area of concern.

Oral Use As Dietary Supplement: Generally recognized as safe (GRAS) for human consumption by the FDA (21CFR182.20). Dilute one drop oil in 2 tsp. honey or in 8 oz. of beverage (i.e. soy/rice milk). However, more dilution may be necessary due to this oil's potential for irritating mucus membranes. Not for children under 6-years-old; use with caution and in greater dilution for children 6-years-old and over.

Safety Data: This type of thyme oil may be somewhat irritating to the mucous membranes and dermal tissues (skin). This type of thyme should be avoided during pregnancy. Use with caution when dealing with high blood pressure.

Blend Classification: Equalizer and Enhancer.

Blends With: Bergamot, melaleuca, oregano, and rosemary.

Odor: Type: Middle Note (50-80% of the blend); Scent: Fresh, medicinal, herbaceous; Intensity: 4.

VETIVER ❶▲❶
(Vetiveria zizanioides)

Botanical Family: Gramineae (grasses)

Extraction Method: Steam distilled from roots

Chemical Constituents: Sesquiterpene Alcohols (up to 42%): isovalencenol (<15%), bicyclovetiverol (<13%), khusenol (<11%), tricyclovetiverol (<4%), vetiverol, zizanol, furfurol; Sesquiterpene Ketones (<22%): α- & β-vetivones (<12%), khusimone (<6%), nootkatone (<5%); Sesquiterpenes (<4%): vitivene, tricyclovetivene, vetivazulene, β- & δ-cadinenes; Sesquiterpene Esters: vetiveryl acetate; Carboxylic Acids: benzoic, palmitic, and vetivenic acids.

Properties: Antiseptic, antispasmodic, calming, grounding, immune stimulant, rubefacient (locally warming), sedative (nervous system), stimulant (circulatory, production of red corpuscles).

Common Primary Uses*: ⊕⊗ADD/ADHD, ⊕⊗Balance, ⊕⊗Termite Repellent, ⊕Vitiligo

Historical Uses: The distillation of vetiver is a painstaking, labor-intensive activity. The roots and rootlets of vetiver have been used in India as a perfume since antiquity.

Other Possible Uses: Vetiver may help acne, anorexia, anxiety, arthritis, breasts (enlarge), cuts, depression (including postpartum), insomnia, muscular rheumatism, nervousness (extreme), skin care (oily, aging, tired, irritated), sprains, and stress.

Body System(s) Affected: Emotional Balance, Hormonal and Nervous Systems, Skin.

Aromatic Influence: Vetiver has a heavy, smoky, earthy fragrance reminiscent of patchouli with lemon-like undertones. Vetiver has been valuable for relieving stress and helping people recover from emotional traumas and shock. As a natural tranquilizer, it may help induce a restful sleep. It is known to affect the parathyroid gland.

Application: Can be applied neat (with no dilution) when used topically. Apply to reflex points and/or directly on area of concern; diffuse. Also excellent in baths or in massage blends. A very small amount of vetiver oil is all that is needed in most applications.

Oral Use As Dietary Supplement: Approved by the FDA (21CFR172.510) for use as a Food Additive (FA) and Flavoring Agent (FL). Dilute one drop oil in 1 tsp. honey or in 4 oz. of beverage (i.e. soy/rice milk). Not for children under 6-years-old; use with caution and in greater dilution for children 6-years-old and over.

Safety Data: Use with caution during pregnancy.

Blends With: Clary sage, lavender, rose, sandalwood, and ylang ylang.

Odor: Type: Base Note (5-20% of the blend); Scent: Heavy, earthy, balsamic, smoky, sweet undertones; Intensity: 5.

WHITE FIR ⊕⊛⊕
(Abies alba)

Botanical Family: Pinaceae (conifer)

Extraction Method: Steam distillation from needles

Chemical Constituents: Monoterpenes (75-95%): l-limonene (34%), α-pinene (24%), camphene (21%), santene, δ-3-carene; Esters: bornyle acetate (up to 10%).

Properties: Analgesic, antiarthritic, anticatarrhal, antiseptic (pulmonary), expectorant, and stimulant.

Common Primary Uses*: ⊕⊕Bronchitis, ⊕Bursitis, ⊕Cartilage Inflammation, ⊕⊕Energizing, ⊕Frozen Shoulder, ⊕Furniture Polish, ⊕Muscle Fatigue, ⊕Muscle Pain, ⊕Overexercised Muscles, ⊕Sprains

Historical Uses: The fir tree is the classic Christmas tree (short with the perfect pyramidal shape and silvery white bark). Though highly regarded for its fragrant scent, the fir tree has been prized through the ages for its medicinal virtues in regards to respiratory complaints, fever, and muscular and rheumatic pain.

French Medicinal Uses: Bronchitis[1], respiratory congestion, energy.

Other Possible Uses: Fir creates the symbolic effect of an umbrella protecting the earth and bringing energy in from the universe. At night the animals in the wild lie down under the tree for the protection, recharging, and rejuvenation the trees bring them. Fir may be beneficial for reducing aches/pains from colds and the flu, fighting airborne germs/bacteria, arthritis, asthma, supporting the blood, bronchial obstructions, coughs, fevers, oxygenating

---

1 In patients with chronic bronchitis, rosemary, basil, fir, and eucalyptus oils were found to demonstrate an antioxidant effect. (Siurin et al., 1997).

---

*See Personal Usage Guide section for more details on these primary uses.   ⊕=Neat, ⊕=Dilute for Children/Sensitive Skin, ⊕=Dilute

the cells, rheumatism, sinusitis, and urinary tract infections.

Body System(s) Affected: Respiratory System.

Aromatic Influence: It creates a feeling of grounding, anchoring, and empowerment. It can stimulate the mind while allowing the body to relax.

Application: Can be applied neat (with no dilution) when used topically. Apply to reflex points and/or directly on area of concern; diffuse.

Oral Use As Dietary Supplement: Approved by the FDA (21CFR172.510) for use as a Food Additive (FA) and Flavoring Agent (FL). Dilute one drop oil in 1 tsp. honey or in 4 oz. of beverage (i.e. soy/rice milk). Not for children under 6-years-old; use with caution and in greater dilution for children 6-years-old and over.

Safety Data: Can irritate sensitive skin.

Blend Classification: Equalizer.

Blends With: Frankincense and lavender.

Odor: Type: Middle Notes (50-80% of the blend); Scent: Fresh, woody, earthy, sweet; Intensity: 3.

WILD ORANGE (SEE ORANGE, WILD)

WINTERGREEN Ⓣ Ⓐ
(Gaultheria procumbens)

Botanical Family: Ericaceae (heather)

Extraction Method: Steam distillation from leaves

Chemical Constituents: Phenolic Esters: methyl salicylate (>90%); Carboxylic Acids: salicylic acid.

Properties: Analgesic, anti-inflammatory[2], anti-rheumatic, antiseptic, antispasmodic, disinfectant, diuretic, stimulant (bone), and warming.

Common Primary Uses*: ⓉArthritic Pain, ⓉBone Pain, ⓉBone Spurs, ⓉCartilage Injury, ⓉDandruff, ⓉFrozen Shoulder, ⓉJoint Pain, ⓉMuscle Development, ⓉMuscle Tone, ⓉPain, ⓉRotator Cuff (Sore)

Historical Uses: Wintergreen oil has a strong, penetrating aroma. The American Indians and early European settlers enjoyed a tea that was flavored with birch bark or wintergreen. According to Julia Lawless, "this has been translated into a preference for 'root beer' flavourings [sic]." A synthetic methyl salicylate is now widely used as a flavoring agent, especially in root beer, chewing gum, toothpaste, etc. In fact, the true essential oil is produced in such small quantities (compared to the very extensive uses of the synthetic methyl salicylate) that those desiring to use wintergreen essential oil for therapeutic uses should verify the source of their oil to make sure they have a true oil, not a synthetic one.

French Medicinal Uses: Rheumatism, muscular pain, cramps, arthritis, tendonitis, hypertension, inflammation.

Other Possible Uses: This oil may be beneficial for acne, bladder infection, cystitis, dropsy, eczema, edema, reducing fever, gallstones, gout, infection, reducing discomfort in joints, kidney stones, draining and cleansing the lymphatic system, obesity, osteoporosis, skin diseases, ulcers, and urinary tract disorders. It is known for its ability to alleviate bone pain. It has a cortisone-like action due to the high content of methyl salicylate.

Body System(s) Affected: Muscles and Bones.

Aromatic Influence: It influences, elevates, opens, and increases awareness in sensory system.

Application: Can be applied neat (with no dilution), or dilute 1:1 (1 drop essential oil to 1 drop carrier oil) for children and for those with sensitive skin when using topically. Apply to reflex points and/or directly on area of concern; diffuse. Apply topically on location, and use only small amounts (dilute with fractionated coconut oil for application on larger areas).

Safety Data: Avoid during pregnancy. Not for use by people with epilepsy. Some people are very allergic to methyl salicylate. Test a small area of skin first for allergies.

---

2 Methyl salicylate (found in wintergreen or birch oils) was found to inhibit leukotriene C4 (a chemical messenger involved in the inflammatory response), while also demonstrating gastroprotective against ethanol-induced gastric injury in rats (Trautmann, et al., 1991).

Ⓣ=Topical, Ⓐ=Aromatic, Ⓘ=Internal

Blend Classification: Personifier and Enhancer.

Blends With: Basil, bergamot, cypress, geranium, lavender, lemongrass, marjoram, and peppermint.

Ylang Ylang 🅣🅐🅘
(Cananga odorata)

Botanical Family: Annonaceae (tropical trees and shrubs—custard-apple)

Extraction Method: Steam distilled from flowers

Chemical Constituents: Sesquiterpenes (up to 55%): β-caryophyllene (<22%), germacrene-D (<20%), α-farnesene (<12%), humulene (<5%); Esters (<50%): benzyl acetate & benzoate (<25%), methyl salicylate & benzoate (<17%), farnesyl acetate (<7%), geranyl acetate (<4%), linalyl acetate; Alcohols (<45%): linalol (<40%), geraniol; Ethers: paracresyl methyl ether (<15%); Phenols (<10%): methyl p-cresol (<9%), methyl chavicol (estragole), eugenol, isoeugenol; Oxides: caryophyllene oxide (<7%); Sesquiterpene Alcohols: farnesol.

Properties: Antidepressant, antiseptic, antispasmodic, sedative[1], and tonic.

Common Primary Uses*: 🅐🅣Aphrodisiac, 🅐🅣Arrhythmia, 🅐🅣Calming, 🅣Colic, 🅐🅣Crying, 🅣🅐Diabetes, 🅣Exhaustion, 🅐🅣Fear, 🅣Hair (Loss), 🅐🅣High Blood Pressure[2,3], 🅐🅣Hormonal Balance, 🅐🅣Hyperpnea, 🅐🅣Libido (Low), 🅐🅣Palpitations, 🅐🅣Relaxation, 🅐🅣Sedative, 🅐🅣Stress, 🅐🅣Tachycardia, 🅐🅣Tension

Historical Uses: Interestingly enough, the original wild flowers had no fragrance. Through selection and cloning, we have this unique fragrance today. Ylang ylang has been used to cover the beds of newlywed couples on their wedding night, for skin treatments, to soothe insect bites, and in hair preparations to promote thick, shiny, lustrous hair (it is also reported to help control split ends). It has been used to treat colic, constipation, indigestion, stomachaches, and to regulate the heartbeat and respiration.

French Medicinal Uses: Anxiety, arterial hypertension, depression, diabetes, fatigue (mental), frigidity, hair loss, hyperpnea (reduces), insomnia, palpitations, tachycardia.

Other Possible Uses: Ylang ylang may help with rapid breathing, balancing equilibrium, frustration, balancing heart function, impotence, infection, intestinal problems, sex drive problems, shock, and skin problems.

Body System(s) Affected: Emotional Balance, Cardiovascular and Hormonal Systems.

Aromatic Influence: It influences sexual energy and enhances relationships. It may help stimulate the adrenal glands. It is calming and relaxing and may help alleviate anger.

Application: Can be applied neat (with no dilution) when used topically. Apply to reflex points and/or directly on area of concern; diffuse. It may be beneficial when applied over the thymus (to help stimulate the immune system).

Oral Use As Dietary Supplement: Generally recognized as safe (GRAS) for human consumption by the FDA (21CFR182.20). Dilute one drop oil in 1 tsp. honey or in 4 oz. of beverage (i.e. soy/rice milk). Not for children under 6-years-old; use with caution and in greater dilution for children 6-years-old and over.

Safety Data: Repeated use can possibly result in contact sensitization.

Blend Classification: Personifier and Modifier.

Blends With: Bergamot, geranium, grapefruit, lemon, marjoram, sandalwood, and vetiver.

Odor: Type: Middle to Base Notes (20-80% of the blend); Scent: Sweet, heavy, narcotic, cloying, tropical floral, with spicy-balsamic undertones; Intensity: 5.

---

1   In human trials, ylang ylang aroma was found to increase calmness (Moss et al., 2008).

2   Inhaled ylang ylang oil was found to decrease blood pressure and pulse rate and to enhance attentiveness and alertness in volunteers compared to an odorless control (Hongratanaworakit et al., 2004).

3   Subjects who had ylang ylang oil applied to their skin had decreased blood pressure, increased skin temperature, and reported feeling more calm and relaxed compared to subjects in a control group (Hongratanaworakit et al., 2006).

---

*See Personal Usage Guide section for more details on these primary uses.   🅣=Neat, 🅣=Dilute for Children/Sensitive Skin, 🅣=Dilute

ESSENTIAL OIL BLENDS

ESSENTIAL OIL BLENDS

This section contains proprietary blends and detailed information about each. Other commercial blends exist on the market, but many find the blends referred to in this section to be superior in synergy and potency. Many of these product names are trademarks of dōTERRA Int., LLC; and although these product names appear throughout other sections of this book without the trademark symbol, they still refer to these same trademarked products.

For further information and research on many of the single oils contained in these blends, see the Single Essential Oils section of this book.

AROMATOUCH™
Massage Blend

The oils in this blend were selected specifically for their abilities to relax, calm, and relieve the tension of muscles, to soothe irritated tissue, and to increase circulation. The AromaTouch™ massage blend has an anti-inflammatory effect on soft tissue and enhances all aspects of massage.

SINGLE OILS CONTAINED IN THIS BLEND:

Basil: has anti-inflammatory and antispasmodic properties. It is relaxing to spastic muscles, including those that contribute to headaches and migraines.

Grapefruit: has calming and sedative properties. It may help with fatigue and stress.

Cypress: is anti-infectious, mucolytic, antiseptic, lymphatic decongestive, refreshing, and relaxing. It may help improve lung circulation as well as help relieve other respiratory problems. It may also help relieve muscle cramps and improve overall circulation.

Marjoram: is an antispasmodic and is relaxing, calming, and appeasing to the muscles that constrict and sometimes contribute to headaches. It may be useful for muscle spasms, sprains, bruises, migraines, and sore muscles.

Lavender: is an oil that has traditionally been known to balance the body and to work

wherever there is a need. It has antispasmodic and analgesic properties. It may help with sprains, sore muscles, headaches, and general healing.

Peppermint: is an anti-inflammatory to the nerves and helps reduce inflammation in damaged tissue. It is soothing, cooling, and dilating to the systems of the body. It may help to reduce fevers, candida, nausea, vomiting, and also help to strengthen the respiratory system.

Body System(s) Affected: The oils in this blend may help it be effective for dealing with various problems related to the Respiratory System, Cardiovascular System, and to Muscles and Bones.

Application: Best if applied on location for all muscles. It may also be applied over the heart or diluted with fractionated coconut oil for a full body massage. It is also beneficial when placed in bathwater.

Companion Oils: Basil, helichrysum, marjoram, and wintergreen.

BALANCE
Grounding Blend

This blend brings a feeling of calmness, peace, and relaxation. It can aid in harmonizing the various physiological systems of the body and promote tranquility and a sense of balance.

SINGLE OILS CONTAINED IN THIS BLEND:

Spruce: grounds the body, creating the balance and the opening necessary to receive and to give. It may help dilate the bronchial tract to improve the oxygen exchange. It may also help a person to release emotional blocks.

Rosewood: is soothing to the skin, appeasing to the mind, relaxing to the body, and creates a feeling of peace and gentleness.

Blue Tansy: may help cleanse the liver and calm the lymphatic system to help rid oneself of anger and promote a feeling of self-control.

Frankincense: contains sesquiterpenes, which may help oxygenate the pineal and pituitary glands. As one of the ingredients for the holy incense, frankincense was used anciently to help enhance one's communication with the creator. It may help promote a positive attitude.

Carrier Oil Contained in This Blend: Fractionated coconut oil.

Body System(s) Affected: The oils in this blend may help it be effective for dealing with various problems related to Muscles and Bones, Skin, the Nervous System, and Emotional Balance.

Aromatic Influence: This blend of oils may help balance the body and mind. Diffuse wherever and whenever possible.

Application: This blend works best on the bottoms of the feet. Put six drops of Balance on bottoms of feet. Put Balance on heart, wrists, and solar plexus from neck to thymus. To balance left and right brain, put Balance on left fingers, and rub on right temple; or put Balance on right fingers, and rub on left temple; or cross arms, and rub reflex points on bottoms of feet. To relieve pain along the spine, apply Balance to reflex points on feet and on spine. Wear as perfume or cologne.

BREATHE
Respiratory Blend

Many of the oils in this blend have been studied for their abilities to open and soothe the tissues of the respiratory system and also for their abilities to combat airborne bacteria and viruses that could be harmful to the system.

SINGLE OILS CONTAINED IN THIS BLEND:

Laurel Leaf (Bay): has antiseptic and antifungal properties. It may also help with asthma, bronchitis, and viral infections.

Peppermint: is antiseptic, antispasmodic, and anti-inflammatory. It is soothing, cooling, and dilating to the system.

Eucalyptus radiata: may have a profound antiviral effect upon the respiratory system. It may also help reduce inflammation of the nasal mucous membrane.

Melaleuca alternifolia: has antibacterial, antifungal, antiviral, and expectorant properties. It may also help with bronchitis, coughs, and inflammation.

Lemon: promotes health, healing, physical energy, and purification. Its fragrance is invigorating, enhancing, and warming. It is an antiseptic and is great for the respiratory system.

Ravensara: is a powerful antiviral, antibacterial, antifungal, and anti-infectious oil. It may help dilate, open, and strengthen the respiratory system. As a cross between clove and nutmeg, it may also help support the adrenal glands.

Body System(s) Affected: The oils in this blend may help it be effective for dealing with various problems related to the Respiratory System and to the Skin.

Aromatic Influence: This blend of oils is excellent for opening the respiratory system when the blend is diffused or inhaled and is perfect for nighttime diffusion, allowing for restful sleep.

Application: Apply topically to the chest, the back, or the bottoms of the feet. Diffuse.

Safety Data: Can be irritating to sensitive skin. Dilute for young or sensitive skin.

Companion Oils: Run hot steaming water in sink; put Breathe and wintergreen in water; put towel over head; and inhale to open sinuses that have been blocked by flu, colds, or pneumonia. Also try On Guard.

CITRUS BLISS
Invigorating Blend

This uniquely exhilarating blend brings together all of the uplifting and stress-reducing benefits of citrus essential oils in a sweetly satisfying way. In addition to their elevating properties, many of the citrus oils in this blend have been studied for their ability to cleanse and to disinfect.

SINGLE OILS CONTAINED IN THIS BLEND:

Wild Orange: brings peace and happiness to the mind and body and joy to the heart, which feelings provide emotional support to help one overcome depression.

Oil Blends

Lemon: promotes health, healing, physical energy, and purification. Its fragrance is invigorating, enhancing, and warming.

Grapefruit: is an antidepressant, an antiseptic, and a diuretic. It is balancing and uplifting to the mind and may help to relieve anxiety.

Mandarin: is appeasing, gentle, and promotes happiness. It is also refreshing, uplifting, and revitalizing. Because of its sedative properties, it is very good for combating stress and irritability.

Bergamot: has uplifting properties. It may also help with depression and agitation.

Tangerine: contains esters and aldehydes, which are sedating and calming to the nervous system. It is also a diuretic and a decongestant of the lymphatic system.

Clementine: is soothing and sedating and may help ease tension.

Vanilla Bean Extract: is calming and may help ease tension.

Body System(s) Affected: The oils in this blend may help it be effective for dealing with various problems related to the Immune System and to Emotional Balance.

Aromatic Influence: This blend of oils may create an enjoyable aromatic fragrance in the home or workplace. Simple diffusion can be achieved by applying a few drops of this blend on a cotton ball and placing it on a desk at work or placing it in an air vent.

Application: May be applied on the ears, heart, and wrists or may be worn as a perfume or cologne. It may be diluted with fractionated coconut oil for a full-body massage. It may also be added to water for a relaxing bath. Mixed with water, this blend can also be used to disinfect countertops and other surfaces.

Safety Data: May cause skin irritation. Avoid exposure to direct sunlight for up to 12 hours after use.

CLEAR SKIN ROLL-ON
Topical Blend

This new formulation of the Clear Skin blend contains oils that have been selected for their unique abilities to help protect the skin from bacterial and fungal proliferation and from other skin problems such as eczema and acne. This blend can be applied topically to infected areas.

SINGLE OILS CONTAINED IN THIS BLEND:

Rosewood: is known for its antiseptic properties and is often used to help clear infections and to support the revitalization of skin tissue.

Melaleuca: is one of the most studied antibacterial and antifungal oils. Melaleuca also has anti-inflammatory properties and can help support the skin in the recovery process after injuries.

Eucalyptus globulus: is often used for inflammation and skin infections and sores. It is used medicinally in France to treat candida and other fungal infections and has also demonstrated strong antibacterial properties.

Geranium: has antibacterial and anti-inflammatory properties and is often used to help alleviate the effects of acne and eczema. It may also help balance sebum levels in the skin.

Lemongrass: is known for its antiseptic properties and is often used to help clear infections and to support the revitalization of skin tissue.

OTHER OILS CONTAINED IN THIS BLEND:

Black Cumin Seed Oil: has been used since ancient times for a myriad of health concerns. In addition to its antioxidant and anti-inflammatory properties, black cumin seed oil also has a high content of linoleic acid, an essential fatty acid used by the body to help maintain healthy skin and hair. Linoleic acid has been studied for its ability to reduce acne microcomedones[1] and to enhance cellular migration during wound healing[2].

Body System(s) Affected: The oils in this blend may help it be effective for dealing with

1 Letawe et al., 1998.
2 Ruthig et al., 1999.

various problems related to the Skin and the Immune System.

Application: Apply on location daily as needed.

Safety Data: Repeated use may possibly result in contact sensitization. Use with caution during pregnancy.

DEEP BLUE™
Soothing Blend—Also available as a roll-on

This remarkable blend contains oils that are well-known and are frequently studied for their abilities to soothe inflammation, alleviate pain, and reduce soreness.

SINGLE OILS CONTAINED IN THIS BLEND:

Wintergreen: contains 99% methyl salicylate, which gives it cortisone-like properties. It may be beneficial for arthritis, rheumatism, tendinitis, and any other discomfort that is related to the inflammation of bones, muscles, and joints.

Camphor: is analgesic (pain-relieving) and anti-inflammatory. It may be beneficial for arthritis, rheumatism, muscle aches and pains, sprains, and bruises.

Peppermint: is anti-inflammatory to the prostate and to damaged tissues. It has a soothing and cooling effect that may help with arthritis and rheumatism.

Blue Tansy: is analgesic and anti-inflammatory. It may also help with low blood pressure, arthritis, and rheumatism.

German Chamomile: is antioxidant, anti-inflammatory, and analgesic. It may also help relieve congestion and arthritis.

Helichrysum: may help cleanse the blood and improve circulatory functions. It is anticatarrhal in structure and nature. As a powerful anti-inflammatory, it may even help reduce inflammation in the meninges of the brain. On a spiritual level, it may help one let go of angry feelings that prevent one from forgiving and moving forward.

Osmanthus: is one of the 10 famous traditional flowers of China. The blossoms are highly aromatic and are used in the world's rarest and most expensive per-

fumes. It is used in Chinese medicine to "reduce phlegm and remove blood stasis."

Body System(s) Affected: The oils in this blend may help it be effective for dealing with various problems related to the Nervous System and to Muscles and Bones.

Application: Apply as a compress on spine and on reflex points on feet. Apply on location for muscle cramps, bruises, or any other pain.

Companion Oils: Add frankincense (to enhance) or wintergreen (for bone pain).

DigestZen™
Digestive Blend

This blend may be useful for improving digestive function. The oils in this blend have been studied for their abilities in balancing the digestive system and in soothing many of that system's ailments.

SINGLE OILS CONTAINED IN THIS BLEND:

Ginger: is warming, uplifting, and empowering. Emotionally, it may help influence physical energy, love, and courage. Because of its calming influence on the digestive system, it may help reduce feelings of nausea and motion sickness.

Peppermint: is an anti-inflammatory to the prostate and nerves. It is soothing, cooling, and dilating to the system. It may also be beneficial for counteracting food poisoning, vomiting, diarrhea, constipation, flatulence, halitosis, colic, nausea, and motion sickness.

Tarragon: may help to reduce anorexia, dyspepsia, flatulence, intestinal spasms, nervous and sluggish digestion, and genital urinary tract infection.

Fennel: may help improve digestive function by supporting the liver. It may also help balance the hormones.

Caraway: is antiparasitic and antispasmodic. It may also help with indigestion, gas, and colic.

Coriander: is antispasmodic and has anti-inflammatory properties. It may also help with indigestion, flatulence, diarrhea, and other spasms of the digestive tract.

Anise: may help calm and strengthen the digestive system.

Body System(s) Affected: The oils in this blend may help it be effective for dealing with various problems related to the Digestive System.

Application: May be applied to reflex points on the feet and on the ankles. It may also be applied topically over the stomach, as a compress on the abdomen, and at the bottom of the throat (for gagging). As a dietary supplement, dilute one drop in 4 oz. of water or soy/rice milk, and sip slowly. May also be used in a retention enema for ridding the colon of parasites and for combating digestive candida. Apply to animal paws for parasites.

Safety Data: Use with caution during pregnancy (only a drop massaged on the outer ear for morning sickness). Not for use by people with epilepsy.

Companion Oils: Peppermint.

ELEVATION™
Joyful Blend

This uplifting combination of essential oils creates an energetic aroma that can help stimulate the body's chemistry when a person is feeling lethargic or sad.

SINGLE OILS CONTAINED IN THIS BLEND:

Lavandin: may help dispel feelings of depression or anxiety.

Tangerine: is sedative in nature. It may help calm and relieve feelings of stress while enhancing energy.

Elemi: is antidepressant and sedative. It may help relieve stress and is calming to the nerves.

Lemon Myrtle: has a strong lemony aroma that is elevating and refreshing.

Melissa: may help with depression and anxiety and has an uplifting lemony aroma.

Ylang Ylang: is calming and relaxing. It brings a feeling of self-love, confidence, joy, and peace.

Osmanthus: is one of the 10 famous traditional flowers of China. The blossoms are highly aromatic and are used in the

world's rarest and most expensive perfumes. Its heady, uplifting fragrance (a very rich, sweet floral fruit bouquet) has been known to make everyone smile.

Sandalwood: is calming and sedative. It helps balance and harmonize the emotions and may help ease nervous tension.

Body System(s) Affected: The oils in this blend may help it be effective for dealing with various problems related to Emotional Balance.

Aromatic Influence: The fragrance of this blend of oils is uplifting, refreshing, and helps promote feelings of self-worth. It can help dispel feelings of depression, sorrow, and anxiety.

Application: Rub over heart, ears, neck, thymus, temples, across brow, and on wrists. Apply on heart reflex points. Put in bathwater. Use as compress; dilute with fractionated coconut oil for a full-body massage. Place on areas of poor circulation. Wear as perfume or cologne, especially over the heart. Put two drops on a wet cloth, and put the cloth in the dryer with washed laundry for great-smelling clothes.

Safety Data: Avoid exposure to direct sunlight for up to 12 hours after use.

IMMORTELLE™
Anti-Aging Blend

This soothing blend may be useful for maintaining skin health and vitality. The oils in this blend have been studied for their abilities to help reduce inflammation, protect the skin from UV radiation, and promote healthy cellular function and proper hydration of the skin.

SINGLE OILS CONTAINED IN THIS BLEND:

Frankincense: has been studied for its anti-inflammatory properties. Its anti-infectious property also helps protect the skin from harmful microbes. Frankincense is also soothing to the skin and nerves.

Sandalwood: has been found in several animal studies to protect the skin from the harmful effects of ultraviolet (UV-b) radiation. It may also be useful in skin regeneration, and in stopping skin infections.

Lavender: has been studied for its ability to reduce inflammation and allergic reactions in the skin. It has also been used to help the skin recover from burns, blisters, infections, and other injuries, as well as to help reduce conditions related to dry skin.

Myrrh: is known to be soothing to the skin, and is often used to relieve chapped or cracked skin. It has been studied for its anti-inflammatory properties, and is also used to fight many bacterial, fungal, and viral infections of the skin.

Helichrysum: is used to help relieve skin conditions such as eczema and psoriasis. It has antioxidant properties, and is often used for tissue regeneration, pain relief, and healing. It has also been used as a natural sun screen

Rose: is often used to help stop the breakdown of collegen in the skin that can lead to a loss of elasticity and wrinkles. It has also been used to help prevent scarring, and to help the body overcome various skin diseases and infections.

Body System(s) Affected: The oils in this blend may help it be effective for dealing with various problems related to the Skin.

Application: Apply directly on areas of concern. Use along with Essential Skin Care.

Safety Data: Use with caution during pregnancy.

On Guard™
Protective Blend

The oils in this blend have been studied for their strong abilities to kill harmful bacteria, mold, and viruses. This blend can be diffused into the air or be used to clean and purify household surfaces.

SINGLE OILS CONTAINED IN THIS BLEND:

Wild Orange: is antibacterial, antifungal, antidepressant, and antiseptic. It is a powerful disinfectant and very effective against colds and flu.

Clove Bud: is antibacterial, antifungal, anti-infectious, antiparasitic, a strong antiseptic, antiviral, and an immune stimulant. It may influence healing and help create a feeling of protection and courage.

Cinnamon Bark: has very specific purposes: (1) it is a powerful purifier, (2) it is a

powerful oxygenator, and (3) it enhances the action and the activity of other oils. It may have a stimulating and toning effect on the whole body and particularly on the circulatory system. It is antibacterial, antifungal, anti-infectious, anti-inflammatory, antimicrobial, antiparasitic, antiseptic, antispasmodic, antiviral, astringent, immune stimulant, sexual stimulant, and warming.

Eucalyptus radiata: may have a profound antiviral effect upon the respiratory system. It also has strong antibacterial, anticatarrhal, and antiseptic properties.

Rosemary: may help balance heart function, energize the solar plexus, and reduce mental fatigue. It may improve circulation and help stimulate the nerves. It is antiseptic and anti-infectious.

Body System(s) Affected: The oils in this blend may help it be effective for dealing with various problems related to the Immune System.

Aromatic Influence: Diffuse this blend of oils periodically for 20–25 minutes at a time to help protect the body against the onset of flu, colds, and viruses.

Application: Massage throat, stomach, intestines, and bottoms of feet. Dilute one drop in 15 drops of fractionated coconut oil: massage the thymus to stimulate the immune system, and massage under the arms to stimulate the lymphatic system. It is best applied to the bottoms of the feet, as it may be caustic to the skin. Dilute with fractionated coconut oil when used on sensitive/young skin.

Safety Data: Repeated use can result in extreme contact sensitization. Can cause extreme skin irritation. Use with caution during pregnancy.

PastTense™ Alleviating Roll-on
Headache Relief Blend

The oils in this blend are known to help relieve the pain and tension associated with headaches.

SINGLE OILS CONTAINED IN THIS BLEND

Wintergreen: has pain-relieving, anti-inflammatory, and antispasmodic properties. It may help with muscle and bone pain.

Lavender: may help relieve pain and inflammation. It is an antispasmodic and may help with migraine headaches and tension.

Peppermint: has pain relieving, anti-inflammatory, and antispasmodic properties. It is often used to help relieve headaches and has a cooling effect on the skin.

Frankincense: has sedative properties and may help reduce inflammation, headaches, and high blood pressure.

Cilantro: has anti-inflammatory and analgesic properties. It is a circulatory stimulant and helps alleviate aches, pains, and stiffness.

Roman Chamomile: has calming properties and is anti-inflammatory and antispasmodic. It also helps soothe the nerves.

Marjoram: is often used to soothe muscle aches and pains. It also has sedative properties and may help increase blood flow.

Basil: is often used to relieve muscle aches and pains and deep muscle spasms.

Rosemary: is often used to help relieve headaches. It may also help relieve sinus congestion and infections that can contribute to sinus headaches.

Body System(s) Affected: The oils in this blend may help it be effective for dealing with various problems related to the Nervous System and to the Muscles and Bones.

Application: Use the roll-on applicator to apply this blend to the temples, the forehead, the back of the neck, and to the reflex areas on the hands and feet.

Safety Data: Repeated use can result in extreme contact sensitization. Can cause extreme skin irritation. Use with caution during pregnancy.

PURIFY™
Cleansing Blend

Several of the oils contained in this blend are well-known and are often used to help remove odors from the air. Others have been studied for their powerful abilities to disinfect and to remove harmful microorganisms.

SINGLE OILS CONTAINED IN THIS BLEND:

Lemon: is antiseptic and antiviral. It may help as an air disinfectant and as a water purifier. Its uplifting aroma promotes healing and purification.

Lime: has antibacterial, antiviral, and antiseptic properties.

Pine: has antimicrobial and antiseptic properties. It may also help with cuts and with infections of the urinary system.

Citronella: has antiseptic, antibacterial, antispasmodic, anti-inflammatory, deodorizing, insecticidal, purifying, and sanitizing properties.

Melaleuca: may help balance heart function and act as a cleanser and detoxifier of the blood. It has antibacterial, antifungal, anti-infectious, antiseptic, antiviral, and immune-stimulant properties.

Cilantro: is relaxing, uplifting, refreshing, and may help memory. It may help with burns, bites, and stings. Cilantro and coriander are distilled from the same plant—cilantro oil, however, is distilled from the leaves of the plant, while coriander oil is distilled from the seeds of the plant.

Body System(s) Affected: The oils in this blend may help it be effective for dealing with various problems related to the Digestive System, to Emotional Balance, and to the Skin.

Aromatic Influence: This blend is great for air purification when diffused. When illness is in the home, diffuse for one hour and then wait for two hours. Repeat this pattern as desired. Diffuse in the office, barn, or garbage areas; or put it on a cotton ball, and place it in an air vent to freshen the car.

Application: Apply to reflex points on the body, ears, feet, and temples. Apply topically for infections and cleansing. Put on cotton balls and place in air vents for an insect repellent at home or at work. Can also be added to paint to help reduce fumes.

Safety Data: Repeated use can possibly result in contact sensitization. Can be irritating to sensitive skin.

Companion Oils: Citrus Bliss, On Guard.

SERENITY
Calming Blend

This relaxing blend contains essential oils that are often used to help calm and soothe feelings of stress, excitement, and anxiety in order to help the body maintain its natural state of health.

SINGLE OILS CONTAINED IN THIS BLEND:

Lavender: has calming and sedative properties. It may help lift feelings of depression and anxiety.

Sweet Marjoram: may help relax and calm the body and mind and also help promote peace.

Roman Chamomile: is calming and relaxing. It may help relieve muscle tension as well as calm nerves and soothe emotions.

Ylang Ylang: has calming and sedative properties. It brings a feeling of self-love, confidence, joy, and peace.

Sandalwood: is calming and sedative. It helps balance and harmonize the emotions and may help ease nervous tension.

Vanilla Bean Extract: is calming and may help ease tension.

Body System(s) Affected: The oils in this blend may help it be effective for dealing with various problems related to the Nervous System and to Emotional Balance.

Aromatic Influence: This blend of oils is perfect for calming the nerves or emotions at the end of a long day or in times of stress. As the body is able to relax, more blood is able to circulate to the brain.

Application: Apply under nose and to back, feet, and back of neck. Put in bathwater. Apply to navel, feet, or back of neck for insomnia. Wear as perfume or cologne.

Companion Oils: Lavender.

SLIM & SASSY™
Metabolic Blend

This blend is specially designed to help control hunger and to help limit excessive calorie intake. The oils in this blend are calming to the stomach and work to improve emotional well-being. Slim & Sassy is most effective when combined with exercise and healthy eating.

SINGLE OILS CONTAINED IN THIS BLEND:

Grapefruit: is balancing and uplifting to the mind. It has been used medicinally by the French to help with cellulite and digestion.

Lemon: is invigorating, enhancing, and warming. It promotes health, healing, and energy.

Peppermint: is purifying and stimulating to the human mind. It may also help soothe digestive difficulties.

Ginger: may help increase physical energy and promote healthy digestion.

Cinnamon: enhances the action of other oils. It may improve circulation, digestion, and energy levels.

Body System(s) Affected: Emotional Balance, Digestive System.

Aromatic Influence: This blend of oils is calming to the stomach and uplifting to the mind.

Application: Add 8 drops of Slim & Sassy to 16 oz. of water, and drink throughout the day between meals. Apply to palms of hands: cup hands over nose and mouth, and breathe deeply. Diffuse into the air.

Safety Data: Because this blend contains citrus oils, it may increase skin photosensitivity. It is best to avoid sunlight or UV rays for 12 hours after topical application. Do not apply directly in eyes, ears, or nose. Consult your doctor before using if you are pregnant or have a medical condition.

Companion Oils: Grapefruit, orange, lemongrass, thyme, lavender, Elevation, rosemary, fennel.

SOLACE™
Monthly Blend for Women

This unique blend combines many different oils often used to help alleviate symptoms often associated with PMS, menopause, and aging.

SINGLE OILS CONTAINED IN THIS BLEND:

Clary Sage: is often used to help balance estrogen and other hormones associated with PMS and menopause symptoms.

Oil Blends

Lavender: has soothing properties and is often used to help balance and calm emotions associated with PMS.

Bergamot: helps relieve feelings of stress and agitation, relieves tension, and helps balance emotions.

Roman Chamomile: is antispasmotic and has calming and relaxing properties. It is often used to help balance emotions and relieve symptoms related to menopause.

Cedarwood: is calming and helps sooth nervous tension.

Ylang Ylang: has calming and sedative properties. It brings a feeling of self-love, confidence, joy, and peace, and is often used to help balance hormones.

Geranium: may help with hormonal balance, and is often used to combat bone problems such as osteoporosis. It has a calming influence and is used in treating symptoms associated with PMS.

Fennel: is often used to help alleviate issues associated with menopause and pre-menopause. It has hormone balancing properties, and may be helpful in soothing symptoms related to PMS. It is also often used to help alleviate skin issues related to aging.

Carrot Seed: is often used to help regulate menstruation and soothe symptoms related to PMS.

Palmarosa: helps reduce stress and tension, and uplifts the emotions. It is often used to help alleviate many different skin problems.

Vitex: has been studied for its abilities to regulate estrogen levels, and to alleviate symptoms associated with PMS and menopause[1].

Body System(s) Affected: Hormonal System, Emotional Balance, Skin.

Aromatic Influence: Helps to balance mood and calm stress and tension.

Application: Diffuse or inhale from the hands. Apply to the chest, abdomen, or back of neck as needed.

1 Meier et al., 2000

Safety Data: Repeated use may result in contact sensitization—dilute with fractionated coconut oil if this occurs. Consult your doctor before using if you are pregnant or have a medical condition.

Companion Oils: Whisper.

TerraShield™
Repellent Blend

This proprietary blend contains 15 essential oils that have been proven to more effectively repel biting insects than other synthetic repellents. A small amount of this blend will provide powerful coverage for up to 6 hours.

Single Oils Contained in This Blend:

Lemon Eucalyptus: is insecticidal. It may also help repel cockroaches, silverfish, and other insects.

Citronella: is insect repellent and insecticidal.

Lemongrass: is a strong insect repellent and is insecticidal to many insects.

Proprietary Blend of 12 Other Oils.

Aromatic Influence: It is highly repellent to many flying and crawling insects and bugs.

Application: Diffuse into the air, or apply a small amount of this oil on the skin. Place a few drops on ribbons and strings, and place near air vents, windows, or openings where bugs might come in.

Whisper™
Blend for Women

This exquisite blend of oils works harmoniously with an individual's unique chemistry to create an appealing aroma—without the harmful chemicals found in many of today's perfumes.

Single Oils Contained in This Blend:

Patchouli: may help calm and relax, relieving feelings of anxiety.

Bergamot: may help relieve feelings of anxiety, stress, and tension. Its aroma is uplifting and refreshing.

Sandalwood: helps to alleviate feelings of depression. It helps one accept others with an open heart, while diminishing one's own egocentricity.

Rose: is stimulating and elevating to the mind. Its beautiful fragrance is felt to be aphrodisiac-like in nature.

Jasmine: is very uplifting to the emotions. It produces feelings of confidence, energy, and optimism.

Cinnamon Bark: has antidepressant and stimulating properties.

Cistus: is stimulating to the senses of touch, sight, and sound. It may also help quiet the nerves and promote feelings of peace.

Vetiver: is antispasmodic and locally warming. Vetiver has been valuable for relieving stress and helping people recover from emotional traumas and shock.

Ylang Ylang: has calming and sedative properties. It brings a feeling of self-love, confidence, joy, and peace.

Geranium: may help with hormonal balance, liver and kidney functions, and the discharge of toxins from the liver.

Cocoa Bean Extract: has a pleasurable, soothing aroma.

Vanilla Bean Extract: is calming and may help ease tension.

Body System(s) Affected: Emotional Balance, Skin.

Aromatic Influence: The subtle aroma of this blend enhances the aura of beauty, femininity, and allure.

Application: Diffuse or wear as a perfume. Add 5–6 drops to 1 Tbs of fractionated coconut oil for use in massage.

Companion Oils: Elevation, Solace, Zendocrine.

ZENDOCRINE™
Detoxification Blend

This blend contains oils that have been studied for their abilities to help support organ cleansing and healthy tissue function.

SINGLE OILS CONTAINED IN THIS BLEND:

Clove: contains high levels of eugenol, which has been found to be an effective antioxidant. Clove is also used in France as a treatment for endocrine disorders such as impotence.

Grapefruit: has demonstrated an ability to stimulate the adrenal glands. It is also often used to help cleanse the kidneys and the lymphatic system.

Rosemary: has demonstrated strong antioxidant effects and has been used to help mitigate the effects of endocrine disorders such as diabetes and stress-related chronic fatigue.

Geranium: may help with hormonal balance, liver and kidney function, pancreas support, and the discharge of toxins from the liver.

Body System(s) Affected: Hormonal System, Emotional Balance, Skin and Hair.

Application: Take 3–5 drops of the Zendocrine oil blend in capsules either alone or with the Zendocrine supplement capsules up to once a day. Massage on bottoms of feet.

Safety Data: Because this blend contains citrus oils, it may increase skin photosensitivity. It is best to avoid sunlight or UV rays for 12 hours after topical application. Repeated use can result in contact sensitization. Consult your doctor before using if you are pregnant, epileptic, or have a medical condition.

Companion Oils: Whisper.

Oil Blends

ESSENTIAL OIL INSPIRED WELLNESS SUPPLEMENTS

ESSENTIAL OIL INSPIRED WELLNESS SUPPLEMENTS

This section contains proprietary essential oil–inspired supplements and detailed information about each one. Other commercial supplements exist on the market, but many find the supplements referred to in this section to be superior. Many of these product names are trademarks of dōTERRA Int., LLC; and although these product names appear throughout other sections of this book without the trademark symbol, they still refer to these same trademarked products.

ALPHA CRS+®

Alpha CRS+ is a multi-nutrient supplement designed to increase cellular health, vitality, and energy.

INGREDIENTS:

Boswellia serrata **Extract (beta-Boswellic Acids):** Boswellic acids are a family of water-soluble triterpene molecules extracted from the resin of plants in the genus *Boswellia*, such as frankincense. Boswellic acids have been studied for years for their strong anti-inflammatory[1,2,3] and anticancerous[4,5,6] properties as well as for their potential to support joint health and to help prevent arthritis[7,8]. This extract contains six highly-bioavailable beta-boswellic acids.

Scuttelaria Root Extract (Baicalin): Baicalin is a polyphenol extracted from the scuttelaria, or Chinese skullcap, root. Besides being known for its antioxidant properties[9], baicalin has also been studied for its anticancer benefits[10,11].

Milk Thistle Extract (Silymarin): Silymarin is a complex of polyphenols extracted from the milk thistle plant. Animal and cellular studies have suggested a toxin-protective effect on the liver from these polyphenols, especially the polyphenol silibinin[12,13].

Pineapple Extract (Bromelain Protease Enzymes): Bromelain protease enzymes extracted from the pineapple plant have been studied for their anti-inflammatory[14,15] properties and for their potential to reduce joint pain and arthritis[16].

Polygonum Capsudatum Extract (Resveratrol): Resveratrol is a polyphenol created by plants in a defensive response to bacteria or fungi. In addition to its antioxidant properties[17], resveratrol has also been studied for its ability to inhibit skin[18] and leukemia[19] cancer cell growth and to improve mitochondrial function in cells[20].

Turmeric Root Extract (Curcumin): Curcumin is a polyphenol found in turmeric root (a spice commonly used in curry). In recent studies, curcumin was found to prevent and bind amyloid-beta plaques[21] and to reduce oxidative stress and DNA damage caused by ameloid-beta in neuronal cells[22]. Ameloid-beta, and its accumulation in the brain in plaque form, has been hypothesized as a possible cause of Alzheimer's disease.

Red Raspberry Extract (Ellagic Acid): Ellagic acid is found in raspberries, pomegranates, walnuts, and other fruits and vegetables. This well-researched polyphenol has been studied for its ability to prevent low-density lipoprotein (LDL) oxidation (a known risk factor for cardiovascular disease)[23,24] and atherosclerotic lesions[25],

1 Ammon, 2002.
2 Banno et al., 2006.
3 Gayathri et al., 2007.
4 Bhushan et al., 2007.
5 Huang et al., 2000.
6 Liu et al., 2002.
7 Roy et al., 2006.
8 Goel et al., 2010.
9 Jung et al., 2008.
10 Zhou et al, 2008.
11 Franek et al, 2005.

12 Al-Anati et al., 2009.
13 Abenavoli et al., 2010.
14 Fitzhugh et al., 2008.
15 Brien et al., 2004.
16 Walker et al., 2002.
17 Chakraborty et al, 2008.
18 Jang et al, 1997.
19 Lee et al, 2005.
20 Lagouge et al, 2006.
21 Yang et al., 2005.
22 Park et al., 2008.
23 Anderson et al, 2001.
24 Chang et al, 2008.
25 Yu et al, 2005.

which ability could help prevent athero-sclerosis.

Grape Seed Extract (Proanthocyanidins): Proanthocyanidins extracted from grape seeds were found in one recent study to significantly decrease oxidized LDL in people with high cholesterol[26].

Marigold Flower Extract (Lutein): Lutein is created in many plants as an antioxidant and a light absorber. In humans, lutein is found in high concentration in the macula, the area of the eye where central vision occurs. Lutein supplementation has been found in at least one study to improve the visual acuity and macular pigment optical density in patients with age-related macular degeneration[27].

Tomato Fruit Extract (Lycopene): Lycopene is a red-colored pigment found in many red plants. It has been studied for its potential role in reducing the risk of prostate cancer[28].

***Bacopa monnieri* Extract:** *Bacopa monnieri* is an herb that has long been used in Ayurvedic medicine for its ability to enhance cognitive ability, and it has been studied for its potential to aid with cognitive function[29]. Extracts from this plant have also been recently studied for their neuroprotective abilities in regulating the serotonin receptor 5-HT(2C)[30].

Acetyl-L-Carnitine: is a substance created by the body that transports fatty acids to the mitochondria to help break down fats into energy. Supplementation with L-carnitine (the bioactive form of carnitine) was found in several studies to reduce fatigue as well as to increase muscle mass and to decrease fat mass in certain populations[31,32,33,34].

Alpha Lipoic Acid: plays an important role in the aerobic metabolism of cells. It has a strong antioxidant ability[35] and has been studied for its effects on Alzheimer's disease patients[36] and as a treatment for neuropathy in diabetic patients[37 38]. Lipoic acid and acetyl-l-carnitine have also been studied together for their ability to reduce the oxidative mitochondrial decay in the brain associated with aging[39,40].

Coenzyme Q(10): is a substance that plays a critical role in the electron transport chain that helps create cellular energy. Besides having antioxidant properties, coenzyme Q(10) has also been studied for its neuroprotective effect in Parkinson's disease[41,42,43] and for its ability to help alleviate symptoms of chronic heart failure[44,45] and other cardiovascular problems[46 47].

Quercetin: is a polyphenol commonly found in apples, citrus fruits, green vegetables, and many berries. It has been studied for its ability to selectively kill prostate cancer cells without harming surrounding healthy cells[48,49].

Tummy Taming Blend: This exclusive blend combines peppermint leaf, ginger root extract, and caraway seed to help keep the stomach calm.

Other Ingredients: Vegetable hypromellose, vegetable cellulose, silica.

Suggested Use: Adults take three capsules per day with food.

Companion Products: xEO Mega, Microplex VMz.

DigestZen® GX Assist®

GX Assist is a proprietary blend of essential oils with caprylic acid that is designed to help support the gastrointestinal tract in eliminating pathogens.

26 Bagchi et al, 2003.
27 Richer et al., 2004.
28 Giovannucci et al., 2002.
29 Lohidasan et al., 2009.
30 Krishnakumar et al., 2009.
31 Ciacci et al., 2007.
32 Malaguarnera et al., 2007.
33 Pistone et al., 2003.
34 Brass et al., 2001.

35 Zembron-Lacne et al., 2007
36 Hager et al., 2007.
37 Ziegler et al., 2006.
38 Tang et al., 2007.
39 Long et al., 2009.
40 Hagen et al., 2002.
41 Hargreaves et al., 2008.
42 Kooncumchoo et al., 2006.
43 Winkler-Stuck et al., 2004.
44 Belardinelli et al., 2005.
45 Keogh et al., 2003.
46 Kuettner et al., 2005.
47 Tiano et al., 2007.
48 Paliwal et al., 2005.
49 Aalinkeel et al., 2008.

Wellness Supplements

Ingredients

Oregano Essential Oil: has antibacterial, anti-fungal, antiparasitic, and antiviral properties.

Melaleuca Essential Oil: has demonstrated strong antifungal properties as well as antibacterial, antiparasitic, and antiviral abilities. It may also help reduce inflammation.

Lemon Essential Oil: is often used for its antiseptic and antiviral properties.

Lemongrass Essential Oil: has demonstrated antiseptic and anti-inflammatory properties.

Peppermint Essential Oil: has demonstrated antibacterial and antiviral properties.

Thyme Essential Oil: is highly antibacterial, as well as antifungal.

Caprylic Acid: is a fatty acid naturally found in coconut milk, breast milk, and other sources. It has demonstrated antimicrobial properties against pathogens such as *E. Coli*[1], *Salmonella*[2,3], and *Strep*[4], among others.

Suggested Use: Take 1-3 softgels a day with meals for 10 days each month.

Companion Product: PB Assist

DigestZen® TerraZyme™

TerraZyme is a potent blend of food-derived enzymes and mineral cofactors that can aid in the digestion and absorption of critical nutrients that are lacking in many of today's diets.

Ingredients:

Protease (Aspergillus): aids in breaking proteins down into smaller amino acid units for use by the body to create necessary protein structures.

Amylase (Aspergillus): begins the process of breaking down complex carbohydrates such as starches into simpler sugars such as maltose.

Lipase (Rhizopus): aids in breaking down large lipids and fats to help release energy and to create smaller units that can be used to build critical lipid-based

structures such as hormones and the cell membrane.

Alpha Galactosidase (Aspergillus): aids in breaking down glycolipids and glycoproteins.

Cellulase (Trichoderma): breaks down cellulose into simpler sugars such as glucose for use as energy.

Maltase (Barley Malt): converts the disaccharide maltose into glucose for use by the body for energy.

Sucrase (Saccharomyces): converts the disaccharide sucrose into fructose and glucose for use by the body for energy.

Tummy Taming Blend: This exclusive blend combines peppermint leaf, ginger root extract, and caraway seed to help keep the stomach calm.

Enzyme Assimilation System: This patented system contains special mineral cofactors necessary for optimum enzymatic action, enhancing nutrient bioavailability to the body. These mineral cofactors include coral calcium, magnesium yeast, manganese yeast, zinc yeast, and 72 organic trace minerals.

Other Ingredients: Vegetable hypromellose, vegetable cellulose.

Suggested Use: Take 1 to 3 capsules with meals.

Companion Products: DigestZen Essential Oil Blend, DigestZen Zendocrine Capsules.

DigestZen® Zendocrine™ Capsules

Zendocrine is a proprietary blend of whole-food based nutrients that can help promote healthy endocrine gland functions and the filtering of toxins by the body's systems.

Ingredients:

Psyllium Seed Husk Powder: contains a high level of soluble fiber that can help keep the digestive tract and the colon functioning properly.

1 Marounek et al., 2003.
2 Skrivanova et al., 2004.
3 Johny et al., 2009.
4 Nair et al., 2009.

Barberry Leaf: contains the alkaloid berberine, which has been studied for its ability to aid the pancreas in regulating insulin production, thus promoting healthy blood sugar levels[5].

Turkish Rhubarb Stem: has been used in traditional Chinese medicine to promote healthy bowel movement, aiding in clearing the intestines and colon of waste.

Kelp: is naturally high in the essential element iodine, which is necessary for proper thyroid functioning.

Milk Thistle Seed (Silymarin): Silymarin is a complex of polyphenols extracted from the milk thistle plant. Animal and cellular studies have suggested a toxin-protective effect in the liver of these polyphenols, especially the polyphenol silibinin[6,7].

Osha Root: was used by native Americans as a purifier and was chewed to help resolve sore throat and upper respiratory tract ailments.

Safflower Petals: are used in traditional Chinese medicine to aid the endocrine system in promoting healthy menstrual functioning in women.

Acacia Gum Bark: is known as a natural astringent that can decrease diarrhea and bloody discharges.

Burdock Root: has been used traditionally to help clear the body of toxins and has been used as a diuretic to help eliminate uric acid. It has also been studied for its ability to help protect liver cells from toxins[8].

Clove Bud: has very potent antimicrobial[9,10,11,12] and antioxidant[13] properties that can help protect cells from toxins.

Dandelion Root (Inulin): has been studied for its ability to protect liver cells from toxin-induced damage[14,15].

Garlic Fruit: is known for its antibacterial and antiseptic properties and has been studied for its potential to help decrease problems related to diabetes[16,17].

Marshmallow Root: has been used traditionally to soothe coughs and irritations of the upper respiratory tract and to soothe irritations of tissues of the gastrointestinal tract, due to its ability to both coat the mucous membrane linings and to stimulate epithelial cell function within these membranes[18].

Red Clover Leaf (Isoflavones): contains high levels of isoflavones, which are structurally similar to natural estrogens in the body. These isoflavones have been studied for their abilities to help regulate healthy estrogen-mediated functions in postmenopausal women[19].

Other Ingredients: Organic evaporated cane juice, organic brown rice syrup.

Enzyme Assimilation System: This patented system contains special enzymes and mineral cofactors that may enhance digestion and nutrient absorption in the small intestine and blood stream, including amylase (breaks complex carbohydrates into sugars), protease (breaks proteins into smaller amino acids), cellulase (breaks cellulose into sugars), and lipase (breaks fats and lipids into their component parts).

Suggested Use: Take 2 capsules daily—1 one with morning meal and 1 one with evening meal.

Companion Products: DigestZen Essential Oil Blend, DigestZen TerraZyme.

xEO Mega®

xEO Mega is a blend of essential fatty acids. It includes essential fatty acids from both marine and land sources, the potent antioxidant astaxanthin, and a unique essential oil blend that helps enhance the benefits of the essential fatty acids.

Ingredients:

Fish Oil Concentrate (EPA, DHA): Eicosapentaenoic acid (or EPA) is an omega-3

Wellness Supplements

5 Zhou et al., 2009.
6 Al-Anati et al., 2009.
7 Abenavoli et al., 2010.
8 Lin et al., 2000.
9 Fabio et al., 2007.
10 Smith-Palmer et al., 2004.
11 Hitokoto et al., 1980.
12 Benencia et al., 2000.
13 Chaieb et al., 2007.
14 Domitrović et al., 2010.
15 Mahesh et al., 2010.

16 Younis et al., 2010.
17 Drobiova et al., 2009.
18 Deters et al., 2010.
19 Lipovac et al., 2010.

fatty acid. It is largely known for its anti-inflammatory benefits but has also been found in several studies to help individuals suffering from depression[1,2,3,4]. Docosahexaenoic acid (or DHA) is another omega-3 fatty acid that is found in high concentrations in the brain and in the retina of the eye, where it is part of several important phospholipids. DHA has also been studied for its ability to help inhibit colon[5] and prostate[6] cancer cells. Taken together in fish oil, there is strong evidence that EPA and DHA can help with high blood pressure[7,8,9] and cardiovascular disease[10,11], especially in high-risk individuals. When taken together by pregnant women, EPA and DHA have also been found to have beneficial effects on these women's children, such as reduced allergies[12,13] and improved neurological development[14].

Astaxanthin: Astaxanthin is a natural cerotenoid that can be found in many marine plants (and in the animals that eat these plants), but it is found in the most abundance in marine algae. This dark, red-colored cerotenoid pigment has been well studied for its potent antioxidant abilities[15,16] and has demonstrated a unique potential to cross the blood-brain barrier in mammals, making it a prime candidate for treating diseases of the central nervous system caused by oxidative damage[17].

Flaxseed Oil (ALA): Alpha-linolenic acid, or ALA, is a substance that is readily able to be synthesized into EPA or DHA by the human body.

Borage Seed Oil (GLA): Borage seed oil has one of the highest contents of the omega-6 fatty acid gamma-linolenic acid. GLA has been studied for its ability to aid with dermatitis[18,19] and other skin conditions[20,21].

Cranberry Seed Oil (ALA): In addition to being high in alpha-linolenic acid, cranberry seed oil is also high in vitamin E, a potent antioxidant.

Pomegranate Seed Oil (CLNA): 9cis, 11trans, 13cis-conjugated linolenic acid (or punicic acid) is a conjugated linolenic acid (CLNA) that is found in pomegranate seed oil. This isomer of linolenic acid has been studied for its antioxidant[22] and anti-inflammatory[23] properties.

Vitamin D (cholecalciferol): plays an important role in bone health and strength and helps modulate hormone secretion and immune function.

Vitamin E (d-alpha & mixed tocopherols): is a potent antioxidant and may play a role in cellular communication.

Clove Bud Essential Oil: is highly antioxidant as well as anti-inflammatory. It may also help relieve pain and skin problems.

Frankincense Essential Oil: is an immune stimulant and is anti-inflammatory. It may also help with blood pressure and depression.

Thyme Essential Oil: Thymol in thyme is highly antioxidant. Thyme oil may help with depression and fatigue.

Cumin Essential Oil: is a digestive aid and may help with indigestion and flatulence.

Orange Essential Oil: aids the digestive system and may help with indigestion and diarrhea.

Peppermint Essential Oil: is anti-inflammatory and antispasmodic. It may help with intestinal cramping and spasms as well as with feelings of nausea.

1   Su et al., 2008.
2   Osher et al., 2005.
3   Lucas et al., 2009.
4   Frangou et al., 2006.
5   Kato et al., 2002.
6   Shaikh et al., 2008.
7   Erkkila et al., 2008.
8   Mori et al., 1999.
9   Morris et al., 1993.
10 Erkkila et al., 2004.
11 Bucher et al., 2002.
12 Furuhjelm et al., 2009.
13 Dunstan et al., 2003.
14 Helland et al., 2003.
15 Palozza et al., 1992.
16 Naguib et al., 2000.
17 Tso et al., 1994.

18 Senapati et al., 2008.
19 Kanehara et al., 2007.
20 De Spirt et al., 2009.
21 Chen et al., 2006.
22 Saha et al., 2009.
23 Boussetta et al., 2009.

Ginger Essential Oil: is calming to the digestive system. It may help alleviate feelings of nausea and indigestion.

Caraway Seed Essential Oil: is antispasmodic and antiparasitic. It may also help with indigestion and diarrhea and may be calming to the intestinal muscles.

German Chamomile Essential Oil: is anti-inflammatory and aids the digestive system. It may also aid liver function and help alleviate gastritis.

Other Ingredients: Fatty acid of coconut, vegetable cellulose, silica, fatty acid of palm.

Suggested Use: Adults take two to four softgels per day with food.

Companion Products: Alpha CRS, Microplex VM.

MICROPLEX VMz™

This unique multivitamin combines natural vitamins and minerals with a complex of whole-food nutrients and minerals that are bound to a glycoprotein matrix to help enhance their bio-availability. These nutrients help support healthy cell, tissue, and system function. Additionally, this supplement contains a proprietary whole-food blend and a patented enzyme assimilation system to help further enhance nutrient bioavailability.

INGREDIENTS:

Vitamin A (natural alpha and beta carotene): plays a role in vision, skin health, and DNA transcription.

Vitamin C (natural calcium ascorbate): provides stability to collagen (the main protein in connective tissue) and helps synthesize neurotransmitters and carnitine (which helps create energy through the breakdown of fatty acids).

Vitamin D (as glycoprotein matrix): plays an important role in bone health and strength and helps modulate hormone secretion and immune function.

Vitamin E (natural mixed tocopherols): is a potent antioxidant and may play a role in cellular communication.

Vitamin K (as glycoprotein matrix): is required by the liver to create the proteins involved in blood clotting and in bone structure.

Vitamin B1 (as glycoprotein matrix): plays a critical role in generating energy from carbohydrates within the cell and is critical to healthy heart and nerve cell function.

Vitamin B2 (as glycoprotein matrix): plays an important role in the creation of energy from lipids and carbohydrates in the cell as well as in the synthesis of several other important cellular chemicals.

Vitamin B3 (as glycoprotein matrix): plays a role in cellular metabolism. Deficiency of niacin can result in dermatitis, diarrhea, confusion, and dementia.

Vitamin B5 (as glycoprotein matrix): plays an important role in the creation of energy within the cell and in the creation of cholesterol, various fatty acids, and acetylcholine (a neurotransmitter that allows cells within the nervous system to communicate with each other).

Vitamin B6 (as glycoprotein matrix): is a necessary coenzyme to several enzymes involved in metabolism as well as to the creation of neurotransmitters such as serotonin and epinephrine.

Folate (as glycoprotein matrix): is necessary for cells to create nucleotides (the building blocks of DNA and RNA).

Vitamin B12 (as glycoprotein matrix): plays a key role in the synthesis of DNA by regenerating folate and is also critical to maintaining a healthy myelin sheath that preserves the normal functioning of the nervous system.

Biotin (as glycoprotein matrix): helps metabolize fatty acids and is important to the synthesis of glucose from various substances.

Calcium (as natural coral and ascorbate): plays a critical role in bone structure and has a role in muscle contraction and nerve cell communication as well.

Iron (as yeast): is part of the structure of heme (a critical part of the protein hemoglobin that allows red blood cells to transport oxygen throughout the body) as well as

Wellness Supplements

several other proteins. It also plays a role in several other important enzymatic reactions within the body.

Magnesium (as yeast): is required to create many different enzymes in the body, including those that create and use ATP (cellular energy) and that create DNA and RNA.

Zinc (as yeast): is an important component of many enzymes and proteins found in the body and also plays a role in cellular communication.

Selenium (as yeast): plays a role as a cofactor for several enzymes within the body, including several in the thyroid.

Copper (as yeast): is found in several different enzymes, including superoxide dismutase.

Manganese (as yeast): is an important component in several different enzymes.

Chromium (as glycoprotein matrix): is believed to play a role in sugar and lipid metabolism within the body.

Vanadium (as yeast): may play a role in proper glucose regulation.

Proprietary Whole-Food Blend: This unique blend contains cayenne fruit powder (high in vitamin A and other vitamins and minerals), kelp powder (high in iodine for thyroid health), horsetail powder, and 72 organic trace minerals.

Enzyme Assimilation System: This patented system contains special enzymes and mineral cofactors that may enhance digestion and nutrient absorption in the small intestine and blood stream, including amylase (breaks complex carbohydrates into sugars), protease (breaks proteins into smaller amino acids), cellulase (breaks cellulose into sugars), and lipase (breaks fats and lipids into their component parts).

Tummy Taming Blend: This exclusive blend combines peppermint leaf, ginger root extract, and caraway seed to help keep the stomach calm.

Other Ingredients: Vegetable hypromellose, vegetable cellulose, silica.

Suggested Use: Adults take four capsules per day with food.

Companion Products: Alpha CRS, EO Mega.

ON GUARD™ PROTECTING THROAT DROPS

On Guard Protecting Throat Drops offer the relief of a throat drop, soothing dry and scratchy throats, combined with the immune-protectant power of the essential oils that make up the On Guard blend.

INGREDIENTS:

Wild Orange Essential Oil: is calming, uplifting, and antiseptic.

Clove Bud Essential Oil: is antibacterial, antiseptic, and may influence healing.

Cinnamon Bark Essential Oil: is antibacterial and antimicrobial. It also enhances the action and activity of other oils.

Eucalyptus radiata **Essential Oil:** is analgesic, antibacterial, and anti-infectious.

Rosemary Essential Oil: is anti-infectious, analgesic, antibacterial, anti-inflammatory, anticatarrhal, and supportive of the respiratory system.

Myrrh Essential Oil: is anti-infectious, anti-inflammatory, antiseptic, and combats coughs and sore throats.

Other Ingredients: Organic evaporated cane juice, organic brown rice syrup.

Suggested Use: Dissolve one throat drop in mouth as needed.

Companion Products: On Guard Foaming Hand Wash, On Guard Toothpaste, On Guard essential oil blend.

PB ASSIST+®

PB Assist+ is a proprietary blend of six strains of probiotic intestinal flora that help support healthy colonies of friendly microflora in the digestive tract. These probiotics are safely delivered to the intestines using a special double-coated capsule that protects the flora as they pass through the stomach. Each strain has shown superior adhesion and colonization.

INGREDIENTS:

Lactobacillus acidophilus: is a bacteria that converts sugars (such as lactose in dairy products) into lactic acid. It may also help to control the growth of *Candida albicans*, helping to prevent oral and vaginal yeast infections. It is commonly used to create yogurt.

Lactobacillus salivarious: is a bacteria commonly found in the intestines. *L. salivarious* has been studied for its ability to help reduce inflammation and prevent the adhesion and growth of harmful bacteria in the digestive system.

Bifidobacterium bifidus: is an intestinal bacteria that helps promote healthy digestive function. It is also used in the production of some yogurts.

Bifidobacterium longum: is found in the intestines and can help support healthy digestion and immune function.

Lactobacillus plantarum: is found in saliva and has the ability to break down gelatin. It is found in foods such as sauerkraut, pickles, and sourdough breads.

Lactobacillus casei: produces lactic acid that can help promote growth of friendly microflora. It is commonly used to make cheddar cheese and other foods.

Fructo-Oligosaccharide (FOS): promotes friendly bacteria growth and adhesion while inhibiting growth of pathogenic bacteria.

Other Ingredients: Vegetable glycerin, vegetable cellulose, vegetable stearate, silica, chlorophyllin.

Suggested Use: Take one double-layer capsule 3 times daily with food for five days each month. Can also be used more frequently when digestive flora has been compromised by antibiotics or other stressors.

Companion Product: GX Assist.

SLIM & SASSY® TRIM SHAKES (CHOCOLATE & VANILLA)

Slim & Sassy Trim Shakes are a high-fiber, high-protein meal alternative drink powder with a low glycemic index and low calories. These shakes

also contain extracts from the ashwagandha plant (*Withania somnifera*) that have shown potential to decrease blood serum levels of cortisol[1] and to reduce stress[2,3]. Cortisol—a hormone created by the adrenal glands—is released into the blood as the result of stress or anxiety, and it also plays a role in the body's sleep/wake cycle. When an individual is exposed to constant or chronic stress, levels of cortisol remain elevated in the body, disrupting the body's ability to relax and its ability to sleep naturally. Chronic stress and abnormally-elevated cortisol levels have also been associated with increased cravings and with increased levels of obesity and abdominal weight[4,5].

INGREDIENTS:

Protein Blend: is a blend of whey, pea, and rice proteins that helps support the body's protein needs—which is critical during exercise and dieting to help maintain and build lean body tissues such as muscle[6].

Fiber Blend: contains a mixture of insoluble fiber and prebiotic soluble fiber that can help promote beneficial GI tract bacteria function and elimination. These dietary fibers include maltodextrin, guar gum, and oligofructose.

Ashwagandha (*Withania somnifera*) Root and Leaf Extracts: have demonstrated a potential to help reduce stress[7,8] and to help lower blood serum cortisol levels[9]. Cortisol—a hormone created by the adrenal glands—is released into the blood as the result of stress or anxiety, and it also plays a role in the body's sleep/wake cycle. When an individual is exposed to constant or chronic stress, levels of cortisol remain elevated in the body, disrupting the body's ability to relax and its ability to sleep naturally. Chronic stress and abnormally-elevated cortisol levels have also been associated with increased cravings

1 Abedon, 2008.
2 Archana et al., 1999
3 Bhattacharya et al., 1987
4 De Vriendt et al., 2009.
5 Wallerius et al., 2003.
6 Walker et al., 2010.
7 Archana et al., 1999
8 Bhattacharya et al., 1987
9 Abedon, 2008.

and with increased levels of obesity and abdominal weight[1,2].

Vitamins and Minerals: include nutrients that have been shown to support cellular energy levels and muscle and bone health. The vitamins and minerals included in this supplement are listed below:

Calcium (dicalcium phosphate): helps support bone density and muscle contraction.

Magnesium (magnesium oxide): supports ATP production and use for energy.

Vitamin C (ascorbic acid): is antioxidant and supports blood vessel and cartilage health.

Vitamin E (vitamin E acetate): is antioxidant.

Vitamin B7 (biotin): helps support metabolism of fats and aerobic energy generation.

Vitamin B3 (niacinamide): helps support cellular energy creation.

Iodine (potassium iodide): plays a role in two important thyroid hormones.

Zinc (zinc oxide): is an important component in many critical cellular enzymes and proteins.

Vitamin A (vitamin A acetate): plays a role in vision, skin health, and DNA transcription.

Copper (copper gluconate): is found in several enzymes, including superoxide dismutase.

Vitamin B5 (D-calcium pantothenate): plays a role in the metabolism of fatty acids.

Vitamin D3: plays an important role in bone health and strength.

Vitamin B6 (pyridoxine hydrochloride): is important in the creation of enzymes that aid in the creation of energy.

Vitamin B2 (riboflavin): plays an important role in the creation of energy from lipids (fat) and carbohydrates in the cell.

Vitamin B1 (thiamine mononitrate): plays a critical role in generating energy from carbohydrates within the cell.

Vitamin B12: plays a key role in the synthesis of DNA and in nerve cell protection.

Folic acid: is a critical nutrient for the creation of DNA and RNA in cells.

Stevia: is a natural herb with a very sweet taste (said to be many times sweeter than sugar). This naturally-sweet herb has been found in at least one study to increase glucose tolerance while decreasing plasma glucose levels in normal volunteers[3].

Other Ingredients: sunflower, natural flavors, cocoa powder (chocolate flavor only).

Suggested Use: Blend one scoop of powder with 8 oz. of water, nonfat milk, almond milk, rice milk, or soy milk. Use up to twice a day as a meal alternative.

Companion Products: Slim & Sassy, Life Long Vitality supplements, TerraZyme, Zendocrine capsules, Zendocrine.

WOMEN'S BONE NUTRIENT LIFETIME COMPLEX™

This unique complex combines bioavailable vitamins and minerals that have demonstrated a role in promoting bone health, and in preventing age and nutritional related calcium loss and bone demineralization .

INGREDIENTS:

Vitamin C (as glycoprotein matrix): provides stability to collagen (the main protein in connective tissue) and helps synthesize neurotransmitters and carnitine (which helps create energy through the breakdown of fatty acids).

Vitamin D-2 (as ergocalciferol) and Vitamin D-3 (as cholacalciferol): play an important role in bone health and strength and helps modulate hormone secretion and immune function.

1 De Vriendt et al., 2009.
2 Wallerius et al., 2003.

3 Curi et al., 1986.

Biotin (as d-biotin): helps metabolize fatty acids and is important to the synthesis of glucose from various substances.

Calcium (as coral calcium): plays a critical role in bone structure, density, and strength. It has a role in muscle contraction and nerve cell communication as well.

Magnesium (as yeast): is required to create many different enzymes in the body, including those that create and use ATP (cellular energy) and that create DNA and RNA.

Zinc (as yeast): is an important component of many enzymes and proteins found in the body and also plays a role in cellular communication.

Copper (as yeast): is found in several different enzymes, including superoxide dismutase.

Manganese (as yeast): is an important component in several different enzymes.

Boron (as yeast): has been studied for its role in decreasing calcium loss and bone demineralization in women, and may play a role in hormone balance[4] and Vitamin D activation[5].

Other Ingredients: Vegetable hypromellose, rice flour, vegetable stearate.

Suggested Use: Teens and adults take four capsules per day with food.

Companion Products: Women's Phytoestrogen Lifetime Complex, Solace Oil Blend.

WOMEN'S PHYTOESTROGEN LIFETIME COMPLEX™

This complex was designed to help women maintain a healthy estrogen balance with a potent blend of phytoestrogens (plant-derived estrogen-mimicking compounds) from soy, pomegranate and flax seeds.

INGREDIENTS:

Soy Extract (64% isoflavones with a minimum 50% genistein): Isoflavones such as genistein act as phytoestrogens in the body that bind with the estrogen receptor beta (ER-β) within cells. Unlike estrogen receptor alpha (ER-α), which is found in high

concentrations in all parts of the female reproductive tract and mammary tissues, beta receptors are found in much smaller concentrations in uterine and mammary tissues[6]. This seems to indicate that soy phytoestrogens do not directly act on cells in uterus and breast tissue. This can be important as over-estrogenation of cells in the mammary tissues has been linked to an increased risk for breast cancer. Isoflavones from soy have also been found to reduce levels of potentially carcinogenic estrogen metabolites in postmenopausal women[7,8], and also to enhance levels of protective estrogen metabolites[9].

Flax Seed Extract (40% lignan): Flax seed contains several potent lignans which are metabolized by gastrointestinal bacteria into the active phytoestrogenic lignans, enterodiol and enterolactone. Both of these lignans have been studied for their antiproliferative effect on breast cancer cells[10,11], and evidence had been found that they may help lower blood triglyceride levels while raising levels of the good high density lipoproteins (HDL) in the blood[12,13].

Pomegranate Extract (40% ellagic acid): contains strong antioxidants in addition to several phytoestrogens that are being studied for their roles in regulating hormone balance and their potential roles in reducing breast cancer growth[14].

Other Ingredients: Flaxseed powder, vegetable hypromellose, silica.

Suggested Use: Pre-menopausal women take 1–2 capsules per day with food. Post-menopausal women take 2 capsules per day with food.

Safety Data: If pregnant, lactating, or experiencing any health conditions, consult a physician before using.

Companion Products: Women's Bone Complex Lifetime Complex, Solace Oil Blend.

4 Nielsen et al., 1987
5 Samman et al., 1998.

6 Couse et al., 1997.
7 Xu et al., 2000.
8 Xu et al., 1998
9 Lu et al., 2000.
10 Truan et al., 2012.
11 Mabrok et al., 2012.
12 Zhang et al., 2008.
13 Penalvo et al., 2012.
14 Strati et al., 2009.

Wellness Supplements

Essential Living & Spa Products

ESSENTIAL LIVING AND SPA PRODUCTS

CLEAR SKIN™ FOAMING FACE WASH

The Clear Skin Foaming Face Wash has been formulated to help clarify the skin and to create a hostile environment for detrimental skin bacteria.

KEY INGREDIENTS:

Rosewood Essential Oil: is known for its antiseptic properties and is often used to help clear infections and to support the revitalization of skin tissue.

Melaleuca Essential Oil: is one of the most studied antibacterial and antifungal oils. Melaleuca also has anti-inflammatory properties and can help support the skin in the recovery process after injuries.

Eucalyptus globulus **Essential Oil:** is often used for inflammation and skin infections and sores. It is used medicinally in France to treat candida and other fungal infections and has also demonstrated strong antibacterial properties.

Geranium Essential Oil: has antibacterial and anti-inflammatory properties and is often used to help alleviate the effects of acne and eczema. It may also help balance sebum levels in the skin.

Lemongrass Essential Oil: is known for its antiseptic properties and is often used to help clear infections and to support the revitalization of skin tissue.

Black Cumin Seed Oil: has been used since ancient times for a myriad of health concerns. In addition to its antioxidant and anti-inflammatory properties, black cumin seed oil also has a high content of linoleic acid, an essential fatty acid used by the body to help maintain healthy skin and hair. Linoleic acid has been studied for its ability to reduce acne microcomedones[1] and to enhance cellular migration during wound healing[2].

White Willow Bark Extract: has been used for centuries for its anti-inflammatory and analgesic properties. This natural extract has also been used topically as an aid for acne and acne lesions by promoting the shedding of dead skin cells from the skin's surface.

Glycyrrhiza inflata **Root Extract:** *Glycyrrhiza inflata* is a species of plant found in China that is closely related to the licorice plant. The root of this plant contains substances that have been studied for their antioxidant[3] and anti-inflammatory[4,5] properties as well as for their ability to help reduce dermatitis[6] and to balance sebum production in the skin[7].

Candida bombicola **Ferment:** *Candida bombicola* is a harmless yeast that has the ability to produce natural, biodegradeable biosurfactants (natural substances that act as detergents to cleanse oils and sebum from the skin)[8].

Vitamin A: plays a critical role in the creation and growth of normal skin cells in the epidermis.

Other Ingredients: water, sodium cocoyl glutamate, sodium cocoyl methyl taurate, sodium lauroamphoacetate, butylene glycol, PEG-40 hydrogenated caster oil, *Salix alba* (willow) bark extract, *Taraktgenos kurzii* seed oil, *Leptospermum scoperium* branch/leaf oil, potassium lauroyl wheat amino acids, palm glycerides, *Magnolia graniflora* bark extract, retinyl palmitate, algae extract, *Artemisia vulgaris* extract, sodium PCA, zinc PCA, dipotassium glycyrrhizate, capryloyl glycine, cetyl hydroxyethylcellulose, disodium EDTA, caprylyl glycol, ethylhexylglycerin, hexylene glycol, phenoxyethanol.

Suggested Use: Moisten the skin, and apply a small amount of face wash on the face and

---

1 Letawe et al., 1998.
2 Ruthig et al., 1999.
3 Veratti et al., 2001.
4 Shetty et al., 2011.
5 Ishida et al., 2012
6 Saeedi et al., 2003.
7 Kambara et al., 2003.
8 Saerens et al., 2011.

neck; then rinse away. Use both morning and evening.

Companion Products: Clear Skin Topical Blend.

DEEP BLUE® RUB

This unique massage and sports cream contains the Deep Blue essential oil blend. This blend is comprised of oils that have been studied for their abilities to help reduce muscle, joint, and bone pain and inflammation. Additionally, this rich, moisturizing cream stimulates sensations of warmth and coolness to help soothe tissue soreness and stiffness.

KEY INGREDIENTS:

Wintergreen Essential Oil: contains 99% methyl salicylate, which gives it cortisone-like properties. It may be beneficial for arthritis, rheumatism, tendinitis, and any other discomfort that is related to the inflammation of bones, muscles, and joints.

Camphor Essential Oil: is analgesic (pain-relieving) and anti-inflammatory. It may be beneficial for arthritis, rheumatism, muscle aches and pains, sprains, and bruises.

Peppermint Essential Oil: is anti-inflammatory to the prostate and to damaged tissues. It has a soothing and cooling effect that may help with arthritis and rheumatism.

Blue Tansy Essential Oil: is analgesic and anti-inflammatory. It may also help with low blood pressure, arthritis, and rheumatism.

German Chamomile Essential Oil: is antioxidant, anti-inflammatory, and analgesic. It may also help relieve congestion and arthritis.

Helichrysum Essential Oil: may help cleanse the blood and improve circulatory functions. It is anticatarrhal in structure and nature. As a powerful anti-inflammatory, it may even help reduce inflammation in the meninges of the brain. On a spiritual level, it may help one let go of angry feelings that prevent one from forgiving and moving forward.

Osmanthus Essential Oil: comes from one of the 10 famous traditional flowers of China. The blossoms are highly aromatic and are used in the world's rarest and most expensive perfumes. It is used in Chinese medicine to "reduce phlegm and remove blood stasis."

Eucalyptus globulus **Essential Oil:** is anti-inflammatory and has pain-relieving properties. It is often used to help alleviate aches, pains, and skin infections.

Menthol: is the main constituent of peppermint oil and is known for its ability to cool the body and skin.

Capsicum frutescens **Fruit Extract:** comes from a species of chili pepper. This extract causes a gentle warming sensation on the skin.

Other Ingredients: Water, glycerin, cetearyl alcohol, *Prunus amygdalus dulcis* (sweet almond) oil, stearic acid, glyceryl stearate, PEG-100 stearate, butylene glycol, caprylic/capric triglyceride, sodium PCA, allantoin, *Gardenia florida* fruit extract, glycine, squalane, *Aloe barbadensis* leaf juice, retinyl palmitate, *Chlorella vulgaris* extract, hydroxyethyl acrylate/sodium acryloyldimethyl taurate copolymer, polysorbate 60, ceteareth-20, dimethicone, acrylates/C10-20 alkyl acrylate crosspolymer, xanthan gum, alcohol, caprylyl glycol, tetrasodium glutamate diacetate, ethylhexylglygerin, hexylene glycol, henoxyethanol.

Suggested Use: Massage a small amount of this cream on tired and sore muscles and joints.

Companion Products: Deep Blue essential oil blend.

ESSENTIAL SKIN CARE: *ANTI-AGING MOISTURIZER*

The Essential Skin Care Anti-Aging Moisturizer has been specially formulated to combat many of the visible signs of aging by reducing wrinkles and fine lines and improving skin elasticity and tone.

KEY INGREDIENTS:

Lavender Essential Oil: is calming and balances the body wherever there is a need.

Essential Living & Spa

Jasmine Essential Oil: is uplifting to the emotions and helps reduce anxiety, apathy, and depression.

Geranium Essential Oil: is hydrating and helps to ease nervous tension and stress.

Frankincense Essential Oil: helps repair cells and reduce signs of aging.

Palmitoyl Oligopeptides and Tetrapeptide-7 (Matrikine Messaging): The space in between skin (and other tissue) cells is filled with water and a mixture of fibrous proteins and polysaccharides called the extracellular matrix. These proteins and polysaccharides help give skin tissue its strength and elasticity and provide a framework for new cell growth and migration. Examples of extracellular proteins commonly found in skin tissue include collagen (provides strength, volume, and rigidity) and elastin (provides flexibility and resilience).

Enzymes on the outside of the cell membranes have the ability to break down some of these extracellular proteins into smaller peptide units when activated. Some of these smaller peptide units, in turn, have the ability to send further signals to surrounding cells to start, or turn off, the creation of new proteins and other structures. These small peptide messengers are called matrikines[1].

Studies have shown that certain matrikines, such as the tripeptide glycyl-histidyl-lysine (GHK), have the ability to activate and regulate synthesis of extracellular matrix proteins[1], while others can help stimulate the creation of an extracellular matrix framework that facilitates new cell growth and the healing of skin wounds[2,3].

With aging, extracellular proteins and fibers begin to break down, and synthesis of new structures is limited. Because of this loss of proteins and other structures in the extracellular matrix, the skin begins to lose its rigidity, structure, resilience, and elasticity, resulting in the appearance of fine lines and wrinkles.

In vitro studies and limited clinical trials have demonstrated evidence that the palmitoylated matrikines used in this Anti-Aging Moisturizer may have the ability to activate synthesis of extracellular matrix structures, such as collagen, fibronectin, and hyaluronic acid, that can lead to a fuller, tighter skin structure and can reduce the appearance of fine lines and wrinkles.

Sodium Hyaluronate (Patented Hyaluronic Acid Spherulites): Hyaluronic acid (also called hyaluronan, or hyaluronate) is not a true acid but is actually a special type of polysaccharide structure (called a glycosaminoglycan) that can form huge molecular chains that have the ability to absorb and hold water. Hyaluronic acid is found in large amounts in the extracellular matrix, where it helps provide structure and may help regulate transport of macromolecules between the cells. It is also found in the joints, where its viscous properties allow it to be used to cushion and lubricate the joint[4].

Hyaluronic acid is also found in high concentrations in the skin tissue, where it helps provide structure, support, and turgidity in the skin. Researchers in Italy have found that hyaluronic acid content in the skin decreases with aging and is nearly absent in the skin of individuals over 60-years-old[5]. This decline in hyaluronic acid has been hypothesized to be one of the main causes of skin issues related to aging.

Because of hyaluronic acid's unique ability to absorb water—causing it to swell to many times its original size—it has been used for years as an injectable cosmetic treatment for increasing volume in the skin in problem areas to reduce wrinkles and also for increasing volume in the lips and other areas. The unique formulation of the patented hyaluronic acid spherulites used in this Anti-Aging Moisturizer, however, actually allows these spherulites to naturally penetrate the outer layers of the skin without the need for invasive injections. These spherulites can then

1 Maquart et al., 1999.
2 Siméon et al., 1999.
3 Tran et al., 2004.

4 Laurent et al., 1995.
5 Ghersetich et al., 1994

absorb water, allowing them to increase the volume of the skin and also to help improve the moisture-barrier functionality of the skin so it can stay hydrated.

Grapeseed Oil: has an extremely high content of the omega-6 fatty acid, linoleic acid. Both animal studies[6] and clinical trials[7] have found that application of an oil high in linoleic acid can help enhance the skin-moisture barrier. Linoleic acid has also been studied for its ability to reduce acne microcomedones[8] and to enhance cellular migration during wound healing[9].

Summer Snowflake Bulb Extract: Many plants and animals enter a dormant stage, where they cease many metabolic activities in order to conserve energy and resources during times of harsh environmental conditions, such as drought or freezing temperatures. This dormancy allows the plant or animal to survive these harsh conditions and continue to live longer than it would otherwise be able.

Over the past several decades, researchers have begun to discover that several substances available in the dormant parts of plants—such as within the bulb—demonstrate an ability to prevent cell growth and cell division in human tissues as well[10,11]. This can be important for skin health, as researchers have found that human cells appear to only have the ability to replicate a certain number of times, and that as they approach their limit, the cells becomes less functional[12]. Because of this limitation, it has been theorized that slowing the process of cell replication can slow the process of loss of cell function associated with aging.

In this Anti-Aging Moisturizer, an extract from the bulbs of dormant Summer Snowflake flowers (Leucojum Aestivum) has been included. This extract has shown promising potential to slow replication of skin fibroblast cells, as well as the ability

to increase the activity of a potent anti-oxidant—mitochondrial superoxide dismutase. Both of these abilities may help promote more youthful skin cell function.

Acetyl Octapeptide-3 (Proprietary Octapeptide): Around the eyes and forehead, fine lines and wrinkles are often the result of tense, contracting muscle fibers repeatedly pulling the skin into folds and creases (often called frown lines).

Muscle fiber contraction is dependent on a complex signaling process from the motor neurons of nerve cells. Within each motor neuron are small, round structures called synaptic vesicles that each contain many copies of the signaling molecule, acetylcholine. When stimulated, a protein on the synaptic vesicle wall called VAMP (vesicle-associated membrane protein) will bind with two proteins on the motor neuron cell membrane called syntaxin (or T-SNARE) and SNAP25. When these proteins bind together, the synaptic vesicle is pulled in close to the motor neuron cell membrane, and the synaptic vesicle fuses with the neuron cell membrane, opening the vesicle and releasing the acetylcholine outside of the cell. The acetylcholine then binds with a protein receptor on the cell membrane of surrounding muscle fiber cells, signaling to them to contract[13,14,15].

This Anti-Aging Moisturizer contains the biomimetic peptide, Acetyl Octapeptide-3, which mimics the part of the SNAP25 protein that binds with the VAMP protein on the synaptic vesicle. Because this proprietary peptide temporarily binds with the VAMP protein, the VAMP protein is blocked from being able to bind with the proteins that allow the synaptic vesicles to release acetylcholine into the extracellular matrix. This results in the muscle fibers remaining more relaxed, preventing them from pulling the skin around the eyes and forehead into the distinctive lines and wrinkles associated with aging.

Essential Living & Spa

---

6 Darmstadt et al., 2002.
7 Darmstadt et al., 2005.
8 Letawe et al., 1998.
9 Ruthig et al., 1999.
10 Ceriotti et al., 1967
11 Jimenez et al., 1976.
12 Hayflick, 1979.

13 Südhof, 1995.
14 Kee et al., 1995
15 Pevsner et al., 1994.

Vitamin Blend: This moisturizer includes tocopherol acetate (Vitamin E—antioxidant and cellular communication) and tetrahexyldecyl ascorbate (stabilized vitamin C—provides stability to collagen).

Other Ingredients: Water, cetearyl alcohol, glycerin, glyceryl stearate, sodium stearoyl lactylate, sucrose palmitate, glyceryl linoleate, caprylic/capric triglyceride, olea europaea (olive) fruit unsaponifiables, betaine, ethylhexylglycerin, brassica oleracea gemmifera (brussels sprouts) extract, brassica juncea (mustard) sprout extract, brassica oleracea italica (broccoli) sprout extract, brassica oleracea botrytis (cauliflower) sprout extract, brassica oleracea capitata (cabbage) sprout extract, brassica oleracea acephala sprout extract, wasabia japonica root extract, glycerin, lecithin, xanthan gum, silica, C12-15 alkyl benzoate, tribehenin, ceramide 2, PEG-10 rapeseed sterol, dimethicone, carrageenan, tetrasodium EDTA, ergothioneine, phenoxyethanol, butylene glycol, carbomer, polysorbate 20, hexylene glycol, caprylyl glycol.

Suggested Use: After using the cleanser and toner, gently apply moisturizer to face and neck.

Companion Products: Facial Cleanser, Invigorating Scrub, Pore-Reducing Toner, Tightening Serum.

ESSENTIAL SKIN CARE: *FACIAL CLEANSER*

The Essential Skin Care Facial Cleanser works to gently cleanse the face while leaving the skin feeling soft, smooth, and fresh.

KEY INGREDIENTS:

Melaleuca Essential Oil: promotes cleansing and purity.

Peppermint Essential Oil: is purifying and stimulating to the conscious mind.

Cruciferous Vegetable Extracts: Plants in the Brassicaceae (or Cruciferae) family, such as broccoli, cabbage, and brussels sprouts, have extremely high concentrations of substances called isothiocyanates. Isothiocyanates, such as sulforaphane and phenethyl isothiocyanate, have been studied for years for their potential anti-inflammatory[1], antioxidant[2], and anticancer[3,4,5,6] properties. A strong association has been found between cruciferous vegetable consumption and decreased risk of cancer in individuals of a certain genotype, due to the ability of isothiocyanates to increase the action of glutathione s-transferase (an enzyme that detoxifies carcinogens)[7,8,9].

The isothiocyanates incorporated in this product have been extracted from seven different cruciferous vegetable plant sprouts. This specific combination of isothiocyanates has also shown promising UVB protection in tests, indicating that it has the potential to decrease redness and damage in skin exposed to the UVB rays found in sunlight.

Vitamin Blend: This unique blend of vitamins provides nutrients essential for healthy skin cell function. It includes tocopherol acetate (Vitamin E—antioxidant and cellular communication), tetrahexyldecyl ascorbate (stabilized vitamin C—provides stability to collagen), Retinyl palmitate (Vitamin A palmitate—supports skin cell health), and D-panthenol triacetate (provitamin B5—may decrease skin irritation and pore size[10,11]).

Other Ingredients: Water, sodium cocoyl isethionate, stearic acid, cetearyl alcohol, glycol stearate, laureth-4, phenoxyethanol, caprylyl glycol, ethylhexylglycerin, hexylene glycol, macadamia (ternifolia) nut oil, brassica oleracea gemmifera (brussels sprouts) extract, brassica juncea (mustard) sprout extract, brassica oleracea italica (broccoli) sprout extract, brassica oleracea botrytis (cauliflower) sprout extract, brassica oleracea capitata (cabbage) sprout extract, brassica oleracea acephala sprout extract, wasabi japonica root extract, glycerin, leci-

1 Traka et al., 2008.
2 Fowke et al., 2006.
3 Ambrosone et al., 2004.
4 Navarro et al., 2009.
5 vanPoppel et al., 1999.
6 Xiao et al., 2010.
7 Moore et al., 2007.
8 Moy et al., 2009.
9 Navarro et al., 2009.
10 Kuo et al., 2007)
11 Leung, 1995.

thin, cucurbita pepo seed extract, sea water, hydroxypropyl guar, polyether-1, disodium EDTA, dipotassium glycyrrhizate, citric acid, sodium hydroxide.

Suggested Use: Apply to dry face and neck, rubbing skin in a circular motion with fingertips. Rinse face and neck with warm water; dry skin with a towel.

Companion Products: Hydrating Cream, Invigorating Scrub, Pore-Reducing Toner, Tightening Serum.

ESSENTIAL SKIN CARE: HYDRATING CREAM

The Essential Skin Care Hydrating Cream combines essential oils known for their abilities to soothe and balance the skin's natural moisture levels with a complex of signaling molecules that promote the production of collagen and other intracellular matrix proteins that are crucial for fuller, smoother-appearing skin.

KEY INGREDIENTS:

Lavender Essential Oil: has been studied for its ability to reduce inflammation and allergic reactions in the skin. It has also been used to help the skin recover from burns, blisters, infections, and other injuries and to help reduce conditions related to dry skin.

Geranium Essential Oil: is soothing to the skin and may help to balance the skin's level of sebum (a fatty, waxy substance secreted by the skin that helps the skin feel moist and supple).

Frankincense Essential Oil: has been studied for its anti-inflammatory and anti-infectious properties. Frankincense is also soothing to the skin and nerves.

Jasmine Essential Oil: is often used to help soothe dry, irritated, or sensitive skin.

Milk Peptide Complex™: is a matrix of signalling molecules derived from milk proteins. These molecules, such as transforming growth factor-beta (TGF beta), signal the cells to produce extracellular matrix proteins such as collagen and

fibronectin[12,13], which can help promote fuller, smoother-looking skin.

Theobroma cacao **(Cocoa) Seed Butter:** is extracted from dried cocoa beans and is widely used for its ability to help moisturize the skin.

Other Ingredients: Water, butylene glycol, betaine, caprylic/capric triglyceride, glycerin, glyceryl stearate, *Hordeum distichon* (barley) extract, behenyl alcohol, cetearyl alcohol, dimethicone, isododecane, biosaccharide gum-1, nylon-12, phytosteryl isostearate, *Theobroma cacao* (cocoa) seed butter, *Phellodendron amurense* bark extract, *Santalum album* (sandalwood) extract, erythritol, algae extract, *Artemisia vulgaris* extract, phospholipids, hydrolyzed oat protein, tetrahexyldecyl ascorbate, tocopheryl acetate, ascophyllum nodosum extract, hydroxyethylcellulose, acetyl dipeptide-1 cetyl ester, adenosine triphosphate, niacinamide, homarine HCL, panthenyl triacetate, retinyl palmitate, xanthan gum, cetearyl methicone, sorbitan laurate, sodium stearoyl lactylate, ammonium acryloyldimethyltaurate/VP copolymer, phenoxyethanol, caprylyl glycol, ethylhexylglycerin, hexylene glycol, tetrasodium EDTA, phenoxyethanol.

Suggested Use: Apply this cream morning and night on clean neck and face.

Companion Products: Invigorating Scrub, Facial Cleanser, Pore-Reducing Toner, Tightening Serum.

ESSENTIAL SKIN CARE: *INVIGORATING SCRUB*

The Essential Skin Care Invigorating Scrub exfoliates and polishes skin with a combination of fragrant and nourishing essential oils, vegetable extracts, and other natural ingredients.

KEY INGREDIENTS:

Grapefruit Essential Oil: is balancing and uplifting to the mind. It is antiseptic, disinfectant, and astringent.

Peppermint Essential Oil: is cooling and stimulating. It is antibacterial and invigorating.

12 Varga et al., 1986.
13 Raghow et al., 1987.

Jojoba Beads (Hydrogenated Jojoba Oil): Although called an oil, jojoba oil is actually a natural liquid wax extracted from jojoba (*Simmondsia chinensis*) plants found in the south-western U.S. and northern Mexico. This liquid wax closely resembles the skin's natural oils (or sebum). Hydrogenating jojoba oil (by combining this liquid wax with pressurized hydrogen) solidifies the oil, allowing the creation of a waxy bead that can be used to gently and naturally exfoliate the skin.

Ascophyllum nodosum **Extract (Brown Algae Extract):** *Ascophyllum nodosum* is a common brown seaweed found in the north Atlantic. This seaweed is rich in antioxidant polyphenols and also contains the polysaccharide fucoidan, which has been studied for its ability to inhibit the enzymes that break down collagen and elastin in the skin[1,2].

The aqueous extract found in this Invigorating Scrub has also demonstrated an ability to inhibit the enzyme tyrosinase—an enzyme necessary for the production of the skin pigment melanin. This action may help decrease the appearance of pigmented spots on the skin, helping to promote a more even skin tone.

Palmaria palmata **Extract (Red Algae Extract):** *Palmaria palmata* is a common red seaweed (often called dulse) found in the northern Atlantic and Pacific. This seaweed is rich in antioxidant polyphenols[3].

Melanocytes are pigment-producing cells scattered throughout the bottom layer of the epidermis. These cells use several multi-step processes to convert tyrosine (an amino-acid building block) into the pigment melanin. Key in this process is the enzyme tyrosinase, which catalyses the first two steps of this conversion. Once the melanin is created, it is stored in vesicles that are transported to the ends of the melanocyte's dendritic arms. The melanin is stored there in these vesicles until the melanocyte is stimulated to release the melanin to the surrounding keratinocyte (epidermal skin) cells, where they are seen as pigmentation on the skin.

The aqueous extract from *Palmaria palmata* found in this Invigorating Scrub has demonstrated an ability to block the action of tyrosinase in melanocyte cells, inhibiting their ability to convert tyrosine into melanin, and an ability to inhibit synthesis of several proteins that transport the melanin to the dendritic arms of the melanocyte. Small clinical trials using this extract found that it demonstrated a potential to lighten skin pigmentation, especially in darker age spots[4].

Cruciferous Vegetable Extracts: Plants in the Brassicaceae (or Cruciferae) family, such as broccoli, cabbage, and brussels sprouts, have extremely high concentrations of substances called isothiocyanates. Isothiocyanates, such as sulforaphane and phenethyl isothiocyanate, have been studied for years for their potential anti-inflammatory[5], antioxidant[6], and anticancer[7,8,9,10] properties. A strong association has been found between cruciferous vegetable consumption and decreased risk of cancer in individuals of a certain genotype, due to the ability of isothiocyanates to increase the action of glutathione s-transferase (an enzyme that detoxifies carcinogens)[11,12,13].

The isothiocyanates incorporated in this product have been extracted from seven different cruciferous vegetable plant sprouts. This specific combination of isothiocyanates has also shown promising UVB protection in tests, indicating that it has the potential to decrease redness and damage in skin exposed to the UVB rays found in sunlight.

Vitamin Blend: This unique blend of vitamins provides nutrients essential for healthy skin cell function. It includes tocopherol

1 Moon et al., 2009.
2 Senni et al., 2006.
3 Yuan et al., 2006.

4 Boudier et al., 2008.
5 Traka et al., 2008.
6 Fowke et al., 2006.
7 Ambrosone et al., 2004.
8 Navarro et al., 2009.
9 vanPoppel et al., 1999.
10 Xiao et al., 2010.
11 Moore et al., 2007.
12 Moy et al., 2009.
13 Navarro et al., 2009.

acetate (Vitamin E—antioxidant and cellular communication), tetrahexyldecyl ascorbate (stabilized vitamin C—provides stability to collagen), Retinyl palmitate (Vitamin A palmitate—supports skin cell health), and D-panthenol triacetate (pro-vitamin B5—may decrease skin irritation and pore size[14,15]).

Other Ingredients: Water, sodium lauroamphoacetate, sodium methyl cocoyl taurate, glucose, brassica oleracea gemmifera (brussels sprouts) extract, brassica juncea (mustard) sprout extract, brassica oleracea italica (broccoli) sprout extract, brassica oleracea botrytis (cauliflower) sprout extract, brassica oleracea capitata (cabbage) sprout extract, brassica oleracea acephala sprout extract, wasabi japonica root extract, glycerin, tetrahexyldecyl ascorbate, chondrus crispus (carrageenan), lecithin, glycol stearate, acrylates copolymer, PEG-40 hydrogenated castor oil, PEG-150 pentaerythrityl tetrastearate, phenoxyethanol, caprylyl glycol, ethylhexylglycerin, hexylene glycol.

Suggested Use: Gently massage product over wet skin for up to one minute. Rinse with warm water.

Companion Products: Facial Cleanser, Hydrating Cream, Pore-Reducing Toner, Tightening Serum.

Essential Skin Care: *Pore-Reducing Toner*

The Essential Skin Care Pore-Reducing Toner has been designed to help reduce the visible size of pores while eliminating skin irritation and stress.

Key Ingredients:

Lavender Essential Oil: is calming and promotes a sense of well-being.

Ylang Ylang Essential Oil: is calming and relaxing and may help alleviate anger.

German Chamomile Essential Oil: soothes and clears the mind, creating an atmosphere of peace and patience.

Lysophosphatidic Acid (Soybean Extract): Lysophosphatidic acid is a phospholipid

messenger that has diverse biological functions. One of the most studied functions involves the role lysophosphatidic acid plays in wound healing of the skin by encouraging cell growth and migration[16].

In the epidermis, the cells visible on the surface of the skin are actually converted keratinocyte cells that have lost their nucleus and have become filled with the rigid skin-barrier protein, keratin. This conversion (called keratinization) is essential for creating a healthy skin barrier that helps keep moisture within the skin and that helps keep harmful microorganisms and toxins from entering the body through the skin. Occasionally, however, these keratinocyte cells do not completely convert, retaining their nuclei and not completely filling with keratin. This condition is called parakeratosis and can lead to several dermatological problems, such as psoriasis, if it happens too often[17].

Recent studies on the cosmetic concern of large, visible facial skin pores have found evidence that incomplete keratinization (or parakeratosis) is significantly more evident on individuals with larger pore sizes than on individuals with smaller pores.

It has been hypothesized that lysophosphatidic acid's role in promoting skin cell differentiation[18] (potentially preventing parakeratosis in keratinocyte cells), as well as its ability to promote the synthesis of proteins involved in cell adhesion[19] (potentially allowing for more tightly packed cells), can lead to more healthy skin with smaller, less visible pores. A small clinical trial with the lysophosphatidic acid contained in this Pore-Reducing Toner has demonstrated the efficacy of this hypothesis, finding that topical application of lysophosphatidic acid reduced pore size and total pore area on the skin of volunteers (as compared to a placebo).

Curcurbita pepo (Pumpkin Seed) Extract: When nerve cells in the skin are stimulated by an irritant, they release specific

14 Kuo et al., 2007)
15 Leung, 1995.

16 Balazs et al., 2001.
17 Scheinfeld et al., 2005.
18 Piazza et al., 1995.
19 Amano et al., 2004.

Essential Living & Spa

chemicals that stimulate the release of histamine into the surrounding tissue. Histamine, in turn, can stimulate the surrounding blood vessels to open, allowing blood and plasma to flow into the skin tissue (causing reddening and swelling), potentially causing further irritation to the nerve cells (causing itching or stinging). While this inflammation process is a natural part of wound healing and cleansing, it can also happen too much or too often—causing dermatological problems such as an allergic reaction, eczema, or psoriasis.

The pumpkin seed extract included in this Pore-Reducing Toner is an amino acid called cucurbitine. Cucurbitine has shown a promising ability to soothe skin and to limit localized skin inflammation in two ways. First, it has demonstrated an ability in laboratory tests to block the enzyme that creates histamine (histidine decarboxylase) from creating excess histamine[1]. Second, cucurbitine has demonstrated an ability to inhibit the release of histamine into the skin tissue. Both of these effects have demonstrated an ability in small clinical trials to soothe red, irritated skin faster than a placebo.

Cruciferous Vegetable Extracts: Plants in the Brassicaceae (or Cruciferae) family, such as broccoli, cabbage, and brussels sprouts, have extremely high concentrations of substances called isothiocyanates. Isothiocyanates, such as sulforaphane and phenethyl isothiocyanate, have been studied for years for their potential anti-inflammatory[2], antioxidant[3], and anticancer[4,5,6,7] properties. A strong association has been found between cruciferous vegetable consumption and decreased risk of cancer in individuals of a certain genotype, due to the ability of isothiocyanates to increase the action of glutathione s-transferase (an enzyme that detoxifies

carcinogens)[8,9,10].

The isothiocyanates incorporated in this product have been extracted from seven different cruciferous vegetable plant sprouts. This specific combination of isothiocyanates has also shown promising UVB protection in tests, indicating that it has the potential to decrease redness and damage in skin exposed to the UVB rays found in sunlight.

Vitamin Blend: This unique blend of vitamins provides nutrients essential for healthy skin cell function. It includes tocopherol acetate (Vitamin E—antioxidant and cellular communication), tetrahexyldecyl ascorbate (stabilized vitamin C—provides stability to collagen), Retinyl palmitate (Vitamin A palmitate—supports skin cell health), and D-panthenol triacetate (pro-vitamin B5—may decrease skin irritation and pore size[11,12]).

Other Ingredients: Sea water, glycerin, inulin, witch hazel (hamamelis virginiana) distillate, brassica oleracea gemmifera (brussels sprouts) extract, brassica juncea (mustard) sprout extract, brassica oleracea italica (broccoli) sprout extract, brassica oleracea botrytis (cauliflower) sprout extract, brassica oleracea capitata (cabbage) sprout extract, brassica oleracea acephala sprout extract, wasabi japonica root extract, lysolecithin, dipotassium glycyrrhizate, aloe barbadensis leaf juice, tetrahexyldecyl ascorbate, retinyl palmitate, panthenyl triacetate, tocopheryl acetate, lecithin, caprylyl glycol, PEG-40 hydrogenated castor oil, ethylhexylglycerin, hexylene glycol, chlorphenesin, allantoin, phytic acid, phenoxyethanol.

Suggested Use: After cleansing, gently apply toner to face with a cotton pad.

Companion Products: Facial Cleanser, Hydrating Cream, Invigorating Scrub, Tightening Serum.

1 Renimel et al., 1995.
2 Traka et al., 2008.
3 Fowke et al., 2006.
4 Ambrosone et al., 2004.
5 Navarro et al., 2009.
6 vanPoppel et al., 1999.
7 Xiao et al., 2010.

8 Moore et al., 2007.
9 Moy et al., 2009.
10 Navarro et al., 2009.
11 Kuo et al., 2007)
12 Leung, 1995.

Essential Skin Care: *Tightening Serum*

The Essential Skin Care Tightening Serum has been formulated to hydrate and tighten the skin in order to reduce the appearance of fine lines and wrinkles.

Key Ingredients:

Frankincense Essential Oil: helps to focus energy and improve concentration and may help reduce signs of aging.

Sandalwood Essential Oil: supports the cardiovascular system and may assist in skin regeneration.

Myrrh Essential Oil: helps improve skin conditions, wounds, and wrinkles.

Acacia senegal **and Hydrolyzed Rhizobian Gums (Rhizobian & Acacia Gum Extracts):** As the skin ages, skin tissue structures such as collagen, elastin, and hyaluronic acid begin to break down or aren't synthesized by cells as quickly as before. The loss and breakage of these structural molecules in the skin tissue result in sagging, wrinkling, and less rigid skin[13].

The two gum extracts included in this Tightening Serum consist of long polysaccharide molecules that have the ability to bind together to form a linked network of molecules. As this Tightening Serum dries, this linked network of molecules contracts, physically pulling the skin tighter to help reduce wrinkling and fine lines.

Avena sativa **(Oat) Kernel Extract:** This ingredient is comprised of a complex sugar structure extracted from oat kernels. This structure has the ability to form a continuous network with elastic qualities that can loosely bind to lipid structures in the epidermal cell membranes. These properties allow this network of molecules to gently tighten the skin, reducing the appearance of fine lines and wrinkles.

Perfluorodecalin (Proprietary Perfluorocarbon): As the skin ages, it can lose its ability to retain moisture, leading to less firm skin and increasing the visibility of fine lines and wrinkles.

Perfluorodecalin is a fluorocarbon molecule that has been studied for decades for its amazing oxygen-carrying properties and its potential to help heal wounds. When used in a cosmetic formulation during a small clinical trial, perfluorodecalin was shown to enhance the barrier function of the skin, allowing it to retain moisture and bringing about a visible reduction in fine lines and wrinkles[14].

Ascophyllum nodosum **Extract (Brown Algae Extract):** *Ascophyllum nodosum* is a common brown seaweed found in the North Atlantic. This seaweed is rich in antioxidant polyphenols and also contains the polysaccharide fucoidan, which has been studied for its ability to inhibit the enzymes that break down collagen and elastin in the skin[15,16].

The aqueous extract found in this Invigorating Scrub has also demonstrated an ability to inhibit the enzyme tyrosinase—an enzyme necessary for the production of the skin pigment melanin. This action may help decrease the appearance of pigmented spots on the skin, helping to promote a more even skin tone.

Nanopeptide-1 (Biomimetic Peptides): Lentigines are spots of pigmentation on the skin associated with UV damage causing activation of the melanocyte (pigment-forming) cells in the skin[17,18]. As the skin ages and cells are replenished at a much slower rate, lentigines stay visible and become more prominent. These persistent lentigines are often called "age spots."

Within the body, one hormone that induces the production of the pigment melanin is alpha-MSH (melanocyte-stimulating hormone, or melanocortin). When this hormone binds to the melanocortin 1 receptor (MC1-R) on melanocytes, it stimulates the enzyme tyrosinase to begin the conversion of tyrosine (an amino-acid building block) into the pigment melanin[19].

The biomimetic peptide contained

Essential Living & Spa

---

13 Ghersetich et al., 1994

14 Stanzl et al., 1996.
15 Moon et al., 2009.
16 Senni et al., 2006.
17 Hölzle, 1992
18 Bastiaens et al., 2004.
19 Kadekaro et al., 2003.

in this Tightening Serum contains the portion of alpha-MSH that binds to the melanocortin 1 receptor. Instead of stimulating melanin production, however, this unique peptide temporarily inhibits melanin production by the melanocyte cells. In vitro studies have indicated that this biomimetic peptide demonstrated the ability to reduce melanin synthesis by melanocyte cells. This finding leads to the potential of this peptide to be able to help control pigmentation in the skin, allowing for more even skin tone.

Vitamin Blend: This unique blend of vitamins provides nutrients essential for healthy skin cell function. It includes tocopherol acetate (Vitamin E—antioxidant and cellular communication), tetrahexyldecyl ascorbate (stabilized vitamin C—provides stability to collagen), Retinyl palmitate (Vitamin A palmitate—supports skin cell health), and D-panthenol triacetate (pro-vitamin B5—may decrease skin irritation and pore size[1,2]).

Other Ingredients: Water, glycerin, betaine, ascophyllum nodosum extract, tocopheryl acetate, ergothioneine, retinyl palmitate, panthenyl triacetate, tetrahexyldecyl ascorbate, xanthan gum, sclerotium gum, allantoin, phytic acid, phenoxyethanol, caprylyl glycol, ethylhexylglycerin, hexylene glycol, carbomer, PEG-40 hydrogenated castor oil.

Suggested Use: Use fingers to apply on face and neck in an upward, outward motion. Follow with Anti-Aging Moisturizer.

Companion Products: Facial Cleanser, Hydrating Cream, Invigorating Scrub, Pore-Reducing Toner.

ON GUARD™ FOAMING HAND WASH

On Guard Foaming Hand Wash is a healthy, all-natural hand soap that is gentle enough for even those with sensitive skin to use. It leaves hands feeling clean, soft, and fresh while it protects against harmful microorganisms.

KEY INGREDIENTS:

Sweet Orange Essential Oil: is calming and uplifting to the mind and body.

Clove Bud Essential Oil: is antibacterial, antiviral, and disinfectant.

Cinnamon Bark Essential Oil: is antibacterial and antimicrobial. It also enhances the action and activity of other oils.

Rosemary Oil: is antibacterial, stimulates memory, and opens the conscious mind.

Other Ingredients: Water, sodium cocoyl glutamate, sodium lauroamphoacetate, polysorbate 20, phenoxyethanol, caprylyl glycol, ethylhexylglycerin, hexylene glycol, cetyl hydroxyethyl cellulose, sodium hydroxide, disodium EDTA, citric acid.

Suggested Use: Dispense onto hands by pushing the pump down 1–2 times; work soap into a lather with warm water; rinse hands thoroughly.

Companion Products: On Guard Protecting Throat Drops, On Guard Natural Whitening Toothpaste, On Guard essential oil blend.

ON GUARD™ NATURAL WHITENING TOOTHPASTE

This natural toothpaste offers the protective benefits of On Guard essential oil blend along with peppermint, wintergreen, and myrrh essential oils.

KEY INGREDIENTS:

Peppermint Essential Oil: contains high levels of menthol, which has been well documented in research studies for its ability to inhibit bacteria known to cause dental cavities.

On Guard Essential Oil Blend: contains wild orange, clove bud, cinnamon bark, *Eucalyptus radiata*, and rosemary essential oils. These oils have all been studied for their powerful antimicrobial and antiseptic properties. Several of these oils are also often used to help alleviate inflammation and ease gum and tooth pain.

Wintergreen Essential Oil: has antiseptic and anti-inflammatory properties.

1 Kuo et al., 2007)
2 Leung, 1995.

Myrrh Essential Oil: has antiseptic properties and is often used to help support healthy gums and mouth tissues.

Hydroxyapatite: Hydroxyapatite is the main component of the hard crystal structure that makes up tooth enamel. While naturally strong, tooth enamel can be demineralized by conditions of acidity in the mouth (caused by eating sugar or acidic foods), weakening the enamel and allowing for small lesions and gaps to be created. There is some evidence that use of a polishing agent containing calcium hydroxyapatite can help restore tooth enamel from small lesions in vitro[3].

Other Ingredients: Glycerin, water, hydrated silica, xylitol, calcium carbonate, cellulose gum, *Stevia rebaudiana* (stevia) extract, sodium lauroyl sarcosinate, carrageenan, titanium dioxide.

Suggested Use: Use along with regular flossing to brush teeth after meals or to brush morning and night. After brushing, place a small amount of water with 1–2 drops of On Guard oil blend in the mouth and swish for 30–60 seconds.

Companion Products: On Guard Foaming Hand Wash, On Guard Protecting Throat Drops, On Guard essential oil blend.

SanoBella™ Protecting Shampoo

SanoBella™ Protecting Shampoo has been specially formulated to restore luminosity, shine, and overall health to hair, especially hair that has been chemically treated or heat styled. This shampoo combines the benefits of essential oils with extracts of rice, soybean, and African palm oil to naturally cleanse and repair damaged hair and to protect hair against future damage.

Key Ingredients:

Extracts of Rice, Soybean, and African Palm Oil: help maintain hair color and contain antioxidants that help prevent the oxidation of cuticle lipids.

Emulsion of Silica: protects hair from chemical treatments and styling damage by deeply conditioning and smoothing the cuticle.

Wild Orange Essential Oil: is calming and uplifting to the mind and body and has a pleasant, citrusy, sweet aroma. Orange oils are well-known for their abilities to degrease and degum, making them especially effective for cleansing the hair.

Mandarin Orange (*Citrus nobilis*) Essential Oil: is moisturizing, uplifting, and has a sweet, refreshing aroma. Orange oils are well-known for their abilities to degrease and degum, making them especially effective for cleansing the hair.

Orange (*Citrus aurantium dulcis*) Essential Oil: The aroma of orange brings peace and happiness to the mind and body and joy to the heart. Orange oils are well-known for their abilities to degrease and degum, making them especially effective for cleansing the hair.

Lime Essential Oil: Has a fresh, lively fragrance that is stimulating and refreshing. It can be used to cleanse the hair.

Other Ingredients: Water, sodium methyl cocoyl taurate, sodium lauroamphoacetate, laurylamidopropyl betaine, sodium cocoyl isethionate, guar hydroxypropyltrimonium chloride, acrylates copolymer, citrus sinensis (wild orange) oil, citrus nobilis (mandarin orange) oil, citrus aurantium dulcis (orange) oil, citrus aurantifolia (lime) oil, glycine soja (soybean) seed extract, elaeis guineensis (palm) fruit extract, oryza sativa (rice) extract, panthenol, trimethylsiloxyamodimethicone, C11-15 pareth-7, C12-16 pareth-9, glycerin, trideceth-12, butylene glycol, fragrance, ethylhexylglycerin, hexylene glycol, caprylyl glycol, disodium EDTA, phenoxyethanol, mica, and titanium dioxide.

Suggested Use: Use as directed on bottle.

Companion Products: SanoBella™ Smoothing Conditioner.

---

3 Nishio et al., 2004.

SANOBELLA™ SOOTHING CONDITIONER

SanoBella™ Soothing Conditioner has been specially formulated to restore luminosity, shine, fullness, and overall health to hair, especially hair that has been chemically treated or heat styled. It is also designed to help reduce static, temporarily repair spit ends, and decrease blow-drying time. This conditioner combines the benefits of essential oils with extracts of rice, soybean, African palm oil, and a nanotechnic silk derivative to naturally condition and repair damaged hair and to protect hair against future damage.

KEY INGREDIENTS:

Nanotechnic Silk Derivative: improves the overall appearance of hair by re-sealing damaged areas of the hair cuticle.

Extracts of Rice, Soybean, and African Palm Oil: help maintain hair color and contain antioxidants that help prevent the oxidation of cuticle lipids.

Emulsion of Silica: protects hair from chemical treatments and styling damage by deeply conditioning and smoothing the cuticle.

Lavender Essential Oil: helps nourish the scalp and hair follicles. Medicinally, it has been used by the French to prevent hair loss.

Peppermint Essential Oil: is invigorating and helps improve the overall health of the scalp and hair.

Other Ingredients: Water, cetearyl alcohol, behentrimonium chloride, centrimonium chloride, hydroxyethylcellulose, behenyl alcohol, lavandula angustifolia (lavender) oil, mentha piperita (peppermint) oil, crambe abyssinica seed oil, butylene glycol, glycine soja (soybean) seed extract, elaeis guineensis (palm) fruit extract, oryza sativa (rice) extract, menthol, glycerin, hydrogenated polyisobutene, PEG-2, polyquaternium-7, sericin, guar hydroxypropyltrimonium chloride, trimethylsiloxyamodimethicone, panthenol, C11-15 pareth-7, C12-16 pareth-9, trideceth-12, caprylyl glycol, ethylhexylglycerin, hexylene glycol, disodium EDTA, and phenoxyethanol.

Suggested Use: Use as directed on bottle.

Companion Products: SanoBella™ Protecting Shampoo.

SPA: CITRUS BLISS INVIGORATING BATH BAR

This invigorating soap combines the skin protecting abilities of sunflower, safflower, palm, coconut, and jojoba oils with naturally exfoliating oatmeal kernels and the stimulating aroma of Citrus Bliss essential oil blend.

KEY INGREDIENTS:

Citrus Bliss Invigorating Oil Blend: combines the uplifting and stress-reducing benefits of many different citrus oils in a sweetly satisfying way. In addition to their elevating properties, many of the oils in this blend have been studied for their ability to cleanse and disinfect. This blend contains wild orange, lemon, grapefruit, mandarin, bergamot, tangerine, and clementine essential oils blended with the soothing aroma of vanilla beans.

Oatmeal (*Avena sativa*) Kernel: is widely used for its gentle exfoliating and skin soothing properties.

Sodium Cocoate (Saponified Coconut Oil): is the soap form of coconut oil (saponification is the process of transforming oils into soap). Coconut oil is often used in soaps, creams, and lotions for its moisturizing and skin-softening abilities.

Sodium Safflowerate (Saponified Safflower Oil): is the soap form of safflower oil. Safflower oil is known for its skin softening properties.

Other Ingredients: Sodium sunflowerate (saponified sunflower oil), sodium palmate (saponified palm oil), sodium hydroxide, *Vanilla planifolia* (vanilla bean), *Simmondsia chinensis* (jojoba) seed oil, *Rosmarinus officinalis* (rosemary) extract.

Suggested Use: Use in bath or shower for a rich, invigorating lather.

Companion Products: Essential Skin Care.

Spa: *Hand and Body Lotion*

This lotion offers unique moisturizing and skin-protecting abilities with natural, botanical ingredients. It has been formulated so that you can mix in your desired essential oil or blend to create your own custom lotion for many different uses.

Key Ingredients:

Cruciferous Vegetable Extracts: Plants in the Brassicaceae (or Cruciferae) family, such as broccoli, cabbage, and brussels sprouts, have extremely high concentrations of substances called isothiocyanates. Isothiocyanates, such as sulforaphane and phenethyl isothiocyanate, have been studied for years for their potential anti-inflammatory[1], antioxidant[2], and anticancer[3,4,5,6] properties. A strong association has been found between cruciferous vegetable consumption and a decreased risk of cancer in individuals of a certain genotype, due to the ability of isothiocyanates to increase the action of glutathione s-transferase (an enzyme that detoxifies carcinogens)[7,8,9].

The isothiocyanates incorporated in this product have been extracted from seven different cruciferous vegetable plant sprouts. This specific combination of isothiocyanates has also shown promising UVB protection in tests, indicating that it has the potential to decrease redness and damage in skin exposed to the UVB rays found in sunlight.

Chlorella vulgaris **(Green Algae) Extract:** *Chlorella vulgaris* is a common green algae that is high in essential amino acids that are the building blocks of cellular proteins vital for skin tone and elasticity. Extracts of *Chlorella vulgaris* have also been studied for their abilities to inhibit inflammation[10] and skin papilloma tumor formation[11].

Dipotassium Glycyrrhizate (Licorice Root Extract): is often used for its skin soothing and skin conditioning properties. Its related licorice root extract— glycyrrhizin—has also been studied extensively for its anti-inflammatory properties.

Olea Europea **(Olive) Fruit Unsaponifiables:** contains many of the same natural compounds found in sebum—the substance secreted by the skin that helps provide protection and moisture retention for the skin's cells.

Vitamin C (Tetrahexyldecyl Ascorbate): has natural antioxidant properties and helps support collagen stability (the main protein in connective tissue).

Vitamin E (Tocopheryl Acetate): is a potent antioxidant.

Other Ingredients: Water, glyceryl stearate, cetearyl alcohol, sodium stearoyl lactylate, butylene glycol, glycerin, *Santalum album* (sandalwood) wood extract, *Phellodendron amurense* bark extract, *Hordeum distichon* (barley) extract, *Aloe barbadensis* leaf juice, panthenyl triacetate, ergothioneine, retinyl palmitate, capric/caprylic triglycerides, linoleic acid, soy sterols, soy phospolipids, *Brassica juncea* (mustard) sprout extract, *Brassica oleracea italica* (broccoli) sprout extract, *Brassica oleracea capitata* (cabbage) sprout extract, *Brassica oleracea botrytis* (cauliflower) sprout extract, *Brassica oleracea acephala* sprout extract, *Brassica oleracea gemmifera* (brussels sprouts) extract, *Wasabi japonica* root extract, sodium PCA, sodium hyaluronate, tetrasodium EDTA, dimethicone, phenoxyethanol, caprylyl glycol, ethylhexylglycerin, hexylene, glycol, phenoxyethanol, carbomer, xanthan gum.

Suggested Use: Place the desired amount of lotion in the palm of the hand, and mix in your desired essential oil or blend. Apply lotion mixture to the hands or body as needed.

Companion Products: Essential Skin Care.

1 Traka et al., 2008.
2 Fowke et al., 2006.
3 Ambrosone et al., 2004.
4 Navarro et al., 2009.
5 vanPoppel et al., 1999.
6 Xiao et al., 2010.
7 Moore et al., 2007.
8 Moy et al., 2009.
9 Navarro et al., 2009.
10 Yasukawa et al., 1996.
11 Singh et al., 1999.

SPA: *SERENITY CALMING BATH BAR*

This soothing soap combines the skin protecting abilities of sunflower, safflower, palm, coconut, and jojoba oils with the moisturizing properties of shea butter and the calming aroma of Serenity essential oil blend.

KEY INGREDIENTS:

Serenity Calming Oil Blend: combines essential oils that are widely known—and have been studied—for their abilities to calm and soothe feelings of stress and anxiety in order to help the body maintain its natural state of health. This blend contains lavender, sweet marjoram, Roman chamomile, ylang ylang, and sandalwood oils blended with the soothing aroma of vanilla beans.

Butyrospermum parkii **(Shea) Butter:** is widely used in soaps, lotions, and creams for its natural moisturizing properties.

Sodium Cocoate (Saponified Coconut Oil): is the soap form of coconut oil (saponification is the process of transforming oils into soap). Coconut oil is often used in soaps, creams, and lotions for its moisturizing and skin-softening abilities.

Sodium Safflowerate (Saponified Safflower Oil): is the soap form of safflower oil. Safflower oil is known for its skin softening properties.

Other Ingredients: Sodium sunflowerate (saponified sunflower oil), sodium palmate (saponified palm oil), sodium hydroxide, *Vanilla planifolia* (vanilla bean), *Simmondsia chinensis* (jojoba) seed oil, *Batschia canescens* (alkanet) root, *Rosmarinus officinalis* (rosemary) extract.

Suggested Use: Use in bath or shower for a luxurious, soothing lather.

Companion Products: Essential Skin Care.

PERSONAL USAGE GUIDE

PERSONAL USAGE GUIDE NOTES AND EXPLANATIONS

This personal usage guide is a compilation of many different health conditions and the various essential oils, blends, and other supplements that are commonly used and recommended for each condition.

Under each condition, the oils, blends, and other supplements have been grouped as Primary Recommendations, Secondary Recommendations, and Other Recommendations for that condition. The criteria for grouping within these categories includes the recommendations of experts within the field of essential oils, supporting scientific research studies, and French medicinal uses for the oils. However, since each individual may have different underlying causes for his or her specific condition, what may work for one individual may be different than what works for another.

Also listed under each condition are recommendations for how to use or apply these oils or supplements for that particular condition. The three main application and usage methods are aromatic, topical, and internal. The recommended methods are indicated next to each oil as a small **Ⓐ** for Aromatic, **Ⓣ** for Topical, and **Ⓘ** for Internal.

Ⓐ: Aromatic means that the oils are breathed or inhaled through the mouth and nose. This could include breathing the aroma of the oil directly from the bottle or breathing in oil that has been applied to the hands or to another material such as a tissue or cotton wick. It could also mean breathing the vapor or mist of an oil that has been diffused or sprayed into the surrounding air.

Ⓣ: Topical means that the oils are applied directly onto the skin, hair, or other surface of the body. This can be through direct application of the oils to the skin or by using the oils in massages, baths, or within a cream, lotion, or soap. While some oils can be applied neat (without dilution), others may need to be diluted before topical application, especially for young or sensitive skin. Refer to the Single Essential Oils section of this book or the Dilution Reference Chart (following these notes) for recommended dilutions for the oils listed in this book.

Ⓘ: Internal means that the oils or supplements are taken orally. This can be done either by adding the oil to a food or beverage that is then consumed or by swallowing a capsule that has the essential oil or supplement inside.

For more information on specific ways essential oils can be applied or used, see the Science and Application of Essential Oils section in this book.

Below are some additional things to keep in mind as you use and apply the essential oils, blends, and supplements listed in this section.

— If essential oils get into your eyes by accident or if they burn the skin a little, do not try to remove the oils with water. This will only drive the oils deeper into the tissue. It is best to dilute the essential oils on location with a pure vegetable oil (such as fractionated coconut oil).

— The FDA has approved some essential oils for internal use and given them the following designations: GRAS (Generally Recognized As Safe for human consumption), FA (Food Additive), or FL (Flavoring agent). *These designations are listed under Oral Use As Dietary Supplement for each single oil in the Single Essential Oils section of this book.*

— Using some oils such as lemon, orange, grapefruit, bergamot, etc., before or during exposure to direct sunlight or UV rays (tanning beds, for example) may cause a rash, pigmentation, or even severe burns. Please see the safety information under each oil in the Single Essential Oil chapter of this book for further information; then either dilute these oils and test a small area, or avoid their use altogether.

— Caution should be used with oils such as clary sage and fennel during pregnancy. These oils contain active constituents with hormone-like activity and could possibly stimulate adverse reactions in the mother, although there are no recorded cases in humans.

— Particular care should be taken when using cassia, cinnamon, lemongrass, oregano, and thyme, as they are some of the strongest and most caustic oils. It is best to dilute them with a pure vegetable oil.

— When a blend or recipe is listed in this section, rather than mix the oils together, it may be more beneficial to layer the oils: that is, apply a drop or two of one oil, rub it in, and then apply another oil. If dilution is necessary, a pure vegetable oil can be applied on top. *Effectiveness is in the layering.*

— Less is often better: use one to three drops of oil and no more than six drops at a time. Stir, and rub on in a clockwise direction.

— When applying oils to infants and small children, dilute one to two drops pure essential oil with 1–3 teaspoon (tsp.) of a pure vegetable oil (such as fractionated coconut oil). If the oils are used in the bath, always use a bath gel base as a dispersing agent for the oils. See CHILDREN AND INFANTS in this section for more information about the recommended list of oils for babies and children.

— The body absorbs oils the fastest through inhalation (breathing) and second fastest through application to the feet or ears. Layering oils can increase the rate of absorption.

— When the cell wall thickens, oxygen cannot get in. The life expectancy of a cell is 120 days (4 months). Cells also divide, making duplicate cells. If the cell is diseased, new diseased cells will be made. When we stop the mutation of the diseased cells (create healthy cells), we stop the disease. Essential oils have the ability to penetrate and carry nutrients through the cell wall to the nucleus and improve the health of the cell.

— *Use extreme caution when diffusing cassia or cinnamon* as they may burn the nostrils if you put your nose directly next to the nebulizer of the diffuser where the mist is coming out.

— When traveling by air, you should always have your oils hand-checked. X-ray machines may interfere with the frequency of the oils.

— Keep oils away from the light and heat—although they seem to do fine in temperatures up to 90 degrees. If stored properly in a cool, dark environment, they can maintain their maximum potency for many years.

DILUTION REFERENCE CHART

SINGLE OIL NAME	RECOMMENDED DILUTION		
	ADULTS	CHILD/SENSITIVE	EXPECTANT MOTHER
Basil	N	1:1	A
Bergamot	N**	N**	N**
Birch	N	1:1	A
Cassia	1:4	C	A
Cinnamon	1:3	C	A
Clary Sage	N	N	C
Clove	1:1	1:4	C
Coriander	N	N	N
Cypress	N	N	C
Eucalyptus	N	1:1	N
Fennel	N	1:1	C
Frankincense	N	N	N
Geranium	N	N	N
Ginger	N*	1:1	N
Grapefruit	N	N	N
Helichrysum	N	N	N
Lavender	N	N	N
Lemon	N*	N*	N*
Lemongrass	N	1:1	1:1
Lime	N*	N*	N*
Marjoram	N	1:1	C
Melaleuca	N	N	N
Melissa	N	N	N
Myrrh	N	N	C
Oregano	1:3	C	C

SINGLE OIL NAME	RECOMMENDED DILUTION		
	ADULTS	CHILD/SENSITIVE	EXPECTANT MOTHER
Patchouli	N	N	N
Peppermint	N	1:1	C
Roman Chamomile	N	1:1	N
Rose	N	N	N
Rosemary	N	1:1	A
Sandalwood	N	N	N
Thyme	1:4	C	A
Vetiver	N	N	C
White Fir	N	1:1	1:1
Wild Orange	N*	N*	N*
Wintergreen	N	1:1	A
Ylang Ylang	N	N	N
OIL BLEND NAME			
AromaTouch	N	N	N
Balance	N	N	N
Breathe	N	1:1	N
Citrus Bliss	N*	N*	N*
Clear Skin Topical	N	1:1	C
Deep Blue	N	1:1	N
DigestZen	N	N	C
Elevation	N*	N*	N*
Immortelle	N	N	C
On Guard	N	1:1	C
PastTense	N	1:1	C
Purify	N	N	N
Serenity	N	N	N
Slim & Sassy	N*	N*	C
Solace	N	1:1	C
TerraShield	N	N	N
Whisper	N	N	N
Zendocrine	1:1	1:4	C

N: Can be used neat (without dilution).

1:1: For ratios like this, the first number is the proportion of essential oil to use, and the second number is the proportion of carrier oil (such as fractionated coconut oil) to use. For this ratio, you would blend 1 part essential oil with 1 part carrier oil before applying.

C: Use with extreme caution and dilute heavily.

A: Avoid.

Photosensitivity:

*: Avoid sunlight for up to 12 hours after use.

**: Avoid sunlight for up to 72 hours after use.

PERSONAL USAGE GUIDE

ADD/ADHD:

Attention deficit disorder or attention deficit/ hyperactivity disorder is a psychological condition characterized by inattentiveness, restlessness, and difficulty concentrating. Although most individuals exhibit all of these symptoms at some point, ADD is characterized by a frequency and duration of these symptoms that are inappropriate to an individual's age.

Oils: Ⓐ Ⓣ Serenity, Ⓣ vetiver, Ⓐ Ⓣ lavender

Blend 1: Combine equal parts lavender and basil. Diffuse, or apply 1–3 drops on the crown of the head.

Ⓐ: Diffuse into the air. Inhale oil applied to a tissue or cotton wick.

Ⓣ: Dilute as recommended, and apply 1–3 drops on the bottoms of the feet and/or on the spine.

AIDS/HIV: *SEE ALSO ANTIVIRAL*

Acquired immune deficiency syndrome (AIDS) is a disease of the human immune system. AIDS progressively inhibits the effectiveness of the immune system, leaving the human body susceptible to both infections and tumors. AIDS is caused by the human immunodeficiency virus (HIV), which is acquired by direct contact of the bloodstream or mucous membrane with a bodily fluid (such as blood, breast milk, vaginal fluid, semen, and preseminal fluid) containing HIV.

Oils: Ⓣ Ⓐ helichrysum[1], Ⓣ On Guard, Ⓣ Ⓐ lemon, Ⓣ Balance

Ⓐ: Diffuse into the air. Inhale oil applied to a tissue or cotton wick.

Ⓘ: Take 1–2 drops in a capsule.

Ⓣ: Dilute as recommended, and apply 1–3 drops on the bottoms of the feet and/or on the spine.

ABSCESS: *SEE ORAL CONDITIONS:ABSCESS*

ABUSE:

Abuse is the harmful treatment or use of something or someone. Abuse has many different forms: physical, sexual, verbal, spiritual, psychological, etc. Abuse in all of its forms often has long-lasting negative effects on the person or thing abused.

Oils: Ⓣ Elevation, Ⓣ lavender, Ⓣ melissa, Ⓣ sandalwood

Ⓣ: Apply oil topically over the heart, rub on each ear, and then cup hands and inhale deeply to help release negative emotions associated with abuse.

ACNE:

Acne is a skin condition, generally of the face, commonly found in adolescents and young adults. Acne is characterized by red, irritating blemishes (pimples) on the skin. Most commonly, acne is found on the oil-producing parts of the body such as the face, chest, back, upper arms, and back of neck. Acne is a blockage of a skin pore by dead skin cells, tiny hairs, and oil secreted by the sebaceous glands located near the hair follicles in the face, neck, and back. This blockage occurs deep within the skin. Acne is not currently believed to be caused by dirt on the face or by eating certain foods, and research has indicated that over-scrubbing the face may actually make acne worse.

Oils: Ⓣ Clear Skin, Ⓣ melaleuca[2,3,4], Ⓣ lavender, Ⓣ geranium, Ⓣ sandalwood, Ⓣ thyme, Ⓣ vetiver, Ⓣ lemon, Ⓣ lemongrass, Ⓣ marjoram, Ⓣ patchouli

Other Products: Ⓣ Clear Skin Foaming Face Wash

—INFECTIOUS:

Oils: Ⓣ Clear Skin, Ⓣ melaleuca[2,3,4], Ⓣ clove

Other Products: Ⓣ Clear Skin Foaming Face Wash

---

2 Tea tree oil and several of its main components were found to be active against *Propionibacterium acnes*, a bacteria involved in the formation of acne. This oil was also found to be active against two types of staphylococcus bacteria (Raman et al., 1995).

3 A topical gel containing 5% tea tree oil was found to be more effective than a placebo at preventing acne lesions and severity in patients suffering from acne vulgaris (Enshaieh et al., 2007).

4 A gel with 5% tea tree oil was found to be as effective as a 5% benzoyl peroxide (a common chemical used to treat acne) lotion, with fewer side effects (Bassett et al., 1990).

---

1 Arzanol, extracted from helichrysum, inhibited HIV-1 replication in T cells and also inhibited the release of pro-inflammatory cytokines (chemical messengers) in monocytes (Appendino et al., 2007).

Primary Recommendations • Secondary Recommendations • Other Recommendations / Ⓐ=Aromatic, Ⓣ=Topical, Ⓘ=Internal

T: Dilute as recommended, and apply one of the above oils on location. Place about 10 drops of an oil in a 1–2 ounce spray bottle filled with water, and mist your face several times per day.

ADDICTIONS:

Addiction is an obsession, compulsion, or extreme psychological dependence that interferes with an individual's ability or desire to function normally. Common addictions include drugs, alcohol, coffee, tobacco, sugar, video games, work, gambling, money, explicit images, compulsive overeating, etc.

—ALCOHOL:

Oils: **TA**rosemary, **TA**Purify, **TA**Serenity, **TA**helichrysum, **TA**lavender, **TA**orange

—DRUGS:

Oils: **TA**Purify, **TA**Serenity, **TA**grapefruit (withdrawal), **TA**lavender, **TA**basil, **TA**eucalyptus, **TA**marjoram, **TA**orange, **TA**sandalwood, **TA**Roman chamomile, **TA**wintergreen

—SMOKING:

Oils: **T**clove or **T**On Guard on tongue

—SUGAR:

Oils: **T**Purify, **T**Serenity

—WITHDRAWAL:

Oils: **TA**lavender, **TA**grapefruit, **TA**orange, **TA**sandalwood, **TA**marjoram

—WORK:

Oils: **A**lavender, **A**basil, **A**marjoram, **A**geranium

A: Diffuse into the air. Inhale the aroma of the oil directly.

T: Dilute as recommended, and apply to temples or to reflex points.

ADDISON'S DISEASE: *SEE ADRENAL GLANDS:ADDISON'S DISEASE*

ADENITIS:

Adenitis is an acute or chronic inflammation of the lymph glands or lymph nodes.

Oils: **T**rosemary

T: Dilute as recommended, and apply on location.

ADRENAL GLANDS:

The adrenal glands are two small glands located on top of the kidneys. The inner part of the adrenal gland, called the medulla, is responsible for producing adrenalin, a hormone that helps control blood pressure, heart rate, and sweating. The outer part of the adrenal gland, called the cortex, is responsible for producing corticosteroids, hormones that help control metabolism and help regulate inflammation, water levels, and levels of electrolytes such as sodium and potassium. An imbalance in adrenal function can lead to problems such as Addison's disease (a lack of adrenal hormones in the body due to suppressed adrenal functioning) or Cushing's syndrome (and over-abundance of corticosteroids, typically due to over-active adrenal functioning).

Oils: **T**basil, **T**rosemary, **T**clove, **T**Elevation

Other Products: **I**Alpha CRS+, **I**Microplex VMz, **I**xEO Mega

—ADDISON'S DISEASE:

Addison's disease is a condition where the function of the adrenal glands is either severely limited or completely shut down in their ability to produce hormones. This is most often caused by an autoimmune disorder where the body's own immune system attacks the cells in the adrenal glands, but it can also be caused by cancer, tuberculosis, or other diseases. The loss of hormones from the adrenal cortex can cause extreme dehydration due to fluid loss and low levels of sodium. Early symptoms can include tiredness, dizziness when standing up, thirst, weight loss, and dark patches of pigmentation appearing on the skin. If untreated, this disease can eventually lead to kidney failure, shock, and death.

Oils: **T**Elevation

Other Products: **I**Microplex VMz , **I**Alpha CRS+ (for cellular support), **I**xEO Mega

—CUSHING'S SYNDROME:

Cushing's syndrome is a condition where there is an over-abundance of corticosteroids (such as cortisol) in the body, typically caused by an over-production of these steroids by the adrenal glands. This over-production in the adrenal glands can be caused by a growth in the adrenal glands or by a tumor in the thyroid leading to the production of too much

Primary Recommendations • Secondary Recommendations • Other Recommendations / **A**=Aromatic, **T**=Topical, **I**=Internal

126

corticotropin (the hormone that stimulates production of corticosteroids in the adrenal gland). This syndrome can also be caused by taking artificial cortisone or cortisone-like substances. Symptoms of excessive corticosteroids include weight gain, muscle loss, and weakness, bruising, and osteoporosis.

Oils: ᵀElevation, ᵀlemon, ᵀbasil, ᵀOn Guard

Other Products: ❶Microplex VMz , ❶Alpha CRS+ (for cellular support), ❶xEO Mega

—SCHMIDT'S SYNDROME (POLYGLANDULAR DEFICIENCY SYNDROME (OR AUTOIMMUNE POLYENDOCRINE SYNDROME) TYPE 2):

This syndrome refers specifically to an autoimmune disorder that causes Addison's disease as well as decreased thyroid function. *See Addison's Disease (above) and Thyroid: Hypothyroidism for oils and products to help support the adrenal glands and thyroid.*

Stimulate glands: ᵀbasil, ᵀrosemary, ᵀclove, ᵀgeranium

Strengthen glands: ᵀpeppermint

Ⓣ: Apply as a warm compress over kidney area. Dilute as recommended, and apply on location or on reflex points on the feet.

Ⓘ: Take capsules as directed on package.

AGING: *SEE ALSO ALZHEIMER'S DISEASE, ANTIOXIDANT, CELLS, FEMALE-SPECIFIC CONDITIONS:MENOPAUSE, HAIR:LOSS, AND SKIN:WRINKLES FOR OTHER AGE-RELATED ISSUES.*

Oils: ᵀImmortelle, ᵀᴬfrankincense, ᵀᴬsandalwood

Other Products: ᵀAnti-Aging Moisturizer, ᵀFacial Cleanser, ᵀInvigorating Scrub, ᵀPore-Reducing Toner, ᵀTightening Serum. ❶Alpha CRS+, ❶xEO Mega, ❶Microplex VMz , ❶PB Assist+

Ⓘ: Take capsules as directed on package.

Ⓣ: Dilute as recommended, and apply to skin. Combine with carrier oil, and massage into skin. Use Essential Skin Care products as directed on packaging.

Ⓐ: Diffuse, or inhale from a tissue or cotton wick.

AGITATION: *SEE CALMING*

AIRBORNE BACTERIA: *SEE ANTIBACTERIAL*

AIR POLLUTION:

Air Pollution is the presence in the atmosphere of chemicals, biological material, or other matter that can potentially harm humans, the environment, or other living organisms.

Oils: ᴬPurify, ᴬOn Guard, ᴬlemon, ᴬlemongrass, ᴬpeppermint, ᴬrosemary, ᴬeucalyptus, ᴬcypress, ᴬgrapefruit

—DISINFECTANTS:

Oils: ᴬPurify, ᴬlemon, ᴬeucalyptus, ᴬclove, ᴬgrapefruit, ᴬpeppermint, ᴬwintergreen

Blend 1: Combine lemongrass and geranium oil, and diffuse into the air[1].

Ⓐ: Diffuse into the air.

ALCOHOLISM: *SEE ADDICTIONS:ALCOHOL*

ALERTNESS:

Alertness is the state of being watchful or paying close attention. It includes being prepared to react quickly to danger, emergencies, or any other situation.

Oils: ᴬᵀpeppermint[2], ᴬylang ylang[3], ᴬᵀlemon, ᴬᵀbasil, ᴬᵀrosemary

Ⓐ: Diffuse into the air. Inhale oil applied to a tissue or cotton wick.

Ⓣ: Dilute as recommended, and apply to the temples and bottoms of the feet.

ALLERGIES:

An allergy is a damaging immune system response to a substance that does not bother most other people. Common allergies are to food, insect bites, pollen, dust, medicine, pets, and mold. Allergy symptoms vary greatly, but common allergic responses include itching, swelling, runny nose, asthma, and sneezing. Both host factors (gender, race, heredity) and environmental factors can cause allergies.

---

1 A formulation of lemongrass and geranium oil was found to reduce airborne bacteria by 89% in an office environment after diffusion for 15 hours (Doran et al., 2009).
2 In human trials, the aroma of peppermint was found to enhance memory and increase alertness (Moss et al., 2008).
3 Inhaled ylang ylang oil was found to decrease blood pressure and pulse rate and to enhance attentiveness and alertness in volunteers compared to an odorless control (Hongratanaworakit et al., 2004).

Oils: [T]melaleuca[1,2,3,4], [T]lavender[5], [A]peppermint[6], [T]Roman chamomile, [T,A]melissa, [T,A]patchouli, [T]eucalyptus

Other Products: [I]Microplex VMz , [I]Alpha CRS+

—COUGHING:

Oils: Purify

—HAY FEVER

Oils: [T]lavender[7], [A]eucalyptus, [A]rose, [T]peppermint

Recipe 1: Apply 1 drop of peppermint on the base of the neck two times a day. Tap the thymus (located just below the notch in the neck) with pointer fingers. Diffuse peppermint.

Recipe 2: For allergy rashes and skin sensitivity, apply 3 drops lavender, 6 drops Roman chamomile, 2 drops myrrh, and 1 drop peppermint on location.

[T]: Dilute as recommended, and apply to sinuses and to bottoms of feet.

[A]: Diffuse into the air. Inhale oil applied to a tissue or cotton wick.

ALZHEIMER'S DISEASE: SEE ALSO BRAIN, MEMORY

Alzheimer's is a progressive and fatal disease that attacks and kills brain cells, causing a loss of memory and other intellectual capacities. Alzheimer's is most commonly diagnosed in individuals over the age of 65. As the disease progresses, sufferers often experience mood swings, long-term memory loss, confusion, irritability, aggression, and a decreased ability to communicate.

Supplements: [I]Alpha CRS+[8,9]

---

1 Tea tree oil was found to reduce swelling during a contact hypersensitivity response in the skin of mice sensitized to the chemical hapten (Brand et al., 2002).
2 Tea tree oil applied to histamine-induced edema (swelling) in mice ears was found to significantly reduce swelling (Brand et al., 2002).
3 Tea tree oil was found to reduce inflammation in the skin of nickel-sensitive human skin exposed to nickel (Pearce et al., 2005).
4 Tea tree oil applied to histamine-induced weal and flare in human volunteers was found to decrease the mean weal volume when compared to a control (Koh et al., 2002).
5 Lavender oil was found to inhibit immediate-type allergic reactions in mice and rats by inhibiting mast cell degranulation (Kim et al., 1999).
6 L-menthol (from peppermint) was found to inhibit production of inflammation mediators in human monocytes (a type of white blood cell involved in the immune response) (Juergens et al., 1998).
7 Lavender oil was found to inhibit immediate-type allergic reactions in mice and rats by inhibiting mast cell degranulation (Kim et al., 1999).
8 In a recent study at UCLA, the polyphenol curcumin was found to inhibit amyloid beta accumulation and to cross the blood-brain barrier of mice and bind amyloid plaques. Amyloid beta plaques are theorized to have a role in the development of Alzheimer's disease (Yang et al., 2005).
9 Curcumin was found to reduce the effects of amyloid beta-caused oxidative stress and DNA damage in neuronal cells (Park et al., 2008).

—BLOOD-BRAIN BARRIER:

Studies have shown that sesquiterpenes can pass the blood-brain barrier. Oils high in sesquiterpenes include sandalwood, ginger, myrrh, vetiver, ylang ylang, and frankincense.

Oils: [A,T]frankincense, [A,T]sandalwood

[I]: Take capsules as directed on package.

[A]: Diffuse oils into the air.

[T]: Dilute as recommended, and apply over brain stem area on back of neck.

AMNESIA: SEE MEMORY

ANALGESIC: SEE PAIN

ANEURYSM: SEE ALSO BLOOD

An Aneurysm is a swelling or dilation of a blood vessel in the area of a weakened blood vessel wall.

Oils: [T,A]cypress, [T,A]melaleuca, [T,A]clary sage, [T,A]helichrysum, [T,A]frankincense

Blend 1: Combine 5 drops frankincense, 1 drop helichrysum, and 1 drop cypress. Diffuse.

Herbs: Cayenne pepper, garlic, hawthorn berry

[T]: Dilute as recommended, and apply to temples, heart, and reflex points for heart on the feet.

[A]: Diffuse into the air. Inhale oil applied to a tissue or cotton wick.

ANGER: SEE CALMING

ANGINA: SEE CARDIOVASCULAR SYSTEM:ANGINA

ANIMALS:

Only 1–2 drops of oil are necessary on most animals, as they respond more quickly to the oils than do humans. Fractionated coconut oil can be added to extend the oil over larger areas and to heavily dilute the essential oil for use on smaller animals, especially cats.

—BLEEDING:

Oils: [T]helichrysum, [T]geranium

—BONES (PAIN):

Oils: [T]wintergreen, [T]Deep Blue, [T]lemongrass

—CALM:

Oils: 🅐🅣Serenity, 🅐🅣lavender, 🅐🅣Citrus Bliss

—CANCER, SKIN

Oils: 🅣sandalwood [10,11,12,13,14,15], 🅣frankincense

—CATS:

Valerie Worwood says that you can treat a cat like you would a child (*see Children/Infants*). Dilute oils heavily with carrier oil. ***Avoid melaleuca, and use oils with extreme caution.***

—COLDS AND COUGHS:

Oils: 🅣eucalyptus, 🅣melaleuca (not for cats). Apply on fur or stomach.

—COWS:

Oils: For scours, use 5 drops 🅣DigestZen on stomach (dilute with fractionated coconut oil to cover a larger area). Repeat 2 hours later.

—DOGS:

–ANXIETY/NERVOUSNESS

Oils: 🅣Serenity, 🅣lavender, 🅣Balance. Rub 1–2 drops between hands, and apply to muzzle, between toes, on tops of feet for the dog to smell, and on edges of ears.

–ARTHRITIS:

Oils: 🅣frankincense [16,17]

Blend 1: Blend equal parts rosemary, lavender, and ginger. Dilute with fractionated coconut oil, and apply topically on affected joints.

–BONE INJURY:

Oils: 🅣wintergreen

–DERMATITIS:

Oils: 🅣melaleuca [18]

–HEART PROBLEMS:

Oils: 🅣peppermint (on paws), 🅣On Guard (apply on back with warm compress)

–SLEEP:

Oils: 🅣lavender (on paws), 🅣Serenity (on stomach)

–STROKE:

Oils: 🅣frankincense (on brain stem/back of neck), 🅣Balance (on each paw)

–TICKS AND BUG BITES:

Oils: 🅣Purify (drop directly on tick, or dilute and apply to wound)

–TRAVEL SICKNESS:

Oils: 🅣peppermint (dilute, and rub on stomach)

—EARACHE:

Blend 2: Combine 1 drop melaleuca, 1 drop lavender, and 1 drop Roman chamomile in 1 tsp. fractionated coconut oil. Apply 1–2 drops to inside and outside of ear.

—EAR INFECTIONS:

Oils: 🅣Purify. Dip cotton swab in oil, and apply to inside and front of ear.

—FLEAS:

Oils: 🅣lemongrass, 🅣eucalyptus. Add 1–2 drops of oil to shampoo.

—HORSES:

–ANXIETY/NERVOUSNESS

Oils: 🅣Serenity. Rub 1–2 drops between hands, and apply to nose, knees, tongue, and front of chest.

–HOOF ROT:

Blend 3: Combine 1 drop Roman chamomile, 1 drop thyme, and 1 drop melissa in 1 tsp. fractionated coconut oil, and apply on location.

---

10 Sandalwood oil was found to decrease skin papilloma (tumors) in mice (Dwivedi et al., 1997).

11 Alpha-santalol, derived from sandalwood EO, was found to delay and decrease the incidence and multiplicity of skin tumor (papilloma) development in mice (Dwivedi et al., 2003).

12 Various concentrations of alpha-santalol (from sandalwood) were tested against skin cancer in mice. All concentrations were found to inhibit skin cancer development (Dwivedi et al., 2005).

13 A solution of 5% alpha-santalol (from sandalwood) was found to prevent skin-tumor formation caused by ultraviolet-b (UVB) radiation in mice (Dwivedi et al., 2006).

14 Oral sandalwood oil use enhanced GST activity (a protein in cell membranes that can help eliminate toxins) and acid-soluble SH levels. This suggests a possible chemopreventive action on carcinogenesis (Banerjee et al., 1993).

15 Pre-treatment with alpha-santalol before UVB (ultraviolet-b) radiation significantly reduced skin tumor development and multiplicity and induced proapoptotic and tumor-suppressing proteins (Arasada et al., 2008).

16 An acetone extract of frankincense was found to decrease arthritic sores, reduce paw edema (swelling), and suppress pro-inflammatory cytokines (cellular messengers) (Fan et al., 2008).

17 Boswellic acid, from frankincense, was found in vitro to prevent expression and activity of several proteins involved in inflammatory response. In vivo, Boswellic acid was found to protect against experimental arthritis (Roy et al., 2006).

18 A cream with 10% tea tree oil was found to be more effective at treating dermatitis in dogs than a commercially-available skin cream (Reichling et al., 2004).

Primary Recommendations • Secondary Recommendations • Other Recommendations / 🅐=Aromatic, 🅣=Topical, 🅘=Internal

—INFECTION:

    Oils: [T]On Guard

—LEG FRACTURES:

    Oils: [T]ginger. Dilute oil, and apply oil to leg with a hot compress wrapped around the leg. Massage leg after the fracture is healed with a blend of [T]rosemary and [T]thyme diluted with fractionated coconut oil. This may strengthen the ligaments and prevent calcification.

—MUSCLE TISSUE

    Oils: Apply equal parts [T]lemongrass and [T]lavender on location, and wrap to help regenerate torn muscle tissue.

—WOUNDS:

    Oils: [T]helichrysum

—PARASITES:

    Oils: [T]lavender, [T]DigestZen. Rub on paws to release parasites.

[T]: Apply as directed above. Dilute as recommended, and apply on location.

[A]: Diffuse into the air.

ANOREXIA: *SEE EATING DISORDERS: ANOREXIA*

ANTIBACTERIAL: *SEE ALSO DISINFECTANT*

The term antibacterial refers to anything that kills bacteria or that limits its ability to grow or reproduce.

STAPHYLOCOCCUS AUREUS BACTERIA

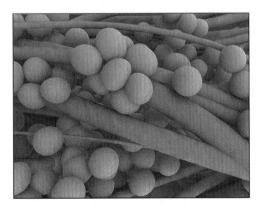

Oils: [T]On Guard, [T]melaleuca[1,2,3,4,5,6,7,8,9,10,11], [T][A]thyme[4,5,12,13,14], [T][A]cinnamon[5,12], [T]peppermint[4,15,16], [A][T]Purify, [T][A]lime, [T][A]lemongrass[12,17,18], [T]helichrysum[19,20], [T][A]geranium[8,17], [T]rosemary[16], [T][A]clove, [T]oregano[21], [A]Breathe, [T]cypress, [T]basil, [T]cassia, [T][A]lemon, [T]eucalyptus, [T]grapefruit, [T]marjoram, [T]clary sage, [T]lavender, [T]frankincense

Blend 1: For an antibiotic blend, place 12 drops of On Guard, 6 drops oregano, and 2 drops frankincense in a size "00" capsule, and ingest every 4–8 hours.

Other Products: [T]On Guard Foaming Hand Wash to help eliminate bacteria on the skin,

---

1 Tea tree oil was found to disrupt the cellular membrane and inhibited respiration in *Candida albicans*, Gram-negative *E. coli*, and Gram-positive *Staphylococcus aureus* (Staph) (Cox et al., 2000).

2 In a human trial, most patients receiving treatment with *Melaleuca alternifolia* oil placed topically on boils experienced healing or reduction of symptoms, while of those receiving no treatment (control), half required surgical intervention, and all still demonstrated signs of the infection (Feinblatt et al., 1960).

3 Gram-positive strains of *Staphylococcus aureus* and *Enterococcus faecalis* were shown to have very low frequencies of resistance to tea tree oil (Hammer et al., 2008).

4 Tea tree, peppermint, and sage oils were found to inhibit oral bacteria, with thymol and eugenol being the most active components of these oils (Shapiro et al., 1994).

5 Cinnamon oil exhibited a strong antimicrobial activity against two detrimental oral bacteria. Manuka, tea tree, and the component thymol also exhibited antimicrobial potency (Filoche et al., 2005).

6 MRSA (methicillin-resistant staph) and MSSA (methicillin-sensitive staph) in biofilms (plaque/microcolonies) were eradicated by a 5% solution of tea tree oil, as were 5 of 9 CoNS (coagulase-negative staph) (Brady et al., 2006).

7 66 isolates of *Staphylococcus aureus* (Staph), including 64 methicillin-resistant (MRSA) and 33 mupirocin-resistant strains, were inhibited by tea tree essential oil (Carson et al., 1995).

8 A combination of Citricidal and geranium oil demonstrated strong antibacterial effects on MRSA. Geranium and tea tree demonstrated strong antibacterial effects on *Staphylococcus aureus* (Edwards-Jones et al., 2004).

9 Tea tree oil and its component terpinen-4-ol demonstrated antibacterial activity against *Staphylococcus aureus* (Staph) bacteria, superior to the activities of several antibiotic drugs—even against antibiotic-resistant strains (Ferrini et al., 2006).

10 Tea tree oil demonstrated ability to kill *Staphylococcus aureus* (Staph) bacteria both within biofilms and in the stationary growth phase at concentrations below 1% (Kwieciński et al., 2009).

11 Turpin-4-ol, found in tea tree oil, was found to effectively inhibit MRSA and CoNS, while not exhibiting toxicity to human fibroblast cells (Loughlin et al., 2008).

12 Cinnamon bark, lemongrass, and thyme oils were found to have the highest level of activity against common respiratory pathogens among 14 essential oils tested (Inouye et al., 2001).

13 Thyme oil demonstrated a strong antibacterial effect against Staph and *E. coli* bacteria (Mohsenzadeh et al., 2007).

14 Oils with aldehydes or phenols as major components demonstrated a high level of antibacterial activity (Inouye et al., 2001).

15 Peppermint and spearmint oil inhibited resistant strains of *Staphylococcus*, *E. coli*, *Salmonella*, and *Helicobacter pylori* (Imai et al., 2001).

16 Peppermint and rosemary oils were each found to be more effective at preventing dental biofilm (plaque) formation than chlorhexidine (an antiseptic) (Rasooli et al., 2008).

17 A formulation of lemongrass and geranium oil was found to reduce airborne bacteria by 89% in an office environment after diffusion for 15 hours (Doran et al., 2009).

18 Lemongrass and lemon verbena oil were found to be bactericidal to *Helicobacter pylori* at very low concentrations. Additionally, it was found that this bacteria did not develop a resistance to lemongrass oil after 10 passages, while this bacteria did develop resistance to clarithromycin (an antibiotic) under the same conditions (Ohno et al., 2003).

19 Helichrysum oil was found to exhibit definite antibacterial activity against six tested Gram (+/-) bacteria (Chinou et al., 1996).

20 Helichrysum was found to inhibit both the growth and some of the enzymes of the *Staphylococcus aureus* (staph) bacteria (Nostro et al., 2001).

21 Oregano oil was found to inhibit MRSA (Nostro et al., 2004).

Primary Recommendations • Secondary Recommendations • Other Recommendations / [A]=Aromatic, [T]=Topical, [I]=Internal

⚬PB Assist+, ⚬GX Assist to help support the intestinal tract against harmful bacteria.

—Airborne Bacteria:

Oils: ⚪cinnamon[12], ⚪lemongrass[17], ⚪geranium[17], ⚪On Guard, ⚪Purify, ⚪oregano

—Cleansing:

Oils: Purify

—MRSA (Methicillin Resistant *Staphylococcus aureus*):

Oils: ⚫melaleuca[6,7,8,11], ⚫oregano[21], ⚫geranium[8], ⚫On Guard, ⚫frankincense, ⚫peppermint[15], ⚫lemon, ⚫thyme, ⚫cinnamon, ⚫clove, ⚫eucalyptus, ⚫lemongrass, ⚫orange, ⚫grapefruit, ⚫lavender

Recipe 1: Place 2–5 drops each of oregano, On Guard, and frankincense (followed by lemon and peppermint) on bottoms of feet every 2 hours.

—Staph (*Staphylococcus aureus*) Infection:

Oils: ⚫⚫On Guard, ⚫⚫melaleuca[1,3,6,7,9,10,11], ⚫oregano[21], ⚫helichrysum[19,20], ⚫thyme[13], ⚫geranium[8], ⚫Purify, ⚫lavender **Note:** peppermint may make a staph infection more painful.

Ⓣ: Dilute as recommended, and apply on location. Dilute and apply to liver area and bottoms of the feet. Use hand wash as directed on packaging.

Ⓐ: Diffuse into the air. Combine a few drops in a small spray bottle with distilled water, and spray into the air.

Ⓘ: Place oils in empty capsules and swallow. Take supplements as directed.

Anticatarrhal: *see Congestion:Catarrh*

Anticoagulant: *see Blood:Clots*

Antidepressant: *see Depression*

Antifungal:

Fungi are a broad range of organisms such as yeast, mold, and mushrooms. While many fungi are safe and beneficial, some create mycotoxins, which are chemicals that can be toxic to plants, animals, and humans. Examples of fungi that can be detrimental to humans include black mold, *Candida*, and ringworm.

Oils: ⚫⚪Clear Skin, ⚫melaleuca[22,23,24,25,26,27,28], ⚫⚪⚪oregano[29,30,31,32], ⚫thyme[32,33,34], ⚫⚪cinnamon[29,32,35], ⚫clove[29,34,36], ⚫⚪On Guard, ⚫lavender[37,38], ⚫peppermint[39], ⚫rosemary[40], ⚫lemon[41], ⚪Purify, patchouli⚫⚪, ⚫lemongrass, ⚫geranium

Other Products: ⚫On Guard Foaming Hand Wash, ⚬PB Assist+, ⚬GX Assist

—Athlete's Foot:

Athlete's foot (tinea pedis) is a fungal infection that develops on the skin of the feet. This infection causes itching, redness, and scaling of the skin, and in severe cases it can cause painful blistering or cracking of the skin.

---

22 Tea tree oil was found to inhibit 301 different types of yeasts isolated from the mouths of cancer patients suffering from advanced cancer, including 41 strains that are known to be resistant to antifungal drugs (Bagg et al., 2006).

23 Eleven types of *Candida* were found to be highly inhibited by tea tree oil (Banes-Marshall et al., 2001).

24 Tea tree oil was found to disrupt the cellular membrane and to inhibit respiration in *Candida albicans* (Cox et al., 2000).

25 Melaleuca oil at concentrations of .16% was found to inhibit the transformation of *C. albicans* from single-cell yeast to the pathogenic mycelial (multi-cellular strands) form (D'Auria et al., 2001).

26 Tea Tree oil was found to alter the membrane properties and functions of *Candida albicans* cells, leading to cell inhibition or death (Hammer et al., 2004).

27 Terpinen-4-ol, a constituent of tea tree oil, and tea tree oil were found to be effective against several forms of vaginal *Candida* infections in rats, including azole-resistant forms (Mondello et al., 2006).

28 Melaleuca oil inhibited several *Candida* species in vitro (Vazquez et al., 2000).

29 In a test of nine oils, clove, followed by cinnamon, oregano, and mace oil, was found to be inhibitory to two toxin-producing fungi. It was also shown that whole and ground cloves stored with grain reduced the amount of aflatoxin contamination (Juglal et al., 2002).

30 The vapor of oregano oil was found to be fungicidal against the *Trichophyton mentagrophytes* fungi (a fungi that causes a skin infection known as Malabar itch) (Inouye et al., 2006).

31 Mice infected with *Candida albicans* who were fed origanum oil or carvacrol diluted in olive oil had an 80% survival rate after 30 days, while infected mice fed olive oil alone all died after 10 days (Manohar et al., 2001).

32 Cinnamon, thyme, oregano, and cumin oils inhibited the production of aflatoxin by aspergillus fungus (Tantaoui-Elaraki et al., 1994).

33 Thyme oil was found to inhibit *Candida* species by causing lesions in the cell membrane, as well as inhibiting germ tube (an outgrowth that develops when the fungi is preparing to replicate) formation (Pina-Vaz et al., 2004).

34 Eugenol from clove and thymol from thyme were found to inhibit the growth of *Aspergillus flavus* and *Aspergillus versicolor* at concentrations of .4 mg/ml or less (Hitokoto et al., 1980).

35 Vapor of cinnamon bark oil and cinnamic aldehyde was found to be effective against fungi involved in respiratory tract mycoses (fungal infections) (Singh et al., 1995).

36 Clove oil was found to have very strong radical scavenging activity (antioxidant). It was also found to display an antifungal effect against tested *Candida* strains (Chaieb et al., 2007).

37 Lavandula oil demonstrated antifungal activity against three pathogenic fungi (Behnam et al., 2006).

38 Lavender oil demonstrated both fungistatic (stopped growth) and fungicidal (killed) activity against *Candida albicans* (D'Auria et al., 2005).

39 Peppermint oil was found to have a higher fungistatic and fungicidal activity against various fungi (including *Candida*) than the commercial fungicide bifonazole (Mimica-Dukić et al., 2003).

40 Rosemary oil was found to inhibit aflatoxin production by aspergillus fungi (a highly toxic and carcinogenic substance produced by these fungi) (Rasooli et al., 2008).

41 Lemon oil was found to be an effective antifungal agent against two bread-mold species (Caccioni et al., 1998).

Primary Recommendations • Secondary Recommendations • Other Recommendations / Ⓐ=Aromatic, Ⓣ=Topical, Ⓘ=Internal

Oils: 🅣melaleuca[1], 🅐🅣oregano[30], 🅣🅐Clear Skin, 🅣cypress, 🅣thyme, 🅣geranium, 🅣lavender

—Candida:

Candida refers to a genus of yeast that are normally found in the digestive tract and on the skin of humans. These yeast are typically symbiotically beneficial to humans. However, several species of *Candida*, most commonly *Candida albicans*, can cause infections such as vaginal candidiasis or thrush (oral candidiasis) that cause localized itching, soreness, and redness *(see Vaginal:Candida for further application methods)*. In immune-system compromised individuals, these infection-causing species of *Candida* can spread further, leading to serious, life-threatening complications.

Oils: 🅣melaleuca[2,3,4,5,6,7], 🅣🅞oregano[8], 🅣clove[9], 🅣On Guard, 🅣🅐peppermint[10], 🅣thyme[11], 🅣lavender[12], 🅣eucalyptus, 🅣rosemary, 🅣🅞DigestZen

—Mold:

Mold are a type of microscopic multi-cellular fungi that grow together to form filaments. Mold is found throughout the world and can survive in extreme conditions. While most mold does not adversely affect humans, an over-abundance of mold spores can cause allergies or other problems within the respiratory system. Additionally, some types of mold

produce toxins that can be harmful to humans or to animals.

Oils: 🅐On Guard, 🅐🅣clove[13,14], 🅐🅣thyme[14,15], 🅐🅣cinnamon[13,15], 🅐🅣oregano[13,15], 🅐🅣rosemary[16], 🅐Purify

—Ringworm:

Ringworm (or tinea) is a fungal infection of the skin that can cause itching, redness, and scaling of the skin. The name comes from the ring-shaped patches that often form on the skin.

Oils: 🅣melaleuca, 🅐🅣oregano[17], 🅣Clear Skin, 🅣peppermint, 🅣thyme, 🅣geranium, 🅣lavender

Blend 1: Combine 2 drops lavender, 2 drops melaleuca, and 2 drops thyme. Apply 1–2 drops on ringworm three times a day for 10 days. Then mix 30 drops melaleuca with 2 Tbs. fractionated coconut oil, and use daily until ringworm is gone.

—Thrush:

Thrush is another name for oral candidiasis *(see Candida above)*. Thrush results in uncomfortable or painful white or yellow patches in the mouth.

Oils: 🅣melaleuca[18], 🅣lavender, 🅣Clear Skin, 🅣eucalyptus, 🅣marjoram, 🅣thyme

🅣: Dilute as recommended, and apply on location. Apply as a warm compress over affected area.

🅐: Diffuse into the air.

🅘: Take capsules as directed on package.

ANTIHEMORRHAGING: *SEE BLOOD:HEMORRHAGING*

ANTIHISTAMINE: *SEE ALLERGIES*

1 Patients with tinea pedis (athlete's foot) were found to have a higher rate of cure and a higher clinical response when treated topically with 25 or 50% tea tree oil solution compared to control (Satchell et al., 2002).

2 Eleven types of *Candida* were found to be highly inhibited by tea tree oil (Banes-Marshall et al., 2001).

3 Tea tree oil was found to disrupt the cellular membrane and to inhibit respiration in *Candida albicans* (Cox et al., 2000).

4 Melaleuca oil at concentrations of .16% was found to inhibit the transformation of *C. albicans* from single-cell yeast to the pathogenic mycelial (multi-cellular strands) form (D'Auria et al., 2001).

5 Tea Tree oil was found to alter the membrane properties and functions of *Candida albicans* cells, leading to cell inhibition or death (Hammer et al., 2004).

6 Terpinen-4-ol, a constituent of tea tree oil, and tea tree oil were found to be effective against several forms of vaginal *Candida* infections in rats, including azole-resistant forms (Mondello et al., 2006).

7 Melaleuca oil inhibited several *Candida* species in vitro (Vazquez et al., 2000).

8 Mice infected with *Candida albicans* who were fed origanum oil or carvacrol diluted in olive oil had an 80% survival rate after 30 days, while infected mice fed olive oil alone all died after 10 days (Manohar et al., 2001).

9 Clove oil was found to have very strong radical scavenging activity (antioxidant). It was also found to display an antifungal effect against tested *Candida* strains (Chaieb et al., 2007).

10 Peppermint oil was found to have a higher fungistatic and fungicidal activity against various fungi (including *Candida*) than the commercial fungicide bifonazole (Mimica-Dukić et al., 2003).

11 Thyme oil was found to inhibit *Candida* species by causing lesions in the cell membrane as well as inhibiting germ tube (an outgrowth that develops when the fungi is preparing to replicate) formation (Pina-Vaz et al., 2004).

12 Lavender oil demonstrated both fungistatic (stopped growth) and fungicidal (killed) activity against *Candida albicans* (D'Auria et al., 2005).

13 In a test of nine oils, clove, followed by cinnamon, oregano, and mace oil, was found to be inhibitory to two toxin-producing fungi. It was also shown that whole and ground cloves stored with grain reduced the amount of aflatoxin contamination (Juglal et al., 2002).

14 Eugenol from clove and thymol from thyme were found to inhibit the growth of *Aspergillus flavus* and *Aspergillus versicolor* at concentrations of .4 mg/ml or less (Hitokoto et al., 1980).

15 Cinnamon, thyme, oregano, and cumin oils inhibited the production of aflatoxin by aspergillus fungus (Tantaoui-Elaraki et al., 1994).

16 Rosemary oil was found to inhibit aflatoxin production by aspergillus fungi (a highly toxic and carcinogenic substance produced by these fungi) (Rasooli et al., 2008).

17 The vapor of oregano oil was found to be fungicidal against the *Trichophyton mentagrophytes* fungi (a fungi that causes a skin infection known as Malabar itch) (Inouye et al., 2006).

18 Tea tree oil was found to inhibit 301 different types of yeasts isolated from the mouths of cancer patients suffering from advanced cancer, including 41 strains that are known to be resistant to antifungal drugs (Bagg et al., 2006).

ANTI-INFECTIOUS: *SEE INFECTION, ANTIBACTERIAL, ANTIVIRAL, ANTIFUNGAL*

ANTI-INFLAMMATORY: *SEE INFLAMMATION*

ANTIMICROBIAL: *SEE ANTIBACTERIAL, ANTIFUNGAL, ANTIVIRAL*

ANTIOXIDANT:

As part of its normal metabolic processes, the body uses and creates oxidative molecules, each capable of transferring electrons to itself from other molecules or substances. This type of reaction can create molecules known as free radicals (Davies, 1995). If left unchecked in the body, these free radicals can bind or react with different molecular structures, altering their abilities to function normally. Under normal, healthy conditions, the body's own systems are able to create or metabolize enough antioxidant materials to neutralize the ability of these oxidative molecules to create free radicals. But when the body comes under stress—including physical stress, psychological stress, poor nutrition, or disease—the amount of oxidative molecules being produced can increase, and the delicate balance between oxidative molecules and antioxidants can be thrown off, potentially overwhelming the body's own antioxidant mechanisms. This "oxidative stress" (Sies, 1997) creates a condition optimal for the formation of many free radicals, which in turn can potentially cause enough damage to the cell's normal structures to cause cell death, mutation, or loss of its ability to function normally within the body (Rhee, 2006; Vertuani et al., 2004).

Oils: ⊕Ⓐclove[19,20], ⓄⓉⒶthyme[19,21,22,23],

⊕Ⓐrosemary[24,25,26,27], ⊕Ⓐpeppermint[28,29,30], ⊕Ⓐmelaleuca[31,32], ⊕Ⓐhelichrysum[33], ⊕ⒶPurify, ⊕ⒶOn Guard, ⊕ⒶBreathe, ⊕ⒶDeep Blue, Ⓐcinnamon, ⊕Ⓐfrankincense, ⊕Ⓐoregano, ⊕ⒶRoman chamomile

Other Products: ❶Alpha CRS+, which contains polyphenols that act as powerful antioxidants, such as quercetin[34], epigallocatechin gallate[35,36], ellagic acid[37], resveratrol[38], baicalin[39], and others[40,41,42].

❶: Take capsules as directed. Use oils recommended as flavoring agents in cooking. Place 1 drop of oil in an empty capsule, and ingest it as a dietary supplement.

---

24 Extracts from rosemary were found to have high antioxidant properties. Rosmarinic acid and carnosic acid from rosemary were found to have the highest antioxidant activities of studied components of rosemary (Almela et al., 2006).

25 An ethanol extract of rosemary was found to have an antiproliferative effect on human leukemia and breast carcinoma cells, as well as an antioxidant effect (Cheung et al., 2007).

26 Extracts from rosemary were found to have high antioxidant levels. Additionally, a methanol extract with 30% carnosic acid, 16% carnosol, and 5% rosmarinic acid were found to be effective against gram-positive and negative bacteria, and yeast (Moreno et al., 2006).

27 In patients with chronic bronchitis, rosemary, basil, fir, and eucalyptus oils were found to demonstrate an antioxidant effect. Lavender was found to promote normalization of lipid levels (Siurin, 1997).

28 Peppermint oil was found to be an effective antibacterial and antioxidant agent (Mimica-Dukić et al., 2003).

29 Peppermint oil fed to mice prior to exposure to gamma radiation was found to decrease levels of damage from oxidation when compared to mice not pretreated with peppermint (Samarth et al., 2006).

30 Peppermint extract fed orally to mice demonstrated the ability to protect the testis from gamma radiation damage (Samarth et al., 2009).

31 *Melaleuca alternifolia* oil was found to reduce reactive oxygen species (ROS) production in neutrophils (a type of white blood cell), indicating an antioxidant effect and decreased Interleukin 2 (a chemical messenger that helps trigger an inflammatory response) secretion, while increasing the secretion of Interleukin 4 (a chemical messenger involved in turning off the inflammatory response) (Caldefie-Chézet et al., 2006).

32 *Melaleuca alternifolia* oil was found to mediate the Reactive Oxygen Species (ROS) production of leukocytes (white blood cells), indicating a possible anti-inflammatory activity (Caldefie-Chézet et al., 2004).

33 Arzanol (extracted from helichrysum), at non-cytotoxic concentrations, showed a strong inhibition of TBH-induced oxidative stress in VERO cells (Rosa et al., 2007).

34 Quercetin was found to increase plasma antioxidant status in healthy volunteers who took it as a supplement over four weeks (Boots et al., 2008).

35 Epigallocatechin-3-gallate (EGCG) supplementation was found to improve the antioxidant status of heat-stressed Japanese quail (Tuzcu et al., 2008).

36 Epigallocatechin-3-gallate (EGCG) was found to improve body weight and increase enzymatic and non-enzymatic antioxidants in bleomycin-induced pulmonary fibrosis in rats (Sriram et al., 2008).

37 Ellagic acid supplementation was found to significantly decrease mitochondrial and microsomal lipid peroxidation in endrin-induced hepatic lipid peroxidation (Bagchi et al., 1993).

38 Resveratrol was found to act as an antioxidant and to reverse the anti-apoptotic effects of repetitive oxidative stress on lung fibroblasts in vitro (Chakraborty et al., 2008).

39 Baicalin was found to be an effective antioxidant, and to counteract oxidative stress induced to retinal cells and brain membranes of rats (Jung et al., 2008).

40 Extracts from bilberry and blueberry were found to have higher ORAC values than strawberry, cranberry, elderberry, or raspberry and were found to significantly inhibit both H2O2 and TNF alpha induced VEGF expression by human keratinocytes (Roy et al., 2002).

41 Catechins and procyanidins extracted from various berries were found to provide substantial antioxidant protection (Maatta-Riihinet et al., 2005).

42 Oral supplementation of bilberry extract was found to reduce the degree of oxidative stress and kidney damage by potassium bromate oxidization in mice (Bao et al., 2008).

---

19 Clove oil was found to have very strong radical scavenging activity (antioxidant). It was also found to display an antifungal effect against tested *Candida* strains (Chaieb et al., 2007).

20 Various essential oils demonstrated an antioxidant effect toward skin lipid squalene oxidized by UV irradiation, with a blend of thyme and clove oil demonstrating the highest inhibitory effect (Wei et al., 2007).

21 Extracts from Eucalyptus and Thyme were found to have high Nitrous Oxide (NO) scavenging abilities and inhibited NO production in macrophage cells. This could possibly explain their role in aiding respiratory inflammatory diseases (Vigo et al., 2004).

22 Older rats whose diets were supplemented with thyme oil were found to have a higher level of the antioxidant enzymes superoxide dismutase and glutathione peroxidase in the heart, liver, and kidneys than older rats without this supplementation (Youdim et al., 1999).

23 Aging rats fed thyme oil or the constituent thymol were found to have higher levels of the antioxidant enzymes superoxide dismutase and glutathione peroxidase in the brain than aging rats not fed the oil or constituent (Youdim et al., 2000).

Primary Recommendations • Secondary Recommendations • Other Recommendations / Ⓐ=**Aromatic**, Ⓣꞏ=**Topical**, ❶=**Internal**

133

Ⓐ: Diffuse into the air. Inhale directly from bottle. Apply oil to hands, tissue, or cotton wick, and inhale.

Ⓣ: Dilute as recommended, and apply on the skin and reflex points on the feet. Dilute in a carrier oil, and massage into the skin. Apply as a hot compress.

ANTIPARASITIC: *SEE PARASITES*

ANTIRHEUMATIC: *SEE ARTHRITIS:RHEUMATOID ARTHRITIS*

ANTISEPTIC: *SEE ANTIBACTERIAL, ANTIFUNGAL, ANTIVIRAL*

ANTIVIRAL:

The term "antiviral" refers to something that is able to inhibit or stop the development, function, or replication of an infection-causing virus.

Oils: **ⓉⒶ**helichrysum[1,2], **ⓉⒶ**melaleuca[3], **ⓉⒶ**clove[4], **ⓉⒶ**On Guard, **ⓉⒶ**melissa[5], **Ⓐ**Breathe, **ⓉⒶ**lime, **Ⓣ**cinnamon, **ⒶⓉ**lemon, **ⓉⒶ**oregano, **ⓉⒶ**peppermint[6], **ⒶⓉ**eucalyptus[7], **Ⓣ**thyme, **Ⓐ**orange, **Ⓐ**grapefruit, **ⓉⒶ**clary sage, **ⓉⒶ**myrrh, **Ⓐ**geranium, **ⓉⒶ**lavender, **ⓉⒶ**sandalwood, **Ⓣ**rosemary, **ⓉⒶ**cypress

Other Products: **Ⓣ**On Guard Foaming Hand Wash to help protect against skin-borne microorganisms. **Ⓣ**On Guard Protecting Throat Drops to soothe irritated and sore throats. **Ⓘ**Alpha CRS+, **Ⓘ**xEO Mega, **Ⓘ**Microplex VMz to help support the immune system.

—AIRBORNE VIRUSES:

Oils: **Ⓐ**On Guard

—EBOLA VIRUS:

Oils: **Ⓣ**cinnamon, **Ⓣ**oregano

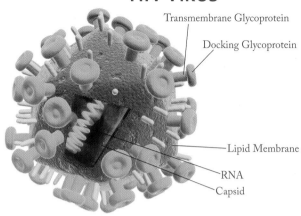

HIV VIRUS

Transmembrane Glycoprotein

Docking Glycoprotein

Lipid Membrane

RNA

Capsid

—EPSTEIN-BARR VIRUS:

Oils: **Ⓣ**On Guard

—HERPES SIMPLEX:

Oils: **Ⓣ**peppermint[6], **Ⓣ**clove[8], **Ⓣ**helichrysum[9], **Ⓣ**melaleuca[3], **Ⓣ**lavender, **Ⓣ**eucalyptus, **Ⓣ**cypress, **Ⓣ**lemon

—HIV: *SEE ALSO AIDS*

Oils: **ⓉⒶ**helichrysum, **Ⓣ**On Guard, **ⓉⒶ**lemon, **Ⓣ**Balance

—RESPIRATORY:

Oils: **Ⓐ**eucalyptus, **Ⓐ**On Guard

—SPINE:

Blend 1: 5 drops oregano and 5 drops thyme. Apply to bottoms of feet and along the spine.

Ⓣ: Dilute as recommended, and apply on location or to reflex points on the bottoms of the feet. Use hand wash as directed on packaging.

Ⓐ: Diffuse into the air. Inhale oil applied to a tissue or cotton wick.

Ⓘ: Take capsules as directed on package.

ANXIETY:

Anxiety is the body's way of preparing itself to deal with a threat or to deal with future stressful events. While this response is normal and happens as part of the body's natural response to stress, this response can also happen at inappropriate times or too frequently, as in the case of anxiety disorders.

---

1 Arzanol, extracted from helichrysum, inhibited HIV-1 replication in T cells and also inhibited the release of pro-inflammatory cytokines (chemical messengers) in monocytes (Appendino et al., 2007).

2 Helichrysum was found to have significant antiviral activity against the herpes virus at non-cytotoxic concentrations (Nostro et al., 2003).

3 Tea tree and eucalyptus oil demonstrated an ability to inhibit the *Herpes simplex* virus (Schnitzler et al., 2001).

4 Eugenol (found in clove oil) was found to be virucidal to *Herpes simplex* and to delay the development of herpes-induced keratitis (inflammation of the cornea) in mice (Benencia et al., 2000).

5 Melissa oil demonstrated inhibition of *Herpes simplex* type 1 and 2 viruses (Schnitzler et al., 2008).

6 Peppermint oil demonstrated a direct virucidal activity against herpes type 1 and 2 viruses (Schuhmacher et al., 2003).

7 Tea tree and eucalyptus oil demonstrated an ability to inhibit the *Herpes simplex* virus (Schnitzler et al., 2001).

8 Eugenol (found in clove oil) was found to be virucidal to *Herpes simplex* and to delay the development of herpes-induced keratitis (inflammation of the cornea) in mice (Benencia et al., 2000).

9 Helichrysum was found to have significant antiviral activity against the herpes virus at non-cytotoxic concentrations (Nostro et al., 2003).

Primary Recommendations • Secondary Recommendations • Other Recommendations / **Ⓐ**=Aromatic, **Ⓣ**=Topical, **Ⓘ**=Internal

134

Anxiety can include both physical and mental symptoms such as fear, nervousness, nausea, sweating, increased blood pressure and heart rate, feelings of apprehension or dread, difficulty concentrating, irritability, restlessness, panic attacks, and many others.

Oils: ⒶⓉlavender[10,11,12,13,14,15], Ⓐorange[15,16,17], Ⓐlemon[18,19], ⒶⓉSerenity, ⓉAromaTouch, ⒶElevation, ⓉBalance (on back of neck) and ⓉBreathe (on chest), ⒶⓉylang ylang, ⒶⓉmelissa[20], ⒶⓉfrankincense, ⒶⓉsandalwood, ⒶCitrus Bliss, ⒶⓉbergamot, ⒶⓉgeranium, ⓉⒶlime, ⒶⓉclary sage, ⒶⓉrose, ⒶⓉbasil, ⒶⓉcypress, ⒶⓉmarjoram

Other Products: ⓉTherapeutic Bath Salts. Add 1–2 drops of essential oil to 1/4 cup bath salts, and dissolve in warm bathwater for an anxiety-relieving bath.

Ⓐ: Diffuse into the air. Inhale directly from bottle. Apply oil to hands, tissue, or cotton wick, and inhale.

Ⓣ: Place 1–2 drops in 1 Tbs. fractionated coconut oil and massage into the skin. Dilute as recommended, and apply to back of neck, temples, or reflex points on feet. Add 1–2 drops to 1/4 cup bath salts, and dissolve in warm bathwater.

APATHY: *SEE DEPRESSION*

---

10 Exposure to lavender odor was found to decrease anxiety in gerbils in the elevated plus maze, with a further decrease in anxiety in females after prolonged (2 week) exposure (Bradley et al., 2007).

11 Subjects receiving a lozenge containing lavender oil, hops extract, lemon balm, and oat were found to have increases in alpha 1, alpha 2, and beta 1 electrical output (Dimpfel et al., 2004).

12 In patients admitted to an intensive care unit, those receiving lavender aromatherapy reported a greater improvement in mood and perceived levels of anxiety compared to those receiving massage or a period of rest (Dunn et al., 1995).

13 Female patients being treated for chronic hemodialysis demonstrated less anxiety when exposed to lavender aroma compared to control (Itai et al., 2000).

14 Lavender oil was found to demonstrate anticonflict effects in mice similar to the anxiolytic (antianxiety) drug diazepam (Umezu, 2000).

15 Patients waiting for dental treatment were found to be less anxious and to have a better mood when exposed to the odor of lavender or orange oil as compared to control (Lehrner et al., 2005).

16 Bitter orange peel oil taken orally by mice was found to reduce anxiety, increase sleeping time, and increase the time before a chemically-induced seizure started (Carvalho-Freitas et al., 2002).

17 Female patients waiting for dental treatment were found to be less anxious, more positive, and more calm when exposed to orange oil odor than patients who were not exposed to the orange oil odor (Lehrner et al., 2000).

18 Rats exposed long-term to lemon essential oil were found to demonstrate different anxiety and pain threshold levels than untreated rats. It was also found that exposure to lemon oil induced chemical changes in the neuronal circuits involved in anxiety and pain (Ceccarelli et al., 2004).

19 Lemon oil was found to have an antistress effect on mice involved in several behavioral tasks (Komiya et al., 2006).

20 Results of a clinical trial indicate that a combination of melissa and valerian oils may have anxiety-reducing properties at some doses (Kennedy et al., 2006).

APHRODISIAC:

An Aphrodisiac is a substance used to stimulate feelings of love or sexual desire. Many books of aromatherapy tout the aphrodisiac qualities of a number of oils. Perhaps an aphrodisiac to one individual may not be to another. The most important factor is to find an oil that brings balance to the mind and body. A balanced individual is more likely to extend love.

Oils: ⒶⓉsandalwood, ⒶⓉylang ylang, ⒶⓉrose, ⒶⓉjasmine, ⒶⓉWhisper, Ⓐcinnamon, ⒶⓉginger, ⒶⓉclary sage,

Ⓐ: Diffuse into the air. Dissolve 2–3 drops in 2 tsp. pure grain or perfumers alcohol, combine with distilled water in a 1 or 2 oz. spray bottle, and spray into the air or on clothes or bed linens.

Ⓣ: Dilute as recommended and wear on temples, neck, or wrists as a perfume or cologne. Combine 3–5 drops of your desired essential oil with 1 Tbs. fractionated coconut oil to use as a massage oil. Combine 1–2 drops with 1/4 cup Therapeutic Bath Salts, and dissolve in warm bathwater for a romantic bath.

APPETITE:

Appetite is the body's desire to eat, expressed as hunger. Appetite is important in regulating food intake to provide the body with the necessary nutrients to sustain life and maintain energy.

—LOSS OF APPETITE:

Oils: Ⓐlavender[21], Ⓐginger, Ⓐlemon, Ⓐorange

—SUPPRESSANT:

Oils: ⒾⒶSlim & Sassy, Ⓐgrapefruit[22]

Other Products: ⒾSlim & Sassy Trim Shake

Ⓘ: Add 8 drops of Slim & Sassy to 16 oz. of water, and drink throughout the day between meals. Drink Trim Shake 1–2 times a day as a meal alternative.

Ⓐ: Diffuse into the air. Inhale oil applied to a tissue or cotton wick.

---

21 Lavender oil was found to inhibit sympathetic nerve activity while exciting parasympathetic nerve activity and increasing appetite and weight gain in rats. Linalool, a component of lavender, was shown to have similar effects (Shen et al., 2005).

22 The scent of grapefruit oil and its component, limonene, was found to affect the autonomic nerves by exciting sympathetic nerve activity and inhibiting parasympathetic nerve activity. It was also found to reduce appetite and body weight in rats exposed to the oil for 15 minutes three times per week (Shen et al., 2005).

Primary Recommendations • Secondary Recommendations • Other Recommendations / Ⓐ=Aromatic, Ⓣ=Topical, Ⓘ=Internal

ARTERIES: *SEE ALSO BLOOD, CARDIOVASCULAR SYSTEM*

Arteries are the vessels of the circulatory system that function to carry blood away from the heart.

—ARTERIAL VASODILATOR:

A vasodilator is a substance that causes a blood vessel to dilate (increase in diameter) through the relaxation of the endothelial cells lining the vessel walls. This gives the blood more room to flow and lowers blood pressure.

Oils: ❶eucalyptus[1], ❶rosemary[1], ❶marjoram

—ATHEROSCLEROSIS:

Atherosclerosis is a hardening of the arteries due to a build-up of plaques along the arterial wall.

Oils: ❶🅐lemon[2],❶🅐lavender[3], ❶rosemary, ❶ginger, ❶thyme, ❶wintergreen

❶: Dilute as recommended, and apply to carotid arteries in neck, over heart, and reflex points on the feet.

🅐: Diffuse into the air. Inhale directly from bottle. Apply oil to hands, tissue, or cotton wick, and inhale.

ARTHRITIS: *SEE ALSO INFLAMMATION, JOINTS*

Arthritis is the painful swelling, inflammation, and stiffness of the joints.

Oils: ❶🅐frankincense[4,5], ❶🅐rosemary[6], ❶🅐marjoram[6], ❶Deep Blue, ❶🅐eucalyptus[6], ❶🅐white fir, ❶🅐peppermint[6], ❶🅐lavender[6], ❶🅐cypress, ❶🅐ginger, ❶🅐Roman chamomile, ❶🅐helichrysum, ❶🅐wintergreen, ❶🅐basil, ❶🅐clove

Blend 1: Combine equal parts wintergreen and Deep Blue. Apply on location.

Other Products: ❶Alpha CRS+[7]

—ARTHRITIC PAIN:

Oils: ❶Deep Blue, ❶wintergreen, ❶ginger

—OSTEOARTHRITIS:

Osteoarthritis is a degenerative arthritis where the cartilage that provides lubrication between the bones in a joint begins to break down, becoming rough and uneven. This causes the bones in the joint to wear and create rough deposits that can become extremely painful.

Oils: ❶rosemary, ❶marjoram, ❶Deep Blue, ❶geranium, ❶wintergreen, ❶thyme, ❶basil, ❶lavender, ❶eucalyptus

Other Products: ❶Alpha CRS+

—RHEUMATOID ARTHRITIS:

Rheumatoid arthritis is arthritis caused by inflammation within the joint, causing pain and possibly causing the joint to degenerate.

Oils: ❶marjoram, ❶lavender, ❶cypress, ❶Deep Blue, ❶geranium, ❶bergamot, ❶clove[8], ❶ginger[8], ❶lemon, ❶rosemary, ❶wintergreen, ❶cinnamon, ❶eucalyptus, ❶oregano (chronic), ❶peppermint, ❶🅐Roman chamomile, ❶thyme

Other Products: ❶Alpha CRS+[7]

❶: Dilute as recommended, and apply on location. Apply as a warm compress over affected area. Dilute 1–2 drops in 1 Tbs. fractionated coconut oil, and use as a massage oil. Add 1–2 drops to 1/4 cup Therapeutic Bath Salts, and dissolve in warm bathwater for a soaking bath.

🅐: Diffuse into the air.

ASTHMA:

Asthma is a disease that causes the lung's airways to narrow, making it difficult to breathe. Episodes (or attacks) of asthma can be triggered by any number of things, including smoke, pollution, dust mites, and other allergens. Asthma causes reoccurring periods of tightness in the chest, coughing, shortness of breath, and wheezing.

---

1 Treatment of rats with 1,8-cineole (or eucalyptol found in eucalyptus and rosemary) demonstrated an ability to lower mean aortic pressure (blood pressure), without decreasing heart rate, through vascular wall relaxation (Lahlou et al., 2002).

2 Lemon oil and one of its components, gamma-terpinene, were found to inhibit oxidation of low-density lipoprotein (LDL). Oxidation of LDL has been found to increase the risk of atherosclerosis and cardiac disease (Grassmann et al., 2001).

3 Inhalation of lavender and monarda oils was found to reduce cholesterol content and atherosclerotic plaques in the aorta (Nikolaevskiĭ et al., 1990).

4 Boswellic acid, from frankincense, was found in vitro to prevent expression and activity of several proteins involved in inflammatory response. In vivo, Boswellic acid was found to protect against experimental arthritis (Roy et al., 2006).

5 An acetone extract of frankincense was found to decrease arthritic scores, reduce paw edema (swelling) and suppress pro-inflammatory cytokines (cellular messengers) (Fan et al., 2005).

6 In patients suffering from arthritis, it was found that a blend of lavender, marjoram, eucalyptus, rosemary, and peppermint blended with carrier oils reduced perceived pain and depression compared to control (Kim et al., 2005).

7 Epigallocatechin-3-gallate was found to ameliorate experimental rheumatoid arthritis in the short term (Morinobu et al., 2008).

8 Eugenol and ginger oil taken orally were found to reduce paw and joint swelling in rats with induced severe arthritis (Sharma et al., 1994).

Oils: [A][T]eucalyptus[9,10], [A][T]frankincense, [A][T]peppermint[11], [A][T]thyme, [A][T]Breathe, [A][T]oregano, [A][T]lemon, [A][T]myrrh, [A][T]lavender, [A][T]geranium, [A][T]cypress, [A][T]clary sage, [A][T]ylang ylang, [A][T]rose, [A][T]helichrysum, [A][T]marjoram, [A][T]rosemary

—Attack

Oils: [A]Breathe, [A]eucalyptus, [A]frankincense (calming), [A]lavender, [A]marjoram

[A]: Diffuse into the air. Inhale directly from bottle. Apply oil to hands, tissue, or cotton wick, and inhale.

[T]: Dilute as recommended and apply to the chest, throat, or back. Add 2–3 drops to 1 Tbs. fractionated coconut oil, and massage onto chest, shoulders, and back.

Athlete's Foot: *see Antifungal:Athlete's Foot*

Attention Deficit Disorder: *see ADD/ADHD*

Autism:

Autism is a developmental disorder that impairs the normal development of communication, sociality, and human interaction.

—Reduce Anxiety/Fear: *see also Anxiety*

Oils: [T]geranium, [T]clary sage, [T]bergamot

—Stimulate the Senses: *see also Stimulating*

Oils: [T]peppermint, [T]basil, [T]lemon, [T]rosemary

[T]: Add 1–2 drops to 1 Tbs. fractionated coconut oil, and massage into skin.

Comments: Only apply these oils when the autistic child is willing and open to receive them. If the experience is forced or negative, the autistic child will associate these oils with a negative experience when used again.

Auto-Immune Diseases: *see Grave's Disease, Hashimoto's Disease, Lupus*

---

9 Extracts from eucalyptus and thyme were found to have high nitrous oxide (NO) scavenging abilities and inhibited NO production in macrophage cells. This could possibly explain their role in aiding respiratory inflammatory diseases (Vigo et al., 2004).

10 Therapy with 1,8 cineole (eucalyptol, found in eucalyptus) in both healthy and bronchitis-afflicted humans was shown to reduce production of LTB4 and PGE2, both metabolites of arachidonic acid (a known chemical messenger involved in inflammation), in white blood cells (Juergens et al., 1998).

11 L-menthol (found in peppermint) was found to inhibit production of inflammation mediators in human monocytes (a type of white blood cell involved in the immune response) (Juergens et al., 1998).

Awake: *see Alertness, Jet Lag*

Babies: *see Children and Infants*

Back:

Oils: [T]Deep Blue, [T]Balance, [T]cypress, [T]eucalyptus, [T]geranium, [T]lavender, [T]Roman chamomile, [T]oregano, [T]peppermint, [T]rosemary, [T]thyme

—Calcified Spine

Calcification occurs when calcium builds up in tissue and causes the tissue to harden. As people age, calcification can cause the ligaments of the spine to thicken and harden, making the spinal canal narrow and create pressure on the spinal nerve.

Oils: [T]Deep Blue, [T]geranium, [T]rosemary

—Deteriorating Spine:

Deteriorating disc disease occurs as people age and their spinal discs begin to deteriorate. As deterioration progresses, movement becomes restricted and pain in the neck and back increases. Although most commonly associated with aging, disc deterioration can be caused by back injuries as well.

Oils: [T]Deep Blue

—Herniated Discs:

In between the bones of the spine are cushioning discs that keep the spine flexible and act as shock absorbers. A herniated disc is caused when one of the discs of the spine is damaged and either bulges or breaks open. When the herniated disc presses on a nerve, it causes pain in the buttock, thigh, and calf. Herniated discs can be caused by spinal injuries or by the wear and tear that come with age as the discs begin to dry out

Oils: [T]Deep Blue, [T]Balance (3 drops on location), [T]peppermint, [T]cypress (strengthens blood capillary walls, improves circulation, anti-inflammatory)

—Lumbago/Lower Back Pain:

Oils: [T]sandalwood, [T]Deep Blue

—Muscular Fatigue:

Oils: [T]clary sage, [T]marjoram, [T]lavender, [T]rosemary

Primary Recommendations • Secondary Recommendations • Other Recommendations / [A]=Aromatic, [T]=Topical, [I]=Internal

—PAIN:

Oils: ⊕Balance, ⊕Deep Blue

Blend 1: Combine 5–10 drops each of lavender, eucalyptus, and ginger, and apply 2–3 drops on location or as a warm compress.

Blend 2: Combine 5–10 drops each of peppermint, rosemary, and basil, and apply 2–3 drops on location or as a warm compress.

—STIFFNESS:

Oils: ⊕marjoram, ⊕Balance

—VIRUSES ALONG SPINE:

Oils: ⊕oregano, ⊕eucalyptus

🅣: Dilute as recommended, and apply along the spine, on affected muscles, or on reflex points on the feet. Dilute 1–3 drops in 1 Tbs. fractionated coconut oil, and massage into muscles on the back or along the spine. Apply as a warm compress over affected area.

🅘: Take capsules as directed.

SPINE

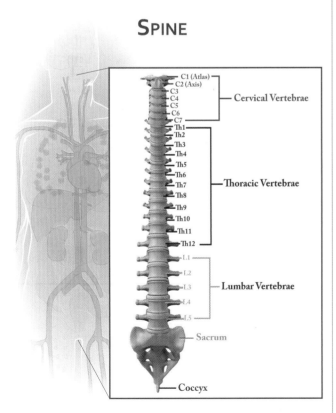

- C1 (Atlas)
- C2 (Axis)
- C3
- C4
- C5
- C6
- C7 — Cervical Vertebrae
- Th1
- Th2
- Th3
- Th4
- Th5
- Th6
- Th7 — Thoracic Vertebrae
- Th8
- Th9
- Th10
- Th11
- Th12
- L1
- L2
- L3 — Lumbar Vertebrae
- L4
- L5
- Sacrum
- Coccyx

BACTERIA: *SEE ANTIBACTERIAL*

BALANCE:

Oils: ⊕🅐Balance, ⊕🅐frankincense, ⊕🅐vetiver, ⊕🅐ylang ylang

—ELECTRICAL ENERGIES:

Oils: ⊕Balance, ⊕frankincense

Application Methods:

🅣: Dilute as recommended, and apply on location. Apply 3–6 drops Balance to the bottom of each foot, and, if desired, apply some to the neck and shoulders. Hold the palm of each hand to the bottom of each corresponding foot (left to left and right to right) for 5–15 minutes to help balance electrical energies.

🅐: Diffuse into the air.

BALDNESS: *SEE HAIR:LOSS*

BATH:

Using essential oils in the bath can be a wonderful way to receive and possibly enhance the benefits of the oils.

Oils: ⊕lavender, ⊕geranium, ⊕Roman chamomile, ⊕ylang ylang

Some common ways to use essential oils in the bath include the following:

Direct: Add 1–3 drops of oil directly to bathwater while the bath is filling. Oils will be drawn to your skin quickly from the top of the water, so use non-irritating oils such as lavender, ylang ylang, etc., or dilute the oil with fractionated coconut oil to safe topical application dilutions.

Bath Gel: To disperse the oil throughout the bathwater, add 5–10 drops of your favorite essential oil to one-half ounce of unscented bath and shower gel.

Bath Salts: For a relaxing mineral bath, add 1–5 drops of your desired essential oil to 1/4–1/2 cup of Therapeutic Bath Salts or Epsom salts; mix well. Dissolve salts in warm bathwater while the tub is filling.

BED WETTING: *SEE BLADDER:BED WETTING*

BELL'S PALSY: *SEE NERVOUS SYSTEM:BELL'S PALSY*

BIRTHING: *SEE PREGNANCY/MOTHERHOOD*

BITES/STINGS: *SEE ALSO INSECTS/BUGS:REPELLENT*

Oils: ⊕thyme, ⊕basil, ⊕lemon, ⊕cinnamon, ⊕lavender

—**ALLERGIC:**

Oils: ⊕Purify

—**BEES AND HORNETS**

Oils: ⊕Roman chamomile, ⊕basil, ⊕Purify, ⊕lavender, ⊕lemongrass, ⊕lemon, ⊕peppermint, ⊕thyme

Recipe 1: Remove the stinger, and apply a cold compress of Roman chamomile to the area for several hours or for as long as possible.

—**GNATS AND MIDGES:**

Oils: ⊕lavender

Recipe 2: Mix 3 drops thyme in 1 tsp. cider vinegar or lemon juice. Apply to bites to stop irritation.

—**MOSQUITOES:**

Oils: ⊕lavender, ⊕helichrysum

—**SNAKES:**

Oils: ⊕basil

—**SPIDERS:**

Oils: ⊕basil, ⊕Purify (with melaleuca), ⊕lavender, ⊕lemongrass, ⊕lemon, ⊕peppermint, ⊕thyme

Recipe 3: Mix 3 drops lavender and 2 drops Roman chamomile with 1 tsp. alcohol. Apply to area three times per day.

—**TICKS:**

Oils: After getting the tick out, apply 1 drop lavender every 5 minutes for 30 minutes:

Removing Ticks:

Do not apply mineral oil, Vaseline, or anything else to remove the tick, as this may cause it to inject the spirochetes into the wound.

Be sure to remove the entire tick. Get as close to the mouth as possible, and firmly tug on the tick until it releases its grip. Don't twist. If available, use a magnifying glass to make sure that you have removed the entire tick.

Save the tick in a jar, and label it with the date, where you were bitten on your body, and the location or address where you were bitten for proper identification by your doctor, especially if you develop any symptoms.

Do not handle the tick.

Wash hands immediately.

Check the site of the bite occasionally to see if any rash develops. If it does, seek medical advice promptly.

—**WASPS:**

Recipe 4: Combine 1 drop basil, 2 drops Roman chamomile, 2 drops lavender, and 1 tsp. apple cider vinegar. Apply to area three times a day.

⊕: Dilute as recommended, and apply on location.

BLADDER: *SEE ALSO URINARY TRACT*

The Urinary Bladder is a hollow organ that collects urine before it is disposed by urination. The bladder sits on the pelvic floor.

—**BED WETTING AND INCONTINENCE:**

Oils: ⊕cypress (rub on abdomen at bedtime).

—**CYSTITIS/INFECTION:**

Oils: ⊕lemongrass, ⊕⊕On Guard, ⊕sandalwood, ⊕thyme, ⊕basil, ⊕cinnamon, ⊕clove, ⊕eucalyptus, ⊕frankincense, ⊕lavender, ⊕bergamot, ⊕fennel, ⊕marjoram, ⊕oregano

⊕: Dilute as recommended, and apply on abdomen and on reflex points on the feet. Add 1–2 drops to warm bathwater; bathe for 10–15 minutes.

❶: Add 1 drop to 8 oz. juice or water; drink three times a day.

BLEEDING: *SEE BLOOD:BLEEDING*

BLISTER (ON LIPS FROM SUN):

Oils: ⊕lavender

⊕: Apply oil to blister often to help take the fever out and return the lip to normal.

BLOATING: *SEE DIGESTIVE SYSTEM:BLOATING*

Primary Recommendations • Secondary Recommendations • Other Recommendations / ⓐ=Aromatic, ⊕=Topical, ❶=Internal

BLOOD:

Blood is the fluid inside the body that transports oxygen and nutrients to the cells and carries waste away from the cells. It also transports cells involved in the immune and inflammatory response, hormones and other chemical messengers that regulate the body's functions, and platelets that help facilitate the blood clotting necessary to repair damaged blood vessels. Blood is primarily composed of plasma (water with dissolved nutrients, minerals, and carbon dioxide) that carries red blood cells (the most numerous type of cells in blood, responsible for transporting oxygen), white blood cells (cells involved in the immune system and immune response), and platelet cells. Blood is circulated in the body by the pumping action of the heart propelling blood through various blood vessels. Proper and healthy circulation and function of blood throughout the body is critical for health and even for the sustaining of life.

—BLOOD PRESSURE

Oils: **O**lemon (will regulate pressure—either raise or lower as necessary), **OAO**lime

–HIGH (HYPERTENSION)

Oils: **AOT**ylang ylang[1,2], **TO**marjoram[3], **TOA**eucalyptus[3], **TOA**lavender, **TOA**clove, **TOA**clary sage, **OA**lemon, **TOA**wintergreen **Note:** Avoid rosemary, thyme, and possibly peppermint.

Bath 1: Place 3 drops ylang ylang and 3 drops marjoram in bathwater, and bathe in the evening twice a week.

Blend 1: Combine 10 drops ylang ylang, 5 drops marjoram, and 5 drops cypress in 1 oz. fractionated coconut oil. Rub over heart and reflex points on left foot and hand.

Blend 2: Combine 5 drops geranium, 8 drops lemongrass, and 3 drops lavender in 1 oz. fractionated coconut oil. Rub over heart and reflex points on left foot and hand.

---

1   Subjects who had ylang ylang oil applied to their skin had decreased blood pressure, increased skin temperature, and reported feeling more calm and relaxed than did subjects in a control group (Hongratanaworakit et al., 2006).

2   Inhaled ylang ylang oil was found to decrease blood pressure and pulse rate and to enhance attentiveness and alertness in volunteers compared to an odorless control (Hongratanaworakit et al., 2004).

3   Treatment of rats with 1,8-cineole (or eucalyptol, found in eucalyptus, rosemary, and marjoram) demonstrated an ability to lower mean aortic pressure (blood pressure), without decreasing heart rate, through vascular wall relaxation (Lahlou et al., 2002).

–LOW

Oils: **AT**rosemary

A: Diffuse into the air. Inhale the aroma directly.

I: Place 1–3 drops of oil in an empty capsule; ingest up to 3 times per day.

T: Dilute as recommended, and apply on location, on reflex points on feet and hands, and over heart.

—BLEEDING (STOPS):

Oils: **T**helichrysum, **T**geranium, **T**rose

T: Dilute as recommended, and apply on location.

—BROKEN BLOOD VESSELS

Oils: **T**helichrysum, **T**grapefruit

T: Dilute as recommended, and apply on location, on reflex points on feet and hands, and over heart.

—CHOLESTEROL:

Cholesterol is a soft, waxy substance found in the bloodstream and in all of the body's cells. The body requires some cholesterol to function properly, but high levels of cholesterol narrow and block the arteries and increase the risk of heart disease.

Oils: **T**helichrysum

T: Dilute as recommended, and apply on reflex points on feet and hands, and over heart.

—CIRCULATION: *SEE CARDIOVASCULAR SYSTEM*

—CLEANSING

Oils: **T**helichrysum, **T**geranium, **T**Roman chamomile

T: Dilute as recommended, and apply on reflex points on feet and hands, and over heart.

—CLOTS:

Blood Clots occur as a natural bodily defense to repair damaged blood vessels and to keep the body from losing excessive amounts of blood. However, clotting can become dangerous if an internal blood clot breaks lose in the circulatory system and blocks the flow of blood to vital organs.

Primary Recommendations • Secondary Recommendations • Other Recommendations / **A**=Aromatic, **T**=Topical, **I**=Internal

140

Oils: ⊕⊕clove[4], ⊕⊕⊕fennel[5], ⊕⊕thyme, ⊕grape-fruit

Ⓘ: Place 1–3 drops of oil in an empty capsule; ingest up to 3 times per day.

Ⓣ: Dilute as recommended, and apply on location, on reflex points on feet and hands, and over heart.

Ⓐ: Diffuse into the air. Inhale the aroma directly.

—HEMORRHAGING:

Hemorrhaging is excessive or uncontrollable blood loss.

Oils: ⊕helichrysum, ⊕ylang ylang, ⊕rose

Ⓣ: Dilute as recommended, and apply on location.

—LOW BLOOD SUGAR:

The term "blood sugar" refers to the amount of glucose in the bloodstream. When the blood glucose drops below its normal level, this is called "low blood sugar" or "hypoglycemia." Since glucose is such an important source of energy for the body, low blood sugar can result in light-headedness, hunger, shakiness, weakness, confusion, nervousness, difficulty speaking, and anxiety.

Oils: ⊕On Guard, ⊕cinnamon, ⊕clove, ⊕thyme

Ⓣ: Dilute as recommended, and apply on location, on reflex points on feet and hands, and over heart.

—STIMULATES BLOOD CELL PRODUCTION

Oils: ⊕⊕peppermint[6], ⊕⊕lemon

Ⓘ: Place 1–3 drops of oil in an empty capsule; ingest up to 3 times per day.

Ⓣ: Dilute as recommended, and apply on location, on reflex points on feet and hands, and over heart.

—VESSELS: *SEE ARTERIES, CAPILLARIES, VEINS*

BODY SYSTEMS: *SEE CARDIOVASCULAR SYSTEM, DIGESTIVE SYSTEM, ENDOCRINE SYSTEM, LYMPHATIC SYSTEM, MUSCLES/CONNECTIVE TISSUE, BONES, NERVOUS SYSTEM, RESPIRATORY SYSTEM, SKIN*

BOILS: *SEE ALSO ANTIBACTERIAL*

A boil is a skin infection that forms in a hair follicle or oil gland. The boil starts as a red, tender lump that after a few days forms a white or yellow point in the center as it fills with pus. Boils commonly occur on the face, neck, armpits, buttock, and shoulders and can be very painful.

Oils: ⊕melaleuca[7], ⊕lavender, ⊕Purify, ⊕lemongrass, ⊕lemon, ⊕frankincense, ⊕clary sage

Ⓣ: Dilute as recommended, and apply on location.

BONES:

Oils: ⊕wintergreen, ⊕white fir, ⊕cypress, ⊕lavender, ⊕lemongrass, ⊕marjoram, ⊕peppermint, ⊕sandalwood

Other Products: ⊕Microplex VMz contains nutrients essential for bone development, such as calcium, magnesium, zinc, and vitamin D.

—BONE SPURS:

A bone spur (osteophyte) is a bony projection formed on a normal bone. Bone spurs form as the body tries to repair itself by building extra bone in response to continued pressure, stress, or rubbing. Bone spurs can cause pain if they rub against soft tissues or other bones.

Oils: ⊕wintergreen, ⊕cypress, ⊕marjoram

—BROKEN:

Oils: ⊕Deep Blue (for pain), ⊕⊕frankincense

Recipe 1: Apply wintergreen and cypress oils at night before bed. Apply helichrysum, oregano, and Balance in the morning.

Blend 1: Combine equal parts lemongrass, clove, eucalyptus, and melaleuca. Apply on location.

---

4 Clove oil demonstrated an ability to prevent the aggregation of platelets that can lead to blood clots and thrombosis both in vivo and in vitro (Saeed et al., 1994).

5 Both fennel oil and its constituent, anethole, were found to significantly reduce thrombosis (blood clots) in mice. They were also found to be free from the prohemorrhagic (increased bleeding) side effect that aspirin (acetylsalicylic acid) has (Tognolini et al., 2007).

6 In mice exposed to whole-body gamma irradiation, only 17% of mice who had been fed peppermint oil died, while 100% of mice who did not receive peppermint oil died. It was also found that the mice pre-fed peppermint oil were able to return blood cell levels to normal after 30 days, while the control mice were not able to (and consequently died), suggesting a protective or stimulating effect of the oil on blood stem cells (Samarth et al., 2004).

7 In a human trial, most patients receiving treatment with *Melaleuca alternifolia* oil placed topically on boils experienced healing or reduction of symptoms; while of those receiving no treatment (control), half required surgical intervention, and all still demonstrated signs of the infection (Feinblatt, 1960).

Primary Recommendations • Secondary Recommendations • Other Recommendations / Ⓐ=Aromatic, Ⓣ=Topical, Ⓘ=Internal

SKELETAL SYSTEM

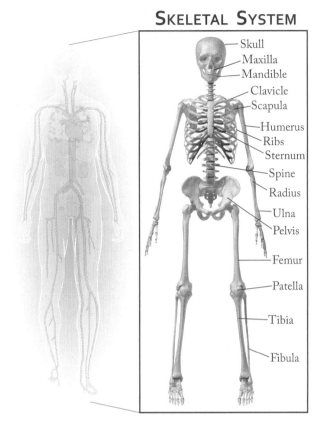

Skull
Maxilla
Mandible
Clavicle
Scapula
Humerus
Ribs
Sternum
Spine
Radius
Ulna
Pelvis
Femur
Patella
Tibia
Fibula

Other Products: ❶Microplex VMz contains essential bone nutrients calcium, magnesium, zinc, and vitamin D.

—BRUISED

Oils: ❶Deep Blue, ❶helichrysum

—CARTILAGE:

Cartilage is a type of connective tissue in the body that provides structure and support for other tissues without being hard and rigid like bone. Unlike other connective tissues, cartilage does not have blood vessels. Cartilage is found in many areas of the body, including the joints, ears, nose, bronchial tubes, and intervertebral discs.

Oils: ❶sandalwood (helps regenerate), ❶white fir (inflammation)

—DEVELOPMENT:

Other Products: ❶Microplex VMz contains essential bone nutrients necessary for development, such as calcium, magnesium, zinc, and vitamin D.

—OSTEOMYELITIS: *SEE ALSO ANTIBACTERIAL, ANTIFUNGAL*

Osteomyelitis is a bone infection that is usually caused by bacteria. The infection often starts in another area of the body and then spreads to the bone. Symptoms include fever, pain, swelling, nausea, drainage of pus, and uneasiness. Diabetes, hemodialysis, recent trauma, and IV drug abuse are risk factors for osteomyelitis.

Recipe 1: Apply equal parts lemongrass, clove, eucalyptus, and melaleuca, either blended together or applied individually on location.

—OSTEOPOROSIS:

Osteoporosis is a disease characterized by a loss of bone density, making the bones extremely fragile and susceptible to fractures and breaking. Osteoporosis is significantly more common in women then in men, especially after menopause; but the disease does occur in both genders.

Oils: ❶clove, ❶geranium, ❶peppermint, ❶wintergreen, ❶white fir, ❶Deep Blue, ❶thyme, ❶rosemary, ❶lemon, ❶cypress

Other Products: ❶Women's Bone Nutrient Lifetime Complex, ❶Women's Phytoestrogen Lifetime Complex

—PAIN:

Oils: ❶Deep Blue, ❶wintergreen, ❶white fir

—ROTATOR CUFF: *SEE JOINTS:ROTATOR CUFF*

❶: Dilute as recommended, and apply on location or on reflex points on feet.

❶: Take capsules as directed. Place 1–2 drops of oil in an empty capsule; swallow.

BOWEL: *SEE DIGESTIVE SYSTEM*

BRAIN:

The brain is the central part of the nervous system. It is responsible for processing sensory stimuli and for directing appropriate behavioral responses to each stimulus, or set of stimuli. The brain also stores memories and is the center of thought.

Oils: (A)(T)lavender[1,2], (A)(T)lemon[3], (A)(T)lemongrass, (A)(T)clary sage, (A)(T)cypress, (A)(T)geranium

Other Products: (O)xEO Mega for omega-3 fatty acids essential for proper brain function, (O)Microplex VMz for vitamins and minerals critical for brain health.

(A): Diffuse into the air. Inhale directly from bottle. Apply oil to hands, tissue, or cotton wick, and inhale.

(T): Dilute as recommended, and rub onto the brain stem area, back of neck, temples, behind ears down to jaw, or on reflex points on the feet. Apply as a cold compress.

(I): Take capsules as directed on package. Place 1–2 drops of oil in an empty capsule; swallow capsule.

—Activates Right Brain

Oils: (A)(T)geranium, (A)(T)grapefruit, (A)(T)helichrysum, (A)(T)wintergreen, (A)(T)Roman chamomile

(A): Diffuse into the air. Inhale directly from bottle. Apply oil to hands, tissue, or cotton wick, and inhale.

(T): Dilute as recommended, and rub onto the brain stem area, or on reflex points on the feet.

—Aging:

Oils: (O)(T)thyme[4], (A)(T)frankincense

(I): Place 1–2 drops of oil in an empty capsule; swallow capsule.

(T): Dilute as recommended, and rub onto the brain stem area, back of neck, temples, behind ears down to jaw, or on reflex points on the feet.

—Broken Blood Vessels: *see Blood:Broken Blood Vessels*

—Concentration: *see Concentration*

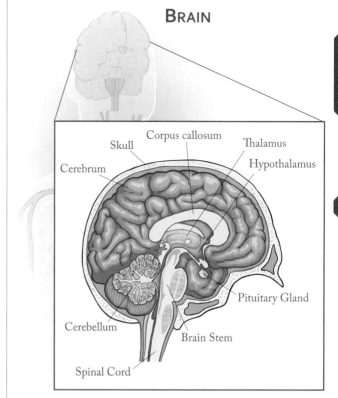

Brain

Corpus callosum
Skull
Thalamus
Cerebrum
Hypothalamus
Pituitary Gland
Cerebellum
Brain Stem
Spinal Cord

—Concussion:

A Concussion is a type of brain injury that causes temporary or permanent impairment in the brain's functioning. Concussions most commonly occur as a result of a blow to the head. Concussion symptoms include headaches, dizziness, blurred vision, vomiting, disorientation, difficulty focusing attention, ringing in the ears, selective memory loss, etc.

Oils: (A)(T)frankincense[5], (T)cypress

(A): Diffuse into the air. Inhale directly from bottle. Apply oil to hands, tissue, or cotton wick, and inhale.

(T): Dilute as recommended, and rub onto the brain stem area, back of neck, temples, behind ears down to jaw, or on reflex points on the feet. Apply as a cold compress.

1 Subjects who smelled a cleansing gel with lavender aroma were more relaxed and able to complete math computations faster (Fielt et al., 2005).

2 Subjects exposed to 3 minutes of lavender aroma were more relaxed and were able to perform math computations faster and more accurately. Subjects exposed to rosemary aroma were more alert and completed math computations faster (but not more accurately) (Diego et al., 1998).

3 Several constituents of lemon oil and their metabolites (chemicals made from these constituents by the body) were found to increase the release of monoamines (various chemicals responsible for neurotransmission and neuromodulation) in rat brain tissue, indicating a possible effect on brain nerve cell behavior (Fukumoto et al., 2006).

4 Aging rats fed thyme oil or the constituent thymol were found to have higher levels of the antioxidant enzymes superoxide dismutase and glutathione peroxidase in the brain than did aging rats not fed the oil or constituent (Youdim et al., 2000).

5 Incensole acetate, isolated from frankincense resin, was found to demonstrate an anti-inflammatory and neuroprotective effect in mice with a closed head injury (Moussaieff et al., 2008).

—INJURY

Oils: Ⓐ🅣frankincense[5], Ⓐ🅣bergamot[1], Ⓐ🅣peppermint[2], Ⓐ🅣lemon[3], Ⓐ🅣Balance, Ⓐ🅣lemongrass

Ⓐ: Diffuse into the air. Inhale the aroma of the oil directly.

🅣: Dilute as recommended, and rub onto the brain stem area, back of neck, temples, behind ears down to jaw, or on reflex points on the feet.

—INTEGRATION

Oils: Ⓐ🅣Balance, Ⓐ🅣helichrysum, Ⓐ🅣geranium, Ⓐ🅣clary sage, Ⓐ🅣cypress, Ⓐ🅣lemongrass

Ⓐ: Diffuse into the air. Inhale the aroma of the oil directly.

🅣: Dilute as recommended, and rub onto the brain stem area, back of neck, temples, behind ears down to jaw, or on reflex points on the feet.

—LEARNING AND MEMORY: *SEE MEMORY*

—MENTAL FATIGUE:

Oils: Ⓐ🅣frankincense

—MYELIN SHEATH:

The myelin sheath is an insulating layer of protein and fatty substances that forms around nerves (including those in the brain), increasing the speed of nerve impulses. Damage to the myelin sheath interrupts these nerve impulses and can cause diseases such as multiple sclerosis, peripheral neuropathy, central pontine myelinolysis, and other neurological diseases.

Oils: Ⓐ🅣peppermint, Ⓐ🅣frankincense, Ⓐ🅣lemongrass, Ⓐ🅣Balance, ⓉⒶgeranium

Other Products: xEO Mega, which contains the omega-3 fatty acid DHA that helps support the myelin sheath

Ⓐ: Diffuse into the air. Inhale directly from bottle. Apply oil to hands, tissue, or cotton wick, and inhale.

🅣: Apply as a cool compress over the brain stem area, back of neck, temples, behind ears down to jaw, or on reflex points on the feet.

—OXYGENATE:

Oils: Ⓐeucalyptus[4], Ⓐrosemary[4], Ⓐ🅣helichrysum, Ⓐ🅣sandalwood, Ⓐmarjoram[4]

Recipe 1: Place three drops each of helichrysum and sandalwood on the back of the neck, on the temples, and behind the ears down to the jaw once or twice a day.

Ⓐ: Diffuse into the air. Inhale the aroma directly.

🅣: Dilute as recommended, and rub onto the brain stem area, back of neck, temples, behind ears down to jaw, or on reflex points on the feet.

—STROKE: *SEE STROKE*

—TUMOR: *SEE CANCER:BRAIN*

BREAST: *SEE ALSO CANCER:BREAST. FOR ISSUES RELATED TO LACTATION AND MOTHERHOOD, SEE PREGNANCY/ MOTHERHOOD*

Oils: 🅣clary sage, 🅣geranium, 🅣lemongrass, 🅣fennel, 🅣cypress, 🅣vetiver

—ENLARGE AND FIRM:

Oils: 🅣clary sage

🅣: Dilute as recommended, and apply on location or on reflex points on feet.

BREATHING: *SEE RESPIRATORY SYSTEM:BREATHING*

BRONCHITIS: *SEE ALSO ANTIBACTERIAL, ANTIFUNGAL, ANTIVIRAL, CONGESTION, INFLAMMATION, RESPIRATORY SYSTEM*

Bronchitis is the inflammation of the bronchi (the tubes that lead from the trachea to the lungs). Symptoms include coughing, breathlessness, and thick phlegm.

---

1 Bergamot essential oil was found to exert neuroprotective effects against brain injury in rats with induced cerebral ischemia (Amantea et al., 2009).

2 Pretreatment of human and rat astrocyte cells (cells found in the nerve and brain that support the blood-brain barrier and help repair the brain and spinal cord following injuries) with peppermint oil was found to inhibit heat-shock induced apoptosis of these cells (Koo et al., 2001).

3 Pretreatment of human and rat astrocyte cells (cells found in the nerve and brain that support the blood-brain barrier and help repair the brain and spinal cord following injuries) with lemon oil was found to inhibit heat-shock induced apoptosis (Koo et al., 2002).

4 Imaging of the brain demonstrated that inhalation of 1,8-cineol (eucalyptol, a constituent of many essential oils, especially eucalyptus, rosemary, and marjoram) increased global cerebral blood flow after an inhalation time of 20 minutes (Nasel et al., 1994).

Oils: ⒶⓉeucalyptus[5,6,7], ⒶⓉthyme[5], ⒶⓉwhite fir, ⒶⓉbasil, ⒶⓉBreathe, ⒶⓉOn Guard, ⒶⓉclary sage, ⒶⓉcypress, ⒶⓉmelaleuca, ⒶⓉmarjoram, ⒶⓉpeppermint, ⒶⓉrosemary, ⒶⓉwintergreen, ⒶⓉmyrrh, ⒶⓉclove, ⒶⓉfrankincense, ⒶⓉginger, ⒶⓉlavender, ⒶⓉlemon, ⒶⓉsandalwood, ⒶⓉbergamot

—CHRONIC

Oils: ⓉⒶeucalyptus, ⓉⒶoregano, ⓉⒶsandalwood

—CHILDREN

Oils: ⓉⒶeucalyptus, ⓉⒶmelaleuca, ⓉⒶlavender, ⓉⒶRoman chamomile, ⓉⒶrosemary

—CLEAR MUCUS:

Oils: ⓉⒶsandalwood, ⓉⒶthyme, ⓉⒶbergamot, ⓉⒶOn Guard,

Ⓐ: Diffuse into the air. Inhale directly from bottle. Apply oil to hands, tissue, or cotton wick, and inhale.

Ⓣ: Dilute as recommended, and apply to chest, sinuses, neck, or reflex points on the feet. Add 2–3 drops to water; gargle.

BRUISES: SEE ALSO CAPILLARIES

A bruise is an injury to tissue that results in blood capillaries breaking and spilling blood into the tissue. This can cause swelling, soreness, and a visible discoloration when the bruise is near the skin.

Oils: Ⓣhelichrysum, Ⓣgeranium, Ⓣfennel, ⓉDeep Blue (for pain), ⓉOn Guard, Ⓣlavender

Ⓣ: Dilute as recommended, and apply 1–2 drops on location.

BUGS: SEE INSECTS/BUGS

BULIMIA: SEE EATING DISORDERS:BULIMIA

BUNIONS: SEE BURSITIS:BUNION

---

5 Extracts from eucalyptus and thyme were found to have high nitrous oxide (NO) scavenging abilities and inhibited NO production in macrophage cells. This could possibly explain their role in aiding respiratory inflammatory diseases (Vigo et al., 2004).

6 Eucalyptus oil was found to have an anti-inflammatory and mucin-inhibitory effect in rats with lipopolysaccharide-induced bronchitis (Lu et al., 2004).

7 Therapy with 1,8 cineole (eucalyptol) in both healthy and bronchitis-afflicted humans was shown to reduce production of LTB4 and PGE2 (both metabolites of arachidonic acid, a known chemical messenger involved in inflammation) in white blood cells (Juergens et al., 1998).

BURNS:

A burn is an injury to tissue caused by heat, chemicals, or radiation. The tissue most often affected by burns is the skin. Minor burns can cause redness and pain over a small area and do not break the skin. For minor heat burns, immediately immerse the affected skin in cool water to stop the heat from causing more damage to the tissue. More serious burns that involve areas of the body larger than the palm of the hand or that involve blistering, swelling, intense pain that lasts for more than a day, or visible skin damage should be attended to by a medical professional. Skin damaged by burns is more prone to developing infection as it cannot act as a barrier against invading microorganisms.

Oils: Ⓣlavender, Ⓣgeranium, Ⓣmelaleuca, Ⓣpeppermint, Ⓣhelichrysum, ⓉRoman chamomile

Other Products: ⓉMicroplex VMz to help replace minerals depleted from the skin and tissues surrounding a burn.

—INFECTED:

Oils: ⓉPurify

—PAIN:

Oils: Ⓣlavender

—HEALING:

Oils: Ⓣlavender

Blend 1: Blend together 1 drop geranium and 1 drop helichrysum; apply on location.

—PEELING:

Oils: Ⓣlavender

—SUNBURN:

Oils: Ⓣlavender, Ⓣmelaleuca, ⓉRoman chamomile

Recipe 1: Place 10 drops lavender in a 4 oz. misting spray bottle filled with distilled water. Shake well, and spray on location to aid with pain and healing.

—SUN SCREEN:

Oils: Ⓣhelichrysum

Ⓣ: Dilute as recommended, and apply on location. Add 2–3 drops oil to 1 oz. water in a spray bottle; shake well, and mist on location.

BURSITIS:

Bursitis is the inflammation of the fluid-filled sack located close to joints that provides lubrication for tendons, skin, and ligaments rubbing against the bone. Bursitis is caused by infection, injury, or diseases such as arthritis and gout. Bursitis causes tenderness and pain which can limit movement.

Oils: ⊕Balance, ⊕white fir, ⊕basil, ⊕cypress, ⊕Deep Blue, ⊕ginger, ⊕Roman chamomile, ⊕marjoram, ⊕wintergreen

Recipe 1: Apply 1–3 drops each of Balance, white fir, and basil on location. Alternate cold and hot packs (10 min. cold and then 15 min. hot) until pain subsides.

Recipe 2: Apply 6 drops marjoram on shoulders and arms, and wait six minutes. Then apply 3 drops of wintergreen, and wait six minutes. Then apply 3 drops cypress.

—BUNION:

A bunion is bursitis of the big toe. It is often caused by constrictive shoes that force the big toe to point inward and the base of the big toe to jut outward. This misplacement can irritate the bursa at the base of the toe and cause it to become inflamed, causing further irritation.

Oils: ⊕cypress

⊕: Dilute as recommended, and apply 1–2 drops on location.

CALLOUSES: *SEE SKIN:CALLOUSES*

CALMING: *SEE ALSO ANXIETY*

Oils: ⊕lavender[1,2,3], ⊕ylang ylang[4,5], ⊕melissa[6], ⊕Serenity, ⊕Citrus Bliss, ⊕myrrh

---

—AGITATION:

Oils: ⊕lavender[2], ylang ylang[4,5], ⊕geranium[7], ⊕bergamot, ⊕Serenity, ⊕sandalwood, ⊕Balance, ⊕marjoram, ⊕myrrh, ⊕clary sage, ⊕rose, ⊕frankincense, ⊕Elevation

—ANGER:

Oils: ⊕Serenity, ⊕lavender, ⊕ylang ylang, ⊕Balance, ⊕Elevation, ⊕bergamot, ⊕geranium, ⊕frankincense, ⊕sandalwood, ⊕cypress, ⊕lemon, ⊕myrrh, ⊕marjoram, ⊕helichrysum, ⊕rose, ⊕orange

—HYPERACTIVITY:

Oils: ⊕lavender[8], ⊕Serenity, ⊕Balance, ⊕Roman chamomile, ⊕Citrus Bliss

—SEDATIVE:

Oils: ⊕lavender[9,10], ⊕Serenity, ⊕Citrus Bliss, ⊕bergamot, ⊕ylang ylang, ⊕geranium, ⊕vetiver, ⊕frankincense, ⊕sandalwood, ⊕orange, ⊕rose, ⊕lemongrass, ⊕clary sage, ⊕marjoram

Ⓐ: Diffuse into the air. Inhale directly from bottle. Apply oil to hands, tissue, or cotton wick, and inhale.

Ⓣ: Dilute as recommended, and apply 1–2 drops to back of neck, temples, chest, shoulders, back, or reflex points on the feet. Place 1–2 drops in 1 Tbs. fractionated coconut oil, and massage into the back, shoulders, neck, or arms.

CANCER:

Cancer can be any of many different conditions where the body's cells duplicate and grow uncontrollably, invade healthy tissues, and possibly spread throughout the body. It is estimated that 95% of cancers result from damage to DNA during a person's lifetime rather than from a pre-existing genetic condition (American Cancer Society, 2008). The most important factor leading to this DNA damage is DNA mutation. DNA mutation can be caused by radiation, environmental chemicals we take into our bodies, free radical damage, or DNA

---

1   *Lavandula angustifolia* essential oil demonstrated ability to inhibit GABA-A receptor channels of rat brain cells (Huang et al., 2008).
2   Inhaling lavender oil was found to be effective at alleviating agitated behaviors in older Chinese patients suffering from dementia (Lin et al., 2007).
3   Female patients waiting for dental treatment were found to be less anxious, more positive, and more calm when exposed to orange oil odor than were patients who were not exposed to the orange oil odor (Lehrner et al., 2000).
4   In human trials, the aroma of peppermint was found to enhance memory and to increase alertness, while ylang ylang aroma was found to increase calmness (Moss et al., 2008).
5   Subjects who had ylang ylang oil applied to their skin had decreased blood pressure, increased skin temperature, and reported feeling more calm and relaxed, as compared to subjects in a control group (Hongratanaworakit et al., 2006).
6   Melissa (lemon balm) oil applied topically in a lotion was found to reduce agitation and to improve quality of life factors in patients suffering severe dementia, as compared to those receiving a placebo lotion (Ballard et al., 2002).

7   Geraniol and eugenol, two components of rose oil (among others), were found to demonstrate antianxiety effects on mice in several tests (Umezo et al., 2008).
8   Exposure to inhaled lavender oil and to its constituents, linalool and linalyl acetate, was found to decrease normal movement in mice as well as to return mice to normal movement rates after caffeine-induced hyperactivity (Buchbauer et al., 1991).
9   Swiss mice fed lavender oil diluted in olive oil were found to be more sedate in several common behavioral tests (Guillemain et al., 1989).
10 Linalool, found in several essential oils, was found to inhibit induced convulsions in rats by directly interacting with the NMDA receptor complex (Brum et al., 2001).

Primary Recommendations • Secondary Recommendations • Other Recommendations / Ⓐ=Aromatic, Ⓣ=Topical, Ⓘ=Internal

copying or division errors. If the body is working properly, it can correct these mutations either by repairing the DNA or by causing the mutated cell to die. When the DNA mutation is severe enough that it allows the cell to bypass these controls, however, the mutated DNA can be copied to new cells that continue to replicate and create more and more new cells uncontrollably, leading to a cancerous growth within an individual.

Oils: Ⓐ⬤Ⓣfrankincense[11,12,13,14,15,16,17,18,19,20,21,22,23], Ⓣ⬤Ⓐsandalwood[24,25,26,27,28,29,30] Ⓐ⬤lavender[31,32,33,34,35],

Ⓣ⬤Ⓐrosemary[36,37,38,39], Ⓐ⬤Ⓣlemongrass[40,41,42,43,44], Ⓐ⬤Ⓣclove[45], Ⓐ⬤Ⓣbasil[46], Ⓣ⬤Ⓐgeranium[42], Ⓐ⬤Ⓣclary sage[47], ⬤citrus oils[48], ⬤rose

Other Products: ⬤Alpha CRS+ contains multiple nutrients that have been studied for their abilities to combat different types of cancer, including polyphenols (such as resveratrol[49,50,51], baicalin[52,53,54], EGCG[55,56], quercetin[41,57,58,59,60,61], ellagic acid[62], and catechin[41,49,50,51]) and coenzyme Q10. ⬤xEO Mega and ⬤Mi-

---

11 Ethanol extract of *Boswellia serrata* demonstrated antiproliferative effects on 5 leukemia and two brain tumor cell lines. It was more potent than one type of Boswellic acid (AKBA) on three leukemia cell lines (Hostanska et al., 2002).

12 Boswellic acids were found to have an antiproliferative and apoptotic effect on human colon cancer cells (Liu et al., 2002).

13 Boswellic acids from frankincense were found to induce apoptosis (cell death) in human leukemia cell lines (Xia et al., 2005).

14 Boswellic acid was found to inhibit DNA and RNA synthesis in human leukemia cells, leading to inhibited cell growth (Shao et al., 1998).

15 Boswellic acid was found to cause differentiation in promyelocytic leukemia cells, while inhibiting growth of these cells in mice (Jing et al., 1992).

16 Boswellic acid was shown to induce apoptosis in three leukemia cell lines and to induce differentiation in one leukemia cell line (Jing et al., 1999).

17 An extract from *Boswellia carterii* was found to induce apoptosis (cell death) in 2 leukemia cell lines (Hunan et al., 1999).

18 Boswellic acid reduced induced inflammation and tumors in mice and was found to inhibit DNA synthesis in human leukemia cells in culture (Huang et al., 2000).

19 An extract from frankincense was found to produce apoptosis in human leukemia cells (Bhushan et al., 2007).

20 Boswellic acids demonstrated an antiproliferative and apoptotic effect on liver cancer cells (Liu et al., 2002).

21 Boswellic acid was found to inhibit the androgen receptors involved in the development and progression of prostate cancer (Yuan et al., 2008).

22 Boswellic acid induced apoptosis in prostate cancer cells (Lu et al., 2008).

23 Boswellic acid was found to prevent and inhibit invasion and metastasis of melanoma (skin pigment) and fibrosarcoma (connective tissue cancer) cells (Zhao et al., 2003).

24 Oral sandalwood oil use enhanced GST activity (a protein in cell membranes that can help eliminate toxins) and acid-soluble SH levels. This suggests a possible chemopreventive action on carcinogenesis (Banerjee et al., 1993).

25 Alpha-santalol was found to induce apoptosis in human skin cancer cells (Kaur et al., 2005).

26 A solution of 5% alpha-santalol (from sandalwood) was found to prevent skin-tumor formation caused by ultraviolet-b (UVB) radiation in mice (Dwivedi et al., 2006).

27 Various concentrations of alpha-santalol (from sandalwood) were tested against skin cancer in mice. All concentrations were found to inhibit skin cancer development (Dwivedi et al., 2005).

28 Alpha-santalol, derived from sandalwood EO, was found to delay and decrease the incidence and multiplicity of skin tumor (papilloma) development in mice (Dwivedi et al., 2003).

29 Sandalwood oil was found to decrease skin papilloma (tumors) in mice (Dwivedi et al., 1997).

30 Pretreatment with alpha-santalol (found in sandalwood) before UVB (ultraviolet-b) radiation significantly reduced skin tumor development and multiplicity and induced proapoptotic and tumor-suppressing proteins (Arasada et al., 2008).

31 In tests for mutagenicity, both tea tree and lavender oils were found to not be mutagenic. In fact, lavender oil was found to have strong antimutagenic activity, reducing mutations of cells exposed to a known mutagen (Evandri et al., 2005).

32 Perillyl alcohol (found in caraway, lavender, and mint), EGCG (polyphenol from green tea), squalene (a triterpene derived from sharks and other vegetable material), and EPA (an essential fatty acid from fish or microalgae) were found to inhibit hyperproliferation of mammary epithelial cells prior to tumorigenisis (Katdare et al., 1997).

33 Rats fed diets containing perillyl alcohol (derived from lavender plants) were found to have less incidence of colon tumors and less multiplicity of tumors in the colon compared to control. Colon tumors of animals fed perillyl alcohol were found to exhibit increased apoptosis of cells compared to control (Reddy et al., 1997).

34 Mice treated with perillyl alcohol (found in lavender and mint plants) had a 22% reduction in tumor incidence and a 58% reduction in tumor multiplicity during a mouse lung tumor bioassay (Lantry et al., 1997).

35 Rats with liver tumors that were treated with perillyl alcohol had smaller tumor sizes than untreated rats due to apoptosis in cancer cells in treated rats (Mills et al., 1995).

36 Rosemary extract injected in rats was found to decrease mammary adenocarcinomas in rats (Singletary et al., 1996).

37 An ethanol extract of rosemary was found to have an antiproliferative effect on human leukemia and breast carcinoma cells, as well as an antioxidant effect (Cheung et al., 2007).

38 Carnosic acid (derived from rosemary) was found to inhibit the proliferation of human leukemia cells in vitro (Steiner et al., 2001).

39 Rosemary extracts induced CYP (cytochrome 450) activity in liver cells, suggesting a possibility of increased ability to remove toxins (Debersac et al., 2001).

40 Citral (found in lemongrass, melissa, and verbena oils) was found to induce apoptosis in several cancer cell lines (hematopoietic cells=stem cells that create blood cells) (Dudai et al., 2005).

41 Lemongrass oil was found to inhibit multiple cancer cell lines, both in vitro and in vivo, in mice (Sharma et al., 2009).

42 Geraniol (found in geranium and lemongrass oil, among others) was found to inhibit colon cancer cell growth while inhibiting DNA synthesis in these cells (Carnesecchi et al., 2001).

43 Lemongrass oil and its constituent, isointermedeol, were found to induce apoptosis in human leukemia cells (Kumar et al., 2008).

44 An extract from lemongrass was found to inhibit hepatocarcinogenesis (liver cancer genesis) in rats (Puatanachokchai et al., 2002).

45 Beta-caryophyllene (found in clove) was found to increase the anticancer activities of paclitaxel (a chemotherapy drug derived from the yew tree) (Legault et al., 2007).

46 Basil and its component, linalool, were found to reduce spontaneous mutagenesis in bacteria cells (Berić et al., 2008).

47 Sclareol, from clary sage oil, was found to have a cytostatic effect in human leukemia cell lines (Dimas et al., 1999).

48 In a study of older individuals, it was found that there was a dose-dependent relationship between citrus peel (which are high in d-limonene) consumption and a lower degree of squamous cell carcinoma (SCC) of the skin (Hakim et al., 2000).

49 Resveratrol was found to act as an antioxidant and antimutagen in addition to inhibiting several types of cancer cells (Jang et al., 1997).

50 Human leukemia cells were found to be irreversibly inhibited by resveratrol, while the effects of resveratrol on nonmalignant human lymphoblastoid cells was largely reversible, suggesting a selective growth inhibition of leukemia cells (Lee et al., 2004).

51 A combination of resveratrol, quercetin, and catechin administered orally was found to reduce primary tumor growth of breast cancer tumors in nude mice (Schlachterman et al., 2008).

52 Baicalin was found to inhibit cyclobutane pyrimidine dimers (a precursor to skin cancer) in fibroblast cells exposed to UVB radiation (Zhou et al., 2008).

53 Baicalin was found to inhibit several different breast cancer cell lines (Franek et al., 2005).

54 Baicalin was found to inhibit two prostate cancer cell lines in vitro (Miocinovic et al., 2005).

55 The polyphenol EGCG from green tea was found to inhibit the ability of bronchial tumor cells to migrate in vitro (Hazgui et al., 2008).

56 EGCG was found to inhibit pancreatic cancer growth, invasion, metastasis and angiogenesis (ability to create blood vessels) in mice (Shankar et al., 2008).

57 A combination of low-frequency ultrasound followed by treatment with quercetin was found to selectively kill cancerous skin and prostate cancer cells, while having no effect on nonmalignant skin cells (Paliwal et al., 2005).

58 Quercetin was found to inhibit and induce apoptosis in cancerous prostate cells, but not in normal prostate epithelial cells in vitro (Aalinkeel et al., 2008).

59 In a large human study, it was found that increased flavonoid intake in male smokers was found to decrease the risk of developing pancreatic cancer (Bobe et al., 2008).

60 Flavonol intake was found to reduce the risk of developing pancreatic cancer among smokers (Nothlings et al., 2007).

61 Flavonol intake (including flavonols such as epicatechin, catechin, quercetin, and kaempferol) was found to be inversely associated with lung cancer among tobacco smokers (Cui et al., 2008).

62 Oral supplementation with ellagic acid was found to decrease the number of induced esophageal tumors in rats, compared to a control (Mandal et al., 1990).

Primary Recommendations • Secondary Recommendations • Other Recommendations / Ⓐ=Aromatic, Ⓣ=Topical, ⬤=Internal

croplex VM to help support cellular and immune function.

Note: Health care professionals are emphatic about avoiding heavy massage when working with cancer patients. Light massage may be used—but never over the trauma area.

—BONE:

    Oils: ⓣfrankincense

—BRAIN:

    Oils: ⒶⓉfrankincense[1], ⒶⓉmyrrh[2], ⒶⓉclove

    Recipe 1: Combine 15 drops frankincense, 6 drops clove, and 1 Tbs. fractionated coconut oil. Massage lightly on spine every day. Diffuse 15 drops frankincense and 6 drops clove for 30 minutes, three times a day.

    Recipe 2: Diffuse frankincense, and massage the brain stem area lightly with frankincense neat.

—BREAST:

    Oils: ⓉⒶrosemary[36,37], ⓉⒶlavender[32] ⒶⓉfrankincense, ⒶⓉclove, ⒶⓉsandalwood, ⒶⓉoregano, ⒶⓉlemongrass, ⒶⓉmarjoram

—CERVICAL:

    Oils: ⓉⒶfrankincense, ⓉⒶgeranium, ⓉⒶwhite fir, ⓉⒶcypress, ⓉⒶclove, ⓉⒶlavender, ⓉⒶlemon

—COLON:

    Oils: ⒾⓉⒶlavender[33], ⓉⒶgeranium[42], ⓉⒶfrankincense[2], ⓉⒶlemongrass[42],

—LEUKEMIA:

    Oils: ⓉⒶfrankincense[13,14,15,16,17,18,19], ⓉⒶlemongrass[43], ⓉⒶrosemary[37], ⓉⒶclary sage[47],

—LIVER:

    Oils: ⓉⒶfrankincense[20], ⓉⒶlemongrass[44], ⓉⒶlavender[35], ⓉⒶrosemary[39],

—LUNG:

    Oils: ⓉⒶfrankincense (apply to chest, or mix 15 drops with 1 tsp. fractionated coconut oil for nightly rectal retention enema), ⓉⒶlavender[34]

—PROSTATE

    Oils: ⓉⒶfrankincense[21,22] (blend 15 drops with 1 tsp. fractionated coconut oil for nightly rectal retention enema)

—SKIN/MELANOMA:

    Oils: ⒾⓉsandalwood[25,26,27,28,29,30], Ⓣfrankincense[23], Ⓘcitrus oils[48]

—THROAT:

    Oils: ⓉⒶfrankincense, ⓉⒶlavender

—UTERINE:

    Oils: ⓉⒶgeranium, ⓣfrankincense

ⓣ: Dilute as recommended, and apply 1–5 drops on location and on reflex points on the feet and hands. Apply as a warm compress over affected area.

Ⓐ: Diffuse into the air. Inhale oil directly or applied to hands, tissue, or a cotton wick.

Ⓘ: Take capsules as recommended on package. Add 1–2 drops of oil in an empty capsule; swallow capsule.

CANDIDA: *SEE ANTIFUNGAL:CANDIDA*

CANKER SORES:

Canker sores are small, round sores that develop in the mouth, typically inside the lips and cheeks or on the tongue.

Oils: ⓣmelaleuca, ⓣoregano, ⓣOn Guard, ⓣRoman chamomile, ⓣmyrrh

ⓣ: Dilute as recommended, and apply 1 drop on location.

CAPILLARIES:

Capillaries are the small, thin blood vessels that allow the exchange of oxygen and other nutrients from the blood to cells throughout the body and allow the exchange of carbon dioxide and other waste materials from these tissues back to the blood. The capillaries connect the arteries (that carry blood away from the heart) and veins (that carry blood back to the heart).

—Broken Capillaries:

    Oils: ⓣgeranium, ⓣcypress, ⓣoregano, ⓣthyme, ⓣRoman chamomile

---

1 Ethanol extract of *Boswellia serrata* demonstrated antiproliferative effects on 5 leukemia and two brain tumor cell lines. It was more potent than one type of Boswellic acid (AKBA) on three leukemia cell lines (Hostanska et al., 2002).

2 Treatment with elemene (found in myrrh oil) was found to increase survival time and to reduce tumor size in patients with malignant brain tumor, as compared to treatment with chemotherapy (Tan et al., 2000).

Blend 1: Apply 1 drop lavender and 1 drop Roman chamomile on location.

🅣: Dilute as recommended, and apply 1–2 drops on location.

Carbuncles: *see Boils*

Cardiovascular System:

The cardiovascular—or circulatory—system is the system responsible for transporting blood to the various tissues throughout the body. It is comprised of the heart and blood vessels such as arteries, veins, and capillaries.

Oils: 🅣🅐orange, 🅣🅐cypress, 🅣🅐cinnamon, 🅣🅐sandalwood, 🅣🅐thyme[3]

Other Products: 🅘Alpha CRS+ contains several polyphenols (including proanthocyanidin polyphenols from grape seed[4], the polyphenols EGCG[5,6,7], and ellagic acid[8,9,10]) and coenzyme Q10[11,12,13,14], which have been found to have beneficial cardiovascular effects.

🅣: Dilute oils as recommended, and apply oils to area: to carotid arteries, heart, feet, under left ring finger, above elbow, behind ring toe on left foot, and to reflex points on the feet. Add 1–2 drops to bathwater for a bath. Add 1–2 drops to 1 Tbs. fractionated coconut oil

---

3 Older rats whose diets were supplemented with thyme oil were found to have a higher level of the antioxidant enzymes superoxide dismutase and glutathione peroxidase in the heart, liver, and kidneys, as compared to older rats without this supplementation (Youdim et al., 1999).

4 An extract of proanthocyanidin polyphenols from grape seed taken as a supplement was found to significantly oxidize LDL (a risk factor for cardiovascular disease) in people with high cholesterol (Bagchi et al., 2003).

5 People who habitually consumed beverages containing EGCG were found to have significantly lower incidences of cardiovascular events (Basu et al., 2007).

6 Supplementation with EGCG was found to lower blood pressure in humans (Brown et al., 2008).

7 EGCG was found to reduce heart weight and cardiac marker enzyme activities in induced heart attacks in rats (Devika et al., 2008).

8 Ellegic acid was found to reduce induced LDL oxidization in vitro (Anderson et al., 2001).

9 Ellegic acid was found to significantly inhibit oxidized LDL proliferation of rat aortic smooth muscle cells (Chang et al., 2008).

10 Supplementation with ellegic acid was found to significantly reduce the amount of atherosclerotic lesions in rabbits fed a high-cholesterol diet (Yu et al., 2005).

11 In patients with coronary artery disease, supplementation with CoQ10 was found to improve extracellular superoxide dismutase activity, endothelium-dependent vasodilation, and peak oxygen volume capacity at a level significantly higher as compared to control (Tiano et al., 2007).

12 Oral supplementation with CoQ10 was found to improve endothelial function (cells that line the blood vessels) and aerobic capacity of the cardiovascular system in patients with chronic heart failure (Belardinelli et al., 2006).

13 Supplementation with CoQ10 was found to improve endothelial dysfunction of the brachial artery in 25 male patients with manifest endothelial dysfunction (Kuettner et al., 2005).

14 Chronic heart failure patients receiving CoQ10 supplementation were found to have an improvement in left-ventricle contractility without any side effects (Belardinelli et al., 2005).

CARDIOVASCULAR SYSTEM

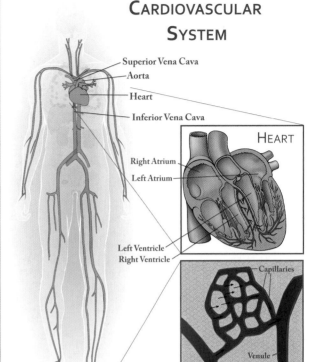

Superior Vena Cava
Aorta
Heart
Inferior Vena Cava

HEART

Right Atrium
Left Atrium

Left Ventricle
Right Ventricle

Capillaries

Venule

Arteriole

CAPILLARY BED

for massage oil, and massage on location or on chest, neck, or feet.

🅐: Diffuse into the air. Inhale oil applied to hands, tissue, or cotton wick.

—Angina:

Angina is pain in the chest due to a lack of blood flow to the heart. Angina is felt as a squeezing, tightening, aching, or pressure in the chest. The pain can also extend to the arms, back, jaw, neck, and teeth.

Oils: 🅣🅐ginger, 🅣🅐orange (for false angina)

🅣: Massage gently onto chest and feet, and apply on carotid artery.

🅐: Diffuse into the air.

—Arrhythmia:

Arrhythmia is any abnormal heart rhythm. *See also Palpitations and Tachycardia below.*

Oils: 🅐🅣ylang ylang[15], 🅐🅣lavender, 🅐🅣Deep Blue

🅐: Diffuse into the air. Inhale the aroma.

---

15 Inhaled ylang ylang oil was found to decrease blood pressure and pulse rate and to enhance attentiveness and alertness in volunteers compared to an odorless control (Hongratanaworakit et al., 2004).

Primary Recommendations • Secondary Recommendations • Other Recommendations / 🅐=Aromatic, 🅣=Topical, 🅘=Internal

T: Dilute oils as recommended, and apply oils to carotid arteries, heart, feet, under left ring finger, above elbow, behind ring toe on left foot, and to reflex points on the feet.

—ATHEROSCLEROSIS:

Atherosclerosis is a hardening of the arteries due to a buildup of plaques (called atheromas) along the arterial wall.

Oils: lemon[1], lavender[2], rosemary, ginger, thyme, wintergreen

A: Diffuse into the air.

I: Take lemon in a capsule or with water.

T: Massage gently onto chest and feet, and apply on carotid artery.

—BLOOD PRESSURE: *SEE BLOOD:BLOOD PRESSURE*

—CARDIOTONIC:

Oils: lavender, thyme

T: Dilute oils as recommended, and apply oils to carotid arteries, heart, feet, under left ring finger, above elbow, behind ring toe on left foot, and to reflex points on the feet.

A: Diffuse into the air. Inhale the aroma.

—CIRCULATION:

Oils: cypress, thyme, peppermint, clary sage, wintergreen, Citrus Bliss, rosemary, geranium, cinnamon, helichrysum, Serenity, basil

T: Add 1–2 drops to 1 Tbs. fractionated coconut oil for massage oil, and massage on location or on chest, neck, or feet.

A: Diffuse into the air. Inhale the aroma.

—HEART:

Oils: ylang ylang, marjoram geranium, cypress, Balance, ginger, lavender, rosemary, Deep Blue

T: Dilute oils as recommended, and apply oils to carotid arteries, heart, feet, under left ring finger, above elbow, behind ring toe on left foot, and to reflex points on the feet.

A: Diffuse into the air. Inhale the aroma.

—HEART TISSUE

Oils: marjoram, lavender, peppermint, rosemary, cinnamon, rose

T: Dilute oils as recommended, and apply oils to carotid arteries, heart, feet, under left ring finger, above elbow, behind ring toe on left foot, and to reflex points on the feet.

A: Diffuse into the air. Inhale the aroma.

—HIGH CHOLESTEROL: *SEE CHOLESTEROL*

—HYPERTENSION: *SEE BLOOD:BLOOD PRESSURE*

—PALPITATIONS:

Palpitations are rapid and forceful contractions of the heart.

Oils: ylang ylang, orange, lavender, melissa, peppermint

T: Dilute oils as recommended, and apply oils to carotid arteries, heart, feet, under left ring finger, above elbow, behind ring toe on left foot, and to reflex points on the feet.

A: Diffuse into the air. Inhale the aroma.

—PHLEBITIS:

Phlebitis is the inflammation of a superficial vein, typically in the legs or groin area. Wearing support hose or a compression bandage over the affected area can help aid in healing.

Oils: helichrysum, lavender, cypress, geranium, grapefruit, Balance

T: Add 1–2 drops to 1 Tbs. fractionated coconut oil for massage oil, and gently massage on location or on feet.

A: Diffuse into the air. Inhale the aroma.

—PROLAPSED MITRAL VALVE:

Oils: marjoram

T: Dilute oils as recommended, and apply oils to carotid arteries, heart, feet, under left ring finger, above elbow, behind ring toe on left foot, and to reflex points on the feet.

A: Diffuse into the air. Inhale the aroma.

—TACHYCARDIA:

Tachycardia is an abnormally rapid resting heart rate, indicating a possible over-working of the heart.

Oils: lavender, ylang ylang, orange

---

1 Lemon oil and one of its components, gamma-terpinene, were found to inhibit oxidation of low-density lipoprotein (LDL). Oxidation of LDL has been found to increase the risk of atherosclerosis and cardiac disease (Grassmann et al., 2001).

2 Inhalation of lavender and monarda oils was found to reduce cholesterol content and atherosclerotic plaques in the aorta (Nikolaevskiĭ et al., 1990).

Primary Recommendations • Secondary Recommendations • Other Recommendations / **A**=Aromatic, **T**=Topical, **I**=Internal

150

T: Dilute oils as recommended, and apply oils to carotid arteries, heart, feet, under left ring finger, above elbow, behind ring toe on left foot, and to reflex points on the feet.

A: Diffuse into the air. Inhale the aroma.

CARPAL TUNNEL SYNDROME:

Carpal tunnel syndrome is a painful condition of the hand, wrist, and fingers. This condition is caused by inflamed carpal ligaments in the wrist causing pressure on the median nerve. The carpal ligaments can become inflamed due to one of many possible factors: wrist trauma or injury, fluid retention, work stress, or certain strenuous wrist activities. Symptoms include tingling or numbness of the fingers and hand, pain starting in the wrist and extending to the arm or shoulder or to the palms or fingers, a general sense of weakness, and difficulty grasping small objects.

Oils: **O**frankincense, **O**basil, **O**marjoram, **O**lemongrass, **O**oregano, **O**cypress, **O**eucalyptus, **O**lavender

Recipe 1: Apply 1 drop basil and 1 drop marjoram on the shoulder, and massage oils into the skin. Then apply 1 drop lemongrass on the wrist and 1 drop oregano on the rotator cuff in the shoulder, and massage into the skin. Next apply 1 drop marjoram and 1 drop cypress on the wrists and 1 drop cypress on the neck down to the shoulder, and massage into the skin. Lastly, apply peppermint from the shoulder down the arm to the wrist and then out to the tips of each finger, and massage into the skin.

T: Dilute oils as recommended, and apply oils on area of concern Add 1–2 drops to 1 Tbs. fractionated coconut oil for massage oil, and massage on location.

CARTILAGE: *SEE BONES:CARTILAGE, MUSCLES/CONNEC-TIVE TISSUE:CARTILAGE INJURY*

CATARACTS: *SEE EYES:CATARACTS*

CATARRH: *SEE CONGESTION:CATARRH*

CAVITIES: *SEE ORAL CONDITIONS:CAVITIES*

CELLS:

Other Products: **O**Alpha CRS+ and **O**Microplex VM for antioxidant support to help protect cells and DNA and for necessary nutrients and **O**xEO Mega for omega-3 fatty acids necessary for cellular health

—DNA & MUTATION:

DNA is the genetic material of the cell, DNA contains all of the codes that enables the cell to build the materials needed for proper cell structure and function. Mutation of DNA can lead to cell death or to cancer.

–ANTIMUTAGENIC OILS:

Oils: **OA**peppermint[3], **OA**lavender[4], **OA** rosemary[5], **OA**basil[6]

T: Dilute oils as recommended, and apply oils on area of concern Add 1–2 drops to 1 Tbs. fractionated coconut oil for massage oil, and massage on location.

A: Diffuse into the air. Inhale oil applied to hands, tissue, or cotton wick.

CELLULITE: *SEE ALSO WEIGHT*

Cellulite refers to deposits of fat under the skin of the thighs, abdomen, and buttocks that cause the skin to appear dimpled.

Oils: **OO**Slim & Sassy, **O**grapefruit, **O**rosemary, **O**basil, **O**orange, **O**lemon, **O**lime, **O**cypress, **O**lavender, **O**oregano, **O**fennel, **O**geranium

Recipe 1: Add 5 drops grapefruit and 5 drops lemon to 1 gallon drinking water. Adjust to taste, and drink throughout the day.

I: Add 8 drops of Slim & Sassy to 16 oz. of water, and drink throughout the day between meals.

T: Dilute as recommended, and apply 1–2 drops on location. Add 1–2 drops to 1 Tbs. fractionated coconut oil, and massage on location.

3 Infusions from peppermint and valerian were shown to have antimutagenic properties on fruit flies exposed to the mutagen hydrogen peroxide (Romero-Jiménez et al., 2005).

4 In tests for mutagenicity, both tea tree and lavender oils were found to not be mutagenic. In fact, lavender oil was found to have strong antimutagenic activity, reducing mutations of cells exposed to a known mutagen (Evandri et al., 2005).

5 An ethanol extract of rosemary demonstrated a protective effect against the oxidative damage to DNA in cells exposed to H2O2 and light-excited methylene blue (Slamenova et al., 2002).

6 Basil and its component, linalool, were found to reduce spontaneous mutagenesis in bacteria cells (Berić et al., 2008).

Primary Recommendations • Secondary Recommendations • Other Recommendations / **A**=Aromatic, **T**=Topical, **I**=Internal

151

CHARLEY HORSE: *SEE MUSCLES/CONNECTIVE TISSUE:CRAMPS/CHARLEY HORSES*

CHEMICALS: *SEE DETOXIFICATION*

CHILDBIRTH: *SEE PREGNANCY/MOTHERHOOD*

CHILDHOOD DISEASES: *SEE ALSO ANTIVIRAL, ANTIBACTERIAL*

—**CHICKEN POX:** *SEE ALSO SHINGLES*

Chicken pox is a common childhood illness caused by the virus varicella zoster. Symptoms of chicken pox include mild fever, weakness, and a rash. The rash appears as red spots that form into blisters that eventually burst and then crust over. Chicken pox can occur between 10 and 21 days after contact with the virus and is contagious up to five days before and five days after the rash appears. Chicken pox is highly contagious and can be contracted by anyone, but it is most common in children under the age of 15.

Oils: ᵀlavender, ᵀᴬmelaleuca, ᵀRoman chamomile, ᵀeucalyptus, ᴬlemon, ᴬbergamot

Recipe 1: Add 10 drops lavender and 10 drops Roman chamomile to 4 oz. calamine lotion. Mix, and apply twice a day over body.

Recipe 2: Add 2 drops lavender to 1 cup bicarbonate of soda (baking soda). Dissolve in warm bathwater, and bathe to help relieve itching.

—**MEASLES:**

Measles is a viral infection of the respiratory system that causes coughing, runny nose, red eyes, fever, and a rash on the skin.

Oils: ᴬᵀeucalyptus, ᴬᵀmelaleuca, ᴬᵀlavender

—**MUMPS:**

Mumps is a viral infection that causes fever, chills, headache, and painful swelling of the saliva glands.

Oils: ᵀᴬmelaleuca, ᵀlavender, ᴬlemon

—**RUBELLA (GERMAN MEASLES):**

Rubella, or German measles, is a viral infection that causes rash, fever, runny nose, and joint pain.

Oils: ᵀmelaleuca, ᵀlavender

—**WHOOPING COUGH:**

Whooping cough, or pertussis, is a bacterial infection that causes cold-like symptoms, followed by severe coughing fits.

Oils: ᵀoregano, ᵀᴬbasil, ᵀᴬthyme, ᵀclary sage, ᵀcypress, ᵀlavender, ᵀRoman chamomile, ᵀgrapefruit, ᴬeucalyptus, ᴬmelaleuca, ᴬpeppermint, ᴬrose

Ⓣ: Dilute as recommended, and apply on location or on chest, neck, back, or reflex points on the feet. Add 1–2 drops to 1 quart warm water, and use water for a sponge bath.

Ⓐ: Diffuse into the air. Diffuse other antiviral oils such as lemon as well. *See Antiviral.*

CHILDREN AND INFANTS:

When using essential oils on children and infants, it is always best to dilute the pure essential oil with a carrier oil. For older children, dilute 1–2 drops essential oil in 1/2–1 tsp. of carrier oil. For newborns and infants, dilute 1–2 drops in 2 Tbs. of carrier oil. If the oils are used in a bath, always use a bath gel base as a dispersing agent for the essential oils.

Keep the oils out of children's reach. If an oil is ever ingested, give the child an oil-soluble liquid such as milk, cream, or half & half. Then call your local poison control center, or seek emergency medical attention. A few drops of pure essential oil shouldn't be life-threatening, but it is best to take these precautions.

Several oils that are generally considered safe for children include cypress, frankincense, geranium, ginger, lavender, lemon*, marjoram, melaleuca, orange*, rosemary**, sandalwood, thyme, and ylang ylang.

*These oils are photosensitive; always dilute, and do not use when skin will be exposed soon to direct sunlight.

**This oil should never be used undiluted on infants or children

—**COLIC:**

Colic is any extended period of crying and fussiness that occurs frequently in an infant. While the exact cause is not known, it has been speculated that the cause may be from indigestion, the build-up of gas, lactose intolerance, or a lack of needed probiotic bacteria in the intestines.

Oils: ⊕marjoram, ⊕bergamot, ⊕ylang ylang, ⊕ginger, ⊕Roman chamomile, ⊕rosemary, ⊕melissa

Blend 1: Combine 2 Tbs. almond oil with 1 drop Roman chamomile, 1 drop lavender, and 1 drop geranium. Mix, and apply to stomach and back.

⊕: Dilute 1–2 drops of oil in 2 Tbs. fractionated coconut oil, and massage a small amount of this blend gently on stomach and back.

—COMMON COLD: *SEE ANTIVIRAL*

A cold is a viral infection that causes a stuffy or runny nose, congestion, cough, and sneezing.

Oils: ⒶⓉthyme, ⒶⓉlemon, ⒶⓉsandalwood, ⒶⓉrosemary, ⒶⓉrose

⊕: Dilute 1–2 drops of oil in 2 Tbs. fractionated coconut oil, and massage a little on neck and chest.

Ⓐ: Diffuse into the air.

—CONSTIPATION:

Constipation is when feces becomes too hard and dry to expel easily from the body.

Oils: ⊕rosemary[1], ⊕ginger, ⊕orange

⊕: Dilute 1–2 drops of oil in 2 Tbs. fractionated coconut oil, and massage on stomach and feet.

—CRADLE CAP:

Cradle cap is a scaling of the skin on the head that commonly occurs in young infants. The scaling is yellowish in color and often disappears by the time the infant is a few months old.

Recipe 1: Combine 2 Tbs. almond oil with 1 drop lemon and 1 drop geranium. Apply a small amount of this blend on the head.

—CROUP:

Croup is a viral respiratory infection that causes inflammation of the area around the larynx (voice box) and a distinctive-sounding

cough. Often, taking an infant or child outside to breath cool night air can help open the restricted airways, as can humidity.

Oils: ⒶⓉmarjoram, ⒶⓉthyme, ⒶⓉsandalwood

Ⓐ: Diffuse into the air.

Ⓣ: Dilute 1–2 drops in 2 Tbs. fractionated coconut oil, and massage on chest and neck.

—CRYING:

Oils: ⒶⓉylang ylang, ⒶⓉlavender, ⒶⓉRoman chamomile, ⒶⓉgeranium, ⒶⓉcypress, ⒶⓉfrankincense

Ⓐ: Diffuse into the air.

Ⓣ: Dilute 1–2 drops in 2 Tbs. fractionated coconut oil. Massage.

—DIAPER RASH:

Diaper rash is a red rash of the skin in the diaper area caused by prolonged skin exposure to the moisture and different pH of urine and feces. Often, more frequent bathing of the area and diaper changes will help alleviate the rash.

Oils: ⊕lavender

Blend 2: Combine 1 drop Roman chamomile and 1 drop lavender with 1 tsp. fractionated coconut oil, and apply on location.

⊕: Dilute 1–2 drops in 2 Tbs. fractionated coconut oil, and apply a small amount of this mixture on location.

—DIGESTION (SLUGGISH):

Oils: ⊕lemon, ⊕orange

⊕: Dilute 1–2 drops in 2 Tbs. fractionated coconut oil, and massage a small amount on feet and stomach.

—DRY SKIN:

Oils: ⊕sandalwood

⊕: Dilute 1–2 drops in 2 Tbs. fractionated coconut oil, and apply a small amount on location.

—EARACHE:

Oils: ⊕melaleuca, ⊕Roman chamomile, ⊕lavender, ⊕thyme

Blend 3: Combine 2 Tbs. fractionated coconut oil with 2 drops lavender, 1 drop Roman chamomile, and 1 drop melaleuca. Put a

---

1 The use of rosemary, lemon, and peppermint oils in massage demonstrated an ability to reduce constipation and increase bowel movements in elderly subjects, compared to massage without the oils (Kim et al., 2005).

drop on a cotton ball or cotton swab, and apply in ear, behind the ear, and on reflex points on the feet.

T: Dilute 1–2 drops in 2 Tbs. fractionated coconut oil, and apply a small amount behind the ear. Place a drop on a cotton ball, and place in the ear.

—FEVER:

Oils: **T**lavender, **A**peppermint

T: Dilute 1–2 drops in 2 Tbs. fractionated coconut oil, and massage a small amount on the neck, feet, behind ears, and on back.

A: Diffuse into the air.

—FLU:

Flu, or influenza, is a viral infection that affects the respiratory system. Symptoms may include coughing, sneezing, fever, runny nose, congestion, muscle aches, nausea, and vomiting.

Oils: **TA**cypress, **TA**lemon

T: Dilute 1 drop oil in an unscented bath gel, and use for a bath.

A: Diffuse into the air.

—HYPERACTIVE: *SEE CALMING, ADD/ADHD*

—JAUNDICE:

Jaundice is a condition where the liver cannot clear the pigment bilirubin quickly enough from the blood, causing the blood to deposit the bilirubin into the skin and whites of the eyes, turning them a yellowish color.

Oils: **T**geranium, **T**lemon, **T**rosemary

T: Dilute 1–2 drops in 2 Tbs. fractionated coconut oil, and massage a small amount on the liver area and on the reflex points on the feet.

—PREMATURE:

Since premature babies have very thin and sensitive skin, it is best to avoid the use of essential oils.

—RASHES:

Oils: **T**lavender, **T**Roman chamomile, **T**sandalwood

T: Dilute 1–2 drops in 2 Tbs. fractionated coconut oil, and apply a small amount on location.

—TEETH GRINDING:

Oils: **T**lavender, **TA**Serenity

T: Dilute 1–2 drops in 2 Tbs. fractionated coconut oil, and massage a small amount on the feet.

A: Diffuse into the air.

—TONSILLITIS:

Tonsillitis is inflammation of the tonsils, two lymph-filled tissues located at the back of the mouth that help provide immune support. These may become inflamed due to a bacterial or viral infection.

Oils: **T**melaleuca, **T**lemon, **T**Roman chamomile, **T**lavender, **T**ginger

T: Dilute 1–2 drops in 2 Tbs. fractionated coconut oil, and apply a small amount to tonsils and lymph nodes.

—THRUSH: *SEE ALSO ANTIFUNGAL*

Thrush is an oral fungal infection caused by *Candida albicans*. It causes painful white-colored areas to appear in the mouth.

Oils: **T**melaleuca[1,2], **T**lavender[3], **T**thyme[4], **T**lemon, **T**geranium

T: Dilute 1–2 drops in 2 Tbs. fractionated coconut oil, and apply a small amount on location.

CHILLS: *SEE FEVER, WARMING OILS*

CHOLERA:

Cholera is a potentially severe bacterial infection of the intestines by the *Vibrio cholerae* bacteria. This infection can cause severe diarrhea, leading to dehydration that can cause low blood pressure, shock, or death. Rehydration with an oral rehydration solution is the most effective way to prevent dehydration. If no commercially-prepared oral

1 Tea tree oil was found to inhibit 301 different types of yeasts isolated from the mouths of cancer patients suffering from advanced cancer, including 41 strains that are known to be resistant to antifungal drugs (Bagg et al., 2006).
2 Eleven types of *Candida* were found to be highly inhibited by tea tree oil (Banes-Marshall et al., 2001).
3 Lavender oil demonstrated both fungistatic (stopped growth) and fungicidal (killed) activity against *Candida albicans* (D'Auria et al., 2005).
4 Thyme oil was found to inhibit *Candida* species by causing lesions in the cell membrane as well as inhibiting germ tube (an outgrowth that develops when the fungi is preparing to replicate) formation (Pina-Vaz et al., 2004).

Primary Recommendations • Secondary Recommendations • Other Recommendations / **A**=Aromatic, **T**=Topical, **I**=Internal

154

rehydration solution is available, a solution made from 1 tsp. salt, 8 tsp. sugar, and 1 liter clean water (with some mashed fresh banana, if available, to add potassium) can work in an emergency.

Oils: ⓣrosemary, ⓣclove

ⓣ: Dilute as recommended, and apply to stomach and on reflex points on the feet.

Cholesterol:

Cholesterol is an important lipid that comprises part of the cell membrane and myelin sheath and that plays a role in nerve cell function. It is created by the body and can be found in many foods we eat. An imbalance of certain types of cholesterol in the blood has been theorized to play a role in the formation of plaques in the arteries (atherosclerosis).

Oils: ⓘlemongrass[5], ⓣclary sage, ⓣhelichrysum, ⓐlavender[6]

ⓣ: Dilute as recommended, and apply to liver area and reflex points on the feet.

ⓘ: Place 1–2 drops in a capsule, and swallow.

ⓐ: Diffuse into the air.

Chronic Fatigue:

Chronic fatigue syndrome refers to a set of debilitating symptoms that may include prolonged periods of fatigue that are not alleviated by rest, difficulty concentrating, muscle and joint pain, headaches, and sore throats that cannot be explained by any other known medical condition. While the exact cause of chronic fatigue syndrome is not known, some have theorized that it is caused by a virus (such as the Epstein-Barr virus) left in the body after an illness.

Oils: ⓣⓐOn Guard, ⓣⓐpeppermint, ⓣⓐbasil, ⓣⓐlemongrass, ⓣⓘDigestZen, ⓣⓐrosemary, ⓣⓐlavender

Other Products: ⓘAlpha CRS+ to help support healthy cellular energy levels. ⓘxEO Mega and ⓘMicroplex VMz to help supply necessary nutrients to support cell and immune function.

ⓣ: Dilute as recommended, and apply 1–2 drops to sore muscles or joints, to the back, or to the feet. Add 1–2 drops to warm bathwater for a bath.

ⓘ: Take capsules as directed on package. Add 1–2 drops of oil to an empty capsule; swallow.

ⓐ: Diffuse into the air. Inhale directly from bottle. Apply oil to hands, tissue, or cotton wick, and inhale.

Cigarettes: *see Addictions:Smoking*

Circulatory System: *see Cardiovascular System*

Cirrhosis: *see Liver:Cirrhosis*

Cleansing: *see also Housecleaning*

Oils: ⓣⓐPurify, ⓣⓐOn Guard, ⓐmelaleuca

Other Products: ⓣOn Guard Foaming Hand Wash to cleanse hands and protect against harmful microorganisms.

—Cuts:

Oils: ⓣlavender, ⓣmelaleuca

—Master Cleanse or Lemonade Diet:

Combine 2 Tbs. fresh lemon or lime juice (approximately 1/2 lemon), 2 Tbs. grade B maple syrup, and 1/10 tsp cayenne pepper (or to taste) with 10 oz. distilled water. In case of diabetes, use black strap molasses instead of the maple syrup. Drink 6–12 glasses of this mixture daily, with an herbal laxative tea taken first thing in the morning and just before retiring at night. Refer to the booklet *The Master Cleanser* for more specifics and for suggestions of how to come off of this cleanse.

ⓣ: Dilute as recommended, and apply on location. Dilute 1–3 drops in 1 Tbs. fractionated coconut oil, and use as massage oil. Use hand wash as directed on packaging.

ⓐ: Diffuse into the air.

Cold Sores: *see also Antiviral, Herpes Simplex*

Cold sores are blisters or sores in the mouth area caused by an infection of the herpes simplex virus.

---

5 Supplementation with lemongrass capsules was found to reduce cholesterol in some subjects (Elson et al., 1989).

6 Inhalation of lavender and monarda oils was found to reduce cholesterol content and atherosclerotic plaques in the aorta (Nikolaevskiĭ et al., 1990).

Oils: ❶melaleuca[1], ❶melissa[2], ❶peppermint[3], ❶lemon, ❶On Guard, ❶geranium, ❶lavender, ❶bergamot

❶: Dilute as recommended, and apply 1–2 drops on location.

Colds: *see also Antiviral, Coughs, Congestion*

A cold is a viral infection that causes a stuffy or runny nose, congestion, cough, sore throat, or sneezing.

Oils: ❹❶thyme, ❹❶lemon, ❹❶On Guard, ❹❶ melaleuca, ❹❶sandalwood, ❹eucalyptus, ❹❶rosemary, ❹❶lime, ❹❶peppermint (for nasal congestion), ❹❶Breathe (for respiratory congestion), ❶ginger, ❹❶basil, ❹❶lavender, ❹❶orange, ❹❶oregano

Other Products: ❶Microplex VMz for nutrients essential to support cellular and immune system health.

Recipe 1: When you first notice a sore throat, apply a tiny amount of melaleuca to the tip of the tongue, and then swallow. Repeat this a few times every 5–10 minutes. Then massage a couple of drops on the back of the neck.

❶: Dilute as recommended, and apply 1–2 drops to throat, temples, forehead, back of neck, sinus area, below the nose, chest, or reflex points on the feet.

❹: Diffuse into the air. Place 1–2 drops in a bowl of hot water, and inhale the vapors. Inhale directly from bottle. Apply oil to hands, tissue, or cotton wick, and inhale.

❶: Take capsules as directed on package. Place 1–2 drops of oil in an empty capsule, and swallow.

Colic: *see Children and Infants:Colic*

Colitis: *see Colon:Colitis*

Colon: *see also Cancer:Colon, Digestive System*

The colon, or large intestine, is the last part of the digestive system. Its function is to extract water and

Colon (Large Intestine)

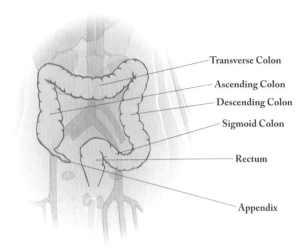

Transverse Colon
Ascending Colon
Descending Colon
Sigmoid Colon
Rectum
Appendix

vitamins created by friendly bacterial flora from the material moving through the digestive system.

Oils: ❶❶DigestZen, ❶❶peppermint

Other Products: ❶PB Assist+ to help restore friendly flora to the intestinal wall. ❶GX Assist to help the digestive system eliminate pathogens. ❶Zendocrine capsules to help support healthy colon functioning. Use Redmond Clay (1–800–367–7258) to help remove fecal matter from the colon.

—**Cancer:** *see Cancer:Colon*

—**Colitis:**

Colitis is inflammation of the large intestine or colon. The exact cause is not known but may involve an auto-immune response. Symptoms can include abdominal pain, tenderness, frequent need to expel stools, diarrhea, and possibly bloody stools and fever in the case of ulcerative colitis.

Oils: ❶❶DigestZen, ❶❹helichrysum, ❶❹peppermint[4], ❶❹thyme, ❶❹clove

—**Diverticulitis:**

Diverticulitis is the inflammation of a diverticula (a small balloon-like sac that sometimes forms along the wall of the large intestine, especially in older individuals), typically due

1 Tea tree and eucalyptus oil demonstrated an ability to inhibit the *Herpes simplex* virus (Schnitzler et al., 2001).
2 Melissa oil demonstrated inhibition of herpes simplex type 1 and type 2 viruses (Schnitzler et al., 2008).
3 Peppermint oil demonstrated a direct virucidal activity against herpes type 1 and type 2 viruses (Schuhmacher et al., 2003).

4 L-menthol was found to inhibit production of inflammation mediators in human monocytes (a type of white blood cell involved in the immune response) (Juergens et al., 1998).

to infection. It causes pain in the abdomen and tenderness on the lower-left-hand part of the stomach.

Oils: ⊕cinnamon, ⊕lavender

Other Products: Use Redmond Clay (1–800-367-7258) to help remove fecal matter from diverticula.

—Polyps: *see also Cancer:Colon*

Polyps are tumors that arise from the bowel surface and protrude into the inside of the colon. Most polyps eventually transform into malignant cancer tumors.

Oils: ⊕⊕peppermint

⊕: Dilute as recommended, and apply 1–2 drops on lower abdomen or on reflex points on the feet. Use 1–2 drops in warm bathwater for a bath.

⊕: Take capsule as directed on package. Place 1–2 drops in an empty capsule; swallow.

⊕: Diffuse into the air. Inhale directly from bottle. Apply oil to hands, tissue, or cotton wick, and inhale.

Coma:

Oils: ⊕frankincense, ⊕Balance, ⊕sandalwood, ⊕cypress, ⊕peppermint

⊕: Dilute as recommended, and massage 1–2 drops on the brain stem area, mastoids (behind ears), temples, and bottoms of feet.

Complexion: *see Skin*

Concentration (Poor):

Oils: ⊕lavender[5,6], ⊕lemon, ⊕peppermint, ⊕orange, ⊕cypress, ⊕eucalyptus, ⊕rosemary, ⊕sandalwood, ⊕ylang ylang

Other Products: ⊕xEO Mega contains omega-3 fatty acids necessary for proper brain cell function.

⊕: Diffuse into the air. Apply, and inhale from hands, tissue, or cotton wick.

⊕: Take capsules as directed on package.

Concussion: *see Brain:Concussion*

Confusion:

Oils: ⊕frankincense, ⊕sandalwood, ⊕Balance, ⊕rosemary, ⊕peppermint, ⊕marjoram, ⊕basil, ⊕ylang ylang, ⊕white fir, ⊕thyme, ⊕geranium, ⊕rose, ⊕ginger

⊕: Diffuse into the air. Inhale directly from bottle. Apply oil to hands, tissue, or cotton wick, and inhale.

Congestion:

Congestion is the blockage of the nasal passages, sinuses, or upper respiratory tract due to inflamed tissues and blood vessels or to an increased output of mucus. Congestion can make it difficult to breathe freely and can sometimes cause pain.

Oils: ⊕⊕eucalyptus[7], ⊕⊕peppermint, ⊕⊕Breathe, ⊕cinnamon, ⊕⊕cypress, ⊕⊕melaleuca, ⊕⊕ginger, ⊕⊕rosemary, ⊕⊕fennel, ⊕⊕citrus oils, ⊕⊕patchouli

—Catarrh:

Catarrh refers to the secretion of mucus and white blood cells from the mucus membranes in the sinuses and nasal passages in response to an infection.

Oils: ⊕⊕cypress, ⊕⊕helichrysum, ⊕⊕Breathe, ⊕⊕On Guard, ⊕⊕eucalyptus ⊕⊕frankincense, ⊕⊕myrrh, ⊕⊕rosemary, ⊕⊕ginger

—Expectorant:

An expectorant is an agent that helps dissolve thick mucus in the trachea, bronchi, or lungs for easier elimination.

Oils: ⊕⊕eucalyptus[7], ⊕⊕marjoram, ⊕⊕frankincense, ⊕⊕helichrysum

—Mucus:

Mucus is the substance produced by epithelial cells to coat the mucous membranes in the respiratory tract, digestive tract, and reproductive system. Mucus plays an important role in helping to protect these surfaces from different substances or from microorganisms they come in contact with. When one of these surfaces becomes infected or inflamed, an excess of mucus is often produced. An excess of

---

5 Subjects who smelled a cleansing gel with lavender aroma were more relaxed and able to complete math computations faster (Field et al., 2005).

6 Subjects exposed to 3 minutes of lavender aroma were more relaxed and able to perform math computations faster and more accurately. Subjects exposed to rosemary aroma were more alert and completed math computations faster (but not more accurately) (Diego et al., 1998).

7 Eucalyptus oil was found to have an anti-inflammatory and mucin-inhibitory effect in rats with lipopolysaccharide-induced bronchitis (Lu et al., 2004).

mucus can lead to difficulty breathing in the sinuses, nasal passages, or respiratory tract. For oils to help combat an excess of mucus, see the entries above.

Oils: ❶❶DigestZen (with ginger - helps digest old mucus)

🅣: Dilute as recommended, and rub 1–2 drops on the chest, neck, back, and feet. Dilute 1–2 drops in 1 Tbs. fractionated coconut oil, and massage on chest, neck, back, and feet.

🅐: Diffuse into the air. Place 1–2 drops in a bowl of hot water, and inhale the vapor. Inhale directly from bottle. Apply oil to hands, tissue, or cotton wick, and inhale.

🅘: Add 1–2 drops of each oil to an empty capsule; swallow.

CONJUNCTIVITIS: SEE EYES:PINK EYE

CONNECTIVE TISSUE: SEE BONES:CARTILAGE, MUSCLES/CONNECTIVE TISSUE

CONSTIPATION: SEE DIGESTIVE SYSTEM:CONSTIPATION

CONVULSIONS: SEE SEIZURE:CONVULSIONS

COOLING OILS:

Typically, oils that are high in aldehydes and esters can produce a cooling effect when applied topically or diffused.

Oils: 🅣🅐peppermint, 🅣🅐eucalyptus, 🅣🅐melaleuca, 🅣🅐lavender, 🅣🅐Roman chamomile, 🅐🅣citrus oils

🅣: Dilute as recommended, and apply 1–2 drops on location. Add 1–2 drops to bathwater, and bathe. Add 1–2 drops to basin of cool water, and sponge over skin.

🅐: Diffuse into the air.

CORNS: SEE FOOT:CORNS

COUGHS:

A cough is a sudden explosive release of air from the lungs to help clear an excess of mucus, an irritant, or other materials from the airway. Coughing can be caused by foreign material entering the airway or by an infection, asthma, or other medical problem. Proper hydration or steam inhalation can

help loosen thick secretions, making them easier to eliminate.

Oils: 🅐🅣Breathe, 🅐🅣melaleuca, 🅐🅣eucalyptus, 🅐🅣frankincense, 🅐🅣On Guard, 🅐🅣peppermint, 🅐🅣white fir, 🅐🅣sandalwood, 🅐🅣thyme, 🅐🅣myrrh, 🅐🅣ginger

Other Products: 🅣On Guard Protecting Throat Drops to soothe irritated and sore throats.

—ALLERGY:

Oils: 🅐Purify

—SEVERE:

Oils: 🅐🅣frankincense

🅐: Diffuse into the air. Use throat drops as directed on package.

🅣: Dilute as recommended, and apply 1–2 drops on the throat and chest.

CRADLE CAP: SEE CHILDREN AND INFANTS:CRADLE CAP

CRAMPS: SEE DIGESTIVE SYSTEM:CRAMPS, FEMALE SPECIFIC CONDITIONS:MENSTRUATION, MUSCLES/CONNECTIVE TISSUE:CRAMPS/CHARLEY HORSES

CROHN'S DISEASE:

Crohn's disease is a chronic inflammation of part of the intestinal wall, thought to be caused by an over-active immune response. It can cause abdominal pain, diarrhea, nausea, and loss of appetite.

Oils: 🅘🅣peppermint[1], 🅘🅣DigestZen, 🅣basil

🅘: Add 1–2 drops of each oil to an empty capsule; swallow.

🅣: Dilute as recommended and apply on stomach and feet.

CUTS: SEE ALSO WOUNDS, ANTIBACTERIAL, BLOOD:BLEEDING

Oils: 🅣helichrysum, 🅣lavender, 🅣melaleuca, 🅣basil[2], 🅣On Guard, 🅣Roman chamomile 🅣cypress

🅣: Dilute as recommended, and apply 1–2 drops on location.

---

1 A combination of peppermint and caraway oil was found to reduce visceral hyperalgesia (pain hypersensitivity in the gastrointestinal tract) after induced inflammation in rats (Adam et al., 2006).

2 Basil (*Ocimum gratissimum*) oil was found to facilitate the healing process of wounds in rabbits to a greater extent than two antibacterial preparations, Cicatrin and Cetavlex (Orafidiya et al., 2003).

CYSTITIS: *SEE BLADDER:CYSTITIS/INFECTION*

DANDRUFF: *SEE HAIR:DANDRUFF*

DECONGESTANT: *SEE CONGESTION*

DEGENERATIVE DISEASE:

A degenerative disease is a disease where the affected tissues or organs are damaged due to internal mechanisms, and not due to infection. Quite a few different diseases can be categorized as degenerative diseases, including Alzheimer's disease, cancer, Parkinson's disease, atherosclerosis, diabetes, osteoporosis, rheumatoid arthritis, and many others. Support the cells and tissues through proper nutrition, reducing stress, exercising regularly, and eliminating toxins. See specific conditions in this guide for oils and other products that can support the body for each condition.

DELIVERY: *SEE PREGNANCY/MOTHERHOOD:DELIVERY*

DENTAL INFECTION: *SEE ORAL CONDITIONS*

DEODORANT:

Oils: (T)Purify, (T)melaleuca, (T)lavender, (T)geranium, (T)eucalyptus, (T)cypress, (T)Elevation, (T)Serenity, (T)Breathe, (T)Whisper,

(T): Dilute as recommended, and apply 1–2 drops on the skin. Dilute 2–3 drops in 1 Tbs. fractionated coconut oil, and apply under the arms. Add 2–3 drops to 4 oz. unscented talcum powder and 2 oz. baking soda, and apply under the arms, on the feet, or on other areas of the body.

DEODORIZING:

Oils: (A)Purify, (A)peppermint, (A)clary sage

(A): Diffuse into the air. Dissolve 8–10 drops in 1 tsp. perfumer's or pure grain alcohol (such as vodka), and combine with distilled water in a 1 oz. spray bottle. Spray into the air or on affected surface.

DEPRESSION:

Depression is a disorder marked by excessive sadness, energy loss, feelings of worthlessness, irritableness, sudden weight loss or gain, trouble sleeping, and loss of interest in activities normally enjoyed. These symptoms can continue for weeks or months if not treated and can destroy an individual's quality of life.

Oils: (A)(T)(I)lemon[3,4,5], (A)(T)frankincense[6], (A)(T)lavender[7,8,9], (A)(T)bergamot[3], (A)(T)Elevation, (A)(T)Balance, (A)(T)Citrus Bliss[3], (A)(T)melissa, (T)(A)rosemary, (A)(T)ylang ylang, (A)(T)grapefruit[3], (A)(T)clary sage, (A)(T)Serenity, (A)(T)(I)lime, (A)(T)geranium, (A)(T)ginger, (A)(T)basil, (A)(T)sandalwood, (T)(A)(I)patchouli

—POSTPARTUM DEPRESSION: *SEE PREGNANCY/ MOTHERHOOD:POSTPARTUM DEPRESSION*

—SEDATIVES:

Oils: (A)(T)lavender[7,10,11,12], (A)(T)ylangylang, (T)(A)melissa[13], (T)(A)Roman chamomile, (A)(T)sandalwood, (A)(T)rose, (A)(T)clary sage, (A)(T)cypress, (A)(T)frankincense, (A)(T)bergamot, (A)(T)marjoram

(A): Diffuse into the air. Inhale directly from bottle. Apply oil to hands, tissue, or cotton wick, and inhale.

(T): Dilute as recommended, and apply 1–2 drops to temple or forehead. Add 5–10 drops to 1 Tbs. fractionated coconut oil, and use as massage oil. Add 1–3 drops to warm bathwater, and bathe.

(I): Add 1–2 drops to 8 oz. distilled water or 4 oz. rice or almond milk, and drink. Add 1–2 drops to empty capsule, and swallow.

3 Lemon oil vapor was found to have strong antistress and antidepressant effects on mice subjected to several common stress tests (Komiya et al., 2006).

4 Lemon oil and its component, citral, were found to decrease depressed behavior in a similar manner to antidepressant drugs in rats involved in several stress tests (Komori et al., 1995).

5 In 12 patients suffering from depression, it was found that inhaling citrus aromas reduced the needed doses of antidepressants, normalized neuroendocrine hormone levels, and normalized immune function (Komori et al., 1995).

6 Incensole acetate was found to open TRPV receptors in mice brains, indicating a possible channel for emotional regulation (Moussaieff et al., 2008).

7 In patients suffering from arthritis, it was found that a blend of lavender, marjoram, eucalyptus, rosemary, and peppermint blended with carrier oils was found to reduce perceived pain and depression compared to control (Kim et al., 2005).

8 Female students suffering from insomnia were found to sleep better and to have a lower level of depression during weeks they used a lavender fragrance when compared to weeks they did not use a lavender fragrance (Lee et al., 2006).

9 Swiss mice fed lavender oil diluted in olive oil were found to be more sedate in several common tests (Guillemain et al., 1989).

10 Exposure to inhaled lavender oil and to its constituents, linalool and linalyl acetate, was found to decrease normal movement in mice as well as to return mice to normal movement rates after caffeine-induced hyperactivity (Buchbauer et al., 1991).

11 *Lavandula angustifolia* essential oil demonstrated ability to inhibit GABA-A receptor channels of rat brain cells (Huang et al., 2008).

12 Inhaling lavender oil was found to lower agitation in older adults suffering from dementia (Lin et al., 2007).

13 Melissa (lemon balm) oil applied topically in a lotion was found to reduce agitation and improve quality of life factors in patients suffering severe dementia compared to those receiving a placebo lotion (Ballard et al., 2002).

Primary Recommendations • Secondary Recommendations • Other Recommendations / (A)=Aromatic, (T)=Topical, (I)=Internal

DERMATITIS: *SEE SKIN:DERMATITIS/ECZEMA*

DESPAIR: *SEE DEPRESSION*

DETOXIFICATION:

Detoxification is the act of clearing toxins out of the body. These toxins may be addictive drugs, alcohol, or any other harmful substance.

Oils: **T**helichrysum, **T**rosemary[1]

T: Dilute as recommended, and apply to liver area, intestines, and reflex points on the feet.

DIABETES:

Diabetes is a disease characterized by the body's inability to properly produce or use the hormone insulin. Insulin, produced in the pancreas, helps regulate the level of sugars in the blood, as well as the conversion of starches and sugar into the energy necessary for life. Common diabetes symptoms include a frequent need to drink and urinate, blurred vision, mental fatigue, and possibly weight loss (depending on the type). Over time, diabetes can lead to additional complications, such as strokes, heart disease, kidney failure, and even the necessity of removing a limb.

Oils: **ITA**rosemary[2], **ITA**cinnamon[3,4], **TA**geranium, **TA**ylang ylang, **TA**eucalyptus, **TA**On Guard, **TA**cypress, **TA**ginger, **TA**fennel, **TA**lavender

Blend 1: Combine 8 drops clove, 8 drops cinnamon, 15 drops rosemary, and 10 drops thyme with 2 oz. fractionated coconut oil. Put on feet and over pancreas.

Blend 2: Combine 5 drops cinnamon and 5 drops cypress. Rub on feet and pancreas.

—PANCREAS SUPPORT:

Oils: **T**cinnamon, **T**geranium

—SORES (DIABETIC):

Those suffering from diabetes have to be especially careful about sores of any kind, especially those on the feet and hands. Diabetes decreases blood flow, so wounds heal much slower. Many who suffer from diabetes experi-ence decreased sensation in their hands and feet, making it more difficult to even notice an injury right away. Even a small sore left untreated can turn into an ulcer, ultimately making amputation necessary.

Oils: **T**lavender, **T**Balance

I: Place 1–2 drops in empty capsule and swallow.

T: Dilute as recommended, and apply on back, chest, feet, and over pancreas.

A: Diffuse into the air.

DIAPER RASH: *SEE CHILDREN AND INFANTS:DIAPER RASH*

DIARRHEA: *SEE DIGESTIVE SYSTEM:DIARRHEA*

DIGESTIVE SYSTEM:

The human digestive system is the series of organs and glands that process food. The digestive system breaks down food, absorbs nutrients for the body to use as fuel, and excretes as bowel movements the part that cannot be broken down.

Oils: **ITA**peppermint[5,6,7,8,9,10,11,12], **ITA**ginger[13,14,15], **TA**lemongrass (purifies)[16],

---

1 Rosemary extracts induced CYP (cytochrome 450) activity in liver cells, suggesting a possibility of increased ability to remove toxins (Debersac et al., 2001).

2 Oral rosemary extract was found to decrease blood glucose levels, while increasing insulin levels in alloxan-diabetic rabbits (Bakirel et al., 2008).

3 Cinnamaldehyde (found in cinnamon oil) was found to significantly reduce blood glucose levels in diabetic wistar rats (Subash et al., 2007).

4 Oral administration of cinnamon oil was found to significantly reduce blood glucose levels in diabetic KK-Ay mice (Ping et al., 2010).

5 A combination of peppermint and caraway oil was found to reduce visceral hyperalgesia (pain hypersensitivity in the gastrointestinal tract) after induced inflammation in rats (Adam et al., 2006).

6 Peppermint oil was found to be as effective as Buscopan (an antispasmodic drug) at preventing spasms during a barium enema (a type of enema used to place barium in the colon for X-ray imaging purposes) (Asao et al., 2003).

7 The use of rosemary, lemon, and peppermint oils in massage demonstrated an ability to reduce constipation and increase bowel movements in elderly subjects, compared to massage without the oils (Kim et al., 2005).

8 Peppermint oil in enteric-coated capsules was found to relieve symptoms of irritable bowel syndrome better than a placebo in patients suffering from IBS (Rees et al., 1979).

9 Patients with IBS symptoms who took a peppermint-oil formulation in an enteric-coated capsule were found to have a significantly higher reduction of symptoms than did patients taking a placebo (Liu et al., 1997).

10 Children suffering from irritable bowel syndrome (IBS) who received peppermint oil in enteric-coated capsules (encapsulated so the capsules wouldn't open until they reached the intestines) reported a reduced severity of pain associated with IBS (Kline et al., 2001).

11 In irritable bowel syndrome patients without bacterial overgrowth, lactose intolerance, or celiac disease, peppermint oil was found over 8 weeks to reduce IBS symptoms significantly more than a placebo (Capello et al., 2007).

12 An enteric-coated capsule with peppermint and caraway oil was found to reduce pain and symptoms in patients with non-ulcer dyspepsia (indigestion), compared to a control (May et al., 1996).

13 Ginger root given one hour before major gynecological surgery resulted in lower nausea and fewer incidences of vomiting compared to control (Nanthakomon et al., 2006).

14 Ginger root given orally to pregnant women was found to decrease the severity of nausea and frequency of vomiting compared to control (Vutyavanich et al., 2001).

15 In a trial of women receiving gynecological surgery, women receiving ginger root had less incidences of nausea than did those receiving a placebo. Ginger root has similar results to the antiemetic drug (a drug effective against vomiting and nausea) metoclopramide (Bone et al., 1990).

16 Lemongrass and lemon verbena oil were found to be bactericidal to *Helicobacter pylori* (a pathogen responsible for gastroduodenal disease) at very low concentrations. Additionally, it was found that this bacteria did not develop a resistance to lemongrass oil after 10 passages, while this bacteria did develop resistance to clarithromycin (an antibiotic) under the same conditions (Ohno et al., 2003).

Primary Recommendations • Secondary Recommendations • Other Recommendations / **A**=Aromatic, **T**=Topical, **I**=Internal

160

ⒾⓉⒶDigestZen, ⒾⓉⒶfennel, ⒾⓉⒶwintergreen[17]**, ⒾⓉⒶmarjoram (stimulates), ⒾⓉⒶoregano**[18]**, ⒾⓉⒶrosemary**[7]**, ⓉⒶclary sage, ⒾⓉⒶgrapefruit, ⒾⓉⒶbasil, ⒾⓉⒶlemon**[7]**, ⓉⒶcinnamon, ⒾⓉⒶclove, ⒾⓉⒶorange, ⒾⓉⒶbergamot**

Regimen 1: Use **Ⓘ**GX Assist for 10 days to help support the digestive system in eliminating pathogenic microorganisms, followed by **Ⓘ**PB Assist+ for 5 days to help rebuild friendly flora to aid digestion and prevent pathogenic bacteria.

Other Products: ⒾTerrazyme for healthy digestion, enyzmatic function, and cellular metabolism. **Ⓘ**Alpha CRS+, **Ⓘ**xEO Mega, **Ⓘ**Microplex VMz to provide essential nutrients, vitamins, and minerals for digestive system cellular support.

Ⓘ: Take capsules as directed on package. Add 1–2 drops of oil to 16 oz. of water, and drink. Add oils as flavoring to food. Place 1–2 drops of oil in an empty capsule, and swallow.

Ⓣ: Dilute oil as recommended, and apply 1–2 drops on stomach or reflex points on feet. Dilute 1–2 drops in 1 Tbs. fractionated coconut oil, and massage over abdomen and lower back. Apply as a warm compress over affected area.

Ⓐ: Diffuse into the air. *See Negative Ions* for oils that produce negative ions when diffused to help stimulate the digestive system. Inhale oil directly or applied to hands, tissue, or cotton wick.

—**Bloating:**

Bloating is an abnormal swelling, increase in diameter, or feeling of fullness and tightness in the abdominal area as gas and liquid are trapped inside. Common causes of bloating can include overeating, menstruation, constipation, food allergies, and irritable bowel syndrome.

Oils: ⓉⒶDigestZen

Ⓣ: Dilute as recommended, and apply to stomach and to reflex points on the feet.

Ⓐ: Diffuse into the air.

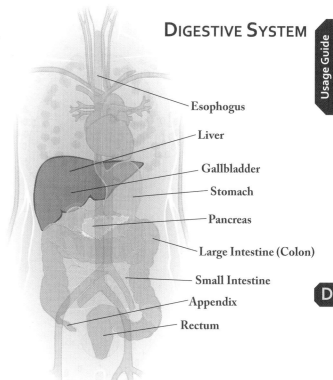

Digestive System

Esophogus
Liver
Gallbladder
Stomach
Pancreas
Large Intestine (Colon)
Small Intestine
Appendix
Rectum

—**Constipation:**

Constipation is a condition characterized by infrequent or difficult bowel movements. A person is considered constipated if he or she has fewer than three bowel movements a week or if the stools are hard and difficult to expel. Common causes of constipation include a lack of fiber, dehydration, ignoring the urge to have a bowel movement, depression, medications, large dairy intake, stress, and abuse of laxatives.

Oils: Ⓣrosemary[19], **Ⓣ**lemon[19], **Ⓣ**peppermint[19], **Ⓣ**marjoram, **Ⓣ**DigestZen, **Ⓣ**ginger, **Ⓣ**fennel, **Ⓣ**orange, **Ⓣ**rose, **Ⓣ**sandalwood

Ⓣ: Dilute as recommended, and apply oils on abdomen. Add 1–2 drops to 1 Tbs. fractionated coconut oil, and massage onto abdomen.

—**Cramps (Abdominal):**

Cramps are sudden, involuntary muscle contractions that often cause severe pain. Abdominal cramps are commonly caused by

17 Methyl salicylate (found in wintergreen or birch oils) was found to inhibit leukotriene C4 (a chemical messenger involved in inflammatory response), while also demonstrating gastroprotective against ethanol-induced gastric injury in rats (Trautmann et al., 1991).

18 Oregano oil administered orally was found to improve gastrointestinal symptoms in 7 of 11 patients who had tested positive for the parasite *Blastocystis hominis* and was also found to cause disappearance of this parasite in 8 cases (Force et al., 2000).

19 The use of rosemary, lemon, and peppermint oils in massage demonstrated an ability to reduce constipation and to increase bowel movements in elderly subjects, compared to massage without the oils.(Kim et al., 2005).

Primary Recommendations • Secondary Recommendations • Other Recommendations / Ⓐ=Aromatic, Ⓣ=Topical, Ⓘ=Internal

stress, menstruation, mild food poisoning, and *Irritable Bowel Syndrome (below)*.

Oils: **◐◍**DigestZen, **◐◍**basil, **◍**clary sage

Recipe 1: Flavor water with 5 drops Digest-Zen, and drink for stomach pains and cramps.

❶: Place 3 drops DigestZen and 3 drops basil in an empty capsule; swallow.

❶: Dilute as recommended, and massage oil onto abdomen over area of pain.

—DIARRHEA:

Diarrhea is an abnormal increase in the frequency of bowel movements, marked by loose, watery stools. Diarrhea is defined as more than three bowel movements a day. Cases of Diarrhea that last more than two days can become a serious problem and cause dehydration. Rehydration with an oral rehydration solution is the most effective way to prevent dehydration. If no commercially-prepared oral rehydration solution is available, a solution made from 1 tsp. salt, 8 tsp. sugar, and 1 liter clean water (with some mashed fresh banana, if available, to add potassium) can work in an emergency. Diarrhea is usually caused by a viral, parasitic, or bacterial infection.

Oils: **◐◍**peppermint, **◐◍**ginger, **◍**geranium, **◍**DigestZen, **◍**orange, **◍**patchouli, **◍**melaleuca, **◍**sandalwood, **◍**lavender, **◍**Roman chamomile, **◍**cypress, **◍**eucalyptus

–CHILDREN:

Oils: **◍**geranium, **◍**ginger, **◍**sandalwood

❶: Place 1–2 drops in an empty capsule, and swallow.

❶: Dilute as recommended, and apply 1–2 drops on abdomen. Apply as a warm compress over affected area.

—GAS/FLATULENCE:

Oils: **◐◍**lavender, **◐◍**ginger, **◍**peppermint, **◍**eucalyptus, **◍**bergamot, **◍**myrrh, **◍**rosemary

❶: Place 1–2 drops in an empty capsule, and swallow.

❶: Dilute as recommended, and apply 1–2 drops on stomach, abdomen, or reflex points on the feet

—GASTRITIS: *SEE ALSO INFLAMMATION*

Gastritis is inflammation of the stomach lining.

Oils: **◐◍**DigestZen, **◐◍**peppermint, **◍**lemongrass[1], **◐◍**fennel

❶: Add 1 drop of oil to rice or almond milk; take as a supplement. Place 1–2 drops in an empty capsule; swallow capsule.

❶: Dilute as recommended, and apply 1–2 drops on stomach. Apply as a warm compress over stomach.

—GIARDIA:

Giardia are parasites that infect the gastrointestinal tract of humans and animals. The form of *Giardia* that affects humans causes severe diarrhea. *See Diarrhea above* for information on rehydration.

Oils: **◐◍**lavender[2]

❶: Place 1–2 drops in an empty capsule; swallow capsule.

❶: Dilute as recommended, and apply 1–2 drops on abdomen or reflex points on the feet.

—HEARTBURN:

Heartburn is a painful burning sensation in the chest or throat. It occurs as a result of backed up stomach acid in the esophagus. Heartburn is often brought on by certain foods, medication, pregnancy, and alcohol.

Oils: **◍**lemon, **◍**peppermint, **◐◍**DigestZen

Blend 1: Blend 2 drops lemon, 2 drops peppermint, and 3 drops sandalwood in 1 Tbs. fractionated coconut oil. Apply to breast bone in a clockwise motion using the palm of the hand. Apply to reflex points on the feet.

---

1   Lemongrass and lemon verbena oil were found to be bactericidal to *Helicobacter pylori* (a pathogen responsible for gastroduodenal disease) at very low concentrations. Additionally, it was found that this bacteria did not develop a resistance to lemongrass oil after 10 passages, while this bacteria did develop resistance to clarithromycin (an antibiotic) under the same conditions (Ohno et al., 2003).

2   Essential oil from *Lavandula angustifolia* demonstrated ability to eliminate protozoal pathogens *Giardia duodenalis*, *Trichomonas vaginalis*, and *Hexamita inflata* at concentrations of 1% or less (Moon et al., 2006).

Primary Recommendations • Secondary Recommendations • Other Recommendations / **Ⓐ**=Aromatic, **Ⓣ**=Topical, **❶**=Internal

162

T: Dilute as recommended, and apply 1–2 drops to chest.

I: Add 1 drop of oil to rice or almond milk; take as a supplement. Place 1–2 drops in an empty capsule; swallow capsule.

—Indigestion:

The term "indigestion" is used to describe abdominal discomfort felt after a meal. Symptoms of indigestion include belching, bloating, nausea, heartburn, a feeling of fullness, and general abdominal discomfort. Indigestion can be caused by overeating or eating too fast, alcoholic or carbonated drinks, particular foods, etc.

Oils: peppermint, ginger, lavender, orange, lime, thyme, myrrh, grapefruit

Other Products: Terrazyme for healthy digestion, enyzmatic function, and cellular metabolism.

I: Add 1–2 drops of oil to 8 oz. of almond or rice milk; drink. Place 1–2 drops of oil in an empty capsule; swallow capsule. Take capsules as directed on package.

T: Dilute oil as recommended, and apply 1–2 drops on stomach or reflex points on feet. Dilute 1–2 drops in 1 Tbs. fractionated coconut oil, and massage over abdomen and lower back. Apply as a warm compress over stomach area.

A: Diffuse into the air.

—Intestines:

The intestines are the largest organs in the digestive track. The intestines include the small intestine, which begins just below the stomach and is responsible for digesting and absorbing nutrients from the food, and the large intestine, which begins at the end of the small intestine and is responsible for reabsorbing water and some vitamins before the undigested food and waste is eliminated.

Oils: basil, marjoram, ginger, rosemary

Other Products: GX Assist to help the digestive system eliminate pathogens. PB Assist+ to provide friendly intestinal flora to aid digestion and help prevent patho-

genic bacteria. Terrazyme for healthy digestion, enyzmatic function, and cellular metabolism.

T: Dilute oil as recommended, and apply 1–2 drops on stomach or reflex points on feet. Dilute 1–2 drops in 1 Tbs. fractionated coconut oil, and massage over abdomen and lower back. Apply as a warm compress over affected area.

I: Take capsules as directed on package. Add 1–2 drops of oil to 16 oz. of water; drink. Add oils as flavoring to food. Place 1–2 drops of oil in a capsule, and swallow.

—Intestinal Parasites:
see Parasites:Intestinal

—Irritable Bowel Syndrome:

Irritable bowel syndrome is an intestinal disorder characterized by reoccurring diarrhea, bloating, gas, constipation, cramping, and abdominal pain. Irritable bowel syndrome is one of the most commonly diagnosed disorders by doctors.

Oils: peppermint[3,4,5,6,7], DigestZen

I: Add 2 drops of each oil to 8 oz. distilled water, and drink 1–2 times per day. Place 2 drops of each oil in an empty capsule; swallow capsule.

T: Dilute 1–2 drops in 1 Tbs. fractionated coconut oil, and apply over the abdomen with a hot compress.

—Nausea/Upset Stomach:

Oils: DigestZen, ginger[8,9,10], peppermint, lavender, Solace, clove

---

3 Peppermint oil in enteric-coated capsules was found to relieve symptoms of irritable bowel syndrome better than a placebo in patients suffering from IBS (Rees et al., 1979).

4 Patients with IBS symptoms who took a peppermint-oil formulation in an enteric-coated capsule were found to have a significantly higher reduction of symptoms than did patients taking a placebo (Liu et al., 1997).

5 Children suffering from irritable bowel syndrome (IBS) who received peppermint oil in enteric-coated capsules (encapsulated so the capsules wouldn't open until they reached the intestines) reported a reduced severity of pain associated with IBS (Kline et al., 2001).

6 In irritable bowel syndrome patients without bacterial overgrowth, lactose intolerance, or celiac disease, peppermint oil was found over 8 weeks to reduce IBS symptoms significantly more than a placebo (Capello et al., 2007).

7 An enteric-coated capsule with peppermint and caraway oil was found to reduce pain and symptoms in patients with non-ulcer dyspepsia (indigestion), compared to a control (May et al., 1996).

8 Ginger root given one hour before major gynecological surgery resulted in lower nausea and fewer incidences of vomiting compared to control (Nanthakomon et al., 2006).

9 Ginger root given orally to pregnant women was found to decrease the severity of nausea and frequency of vomiting compared to control (Vutyavanich et al., 2001).

10 In a trial of women receiving gynecological surgery, women receiving ginger root

---

Primary Recommendations • Secondary Recommendations • Other Recommendations / **A**=Aromatic, **T**=Topical, **I**=Internal

163

Ⓘ: Place 1–2 drops in an empty capsule; swallow capsule. Place 1 drop in 8 oz. rice or almond milk, and drink.

Ⓣ: Dilute as recommended, and apply behind ears, on stomach, or on reflex points on the feet.

Ⓐ: Diffuse into the air. Inhale directly from bottle. Apply oil to hands, tissue, or cotton wick, and inhale.

—PARASITES: *SEE PARASITES*

—STOMACH:

The stomach is the organ mainly responsible for breaking food apart using strong acids. It is located below the esophagus and before the intestines.

Oils: ⓄⓉbasil, ⓄⓉpeppermint, Ⓞlemongrass[1], ⓄⓉginger, ⓄⓉDigestZen

Ⓘ: Place 1–2 drops in an empty capsule, and swallow.

Ⓣ: Dilute as recommended, and apply 1–2 drops on stomach, abdomen, or reflex points on the feet

—ULCERS: *SEE ULCERS*

DISINFECTANT:

A disinfectant is any substance that destroys microorganisms on non-living surfaces.

Oils: ⓉⒶlemon, ⓉⒶPurify, ⓉⒶgrapefruit, Ⓐlemongrass[2], Ⓐgeranium[2]

Other Products: On Guard Foaming Hand Wash to cleanse hands and protect against harmful microorganisms.

Blend 1: Add 10 drops lavender, 20 drops thyme, 5 drops eucalyptus, and 5 drops oregano to a large bowl of water. Use to disinfect small areas.

Ⓣ: Add 1–2 drops of oil to a wet cloth, and use to wipe down counters and other surfaces. Use hand wash as directed on packaging.

Ⓐ: Diffuse into the air.

DIURETIC:

A diuretic is a substance that increases the rate of urination and fluid elimination from the body.

Oils: Ⓣlemongrass, Ⓣrosemary, Ⓣlavender, Ⓣpatchouli, Ⓣgrapefruit, Ⓣcypress, Ⓣfennel, Ⓣorange, Ⓣlemon, Ⓣoregano, Ⓣmarjoram

Ⓣ: Dilute as recommended, and apply oils to kidney area on back and to bottoms of feet.

DIVERTICULITIS: *SEE COLON:DIVERTICULITIS*

DYSENTERY: *SEE ALSO ANTIBACTERIAL, DIGESTIVE SYSTEM:DIARRHEA*

Dysentery is severe, frequent diarrhea, often with blood or mucus, that occurs due to infection by bacteria or amoeba. Dysentery can be fatal due to dehydration if left untreated. *See Digestive System:Diarrhea* for information on rehydrating the body.

Oils: Ⓣmyrrh, Ⓣeucalyptus, Ⓣlemon, ⓉRoman chamomile, Ⓣcypress, Ⓣclove (amoebic), Ⓣmelissa

Ⓣ: Dilute as recommended, and apply on abdomen and on bottoms of feet.

DYSPEPSIA: *SEE DIGESTIVE SYSTEM:INDIGESTION*

EARS:

Oils: ⓉⒶhelichrysum, ⓉⒶPurify, ⓉⒶeucalyptus, ⓉⒶmelaleuca, ⓉⒶgeranium, ⓉⒶBalance, ⓉⒶmarjoram

—EARACHE:

Oils: Ⓣbasil, Ⓣmelaleuca, Ⓣhelichrysum

—HEARING IN A TUNNEL:

Oils: ⓉPurify

—INFECTION:

Oils: Ⓣmelaleuca, ⓉPurify, Ⓣlavender

—INFLAMMATION:

Oils: Ⓣeucalyptus

—TINNITUS:

Tinnitus is a ringing or other audible noise in the ears caused by ear infection, wax buildup, or a block in the eustachian tube.

---

had less incidences of nausea than did women receiving a placebo. Ginger root has similar results to the antiemetic drug (a drug effective against vomiting and nausea) metoclopramide (Bone et al., 1990).

1 Lemongrass and lemon verbena oil were found to be bactericidal to *Helicobacter pylori* (a pathogen responsible for gastroduodenal disease) at very low concentrations. Additionally, it was found that this bacteria did not develop a resistance to lemongrass oil after 10 passages, while this bacteria did develop resistance to clarithromycin (an antibiotic) under the same conditions (Ohno et al., 2003).

2 A formulation of lemongrass and geranium oil was found to reduce airborne bacteria by 89% in an office environment after diffusion for 15 hours (Doran et al., 2009).

Primary Recommendations • Secondary Recommendations • Other Recommendations / Ⓐ=Aromatic, Ⓣ=Topical, Ⓘ=Internal

Ear

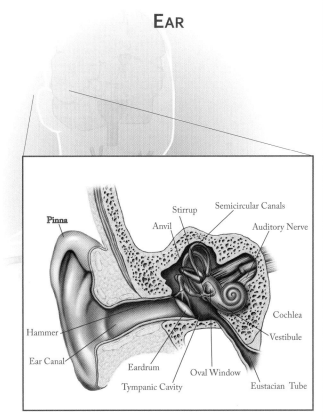

Oils: ⊕helichrysum

⊕: Caution: Never put oils directly into the ear canal. Dilute as recommended, and apply 1–2 drops on surface of the ear and behind the ear on the mastoid bone. Apply 1 drop oil to small cotton ball, and place over opening to ear canal (do not press into the ear canal). Place 1 drop oil on cotton swab, and swab around the ear canal.

Ⓐ: Diffuse into the air.

Eating Disorders:

—Anorexia:

Anorexia is a psychological disorder where a person becomes obsessed with body size and weight, often depriving him or herself of food to avoid gaining weight.

Oils: Ⓐgrapefruit, ⒶCitrus Bliss

Ⓐ: Diffuse into the air. Inhale directly from bottle. Apply oil to hands, tissue, or cotton wick, and inhale.

—Bulimia:

Bulimia is a disorder categorized by periods of overeating, or binging, followed by periods of self-induced vomiting, fasting, or abuse of laxatives and diuretics to purge the body of the food or to compensate for the overeating.

Oils: Ⓐgrapefruit, ⒶCitrus Bliss

Ⓐ: Diffuse into the air. Inhale directly from bottle. Apply oil to hands, tissue, or cotton wick, and inhale.

—Overeating:

Overeating is eating too much food for the body. It can include binging (eating so much at one time that the stomach is overly filled and uncomfortable or painful) or chronic overeating (eating more than the body needs over a long period of time). Consistently overeating can lead to obesity and other health problems.

Oils: ❶ⒶSlim & Sassy, Ⓐgrapefruit[3], Ⓐlemon[3], Ⓐpeppermint, Ⓐginger

Other Products: ❶Slim & Sassy Trim Shake

❶: Add 8 drops of Slim & Sassy to 16 oz. of water, and drink throughout the day between meals. Drink Trim Shake 1–2 times per day as a meal alternative.

Ⓐ: Diffuse into the air. Inhale directly from bottle. Apply oil to hands, tissue, or cotton wick, and inhale.

Eczema: *see Skin:Dermatitis/Eczema*

Edema: *see also Allergies, Diuretic, Inflammation*

Edema is swelling caused by the abnormal accumulation of fluids in a tissue or body cavity. This can be caused by an allergic reaction, inflammation, injury, or as a signal of problems with the heart, liver, or kidneys.

Oils: ⊕⊕grapefruit, ⊕lemongrass, ⊕cypress, ⊕geranium, ⊕rosemary

⊕: Dilute as recommended, and apply 1–2 drops on location.

❶: Add 1–2 drops to 8 oz. of water, and drink every 3 hours.

---

3 The scent of grapefruit oil and its component, limonene, was found to affect the autonomic nerves and to reduce appetite and body weight in rats exposed to the oil for 15 minutes three times per week (Shen et al., 2005).

ELBOW: *SEE JOINTS:TENNIS ELBOW*

EMERGENCY OILS:

The following oils are recommended to have on hand in case of an emergency:

Clove: Use as an analgesic (for topical pain relief) and a drawing salve (to pull toxins/infection from the body). Good for acne, constipation, headaches, nausea, and toothaches.

Frankincense: Enhances effect of any other oil. It facilitates clarity of mind, accelerates all skin recovery issues, and reduces anxiety and mental and physical fatigue. Reduces hyperactivity, impatience, irritability, and restlessness. Helps with focus and concentration.

Lavender: Use for agitation, bruises, burns (can mix with melaleuca), leg cramps, herpes, heart irregularities, hives, insect bites, neuropathy, pain (inside and out), bee stings, sprains, sunburn (combine with frankincense), and sunstroke. Relieves insomnia, depression, and PMS and is a natural antihistamine (asthma or allergies).

Lemon: Use for arthritis, colds, constipation, coughs, cuts, sluggishness, sore throats, sunburn, and wounds. It lifts the spirits and reduces stress and fatigue. Internally it counteracts acidity, calms an upset stomach, and encourages elimination.

Lemongrass: Use for sore and cramping muscles and charley horses (with peppermint; drink lots of water). Apply to bottoms of feet in winter to warm them.

Melaleuca: Use for bug bites, colds, coughs, cuts, deodorant, eczema, fungus, infections (ear, nose, or throat), microbes (internally), psoriasis, rough hands, slivers (combine with clove to draw them out), sore throats, and wounds.

Oregano: Use as heavy-duty antibiotic (internally with olive oil or coconut oil in capsules or topically on bottoms of feet—follow up with lavender and peppermint). Also for fungal infections and for reducing pain and inflammation of arthritis, backache, bursitis, carpal tunnel syndrome, rheumatism, and sciatica. *Always dilute.*

Peppermint: Use as an analgesic (for topical pain relief, bumps, and bruises). Can also be used for circulation, fever, headache, indigestion, motion sickness, nausea, nerve problems, or vomiting.

AromaTouch: Use for relaxation and stress relief. It is soothing and anti-inflammatory and enhances massage.

Breathe: Use for allergies, anxiety, asthma, bronchitis, congestion, colds, coughs, flu, and respiratory distress.

Deep Blue: Use for pain relief. Works well in cases of arthritis, bruises, carpel tunnel, headaches, inflammation, joint pain, migraines, muscle pain, sprains, and rheumatism. Follow with peppermint to enhance affects.

DigestZen: Use for all digestion issues such as bloating, congestion, constipation, diarrhea, food poisoning (internal), heartburn, indigestion, motion sickness, nausea, and stomachache. Also works well on diaper rash.

On Guard: Use to disinfect all surfaces. It eliminates mold and viruses and helps to boost the immune system (bottoms of feet or internally; use daily).

Purify: Use for airborne pathogens, cuts, germs (on any surface), insect bites, itches (all types and varieties), and wounds. Also boosts the immune system.

TerraShield: Deters all flying insects and ticks from human bodies and pets.

EMOTIONS: *SEE ANXIETY, CALMING, DEPRESSION, FEAR, GRIEF/SORROW, STRESS:EMOTIONAL STRESS, UPLIFTING*

EMPHYSEMA:

Emphysema is a chronic pulmonary disease where airflow is restricted through the lungs due to destruction (typically caused by airborne toxins such as those in cigarette smoke) of the wall of the alveoli (small air sacs in the lungs where oxygen and carbon dioxide is exchanged with the blood). This destruction of the alveolar wall causes the alveoli to collapse when air is expelled from the lungs, trapping air inside.

Oils: ^{AT}eucalyptus, ^{AT}Breathe

A: Diffuse into the air.

T: Dilute as recommended, and apply 1–2 drops to chest and back. Apply as a warm compress on chest.

ENDOCRINE SYSTEM: *SEE ALSO ADRENAL GLANDS, OVARIES, PANCREAS, PINEAL GLAND, PITUITARY GLAND, TESTES, THYMUS, THYROID*

The endocrine system is the series of hormone-producing glands and organs that help regulate metabolism, reproduction, blood pressure, appetite, and many other body functions. The endocrine system is mainly controlled by the hypothalamus region of the brain that either produces hormones that stimulate the other endocrine glands directly, or that stimulates the pituitary gland located just below it to release the hormones needed to stimulate the other endocrine glands. These hormones are released into the blood stream where they travel to other areas of the body to either stimulate other endocrine glands or to stimulate tissues and organs of the body directly. Some essential oils may act as hormones or stimulate the endocrine system to produce hormones that have a regulating effect on the body.

Oils: ^{IT}Zendocrine, ^{AT}rosemary, ^{AT}cinnamon

Other Products: ^IZendocrine capsules to help support healthy endocrine cleansing and filtering.

—HORMONAL BALANCE:

Oils: ^{TA}clary sage, ^Aclove, ^{AT}ylang ylang

Other Products: ^IWomen's Phytoestrogen Lifetime Complex,

–FEMALE:

Oils: ^{IA}Whisper

–SEXUAL ENERGY:

Oils: ^{AT}ylang ylang

I: Take capsules as directed on package. Add 3–5 drops of essential oil to an empty capsule; swallow capsule.

A: Diffuse into the air. Inhale directly from bottle. Apply oil to hands, tissue, or cotton wick, and inhale.

ENDOCRINE GLANDS

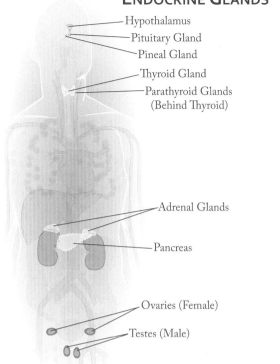

Hypothalamus
Pituitary Gland
Pineal Gland
Thyroid Gland
Parathyroid Glands (Behind Thyroid)
Adrenal Glands
Pancreas
Ovaries (Female)
Testes (Male)

T: Dilute as recommended, and apply 1–2 drops to the reflex points on the feet, lower back, thyroid, liver, kidneys, gland areas, the center of the body, or both sides of the spine and clavicle area. Add 1–2 drops to 1 Tbs. fractionated coconut oil, and use as massage oil.

ENDOMETRIOSIS:

Endometriosis is a chronic disorder in women where endometrium cells (cells from the lining of the uterus) grow outside of the uterus—typically around the ovaries, the ligaments that support the uterus, or the peritoneal (abdominal) cavity. These cells are often still responsive to the monthly hormone cycle that effects the changes in the uterus and can cause abnormal abdominal pain and irregularities in the menstrual cycle.

Oils: ^Tgeranium, ^Tcypress, ^Tclary sage, ^TOn Guard, ^Teucalyptus, ^TWhisper

T: Dilute as recommended, and apply 1–2 drops on lower abdomen or on feet. Apply as a warm compress. Place 1–2 drops in warm bathwater, and bathe.

ENDURANCE:

Oils: ^Apeppermint

Primary Recommendations • Secondary Recommendations • Other Recommendations / **A**=Aromatic, **T**=Topical, **I**=Internal

167

Other Products: ❶Alpha CRS+, ❶xEO Mega, ❶Microplex VMz to provide nutrients and antioxidants that help support healthy cellular function and energy levels.

Ⓐ: Diffuse into the air. Inhale directly from bottle. Apply oil to hands, tissue, or cotton wick, and inhale.

❶: Take capsules as directed on package.

ENERGY:

Oils: ⒶⓉwhite fir, ⒶⓉElevation, ⒶⓉBalance, ⒶⓉpeppermint, ⒶⓉlemon, ⒶⓉbasil, ⒶⓉthyme, ⒶⓉrosemary, ⒶⓉorange, ⒶⓉlemongrass, ⒶⓉeucalyptus

Other Products: ❶Alpha CRS+, ❶xEO Mega, ❶Microplex VMz to provide nutrients and antioxidants that help support healthy cellular function and energy levels.

—EXHAUSTION:

Oils: First, work with one or more of the following nervous system oils to help calm and relax: Ⓣlavender, Ⓣylang ylang, ⓉRoman chamomile, Ⓣfrankincense, Ⓣclary sage. Secondly, use an energizing oil such as Ⓣlemon, Ⓣsandalwood, Ⓣrosemary, ⒶⓉlime, Ⓣbasil, Ⓣgrapefruit.

—FATIGUE:

Oils: ⓉⒶrosemary (nervous fatigue), ⓉⒶthyme (general fatigue)

–MENTAL FATIGUE:

Oils: ⒶⓉSerenity, ⒶⓉlemongrass, ⒶⓉbasil

Blend 1: Blend equal parts basil and lemongrass together. Apply to temples, back of neck, and feet. Diffuse into the air.

–PHYSICAL FATIGUE:

Oils: ⓉⒶSerenity

—PHYSICAL:

Oils: Ⓐlemon, Ⓐcinnamon, Ⓐbergamot

—SEXUAL:

Oils: Ⓐylang ylang

Ⓐ: Diffuse into the air. Inhale directly from bottle. Apply oil to hands, tissue, or cotton wick, and inhale.

Ⓣ: Dilute 1–2 drops in 1 Tbs. fractionated coconut oil, and massage into muscles. Place 1–2 drops in warm bathwater, and bathe. Dilute as recommended, and apply 1–2 drops on temples, back of neck, liver area, or feet.

❶: Take capsules as directed on package.

EPILEPSY: *SEE SEIZURE:EPILEPSY*

EPSTEIN-BARR: *SEE MONO; SEE ALSO ANTIVIRAL:EPSTEIN-BARR VIRUS*

ESTROGEN:

Estrogens are hormones produced by the ovaries that regulate the development of female characteristics and the menstrual cycle in females.

Oils: ⓉⒶSolace, ⓉⒶclary sage

Other Products: ❶Women's Phytoestrogen Lifetime Complex

Ⓣ: Apply on the lower abdomen. Dilute 1–2 drops in 1 Tbs. fractionated coconut oil, and use as massage oil.

❶: Take capsules as directed on package.

Ⓐ: Diffuse into the air. Inhale directly from bottle. Apply oil to hands, tissue, or cotton wick, and inhale.

EXHAUSTION: *SEE ENERGY:EXHAUSTION*

EXPECTORANT: *SEE CONGESTION:EXPECTORANT*

EYES:

Eyes are the organs of the body responsible for detecting and adjusting to light and focusing images of the surrounding environment onto the optical nerve for transfer to the brain for processing.

Oils: Ⓣlemongrass, Ⓣsandalwood, Ⓣcypress, Ⓣlemon, Ⓣfennel, Ⓣeucalyptus, Ⓣlavender, ⓉOn Guard

Other Products: ❶Microplex VMz for nutrients that help support healthy eye cell function.

Recipe 1: Eye Drop Recipe: Combine 5 parts distilled water, 2 parts honey, and 1 part apple cider vinegar (do not use white vinegar). Mix together, and store in a bottle. Does not need to be refrigerated. This special eye drop

EYE

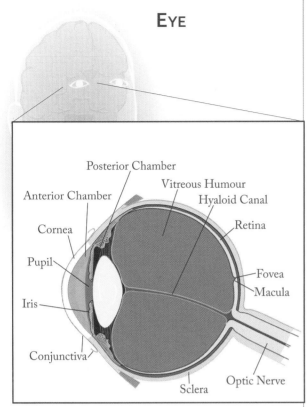

formula is found in Stanley Burroughs' book, *Healing for the Age of Enlightenment* and has proven over the years to be superior to most commercial eye drops. These drops have been used for glaucoma, cataracts, spots, film, and growths of various kinds. Apply drops one at a time to each eye several times a day until condition has cleared.

—BLOCKED TEAR DUCTS:

Tears from the eye normally drain through small tubes called tear ducts. The tear ducts carry tears from the surface of the eye into the nose where they are reabsorbed or evaporate. When these tear ducts are blocked, the eyes become watery and irritated. Blocked tear ducts are most common in babies and in older adults.

Oils: ❶lavender

—CATARACTS:

A cataract is a clouding of the normally transparent lens of the eye. This clouding results in blurry vision, seemingly faded colors, double vision, glare, and difficulty seeing at night. Over time, the clouding can increase and lead to severe vision problems.

Oils: ❶clove, ❶lavender

Blend 1: Combine 8 drops lemongrass, 6 drops cypress, and 3 drops eucalyptus. Apply around the eye area two times a day. Do not get oil in the eyes.

—DRY/ITCHY EYES:

Oils: ❹melaleuca (in humidifier)

—EYE LID DROP/DROOPING EYELID:

A drooping eyelid is characterized by an excessive sagging of the upper eyelid. Drooping can be present at birth as a result of underdeveloped eyelid muscles, or it can occur with aging. Drooping eyelids can cause visual impairment if they droop enough to partially cover the eye.

Blend 2: Combine equal parts helichrysum and peppermint, and apply 1–2 drops on the eyelid. Do not get oil in the eyes.

—IMPROVE VISION:

Oils: ❶frankincense, ❶lemongrass, ❶On Guard, ❶sandalwood, ❶lavender

Blend 3: Combine 10 drops lemongrass, 5 drops cypress, and 3 drops eucalyptus with 2 Tbs. fractionated coconut oil. Apply around the eyes morning and night, or apply on reflex points on the feet or on the ears.

—IRIS INFLAMMATION:

The iris is the colored part of the eye that regulates the amount of light entering the eye through the pupil. When the iris becomes inflamed, it results in a condition called iritis. Iritis is normally related to a disease or infection in another part of the body, but it can also be caused by injury to the eye. Symptoms of iritis include blurred vision, pain, tearing, light sensitivity, red eye, and a small pupil size.

Oils: ❶eucalyptus

—MACULAR DEGENERATION:

Macular degeneration is an eye disease common in individuals 65 and older. It is marked by degeneration of a small, oval-shaped part of the retina called the macula. Because the macula is responsible for capturing the light from the central part of images coming into the eye, macular degeneration causes blurring or a blind spot in the central vision, making it difficult to drive, recognize faces, read, or do any kind of detail work.

Oils: ❶clove

—Pink Eye:

Pink eye, also know as conjunctivitis, is an inflammation or infection of the membranes covering the whites of the eyes (conjunctiva) and the inner part of the eyelids. Swelling, redness, itching, discharge, and burning of the eyes are common symptoms of pink eye. Frequent causes include allergies, bacterial or viral infection, contact lenses, and eye drops.

Oils: ❶❷melaleuca, ❶❷lavender

—Retina (strengthen):

The retina is a layer of nerves lining the back of the eye. The retina is responsible for sensing light and then sending impulses (via the optic nerve) back to the brain so that visual images can be formed.

Oils: ❶cypress, ❶lemongrass, ❶helichrysum, ❶peppermint, ❶lavender, ❶sandalwood

—Swollen Eyes:

Oils: ❶cypress, ❶helichrysum, ❶peppermint (allergies), ❶lavender

❶: Caution: Never put essential oils directly in the eyes! Be careful when applying oils near the eyes. Be sure to have some fractionated coconut oil handy for additional dilution if irritation occurs. Never use water to wash off an oil that irritates. Dilute as recommended, and apply 1–2 drops around eyes or to feet, thumbs, ankles, pelvis, base of neck, or reflex points on the feet.

🅐: Diffuse into the air.

🅘: Take capsules as directed on package.

Facial Oils: see Skin

Fainting: see also Shock

Fainting is a temporary loss of consciousness caused by a momentary disruption of blood flow to the brain. Fainting can result from standing in one place too long, coughing very hard, fear, emotional trauma, heavy bleeding, or severe dehydration. Fainting can sometimes be a symptom of a more serious condition.

Oils: ❶peppermint, ❶rosemary, ❶basil, ❶lavender

🅐: Inhale directly from bottle.

Fatigue: see Energy:Fatigue

Fear: see also Anxiety, Calming

Fear causes the blood vessels to tighten, restricting the amount of oxygen and nutrients that can reach the cells.

Oils: 🅐🅣Balance, 🅐🅣ylang ylang[1], 🅐orange[2], 🅐🅣sandalwood, 🅐🅣clary sage, 🅐🅣geranium, 🅐🅣myrrh, 🅐🅣bergamot, 🅐🅣white fir, 🅐🅣cypress, 🅐🅣marjoram

🅐: Diffuse into the air. Inhale directly from bottle. Apply oil to hands, tissue, or cotton wick, and inhale.

🅣: Dilute as recommended, and apply 1–2 drops to temples, back of neck, or bottoms of feet.

Feet: see Foot

Female Specific Conditions: see also Endometriosis, Pregnancy/Motherhood

—Hemorrhaging: see Blood:Hemorrhaging

—Hot Flashes:

A hot flash is a sudden, intense feeling of heat in the face and upper body, often accompanied by an increased heart rate, sweating, dizziness, headache, weakness, or anxiety. Hot flashes are generally associated with the symptoms of menopause and premenopause.

Oils: 🅣🅐Solace, 🅣Balance, 🅣peppermint, 🅣clary sage

Other Products: 🅘Women's Phytoestrogen Lifetime Complex, 🅘Lifelong Vitality Pack (contains Alpha CRS+, xEO Mega, and Microplex VMz)

Recipe 1: Both morning and evening, apply 1–2 drops each of Balance and peppermint to back of neck; then apply 1–2 drops clary sage to forearms in the morning and to ankles in the evening. Lifelong

---

1   Subjects who had ylang ylang oil applied to their skin had decreased blood pressure, increased skin temperature, and reported feeling more calm and relaxed compared to subjects in a control group (Hongratanaworakit et al., 2006).

2   Female patients waiting for dental treatment were found to be less anxious, more positive, and more calm when exposed to orange oil odor than were patients who were not exposed to the orange oil odor (Lehrner et al., 2000).

Vitality Pack may also be taken to help regulate the hormonal system.

—**HORMONES (BALANCING):**

Oils: ❶🅐Solace, ❶🅐ylang ylang, ❶🅐clary sage

Other Products: ❶Women's Phytoestrogen Lifetime Complex

—**INFERTILITY:**

Infertility is clinically defined as the inability to get pregnant after a year of trying. This could be due to any of several underlying causes.

Oils: ❶clary sage, ❶geranium, ❶melissa, ❶cypress, ❶thyme, ❶fennel, ❶Roman chamomile, ❶ylang ylang

—**MENOPAUSE:**

Menopause is the permanent ending of a female's menstruation and fertility. For most American women, Menopause occurs around age 51 and is often recognized by hot flashes, irregular periods, vaginal dryness, mood swings, difficulty sleeping, thinning hair, abdominal weight gain, and decreased fertility.

Oils: ❶🅐Solace, ❶cypress, ❶lavender, ❶Roman chamomile, ❶orange, ❶clary sage, ❶basil, ❶geranium, ❶rosemary, ❶thyme

Other Products: ❶Women's Phytoestrogen Lifetime Complex, ❶Women's Bone Nutrient Lifetime Complex

–**PREMENOPAUSE:**

Oils: ❶🅐Solace, ❶clary sage, ❶lavender

Other Products: ❶Women's Phytoestrogen Lifetime Complex, ❶Women's Bone Nutrient Lifetime Complex

—**MENSTRUATION:**

Menstruation, also known as a woman's "period," is the regular shedding of the uterus lining and vaginal discharge of blood when a woman is not pregnant. A woman's period lasts between two and seven days and reoccurs on an average of every 28 days.

–**AMENORRHEA:**

Amenorrhea is the absence of menstruation. The following oils may help induce menstrual flow (emmenagogic) and may need to be avoided during pregnancy for this reason. *See Pregnancy/Motherhood* for further safety data.

Oils: ❶🅐Solace, ❶basil, ❶clary sage, ❶peppermint, ❶rosemary ❶marjoram, ❶lavender, ❶Roman chamomile

Other Products: ❶Women's Phytoestrogen Lifetime Complex

–**DYSMENORRHEA:**

Dysmenorrhea is painful menstruation. Apply one or more of these oils to the abdomen. It may also help to use a hot compress.

Oils: ❶🅐Solace, ❶geranium, ❶clary sage, ❶lavender, ❶cypress, ❶peppermint, ❶marjoram, ❶Roman chamomile, ❶basil, ❶rosemary, ❶fennel

Other Products: ❶Women's Phytoestrogen Lifetime Complex

–**IRREGULAR:**

Oils: ❶🅐Solace, ❶peppermint, ❶rosemary, ❶Roman chamomile, ❶clary sage, ❶fennel, ❶lavender, ❶rose

Other Products: ❶Women's Phytoestrogen Lifetime Complex

—**MENORRHAGIA:**

Menorrhagia is abnormally heavy or extended menstrual flow. It may also refer to irregular bleeding at any time. This situation may be a sign of a more serious condition, so please see your doctor.

Oils: ❶🅐Solace, ❶cypress, ❶geranium, ❶Roman chamomile, ❶rose

Other Products: ❶Women's Phytoestrogen Lifetime Complex

–**SCANTY:**

Oils: ❶🅐Solace, ❶peppermint, ❶lavender, ❶melissa

Other Products: ❶Women's Phytoestrogen Lifetime Complex

—**OVARIES:**

Ovaries are the female reproductive organs in which eggs are produced and stored.

Oils: ❶🅐Solace, ❶rosemary, ❶geranium, ❶DigestZen

E

F

Primary Recommendations • Secondary Recommendations • Other Recommendations / 🅐=Aromatic, ❶=Topical, ❶=Internal

Other Products: ❶Women's Phytoestrogen Lifetime Complex

—OVARIAN CYST:

    Oils: ❶basil

—PMS:

Premenstrual syndrome (PMS) is a group of symptoms such as irritability, anxiety, moodiness, bloating, breast tenderness, headaches, and cramping that occurs in the days or hours before menstruation begins and then disappear once menstruation begins. PMS is thought to be caused by the fluctuation in hormones during this time or by the way progesterone is broken down by the body. Caffeine intake from beverages or chocolate is also thought to enhance PMS symptoms.

Oils: ❶ⒶSolace, ❶Ⓐclary sage, ❶Ⓐgeranium, ❶Ⓐfennel, ❶lavender, ❶Ⓐbergamot, ❶Ⓐgrapefruit

Other Products: ❶Women's Phytoestrogen Lifetime Complex, ❶Women's Bone Nutrient Lifetime Complex or ❶Microplex VMz contain calcium, which has been found to help lessen PMS symptoms.

—APATHETIC-TIRED-LISTLESS:

    Oils: ❶ⒶSolace, ❶Ⓐgrapefruit, ❶Ⓐgeranium, ❶Ⓐbergamot, ❶Ⓐfennel

    Other Products: ❶Women's Phytoestrogen Lifetime Complex

—IRRITABLE:

    Oils: ❶ⒶSolace, ❶Ⓐclary sage, ❶Ⓐbergamot, ❶ⒶRoman chamomile

    Other Products: ❶Women's Phytoestrogen Lifetime Complex

—VIOLENT AGGRESSIVE:

    Oils: ❶ⒶSolace, ❶Ⓐgeranium, ❶Ⓐbergamot

    Other Products: ❶Women's Phytoestrogen Lifetime Complex

—WEEPING-DEPRESSION:

    Oils: ❶ⒶSolace, ❶Ⓐclary sage, ❶Ⓐbergamot, ❶Ⓐgeranium

    Other Products: ❶Women's Phytoestrogen Lifetime Complex

—POSTPARTUM DEPRESSION: *SEE PREGNANCY/ MOTHERHOOD:POSTPARTUM DEPRESSION*

Ⓣ: Dilute as recommended, and apply to the abdomen, lower back, shoulders, or reflex points on the feet. Add 1–2 drops to 1 Tbs. fractionated coconut oil, and massage into abdomen, lower back, and shoulders. Apply as a warm compress to the abdomen. Add 1–2 drops to 2 tsp. olive oil, insert into vagina, and retain overnight with a tampon.

Ⓐ: Place in hands and inhale. Diffuse into the air.

❶: Take capsules as directed on package.

FERTILITY: *SEE FEMALE SPECIFIC CONDITIONS:INFERTILITY, MALE SPECIFIC CONDITIONS:INFERTILITY*

FEVER: *SEE ALSO COOLING OILS*

Fever is an increase of the body's core temperature, typically in response to an infection or injury. A fever is the body's natural response to help enhance the immune system's ability to fight the infection.

Oils: ❶ⓉⒶpeppermint, ❶Ⓣlemon, ❶ⓉⒶlime, ❶eucalyptus, ❶clove, ❶ⓉⒶpatchouli, ❶melaleuca, ❶ginger, ❶lavender, ❶basil, ❶white fir, ❶bergamot

—TO COOL THE SYSTEM:

    Oils: ❶clove, ❶ⓉⒶpeppermint, ❶eucalyptus, ❶bergamot

—TO INDUCE SWEATING:

    Oils: ❶basil, ❶fennel, ❶melaleuca, ❶peppermint, ❶rosemary, ❶lavender, ❶cypress

❶: Place 1–2 drops of essential oil into capsule; then swallow capsule. Place 1–2 drops in 8 oz. of rice milk or water, and sip slowly.

Ⓣ: Dilute as recommended, and apply to back or to bottoms of the feet.

Ⓐ: Diffuse into the air.

FIBRILLATION: *SEE CARDIOVASCULAR SYSTEM*

FIBROIDS:

Fibroids are noncancerous growths of muscle and connective tissue in the uterus. Fibroids can be painful and may affect fertility and pregnancy.

Oils: ☻frankincense, ☻helichrysum, ☻oregano, ☻Balance, ☻lavender

☻: Place 3 drops of oil in douche. Dilute as recommended, and apply to reflex points on the feet.

Fibromyalgia:

Fibromyalgia is long-term localized or generalized aches, pain, or tenderness in the muscles, ligaments, or other soft tissue that can interfere with normal movement, sleep, or other activities. There is no known cause of fibromyalgia, and many different factors may contribute to the development of this condition. Some have suggested eliminating refined sugar from the diet. Others have recommended reducing stress, stretching exercises, massage, or better sleep.

Oils: ☻Deep Blue, ☻wintergreen, ☻helichrysum, ☻lavender, ☻rosemary, ☻thyme

Other Products: ❶Alpha CRS+, ❶xEO Mega, ❶Microplex VMz for nutrients needed for healthy muscle and nerve cell function.

☻: Add 1–2 drops of oil to 1 Tbs. fractionated coconut oil, and massage on location. Apply as a warm compress over affected area.

❶: Take capsules as directed on package.

Finger (mashed):

Recipe 1: Apply 1 drop geranium (for bruising), 1 drop helichrysum (to stop the bleeding), 1 drop lavender, 1 drop lemongrass (for tissue repair), and 1 drop Deep Blue (for pain).

Flatulence: *see Digestive System:Gas/Flatulence*

Flu: *see Influenza*

Fluids: *see Edema, Diuretic*

Food Poisoning: *see also Antibacterial, Antifungal, Antiviral, Digestive System, Parasites*

Food poisoning refers to the effects on the digestive tract by pathogenic organisms—or the toxins they produce—that are ingested into the body in food. Symptoms of food poisoning can include stomach pain, cramps, diarrhea, nausea, and vomiting.

Oils: ❶DigestZen[1], ❶On Guard, ❶rosemary

❶: Add 6 drops to 8 oz. of water. Swish around in the mouth, and swallow. Place 1–2 drops in an empty capsule, and swallow.

Foot:

Oils: ☻lemon, ☻lavender, ☻Roman chamomile

—Athlete's Foot: *see Antifungal:Athlete's Foot*

—Blisters:

Oils: ☻lavender, ☻geranium, ☻melaleuca, ☻Purify

—Bunion: *see also Bursitis*

A bunion is bursitis located at the base of the big toe. It is often caused by constrictive shoes that force the big toe to point inward and the base of the big toe to jut outward. This misplacement can irritate the bursa located at the base of the toe and cause it to become inflamed, which causes further irritation.

Oils: ☻cypress

—Calluses:

A callus is a flat, thick growth of skin that develops on areas of the skin where there is constant friction or rubbing. Calluses typically form on the bottoms of the feet, but they can also form on the hands or other areas of the body exposed to constant friction.

Oils: ☻oregano

—Club Foot:

Oils: ☻ginger, ☻rosemary, ☻lavender, ☻Roman chamomile

—Corns:

Corns are painful growths that develop on the small toes due to repetitive friction in that area (often from ill-fitting footwear). If untreated, corns can cause increased pressure on underlying tissue, causing tissue damage or ulcerations.

Oils: ☻clove, ☻peppermint, ☻grapefruit, ☻Citrus Bliss

☻: Dilute as recommended, and apply to area. Combine 1–2 drops with fractionated coconut oil, and massage on location.

---

1 Peppermint and spearmint oils inhibited resistant strains of *Staphylococcus*, *E. coli*, *Salmonella*, and *Helicobacter pylori* (Imai et al., 2001).

Primary Recommendations • Secondary Recommendations • Other Recommendations / ☻=Aromatic, ☻=Topical, ❶=Internal

Forgetfulness: *see Memory*

Free Radicals: *see Antioxidant*

Frigidity: *see Sexual Issues:Female Frigidity*

Fungus: *see Antifungal*

Gallbladder:

The gallbladder is a small sac that stores extra bile from the liver until it is needed to help with digestion in the small intestine. The gallbladder is located just below the liver.

Oils: ⓣgeranium, ⓣrosemary, ⓣlavender

—Infection:

Oils: ⓣhelichrysum

—Stones:

Gallstones are formed by cholesterol that has crystallized from the bile stored in the gallbladder. These stones can sometimes block the duct that comes from the gallbladder or the small opening from the common hepatic duct that allows bile to flow into the small intestine. Gallstones blocking these ducts can be painful and can lead to more serious complications, such as infections or jaundice.

Oils: ⓣgrapefruit, ⓣgeranium, ⓣrosemary, ⓣwintergreen, ⓣlime

ⓣ: Dilute as recommended, and apply 1–2 drops over gallbladder area. Apply as a warm compress over the gallbladder area.

Gallstones: *see Gallbladder:Stones*

Gangrene:

Gangrene is the localized decay of body tissue caused by a loss of blood to that area. Gas gangrene is caused by bacteria invading a deep wound that has lessened the blood supply or cut it off entirely. The bacteria create gases and pus in the infected area, causing severe pain and accelerating decay of the tissue.

Oils: ⓣlavender, ⓣOn Guard, ⓣthyme

ⓣ: Dilute as recommended, and apply 1–3 drops on location.

Gas: *see Digestive System: Gas/Flatulence*

Gastritis: *see Digestive System:Gastritis*

Genitals: *see Female Specific Conditions, Male Specific Conditions/Issues*

Germs: *see Antibacterial, Antifungal, Antiviral*

Gingivitis: *see Oral Conditions:Gum Disease*

Goiter: *see Thyroid:Hyperthyroidism*

Gout:

Gout is a painful inflammation of a joint caused by a buildup of uric acid crystals deposited in the joint. Uric acid is formed during the natural breakdown of dead tissues in the body. An excess of uric acid in the bloodstream can lead to the formation of crystals in the joints or kidneys (kidney stones). Some good ways to prevent the formation of uric acid crystals include maintaining a healthy body weight (which leaves less body tissue to be broken down), exercising, and drinking plenty of water.

Oils: ⓘⓘlemon, ⓣgeranium, ⓣDeep Blue, ⓣwintergreen, ⓣthyme

ⓘ: Place 1–2 drops in 8 oz. of water, and drink. Place 1–2 drops in an empty capsule, and swallow.

ⓣ: Dilute as recommended, and apply on location. Add 1–2 drops to 1 Tbs. fractionated coconut oil, and massage on location.

Grave's Disease: *see Thyroid:Hyperthyroidism*

Grave's disease is an autoimmune disease caused by an abnormally-shaped protein stimulating the thyroid to make and secrete more hormones. This can cause an enlargement of the thyroid (goiter), bulging eyes, increased heart rate, high blood pressure, and anxiety.

Oils: ⓣⓐlemongrass, ⓣⓐmyrrh

Other Products: ⓘMicroplex VMz for nutrients and minerals to help support thyroid function.

ⓣ: Dilute as recommended, and apply on thyroid area or on reflex points on the feet.

ⓐ: Diffuse into the air.

❶: Take capsules as directed on package.

GRIEF/SORROW:

Oils: ❶❶lemon[1,2,3,4], ❶❶Elevation, ❶Balance, ❶❶lavender, ❶❶bergamot[4], ❶❶clary sage, ❶❶eucalyptus, ❶❶helichrysum

Ⓐ: Diffuse into the air. Inhale directly from bottle. Apply oil to hands, tissue, or cotton wick, and inhale. Wear 1–2 drops as perfume or cologne.

❶: Dilute as recommended, and apply 1–2 drops to the forehead, shoulders, or feet. Add 1–2 drops to 1 Tbs. fractionated coconut oil, and massage over whole body.

GUM DISEASE: *SEE ORAL CONDITIONS:GUM DISEASE*

GUMS: *SEE ORAL CONDITIONS:GUMS*

HABITS: *SEE ADDICTIONS*

HAIR:

Other Products: ❶SanoBella Smoothing Conditioner, ❶SanoBella Protecting Shampoo

—BEARD:

Oils: ❶rosemary, ❶lemon, ❶lavender, ❶thyme, ❶cypress

—CHILDREN:

Oils: ❶lavender

—DAMAGED:

Other Products: ❶SanoBella Smoothing Conditioner, ❶SanoBella Protecting Shampoo

—DANDRUFF: *SEE ALSO ANTIFUNGAL*

Dandruff is a scalp condition characterized by the excessive shedding of dead skin cells. A small amount of flaking on the scalp is normal as old skin cells die off and fall away, but dandruff results when the amount of dead

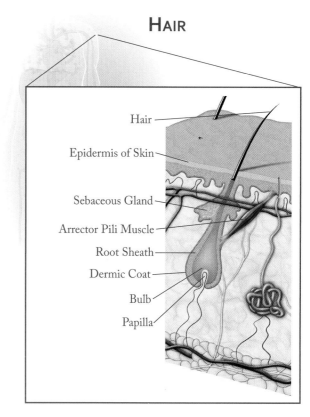

HAIR

Hair

Epidermis of Skin

Sebaceous Gland

Arrector Pili Muscle

Root Sheath

Dermic Coat

Bulb

Papilla

skin cells becomes excessive and visible. Dandruff can be caused by many possible factors: hormonal imbalance, poor hygiene, allergies, excessive use of hair sprays and gels, excessive use of curling irons, cold weather, infrequent shampooing, etc. Many specialists believe that dandruff is caused by a tiny fungus called *Pityrosporum ovale*.

Oils: ❶lavender, ❶wintergreen, ❶cypress, ❶rosemary, ❶thyme

—DRY:

Oils: ❶geranium, ❶sandalwood, ❶lavender, ❶rosemary, ❶wintergreen

Other Products: ❶SanoBella™ Smoothing Conditioner, ❶SanoBella™ Protecting Shampoo

—ESTROGEN BALANCE:

Estrogen is a steroid hormone that causes the development of female characteristics such as breasts and larger hips, helps with calcium uptake and balance, and plays many other important roles. Estrogen also helps hair to grow faster and to stay on the head longer. If estrogen levels fall, hair loss can quickly result.

Oils: ❶clary sage

---

1 Lemon odor was found to enhance the positive mood of volunteers exposed to a stressor (Kiecolt-Glaser et al., 2008).

2 Lemon oil vapor was found to have strong antistress and antidepressant effects on mice subjected to several common stress tests (Komiya et al., 2006).

3 Lemon oil and its component, citral, were found to decrease depressed behavior in a similar manner to antidepressant drugs in rats involved in several stress tests (Komori et al., 1995).

4 In 12 patients suffering from depression, it was found that inhaling citrus aromas reduced the needed doses of antidepressants, normalized neuroendocrine hormone levels, and normalized immune function (Komori et al., 1995).

—**Fragile Hair:**

    Oils: ⓉClary sage, Ⓣlavender, Ⓣthyme, Ⓣsandalwood, Ⓣwintergreen, ⓉRoman chamomile

    Other Products: ⓉSanoBella Smoothing Conditioner, ⓉSanoBella Protecting Shampoo

—**Greasy/Oily Hair:**

    Oils: Ⓣbasil, Ⓣcypress, Ⓣthyme, Ⓣlemon, Ⓣrosemary

    Other Products: ⓉSanoBella Smoothing Conditioner, ⓉSanoBella Protecting Shampoo

—**Growth (stimulate):**

    Oils: Ⓣthyme[1], Ⓣlavender[5], Ⓣrosemary[5], Ⓣylang ylang, Ⓣclary sage, Ⓣgeranium, Ⓣginger, Ⓣlemon, Ⓣgrapefruit

—**Itching:**

    Oils: Ⓣpeppermint, Ⓣlavender

—**Loss:**

One common form of hair loss, especially in males, is androgenic alopecia (also known as male-pattern baldness in males). This condition is thought to be caused by a genetically-predisposed sensitivity within the hair follicles to androgen hormones that causes them to shrink when exposed to this hormone. This shrinking of the hair follicles inhibits their ability to produce hair, leading to a receding hairline and partial baldness on the top and sides of the head in males and thinning hair in females. Another common form of baldness, especially in females, is alopecia areata, which is a condition in which hair loss occurs on all or part of the body. The most common form of alopecia areata involves the loss of round patches of hair on the scalp, leading this condition to be commonly referred to as "spot baldness."

    Oils: Ⓣrosemary[5], Ⓣlavender[5], Ⓣthyme[5], Ⓣylang ylang, Ⓣwintergreen, Ⓣlemon, Ⓣclary sage, Ⓣcypress, ⓉRoman chamomile

Ⓣ: Apply 1–2 drops of oil to hands, and massage into hair and scalp before bath or shower;

---

1 Patients with alopecia areata (hair loss) that massaged carrier oils containing a blend of thyme, rosemary, lavender, and cedarwood oils into their scalps were more likely to show improvement when compared to a control group that massaged carrier oils alone into their scalps (Hay et al., 1998).

then shampoo and rinse hair as normal. Add 1–2 drops of oil to 2 Tbs. of an unscented shampoo or shower gel, and use to shampoo hair. Use SanoBella Shampoo and Conditioner as directed on bottles.

Halitosis: *see Oral Conditions:Halitosis*

Hands:

    Oils: Ⓣgeranium, Ⓣlemon, Ⓣlemongrass, Ⓣsandalwood, Ⓣrosemary, Ⓣeucalyptus

—**Dry:**

    Oils: Ⓣgeranium, Ⓣsandalwood

—**Neglected:**

    Oils: Ⓣgeranium, Ⓣlemon

—**Tingling In:**

    Oils: Ⓣlemongrass

Ⓣ: Dilute as recommended, and apply 1–2 drops to hands. Dilute 1–2 drops in 1 Tbs. almond or olive oil, and use as massage oil to massage into hands.

Hangovers:

A hangover is a set of unpleasant physical effects that comes after heavy alcohol consumption. Common symptoms of a hangover include nausea, headache, lack of energy, diarrhea, and increased sensitivity to light and noise.

    Oils: ⓉⒶlemon, ⓉⒶgrapefruit, ⓉⒶlavender, ⓉⒶrosemary, ⓉⒶsandalwood

Ⓣ: Add 3–4 drops to warm bathwater, and bathe. Dilute as recommended, and apply 1–2 drops to back of neck or over liver. Add 1–2 drops to 1 Tbs. fractionated coconut oil, and massage onto back and neck.

Ⓐ: Inhale directly from bottle. Apply oil to hands, tissue, or cotton wick, and inhale. Drop 1–2 drops in bowl of hot water, and inhale vapors. Diffuse into the air.

Hashimoto's Disease: *see also Thyroid:Hypothyroidism.*

Hashimoto's disease is an autoimmune disorder where the immune system attacks the thyroid, causing it to swell up and become irritated. Hashimoto's disease does not have a unique set of

---

symptoms, but possible symptoms include abnormal fatigue, weight gain, muscle pain and stiffness, a hoarse voice, prolonged menstrual bleeding, constipation, a feeling of tightness in the throat, sensitivity to cold, dry skin, and depression.

Oils: ᵀᴬlemongrass, ᵀᴬmyrrh

Other Products: ᴵMicroplex VMz , ᴵAlpha CRS+ to help provide nutrients essential for thyroid cell health.

🅣: Dilute as recommended, and apply 1–2 drops over thyroid area or on reflex points on the feet.

🅐: Diffuse into the air. Inhale oil applied to hands.

🅘: Take capsules as directed on package.

HAY FEVER: *SEE ALLERGIES:HAY FEVER*

HEAD LICE: *SEE INSECTS/BUGS:LICE*

HEADACHES:

Oils: ᵀᴬPastTense, ᵀᴬpeppermint[2], ᵀᴬrosemary, ᵀᴬDeep Blue, ᵀᴬeucalyptus, ᵀᴬfrankincense, ᵀᴬpatchouli, ᵀᴬbasil, ᵀᴬmarjoram, ᵀᴬlavender, ᵀᴬclove

Recipe 1: Apply 2 drops each of peppermint, eucalyptus, and frankincense to neck, temples, and forehead.

—MIGRAINE HEADACHE:

A migraine is a severe and painful type of headache. Symptoms of migraines include throbbing pain accompanied by nausea, vomiting, and heightened sensitivity to light. Women are much more likely than men to suffer from migraines. Migraines can be triggered by stress, anxiety, sleep or food deprivation, bright lights, loud noises, and hormonal changes.

Oils: ᵀᴬPastTense, ᵀᴬpeppermint, ᵀᴬbasil, ᵀᴬDeep Blue, ᵀᴬwintergreen, ᵀᴬylang ylang

—TENSION HEADACHE:

Tension headaches (also called "stress headaches") are the most common type of headache. Tension headaches are characterized by dull, constant pressure or pain (usually on both sides of the head). Tension headaches can last from thirty minutes to several days and tend to come back when a person is under stress.

Oils: ᵀᴬPastTense, ᵀᴬpeppermint, ᵀᴬDeep Blue

—SUGAR HEADACHE (CAUSED BY LOW BLOOD SUGAR):

Oils: ᵀᴬOn Guard

🅣: Dilute as recommended, and apply 1–2 drops to temples, back of neck, and forehead.

🅐: Diffuse into the air. Inhale directly from bottle. Apply oil to hands, tissue, or cotton wick, and inhale.

HEARING: *SEE EARS*

HEART: *SEE CARDIOVASCULAR SYSTEM:HEART*

HEARTBURN: *SEE DIGESTIVE SYSTEM:HEARTBURN*

HEATSTROKE:

Heatstroke is when the body's temperature rises dangerously high due to the body's inability to dissipate heat, typically because of high environmental temperatures and high levels of exertion. If not corrected, the body can overheat too much, causing organs and body systems to become damaged and possibly shut down—possibly leading to death. Symptoms of heatstroke include perspiration, dizziness, confusion, headaches, and nausea.

Oils: ᵀpeppermint, ᵀlavender

🅣: Dilute as recommended, and apply 3–5 drops on neck and forehead. Cool the body as soon as possible in a cool bathtub, lake, river, or soaked linens.

HEMATOMA: *SEE ALSO BLOOD:HEMORRHAGING.*

A hematoma is a collection of blood outside of the blood vessels. The most common form of a hematoma is a bruise. Hematomas can also form into hard, blood-filled sacs that look like welts and can move to different locations. These often dissolve on their own. Hematomas can also form in other organs as the result of injury or hemorrhaging.

Oils: ᵀhelichrysum

🅣: Dilute as recommended, and apply 1–2 drops on location.

---

2 A combination of peppermint oil and ethanol was found to have a significant analgesic effect with a reduction in sensitivity to headache, while a combination of peppermint, eucalyptus, and ethanol was found to relax muscles and to increase cognitive performance in humans (Göbel et al., 1994).

HEMORRHAGING: *SEE BLOOD:HEMORRHAGING*

HEMORRHOIDS:

Hemorrhoids are swollen, twisted veins that occur in the rectum or anus. They are caused by increased pressure within the veins, often due to pregnancy, frequent lifting, or constipation.

Oils: ⊕cypress, ⊕geranium, ⊕clary sage, ⊕helichrysum, ⊕patchouli, ⊕peppermint, ⊕sandalwood, ⊕frankincense, ⊕myrrh

Blend 1: Mix 1 drop cypress with 1 drop of either helichrysum or geranium, and apply on location.

⊕: Dilute as recommended, and apply 1–2 drops on location. Mix 1–2 drops with 1 tsp. fractionated coconut oil, and apply on location using a rectal syringe.

HEPATITIS: *SEE LIVER:HEPATITIS*

HERNIA: *SEE ALSO BACK:HERNIATED DISCS*

A hernia is the protrudence of a tissue or organ through tissue or muscle outside of the body cavity in which it is normally contained. There are several different types of hernias, and the symptoms vary with each type.

—HIATAL:

A hiatal (hiatus) hernia is when a portion of the stomach protrudes through the diaphragm into the chest cavity above. This can cause pain, acid reflux, and heartburn. It can be caused by a birth defect or may be brought on by heavy lifting, stress, or being overweight.

Oils: ⊕basil, ⊕peppermint, ⊕cypress, ⊕ginger, ⊕geranium, ⊕lavender, ⊕fennel, ⊕rosemary

—INCISIONAL:

An incisional hernia is caused by a protrusion through scar tissue from an abdominal wound or incision that hasn't healed correctly.

Oils: ⊕basil, ⊕helichrysum, ⊕lemongrass, ⊕geranium, ⊕lavender, ⊕ginger, ⊕lemon, ⊕melaleuca

—INGUINAL:

An inguinal hernia is when the intestines protrude into the inguinal canal (a small opening that leads from the abdominal cavity into the

groin area). This can sometimes be seen as a bulge in the groin area and is usually painless, but it may become painful if the blood supply to the herniated portion of the intestine is restricted (strangulated).

Oils: ⊕lemongrass, ⊕lavender

⊕: Dilute as recommended, and apply on location, lower back, and reflex points on the feet.

HERPES SIMPLEX: *SEE ALSO ANTIVIRAL*

Herpes simplex type 1 and type 2 viruses are the two viruses that cause genital and oral herpes infections. These viruses cause painful outbreaks of blisters and sores to occur in the affected area when the virus is active in the skin or mucus membranes, followed by periods of latency when the virus resides in the nerve cells around the infected area.

Oils: ⊕peppermint[1], ⊕melaleuca[2], ⊕helichrysum[3], ⊕clove[4], ⊕lavender, ⊕eucalyptus[2], ⊕lemon, ⊕cypress, ⊕rose, ⊕bergamot

⊕: Dilute as recommended, and apply oil directly on the lesions at the first sign of outbreak.

HICCUPS/HICCOUGHS:

Hiccups, or hiccoughs, are the uncontrollable spasms of the diaphragm that cause a sudden intake of breath and the closure of the glottis (the opening that stops substances from entering the trachea while swallowing). Hiccups are thought to be caused either by a lack of carbon dioxide in the blood or by something irritating the diaphragm.

Oils: ⊛⊕sandalwood

⊛: Diffuse into the air. Inhale directly from bottle. Apply oil to hands, tissue, or cotton wick, and inhale.

⊕: Dilute as recommended, and apply 1–2 drops to the diaphragm area or reflex points on the feet.

HIGH BLOOD PRESSURE:
SEE BLOOD:BLOOD PRESSURE:HIGH

1 Peppermint oil demonstrated a direct virucidal activity against herpes type 1 and type 2 viruses (Schuhmacher et al., 2003).
2 Tea tree and eucalyptus oil demonstrated ability to inhibit *Herpes simplex* virus (Schnitzler et al., 2001).
3 Helichrysum was found to have significant antiviral activity against the herpes virus at non-cytotoxic concentrations (Nostro et al., 2003).
4 Eugenol was found to be virucidal to *Herpes simplex* and to delay the development of herpes-induced keratitis (inflammation of the cornea) in mice (Benencia et al., 2000).

HIVES: *SEE ALSO ALLERGIES, ANTIVIRAL*

Hives are itchy patches of inflamed spots on the skin surrounded by redness, typically caused by an allergic reaction or a viral infection.

Oils: ⊕melaleuca[5,6], ⊕peppermint, ⊕lavender[7]

⊕: Dilute as recommended, and apply 1–2 drops on location. Add 1–2 drops to 1 Tbs. fractionated coconut oil, and massage on location.

HODGKIN'S DISEASE: *SEE ALSO CANCER*

Hodgkin's disease (or Hodgkin's lymphoma) is a type of cancer that affects lymphocytes (white blood cells). It can cause enlarged lymph nodes, fever, sweating, fatigue, and weight loss.

Oils: ⊕clove

⊕: Dilute as recommended, and apply 1–2 drops to the liver, kidney, and reflex points on the feet.

HORMONAL SYSTEM/IMBALANCE:
SEE ENDOCRINE SYSTEM

HOT FLASHES: *SEE FEMALE SPECIFIC CONDITIONS*

HOUSECLEANING:

—BATHROOMS/KITCHENS:

Oils: ⊕lemon, ⊕white fir (for cleaning and disinfecting)

⊕: Place a few drops on your cleaning rag or dust cloth; or place 10 drops in a small spray bottle with distilled water, and mist on surfaces before cleaning.

—CARPETS:

Oils: ⊕lemon, ⊕Purify

⊕: Apply on carpet stains to help remove. To freshen carpet, add 50–70 drops of these (or another favorite oil) to 1/2 cup baking soda. Sprinkle over carpets, wait 15 minutes, and then vacuum.

—DISHES:

Oils: ⊕lemon

⊕: Add a couple of drops to dishwater for sparkling dishes and a great smelling kitchen. Can add to dishwasher as well.

—FURNITURE POLISH:

Oils: ⊕lemon, ⊕white fir, ⊕Citrus Bliss, ⊕Purify

⊕: Place a few drops on a clean rag, and use to polish furniture.

—GUM/GREASE:

Oils: ⊕lemon, ⊕lime

⊕: Place 1–2 drops on gum or grease to help dissolve.

—LAUNDRY:

Oils: ⊕lemon, ⊕Purify

⊕: Add a few drops of oil to the water in the washer. Add a few drops on a washcloth with clothes in the dryer. Add a few drops to a small spray bottle of water, and mist on laundry in the dryer before drying. Any of these methods can increase the antibacterial benefits and help clothes to smell fresh and clean.

—MOLD/FUNGUS: *SEE ALSO ANTIFUNGAL:MOLD*

Oils: Ⓐ⊕On Guard, ⊕Purify

Ⓐ: Diffuse into the air.

⊕: Place a few drops on a cleaning rag, and wipe down the affected area.

—STAINS:

Oils: ⊕lemon (has been used to remove black shoe polish from carpets)

⊕: Apply on location.

HYPERACTIVITY: *SEE CALMING:HYPERACTIVITY*

HYPERPNEA: *SEE RESPIRATORY SYSTEM:HYPERPNEA*

HYPERTENSION:
SEE BLOOD:BLOOD PRESSURE:HIGH

HYPOGLYCEMIA:

Hypoglycemia is a condition of low levels of sugar in the blood. It is most common in people with diabetes but can be caused by drugs or by a tumor in the pancreas that causes the pancreas to create too much insulin. Symptoms of hypoglycemia can

---

5 Tea tree oil applied to histamine-induced weal and flare in human volunteers was found to decrease the mean weal volume when compared to a control (Koh et al., 2002).

6 Tea tree oil applied to histamine-induced edema (swelling) in mice ears was found to significantly reduce swelling (Brand et al., 2002).

7 Lavender oil was found to inhibit immediate-type allergic reactions in mice and rats by inhibiting mast cell degranulation (Kim et al., 1999).

Primary Recommendations • Secondary Recommendations • Other Recommendations / Ⓐ=Aromatic, ⊕=Topical, ⓘ=Internal

include hunger, sweating, weakness, palpitations, shaking, dizziness, and confusion.

Oils: ⓣeucalyptus, ⓣOn Guard, ⓣcinnamon, ⓣclove, ⓣthyme

Other Products: ⓘPB Assist+ to help maintain a healthy digestive system.

ⓣ: Dilute as recommended and apply 1–2 drops over pancreas and on reflex points on the feet.

ⓘ: Take capsules as directed on package.

Hysteria: *see Calming*

Immune System: *see also Allergies, Antibacterial, Antifungal, Antiviral, Cancer, Lymphatic System, Parasites*

The immune system is the body's defense against disease. The immune system protects the body by identifying and killing bacteria, viruses, parasites, other microorganisms, and tumor cells that would harm the body. The immune system is comprised of several different types of white blood cells (lymphocytes) that recognize, process, or destroy foreign objects, the bone marrow that creates several types of white blood cells, the thymus that creates white blood cells and teaches them to recognize foreign objects and distinguish them from the body's cells, lymphatic vessels that help transport lymph and white blood cells, and several other organs, such as the lymph nodes, tonsils, spleen, and appendix, that filter out foreign objects and serve as a place for white blood cells to gather, interact, and share information about infections.

Oils: ⓣⒶOn Guard, ⓣⒶⓘoregano[1], ⓣⒶmelaleuca, ⓣⒶrosemary, ⓣⒶclove, ⓣⒶfrankincense, ⓣⒶgeranium, ⓣⒶlemon, ⓣⒶthyme, ⓣⒶlavender, ⓣⒶlime

Other Products: ⓘAlpha CRS+, ⓘxEO Mega, ⓘMicroplex VMz to provide nutrients essential for healthy immune system function.

—**Stimulates:**

Oils: ⓣⒶⓘoregano[1], Ⓐcinnamon, ⓣⒶfrankincense, ⓣⒶmelaleuca, ⓣOn Guard, ⓣⒶlavender

ⓣ: Dilute as recommended, and apply 1–2 drops to bottoms of feet, along spine, or under arms

(around lymph nodes). Add 1–2 drops to 1 Tbs. fractionated coconut oil, and massage onto back, arms, and feet.

Ⓐ: Diffuse into the air.

ⓘ: Take capsules as recommended. Place 2–3 drops in an empty capsule, and swallow.

Impetigo: *see Skin:Impetigo*

Impotence: *see Male Specific Conditions:Impotence*

Incontinence: *see Bladder:Bed Wetting and Incontinence*

Indigestion: *see Digestive System:Indigestion*

Infection: *see also Antibacterial, Antifungal, Antiviral*

Oils: ⓣⒶcinnamon, ⓣⒶclary sage, ⓣⒶOn Guard, ⓣⒶbergamot, ⓣⒶmyrrh (with oregano), ⓣⒶbasil, ⓣⒶcypress, ⓣⒶrosemary (with myrrh for oral infection), ⓣⒶthyme (for urinary infection), ⓣⒶlemongrass, ⓣⒶlime, ⓣⒶpatchouli, ⓣⒶlavender, ⓣⒶoregano, ⓣⒶfennel, ⓣⒶpeppermint

Other Products: ⓘMicroplex VMz for nutrients that help provide immune support.

—**Infected Wounds:**

Oils: ⓣⒶfrankincense, ⓣⒶmelaleuca

Blend 1: Apply 1 drop thyme on location with hot compress daily. After infection and pus have been expelled, mix 3 drops lavender, 2 drops melaleuca, and 2 drops thyme combined with 1 tsp. fractionated coconut oil, and apply a little of this mixture on location twice daily.

ⓣ: Dilute as recommended, and apply 1–2 drops on location. Mix 1–2 drops with 1 Tbs. fractionated coconut oil, and massage on location or on neck, arms, chest, or feet.

Ⓐ: Diffuse into the air. Add 1–2 drops to a bowl of hot water, and inhale the vapors.

ⓘ: Take capsules as directed on package.

Infertility: *see Female Specific Conditions: Infertility, Male Specific Conditions:Infertility*

---

[1] Growth-retarded pigs receiving a supplementation of oregano leaves and flowers enriched with cold-pressed oregano oil were found to have increased growth, decreased mortality, and higher numbers of immune-system cells and compounds when compared to control pigs who did not receive supplementation (Walter et al., 2004).

INFLAMMATION: *SEE ALSO ANTIOXIDANT*

Inflammation is the body's reaction to infection and injury. It is characterized by redness, swelling, warmth, and pain. Inflammation is an immune system response that allows the body to contain and fight infection or repair damaged tissue by dilating the blood vessels and allowing vascular permeability to increase blood supply to an injured or infected tissue. While a certain amount of inflammation can be beneficial in fighting disease and healing injuries, too much inflammation or chronic inflammation can actually be debilitating.

Oils: ⊤◬frankincense[2,3,4,5,6,7,8,9], ⊤◬melaleuca[10,11,12,13,14,15,16,17,18], ⊤◬eucalyptus[19,20,21,22,23], ⊤oregano, ⊤Deep

Blue, ⊤lavender[24,25], ⊤◬patchouli, ⊤Roman chamomile[26], ⊤myrrh[27,28], ⊤rosemary[29,30,31], ⊤◬peppermint[32,33], ⊤◬wintergreen[34], ⊤clove[35,36], ⊤thyme[37], ⊤geranium[38], ⊤helichrysum[39], ⊤Immortelle ⊤◬Serenity, ⊤◬lemongrass, ⊤◬cypress

Other products: ◐Alpha CRS+ and ◐Microplex VMz for polyphenols and other antioxidants to help relieve oxidative stress associated with inflammation. ◐xEO Mega for omega-3 fatty acids that help balance the inflammatory response.

⊤: Dilute as recommended, and apply 1–2 drops on location and on the back of neck by the base of the skull. Add 3–4 drops to 1 Tbs. fractionated coconut oil, and massage on location.

◐: Take capsules as directed on package. Place 2–3 drops of essential oil in an empty capsule, and swallow. Place 1–2 drops in 8 oz. of rice or almond milk, and drink.

2 Triterpene acids isolated from frankincense were found to exhibit a marked anti-inflammatory activity in TPA-induced inflammation in mice (Banno et al., 2006).

3 Boswellic acids from frankincense were found to inhibit TH1 cytokines while potentiating TH2 cytokines when delivered with sesame seed oil, demonstrating their ability to modulate the immune response (Chevrier et al., 2005).

4 Compounds from *Boswellia serrata* were found to carry out anti-inflammatory activity by switching off the pro-inflammatory cytokines and mediators that initiate the inflammatory process (Gayathri et al., 2007).

5 An acetone extract of frankincense was found to decrease arthritic scores, reduce paw edema (swelling), and suppress pro-inflammatory cytokines (cellular messengers) (Fan et al., 2005).

6 Boswellic acid reduced induced inflammation and tumors in mice and was found to inhibit DNA synthesis in human leukemia cells in culture (Huang et al., 2000).

7 Boswellic extract was found to affect genes related to the inflammatory response in human microvascular cells. Additionally, Boswellic extract was found to reduce inflammation in carrageenan-induced rat paw inflammation (Roy et al., 2005).

8 Boswellic acid, from frankincense, was found in vitro to prevent expression and activity of several proteins involved in inflammatory response. In vivo, Boswellic acid was found to protect against experimental arthritis (Roy et al., 2006).

9 Incensole acetate, isolated from frankincense resin, was found to demonstrate an anti-inflammatory and neuroprotective effect in mice with closed head injuries (Moussaieff et al., 2008).

10 *Melaleuca alternifolia* oil was found to mediate the reactive oxygen species (ROS) production of leukocytes (white blood cells), indicating possible anti-inflammatory activity (Caldefie-Chézet et al., 2004).

11 Tea tree oil applied to histamine-induced edema (swelling) in mice ears was found to significantly reduce swelling (Brand et al., 2002).

12 Tea tree oil applied to histamine-induced edema (swelling) in mice ears was found to significantly reduce swelling (Brand et al., 2002).

13 Tea tree oil was found to reduce swelling during a contact hypersensitivity response in the skin of mice sensitized to the chemical hapten (Brand et al., 2002).

14 Several water-soluble components of tea tree oil were found to suppress the production of superoxide by monocytes (a type of white blood cell involved in the immune system) (Brand et al., 2001).

15 The water soluble terpinen-4-ol component of tea tree was found to suppress the production of pro-inflammatory mediators in human monocytes (a type of white blood cell that is part of the human immune system) (Hart et al., 2000).

16 Inhaled tea tree oil was found to have anti-inflammatory influences on male rats with induced peritoneal inflammation (Golab et al., 2007).

17 Tea tree oil applied to histamine-induced weal and flare in human volunteers was found to decrease the mean weal volume when compared to a control (Koh et al., 2002).

18 Tea tree oil was found to reduce inflammation in nickel-sensitive human skin exposed to nickel (Pearce et al., 2005).

19 Eucalyptus oil was shown to ameliorate inflammatory processes by interacting with oxygen radicals and interfering with leukocyte activation (Grassmann et al., 2000).

20 1,8 cineole (eucalyptol) was found to display an anti-inflammatory effect on rats in several tests and was found to exhibit antinociceptive (pain-reducing) effects in mice, possibly by depressing the central nervous system (Santos et al., 2000).

21 Eucalyptus oil was found to have an anti-inflammatory and mucin-inhibitory effect in rats with lipopolysaccharide-induced bronchitis (Lu et al., 2004).

22 Oils of three eucalyptus species (*citriodora, tereticornis,* and *globulus*) were found to have analgesic (pain-relieving) and anti-inflammatory properties in rats (Silva et al., 2003).

23 Extracts from eucalyptus and thyme were found to have high nitrous oxide (NO) scavenging abilities and to inhibit NO production in macrophage cells. This could possibly explain their role in aiding respiratory inflammatory diseases (Vigo et al., 2004).

24 Oil from *Lavandula angustifolia* was found to reduce writhing in induced writhing in rats and to reduce edema (swelling) in carrageenan-induced paw edema, indicating an anti-inflammatory effect (Hajhashemi et al., 2003).

25 Linalool and linalyl acetate (from lavender and other essential oils) were found to exhibit anti-inflammatory activity in rats subjected to carrageenin-induced edema (inflammation) (Peana et al., 2002).

26 Chamazulene, a chemical in chamomile oil, was found to block formation of leukotriene (a signaling chemical involved in the inflammation process) in neutrophilic (immune system) granulocytes (white blood cells containing granules). It also demonstrated an antioxidant effect (Safayhi et al., 1994).

27 At subtoxic levels, myrrh oil was found to reduce interleukin (chemical signals believed to play a role in the inflammation response) by fibroblast cells in the gums (Tipton et al., 2003).

28 Subtoxic levels of myrrh oil were found to inhibit interleukin (chemical messenger involved in inflammation), in part by inhibiting PGE(2) (Prostaglandin E, a lipid compound that has several messenger functions in the body, including in the inflammatory response) (Tipton et al., 2006).

29 An ethanol extract of rosemary was found to have an antiproliferative effect on human leukemia and breast carcinoma cells as well as an antioxidant effect (Cheung et al., 2007).

30 An ethanol extract of rosemary was found to demonstrate antinociceptive (pain blocking) and anti-inflammatory activity in mice and rats (González-Trujano et al., 2007).

31 Rosemary oil was found to have anti-inflammatory and peripheral-antinociceptive (pain sensitivity blocking) properties in mice (Takaki et al., 2008).

32 A combination of peppermint and caraway oil was found to reduce visceral hyperalgesia (pain hypersensitivity in the gastrointestinal tract) after induced inflammation in rats (Adam et al., 2006).

33 L-menthol was found to inhibit production of inflammation mediators in human monocytes (a type of white blood cell involved in the immune response) (Juergens et al., 1998).

34 Methyl salicylate (found in wintergreen or birch oils) was found to inhibit leukotriene C4 (a chemical messenger involved in inflammatory response), while also demonstrating a gastroprotective effect against ethanol-induced gastric injury in rats (Trautmann et al., 1991).

35 Eugenol (found in clove EO) was found to increase the anti-inflammatory activity of cod liver oil (lowered inflammation by 30%) (Reddy et al., 1994).

36 Topical application of geranium oil was found to reduce the inflammatory response of neutrophil (white blood cell) accumulation in mice (Maruyama et al., 2005).

37 Extracts from eucalyptus and thyme were found to have high nitrous oxide (NO) scavenging abilities and to inhibit NO production in macrophage cells. This could possibly explain their role in aiding respiratory inflammatory diseases (Vigo et al., 2004).

38 Topical application of geranium oil was found to reduce the inflammatory response of neutrophil (white blood cell) accumulation in mice (Maruyama et al., 2005).

39 Arzanol, extracted from helichrysum, inhibited HIV-1 replication in T cells and also inhibited the release of pro-inflammatory cytokines (chemical messengers) in monocytes (Appendino et al., 2007).

A: Diffuse into the air. Add 1–2 drops to a bowl of hot water or humidifier, and inhale the vapors to help relieve inflammation within the respiratory system.

INFLUENZA: *SEE ALSO ANTIVIRAL*

Influenza, commonly referred to as "the flu," is a highly contagious viral infection of the respiratory system. Influenza is marked by a sudden onset of high fever, dry cough, sore throat, muscle aches and pains, headache, fatigue, loss of appetite, nausea, and nasal congestion.

Oils: **A T**Breathe, **A T**melaleuca, **A T I**peppermint, **A T**rosemary, **A T**eucalyptus, **T A**On Guard, **A T**white fir (aches/pains), **A T**lavender, **A T**oregano, **A T**thyme, **A**orange, **A T**clove, **T A**ginger

Other Products: **T**On Guard Foaming Hand Wash to help prevent the spread of influenza viruses. **I**Microplex VMz for nutrients to help support immune function.

A: Diffuse into the air.

T: Dilute as recommended, an apply to thymus area, chest, back, sinuses, or reflex points on the feet. Add 1–2 drops to hot bathwater, and bathe. Dilute 1–2 drops in 1 Tbs. fractionated coconut oil, and massage on chest, back, and feet.

I: Place 1–2 drops of ginger oil in an empty capsule, and swallow to help reduce feelings of nausea. Take capsules as directed on package.

INJURIES: *SEE BONES, BRUISES, CUTS, INFLAMMATION, JOINTS, MUSCLES/CONNECTIVE TISSUE, PAIN, SKIN:SCARRING, TISSUE:SCARRING, WOUNDS*

INSECTS/BUGS: *SEE ALSO BITES/STINGS*

—BEES, WASPS, AND HORNET STINGS:

Oils: **T**Roman chamomile, **T**basil, **T**Purify, **T**lavender, **T**lemongrass, **T**lemon, **T**peppermint, **T**thyme.

Recipe 1: Remove the stinger, and apply a cold compress of Roman chamomile to the area for several hours or as long as possible.

T: Dilute as recommended, and apply 1–2 drops on location after making certain that the stinger is removed.

—GNATS AND MIDGES:

Oils: **T**lavender, **T A**TerraShield.

Recipe 2: Mix 3 drops thyme in 1 tsp. cider vinegar or lemon juice. Apply to bites to stop irritation.

T: Dilute as recommended, and apply 1–2 drops to bite area.

A: Diffuse into the air. Place 1–2 drops on small ribbons, strings, or cloth, and hang around area to help repel mosquitoes.

—ITCHING:

Oils: **T**lavender

T: Dilute as recommended, and apply 1–2 drops to affected area.

—LICE:

Oils: **T**eucalyptus, **T A**TerraShield, **T**rosemary, **T**melaleuca[1,2], **T**geranium, **T**lemon, **T**lavender

T: Dilute as recommended, and rub 1–2 drops into the scalp three times a day, and apply to feet.

—MOSQUITOES:

Oils: **T A**TerraShield, **T A**patchouli[3], **T**lavender, **T**helichrysum

T: Dilute as recommended, and apply 1–2 drops to feet and exposed skin. Add 3–5 drops to 1 Tbs. fractionated coconut oil, and apply to exposed skin. Add 2–3 drops to 1–2 oz. distilled water in a small spray bottle; shake well, and mist onto the skin or into small openings where bugs may come through.

A: Diffuse into the air. Place 1–2 drops on small ribbons, strings, or cloth, and hang around area to help repel mosquitoes.

---

1 Tea tree oil was found to be effective against both lice and dust mites in a mite chamber assay (Williamson et al., 2007).
2 Tea tree oil was found to prevent some blood feeding by lice on treated skin; and while not highly effective at the studied dosages, tea tree oil was found to be more effective than DEET at repelling head lice (Canyon et al., 2007).
3 Clove, citronella, and patchouli oils were found to effectively repel 3 species of mosquitoes (Trongtokit et al., 2005)

Primary Recommendations • Secondary Recommendations • Other Recommendations / **A**=Aromatic, **T**=Topical, **I**=Internal

182

—REPELLENT:

Oils: ⊤⊕TerraShield, ⊤⊕patchouli, ⊤⊕basil, ⊤⊕lavender[4,5], ⊤⊕lemongrass, ⊤⊕eucalyptus, ⊤⊕thyme, ⊤⊕Purify,

Blend 1: Combine 5 drops lavender, 5 drops lemongrass, 3 drops peppermint, and 1 drop thyme. Place neat on feet. Add to 1 cup (8 oz.) of water, and spray on using a fine-mist spray bottle. Or place drops of this blend on ribbons or strings and tie near windows or around picnic or camping area.

Blend 2: Combine equal parts clove, lemon, and orange, and apply 2–3 drops on skin.

Blend 3: Place 5 drops lemon and 5 drop Purify in a small spray bottle with distilled water. Shake well, and mist on your skin to help protect against insects, flies, and mosquitoes.

⊤: Dilute as recommended, and apply 1–2 drops to feet and exposed skin. Add 3–5 drops to 1 Tbs. fractionated coconut oil, and apply to exposed skin. Add 2–3 drops to 1–2 oz. distilled water in a small spray bottle; shake well, and mist onto the skin or into small openings where bugs may come through.

⊕: Diffuse into the air. Place 1–2 drops on small ribbons, strings, or cloth, and hang around area to help repel insects.

—SPIDERS:

Oils: ⊤basil, ⊤Purify (with melaleuca), ⊤lavender, ⊤lemongrass, ⊤lemon, ⊤peppermint, ⊤thyme

⊤: Dilute as recommended, and apply 1–2 drops to affected area. Apply oil as a cold compress.

—TERMITES:

Oils: ⊤⊕patchouli[6], ⊤⊕vetiver[7] (repels), ⊕⊤clove[7] (kills)

⊤: Apply oils around foundation and to soil around wood structures to help repel termites.

⊕: Diffuse into the air.

—TICKS:

Oils: ⊤⊕TerraShield, ⊤lavender[8]

Removing Ticks:

Do not apply mineral oil, Vaseline, or anything else to remove the tick as this may cause it to inject the spirochetes into the wound.

Be sure to remove the entire tick. Get as close to the mouth as possible, and firmly tug on the tick until it releases its grip. Don't twist. If available, use a magnifying glass to make sure that you have removed the entire tick.

Save the tick in a jar, and label it with the date, where you were bitten on your body, and the location or address where you were bitten for proper identification by your doctor, especially if you develop any symptoms.

Do not handle the tick.

Wash hands immediately.

Check the site of the bite occasionally to see if any rash develops. If it does, seek medical advice promptly.

⊤: After getting the tick out, apply 1 drop lavender every 5 minutes for 30 minutes.

INSOMNIA:

Insomnia is difficulty falling or staying asleep. It can be triggered by stress, medications, drug or alcohol use, anxiety, or depression.

Oils: ⊕⊤lavender[9], ⊕⊤orange[10], ⊕⊤Serenity, ⊕⊤Roman chamomile, ⊕⊤cypress, ⊕⊤ylang ylang, ⊕⊤Citrus Bliss, ⊕⊤marjoram, ⊕⊤lemon, ⊕⊤rosemary, ⊕⊤sandalwood, ⊕⊤clary sage, ⊕⊤bergamot

Blend 1: Combine 6 drops Citrus Bliss with 6 drops lavender. Apply blend to big toes, bot-

4 An infestation of the red bud borer pest was reduced by more than 95% in the grafted buds of apple trees by application of the essential oil of *Lavandula angustifolia* (van Tol et al., 2007).

5 Lavender oil was found to be comparable to DEET in its ability to repel ticks (Hyalomma marginatum) (Mkolo et al., 2007).

6 Both patchouli oil and its constituent, patchouli alcohol (patchoulol), were found to be repellent and insecticidal to Formosan termites when applied topically (Zhu et al., 2003).

7 Vetiver oil was found to repel termites and to prevent tunneling (with long-lasting effects), while clove oil was found to be highly termiticidal (Zhu et al., 2001).

8 Lavender oil was found to be comparable to DEET in its ability to repel ticks (Hyalomma marginatum) (Mkolo et al., 2007).

9 Female students suffering from insomnia were found to sleep better and to have a lower level of depression during weeks they used a lavender fragrance when compared to weeks they did not use a lavender fragrance (Lee et al., 2006).

10 Bitter orange peel oil taken orally by mice was found to reduce anxiety, increase sleeping time, and increase the time before a chemically-induced seizure started (Carvalho-Freitas et al., 2002).

Primary Recommendations • Secondary Recommendations • Other Recommendations / ⊕=Aromatic, ⊤=Topical, ⊕=Internal

toms of the feet, 2 drops around the navel, and 3 drops on the back of the neck.

Recipe 1: Combine 2 drops Roman chamomile, 6 drops geranium, 3 drops lemon, and 4 drops sandalwood. Add 6 drops of this blend to your bath at bedtime, and combine 5 drops with 2 tsp. fractionated coconut oil for a massage after the bath.

—FOR CHILDREN:

–1–5 YEARS:

Oils: Ⓐlavender, ⒶRoman chamomile

–5+ YEARS:

Oils: ⒶⓉclary sage, ⒶⓉgeranium, ⒶⓉylang ylang

Ⓐ: Diffuse into the air. Dissolve 3 drops essential oil in 1 tsp. pure grain alcohol (such as vodka) or perfumers alcohol, and combine with distilled water in a 2 oz. spray bottle; shake well, and spray into the air before sleep. Place 1–2 drops on bottom of pillow or stuffed animal.

Ⓣ: Dilute as recommended, and apply 1–2 drops on feet and back of neck. Combine 1–2 drops essential oil with 1 Tbs. fractionated coconut oil, and massage onto back, legs, feet, and arms.

INTESTINAL PROBLEMS: *SEE DIGESTIVE SYSTEM*

INVIGORATING:

Oils: ⓉⒶwintergreen, ⓉⒶeucalyptus, ⓉⒶpeppermint

Ⓣ: Dilute as recommended, and apply 1–2 drops to back of neck or temples.

Ⓐ: Diffuse into the air. Inhale directly from bottle. Apply oil to hands, tissue, or cotton wick, and inhale.

IONS:

An ion is an atom or group of atoms that has acquired a positive or negative electric charge as a result of losing or gaining electrons. Positive ions (cations) form when electrons are lost, and negative ions (anions) form when electrons are gained.

—NEGATIVE IONS:

Negative ions are produced naturally by wind and rain. They help stimulate the parasympathetic nervous system, which controls rest, relaxation, digestion, and sleep. The diffusion

of the following oils can help balance an over-abundance of positive ions and help produce a more stress-free environment.

Oils that ionize negatively when diffused:
grapefruit, bergamot, lavender, lemon

—POSITIVE IONS:

Positive ions are produced by electronic equipment and are typically found in man-made environments. They help stimulate the sympathetic nervous system, necessary for recovering, strengthening, and energizing. If you live in an environment with an over-abundance of negative ions, such as in the country or by the ocean, you may benefit by diffusing the following oils. The production of more positive ions can help bring greater balance to the area and provide a more healthy environment.

Oils that ionize positively when diffused:
clove, cypress, eucalyptus, frankincense, helichrysum, marjoram, rosemary, thyme, ylang ylang

---

IRRITABILITY: *SEE CALMING*

IRRITABLE BOWEL SYNDROME: *SEE DIGESTIVE SYSTEM*

ITCHING:

Itching is a tingling or irritation of the skin that produces a desire to scratch. Itching can be brought on by many factors including stress, bug bites, sunburns, allergic reactions, infections, and dry skin.

Oils: Ⓣlavender, ⓉSerenity, Ⓣpeppermint

Ⓣ: Dilute as recommended, and apply 1–2 drops on location and on ears. Add 2–3 drops to 1 Tbs. fractionated coconut oil, and apply a small amount on location.

JAUNDICE:

Jaundice is a condition characterized by a yellow appearance of the skin and the whites of the eyes. Jaundice is a result of excessive levels in the blood of a chemical called bilirubin. Bilirubin is a pigment that is made when hemoglobin from old or dead red blood cells is broken down. Jaundice occurs when the liver is unable to pass bilirubin from

---

the body as fast as it is being produced. Jaundice is often a symptom of other diseases or conditions.

Oils: ⊕Ⓐgeranium, ⒶⓉlemon, ⊕Ⓐrosemary

Ⓣ: Dilute as recommended, and apply 1–2 drops to liver area, abdomen, and reflex points on the feet.

Ⓐ: Diffuse into the air.

JET LAG: *SEE ALSO INSOMNIA*

Jet lag is the disruption of normal sleep patterns experienced while the body's internal clock adjusts to rapid changes in daylight and nighttime hours when flying to different areas of the world. Jet lag can cause tiredness, fatigue, and insomnia during normal sleeping hours. It is recommended to drink lots of fluids and to avoid alcohol or caffeine while flying to help prevent jet lag. Avoiding naps and forcing yourself to stay awake until your normal bedtime the first day can also help the body recover more quickly.

Oils: ⊕Balance, ⊕peppermint, ⊕eucalyptus, ⊕geranium, ⊕lavender, ⊕grapefruit, ⊕lemongrass

Ⓣ: Use invigorating oils such as peppermint and eucalyptus in the morning and calming oils such as lavender and geranium at night. Dilute as recommended, and apply 1–2 drops to temples, thymus, lower back, and bottoms of feet. Add 2–3 drops to 1 Tbs. fractionated coconut oil, and massage onto back, legs, shoulders, and feet. Add 1–2 drops to warm bathwater, and bathe.

JOINTS: *SEE ALSO ARTHRITIS, BONES, INFLAMMATION, MUSCLES/CONNECTIVE TISSUE*

A joint is an area where two bones come together. Joints can offer limited or no movement between the bones (such as in the skull) or can offer a wide range of motion (such as in the shoulders, hands, and knees).

Oils: ⊕Deep Blue, ⊕wintergreen, ⊕Roman chamomile (inflammation)

Other Products: ⊕Deep Blue Rub to help comfort joint stiffness and soreness.

—ROTATOR CUFF (SORE):

The rotator cuff is the group of muscles and tendons that connect and hold the upper arm in the shoulder joint. The rotator cuff can be-

KNEE JOINT

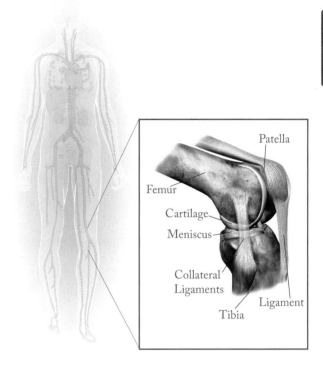

Patella
Femur
Cartilage
Meniscus
Collateral Ligaments
Tibia
Ligament

come sore due to repetitive stressful shoulder motions or injury.

Oils: ⊕wintergreen, ⊕Deep Blue, ⊕lemongrass, ⊕peppermint, ⊕white fir

Other Products: ⊕Deep Blue Rub to help comfort joint stiffness and soreness.

—SHOULDER (FROZEN): *SEE ALSO INFLAMMATION*

A frozen shoulder refers to a condition where the range of motion of the shoulder is severely limited and painful. This can be caused by inflammation, stiffness, abnormal tissue growth within the joint capsule (connective tissue that helps cushion, lubricate, and protect the joint) around the shoulder, arthritis, or inflammation of the bursa (small fluid-filled sacs that cushions muscle, ligament, and tendon tissue from the bones as they move across them). These conditions can be extremely painful and can take a long time to heal.

Oils: ⊕Deep Blue, ⊕white fir, ⊕lemongrass, ⊕basil, ⊕wintergreen, ⊕oregano, ⊕peppermint

Other Products: ⊕Deep Blue Rub to help comfort joint stiffness and soreness.

Regimen 1: Begin by applying 1–2 drops of white fir to the shoulder reflex point on the foot on the same side as the frozen shoulder to help with any inflammation. Check for any improvement in pain and/or range of motion. Repeat these steps using lemongrass (for torn or pulled ligaments), basil (for muscle spasms), and wintergreen (for bone problems). After determining which of these oils gets the best results for improving pain and/or range of motion, apply 1–2 drops of the oil (or oils) to the shoulder. Then apply 1–2 drops of peppermint (to help soothe the nerves) and 1–2 drops oregano (to help enhance muscle flexibility). Finally, apply white fir to the opposite shoulder to create balance as it compensates for the sore one. Drink lots of water.

—Tennis Elbow:

Tennis elbow (epicondylitis) is an injury to the tendons that connect the humerus bone near the elbow to the muscles that pull the hand backwards (lateral) and forward (medial) at the wrist. This type of injury is often associated with the repetitive forehand and backhand motions of playing tennis but can be caused by other activities that stress these tendons as well.

Oils: Deep Blue, eucalyptus, peppermint, helichrysum, wintergreen, rosemary, lemongrass

Other Products: Deep Blue Rub to help comfort joint stiffness and soreness.

Blend 1: Combine 10 drops eucalyptus, 10 drops peppermint, 10 drops rosemary, and 1 Tbs. fractionated coconut oil. Apply on location; then apply an ice pack. Can also try alternating cold and hot packs.

Blend 2: Combine 1 drop each of lemongrass, helichrysum, marjoram, and peppermint. Apply on location; then apply an ice pack.

T: Dilute as recommended, and apply 1–2 drops on location or on reflex points on the feet. Combine 5–10 drops with 1 Tbs. fractionated coconut oil, and massage on location.

Kidneys:

The kidneys are paired organs located just below the rib cage on either side of the spine that func-

tion to filter waste and extra water from the blood. The kidneys convert the waste and extra water into urine that is then excreted through urination. The kidneys also play an important role in hormone production.

Oils: lemongrass, thyme[1], Zendocrine, grapefruit, geranium, clary sage

Other Products: xEO Mega to provide omega-3 fatty acids that help support kidney function. Zendocrine capsules to help support healthy kidney functioning.

T: Dilute as recommended, and apply to kidneys and reflex points on the feet. Apply as a hot compress.

I: Take capsules as directed on package. Add 1–2 drops of essential oil to an empty capsule; swallow capsule.

—Diuretic: *see Diuretic*

—Infection:

Kidney infections occur when bacteria enters the urinary tract. They are marked by fever, abdominal pain, chills, painful urination, dull kidney pain, nausea, vomiting, and a general feeling of discomfort.

Oils: rosemary

T: Dilute as recommended, and apply to kidneys and reflex points on the feet.

I: Drink 1 gallon of distilled water and 2 quarts cranberry juice in one day.

—Inflammation (nephritis):

I: Drink 1 gallon of distilled water and 2 quarts cranberry juice in one day.

—Kidney Stones:

A kidney stone is a solid piece of material that forms as chemicals in the urine crystallize and adhere together in the kidney. Small stones may pass through urination without causing pain. Larger stones with sharp edges and corners, however, can cause an extreme amount of pain as they are passed out of the body through the urinary tract.

Oils: lemon, eucalyptus

---

1 Older rats whose diets were supplemented with thyme oil were found to have a higher level of the antioxidant enzymes superoxide dismutase and glutathione peroxidase in the heart, liver, and kidneys than did older rats without this supplementation (Youdim et al., 1999).

Primary Recommendations • Secondary Recommendations • Other Recommendations / **A**=Aromatic, **T**=Topical, **I**=Internal

186

Usage Guide

KIDNEYS

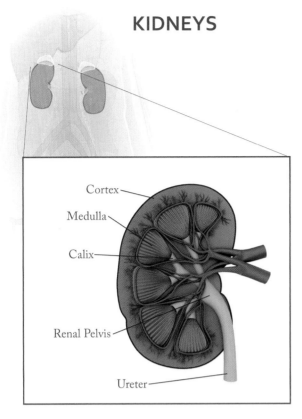

Cortex
Medulla
Calix
Renal Pelvis
Ureter

T: Apply as a hot compress over kidneys. Dilute as recommended, and apply 1–2 drops on location.

I: Add 1–2 drops oil to 8 oz. of water, and drink. To help pass a stone, drink 4 oz. distilled water with juice from 1/2 lemon every 30 minutes for 6 hours; then take 2 Tbs. extra-light virgin olive oil with the juice from 1 full lemon, and repeat daily until stone passes. Drinking plenty of water can help prevent the formation of kidney stones.

KNEE CARTILAGE INJURY:
SEE MUSCLES/CONNECTIVE TISSUE:CARTILAGE INJURY

LABOR: *SEE PREGNANCY/MOTHERHOOD:LABOR*

LACTATION: *SEE PREGNANCY/MOTHERHOOD:LACTATION*

LACTOSE INTOLERANCE:

Lactose intolerance is the inability of the body to fully digest lactose, a sugar found in milk and in other dairy products. Symptoms of lactose intolerance include abdominal pain and bloating, diarrhea, nausea, and gas.

Oils: **AI**lemongrass

I: Add 1–2 drops to 1 tsp. honey, and swallow; or add 1–2 drops to 4 oz. rice or almond milk, and drink. Place 1–2 drops in an empty capsule, and swallow.

T: Dilute as recommended, and apply 1–2 drops on abdomen or reflex points on the feet.

LARYNGITIS: *SEE ALSO ALLERGIES, ANTIVIRAL*

Laryngitis is an inflammation and swelling of the voice box (called the larynx) that causes the voice to sound hoarse or raspy. Laryngitis is most commonly caused by viruses, allergies, or overuse of the voice and will generally go away by itself within two weeks.

Oils: **AT**sandalwood, **A**frankincense, **A**thyme, **A**lavender

A: Diffuse into the air.

T: Dilute as recommended, and apply to neck and reflex points on the feet.

LAUNDRY: *SEE HOUSECLEANING:LAUNDRY*

LEUKEMIA: *SEE CANCER:LEUKEMIA*

LIBIDO: *SEE SEXUAL ISSUES:LIBIDO*

LICE: *SEE INSECTS/BUGS:LICE*

LIGAMENTS: *SEE MUSCLES/CONNECTIVE TISSUE:LIGAMENTS*

LIPOMA: *SEE TUMOR:LIPOMA*

LIPS:

Oils: **T**lavender, **T**melaleuca, **T**lemon

—DRY LIPS:

Blend 1: Combine 2–5 drops geranium with 2–5 drops lavender. Apply 1–2 drops on lips.

T: Dilute as recommended, and apply 1 drop on lips. Combine 1–2 drops essential oil with 1 Tbs. fractionated coconut oil, and apply a small amount to lips.

J

K

L

Primary Recommendations • Secondary Recommendations • Other Recommendations / **A**=Aromatic, **T**=Topical, **I**=Internal

187

LIVER:

The liver is the largest internal organ of the body. It is located in the upper abdomen and helps with digestion, produces cholesterol used to make several hormones and cellular membranes, removes waste products and old cells from the blood, and metabolizes harmful substances and toxins into harmless chemicals. The liver also has amazing regenerative abilities. Left with as little as 25% of its original mass, the liver can regrow what was lost and return to normal size.

Oils: geranium, helichrysum, DigestZen, cypress, grapefruit, Zendocrine, myrrh, Serenity, Roman chamomile

Other Products: xEO Mega, Alpha CRS+, Microplex VMz for omega-3 fatty acids and other nutrients that help support healthy liver cell functions. Zendocrine capsules to help support healthy liver functioning.

—CIRRHOSIS:

Cirrhosis is scarring of the liver that occurs as the liver tries to repair damage done to itself. When extensive liver damage occurs, the massive scar tissue buildup makes it impossible for the liver to function. The most common causes of cirrhosis are fatty liver (resulting from obesity or diabetes) and alcohol abuse; but any damage done to the liver can cause cirrhosis.

Oils: frankincense, myrrh, geranium, rosemary, rose, Roman chamomile

—CLEANSING:

Oils: clove, geranium, helichrysum, myrrh

—HEPATITIS: *SEE ALSO ANTIVIRAL.*

Hepatitis is any swelling or inflammation of the liver. This can interfere with normal liver functioning and can possibly lead to cirrhosis or cancer over time. The most common cause of hepatitis is from one of the five different forms of hepatitis viruses, but it can also be caused by alcohol consumption, other viruses, or medications. Possible symptoms of hepatitis include diarrhea, jaundice, stomach pain, loss of appetite, dark-colored urine, pale bowel movements, nausea, and vomiting.

Oils: myrrh, melaleuca, frankincense[1], rosemary, oregano, thyme, basil, cinnamon, cypress, eucalyptus, peppermint

—VIRAL:

Oils: myrrh, rosemary, basil

Other Products: PB Assist+ to help maintain friendly intestinal flora that help prevent toxins from pathogenic bacteria and viruses.

—JAUNDICE: *SEE JAUNDICE*

—STIMULANT:

Oils: helichrysum

T: Dilute as recommended, and apply 1–2 drops over liver area and on reflex points on the feet. Apply 1–2 drops on spine and liver area for viral infections. Apply as a warm compress over the liver area.

A: Diffuse into the air. Inhale directly from bottle. Apply oil to hands, tissue, or cotton wick, and inhale.

I: Take capsules as directed on package. Add 1–2 drops essential oil to an empty capsule; swallow capsule.

LOSS OF SMELL: *SEE NOSE:OLFACTORY LOSS*

LOU GEHRIG'S DISEASE:

Lou Gehrig's disease (also known as amyotrophic lateral sclerosis) is a progressive and fatal neurological disease that affects nerve cells in the brain and spinal cord. As the disease progresses, motor neurons die and the brain loses its ability to control muscle movement. Later stages of the disease can lead to complete paralysis. Eventually, control is lost of the muscles needed to breathe, to speak, and to eat.

Oils: cypress, Balance, frankincense, sandalwood, Serenity, geranium, rosemary, thyme

Other Products: xEO Mega for omega fatty acids essential for nerve cell function.

T: Dilute as recommended, and apply 1–2 drops on brain stem, neck, spine, and reflex points on the feet. Add 1–2 drops to 1 Tbs. fractionated coconut oil, and apply on back, neck, and feet.

---

1 A methanol extract of *Boswellia carterii* was found to have a high inhibition rate of hepatitis C virus protease (Hussein et al., 2000).

Primary Recommendations • Secondary Recommendations • Other Recommendations / **A**=Aromatic, **T**=Topical, **I**=Internal

188

A: Diffuse into the air. Inhale directly from bottle. Apply oil to hands, tissue, or cotton wick, and inhale.

I: Take capsules as directed on package.

LUMBAGO: *SEE BACK:LUMBAGO/LOWER BACK PAIN*

LUNGS: *SEE RESPIRATORY SYSTEM:LUNGS*

LUPUS:

Lupus is an autoimmune disease that occurs when the immune system begins attacking its own tissues and organs. Lupus can cause pain, damage, and inflammation in the joints, blood vessels, skin, and organs. Common symptoms include joint pain or swelling, fever, muscle pain, and red rashes (often on the face). Lupus is more common in women than in men.

Oils: ᵀclove, ᵀᴬElevation, ᵀOn Guard, ᵀBalance, ᴬᵀmelissa

T: Dilute as recommended, and apply 1–2 drops on adrenal glands, under the arms, on neck, or on bottoms of the feet.

A: Diffuse into the air. Inhale directly from bottle. Apply oil to hands, tissue, or cotton wick, and inhale.

LYMPHATIC SYSTEM: *SEE ALSO IMMUNE SYSTEM*

The lymphatic system is made up of the tissues and organs (bone marrow, thymus, spleen, lymph nodes, etc.) that produce and store the cells used to fight infection and disease. The lymphatic system transports immune cells through a fluid called lymph.

Oils: ᴬcypress, ᵀᴬsandalwood, ᴬᵀDigestZen

Blend 1: Combine 5 drops Roman chamomile, 5 drops lavender, and 5 drops orange with 2 Tbs. fractionated coconut oil, and massage onto the skin over lymph nodes.

Other Products: ᴵAlpha CRS+, ᴵxEO Mega, and ᴵMicroplex VMz for nutrients that help support healthy immune function.

—CLEANSING:

Oils: ᴬᵀlemon, ᵀᴬlime

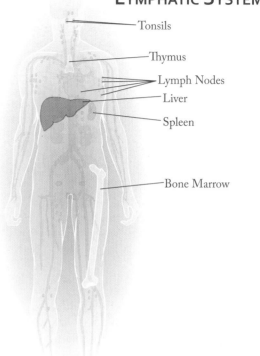

LYMPHATIC SYSTEM

Tonsils — Thymus — Lymph Nodes — Liver — Spleen — Bone Marrow

—DECONGESTANT FOR:

Oils: ᴬᵀcypress, ᵀᴬgrapefruit, ᴬᵀCitrus Bliss, ᵀᴬlemongrass, ᵀhelichrysum, ᴬᵀorange, ᵀᴬrosemary, ᵀᴬthyme

—DRAINAGE OF:

Oils: ᵀhelichrysum, ᵀᴬlemongrass

—ELIMINATES WASTE THROUGH:

Oils: ᵀᴬlavender

—INCREASE FUNCTION OF:

Oils: ᴬᵀlemon

A: Diffuse into the air. Inhale directly from bottle. Apply oil to hands, tissue, or cotton wick, and inhale.

T: Dilute as recommended, and apply 1–2 drops on neck, arms, thyroid area, and reflex points on the feet. Add 1–2 drops to warm bathwater, and bathe.

I: Take capsules as directed on package.

MALARIA:

Malaria is a disease caused by single-celled *Plasmodium* parasites. These parasites are spread by mosquitoes from one infected person to another.

Primary Recommendations • Secondary Recommendations • Other Recommendations / **A**=Aromatic, **T**=Topical, **I**=Internal

189

Symptoms of malaria include light-headedness, shortness of breath, fever, chills, nausea, and, in some cases, coma and death. The best way to prevent malaria is to avoid being bit by using mosquito repellent and mosquito nets, especially between dusk and dawn, in areas of the world where malaria is common.

Oils: ⊕ⒶTerraShield, ⊕Ⓐeucalyptus[1], ⊕Ⓐlemongrass, ⊕Ⓐlavender, ⊕lemon

Ⓣ: Dilute as recommended, and apply 1–2 drops to feet and exposed skin. Add 3–5 drops to 1 Tbs. fractionated coconut oil, and apply to exposed skin. Add 2–3 drops to 1–2 oz. distilled water in a small spray bottle; shake well, and mist onto the skin or into small openings where bugs may come through.

Ⓐ: Diffuse into the air. Place 1–2 drops on small ribbons, strings, or cloth, and hang around area to help repel mosquitoes.

Ⓘ: Mix 1–2 drops lemon with 1 tsp. honey and 8 oz. distilled water, and drink.

MALE SPECIFIC CONDITIONS/ISSUES:

—Genit al Area

–INFECTION:

Oils: ⊕melaleuca, ⊕oregano, ⊕eucalyptus, ⊕lavender

–INFLAMMATION:

Oils: ⊕lavender, ⊕Roman chamomile

–SWELLING:

Oils: ⊕cypress, ⊕lavender, ⊕rosemary, ⊕eucalyptus

—IMPOTENCE:

Impotence, also known as erectile dysfunction, is the frequent inability to have or sustain an erection. This may be caused by circulation problems, nerve problems, low levels of testosterone, medications, or psychological stresses.

Oils: ⊕Ⓐclary sage, ⊕Ⓐclove, ⊕Ⓐginger, ⊕Ⓐsandalwood

—INFERTILITY:

Infertility is clinically defined as the inability to achieve pregnancy after a year of trying.

---

1 A eucalyptus-based repellent containing p-menthane-3,8-diol as the active ingredient was found to be as effective as DEET in repelling the mosquito commonly known to carry a deadly malaria disease (complete protection for 6–7.75 hours) (Trigg, 1996).

Oils: ⊕Ⓐbasil, ⊕Ⓐclary sage, ⊕thyme

—JOCK ITCH: SEE ALSO ANTIFUNGAL:RINGWORM

Jock itch is a type of fungal infection that infects the skin of the genital area, causing itching or painful red patches of skin. It occurs more often during warm weather.

Oils: ⊕melaleuca, ⊕Clear Skin, ⊕lavender, ⊕cypress

Recipe 1: Place 2 drops of any of the above oils in 1 tsp. fractionated coconut oil, and apply to area morning and night. Alternately, place 2 drops oil in a small bowl of water, and wash the area with the water and then dry well each morning and night.

Ⓣ: Dilute as recommended, and apply 1–2 drops on location or on reflex points on the feet. Dilute 1–2 drops in 1 Tbs. fractionated coconut oil, and massage on location. Add 1–2 drops essential oil to warm water, and bathe.

Ⓘ: Place 1–2 drops in an empty capsule, and swallow.

Ⓐ: Diffuse into the air. Inhale directly from bottle. Apply oil to hands, tissue, or cotton wick, and inhale.

MASSAGE: *FOR OILS THAT CAN BE USED FOR AN AROMATIC MASSAGE FOR A SPECIFIC PURPOSE, SEE ALSO ANXIETY, ARTHRITIS, ASTHMA, BACK, BONES, CALMING, CARDIOVASCULAR SYSTEM, COOLING OILS, EDEMA, ENERGY, FEVER, FOOT, HAIR, HANDS, HEADACHES, INFLAMMATION, INVIGORATING, JOINTS, LYMPHATIC SYSTEM, MUSCLES/CONNECTIVE TISSUE, NERVOUS SYSTEM, PAIN, PREGNANCY/MOTHERHOOD, RESPIRATORY SYSTEM, SKIN, SLEEP, STRESS, TISSUE, UPLIFTING, WARMING OILS*

Massage is the manipulation of the soft tissues in the body through holding, moving, compressing, or stroking. Massage can be done to help aid circulation, relax muscles, relieve pain, reduce swelling, speed healing after strains and sprains, restore function to the body, and release tension and stress.

Oils: ⊕AromaTouch—a blend specifically created to aid in therapeutic massage to relax and soothe muscles, to increase circulation, and to stimulate tissues. See other conditions for specific oils that can be used to create a massage oil for that condition.

Other Products: ⊕Deep Blue Rub to help soothe tired, achy, and sore muscles and improve circulation within the tissue.

Blend 1: Combine 5 drops Roman chamomile, 5 drops lavender, and 5 drops orange with 2 Tbs. fractionated coconut oil, and use as massage oil for a relaxing massage.

🅣: Add 1–10 drops of essential oil to 1 Tbs. fractionated coconut oil or another carrier oil such as almond, olive, jojoba, sesame seed, or flaxseed to create a massage oil. *See also the section on the AromaTouch technique in the Science and Application of Essential Oils section of this book.*

MEASLES: *SEE CHILDHOOD DISEASES:MEASLES*

MELANOMA: *SEE CANCER:SKIN/MELANOMA*

MEMORY: *SEE ALSO ALZHEIMER'S DISEASE*

Memory is the mental capacity to retain and recall facts, events, past experiences, and impressions. Memory retention can be enhanced by memory exercises, adequate sleep, and associations with previous knowledge. Aroma also plays a roll in memory. At least one study has indicated that individuals exposed to an aroma while learning had an easier time remembering what they had learned when exposed to the same aroma, while those who were exposed to a differing aroma had a more difficult time remembering what they had learned[2].

Oils: 🅐🅣rosemary[3], 🅐🅣peppermint[4], 🅐🅣frankincense, 🅐🅣basil, 🅐🅣Citrus Bliss, 🅐🅣clove, 🅐🅣lemon, 🅣🅐ginger, 🅐🅣grapefruit, 🅣🅐lime, 🅐🅣bergamot, 🅐🅣rose, 🅐🅣lavender, 🅐🅣lemongrass

Other Products: ⊕xEO Mega, ⊕Microplex VMz for omega-3 fatty acids and other nutrients essential to brain cell health.

—**IMPROVE:**

Oils: 🅐🅣clove, 🅐clary sage

—**STIMULATE:**

Oils: 🅐rosemary

🅐: Diffuse into the air. Inhale directly from bottle. Apply oil to hands, tissue, or cotton wick, and inhale. Wear as a perfume or cologne.

🅣: Dilute as recommended, and apply 1–2 drops on temples or back of neck.

🅘: Take capsules as directed on package.

MENOPAUSE: *SEE FEMALE SPECIFIC CONDITIONS: MENOPAUSE*

MENSTRUATION: *SEE FEMALE SPECIFIC CONDITIONS:MENSTRUATION*

MENTAL: *SEE ALERTNESS, BRAIN, ENERGY, MEMORY, STRESS*

METABOLISM:

Metabolism refers to the processes involved in converting ingested nutrients into substances that can be used within the cells of the body for energy or to create needed cellular structures. This process is carried out by various chemical reactions facilitated by enzymes within the body.

—**BALANCE:**

Oils: 🅐clove, 🅐🅣Balance, 🅐🅣oregano

🅐: Diffuse into the air. Inhale oil applied to tissue or cotton wick.

🅣: Dilute as recommended, and apply 1–2 drops on neck or on bottoms of the feet.

METALS: *SEE DETOXIFICATION*

MICE (REPEL):

Oils: 🅣🅐Purify

🅣: Apply 1–2 drops in small openings or crevices where mice are likely to appear. Add 1–5 drops to small cotton balls, and place in openings where mice may come in.

🅐: Diffuse into the air.

MIGRAINES: *SEE HEADACHES:MIGRAINE HEADACHE*

MILDEW: *SEE ALSO ANTIFUNGAL*

Mildew is a whitish fungus that forms a flat growth on plants and organic material. Mildew attacks clothing, leather, paper, ceilings, walls,

---

2   Subjects who had learned a list of 24 words when exposed to an odor had an easier time relearning the list when exposed to the same odor compared to those who were exposed to an alternate odor (Smith et al., 1992).

3   Volunteers completing a battery of tests were found to be more content when exposed to lavender and rosemary aromas. Rosemary aroma also was found to enhance quality of memory compared to control (Moss et al., 2003).

4   In human trials, the aroma of peppermint was found to enhance memory and to increase alertness (Moss et al., 2008).

---

floors, shower walls, windowsills, and other places with high moisture levels. Mildew can produce a strong musty odor, especially in places with poor air circulation.

Oils: **⊕**Purify

T: Place a few drops in a small spray bottle with distilled water, and spray into air or on surface to help neutralize mildew.

MIND: *SEE ALERTNESS, BRAIN, ENERGY:FATIGUE:MENTAL FATIGUE, MEMORY*

MINERALS (DEFICIENCY):

Minerals are naturally-occurring, inorganic substances with a chemical composition and structure. Some minerals are essential to the human body. A person is considered to have a mineral deficiency when the concentration level of any mineral needed to maintain optimal health is abnormally low in the body.

Other Products: ⊕Microplex VMz contains a balanced blend of minerals essential for optimal cellular health, including calcium, magnesium, zinc, selenium, copper, manganese, chromium, and molybdenum.

I: Take capsules as directed on package.

MISCARRIAGE: *SEE PREGNANCY/MOTHERHOOD: MISCARRIAGE*

MOLES: *SEE SKIN:MOLES*

MONO (MONONUCLEOSIS): *SEE ALSO ANTIVIRAL*

Mononucleosis is a viral disease caused by the Epstein-Barr virus that usually spread through contact with infected saliva, tears, and mucous. Most adults have been exposed to this virus sometime in their lives, but many display no symptoms or only very mild flu-like symptoms. Mononucleosis symptoms are most often seen in adolescents and young adults. Symptoms of this disease include fatigue, weakness, severe sore throat, fever, swollen lymph nodes, swollen tonsils, headache, loss of appetite, and a soft or swollen spleen. Once individuals are exposed to the Epstein-Barr virus, they carry the virus for the rest of their lives. The virus sporadically becomes active, but the symptoms do not appear again. Whenever the virus is

active, however, it can be spread to others—even if the person carrying it shows no symptoms.

Oils: **AT**Breathe, **AT**On Guard

Blend 1: Combine 3 drops oregano, 3 drops On Guard, and 3 drops thyme. Rub the blend on the feet.

T: Dilute as recommended, and apply 1–3 drops on throat and feet.

A: Diffuse into the air. Inhale oil directly from bottle, or inhale oil that is applied to the hands.

MOOD SWINGS:

A mood swing is a rapid change of mood caused by fatigue or by a sudden shift in the body's hormonal balance.

Oils: **A**clary sage, **A**Serenity, **A**lavender, **A**Balance, **A**rosemary, **A**Elevation, **A**geranium, **A**rose, **A**ylang ylang, **A**sandalwood, **A**lemon, **A**peppermint, **A**bergamot, **A**fennel

A: Diffuse into the air. Inhale oil directly or applied to the hands.

MORNING SICKNESS: *SEE PREGNANCY/ MOTHERHOOD:MORNING SICKNESS*

MOSQUITOES: *SEE INSECTS/BUGS:MOSQUITOES*

MOTION SICKNESS: *SEE NAUSEA:MOTION SICKNESS*

MRSA: *SEE ANTIBACTERIAL*

MUCUS: *SEE CONGESTION*

MULTIPLE SCLEROSIS: *SEE ALSO BRAIN:MYELIN SHEATH*

Multiple sclerosis (MS) is an autoimmune disease in which the immune system attacks and gradually destroys the myelin sheath (which covers and insulates the nerves) and the underlying nerve fibers of the central nervous system. This destruction of the myelin sheath interferes with communication between the brain and the rest of the body. Symptoms of MS include partial or complete loss of vision, tingling, burning, pain in parts of the body, tremors, loss of coordination, unsteady gait, dizziness, and memory problems.

Primary Recommendations • Secondary Recommendations • Other Recommendations / **A**=Aromatic, **T**=Topical, **I**=Internal

Oils: **⊙Ⓐ**frankincense, **⊙Ⓐ**sandalwood, **⊙Ⓐ**peppermint, **⊙**cypress, **⊙Ⓐ**Serenity, **⊙**oregano, **⊙**thyme, **⊙**birch, **⊙**rosemary, **⊙**wintergreen

Other Products: **Ⓞ**xEO Mega for omega-3 fatty acids that help support nerve and brain function.

⊙: Dilute as recommended, and apply 1–2 drops to spine, back of neck, and feet. Dilute 1–3 drops in 1 Tbs. fractionated coconut oil, and massage on back and neck.

Ⓞ: Take capsules as directed on package.

Ⓐ: Diffuse into the air. Inhale directly from bottle. Apply oil to hands, tissue, or cotton wick, and inhale.

Mumps: *see Childhood Diseases: Mumps*

Muscles/Connective Tissue: *see also Cardiovascular System: Heart Tissue*

Muscle is the tissue in the body that has the ability to contract, making movement possible. The three main types of muscle in the body are smooth muscle (such as that in the stomach, intestines, and blood vessels), cardiac muscle (found in the heart), and skeletal muscle (attached to the bones). Skeletal muscles are connected to the bones with tough fibrous tissue called tendons and allow for coordinated, controlled movement of the body, such as walking, pointing, or eye movement. Smooth muscles and cardiac muscles move automatically without conscious control to perform their functions.

Oils: **⊙**marjoram, **⊙**Deep Blue, **⊙**peppermint[1], **⊙**AromaTouch, **⊙**birch, **⊙**cypress, **⊙**wintergreen, **⊙**lemongrass, **⊙**lavender

Other Products: **⊙**Deep Blue Rub to help relieve sore muscles, **Ⓞ**Alpha CRS+, **Ⓞ**xEO Mega, **Ⓞ**Microplex VMz for coenzyme Q10 and other nutrients to support muscle cell energy and function.

—**Aches and Pains:** *see also Pain*

Muscle pain usually results from overuse, tension, stress, strain, or injury. However, muscle pain can also be caused by a disease or infection affecting the whole body, such as the flu, fibromyalgia, or a connective tissue disorder.

Oils: **⊙**marjoram, **⊙**Deep Blue, **⊙**birch, **⊙**clove, **⊙**AromaTouch, **⊙**oregano, **⊙**peppermint, **⊙**wintergreen, **⊙**white fir (with inflammation), **⊙**vetiver, **⊙**Roman chamomile, **⊙**helichrysum, **⊙**ginger, **⊙**lavender, **⊙**rosemary, **⊙**thyme

Other Products: **⊙**Deep Blue Rub to help relieve sore muscles.

—**Bruised:** *see Bruises*

—**Cardiac Muscle:** *see also Cardiovascular System: Heart*

Cardiac muscle is the type of muscle found in the walls of the heart.

Oils: **⊙Ⓐ**marjoram, **⊙Ⓐ**lavender, **⊙Ⓐ**peppermint, **⊙Ⓐ**rosemary, **⊙**cinnamon

—**Cartilage Injury:**

Cartilage is a type of connective tissue in the body. It is firmer than other tissues and is used to provide structure and support without being as hard or as rigid as bone. Types of cartilage include hyaline cartilage, elastic cartilage, and fibrocartilage. Hyaline cartilage lines the bones and joints, helping them move smoothly. Elastic cartilage is found in the ear and larynx and is used to keep other tubular structures, such as the nose and trachea, open. Fibrocartilage is the strongest and most rigid cartilage. It is found in the intervertebral discs and other high-stress areas and serves to connect tendons and ligaments to bones. The hyaline cartilage surrounding bones and joints can become torn or injured if the joint is bent or twisted in a traumatic way. This can cause pain, swelling, tenderness, popping, or clicking within the joint and can limit movement.

Oils: **⊙**birch, **⊙**wintergreen, **⊙**marjoram, **⊙**lemongrass, **⊙**white fir, **⊙**peppermint

—**Cramps/Charley Horses:**

A muscle cramp or charley horse is the sudden, involuntary contraction of a muscle. Muscle cramps can occur in any muscle in the body, but they usually occur in the thigh, calf, or arch of the foot. Cramps can be caused by excessive strain to the muscle, injury, overuse, dehydration, or lack of blood flow to the

---

1 A combination of peppermint oil and ethanol was found to have a significant analgesic effect with a reduction in sensitivity to headache; while a combination of peppermint, eucalyptus, and ethanol were found to relax muscles, and increase cognitive performance in humans (Göbel et al., 1994).

Primary Recommendations • Secondary Recommendations • Other Recommendations / **Ⓐ**=Aromatic, **⊙**=Topical, **Ⓞ**=Internal

193

muscle. Muscle cramps can happen during or after a physical activity and while lying in bed.

Oils: ⓉLemongrass with Ⓣpeppermint, Ⓣmarjoram, ⓉDeep Blue, Ⓣrosemary, Ⓣbasil, Ⓣthyme, Ⓣvetiver, ⓉRoman chamomile, Ⓣcypress, Ⓣgrapefruit, Ⓣclary sage, Ⓐlavender

—DEVELOPMENT:

When muscles are stretched or used during exercise, they produce a substance that activates stem cells already present in the tissue. Once these cells are activated, they begin to divide—creating new muscle fiber and thereby increasing the size and strength of the muscles.

    Oils: Ⓣbirch, Ⓣwintergreen, ⓉDeep Blue

—FATIGUE:

Muscle fatigue is the muscle's temporary reduction in strength, power, and endurance. This happens when there is an increase in lactic acid and blood flow to the muscle, a depletion of glycogen, or a deprivation of oxygen to the tissue.

Oils: Ⓣmarjoram, Ⓣwhite fir, Ⓣcypress, Ⓣpeppermint, Ⓣeucalyptus, Ⓣgrapefruit, Ⓣrosemary, Ⓣthyme

Other Products: ⓉDeep Blue Rub

—INFLAMMATION: *SEE INFLAMMATION*

—LIGAMENTS:

A ligament is a sheet or band of tough connective tissue and fibers that connects bones together or helps bind and support a joint.

Oils: Ⓣlemongrass

—OVER EXERCISED:

When a person overexercises, his or her muscles do not get sufficient rest or time to heal. This continued muscle strain can cause muscle sprains, strain, and even tears to soft tissue. It may also cause stiffness and soreness to the neck, upper or lower back, shoulder, arm, or joint.

Oils: Ⓣwhite fir, Ⓣeucalyptus, Ⓣlavender, Ⓣthyme, Ⓣginger

Other Products: ⓉDeep Blue Rub to help provide comfort to tired and sore muscles.

Recipe 1: Add 3 drops marjoram and 2 drops lemon to warm bathwater, and soak.

Blend 1: Combine 2 drops eucalyptus, 2 drops peppermint, and 2 drops ginger with 1 Tbs. fractionated coconut oil, and massage into muscles.

—RHEUMATISM (MUSCULAR): *SEE FIBROMYALGIA*

—SMOOTH MUSCLE:

Oils: Ⓣmarjoram, Ⓣrosemary[1], ⓉⒾpeppermint, Ⓣfennel, Ⓣcypress, Ⓣclary sage, Ⓣmelissa, Ⓣlavender, Ⓣsandalwood, Ⓣbergamot

—SPASMS:

A muscle spasm is a sudden, involuntary contraction or twitching of a muscle. This may or may not cause pain.

Oils: Ⓣbasil, Ⓣmarjoram, ⓉDeep Blue, ⓉRoman chamomile, Ⓣpeppermint, Ⓣcypress, Ⓣclary sage, Ⓣlavender

—SPRAINS:

A sprain is an injury to a ligament caused by excessive stretching. The ligament can have little tears in it or it can be completely torn apart to be considered a sprain. The most common areas to receive a sprain are the ankle, knee, and wrist. After a person receives a sprain, the area will swell rapidly and be quite painful. If the ligament is torn apart, surgery may be required.

Oils: Ⓣmarjoram, Ⓣlemongrass, Ⓣwhite fir, Ⓣhelichrysum, Ⓣrosemary, Ⓣthyme, Ⓣvetiver, Ⓣeucalyptus, Ⓣclove, Ⓣginger, Ⓣlavender

—STRAIN:

A strain is a tear of the muscle tissue due to excessive strain or overstretching. Strains can cause inflammation, pain, and discoloration of the skin around the injured area.

Oils: Ⓣlemongrass, ⓉDeep Blue, Ⓣginger (circulation), Ⓣhelichrysum (pain)

—STIFFNESS:

Oils: ⓉDeep Blue

Other Products: ⓉDeep Blue Rub

---

1   Rosemary oil demonstrated a relaxant effect on smooth muscle from the trachea of rabbits and guinea pigs (Aqel, 1991).

—Tendinitis:

Tendinitis is the inflammation of a tendon due to injury, repetitive exercise or strain, or diseases such as arthritis, gout, and gonorrhea. This can cause swelling and pain in the effected tendon.

Oils: ⊤marjoram, ⊤lavender

—Tension (especially in shoulders and neck):

Muscle tension is a condition in which the muscle remains in a semi-contracted state for an extended period of time. This is usually due to physical or emotional stress.

Oils: ⊤marjoram, ⊤Deep Blue, ⊤peppermint[2], ⊤helichrysum, ⊤lavender, ⊤Roman chamomile

Other Products: ⊤Deep Blue Rub

—Tone:

Apply these oils before exercise to help tone muscles.

Oils: ⊤birch, ⊤cypress, ⊤wintergreen, ⊤marjoram, ⊤basil, ⊤peppermint, ⊤orange, ⊤thyme, ⊤rosemary, ⊤grapefruit, ⊤lavender

⊤: Dilute as recommended, and apply 1–2 drops on location. Add 2–4 drops to 1 Tbs. fractionated coconut oil, and massage into desired muscles or joints. Add 1–2 drops to warm bathwater, and bathe. Apply as hot or cold (for strains or sprains) compress.

Ⓘ: Take capsules as directed on package. Add 1–2 drops essential oil to empty capsule, and swallow.

Ⓐ: Diffuse into the air.

Muscular Dystrophy:

Muscular dystrophy is any of several genetic diseases that cause gradual weakening of the skeletal muscles. The most common forms, Duchenne and Becker muscular dystrophies, are caused by a gene defect that inhibits or alters the production of dystrophin, a protein necessary for proper muscle cell structure.

Oils: ⊤marjoram, ⊤lemongrass, ⊤basil, ⊤rosemary, ⊤AromaTouch, ⊤Deep blue, ⊤geranium, ⊤lavender, ⊤lemon, ⊤orange, ⊤ginger

Other Products: ⊤Deep Blue Rub to help relieve and relax tense and aching muscles.

⊤: Dilute as recommended, and apply 1–2 drops on location. Add 2–4 drops to 1 Tbs. fractionated coconut oil, and massage into desired muscles. Add 1–2 drops to warm bathwater and bathe. Apply as cold compress.

Myelin Sheath: *see Brain:Myelin Sheath*

Nails:

Oils: ⊤lemon, ⊤frankincense, ⊤myrrh, ⊤Citrus Bliss, ⊤melaleuca (infection[3]), ⊤eucalyptus, ⊤lavender, ⊤grapefruit, ⊤rosemary, ⊤cypress, ⊤oregano, ⊤thyme

Blend 1: Combine 2 drops frankincense, 2 drops lemon, and 2 drops myrrh with 2 drops wheat germ oil. Apply 2–3 times per week.

Other Products: Ⓘ Microplex VMz for nutrients essential to healthy nail growth.

⊤: Dilute as recommended, and apply 1–2 drops to nails. Add 1–2 drops to 1 tsp. fractionated coconut oil, and apply to nails.

Ⓘ: Take capsules as directed on package.

Nasal: *see Nose*

Nausea:

Nausea is a sick feeling in the stomach producing an urge to vomit.

Oils: ⒶⒾ⊤ginger[4,5,6], Ⓐpeppermint, Ⓣ Ⓐlavender, Ⓣ ⒶDigestZen, Ⓐ⊤patchouli, Ⓣ Ⓐclove

—Morning Sickness: *see Pregnancy/Motherhood:Morning Sickness*

—Motion Sickness:

Motion sickness is a feeling of illness that occurs as a result of repeated movement, such as that experienced in a car, on a boat, or on

---

2 A combination of peppermint oil and ethanol was found to have a significant analgesic effect with a reduction in sensitivity to headache; while a combination of peppermint, eucalyptus, and ethanol was found to relax muscles and to increase cognitive performance in humans (Göbel et al., 1994).

3 Topical application of 100% tea tree oil was found to have results similar to topical application of 1% clotrimazole (antifungal drug) solution on onychomycosis (also known as tinea, or fungal nail infection) (Buck et al., 1994).

4 Ginger root given orally to pregnant women was found to decrease the severity of nausea and frequency of vomiting compared to control (Vutyavanich et al., 2001).

5 Ginger root given one hour before major gynecological surgery resulted in lower nausea and fewer incidences of vomiting compared to control (Nanthakomon et al., 2006).

6 In a trial of women receiving gynecological surgery, women receiving ginger root had less incidences of nausea compared to a placebo. Ginger root has similar results to the antiemetic drug (a drug effective against vomiting and nausea) metoclopramide (Bone et al., 1990).

Primary Recommendations • Secondary Recommendations • Other Recommendations / Ⓐ=Aromatic, ⊤=Topical, Ⓘ=Internal

a plane. These motions interfere with the body's sense of balance and equilibrium. The most common symptoms of motion sickness include dizziness, fatigue, and nausea.

Oils: (A)peppermint, (A)DigestZen, (A)ginger

—VOMITING:

Oils: (I)(A)ginger [4,5], (A)peppermint, (A)(T)patchouli, (T)(A)fennel, (T)rose, (T)Roman chamomile

(I): Place 1–2 drops essential oil in an empty capsule, and swallow.

(A): Diffuse into the air. Inhale directly from bottle. Apply oil to hands, tissue, or cotton wick, and inhale.

(T): Dilute as recommended, and apply 1–2 drops to the feet, temples and wrists. Dilute 1–2 drops essential oil in 1 Tbs. fractionated coconut oil, and massage on stomach. Apply oil as a warm compress.

NECK:

Oils: (T)lemon, (T)geranium, (T)clary sage, (T)orange, (T)basil, (T)helichrysum

(T): Dilute 1–5 drops oil in 1 Tbs. fractionated coconut oil, and massage on neck.

NERVOUS SYSTEM: *SEE ALSO BACK, BRAIN*

The nervous system is a network of nerve cells that regulates the body's reaction to external and internal stimuli. The nervous system sends nerve impulses to organs and muscles throughout the body. The body relies on these impulses to function. The nervous system is comprised of the central nervous system (the brain and spinal cord) and the peripheral nervous system (all other nerves). The peripheral nervous system is comprised of the somatic nervous system (nerves that connect to the skeletal muscles and sensory nerve receptors in the skin) and the autonomic nervous system (nerves that connect to the cardiac and smooth muscles and other organs, tissues, and systems that don't require conscious effort to control). The autonomic system is divided further into two main parts: the sympathetic and parasympathetic nervous systems. The sympathetic nervous system functions to accelerate heart rate, increase blood pressure, slow digestion, and constrict blood vessels. It activates the "fight or flight" response in order to deal with threatening or stressful situations. The parasympa-

thetic nervous system functions to slow heart rate, store energy, stimulate digestive activity, and relax specific muscles. It allows the body to return to a normal and calm state after experiencing pain or stress.

Oils: (I)(A)peppermint[1] (soothes and strengthens damaged nerves), (I)(A)basil (stimulates), (I)(A)lavender[2,3], (A)(T)lemon[4,5,6], (A)(T)grapefruit[7,8], (I)(A)frankincense[9], (I)(A)bergamot, (T)(A)lemongrass (for nerve damage), (I)(A)marjoram (soothing), (I)(A)geranium (regenerates), (A)(T)Serenity, (I)(A)Roman chamomile, (I)(A)vetiver, (I)(A)cinnamon, (I)(A)ginger, (I)(A)orange, (I)(A)sandalwood

Other Products: (I)xEO Mega for essential omega fatty acids that help support nerve cell health. (I)Microplex VMz for nutrients and minerals necessary for proper nerve cell function. (I)Alpha CRS+ for nutrients that help support nerve cell health and energy.

—BELL'S PALSY:

Bell's palsy is a weakness or paralysis of muscles on one side of the face. Bell's palsy tends to set in quickly, normally in a single day. Symptoms include numbness of one side of the face, loss of ability to taste, drooling, pain in or behind the ear, facial droop, headache, and change in the amount of saliva or tears produced. In most cases Bell's palsy symptoms will begin to improve within a few

---

1 Pretreatment of human and rat astrocyte cells (cells found in the nerve and brain that support the blood-brain barrier and help repair the brain and spinal cord following injuries) with peppermint oil was found to inhibit heat-shock induced apoptosis of these cells (Koo et al., 2001).

2 Lavender oil scent was found to lower sympathetic nerve activity and blood pressure, while elevating parasympathetic nerve activity in rats. It was further found that applying an anosmia-inducing agent (something that causes a loss of smell) eliminated the effects of the lavender oil scent (Tanida et al., 2006).

3 Lavender oil was found to inhibit sympathetic nerve activity, while exciting parasympathetic nerve activity in rats. Linalool, a component of lavender, was shown to have similar effects (Shen et al., 2005).

4 Inhaling the aroma of lemon essential oil was found to decrease pain response in rats and was also found to modulate the neuronal response to formalin-induced pain (Aloisi et al., 2002).

5 Several constituents of lemon oil and their metabolites (chemicals made by these chemicals in the body) were found to affect the release of monoamines (various chemicals responsible for neurotransmission and neuromodulation) in rat brain tissue, indicating a possible effect on brain nerve cell behavior (Fukumoto et al., 2006).

6 Pretreatment of human and rat astrocyte cells (cells found in the nerve and brain that support the blood-brain barrier and help repair the brain and spinal cord following injuries) with lemon oil was found to inhibit heat-shock induced apoptosis of these cells (Koo et al., 2002).

7 The scent of grapefruit oil and its component, limonene, was found to affect the autonomic nerves and reduce appetite and body weight in rats exposed to the oil for 15 minutes three times per week (Shen et al., 2005).

8 Inhalation of essential oils such as pepper, estragon, fennel, and grapefruit was found to have a stimulating effect on sympathetic activity; while inhalation of essential oils of rose or patchouli caused a decrease in sympathetic activity in healthy adults (Haze et al., 2002).

9 Incensole acetate, isolated from frankincense resin, was found to demonstrate an anti-inflammatory and neuro-protective effect in mice with a closed head injury (Moussaieff et al., 2008).

Nervous System

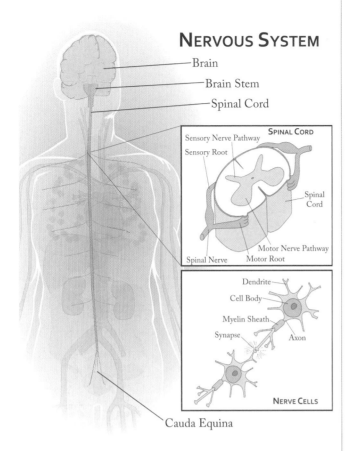

Brain
Brain Stem
Spinal Cord

SPINAL CORD

Sensory Nerve Pathway
Sensory Root
Spinal Cord
Spinal Nerve
Motor Nerve Pathway
Motor Root

Dendrite
Cell Body
Myelin Sheath
Synapse
Axon

NERVE CELLS

Cauda Equina

weeks. But in some few cases the symptoms continue for life.

Oils: ⊕⊘peppermint, ⊕⊘rosemary, ⊕⊘thyme

—**CARPAL TUNNEL SYNDROME:** *SEE CARPAL TUNNEL SYNDROME*

—**HUNTINGTON'S DISEASE:**

Huntington's disease (HD) is a progressive neurodegenerative disorder passed genetically from one generation to the next. As the disease develops, it causes nerve cells in the brain to waste away, resulting in a loss of control over body movement, emotions, and mental reasoning. Early symptoms include unsteady walking and decreased coordination. Later symptoms include sudden involuntary jerking body movements, slurred speech, decreased mental capacity, and psychological and emotional problems. Those carrying the HD gene have a 50 percent chance of passing it on to each of their children.

Oils: ⊕⊘peppermint, ⊕⊘basil

Other Products: ⓞxEO Mega

—**LOU GEHRIG'S DISEASE (ALS):** *SEE LOU GEHRIG'S DISEASE*

—**MULTIPLE SCLEROSIS (MS):** *SEE MULTIPLE SCLEROSIS*

—**NEURALGIA:**

Neuralgia is intense pain felt along the path of a nerve. Neuralgia results from damage or irritation to a nerve. Causes can include certain drugs, diabetes, infections, inflammation, trauma, and chemical irritation.

Oils: ⊕marjoram, ⊕eucalyptus[10], ⊕Roman chamomile, ⊕lavender, ⊕helichrysum

—**NEURITIS:**

Neuritis is the inflammation of a nerve or of a group of nerves. Neuritis causes pain, poor reflexes, and muscle atrophy.

Oils: ⊕eucalyptus[10], ⊕Roman chamomile, ⊕lavender, ⊕clove

—**NEUROTONIC:**

Oils: ⊕melaleuca, ⊕thyme

—**PARALYSIS:**

Paralysis is the loss of one's ability to move and control one or more specific sets of muscles. Paralysis generally occurs as a result of damage to the nervous system, especially damage to the spinal cord. Primary causes include injury, stroke, multiple sclerosis, amyotrophic lateral sclerosis (Lou Gehrig's disease), botulism, spina bifida, and Guillain-Barré syndrome.

Oils: ⊕⊘peppermint, ⊕⊘lemongrass, ⊕⊘geranium, ⊕⊘Balance, ⊕⊘Purify, ⊕⊘cypress, ⊕⊘ginger, ⊕⊘helichrysum

—**PARASYMPATHETIC NERVOUS SYSTEM:** *SEE ALSO IONS:NEGATIVE IONS.*

The parasympathetic nervous system functions to slow heart rate, store energy, stimulate digestive activity, and relax specific muscles. It allows the body to return to a normal and calm state after experiencing pain or stress.

N

---

10 1,8 cineole (eucalyptol) was found to display an anti-inflammatory effect on rats in several tests and was found to exhibit antinociceptive (pain-reducing) effects in mice, possibly by depressing the central nervous system (Santos et al., 2000).

Oils: [A][T]lavender[1,2] (stimulates), [A][T]lemongrass (regulates), [A][T]marjoram (tones), [A][T]Serenity, [A][T]Balance

—PARKINSON'S DISEASE: *SEE PARKINSON'S DISEASE*

—SYMPATHETIC NERVOUS SYSTEM: *SEE ALSO IONS:POSITIVE IONS.*

The sympathetic nervous system functions to accelerate heart rate, increase blood pressure, slow digestion, and constrict blood vessels. It activates the "fight or flight" response in order to deal with threatening or stressful situations.

Oils: [A][T]grapefruit[3,4] (stimulates), [A][T]eucalyptus, [A][T]peppermint, [A][T]ginger

—VIRUS OF NERVES: *SEE ALSO ANTIVIRAL*

Oils: [T]frankincense, [T]clove

[T]: Dilute as recommended, and apply 1–3 drops on location, spine, back of neck, and reflex points on the feet. Add 2–4 drops to 1 Tbs. fractionated coconut oil, and massage on location. Add 1–2 drops to warm bathwater, and bathe.

[A]: Diffuse into the air. Inhale directly from bottle. Apply oil to hands, tissue, or cotton wick, and inhale.

[I]: Take capsules as directed on package.

NERVOUSNESS:

Nervousness is a state of high anxiety, distress, agitation, or psychological uneasiness.

Oils: [A][T]orange

[A]: Diffuse into the air. Inhale directly from bottle. Apply oil to hands, tissue, or cotton wick, and inhale.

[T]: Dilute as recommended, and apply 1–2 drops to temples.

---

1 Lavender oil scent was found to lower sympathetic nerve activity and blood pressure, while elevating parasympathetic nerve activity in rats. It was further found that applying an anosmia-inducing agent (something that causes a loss of smell) eliminated the effects of the lavender oil scent (Tanida et al., 2006).

2 Lavender oil was found to inhibit sympathetic nerve activity, while exciting parasympathetic nerve activity in rats. Linalool, a component of lavender, was shown to have similar effects (Shen et al., 2005).

3 The scent of grapefruit oil and its component, limonene, was found to affect the autonomic nerves and reduce appetite and body weight in rats exposed to the oil for 15 minutes three times per week (Shen et al., 2005).

4 Inhalation of essential oils such as pepper, estragon, fennel, and grapefruit was found to have a stimulating effect on sympathetic activity; while inhalation of essential oils of rose or patchouli caused a decrease in sympathetic activity in healthy adults (Haze et al., 2002).

NOSE:

Oils: [T][A]melaleuca, [T][A]rosemary

—BLEEDING:

A nosebleed (medically called *epistaxis*) is the loss of blood through the nose. Nosebleeds are fairly common and can be caused by many factors. The most common causes of nosebleed are dry air that causes the nasal membrane to dry out and crack, allergies, nose trauma/injury, and colds and other viruses.

Oils: [T]helichrysum, [T]cypress, [T]lemon, [T]frankincense, [T]lavender

Blend 1: Combine 2 drops cypress, 1 drop helichrysum, and 2 drops lemon in 8 oz. (1 cup) ice water. Soak a cloth in the water, and apply the cloth to nose and back of neck.

—NASAL NASOPHARYNX:

The nasopharynx is the upper part of the throat (pharynx) situated behind the nose. The nasopharynx is responsible for carrying air from the nasal chamber into the trachea.

Oils: [A][T]eucalyptus

—NASAL POLYP:

A nasal polyp is an abnormal tissue growth inside the nose. Since nasal polyps are not cancerous, very small polyps generally do not cause any problems. But larger polyps can obstruct the nasal passage and make it difficult to breath or smell and can cause frequent sinus infections. Possible symptoms of polyps include runny nose, decreased sense of smell, decreased sense of taste, snoring, facial pain or headache, itching around the eyes, and persistent congestion.

Oils: [T][A]frankincense, [T][A]oregano, [T][A]Breathe, [T][A]peppermint, [T][A]Purify, [T][A]basil

—OLFACTORY LOSS:

Olfactory loss (or anosmia) is the loss of one's ability to smell. The most common causes for olfactory loss are sinonasal disease, head injury, and infection of the upper respiratory tract.

Oils: [A][T]peppermint, [A][T]basil

—RHINITIS: *SEE ALSO ALLERGIES, ANTIVIRAL, COLDS*

Rhinitis is an inflammation of the nasal mucus membrane (the moist lining inside the

---

nasal cavity where mucus is produced that acts as an air filtration system by trapping incoming dirt particles and moving them away for disposal). Rhinitis can cause runny nose, nasal congestion, sneezing, ear problems, and phlegm in the throat. Rhinitis is commonly caused by viral infections and allergies and can be acute (short-term) or chronic (long-term).

Oils: ⒶⓉeucalyptus, ⒶⓉpeppermint, ⒶⓉbasil

Ⓣ: Dilute as recommended, and apply 1–2 drops on nose (use extreme caution to avoid getting oil in the eye). Dilute as recommended, and apply 1 drop to a cotton swab, and swab the inside of the nose.

Ⓐ: Diffuse into the air, and inhale the vapors through the nose. Inhale directly from bottle. Apply oil to hands, tissue, or cotton wick, and inhale.

NURSING: *SEE PREGNANCY/MOTHERHOOD:LACTATION*

OBESITY: *SEE WEIGHT:OBESITY*

ODORS: *SEE DEODORANT, DEODORIZING*

ORAL CONDITIONS: *SEE ALSO ANTIBACTERIAL, ANTIFUNGAL:THRUSH.*

—ABSCESS:

A tooth abscess is a collection of pus at the root of an infected tooth. The main symptom of a tooth abscess is a painful, persistent, throbbing toothache. The infected tooth may be sensitive to heat, cold, and pressure caused by chewing. Later symptoms may include swelling in the face, swollen lymph nodes in the neck or jaw, and a fever. Abscesses may eventually rupture, leaving a foul-tasting fluid in the mouth. If left untreated, an abscess can spread to other areas of the head and neck.

Oils: Ⓣclove, ⓉOn Guard, ⓉPurify, Ⓣhelichrysum, Ⓣmelaleuca, Ⓣfrankincense, ⓉRoman chamomile, Ⓣwintergreen

Other Products: ⓉOn Guard Toothpaste

Blend 1: Blend 1 drop each of clove, wintergreen, myrrh, and helichrysum to help with infection.

TOOTH

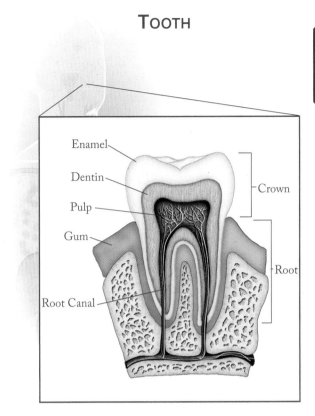

Enamel
Dentin
Pulp
Gum
Root Canal
Crown
Root

—CAVITIES:

A cavity is a decayed area or hole in a tooth caused by bacteria in the mouth. A cavity that is allowed to progress without treatment can result in pain, infection, and loss of the tooth. Good oral hygiene and eating less sugar can help to reduce the risk of cavities.

Oils: ⓉOn Guard, Ⓣmelaleuca[5,6,7], Ⓣpeppermint[8,9], Ⓣeucalyptus[3,10], Ⓣcinnamon[5]

Other Products: ⓉOn Guard Toothpaste

—GUMS:

The gums (also called "gingiva") are the soft pink tissue surrounding the teeth. The gums form a seal around the teeth and are snugly at-

---

5 Among several oils tested, tea tree (melaleuca), manuka, and eucalyptus demonstrated strong antibacterial activity against detrimental oral bacteria (Takarada et al., 2004).

6 Tea tree, peppermint, and sage oils were found to inhibit oral bacteria, with thymol and eugenol being the most active components of these oils (Shapiro et al., 1994).

7 Cinnamon oil exhibited a strong antimicrobial activity against two detrimental oral bacteria. Manuka, tea tree, and the component thymol also exhibited antimicrobial potency (Filoche et al., 2005).

8 Peppermint oil blended with toothpaste was found to be more effective at lower concentrations in inhibiting the formation of dental plaque than chlorhexidine (an antiseptic) in human volunteers (Shayegh et al., 2008).

9 Peppermint and rosemary oils were each found to be more effective at preventing dental biofilm (plaque) formation than chlorhexidine (an antiseptic) (Rasooli et al., 2008).

10 Subjects using a mouthwash containing thymol, menthol, methyl salicylate, and eucalyptol for 6 months were found to not have developed oral bacteria that were resistant to the oils (Charles et al., 2000).

---

tached to the bone underneath to withstand the friction of food passing over them in chewing.

Oils: Ⓣmyrrh, Ⓣlavender, Ⓣmelaleuca, Ⓣhelichrysum, ⓉRoman chamomile

Other Products: ⓉOn Guard Toothpaste

—GUM DISEASE:

Gum disease is an infection of the tissue and bones surrounding the teeth and is caused by a buildup of plaque. Gum disease consists of two parts: first gingivitis and then periodontal disease. Gingivitis is an inflammation of the gums because of bacteria associated with plaque buildup. When infected with gingivitis, the gums become red and swollen and often bleed during teeth brushing. Periodontal disease occurs when gingivitis is left untreated and becomes progressively worse. The inflamed gums begin pulling away from the teeth and leave empty pockets where food particles can easily collect and become infected. As the disease progresses, the gums pull farther away from the teeth and the bacteria eats away at the tissue and bone. As this occurs, the teeth lose their anchoring and can fall out.

Oils: Ⓣmelaleuca [3,4,5], ⓉOn Guard, Ⓣmyrrh, Ⓣhelichrysum, Ⓣrose

Other Products: ⓉOn Guard Toothpaste

—HALITOSIS (BAD BREATH):

Halitosis is the technical term for "bad breath." Common causes of halitosis include smoking, drinking, poor oral hygiene, gum disease, dry mouth, tooth decay, and certain foods.

Oils: Ⓣpeppermint [6,7], ⓉOn Guard, Ⓣpatchouli, Ⓣlavender

Other Products: ⓉOn Guard Toothpaste

—MOUTH ULCERS:

Mouth ulcers are open, often painful, sores that occur in the mouth. Common mouth ulcers include canker sores and cold sores. Stress, anxiety, fatigue, injury, illness, hormonal changes, and food allergies can often trigger mouth ulcers.

Oils: Ⓣbasil, Ⓣmyrrh, Ⓣorange

Other Products: ⓉOn Guard Toothpaste

—TEETH GRINDING:

Teeth grinding (also called bruxism) is the habit of clenching the teeth and rubbing them against one another. Teeth grinding often occurs unconsciously while a person is asleep. If teeth grinding is frequent, it can lead to tooth damage, jaw pain, and headaches.

Oils: ⒶⓉSerenity

—TEETHING PAIN:

Around ages 4–7 months, a baby will get his or her first teeth. Some infants teethe without discomfort; but for other infants, teething can be a painful process. Common symptoms of teething include irritability or fussiness, drooling, chin rash, biting, difficulty sleeping, and low-grade fever.

Oils: Ⓣlavender

—TOOTHACHE:

A toothache is a pain around a tooth. Toothaches can result from many factors, including infection, injury, decay, jaw problems, cavities, damaged fillings, and gum disease. Common symptoms of a toothache include sharp or throbbing pain, swelling around the tooth, fever, headache, and foul-tasting drainage from the infected tooth.

Oils: Ⓣclove, Ⓣmelaleuca, ⓉPurify, ⓉRoman chamomile

Other Products: ⓉOn Guard Toothpaste

—TOOTHPASTE:

Oils: ⓉOn Guard

Other Products: ⓉOn Guard Toothpaste

Recipe 1: Mix 1–2 drops On Guard blend with 1/2 tsp. baking soda to form a paste, and use as toothpaste to brush onto the teeth.

Ⓣ: Dilute as recommended, and apply 1–2 drops on location or along jawbone. Apply the oils with a hot compress on the face. Use On Guard toothpaste as directed. Dilute as recommended, and apply 1–2 drops to a small cotton ball or cotton swab; swab on location. Mix 1–2 drops with 4 oz. of water, and use as mouthrinse. Add 1–2 drops to toothpaste. Place 5–6 drops with 1 oz. distilled water in a small spray bottle, and mist into the mouth.

Ⓐ: Diffuse into the air.

OSTEOMYELITIS: *SEE BONES:OSTEOMYELITIS*

OSTEOPOROSIS: *SEE BONES:OSTEOPOROSIS*

OVARIES:

Ovaries are the female reproductive organs in which eggs are produced and stored.

Oils: ⊕Ⓐrosemary (regulates), ⊕Ⓐgeranium, ⊕ⒶWhisper, ⊕ⒶDigestZen

—OVARIAN CYST:

An ovarian cyst is a fluid-filled sac within the ovary. While ovarian cysts are common, and most cause no problems, they may cause feelings of aching or pressure and can cause pain, bleeding, and other problems if they become too large or become twisted or rupture.

Oils: ⊕Ⓐbasil

⊕: Dilute as recommended, and apply 1–2 drops on abdomen and reflex points on the feet. Add 1–2 drops to 1 Tbs. fractionated coconut oil, and massage into abdomen and lower back. Apply as a warm compress to the abdomen. Add 1–2 drops to 2 tsp. olive oil, insert into vagina, and retain overnight with a tampon.

Ⓐ: Diffuse into the air. Inhale directly from bottle. Apply oil to hands, tissue, or cotton wick, and inhale.

OVEREATING: *SEE EATING DISORDERS:OVEREATING*

OVERWEIGHT: *SEE WEIGHT*

OXYGENATING:

The term "oxygenate" means to supply, to treat, or to infuse with oxygen. All of the cells in the body require oxygen to create the energy necessary to live and function correctly. The brain consumes 20% of the oxygen we inhale.

Oils: Ⓐ⊕sandalwood, Ⓐ⊕frankincense, Ⓐ⊕oregano, Ⓐ⊕fennel

Ⓐ: Diffuse into the air. Inhale directly from bottle. Apply oil to hands, tissue, or cotton wick, and inhale.

⊕: Dilute as recommended, and apply 1–2 drops to forehead, chest, and sinuses.

PAIN:

Oils: ⊕Ⓐlavender[1,2,3,4], ⊕eucalyptus[5,6,7], ⊕Deep Blue, Ⓐlemon[8,9], ⊕rosemary[4,6,7,10,11], ⊕clove[12], ⊕cypress, ⊕white fir, ⊕helichrysum, ⊕geranium, ⊕frankincense, ⊕lemongrass, ⊕marjoram, ⊕melaleuca, ⊕peppermint, ⊕rosemary, ⊕wintergreen

Other Products: ⊕Deep Blue Rub to help soothe muscles and joints. ⓘAlpha CRS+ to help relieve oxidation associated with inflammation that contributes to pain.

—BONE:

Bone pain is a gnawing, throbbing sensation in the bones and has many possible causes, including fractures, cancer, infection, injury, leukemia, and osteoporosis.

Oils: ⊕Deep Blue, ⊕wintergreen, ⊕lavender, ⊕cypress, ⊕white fir, ⊕helichrysum, ⊕peppermint, ⊕sandalwood

—CHRONIC:

Chronic pain is generally defined as pain that lasts three months or longer.

Oils: ⊕Deep Blue, ⊕wintergreen, ⊕cypress, ⊕white fir, ⊕helichrysum, ⊕ginger, ⊕peppermint, ⊕sandalwood

1 Lavender oil was found to work as an anaesthetic (reducing pain) in a rabbit reflex test (Ghelardini et al., 1999).
2 Oil from *Lavandula angustifolia* was found to reduce writhing in induced writhing in rats and to reduce edema (swelling) in carrageenan-induced paw edema, indicating an anti-inflammatory effect (Hajhashemi et al., 2003).
3 The odor of lavender combined with relaxing music was found to lessen the intensity of pain following a vascular wound dressing change (Kane et al., 2004).
4 In patients suffering from arthritis, it was found that a blend of lavender, marjoram, eucalyptus, rosemary, peppermint, and carrier oils reduced perceived pain and depression compared to a control (Kim et al., 2005).
5 A combination of peppermint oil and ethanol was found to have a significant analgesic effect with a reduction in sensitivity to headache; while a combination of peppermint, eucalyptus, and ethanol was found to relax muscles and to increase cognitive performance in humans (Göbel et al., 1994).
6 1,8 cineole (eucalyptol) was found to have antinociceptive (pain-reducing) properties similar to morphine. Beta-pinene was found to reverse the effects of morphine in a degree similar to naloxone (a drug used to counter the effects of morphine overdose) (Liapi et al., 2007).
7 1,8 cineole (eucalyptol) was found to display an anti-inflammatory effect on rats in several tests and was found to exhibit antinociceptive (pain-reducing) effects in mice, possibly by depressing the central nervous system (Santos et al., 2000).
8 Inhaling the aroma of lemon essential oil was found to decrease pain response in rats and was also found to modulate the neuronal response to formalin-induced pain (Aloisi et al., 2002).
9 Rats exposed long-term to lemon essential oil were found to demonstrate different anxiety and pain threshold levels than untreated rats. It was also found that exposure to lemon oil induced chemical changes in the neuronal circuits involved in anxiety and pain (Ceccarelli et al., 2004).
10 An ethanol extract of rosemary was found to demonstrate antinociceptive (pain-blocking) and anti-inflammatory activity in mice and rats (González-Trujano et al., 2007).
11 Rosemary oil was found to have anti-inflammatory and peripheral antinociceptive (pain sensitivity–blocking) properties in mice (Takaki et al., 2008).
12 Beta-caryophyllene (found in clove oil) demonstrated anaesthetic (pain-reducing) activity in rats and rabbits (Ghelardini et al., 2001).

O

P

—GENERAL:

Oils: ☉Deep Blue, ☉wintergreen, ☉lavender, ☉cypress, ☉marjoram, ☉white fir, ☉helichrysum, ☉peppermint, ☉sandalwood

—INFLAMMATION: *SEE ALSO INFLAMMATION*

Oils: ☉rosemary [1,2,3], ☉eucalyptus [1], ☉lavender [4], ☉Deep Blue

Other Products: ☉Deep Blue Rub

—JOINTS:

Oils: ☉Deep Blue, ☉wintergreen, ☉Roman chamomile

Other Products: ☉Deep Blue Rub

—MUSCLE:

Oils: ☉Deep Blue, ☉white fir, ☉clove, ☉lavender, ☉lemongrass (ligaments), ☉cypress, ☉marjoram, ☉helichrysum, ☉peppermint, ☉sandalwood, ☉wintergreen

Other Products: ☉Deep Blue Rub

—TISSUE:

Oils: ☉Deep Blue, ☉helichrysum

Other Products: ☉Deep Blue Rub

Ⓣ: Dilute as recommended, and apply 1–2 drops on location. Combine with carrier oil, and massage into affected muscles and joints. Apply as a warm compress over affected areas.

Ⓘ: Take capsules as directed on package.

Ⓐ: Diffuse into the air. Inhale oil that is applied to a tissue or cotton wick.

PAINTING:

Add one 15 ml bottle of your favorite essential oil (or oil blend) to any five gallon bucket of paint. Stir vigorously, mixing well, and then either spray paint or paint by hand. This should eliminate the paint fumes and after-smell.

PALPITATIONS: *SEE CARDIOVASCULAR SYSTEM:PALPITATIONS*

---

1 1,8 cineole (eucalyptol) was found to display an anti-inflammatory effect on rats in several tests and was found to exhibit antinociceptive (pain-reducing) effects in mice, possibly by depressing the central nervous system (Santos et al., 2000).
2 An ethanol extract of rosemary was found to demonstrate antinociceptive (pain-blocking) and anti-inflammatory activity in mice and rats (González-Trujano et al., 2007).
3 Rosemary oil was found to have anti-inflammatory and peripheral antinociceptive (pain sensitivity–blocking) properties in mice (Takaki et al., 2008).
4 Oil from *Lavandula angustifolia* was found to reduce writhing in induced writhing in rats and to reduce edema (swelling) in carrageenan-induced paw edema, indicating an anti-inflammatory effect (Hajhashemi et al., 2003).

PANCREAS:

The pancreas is a gland organ located behind the stomach. The pancreas is responsible for producing insulin and other hormones and for producing "pancreatic juices" that aid in digestion.

Oils: ☉cypress, ☉rosemary, ☉ⒶBreathe, ☉Ⓐlemon, ☉ⒶOn Guard

—PANCREATITIS:

Pancreatitis is the term used to describe pancreas inflammation. Pancreatitis occurs when the pancreatic juices that are designed to aid in digestion in the small intestine become active while still inside the pancreas. When this occurs, the pancreas literally begins to digest itself. Acute pancreatitis lasts for only a short time and then resolves itself. Chronic pancreatitis does not resolve itself but instead gradually destroys the pancreas.

Oils: ☉Ⓐlemon, ☉Ⓐmarjoram

—STIMULANT FOR:

Oils: ☉helichrysum

—SUPPORT:

Oils: ☉Ⓐcinnamon, ☉Ⓐgeranium, ☉Ⓐfennel

Ⓣ: Dilute as recommended, and apply 1–2 drops over pancreas area or on reflex points on the feet.

Ⓐ: Diffuse into the air. Inhale directly from bottle. Apply oil to hands, tissue, or cotton wick, and inhale.

PANIC: *SEE ANXIETY*

PARALYSIS: *SEE NERVOUS SYSTEM:PARALYSIS*

PARASITES:

A parasite is an organism that grows on or in another organism at the host organism's expense. A parasite cannot live independently and is fed and sheltered by the host organism without making any helpful contribution itself.

Oils: ☉☉oregano [5], ☉☉thyme, ☉☉fennel, ☉☉Roman chamomile, ☉☉DigestZen, ☉☉lavender [6], ☉melaleuca, ☉☉clove

---

5 Oregano oil administered orally was found to improve gastrointestinal symptoms in 7 of 11 patients who had tested positive for the parasite *Blastocystis hominis* and was found to cause disappearance of this parasite in 8 cases (Force et al., 2000).
6 Essential oil from *Lavandula angustifolia* demonstrated ability to eliminate protozoal

—Intestinal:

Intestinal parasites are parasites that infect the intestinal tract. These parasites enter the intestinal tract through the mouth by unwashed or uncooked food, contaminated water, and unclean hands. Symptoms of intestinal parasites include diarrhea, abdominal pain, weight loss, fatigue, gas or bloating, nausea or vomiting, stomach pain, passing a worm in a stool, stools containing blood and mucus, and rash or itching around the rectum or vulva.

Oils: **❶❻**lemon, **❶❻**oregano[7], **❶❻**Roman chamomile

—Worms:

Parasitic worms are worm-like organisms that live inside another living organism and feed off their host organism at the host organism's expense, causing weakness and disease. Parasitic worms can live inside of animals as well as humans.

Oils: **❶❻**DigestZen, **❶❻**lavender, **❶❻**rosemary, **❶❻**thyme, **❶❻**peppermint, **❶❻**Roman chamomile, **❶❻**bergamot, **❻**melaleuca

Blend 1: Combine 6 drops Roman chamomile, 6 drops eucalyptus, 6 drops lavender, and 6 drops lemon with 2 Tbs. fractionated coconut oil. Apply 10–15 drops over abdomen with a hot compress, and apply 1–2 drops on intestine and colon reflex points on the feet.

❶: Place 2–4 drops essential oil in empty capsule, and swallow. Add 1–2 drops to 4 oz. rice or almond milk; drink.

❻: Apply as warm compress over abdomen. Add 2–3 drops to 1 Tbs. fractionated coconut oil, and apply as rectal retention enema for 15 minutes or more. Dilute as recommended, and apply to abdomen and reflex points on the feet.

Parasympathetic Nervous System: *see Nervous System:Parasympathetic Nervous System*

Parkinson's Disease:

Parkinson's disease is a progressive neurodegenerative disease marked by impairment of muscle movement and speech. Symptoms of Parkinson's disease include slowed motion, muscle stiffness, difficulty maintaining balance, impaired speech, loss of automatic movements (such as blinking, smiling, and swinging the arms while walking), and hand tremors.

Oils: **❻**marjoram, **❻**lavender, **❻**clary sage, **❶❻**frankincense, **❶❻**Balance, **❶❻**sandalwood, **❶❻**Serenity, **❶❻**vetiver, **❻**cypress (circulation), **❻❶**bergamot, **❻❶**geranium, **❻**helichrysum, **❶❻**lemon, **❶❻**orange, **❻❶**peppermint, **❻❶**rosemary, **❻❶**thyme

Other Products: **❶**Alpha CRS+ contains Coenzyme Q10, which has been studied for its potential benefits in alleviating Parkinson's disease[8,9,10]. **❶**xEO Mega for essential omega fatty acids that help support healthy nerve cell function.

❻: Add 5–10 drops essential oil to 1 Tbs. fractionated coconut oil and massage on affected muscles, back, legs, and neck. Dilute as recommended and apply 1–2 drops to base of neck or reflex points on the feet. Add 3–5 drops to warm bathwater, and bathe.

❶: Take capsules as directed on package.

❹: Diffuse into the air. Inhale directly from bottle. Apply oil to hands, tissue, or cotton wick, and inhale.

Pelvic Pain Syndrome:

Pelvic pain syndrome is characterized by pain in the pelvis area that continues for several months. Symptoms include severe and steady pain, dull aching, a feeling of pressure deep in the pelvis, painful bowel movements, pain during intercourse, and pain when sitting down.

Oils: **❻**ginger, **❻**geranium, **❻**clove, **❻**bergamot, **❻**thyme, **❻**rose

❻: Place 2–3 drops in warm bathwater, and soak for 10 minutes. Add 5–10 drops to 1 Tbs.

---

8 A study of Parkinson's disease patients found that CoQ10 was significantly lower in the cortex region of their brains than in the brains of healthy patients (Hargreaves et al., 2008).

9 Pretreatment of mice with CoQ10 was found to protect dopaminergic neurons from iron-induced oxidative stress that has been theorized to play a role in the development of Parkinson's disease (Kooncumchoo et al., 2006).

10 A mitochondrial defect in fibroblast cells cultivated from 18 Parkinson's disease patients was found to be ameliorated in 50% of these cells treated with CoQ10 (Winkler-Stuck, 2004).

---

pathogens *Giardia duodenalis*, *Trichomonas vaginalis*, and *Hexamita inflata* at concentrations of 1% or less (Moon et al., 2006).

7 Oregano oil administered orally was found to improve gastrointestinal symptoms in 7 of 11 patients who had tested positive for the parasite *Blastocystis hominis* and was found to cause disappearance of this parasite in 8 cases (Force et al., 2000).

P

Primary Recommendations • Secondary Recommendations • Other Recommendations / **❹**=Aromatic, **❻**=Topical, **❶**=Internal

fractionated coconut oil, and massage on pelvis and upper legs.

PERIODONTAL DISEASE:
SEE ORAL CONDITIONS:GUM DISEASE

PESTS: *SEE INSECTS/BUGS, MICE*

PHLEBITIS: *SEE CARDIOVASCULAR SYSTEM:PHLEBITIS*

PIMPLES: *SEE ACNE*

PINK EYE: *SEE EYES:PINK EYE*

PINEAL GLAND:

The pineal gland is a tiny endocrine gland located close to the center of the brain. It is responsible for producing the hormone melatonin that regulates the sleep/wake cycle. The pineal gland also serves to regulate blood pressure, sexual development, growth, body temperature, and motor function.

Oils: Ⓐfrankincense, Ⓐsandalwood, Ⓐvetiver, Ⓐginger

Ⓐ: Diffuse into the air. Inhale oil directly from bottle. Apply oil to hands, tissue, or cotton wick, and inhale.

PITUITARY GLAND:

The pituitary gland is a small endocrine gland located at the base of the brain that secretes hormones directly into the bloodstream. It is composed of three different lobes, each responsible for producing a different set of hormones. The anterior lobe secretes the human growth hormone (stimulates overall body growth), adrenocorticotropic hormone (controls hormone secretion by the adrenal cortex), thyrotropic hormone (stimulates activity of the thyroid gland), and the gonadotropic hormones (control growth and reproductive activity of the ovaries and testes). The posterior lobe secretes antidiuretic hormone (causes water retention by the kidneys) and oxytocin (stimulates the mammary glands to release milk and causes uterine contractions). The pituitary gland is often referred to as the "master" endocrine gland because it controls the functioning of the other endocrine glands.

Oils: Ⓐfrankincense, Ⓐsandalwood, Ⓐvetiver, Ⓐginger

—BALANCES:

Oils: ⒶⓉylang ylang, ⒶⓉgeranium

—INCREASES OXYGEN:

Oils: ⒶⓉfrankincense, ⒶⓉsandalwood

Ⓐ: Diffuse into the air. Inhale oil directly from bottle. Apply oil to hands, tissue, or cotton wick, and inhale.

Ⓣ: Dilute as recommended, and apply 1–2 drops to forehead, back of neck, and reflex points on big toes.

PLAGUE: *SEE ALSO ANTIBACTERIAL*

Plague is a potentially deadly bacterial disease that is caused by the *Yersinia pestis* bacteria, which is transmitted to humans and animals through close contact or through bites from fleas that have previously bitten infected animals. Symptoms include fever, headaches, and extremely swollen and hot lymph nodes. If left untreated, plague can quickly invade the lungs—causing severe pneumonia, high fever, bloody coughing, and death.

Oils: ⓉⒶclove, ⒶⓉOn Guard, ⓉⒶfrankincense, ⓉⒶoregano

Ⓣ: Dilute as recommended, and apply to neck, chest, and reflex points on the feet.

Ⓐ: Diffuse into the air.

PLAGUE: *SEE ANTIBACTERIAL, ORAL CONDITIONS*

PLEURISY: *SEE ANTIBACTERIAL, RESPIRATORY SYSTEM:PLEURISY*

PMS: *SEE FEMALE SPECIFIC CONDITIONS:PMS*

PNEUMONIA: *SEE ALSO RESPIRATORY SYSTEM, ANTIBACTERIAL, ANTIFUNGAL, ANTIVIRAL*

Pneumonia is an illness characterized by lung inflammation in which the lungs are infected by a bacteria, fungus, or virus. The result is a cough, chest pain, difficulty breathing, fever, shaking chills, headache, muscle pain, and fatigue. Pneumonia is a special concern for young children and individuals over the age of sixty-five. Pneumonia ranges in seriousness from mild to life threatening.

Oils: ⒶⓉBreathe, ⒶⓉOn Guard, ⒶⓉthyme[1,2], Ⓐcinnamon[1,2], ⒶⓉoregano[3], ⒶⓉeucalyptus, ⒶⓉmelaleuca, ⒶⓉlavender, Ⓐlemon, ⒶⓉfrankincense, ⒶⓉmyrrh

Ⓐ: Diffuse into the air. Place 4 drops in 1/2 cup hot water, and inhale steam deeply.

Ⓣ: Dilute as recommended, and apply to chest, back, and reflex points on the feet. Apply as warm compress to the chest. Place 2–3 drops in 1 tsp. fractionated coconut oil; place oil in rectum, and retain overnight.

POISON IVY/OAK:

Poison oak and poison ivy are plants with an oily sap called urushiol that causes an itchy rash when it comes into contact with the skin. Infection by poison oak or poison ivy is recognized by redness and itching of the skin, a rash, red bumps, and later oozing blisters. A rash caused by poison oak or by poison ivy usually lasts from 5–12 days.

Oils: Ⓣrose, Ⓣlavender, ⓉElevation, ⓉRoman chamomile

Ⓣ: Dilute as recommended, and apply 1–2 drops on location. Add 2–3 drops to 1 tsp. fractionated coconut oil, and apply on location.

POLLUTION: *SEE PURIFICATION*

POLYPS: *SEE COLON:POLYPS, NOSE:NASAL POLYP*

POSITIVE IONS: *SEE IONS:POSITIVE IONS*

PREGNANCY/MOTHERHOOD:

Pregnancy is the period of time (generally nine months) in which a woman carries a developing fetus in her uterus.

Oils: ⓉⒶgeranium, ⓉⒶylang ylang, ⓉⒶlavender, ⓉⒶgrapefruit, ⓉⒶRoman chamomile

Other Products: ❶Alpha CRS+, ❶xEO Mega, ❶Microplex VMz for nutrients essential to support cellular health and body function.

—ANXIETY/TENSION: *SEE CALMING*

---

1 Oils with aldehyde or phenol as major components demonstrated a high level of antibacterial activity (Inouye et al., 2001).
2 Cinnamon, thyme, and clove essential oils demonstrated an antibacterial effect on several respiratory tract pathogens (Fabio et al., 2007).
3 Oregano oil was found to kill antibiotic resistant strains of Staph, *E. coli, Klebsiella pneumoniae, Helicobacter pylori,* and *Mycobacterium terrae* (Preuss et al., 2005).

—BABY (NEWBORN):

Oils: Ⓣfrankincense (1 drop on crown), Ⓣmyrrh (1 drop on umbilical cord and navel), ⓉBalance (1 drop on feet and spine)

Ⓣ: Apply as indicated above.

—BREASTS:

In the first trimester of pregnancy, a woman's breasts become sore and tender as the body begins to prepare itself for breast-feeding. During pregnancy the breasts enlarge, the nipples grow larger and become darker, and the breasts may begin to leak colostrum—the first milk the body makes in preparation for the developing baby.

Oils: Ⓣlavender (soothes), Ⓣgeranium (soothes), ⓉRoman chamomile (sore nipples), Ⓣfennel (tones)

Ⓣ: Add 3–5 drops to 1 Tbs. fractionated coconut oil, and massage on location.

—DELIVERY:

Delivery is the act or process of giving birth.

Oils: ⓉⒶlavender (stimulates circulation, calming, antiseptic), Ⓣclary sage, ⓉBalance

Ⓣ: Dilute as recommended, and apply 1–2 drops on hips, bottoms of feet, or abdomen. Add 3–5 drops to 1 Tbs. fractionated coconut oil, and massage on hips, bottoms of feet, or abdomen.

Ⓐ: Diffuse into the air. Inhale directly from bottle. Apply oil to hands, tissue, or cotton wick, and inhale.

–AVOID EPISIOTOMY:

Oils: Ⓣgeranium

Ⓣ: Add 5–10 drops to 1/2 tsp. olive oil, and massage perineum.

–DIFFUSE:

Oils: ⒶSerenity, ⒶElevation

Ⓐ: Diffuse into the air.

–UTERUS:

Oils: Ⓣclary sage

Ⓣ: Apply 1–3 drops around the ankles to help tone uterus.

–TRANSITION:

Oils: Ⓣbasil

Primary Recommendations • Secondary Recommendations • Other Recommendations / Ⓐ=Aromatic, Ⓣ=Topical, ❶=Internal

☂: Dilute as recommended, and apply 1–2 drops to temples or abdomen.

—EARLY LABOR:

Preterm labor is labor that begins before the 37th week of pregnancy. Babies born before the 37th week are considered premature. Signs of preterm labor include contractions every 10 minutes or more often, cramps, low backache, pelvic pressure, and change in vaginal discharge (fluid or blood).

Oils: **☂**lavender

☂: Rub 1–3 drops on stomach to help stop.

—ENERGY:

Blend 1: Combine 2 drops Roman chamomile, 2 drops geranium, and 2 drops lavender in 2 tsp. fractionated coconut oil, and massage into the skin.

—HEMORRHAGING:

Postpartum Hemorrhaging is excessive bleeding following childbirth. It is commonly defined as losing 500 ml of blood after vaginal birth and 1000 ml of blood after a cesarean birth. Postpartum hemorrhaging generally occurs within 24 hours following the birth and can be life threatening if not stopped.

Oils: **☂**helichrysum

☂: Apply 1–3 drops on lower back to help prevent hemorrhaging.

—HIGH BLOOD PRESSURE:

High blood pressure can potentially be dangerous in pregnancy. High blood pressure can cause a decreased flow of blood to the placenta, slowing down the baby's growth; premature placenta separation from the uterus, taking away the baby's oxygen and nutrients and causing heavy bleeding in the mother; premature birth; and the risk of future disease. Pregnancy can in some cases actually cause a woman's blood pressure to increase.

Oils: **☁☂**ylang ylang[1,2], **☂☁**eucalyptus[3], **☂☁**lavender, **☂☁**clove, **☂☁**clary sage, **☂☁**le-

mon. **Note:** Avoid rosemary, thyme, and possibly peppermint.

Bath 1: Place 3 drops ylang ylang in bathwater, and bathe in the evening twice a week.

Blend 2: Combine 5 drops geranium, 8 drops lemongrass, and 3 drops lavender in 1 oz. fractionated coconut oil. Rub over heart and on reflex points on left foot and hand.

☂: Dilute as recommended, and apply on location, on reflex points on feet and hands, and over heart.

☁: Diffuse into the air. Apply oils to hands, and inhale oils from hands cupped over the nose. Inhale oil applied to a tissue or cotton wick.

—LABOR (DURING):

Oils: **☂**clary sage (may combine with fennel)

☂: Apply 3 drops around ankles or on abdomen.

—LABOR (POST):

Oils: **☂**lavender, **☂**geranium

☂: Dilute as recommended, and apply 1–3 drops on abdomen, ankles, or bottoms of feet.

—LACTATION (MILK PRODUCTION):

Lactation is the production and secretion of milk from the mammary glands of females for the nourishment of their young offspring. Lactation is commonly referred to as "breast-feeding."

Oils: **☂**clary sage (start production), **☂**fennel or **☂**basil (increase production), **☂**peppermint (decrease production), **☂**Whisper (contains jasmine that may help decrease production[4])

☂: Dilute as recommended, and apply 1–2 drops on breasts. Apply peppermint with cold compress to help reduce production. *Caution: Fennel should not be used for more than 10 days, as it will excessively increase flow through the urinary tract.*

---

1   Subjects who had ylang ylang oil applied to their skin had decreased blood pressure, increased skin temperature, and reported feeling more calm and relaxed compared to subjects in a control group (Hongratanaworakit et al., 2006).
2   Inhaled ylang ylang oil was found to decrease blood pressure and pulse rate and to enhance attentiveness and alertness in volunteers compared to an odorless control (Hongratanaworakit et al., 2004).
3   Treatment of rats with 1,8-cineole (or eucalyptol—found in eucalyptus, rosemary, and marjoram) demonstrated an ability to lower mean aortic pressure (blood pres-

sure), without decreasing heart rate, through vascular wall relaxation (Lahlou et al., 2002).
4   Jasmine flowers applied to the breast were found to be as effective as the antilactation drug bromocriptine in reducing breast engorgement, milk production, and analgesic (pain-relieving drug) intake in women after giving birth. (Shrivastav et al., 1988).

Primary Recommendations • Secondary Recommendations • Other Recommendations / **☁**=Aromatic, **☂**=Topical, **☽**=Internal

206

—MASTITIS: *SEE ALSO ANTIBACTERIAL.*

Mastitis is a breast infection occurring in women who are breast-feeding. Mastitis causes the breast to become red, swollen, and very painful. Symptoms of mastitis include breast tenderness, fever, general lack of well-being, skin redness, and a breast that feels warm to the touch. Mastitis generally occurs in just one breast, not in both.

Oils: Ⓣlavender, ⓉCitrus Bliss (combine with lavender)

Ⓣ: Dilute as recommended, and apply 1–2 drops on breasts.

—MISCARRIAGE (AFTER):

A miscarriage is a pregnancy that ends on its own within the first 20 weeks. Signs of a miscarriage include vaginal bleeding, fluid or tissue being ejected from the vagina, and pain and cramping in the abdomen or lower back. Miscarriages occur before the baby is developed enough to survive. About half of all pregnancies end in miscarriage, but most happen too early for the mother to be aware that it has occurred. Women who miscarry after about 8 weeks of pregnancy should consult their doctor as soon as possible afterwards to prevent any future complications.

Oils: Ⓣfrankincense, Ⓣgrapefruit, Ⓣgeranium, Ⓣlavender, ⓉRoman chamomile

Ⓣ: Dilute 5–6 drops in 1 Tbs. fractionated coconut oil, and massage on back, legs, and arms. Add 3–4 drops to warm bathwater, and bathe.

—MORNING SICKNESS:

Morning sickness is the nauseated feeling accompanying the first trimester of pregnancy for many women. Morning sickness can often include vomiting. For most women, morning sickness begins around the sixth week of pregnancy and ends around the twelfth week. Although it is called "morning" sickness, the symptoms can occur at any time during the day.

Oils: ⓉⒾⒶginger[5], ⓉⒶpeppermint

Ⓣ: Dilute as recommended, and apply 1–3 drops on ears, down jaw bone, and on reflex points on the feet.

Ⓘ: Place 1–3 drops in empty capsule; swallow capsule.

Ⓐ: Diffuse into the air. Inhale directly from bottle. Apply oil to hands, tissue, or cotton wick, and inhale. Apply 1 drop on pillow to inhale at night.

—PLACENTA:

The placenta is the organ responsible for sustaining life in an unborn baby. The placenta attaches to the uterus wall and connects to the mother's blood supply to provide nutrients and oxygen for the fetus. The placenta plays other essential roles as well: It removes waste created by the fetus, triggers labor and delivery, and protects the fetus against infection.

Oils: Ⓣbasil (to help retain)

Ⓣ: Dilute as recommended, and apply 1–2 drops on lower abdomen and reflex points on the feet.

—POSTPARTUM DEPRESSION:

Postpartum depression is depression sometimes experienced by mothers shortly after giving birth. New mothers may experience symptoms such as irritableness, sadness, uncontrollable emotions, fatigue, anxiety, difficulty sleeping, thoughts of suicide, hopelessness, and guilt. Postpartum depression is typically thought to result from a hormonal imbalance caused by the pregnancy and childbirth.

Oils: ⒶⓉElevation, ⒶⓉlemon[6,7,8], ⒶⓉlavender[9], ⒶⓉfrankincense[10], ⒶⓉclary sage, ⒶⓉgeranium, Ⓐgrapefruit, ⒶⓉbergamot, ⒶⓉBalance, ⒶⓉmyrrh, Ⓐorange

Ⓐ: Diffuse into the air. Inhale directly from bottle. Apply oil to hands, tissue, or cotton wick, and inhale.

---

5   Ginger root given orally to pregnant women was found to decrease the severity of nausea and frequency of vomiting compared to control (Vutyavanich et al., 2001).

6   Lemon oil vapor was found to have a strong antistress and antidepressant effects on mice subjected to several common stress tests (Komiya et al., 2006).

7   Lemon oil and its component, citral, were found to decrease depressed behavior in a similar manner to antidepressant drugs in rats involved in several stress tests (Komori et al., 1995).

8   In 12 patients suffering from depression, it was found that inhaling citrus aromas reduced the needed doses of antidepressants, normalized neuroendocrine hormone levels, and normalized immune function (Komori et al., 1995).

9   Female students suffering from insomnia were found to sleep better and to have a lower level of depression during weeks they used a lavender fragrance when compared to weeks they did not use a lavender fragrance (Lee et al., 2006).

10   Incensole acetate was found to open TRPV receptor in mice brain, a possible channel for emotional regulation (Moussaieff et al., 2008).

Primary Recommendations • Secondary Recommendations • Other Recommendations / Ⓐ=Aromatic, Ⓣ=Topical, Ⓘ=Internal

T: Dilute as recommended, and apply 1–2 drops to temple or forehead. Add 5–10 drops to 1 Tbs. fractionated coconut oil, and use as massage oil. Add 1–3 drops to warm bathwater, and bathe.

—**Preeclampsia:** *see also Pregnancy/Motherhood: High Blood Pressure*

Preeclampsia, also known as toxemia, is pregnancy-induced high blood pressure. Symptoms include protein in the urine, elevated blood pressure levels, sudden weight gain, blurred vision, abdominal pains in the upper-right side, and swelling in the hands and face. Women suffering from preeclampsia are often put on bed rest for the remainder of the pregnancy to ensure the safety of the mother and baby.

Oils: **TA**cypress

T: Dilute 1:1 in fractionated coconut oil, and apply 1–2 drops on bottoms of feet and on abdomen.

A: Diffuse into the air. Inhale directly from bottle. Apply oil to hands, tissue, or cotton wick, and inhale.

—**Self Love:**

Oils: **A**Elevation

A: Diffuse into the air. Wear as perfume.

—**Stretch Marks:** *see Skin:Stretch Marks*

Prostate:

The prostate gland is a small organ just beneath that bladder that is part of the male reproductive system. Its primary function is to create and store fluid that helps nourish and protect the sperm.

Oils: **T**helichrysum, **T**frankincense

—**Benign Prostatic Hyperplasia:**

The size of the prostate begins at about the same size as a walnut but increases in size as a male ages. If the prostate grows too large, it can block passage of urine from the bladder through the urethra. This blockage can lead to increased risk for developing urinary tract stones, infections, or damaged kidneys.

Oils: **T**fennel

—**Prostate Cancer:** *see Cancer:Prostate*

—**Prostatitis:**

Prostatitis is an inflamed prostate, typically due to infection. This can cause pain in the lower back and groin area, painful urination, and the need to urinate frequently.

Oils: **T**thyme, **T**cypress, **T**lavender

T: Dilute as recommended, and apply to the posterior, scrotum, ankles, lower back, or bottoms of feet. Add 5 drops to 1 Tbs. fractionated coconut oil, insert into rectum, and retain throughout the night.

Psoriasis:

Psoriasis is a skin condition characterized by patches of red, scaly skin that may itch or burn. The most commonly affected areas are the elbows, knees, scalp, back, face, palms, and feet. But other areas can be affected as well. Psoriasis doesn't have a known cure or cause, but it is thought an auto-immune disorder may play a role. Psoriasis tends to be less severe in the warmer months.

Oils: **T**helichrysum, **T**thyme, **T**lavender, **T**melaleuca, **T**Roman chamomile, **T**bergamot

Blend 1: Combine 2 drops Roman chamomile with 2 drops lavender, and apply on location.

T: Dilute as recommended, and apply 1–2 drops on location.

Pulmonary: *see Respiratory System:Lungs*

Purification:

Oils: **A**Purify, **A**lemon, **A**lemongrass, **A**eucalyptus, **A**melaleuca, **A**orange, **A**fennel

—**Air:**

Oils: **A**lemon, **A**peppermint, **A**Purify

—**Cigarette Smoke:**

Oils: **A**Purify

—**Dishes:**

Oils: **T**lemon

—**Water:**

Oils: **IT**lemon, **T**Purify, **IT**peppermint

Primary Recommendations • Secondary Recommendations • Other Recommendations / **A**=Aromatic, **T**=Topical, **I**=Internal

208

Ⓐ: Diffuse into the air. Add 10–15 drops to 1 oz. distilled water in a small spray bottle; shake well, and mist into the air.

Ⓣ: Add 1–2 drops to dishwater for sparkling dishes and a great smelling kitchen. Add 1–2 drops to warm bathwater, and bathe. Add 1–2 drops to bowl of water, and use to clean the outside of fruit and vegetables.

Ⓘ: Add 1 drop oil to 12–16 oz. of drinking water to help purify.

PUS: *SEE INFECTION*

RADIATION:

Radiation is energy emitted from a source and sent through space or matter. Different forms of radiation can include light, heat, sound, radio, micro-waves, gamma rays, or X-rays, among others. While many forms of radiation are around us every day and are perfectly safe (such as light, sound, and heat), frequent or prolonged exposure to high-energy forms of radiation can be detrimental to the body, possibly causing DNA mutation, damaged cellular structures, burns, cancer, or other damage.

Oils: ⒾⓉpeppermint, ⒾⓉsandalwood

—GAMMA RADIATION:

Oils: ⒾⓉpeppermint[1,2,3,4,5]

—RADIATION THERAPY:

Radiation treatments can produce tremendous toxicity within the liver. Cut down on the use of oils with high phenol content to prevent increasing liver toxicity. Oils with high phenol content include wintergreen, birch, clove, basil, fennel, oregano, thyme, melaleuca, and cinnamon.

—ULTRAVIOLET RADIATION:

Oils: ⒾⓉsandalwood[6,7], Ⓣfrankincense, Ⓣmelaleuca[8], Ⓣthyme[9], Ⓣclove[9]

—WEEPING WOUNDS FROM:

Oils: Ⓣmelaleuca, Ⓣthyme, Ⓣoregano

Ⓘ: Place 2–3 drops in an empty capsule, and swallow.

Ⓣ: Dilute as recommended, and apply 1–2 drops on location.

RASHES: *SEE SKIN:RASHES*

RAYNAUD'S DISEASE: *SEE ALSO ARTERIES, CARDIOVASCULAR SYSTEM:CIRCULATION*

Raynaud's disease is a condition that causes the arteries supplying blood to the skin to suddenly narrow and inhibit blood circulation. As a result, specific areas of the body feel numb and cool. The most commonly affected areas are the toes, fingers, nose, and ears. During an attack, the skin turns white and then blue. As circulation returns and warms the affected areas, a prickling, throbbing, stinging, or swelling sensation often accompanies it. These attacks are often triggered by cold temperatures and by stress.

Oils: ⒾⓉⒶcypress, ⓉⒶrosemary, ⓉⒶgeranium, ⓉⒶhelichrysum, ⒾⓉfennel, ⓉⒶclove, ⓉⒶlavender

Ⓣ: Dilute as recommended, and apply 1–2 drops on the affected area, to carotid arteries, and on reflex points on the feet.

Ⓐ: Diffuse into the air. Inhale oil directly from bottle, or inhale oil that is applied to hands, tissue, or cotton wick.

---

1 In mice exposed to whole-body gamma irradiation, only 17% of mice who had been fed peppermint oil died; while 100% of mice who did not receive peppermint oil died. It was also found that the mice pre-fed peppermint oil were able to return blood cell levels to normal after 30 days, while control mice were not (and consequently died)—suggesting a protective or stimulating effect of the oil on blood stem cells (Samarth et al., 2004).

2 Peppermint extract fed orally to mice demonstrated the ability to protect the testis from gamma radiation damage (Samarth et al., 2009).

3 Peppermint oil fed to mice prior to exposure to gamma radiation was found to decrease levels of damage from oxidation, as compared to mice not pretreated with peppermint (Samarth et al., 2006).

4 Mice treated with oral administration of peppermint extract demonstrated a higher ability to tolerate gamma radiation than non-treated mice (Samarth et al., 2003).

5 Mice pretreated with peppermint leaf extract demonstrated less bone marrow cell loss than mice not pretreated with peppermint when exposed to gamma radiation (Samarth et al., 2007).

6 Pretreatment with alpha-santalol before UVB (ultraviolet-b) radiation significantly reduced skin tumor development and multiplicity and induced proapoptotic and tumor-suppressing proteins (Arasada et al., 2008)

7 A solution of 5% alpha-santalol (from sandalwood) was found to prevent skin-tumor formation caused by ultraviolet-b (UVB) radiation in mice (Dwivedi et al., 2006).

8 *Melaleuca alternifolia* oil was found to mediate the reactive oxygen species (ROS) production of leukocytes (white blood cells), indicating a possible anti-inflammatory activity (Caldefie-Chézet et al., 2004).

9 Various essential oils demonstrated an antioxidant effect toward skin lipid squalene oxidized by UV irradiation, with a blend of thyme and clove oil demonstrating the highest inhibitory effect (Wei et al., 2007).

Primary Recommendations • Secondary Recommendations • Other Recommendations / Ⓐ=Aromatic, Ⓣ=Topical, Ⓘ=Internal

Relaxation:

Relaxation is a state of rest and tranquility, free from tension and anxiety.

Oils: **AT**lavender[1,2,3,4], **AT**ylang ylang[5], **A**lemon[6], **T**AromaTouch, **AT**Roman chamomile, **AT**geranium, **AT**frankincense, **AT**sandalwood, **AT**clary sage

A: Diffuse into the air. Inhale directly from bottle. Apply oil to hands, tissue, or cotton wick, and inhale. *See also Ions:Negative for oils that produce negative ions when diffused to help promote relaxation.*

T: Add 5–10 drops to 1 Tbs. fractionated coconut oil (or another carrier oil), and use as massage oil. Place 1–2 drops in warm bathwater, and bathe.

Respiratory System:

The respiratory system's primary purposes are to supply the blood with oxygen that is then delivered to all parts of the body and to remove waste carbon dioxide from the blood and eliminate it from the body. The respiratory system consists of the mouth, nose, and pharynx (through which air is first taken in), larynx (voice box), trachea (airway leading from the larynx to the lungs), bronchi (which branch off from the trachea and into the lungs), bronchioles (smaller tubes that branch off from the bronchi), alveoli (tiny sacs filled with capillaries that allow inhaled oxygen to be transferred into the blood and carbon dioxide to be expelled from the blood into the air in the lungs), pleura (which covers the outside of the lungs and the inside of the chest wall), and diaphragm (a large muscle at the bottom of the chest cavity that moves to pull air into the lungs (inhale) and to push air out of the lungs (exhale)).

RESPIRATORY SYSTEM

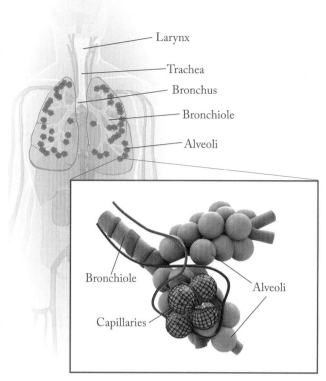

Larynx
Trachea
Bronchus
Bronchiole
Alveoli

Bronchiole
Alveoli
Capillaries

Oils: **AT**Breathe, **AT**eucalyptus[7,8,9], **AT**peppermint[10], **AT**white fir, **AT**cinnamon[11,12], **AT**On Guard, **AT**melaleuca, **AT**clary sage, **AT**fennel, **AT**helichrysum, **AT**marjoram, **T**oregano, **AT**bergamot, **AT**clove, **AT**frankincense, **A**lemon, **AT**rosemary, **AT**lime

Blend 1: Combine 5 drops eucalyptus, 8 drops frankincense, and 6 drops lemon. Apply to bottoms of feet; or add to 1 oz. (2 Tbs.) fractionated coconut oil, and apply as a hot compress on chest.

Recipe 1: Combine 10 drops eucalyptus and 10 drops myrrh with 1 Tbs. fractionated coco-

---

1 Nurses working in an ICU setting demonstrated decreased perception of stress when receiving a topical application of *Lavandula angustifolia* and *Salvia sclarea* essential oils (Pemberton et al., 2008).

2 Subjects who smelled a cleansing gel with lavender aroma were more relaxed and able to complete math computations faster (Field et al., 2005).

3 Subjects exposed to 3 minutes of lavender aroma were more relaxed and able to perform math computations faster and more accurately (Diego et al., 1998).

4 Mice who inhaled lavender were found to have a decreased motility (natural movement) dependent on exposure time. Additionally, mice injected with caffeine (causing a hyperactivity) were found to reduce their movement to near normal levels after inhaling lavender (Buchbauer et al., 1991).

5 Subjects who had ylang ylang oil applied to their skin had decreased blood pressure, increased skin temperature, and reported feeling more calm and relaxed compared to subjects in a control group (Hongratanaworakit et al., 2006).

6 Lemon oil was found to have an antistress effect in mice involved in several behavioral tasks (Komiya et al., 2006).

7 Extracts from eucalyptus and thyme were found to have high nitrous oxide (NO) scavenging abilities and inhibited NO production in macrophage cells. This could possibly explain their role in aiding respiratory inflammatory diseases (Vigo et al., 2004).

8 Eucalyptus oil was found to have an anti-inflammatory and mucin-inhibitory effect in rats with lipopolysaccharide-induced bronchitis (Lu et al., 2004).

9 Therapy with 1,8 cineole (eucalyptol) in both healthy and bronchitis-afflicted humans was shown to reduce production of LTB4 and PGE2—both metabolites of arachidonic acid, a known chemical messenger involved in inflammation—in white blood cells (Juergens et al., 1998).

10 L-menthol was found to inhibit production of inflammation mediators in human monocytes (a type of white blood cell involved in the immune response) (Juergens et al., 1998).

11 Vapor of cinnamon bark oil and cinnamic aldehyde was found to be effective against fungi involved in respiratory tract mycoses (fungal infections) (Singh et al., 1995).

12 Cinnamon bark, lemongrass, and thyme oils were found to have the highest level of activity against common respiratory pathogens among 14 essential oils tested (Inouye et al., 2001).

Primary Recommendations • Secondary Recommendations • Other Recommendations / **A**=Aromatic, **T**=Topical, **I**=Internal

Usage Guide

nut oil. Insert rectally for overnight retention enema.

—ASTHMA: *SEE ASTHMA*

—BREATHING:

Oils: ᴬᵀBreathe, ᴬᵀcinnamon, ᴬᵀfrankincense, ᴬᵀrosemary, ᴬᵀthyme, ᴬᵀmarjoram, ᴬᵀginger

—BRONCHITIS: *SEE BRONCHITIS*

—HYPERPNEA:

Hyperpnea is rapid or heavy breathing that occurs normally as a result of strenuous physical exertion and abnormally in conjunction with fever and disorders.

Oils: ᴬᵀylang ylang

—LUNGS:

The lungs are paired organs located on either side of the heart. The lungs function to exchange oxygen and carbon dioxide (breathing). Oxygen passes into the blood by inhaling, and exhaling expels carbon dioxide. The lungs keep the body supplied with the oxygen necessary to keep cells alive. The lung on the right side of the body contains three lobes (sections) and is slightly larger than the lung on the left side of the body, which has two lobes.

Oils: ᴬᵀBreathe, ᴬᵀeucalyptus, ᴬᵀsandalwood, ᴬᵀfrankincense, ᴬᵀElevation, ᴬᵀOn Guard (for infections)

Other Products: ᴵZendocrine capsules to help support healthy lung functioning.

—OXYGEN:

Oils: ᴬfrankincense, ᴬsandalwood

—PLEURISY:

Pleurisy is an inflammation of the moist membrane (pleura) that surrounds the lungs and lines the rib cage. Pleurisy is characterized by a dry cough, chest pain, and difficulty breathing. Viral infection is the most common cause of pleurisy; but lung infections, chest injuries, and drug reactions are also possible causes. Pleurisy usually lasts between a few days and a couple weeks.

Oils: ᴬᵀcypress, ᴬᵀthyme

—PNEUMONIA: *SEE PNEUMONIA*

Ⓐ: Diffuse into the air. Inhale directly from bottle. Apply oil to hands, tissue, or cotton wick, and inhale.

Ⓣ: Dilute as recommended, and apply to chest, sinuses, neck, or reflex points on the feet. Add 2–3 drops to water, and gargle. Apply to chest as warm compress. Add 20 drops to 1 Tbs. fractionated coconut oil, and insert rectally for overnight retention enema.

RESTLESSNESS: *SEE CALMING*

RHEUMATIC FEVER: *SEE ALSO ANTIBACTERIAL*

Rheumatic fever is the inflammation of the heart and joints in response to a strep throat or scarlet fever infection. This inflammation can cause permanent damage to the heart. Symptoms of rheumatic fever include painful and swollen joints, chest pain, fever, fatigue, the sensation of a pounding heartbeat, shortness of breath, rash, sudden jerky body movements, and unusual displays of emotion. Rheumatic fever is most common in children between ages 5 and 15.

Oils: ᵀginger (for pain)

Ⓣ: Dilute as recommended, and apply 1–2 drops on location.

RHEUMATISM: *SEE ARTHRITIS:RHEUMATOID ARTHRITIS*

RHINITIS: *SEE NOSE:RHINITIS*

RINGWORM: *SEE ANTIFUNGAL:RINGWORM*

SADNESS: *SEE GRIEF/SORROW*

SALMONELLA: *SEE ANTIBACTERIAL, FOOD POISONING*

SCABIES: *SEE SKIN:SCABIES*

SCARRING: *SEE SKIN:SCARRING, TISSUE:SCARRING*

SCHMIDT'S SYNDROME: *SEE ADRENAL GLANDS:SCHMIDT'S SYNDROME*

SCIATICA:

Sciatica is pain resulting from the irritation of the sciatic nerve. The sciatic nerve is the longest nerve in the body. It runs from the spinal cord through the buttock and hip area and down the back of each leg. When the sciatic nerve is pinched or irritated due to something such as a herniated disk, the pain experienced along the sciatic nerve is called "sciatica." Symptoms of sciatica include pain in the area, numbness and weakness along the sciatic nerve, tingling sensations, or a loss of bladder or bowel control.

Oils: ❶peppermint, ❶Roman chamomile, ❶helichrysum, ❶thyme, ❶Deep Blue (for pain), ❶Balance, ❶white fir, ❶sandalwood, ❶lavender, ❶wintergreen

❶: Dilute as recommended, and apply 1–2 drops on lower back, buttocks, or legs. Add 5–10 drops to 1 Tbs. fractionated coconut oil, and massage on spine, back, legs, and bottoms of feet.

SCRAPES: *SEE WOUNDS*

SCURVY:

Scurvy is a disease caused by a deficiency of ascorbic acid (vitamin C). Some results of scurvy are general weakness, anemia, gum disease (gingivitis), skin hemorrhages, spots on the skin (usually the thighs and legs), and bleeding from the mucus membranes.

Oils: ❶ginger

Other Products: ❶Microplex VMz contains vitamin C necessary for preventing scurvy.

❶: Dilute as recommended, and apply 1–2 drops over kidneys, liver, and reflex points on the feet.

❶: Take capsules as directed on package.

SEDATIVE: *SEE CALMING:SEDATIVE*

SEIZURE:

A seizure is an uncontrolled, abnormal electrical discharge in the brain which may produce a physical convulsion, minor physical signs, thought disturbances, or a combination of symptoms. The symptoms depend on what parts of the brain are involved.

Oils: ❶clary sage, ❶lavender, ❶Balance, ❶Serenity, ❶Elevation

Other Products: ❶xEO Mega, ❶Microplex VMz contain omega fatty acids, minerals, and other nutrients that support healthy brain function.

—CONVULSIONS:

A convulsion is the repeated, rapid contracting and relaxing of muscles resulting in the uncontrollable shaking of the body. Convulsions usually last about 30 seconds to 2 minutes and are often associated with seizures.

Oils: ❶lavender[1], ❶clary sage, ❶Balance

—EPILEPSY:

Epilepsy is a neurological condition where the person has recurring, unpredictable seizures. Epilepsy has many possible causes; although in many cases the cause is unknown. Possible causes may include illness, injury to the brain, or abnormal brain development.

Oils: ❶clary sage

—GRAND MAL SEIZURE:

The grand mal seizure, also known as the tonic-clonic seizure, is the most common seizure. The tonic phase lasts about 10–20 seconds. During this stage, the person looses consciousness, and the muscles contract—causing the person to fall down. During the clonic phase, the person experiences violent convulsions. This phase usually lasts less than two minutes.

Oils: ❶Balance (on feet), ❶❶Serenity (around navel), ❶Elevation (over heart)

Other Products: ❶Microplex VMz contains zinc and copper—an imbalance of zinc and copper has been theorized to play a role in grand mal seizures.

❶: Dilute as recommended, and apply 1–2 drops to back of neck, navel, heart, or reflex points on the feet.

❶: Take capsules as directed on package.

❶: Diffuse into the air.

---

1 Linalool (found in several essential oils) was found to inhibit induced convulsions in rats by directly interacting with the NMDA receptor complex (Brum et al., 2001).

Sexual Issues:

—Arousing Desire: *see Aphrodisiac*

—Female Frigidity:

Female frigidity is a female's lack of sexual drive or her inability to enjoy sexual activities. This disorder has many possible physical and psychological causes, including stress, fatigue, guilt, fear, worry, alcoholism, or drug abuse.

Oils: clary sage, ylang ylang, Whisper, rose

—Impotence:

Impotence in men, also known as erectile dysfunction, is the frequent inability to have or sustain an erection. This may be caused by circulation problems, nerve problems, low levels of testosterone, medications, or psychological stresses.

Oils: clary sage, clove, rose, ginger, sandalwood

—Libido (Low):

Libido is a term used by Sigmund Freud to describe human sexual desire. Causes for a lack of sexual desire can be both physical and psychological. Some possible causes include anemia, alcoholism, drug abuse, stress, anxiety, past sexual abuse, and relationship problems.

Oils: ylang ylang, Elevation

–Men:

Oils: cinnamon, ginger, myrrh

–Women:

Oils: clary sage, geranium

A: Diffuse into the air. Dissolve 2–3 drops in 2 tsp. pure grain or perfumers alcohol, combine with distilled water in a 1 or 2 oz. spray bottle, and spray into the air or on clothes or bed linens.

T: Dilute as recommended, and wear on temples, neck, or wrists as perfume or cologne. Combine 3–5 drops of your desired essential oil with 1 Tbs. fractionated coconut oil to use as a massage oil. Combine 1–2 drops with 1/4 cup Therapeutic Bath Salts, and dissolve in warm bathwater for a romantic bath.

I: Place 1–2 drops in an empty capsule, and swallow.

Sexually Transmitted Diseases (STD): *see AIDS/HIV, Herpes Simplex*

Shingles: *see also Antiviral, Childhood Diseases:Chickenpox, Nervous System:Neuralgia*

Shingles is a viral infection caused by the same virus that causes chickenpox. After a person has had chickenpox, the virus lies dormant in the nervous system. Years later, that virus can be reactivated by stress, immune deficiency, or disease and cause shingles. Symptoms of shingles start with tingling, pain, neuralgia, or itching of an area of skin and become visually obvious as red blisters form in that same area along the nerve path, forming a red band on the skin. Blisters most commonly appear wrapping from the middle of the back to the middle of the chest but can form on the neck, face, and scalp as well. Another name for shingles is herpes zoster.

Oils: melaleuca, eucalyptus, lavender, lemon, geranium, bergamot

Blend 1: Combine 10 drops lavender, 10 drops melaleuca, and 10 drops thyme with 1 Tbs. fractionated coconut oil. Apply on feet and on location.

T: Dilute as recommended, and apply 1–2 drops on location. Add 5–10 drops essential oil to 1 Tbs. fractionated coconut oil, and massage on location and on bottoms of feet.

Shock: *see also Cardiovascular System: Circulation, Cardiovascular System:Heart*

Shock is a life-threatening condition where the body suffers from severely low blood pressure. This can be caused by low blood volume due to bleeding or dehydration, inadequate pumping of the heart, or dilation of the blood vessels due to head injury, medications, or poisons from bacterial infections. Shock can cause pale or bluish skin that feels cold or clammy to the touch, confusion, rapid breathing, and a rapid heartbeat. Without the needed oxygen being sent to the body's tissues and cells, the organs can shut down and, in severe cases, can lead to death. Shock often accompanies severe injuries or other traumatic situations. A person suffering from shock should be made to lie down with the feet elevated above the head, be kept warm, and have the head turned to the side in case of vomiting. Check breathing often, and

Primary Recommendations • Secondary Recommendations • Other Recommendations / **A**=Aromatic, **T**=Topical, **I**=Internal

213

ensure that any visible bleeding is stopped. Get emergency medical help as soon as possible.

Oils: ⒶⓉpeppermint, ⓉRoman chamomile, Ⓣhelichrysum (may help stop bleeding), Ⓣmelaleuca, ⒶElevation, ⒶⓉylang ylang, ⓉBalance, ⒶⓉmyrrh, ⒶⓉmelissa, ⒶⓉbasil, Ⓣrosemary

Ⓣ: Dilute as recommended, and apply 1–2 drops on back of neck, feet, over heart, or on front of neck.

Ⓐ: Diffuse into the air. Inhale directly from bottle. Apply oil to hands, tissue, or cotton wick, and inhale.

SHOULDER: *SEE JOINTS:SHOULDER*

SINUSES:

Sinuses are several hollow cavities within the skull that allow the skull to be more lightweight without compromising strength. These cavities are connected to the nasal cavity through small channels. When the mucous membrane lining these channels becomes swollen or inflamed due to colds or allergies, these channels can become blocked—making it difficult for the sinuses to drain correctly. This can lead to infection and inflammation of the mucous membrane within the sinuses (sinusitis). There are sinus cavities behind the cheek bone and forehead and near the eyes and nasal cavity.

Oils: ⒶⓉhelichrysum, ⒶⓉeucalyptus, ⒶⓉBreathe, ⒶⓉpeppermint, ⒶⓉOn Guard

—SINUSITIS:

Oils: ⒶⓉeucalyptus, ⒶⓉrosemary, ⒶⓉBreathe, ⓉDigestZen, ⒶⓉpeppermint, ⒶⓉmelaleuca, ⒶⓉwhite fir, ⒶⓉginger

Recipe 1: For chronic sinusitis, apply 1–2 drops DigestZen around navel four times daily; apply 2 drops peppermint under tongue two times daily.

Ⓐ: Diffuse into the air. Inhale directly from bottle. Apply oil to hands, tissue, or cotton wick, and inhale. Place 1–2 drops in a bowl of hot water, and inhale vapors.

Ⓣ: Dilute as recommended, and apply 1–2 drops along the sides of the nose or forehead (often clears out sinuses immediately).

SKELETAL SYSTEM: *SEE BONES*

SKIN: *SEE ALSO ACNE, ANTIBACTERIAL, ANTIFUNGAL, BOILS, BURNS, FOOT, CANCER:SKIN/MELANOMA*

The skin is the organ the covers the body, offering the first layer of protection to the internal organs and tissues from exposure to the environment and fungal, bacterial, and other types of infection. It helps regulate body heat and helps prevent evaporation of water from the body. The skin also carries nerve endings that allow the body to sense touch, heat, and pain. The skin is comprised of three layers. The upper layer is the epidermis, the middle layer is the dermis, and the deeper layer is the hypodermis (or subcutis layer).

Oils: Ⓣpeppermint, Ⓣmelaleuca, ⓉClear Skin, ⓉImmortelle, Ⓣsandalwood, Ⓣfrankincense, Ⓣlavender, Ⓣmyrrh, Ⓣgeranium, Ⓣrosemary, ⓉBalance, Ⓣylang ylang, Ⓣmarjoram, Ⓣcypress, ⒾZendocrine, Ⓣvetiver, Ⓣhelichrysum, Ⓣlemon, Ⓣorange, Ⓣlime, Ⓣpatchouli

Other Products: Essential Skin Care products: ⓉAnti-Aging Moisturizer, ⓉFacial Cleanser, ⓉHydrating Cream, ⓉInvigorating Scrub, ⓉPore-Reducing Toner, and ⓉTightening Serum **for vibrant, youthful-looking skin.** ⓉClear Skin Foaming Face Wash **to help improve tone and texture of the skin.** ⓉOn

SKIN

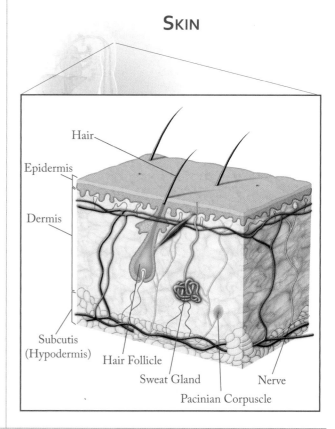

Hair
Epidermis
Dermis
Subcutis (Hypodermis)
Hair Follicle
Sweat Gland
Pacinian Corpuscle
Nerve

Guard Foaming Hand Wash to help protect against harmful microorganisms on the skin. ⓉCitrus Bliss and ⓉSerenity Bath Bars, or ⓉHand and Body Lotion to help cleanse and moisturize the skin. ⓘxEO Mega, ⓘAlpha CRS+, ⓘMicroplex VMz contain omega fatty acids and other nutrients essential for healthy skin cell function. ⓘZendocrine capsules to help support healthy cleansing and filtering of the skin.

Ⓣ: Dilute as recommended, and apply 1–2 drops on location. Add 5–10 drops to 2 Tbs. fractionated coconut oil, and use as massage oil. Add 1 drop essential oil to 1 tsp. unscented lotion, and apply on the skin. Add 1–2 drops to 1 Tbs. bath or shower gel, and apply to skin. Apply foaming hand wash to skin instead of soap, or use bath bars when washing hands or bathing. Use Essential Skin Care products and Hand and Body Lotion as directed on packaging.

Ⓘ: Take capsules as directed on package. Add 3–5 drops of oil to an empty capsule; swallow capsule.

—Acne: *see Acne*

—Boils: *see Boils*

—Burns: *see Burns*

—Callouses:

A callous is a flat, thick growth of skin that develops on areas of the skin where there is constant friction or rubbing. Callouses typically form on the bottoms of the feet but can also form on the hands or other areas of the body exposed to constant friction.

Oils: Ⓣoregano, ⓉClear Skin, ⓉRoman chamomile

Ⓣ: Dilute as recommended, and apply 1–2 drops on area.

—Chapped/Cracked:

Chapped or cracked skin is the result of the depletion of natural oils (sebum) in the skin, leading to dehydration of the skin beneath it. Some common causes for chapped skin include exposure to the cold or wind, repeated contact with soap or chemicals that break down oils, or a lack of essential fatty acids in the body.

Oils: Ⓣmyrrh, ⓉClear Skin, ⓉImmortelle

Other Products: ⓉHand and Body Lotion and ⓉHydrating Cream to help moisturize and protect. ⓘxEO Mega to help supply essential omega fatty acids necessary for healthy skin. ⓉCitrus Bliss and ⓉSerenity Bath Bars contain natural oils that help moisturize and soften the skin.

Ⓣ: Dilute as recommended, and apply 1–2 drops on location. Add 5–10 drops to 1 Tbs. fractionated coconut oil, and massage on location.

Ⓘ: Take capsules as directed on package.

—Corns: *see Foot:Corns*

—Dehydrated:

Oils: Ⓣgeranium, Ⓣlavender, ⓉImmortelle

Other Products: ⓉHand and Body Lotion and ⓉHydrating Cream to help moisturize and protect. ⓉCitrus Bliss and ⓉSerenity Bath Bars contain natural oils that help moisturize and soften.

Ⓣ: Dilute as recommended, and apply 1–2 drops on location. Add 5–10 drops to 2 Tbs. fractionated coconut oil, and use as massage oil. Add 1 drop essential oil to 1 tsp. unscented lotion, and apply on the skin. Add 1–2 drops to 1 Tbs. bath or shower gel, and apply to skin.

—Dermatitis/Eczema:

Dermatitis is any inflammation of the upper layers of the skin that results in redness, itching, pain, or possibly blistering. It can be caused by contact with an allergen or irritating substance, fungal infection, dehydration, or possibly another medical condition.

Oils: ⓉClear Skin, Ⓣhelichrysum, Ⓣthyme, Ⓣgeranium, Ⓣmelaleuca, Ⓣlavender, Ⓣpatchouli, Ⓣbergamot, Ⓣrosemary

Ⓣ: Add 5–10 drops to 1 Tbs. fractionated coconut oil, and apply on location. Dilute as recommended, and apply 1–2 drops on location.

—Diaper Rash: *see Children and Infants:Diaper Rash*

—Dry:

Oils: ⊕geranium, ⊕lavender, ⊕Roman chamomile, ⊕Immortelle, ⊕sandalwood, ⊕lemon

Other Products: ⊕Anti-Aging Moisturizer and ⊕Hydrating Cream to help relieve dryness and reduce the visible signs of aging. ⊕Hand and Body Lotion to help moisturize and protect.

🅣: Add 5–10 drops to 1 Tbs. fractionated coconut oil, and use as massage oil. Add 2–3 drops essential oil to 1 tsp. Hand and Body Lotion, and apply on the skin.

—Energizing:

Oils: ⊕bergamot, ⊕lemon

Other Products: ⊕Invigorating Scrub to polish and exfoliate the skin. ⊕Citrus Bliss Invigorating Bath Bar contains natural oatmeal kernels that help exfoliate.

🅣: Dilute as recommended, and apply 1–2 drops on location. Add 5–10 drops to 2 Tbs. fractionated coconut oil, and use as massage oil. Add 1 drop essential oil to 1 tsp. Hand and Body Lotion, and apply on the skin. Add 1–2 drops to 1 Tbs. bath or shower gel, and apply to skin. Massage Invigorating Scrub over wet skin for up to one minute before rinsing with warm water.

—Facial Oils: *see also Dehydrated, Dry, Energizing, Oily/Greasy, and Revitalizing in this section for other oils that can be used for specific skin types/conditions.*

Oils: ⊕myrrh, ⊕sandalwood, ⊕vetiver

🅣: Add 5–10 drops to 1 Tbs. fractionated coconut oil, and apply to face. Add 1–2 drops essential oil to 1 tsp. unscented lotion, and apply on the skin.

—Fungal Infections: *see Antifungal:Athlete's Foot, Antifungal:Ringworm*

—Impetigo:

Impetigo is a bacterial skin infection that causes sores and blisters full of a yellowish fluid. These sores can be itchy and painful and can easily be spread to other areas of the skin or to another person.

Oils: ⊕geranium, ⊕lavender, ⊕Clear Skin, ⊕myrrh

🅣: Boil 4 oz. of water; cool; and add 5–10 drops essential oil: wash sores with this water, and then cover sores for an hour. Apply oils as a hot compress on location.

—Itching:

An itch is a tingling and unpleasant sensation that evokes the desire to scratch. Itching can be caused by various skin disorders or diseases, parasites such as scabies and lice, allergic reactions to chemicals or drugs, dry skin, insect bites, etc. Scratching the itching area too hard or too often can damage the skin.

Oils: ⊕peppermint, ⊕lavender, ⊕Serenity

Other Products: ⊕Citrus Bliss Invigorating Bath Bar contains natural oatmeal kernels that can help exfoliate skin and soothe itching.

🅣: Dilute as recommended, and apply 1–2 drops on location and on ears. Wash body with Bath Bar.

—Melanoma: *see Cancer:Skin/Melanoma*

—Moles:

Moles are small growths on the skin of pigment-producing skin cells that usually appear brown or black in color. Moles typically appear within a person's first 20 years of life and usually stay with a person throughout his or her life. While moles are not dangerous, melanoma (a type of skin cancer that develops in pigment cells) can resemble a mole at first. Moles that vary in color or that appear to change fairly quickly in size or shape could be cancerous and should be examined.

Oils: ⊕frankincense, ⊕sandalwood, ⊕geranium, ⊕lavender

🅣: Dilute as recommended, and apply 1 drop on location.

—Oily/Greasy:

Oils: ⊕lemon, ⊕Clear Skin, ⊕cypress, ⊕Clear Skin, ⊕frankincense, ⊕geranium, ⊕lavender, ⊕marjoram, ⊕orange, ⊕rosemary

Other Products: ⊕Clear Skin Foaming Face Wash to help balance skin sebum levels. ⊕Facial Cleanser to cleanse the skin and leave it feeling smooth and fresh.

⚬: Add 5–10 drops to 1 Tbs. fractionated coconut oil, and use as massage oil. Use Facial Cleanser as directed on package.

—PSORIASIS: *see Psoriasis*

—RASHES:

A rash is an area of irritated skin, redness, or red bumps on the body. Rashes may be localized or may cover large patches of the body. A rash may be caused by a chemical or allergen irritating the skin or may occur as a symptom of another medical condition or infection.

Oils: ⚬melaleuca, ⚬lavender, ⚬Roman chamomile

⚬: Dilute as recommended, and apply 1–2 drops on location. Add 1–5 drops to 1 Tbs. fractionated coconut oil, and apply on location.

—REVITALIZING:

Oils: ⚬cypress, ⚬lemon, ⚬Immortelle, ⚬Clear Skin, ⚬fennel, ⚬lime

Other Products: ⚬Invigorating Scrub to polish and exfoliate the skin. ⚬Citrus Bliss Invigorating Bath Bar contains natural oatmeal kernels that help exfoliate.

⚬: Add 5–10 drops to 1 Tbs. fractionated coconut oil, and use as massage oil. Add 2–3 drops essential oil to 1 tsp. unscented lotion, and apply on the skin. Massage Invigorating Scrub over wet skin for up to one minute before rinsing with warm water.

—RINGWORM: *see Antifungal:Ringworm*

—SCABIES:

Scabies is an infestation of the skin by mites (*Sarcoptes scabei*) that burrow into the upper layers of the skin, causing small, extremely itchy bumps.

Oils: ⚬On Guard, ⚬Clear Skin, ⚬melaleuca, ⚬peppermint, ⚬lavender, ⚬bergamot

⚬: Add 5–10 drops to 1 Tbs. fractionated coconut oil, and apply a small amount on location morning and night. Dilute as recommended, and apply 1–2 drops on location.

—SCARRING:

Scars are fibrous connective tissue that is used to quickly repair a wound or injury in place of the regular skin or tissue.

Oils: ⚬lavender (burns), ⚬rose (helps prevent), ⚬frankincense (helps prevent), ⚬helichrysum (reduces), ⚬geranium, ⚬myrrh

Blend 1: Combine 5 drops helichrysum and 5 drops lavender with 1 Tbs. sunflower oil or with liquid lecithin (an emulsifier extracted from eggs or soy), and apply on location.

Blend 2: Combine 1 drop lavender, 1 drop lemongrass, and 1 drop geranium; apply on location to help prevent scar formation.

⚬: Dilute as recommended, and apply 1–2 drops on location.

—SENSITIVE:

Oils: ⚬lavender, ⚬geranium

⚬: Dilute as recommended, and apply 1–2 drops on location.

—SKIN ULCERS:

A skin ulcer is an open sore where the epidermis and possibly part or all of the dermis is missing, exposing the deeper layers of the skin. This can be caused by burns, pressure, friction, irritation, or infections damaging the upper layers of the skin.

Oils: ⚬lavender, ⚬myrrh, ⚬Clear Skin, ⚬helichrysum, ⚬Purify

⚬: Dilute as recommended, and apply 1–2 drops on location.

—STRETCH MARKS:

Stretch marks are thin purple or red areas of the skin that appear as the skin is rapidly stretched over a short period of time, stretching and tearing the dermis layer (middle layer) of the skin. Many women notice the appearance of stretch marks in the last few months of pregnancy, but stretch marks can also appear on men or women during any period of rapid weight gain. These marks most often appear on the breasts, stomach, buttocks, thighs, and hips. Stretch marks tend to fade over time, but it is difficult to eliminate them completely.

Primary Recommendations • Secondary Recommendations • Other Recommendations / ▲=Aromatic, ⚬=Topical, ⚫=Internal

Oils: ⊕lavender, ⊕myrrh

⊕: Add 5–10 drops to 1 Tbs. fractionated coconut oil or hazelnut oil, and apply on location.

—SUNBURN: *SEE BURNS:SUNBURN*

—TONES:

Oils: ⊕lemon

⊕: Add 4–5 drops to 1 Tbs. fractionated coconut oil, and use as massage oil (avoid direct sunlight for 24 hours after application).

—VITILIGO:

Vitiligo is white patches of the skin caused by the death or dysfunction of pigment-producing cells in the area. While the exact cause is unknown, vitiligo may be caused by an immune or genetic disorder or may have a relationship to thyroid problems.

Oils: ⊕sandalwood, ⊕vetiver, ⊕frankincense, ⊕myrrh, ⊕Purify

⊕: Dilute as recommended, and apply 1–2 drops behind ears and on back of neck or on reflex points on the feet; then cup hands together, and inhale the aroma from the hands.

—WRINKLES:

A wrinkle is a fold or crease in the skin that develops as part of the normal aging process. Wrinkles are thought to be caused by a breakdown of collagen (a protein that gives structure to cells and tissue) in the skin, causing the skin to become more fragile and loose.

Oils: ⊕Immortelle, ⊕lavender, ⊕fennel, ⊕geranium, ⊕frankincense, ⊕rose, ⊕rosemary, ⊕myrrh, ⊕clary sage, ⊕cypress, ⊕helichrysum, ⊕lemon, ⊕orange, ⊕oregano, ⊕sandalwood, ⊕thyme, ⊕ylang ylang

Other Products: ⊕Anti-Aging Moisturizer to help relieve dryness and reduce the visible signs of aging. ⊕Tightening Serum to help tighten the skin to eliminate fine line and wrinkles. ⊕Hydrating Cream to help promote fuller, smoother looking skin.

Blend 1: Combine 1 drop frankincense, 1 drop lavender, and 1 drop lemon. Rub on morning and night around the eyes (be careful not to get in eyes).

Blend 2: Combine 1 drop sandalwood, 1 drop helichrysum, 1 drop geranium, 1 drop lavender, and 1 drop frankincense. Add to 2 tsp. unscented lotion, and apply to skin.

⊕: Dilute as recommended, and apply 1–2 drops to skin. Add 5–10 drops to 1 Tbs. fractionated coconut oil or other carrier oil such as jojoba, apricot, hazelnut, or sweet almond, and apply on areas of concern. Add 3–5 drops to 1/2 cup Therapeutic Bath Salts, and dissolve in warm bathwater before bathing. Use Essential Skin Care products as directed on packaging.

SLEEP: *SEE ALSO INSOMNIA, IONS:NEGATIVE IONS*

Sleep is a regular period in which the body suspends conscious motor and sensory activity. Sleep is thought to play a role in restoring and healing the body and processing the memories of the day.

Oils: ⊕Ⓐlavender, ⊕ⒶSerenity, ⊕ⒶRoman chamomile, Ⓐmarjoram

Recipe 1: Combine 5 drops geranium and 5 drops lavender with 1/4 cup Therapeutic Bath Salts; dissolve in warm bathwater, and bathe in the evening to help promote a good night's sleep.

⊕: Dilute as recommended, and apply 1–2 drops essential oil to spine, bottoms of feet, or back of neck. Add 1–2 drops to warm bathwater, and bathe before sleeping. Add 5–10 drops to 1 Tbs. fractionated coconut oil, and massage on back, arms, legs, and feet.

Ⓐ: Diffuse into the air. Add 1–2 drops to bottom of pillow before sleeping. Add 2–5 drops to 1 oz. distilled water in a small spray bottle, and mist into the air or on linens before sleeping.

SLIMMING AND TONING OILS: *SEE WEIGHT:SLIMMING/ TONING*

SMELL (LOSS OF): *SEE NOSE:OLFACTORY LOSS*

SMOKING: *SEE ADDICTIONS:SMOKING, PURIFICATION:CIGARETTE SMOKE*

SNAKE BITE: *SEE BITES/STINGS:SNAKES*

SORES: *SEE WOUNDS, ANTIBACTERIAL, ANTIFUNGAL, ANTIVIRAL*

Primary Recommendations • Secondary Recommendations • Other Recommendations / Ⓐ=Aromatic, ⊕=Topical, ⊕=Internal

SORE THROAT: *SEE THROAT:SORE, ANTIBACTERIAL, ANTI-VIRAL, INFECTION*

SPASMS: *SEE MUSCLES/CONNECTIVE TISSUE, DIGESTIVE SYSTEM*

SPINA BIFIDA:

Spina bifida is a birth defect in which the vertebrae of the lower spine do not form correctly, leaving a gap or opening between them. In the most severe cases, this can cause the meninges (the tissue surrounding the spinal cord), or even the spinal cord itself, to protrude through the gap. If the spinal cord protrudes through the gap, it can prevent the nerves from developing normally, causing numbness, paralysis, back pain, and loss of bladder and bowel control and function. This latter type often also develops with a defect in which the back part of the brain develops in the upper neck rather than within the skull, often causing a mental handicap.

Oils: eucalyptus, lavender, Roman chamomile, lemon, orange, rosemary

Other Products: Alpha CRS+ contains 400 mg of folic acid, which has been found to significantly reduce the chance of spina bifida developing in infants if taken as a daily supplement by their mothers before conception[1].

I: Take capsules as directed on package

T: Dilute as recommended, and apply 1–2 drops to bottoms of feet, along spine, on forehead, and on back of neck.

A: Diffuse into the air.

SPINE: *SEE BACK*

SPLEEN: *SEE ALSO LYMPHATIC SYSTEM*

The spleen is a fist-sized spongy tissue that is part of the lymphatic system. Its purpose is to filter bacteria, viruses, fungi, and other unwanted substances out of the blood and to create lymphocytes (white blood cells that create antibodies).

Oils: marjoram

T: Dilute as recommended and apply 1–2 drops over spleen or on reflex points on the feet. Apply as a warm compress over upper abdomen.

SPRAINS: *SEE MUSCLES/CONNECTIVE TISSUE:SPRAINS*

SPURS: *SEE BONES:BONE SPURS*

STAINS: *SEE HOUSECLEANING:STAINS*

STAPH INFECTION: *SEE ANTIBACTERIAL:STAPH INFECTION*

STERILITY: *SEE FEMALE SPECIFIC CONDITIONS:INFERTILITY, MALE SPECIFIC CONDITIONS:INFERTILITY*

STIMULATING:

Oils: peppermint, Elevation, eucalyptus[2], orange, ginger, grapefruit, rose, rosemary[2], basil

A: Diffuse into the air. Inhale directly from bottle. Apply oil to hands, tissue, or cotton wick, and inhale.

T: Dilute as recommended, and apply 1–2 drops to forehead, neck, or bottoms of feet. Add 1–2 drops to an unscented bath gel, and add to warm bathwater while filling; bathe. Add 5–10 drops to 1 Tbs. fractionated coconut oil, and use as massage oil.

STINGS: *SEE BITES/STINGS*

STOMACH: *SEE DIGESTIVE SYSTEM:STOMACH*

STREP THROAT: *SEE THROAT:STREP*

STRESS:

Stress is the body's response to difficult, pressured, or worrisome circumstances. Stress can cause both physical and emotional tension. Symptoms of stress include headaches, muscle soreness, fatigue, insomnia, nervousness, anxiety, and irritability.

1 Centers for Disease Control and Prevention, 2004.

2 Imaging of the brain demonstrated that inhalation of 1,8-cineol (eucalyptol—a constituent of many essential oils, especially eucalyptus, rosemary, and marjoram) increased global cerebral blood flow after an inhalation-time of 20 minutes (Nasel et al., 1994).

Primary Recommendations • Secondary Recommendations • Other Recommendations / A=Aromatic, T=Topical, I=Internal

Oils: [A][T]lavender[1,2], [A][T]lemon[3], [A][T]ylang ylang[4], [A][T]bergamot, [A][T]Elevation, [A][T]Serenity, [A][T]grapefruit, [T]AromaTouch, [T][A]Roman chamomile, [A][T]geranium, [A][T]Balance, [A][T]frankincense, [A][T]marjoram

—Chemical:

Oils: [A][T]lavender, [A][T]rosemary, [A][T]grapefruit, [A][T]geranium, [A][T]clary sage, [A][T]lemon

—Emotional Stress:

Oils: [A][T]Elevation, [A][T]clary sage, [A][T]bergamot, [A][T]geranium, [T][A]Roman chamomile, [A][T]sandalwood

—Environmental Stress:

Oils: [A][T]bergamot, [A][T]cypress, [A][T]geranium

—Mental Stress:

Oils: [A][T]lavender[5], [A][T]grapefruit, [A][T]bergamot, [A][T]sandalwood, [A][T]geranium

—Performance Stress:

Oils: [A][T]grapefruit, [A][T]bergamot, [A][T]ginger, [A][T]rosemary

—Physical Stress:

Oils: [A][T]Serenity, [A][T]lavender, [A][T]bergamot, [A][T]geranium, [A][T]marjoram, [T][A]Roman chamomile, [A][T]rosemary, [A][T]thyme

—Stress Due to Tiredness or Insomnia:

Blend 1: Add 15 drops clary sage, 10 drops lemon, and 5 drops lavender to 2 Tbs. fractionated coconut oil. Massage on skin.

[A]: Diffuse into the air. Inhale directly from bottle. Apply oil to hands, tissue, or cotton wick, and inhale. Wear as perfume or cologne.

[T]: Add 5–10 drops to 1 Tbs. fractionated coconut oil, and massage on skin. Add 1–2 drops to 1/4 cup Therapeutic Bath Salts, and dissolve in warm bathwater before bathing.

Dilute as recommended, and apply 1–2 drops on neck, back, or bottoms of feet.

Stretch Marks: *see Skin:Stretch Marks*

Stroke: *see also Brain, Blood:Clots, Cardiovascular System*

A stroke occurs when the blood supply to the brain is interrupted. Within a few minutes, brain cells begin to die. The affected area of the brain is unable to function, and one or more limbs on one side of the body become weak and unable to move. Strokes can cause serious disabilities, including paralysis and speech problems.

Oils: [A][T]cypress, [A][T]helichrysum, [I]fennel[6]

—Muscular Paralysis:

Oils: [T]lavender

Blend 1: Combine 1 drop basil, 1 drop lavender, and 1 drop rosemary, and apply to spinal column and paralyzed area.

[A]: Inhale oil directly or applied to hands, tissue, or cotton wick. Diffuse into the air.

[T]: Dilute as directed, and apply 1–2 drops to the back of the neck and the forehead.

Sudorific:

A sudorific is a substance that induces sweating.

Oils: [T]thyme, [T]rosemary, [T]lavender, [T]Roman chamomile

[T]: Add 5–10 drops to 1 Tbs. fractionated coconut oil, and apply to skin.

Suicide: *see Depression*

Sunburn: *see Burns:Sunburn*

Sun Screen:

Oils: [T]helichrysum, [T]sandalwood

[T]: Add 5–10 drops to 1 Tbs. fractionated coconut oil, and apply to the skin.

Swelling: *see Edema, Inflammation*

1 Nurses working in an ICU setting demonstrated decreased perception of stress when receiving a topical application of *Lavandula angustifolia* and *Salvia sclarea* essential oils (Pemberton et al., 2008).

2 Subjects placed in a small, soundproof room for 20 minutes were found to have reduced mental stress and increased arousal rate when exposed to the scent of lavender (Motomura et al., 2001).

3 Lemon oil vapor was found to have strong antistress and antidepressant effects on mice subjected to several common behavioral stress tests (Komiya et al., 2006).

4 Subjects who had ylang ylang oil applied to their skin had decreased blood pressure, increased skin temperature, and reported feeling more calm and relaxed compared to subjects in a control group (Hongratanaworakit et al., 2006).

5 Subjects placed in a small, soundproof room for 20 minutes were found to have reduced mental stress and increased arousal rate when exposed to the scent of lavender (Motomura et al., 2001).

6 Both fennel oil and its constituent, anethole, were found to significantly reduce thrombosis (blood clots) in mice. They were also found to be free from the prohemorrhagic (increased bleeding) side effect that aspirin (acetylsalicylic acid) has (Tognolini et al., 2007).

Usage Guide

SYMPATHETIC NERVOUS SYSTEM: *SEE NERVOUS SYSTEM:SYMPATHETIC NERVOUS SYSTEM*

TACHYCARIDA: *SEE CARDIOVASCULAR SYSTEM: TACHYCARIDA*

TASTE (IMPAIRED): *SEE ALSO NOSE:OLFACTORY LOSS*

Taste is the sensation of sweet, sour, salty, or bitter by taste buds on the tongue when a substance enters the mouth. This sensation, combined with the smell of the food, helps create the unique flavors we experience in food.

Oils: Ⓣhelichrysum, Ⓣpeppermint

Ⓣ: Dilute as recommended, and apply 1 drop on the tongue or reflex points on the feet.

TEETH: *SEE ORAL CONDITIONS*

TEMPERATURE: *SEE COOLING OILS, WARMING OILS*

TENDINITIS: *SEE MUSCLES/CONNECTIVE TISSUE:TENDINITIS*

TENNIS ELBOW: *SEE JOINTS:TENNIS ELBOW*

TENSION:

Oils: ⒶⓉSerenity, ⒶⓉlavender, ⓉAromaTouch, ⒶⓉylang ylang, ⓉⒶRoman chamomile, ⒶⓉfrankincense, ⒶⓉbasil (nervous), ⒶⓉbergamot (nervous), ⒶⓉgrapefruit

Ⓐ: Inhale oil applied to hands. Diffuse into the air.

Ⓣ: Add 3–5 drops to 1/2 cup Therapeutic Bath Salts, and dissolve in warm bathwater before bathing. Add 5–10 drops to 1 Tbs. fractionated coconut oil, and use as massage oil.

TESTES:

Testes are the male reproductive organs. The testes are responsible for producing and storing sperm and male hormones such as testosterone. Hormones produced in the testes are responsible for the development of male characteristics: facial hair, wide shoulders, low voice, and reproductive organs.

Oils: ⓉⒶrosemary

—**REGULATION:**

Oils: ⓉⒶclary sage, ⓉⒶsandalwood, ⓉⒶgeranium

Ⓣ: Dilute as recommended, and apply 1–2 drops on location or on reflex points on the feet.

Ⓐ: Diffuse into the air. Inhale directly from bottle. Apply oil to hands, tissue, or cotton wick, and inhale.

THROAT: *SEE ALSO RESPIRATORY SYSTEM, NECK*

Oils: Ⓣcypress, Ⓣoregano

—**CONGESTION:**

Oils: ⓉⒶpeppermint, ⓉⒶmyrrh

—**COUGH:** *SEE RESPIRATORY SYSTEM*

—**DRY:**

Oils: ⓄⓉlemon, ⓄⓉgrapefruit

—**INFECTION IN:**

Oils: ⓉⒶⓄlemon, ⓄⓉⒶOn Guard, ⓉⒶⓄpeppermint, ⓉⒶoregano, ⓉⒶclary sage

—**LARYNGITIS:** *SEE LARYNGITIS*

—**SORE:**

Oils: ⓉⒶmelaleuca, ⓄⓉⒶOn Guard, ⓉⒶoregano, ⓉⒶsandalwood, ⓉⒶⓄlime, ⓉⒶbergamot, ⓉⒶgeranium, ⓉⒶginger, ⓉⒶmyrrh

Other Products: ⓄOn Guard Protecting Throat Drops to soothe irritated and sore throats.

—**STREP:**

Strep throat is a throat infection caused by streptococci bacteria. This infection causes the throat and tonsils to become inflamed and swollen, resulting in a severe sore throat. Symptoms of strep throat include a sudden severe sore throat, pain when swallowing, high fever, swollen tonsils and lymph nodes, white spots on the back of the throat, skin rash, and sometimes vomiting. Strep throat should be closely monitored so that it doesn't develop into a more serious condition such as rheumatic fever or kidney inflammation.

Oils: ⓄⓉⒶOn Guard[7,8], ⓉⒶmelaleuca, ⓉⒶginger, ⓉⒶgeranium, ⓉⒶoregano

—**TONSILLITIS:**

Tonsillitis is inflammation of the tonsils, typically due to infection. Tonsillitis causes the tonsils to become swollen and painful.

---

[7] Cinnamon, thyme, and clove essential oils demonstrated an antibacterial effect on several respiratory tract pathogens including streptococci (Fabio et al., 2007).

[8] *Eucalyptus globulus* oil was found to inhibit several bacteria types, including strep (Cermelli et al., 2008).

Symptoms of Tonsillitis include sore throat, red and swollen tonsils, painful swallowing, loss of voice, fever, chills, headache, and white patches on the tonsils.

Oils: ⓉⒶmelaleuca, ⓉⒶOn Guard, Ⓣginger, ⓉⒶlavender, ⓉⒶlemon, ⓉⒶbergamot, ⓉⒶclove, Ⓐthyme, ⓉⒶRoman chamomile

Ⓘ: Add 1 drop to 8 oz. water (32 oz. for On Guard), and drink.

Ⓣ: Dilute as recommended, and apply 1–2 drops on throat or reflex points on the feet. Add 1–2 drops to 4 oz. (1/2 cup) water, and gargle.

Ⓐ: Diffuse into the air. Inhale directly from bottle. Apply oil to hands, tissue, or cotton wick, and inhale.

THRUSH: *SEE ANTIFUNGAL:CANDIDA, ANTIFUNGAL:THRUSH, CHILDREN AND INFANTS:THRUSH*

THYMUS: *SEE ALSO IMMUNE SYSTEM, LYMPHATIC SYSTEM*

The thymus is an organ responsible for the development of T cells needed for immune system functioning. The thymus is located just behind the sternum in the upper part of the chest.

Oils: ⓉOn Guard

Ⓣ: Dilute as recommended, and apply over thymus or on bottoms of feet.

THYROID: *SEE ALSO ENDOCRINE SYSTEM*

The thyroid is a gland located in the front of the neck that plays a key role in regulating metabolism. The thyroid produces and secretes the hormones needed to regulate blood pressure, heart rate, body temperature, and energy production.

—**DYSFUNCTION:**

Oils: ⓉⒶclove

—**HYPERTHYROIDISM:** *SEE ALSO GRAVE'S DISEASE*

Hyperthyroidism is when the thyroid gland produces too much of its hormones, typically due to the thyroid becoming enlarged. This can result in a noticeably enlarged thyroid gland (goiter), sudden weight loss, sweating, a rapid or irregular heartbeat, shortness of breath, muscle weakness, nervousness, and irritability.

Oils: ⓉⒶmyrrh, ⓉⒶlemongrass

Blend 1: Combine 1 drop myrrh and 1 drop lemongrass, and apply on base of throat and on reflex points on the feet.

—**HYPOTHYROIDISM:** *SEE ALSO HASHIMOTO'S DISEASE*

Hypothyroidism is the result of an underactive thyroid. Consequently, the thyroid gland doesn't produce enough of necessary hormones. Symptoms include fatigue, a puffy face, a hoarse voice, unexplained weight gain, higher blood cholesterol levels, muscle weakness and aches, depression, heavy menstrual periods, memory problems, and low tolerance for the cold.

Oils: ⓉⒶpeppermint, ⓉⒶclove, ⓉⒶlemongrass

Blend 2: Combine 1 drop lemongrass with 1 drop of either peppermint or clove, and apply on base of throat and on reflex points on the feet.

—**SUPPORTS:**

Oils: Ⓣmyrrh

Ⓣ: Dilute as recommended, and apply 1–2 drops on base of throat, hands, or reflex points on the feet.

Ⓐ: Diffuse into the air. Inhale oils applied to hands.

TINNITUS: *SEE EARS:TINNITUS*

TIRED: *SEE ENERGY*

TISSUE:

Tissue refers to any group of similar cells that work together to perform a specific function in an organ or in the body. Some types of tissue include muscle tissue, connective tissue, nervous tissue, or epithelial tissue (tissue that lines or covers a surface, such as the skin or the lining of the blood vessels).

Oils: Ⓣlemongrass, Ⓣhelichrysum, Ⓣbasil, Ⓣmarjoram, Ⓣsandalwood, ⓉRoman chamomile, Ⓣlavender

Other Products: ⓉDeep Blue Rub to help soothe muscle and connective tissues.

—Cleanses Toxins From:

Oils: Ⓣfennel

—Connective Tissue: *see Muscles/Connective Tissue*

—Deep Tissue Pain: *see Pain:Tissue*

—Repair:

Oils: Ⓣlemongrass, Ⓣhelichrysum, Ⓣorange

—Regenerate:

Oils: Ⓣlemongrass, Ⓣhelichrysum, Ⓣgeranium, Ⓣpatchouli

—Scarring:

Scar tissue is the dense and fibrous tissue that forms over a healed cut or wound. The scar tissue serves as a protective barrier but is still inferior to the healthy, normal tissue. In an area of scar tissue, sweat glands are nonfunctional, hair does not grow, and the skin is not as protected against ultraviolet radiation. Scars fade and become less noticeable over time but cannot be completely removed.

Oils: Ⓣlavender (burns), Ⓣrose (helps prevent), Ⓣfrankincense (helps prevent), Ⓣhelichrysum (reduces), Ⓣgeranium, Ⓣmyrrh

Blend 1: Combine 5 drops helichrysum and 5 drops lavender with 1 Tbs. sunflower oil or with liquid lecithin (an emulsifier extracted from eggs or soy), and apply on location.

Blend 2: Combine 1 drop lavender, 1 drop lemongrass, and 1 drop geranium, and apply on location to help prevent scar formation.

Ⓣ: Dilute as recommended, and apply 1–2 drops on location or on reflex points on the feet. Apply as warm compress. Add 5–10 drops to 1 Tbs. fractionated coconut oil, and massage on location.

Tonic:

A tonic is a substance given to invigorate or strengthen an organ, tissue, or system or to stimulate physical, emotional, or mental energy and strength.

—General:

Oils: ⓉⒶlemongrass, ⓉⒶcinnamon, ⓉⒶsandalwood, ⓉⒶclary sage, ⓉⒶgrapefruit, ⓉⒶginger, ⓉⒶgeranium, ⓉⒶmarjoram, ⓉⒶmyrrh, ⓉⒶorange, ⓉⒶRoman chamomile, ⓉⒶylang ylang

—Heart:

Oils: ⓉⒶthyme, ⓉⒶlavender

—Nerve:

Oils: ⓉⒶclary sage, ⓉⒶmelaleuca, ⓉⒶthyme

—Skin:

Oils: Ⓣlemon

—Uterine:

Oils: ⓉⒶthyme

Ⓣ: Add 5–10 drops to 1 Tbs. fractionated coconut oil, and massage on location. Dilute as recommended, and apply 1–2 drops to area or to reflex points on the feet. Add 1–2 drops to warm bathwater before bathing.

Ⓐ: Diffuse into the air. Inhale directly from bottle. Apply oil to hands, tissue, or cotton wick, and inhale.

Tonsillitis: *see Throat:Tonsillitis*

Toothache: *see Oral Conditions:Toothache*

Toxemia: *see also Antibacterial, Pregnancy/Motherhood:Preeclampsia*

Toxemia is the general term for toxic substances in the bloodstream. This is typically caused by a bacterial infection in which bacteria release toxins into the blood.

Oils: ⓉⒶcypress

Ⓣ: Dilute as recommended, and apply 1–2 drops on neck, over heart, or on bottoms of feet. Add 5–10 drops to 1 Tbs. fractionated coconut oil, and massage on neck, back, chest, and legs.

Ⓐ: Diffuse into the air.

Toxins: *see Detoxification*

Travel Sickness: *see Nausea:Motion Sickness*

Tuberculosis (T.B.): *see also Antibacterial, Respiratory System*

Tuberculosis is a bacterial disease spread through the air (via coughing, spitting, sneezing, etc.). Tuberculosis most commonly infects the lungs, but it can infect other bodily systems as well. Symptoms of tuberculosis include a chronic cough (often with blood), fever, chills, weakness and fatigue, weight loss, and night sweats. Tuberculosis is contagious and sometimes deadly.

Oils: ᴬᵀeucalyptus, ᴬᵀcypress, ᴬᵀBreathe, ᴬᵀthyme, ᴬᵀOn Guard, ᴬlemon, ᴬᵀmelissa, ᴬᵀpeppermint, ᴬᵀsandalwood

—**Airborne Bacteria:**

Oils: ᴬOn Guard, ᴬlemongrass[1], ᴬgeranium[1], ᴬPurify, ᴬBreathe

—**Pulmonary:**

Oils: ᴬᵀoregano, ᴬᵀcypress, ᴬᵀeucalyptus, ᴬᵀfrankincense

Ⓐ: Diffuse into the air. Inhale directly from bottle. Apply oil to hands, tissue, or cotton wick, and inhale. Add 2–3 drops to bowl of hot water, and inhale vapors.

Ⓣ: Dilute as recommended, and apply 1–2 drops on chest, back, or reflex points on the feet. Add 1–2 drops to 1 tsp. fractionated coconut oil, and apply as rectal implant. Add 5–10 drops to 1 Tbs. fractionated coconut oil, and massage on chest, back, and feet.

Tumor: *see also Cancer*

A tumor is an abnormal growth of cells in a lump or mass. Some tumors are malignant (cancerous) and some are benign (noncancerous). Benign tumors in most parts of the body do not create health problems. *For information on cancerous (malignant) tumors, see Cancer.*

Oils: ᵀᴬfrankincense, ᵀᴬclove, ᵀᴬsandalwood

—**Lipoma:**

Lipoma is a benign tumor of the fatty tissues that most commonly forms just below the surface of the skin; but it can also form in any other area of the body where fatty tissue is present.

Oils: ᵀfrankincense, ᵀclove, ᵀgrapefruit, ᵀginger

Ⓣ: Dilute as recommended, and apply 1–2 drops on location.

Ⓐ: Diffuse into the air. Inhale directly from bottle. Apply oil to hands, tissue, or cotton wick, and inhale.

Typhoid: *see also Antibacterial*

Typhoid fever is a bacterial infection caused by the bacteria *Salmonella typhi*. Typhoid is spread through food and water infected with the feces of typhoid carriers. Possible symptoms of typhoid include abdominal pain, severe diarrhea, bloody stools, chills, severe fatigue, weakness, chills, delirium, hallucinations, confusion, agitation, and fluctuating mood.

Oils: ᵀᴬcinnamon, ᵀᴬpeppermint, ᵀᴬPurify, ᵀᴬlemon, ᵀᴬBreathe

Ⓣ: Dilute as recommended, and apply over intestines or on reflex points on the feet.

Ⓐ: Diffuse into the air.

Ulcers: *see also Digestive System*

An ulcer is an open sore either on the skin or on an internal mucous membrane (such as that lining the stomach).

Oils: ᴵᵀfrankincense, ᴵᵀmyrrh, ᴵᵀlemon, ᴵᵀoregano, ᴵᵀrose, ᴵᵀthyme, ᴵᵀclove, ᴵᵀbergamot

—**Duodenal:**

A duodenal ulcer is an ulcer in the upper part of the small intestine.

Oils: ᴵᵀfrankincense, ᴵᵀmyrrh, ᴵᵀlemon, ᴵᵀoregano, ᴵᵀrose, ᴵᵀthyme, ᴵᵀclove, ᴵᵀbergamot

—**Gastric:** *see also Digestive System:Gastritis.*

A gastric ulcer is an ulcer in the stomach.

Oils: ᴵᵀgeranium, ᴵᵀpeppermint, ᴵᵀfrankincense, ᴵᵀorange, ᴵᵀbergamot

—**Leg:**

An ulcer on the leg may be due to a lack of circulation in the lower extremities or possibly due to a bacterial, fungal, or viral infection. *See also Circulatory System:Circulation, Antibacterial, Antifungal, Antiviral.*

Oils: ᵀPurify, ᵀlavender, ᵀRoman chamomile, ᵀgeranium

---

1 A formulation of lemongrass and geranium oil was found to reduce airborne bacteria by 89% in an office environment after diffusion for 15 hours (Doran et al., 2009).

—Mouth: *see Canker Sores*

—Peptic:

A peptic ulcer is an ulcer that forms in an area of the digestive system where acid is present, such as in the stomach (gastric), esophagus, or upper part of the small intestine (duodenal). *See also Duodenal, Gastric in this section.*

Recipe 1: Flavor a quart of water with 1 drop cinnamon, and sip all day.

—Varicose Ulcer:

A varicose ulcer is an ulcer on the lower leg where varicose (swollen) veins are located.

Oils: Ⓣmelaleuca, Ⓣgeranium, Ⓣlavender, Ⓣeucalyptus, Ⓣthyme

Ⓘ: Add 1 drop oil to rice or almond milk, and drink. Place oil in an empty capsule and swallow. Add 1 drop or less as flavoring to food after cooking.

Ⓣ: Dilute as recommended, and apply 1–2 drops over area. Apply as warm compress.

Unwind: *see Calming*

Uplifting

Oils: Ⓐlemon[2,3], Ⓐorange, ⒶElevation, ⒶCitrus Bliss, Ⓐbergamot, Ⓐgrapefruit, ⒶWhisper, Ⓐmyrrh, Ⓐwintergreen, Ⓐlavender

Ⓐ: Diffuse into the air. Inhale directly from bottle. Apply oil to hands, tissue, or cotton wick; inhale. Wear as perfume or cologne.

Ureter: *see Urinary Tract*

Urinary Tract:

The urinary tract is the collection of organs and tubes responsible for producing and excreting urine. The urinary tract is comprised of the kidneys, bladder, ureters, and urethra.

Oils: ⓉⒶsandalwood, ⓉⒶthyme, ⓉⒶmelaleuca, ⓉⒶbergamot, ⓉⒶlavender, ⓉⒶrosemary

—General Stimulant:

Oils: ⓉⒶeucalyptus, ⓉⒶbergamot

Urinary Tract

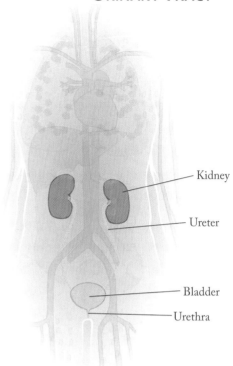

Kidney

Ureter

Bladder

Urethra

—Infection: *see also Bladder:Cystitis/Infection*

Oils: ⓉPurify, ⓉⒶlemongrass, ⓉⒶgeranium, Ⓣbergamot

Blend 1: Combine 1 drop On Guard with 1 drop oregano; apply as a hot compress over abdomen and pubic area.

—Stones In: *see also Kidneys:Kidney Stones*

Stones are solid masses that form as minerals and other chemicals crystallize and adhere together. They can form in the bladder or kidneys. While small stones generally cause no problems, larger stones may block the ureters or urethra, causing intense pain and possibly injury.

Oils: Ⓣfennel, Ⓣgeranium

—Support:

Oils: ⓉⒶgeranium, ⓉⒶcypress, ⓉⒶmelaleuca

Ⓣ: Dilute as recommended, and apply 1–2 drops over lower abdomen, lower back, or pubic area. Add 5–10 drops to 1 Tbs. fractionated coconut oil, and massage on abdomen, lower, back, or pubic area. Apply as a warm compress.

Ⓐ: Diffuse into the air.

---

2 Lemon odor was found to enhance the positive mood of volunteers exposed to a stressor (Kiecolt-Glaser et al., 2008).

3 Lemon oil and its component, citral, were found to decrease depressed behavior in a similar manner to antidepressant drugs in rats involved in several stress tests (Komori et al., 1995).

Uterus: *see also Endometriosis, Female Specific Conditions*

The uterus is the female reproductive organ in which a fetus is formed and develops until birth.

Oils: **T**frankincense, **T**lemon, **T**myrrh, **T**geranium

—Regeneration of Tissue:

Oils: **T**frankincense

—Uterotonic:

An uterotonic is a medication used to stimulate uterus contractions. Uterotonics should be avoided or used with extreme caution during pregnancy as they may be abortive. Uterotonics are used to start or speed up labor, to reduce hemorrhaging, and to cause contractions after a miscarriage.

Oils: **T**thyme

—Uterine Cancer: *See Cancer:Uterine*

T: Dilute as recommended, and apply 1–2 drops on lower abdomen or on reflex points on the feet and ankles. Add 2–5 drops essential oil to 1 tsp. fractionated coconut oil, and insert into vagina for overnight retention (a tampon may be used if necessary to help retain the oil). Apply as a warm compress.

Vaginal:

—Candida: *see also Antifungal:Candida*

Candida refers to a genus of yeast that are normally found in the digestive tract and on the skin of humans. These yeast are typically symbiotically beneficial to humans. However, several species of *Candida*, such as *Candida albicans*, can cause infections, such as vaginal candidiasis, that cause localized itching, soreness, and redness.

Oils: **T**melaleuca[1,2,3,4,5,6,7], **TI**oregano[8], **T**clove[9], **T**On Guard, **T**bergamot, **T**Clear Skin, **T**peppermint[10], **T**thyme[11], **T**lavender[12], **T**eucalyptus, **T**rosemary, **TI**DigestZen

—Infection: *see also Candida (above), Antibacterial, Antifungal, Antiviral*

Vaginal infections occur when there is a disruption in the normal balance of vaginal organisms, such as the sudden presence of yeast, bacteria, or viruses. Common signs of vaginal infection include redness, swelling, itching, pain, odor, change in discharge color or amount, a burning sensation when urinating, and pain or bleeding during intercourse. The most common vaginal infections are yeast infection, trichomoniasis, and bacterial vaginosis.

Oils: **T**rosemary, **T**cinnamon (dilute heavily), **T**melaleuca, **T**oregano, **T**thyme, **T**myrrh, **T**clary sage, **T**cypress, **T**eucalyptus, **T**lavender

—Vaginitis:

Vaginitis is vaginal inflammation, typically due to infection, characterized by redness, swelling, itching, irritation, discharge, and pain of the vaginal area.

Oils: **T**rosemary, **T**cinnamon (dilute heavily), **T**eucalyptus, **T**melaleuca, **T**lavender

---

1   Tea tree oil was found to inhibit 301 different types of yeasts isolated from the mouths of cancer patients suffering from advanced cancer, including 41 strains that are known to be resistant to antifungal drugs (Bagg et al., 2006).

2   Eleven types of *Candida* were found to be highly inhibited by tea tree oil (Banes-Marshall et al., 2001).

3   Tea tree oil was found to disrupt the cellular membrane and to inhibit respiration in *Candida albicans* (Cox et al., 2000).

4   Melaleuca at concentrations of .16% was found to inhibit the transformation of *C. albicans* from single-cell yeast to the pathogenic mycelial (multi-cellular strands) form (D'Auria et al., 2001).

5   Tea Tree oil was found to alter the membrane properties and functions of *Candida albicans* cells, leading to cell inhibition or death (Hammer et al., 2004).

6   Terpinen-4-ol, a constituent of tea tree oil, and tea tree oil were found to be effective against several forms of vaginal *Candida* infections in rats, including azole-resistant forms (Mondello et al., 2006).

7   Melaleuca oil inhibited several *Candida* species in vitro (Vazquez et al., 2000).

8   Mice infected with *Candida albicans* who were fed origanum oil or carvacrol diluted in olive oil had an 80% survival rate after 30 days, while infected mice fed olive oil alone all died after 10 days (Manohar et al., 2001).

9   Clove oil was found to have very strong radical scavenging activity (antioxidant). It was also found to display an antifungal effect against tested *Candida* strains (Chaieb et al., 2007).

10 Peppermint oil was found to have a higher fungistatic and fungicidal activity against various fungi (including *Candida*) than the commercial fungicide bifonazole (Mimica-Dukić et al., 2003).

11 Thyme oil was found to inhibit *Candida* species by causing lesions in the cell membrane and inhibiting germ tube (an outgrowth that develops when the fungi is preparing to replicate) formation (Pina-Vaz et al., 2004).

12 Lavender oil demonstrated both fungistatic (stopped growth) and fungicidal (killed) activity against *Candida albicans* (D'Auria et al., 2005).

Primary Recommendations • Secondary Recommendations • Other Recommendations / **A**=Aromatic, **T**=Topical, **I**=Internal

226

Recipe 1: Valerie Worwood suggests combining 1 drop lavender, 1 drop melaleuca, 1 tsp. vinegar, 1/2 tsp. lemon juice, and 2–1/2 cups of warm water for a douche that can be used three days a week.

🔵: Dilute oils as recommended, and apply 1–2 drops on location. Add 2–3 drops to 1 tsp. fractionated coconut oil, insert using vaginal syringe, and retain using tampon overnight. Add 2–3 drops to 1 tsp. fractionated coconut oil, soak tampon in mixture, insert, and leave in all day or overnight. Add 1–2 drops to warm water, and use in a douche. Add 1–2 drops to warm bathwater, and bathe.

🔵: Place 2–3 drops in an empty capsule, and swallow.

VARICOSE ULCERS: *SEE ULCERS:VARICOSE ULCER*

VARICOSE VEINS:

Varicose veins are twisted, enlarged, blue and purple veins most often found on the legs and ankles. They have several possible causes, including weakened valves causing blood to pool around the vein. In some cases, varicose veins are merely a cosmetic problem because of their appearance, but in other cases they can be quite painful. *See also Hemorrhoids for varicose veins of the anus or rectum.*

Oils: ᵀcypress, ᵀlemongrass, ᵀlemon, ᵀpeppermint, ᵀhelichrysum, ᵀCitrus Bliss, ᵀgeranium, ᵀlavender, ᵀrosemary, ᵀorange

🔵: Dilute as recommended, and apply oils gently from ankles up the legs. *Consistent application of oils for an extended period of time is the key.* Add 3–5 drops to 1 Tbs. fractionated coconut oil, and massage above the veins towards the heart. Wearing support hose and elevating the feet can also help keep blood from pooling in the legs.

VASCULAR SYSTEM: *SEE CARDIOVASCULAR SYSTEM; SEE ALSO ARTERIES, CAPILLARIES, VEINS*

VASODILATOR: *SEE ARTERIES:ARTERIAL VASODILATOR*

VEINS:

A vein is a blood vessel that carries blood from the capillaries back to the heart. Veins may also have one-way valves on the inside that help keep blood

from flowing backwards and pooling in the lower extremities due to gravity.

Oils: ᵀlemongrass, ᵀcypress, ᵀlemon, ᵀhelichrysum

—BLOOD CLOT IN VEIN:

Blend 1: Apply 1 drop cypress and 1 drop helichrysum on location of clot to help dissolve.

🔵: Dilute as recommended, and apply 1–2 drops on location. Add 5–10 drops to 1 Tbs. fractionated coconut oil, and massage on location.

VERTIGO: *SEE ALSO EARS, NAUSEA:MOTION SICKNESS*

Vertigo refers to the sensation that the environment and objects around an individual are moving or spinning, usually causing a loss of balance or feelings of nausea. Vertigo may be caused by ear infections, ear disorders, or motion sickness.

Oils: ᴬᵀginger, ᵀhelichrysum, ᵀgeranium, ᵀbasil, ᵀlavender

Recipe 1: Apply 1–2 drops each of helichrysum, geranium, and lavender to the tops of each ear (massaging slightly); then apply the oils behind each ear, pulling your hands down behind the jaw bone to just below the jaw. Finish by applying 1–2 drops of basil behind and down each ear. This can be performed multiple times a day until symptoms decrease.

🔵: Dilute as recommended, and apply 1–2 drops around ears and on reflex points on the feet.

🅐: Inhale oil directly from bottle. Apply oil to hands, tissue, or cotton wick, and inhale.

VIRAL DISEASE/VIRUSES: *SEE ANTIVIRAL*

VITILIGO: *SEE SKIN:VITILIGO*

VOICE (HOARSE): *SEE ALSO LARYNGITIS*

A hoarse voice is typically caused by laryngitis (inflammation of the larynx due to infection), but it can also be caused by other problems such as an ulcer, sore, polyp, or tumor on or near the vocal cords.

Oils: ᵀbergamot

Recipe 1: Add 1 drop melaleuca, 1 drop rosemary, 1 drop clove, and 1 drop lemon to 1 tsp. honey. Swish around in the mouth for a couple of minutes to liquefy with saliva; then swallow.

🔵: Add 1 drop to 1 tsp. honey, and swallow.

U

V

VOMITING: *SEE NAUSEA:VOMITING*

WARMING OILS:

Oils: ⊤cinnamon, ⊤oregano, ⊤thyme, ⊤marjoram, ⊤rosemary

⊤: Add 5–10 drops to 1 tsp. fractionated coconut oil, and massage briskly into skin.

WARTS:

A wart is a small, firm, hard growth on the skin, usually located on the hands and feet, that is typically caused by a virus.

Oils: ⊤frankincense, ⊤On Guard, ⊤melaleuca, ⊤oregano (layer with On Guard), ⊤clove, ⊤cypress, ⊤cinnamon, ⊤lemon, ⊤lavender

Recipe 1: Combine 5 drops cypress, 10 drops lemon, and 2 Tbs. apple cider vinegar. Apply on location twice daily; bandage. Keep a bandage on until wart is gone.

—GENITAL:

A genital wart is a small, painful wart or cluster of warts located in the genital area or in the mouth or throat. This type of wart is typically spread by contact with the skin through sexual activity.

Oils: ⊤frankincense, ⊤On Guard, ⊤melaleuca, ⊤oregano, ⊤thyme

—PLANTAR:

Plantar warts are painful warts that grow on the bottoms of the feet. They are usually flattened and embedded into the skin due to the pressure caused by walking on them.

Oils: ⊤oregano

⊤: Dilute as recommended, or dilute 1–2 drops of oil in a few drops fractionated coconut oil; then apply 1–2 drops on location daily.

WATER PURIFICATION:

Oils: ❶⊤lemon, ❶⊤Purify, ⊤peppermint, ⊤orange

❶: Add 1 drop of oil to 12–16 oz. of drinking water to help purify.

⊤: Add 1–2 drops to dishwater for sparkling dishes and a great smelling kitchen. Add 1–2 drops to warm bathwater, and bathe. Add 1–2 drops to a bowl of water, and use the water to clean the outsides of fruits and vegetables.

WATER RETENTION: *SEE EDEMA, DIURETIC*

WEAKNESS: *SEE ENERGY*

WEIGHT:

Proper exercise and nutrition are the most critical factors for maintaining a healthy weight. Other factors that may influence weight include an individual's metabolism, level of stress, hormonal imbalances, low or high thyroid function, or the level of insulin being produced by the body.

—OBESITY:

Obesity is the condition of being overweight to the extent that it effects health and lifestyle. By definition, obesity is considered as a body mass index (BMI) of 30 kg/m² or greater.

Oils: Ⓐ❶grapefruit[1] Ⓐ❶Slim & Sassy, Ⓐ❶orange, ⊤rosemary, ❶fennel

Other Products: ❶Slim & Sassy Trim Shake, ❶Alpha CRS+ contains polyphenols resveratrol and epigallocatechin-3-gallate (EGCG), which have been studied for their abilities to help prevent obesity.

—SLIMMING/TONING:

Oils: Ⓐ❶grapefruit[1], ❶Ⓐslim & Sassy, Ⓐ❶orange, Ⓐlemongrass, Ⓐrosemary, ⊤thyme, Ⓐlavender

Other Products: ❶Slim & Sassy Trim Shake.

—WEIGHT LOSS:

Oils: Ⓐ❶Slim & Sassy, Ⓐelevation, ⊤Ⓐpatchouli

Other Products: ❶Slim & Sassy Trim Shake.

Recipe 1: Add 5 drops lemon and 5 drops grapefruit to 1 gallon of water, and drink throughout the day.

Ⓐ: Diffuse oil into the air. Inhale oil directly from bottle; or inhale oil that is applied to hands, tissue, or cotton wick.

❶: Add 8 drops of Slim & Sassy to 16 oz. of water, and drink throughout the day between meals. Add 1 drop of oil to 12–16 oz. of water, and drink. Drink Trim Shake 1–2 times per

---

1 The scent of grapefruit oil and its component, limonene, was found to affect the autonomic nerves and to reduce appetite and body weight in rats exposed to the oil for 15 minutes three times per week (Shen et al., 2005).

Primary Recommendations • Secondary Recommendations • Other Recommendations / Ⓐ=Aromatic, ⊤=Topical, ❶=Internal

day as a meal alternative. Take capsules as directed on package.

WHIPLASH:

Whiplash is the over-stretching or tearing of the muscles, ligaments, and/or tendons in the neck and head. This is typically caused by a sudden collision or force pushing the body in one direction, while the head's tendency to remain in the same place causes the head to quickly rock in the opposite direction the body is going.

Oils: Ⓣ Deep Blue, Ⓣ lemongrass (ligaments), Ⓣ marjoram (muscles), Ⓣ birch, Ⓣ basil, Ⓣ helichrysum, Ⓣ vetiver, Ⓣ clove, Ⓣ peppermint, Ⓣ Roman chamomile

Ⓣ: Dilute as recommended, and apply 1–2 drops on back of neck. Add 5–10 drops to 1 Tbs. fractionated coconut oil, and massage on back of neck, on shoulders, and on upper back.

WHOOPING COUGH: *SEE CHILDHOOD DISEASES: WHOOPING COUGH*

WITHDRAWAL: *SEE ADDICTIONS:WITHDRAWAL*

WOMEN: *SEE FEMALE SPECIFIC CONDITIONS*

WORKAHOLIC: *SEE ADDICTIONS:WORK*

WORMS: *SEE ANTIFUNGAL:RINGWORM, PARASITES:WORMS*

WOUNDS: *SEE ALSO ANTIBACTERIAL, BLOOD:BLEEDING*

A wound is a general term for an injury that involves tissue (typically the skin or underlying skeletal muscles) being torn, cut, punctured, scraped, or crushed.

Oils: Ⓣ clove, Ⓣ melaleuca, Ⓣ helichrysum, Ⓣ lavender, Ⓣ lemongrass, Ⓣ Purify, Ⓣ basil[2], Ⓣ cypress, Ⓣ eucalyptus, Ⓣ frankincense, Ⓣ Roman chamomile, Ⓣ peppermint (after wound has closed), Ⓣ myrrh, Ⓣ rose, Ⓣ sandalwood, Ⓣ thyme, Ⓣ bergamot

Recipe 1: Place 1–3 drops of helichrysum on fresh wound to help stop bleeding. Add 1 drop

clove[3] to help reduce pain. Once bleeding has stopped, apply a drop of lavender (to help start healing), a drop of melaleuca (to help fight infection), and a drop of lemongrass (for possible ligament damage). Bandage the wound. When changing the bandage, apply 1 drop basil or sandalwood to help promote further healing. Add 1 drop Purify or On Guard to help prevent infection.

Blend 1: Add 1 drop lavender to 1 drop Purify and apply to wound.

—CHILDREN/INFANTS:

Oils: Ⓣ Roman chamomile

Recipe 2: Add 1–3 drops each of helichrysum and lavender to 1 tsp. fractionated coconut oil, and apply a small amount to wound.

—BLEEDING:

Oils: Ⓣ helichrysum, Ⓣ rose, Ⓣ lavender, Ⓣ lemon

Blend 2: Combine 1 drop Roman chamomile, 1 drop geranium, and 1 drop lemon, and apply with a warm compress 2–3 times a day for 3–4 days, then reduce to once a day until healed.

—DISINFECT:

Oils: Ⓣ melaleuca, Ⓣ thyme, Ⓣ lavender

—HEALING:

Oils: Ⓣ basil[2], Ⓣ helichrysum, Ⓣ melaleuca, Ⓣ lavender, Ⓣ myrrh, Ⓣ sandalwood

—INFLAMMATION: *SEE INFLAMMATION*

—SCARRING: *SEE SKIN:SCARRING, TISSUE:SCARRING*

—SURGICAL:

Oils: Ⓣ peppermint, Ⓣ melaleuca

Blend 2: Add 3 drops helichrysum, 3 drops frankincense, and 4 drops lavender to 2 tsp. fractionated coconut oil. Apply a few drops when changing bandages.

—WEEPING:

Oils: Ⓣ myrrh, Ⓣ patchouli

Ⓣ: Dilute as recommended, and apply 1–2 drops on location.

WRINKLES: *SEE SKIN:WRINKLES*

V

W

---

2 Basil (*Ocimum gratissimum*) oil was found to facilitate the healing process of wounds in rabbits to a greater extent than two antibacterial preparations, Cicatrin and Cetavlex (Orafidiya et al., 2003).

3 Beta-caryophyllene (found in clove and copal oils) demonstrated anaesthetic (pain reducing) activity in rats and rabbits (Ghelardini et al., 2001).

YEAST: *SEE ANTIFUNGAL:CANDIDA*

YOGA:

    Oils: ⓐsandalwood

    ⓐ: Diffuse into the air.

APPENDIX AND REFERENCES

APPENDIX A: BODY SYSTEMS CHART

The following chart lists all of the products discussed within this book and indicates which body systems they primarily affect. While this chart does not include every system that could possibly be affected by each product, it attempts to list the primary systems that are most often affected. It is provided to give the beginning aromatherapy student a starting point for personal use and analysis.

Product	Cardiovascular System	Digestive System	Emotional Balance	Hormonal System	Immune System	Muscles and Bones	Nervous System	Respiratory System	Skin and Hair
Alpha CRS+	●				●	●	●	●	●
AromaTouch			●	●	●	●	●		
Balance			●			●	●		●
Basil	●				●				
Bergamot		●	●						●
Birch						●			
Breathe								●	
Cassia					●				
Cinnamon Bark					●				
Citrus Bliss			●		●		●		
Citrus Bliss Bath Bar			●		●		●		●
Clary Sage				●					
Clear Skin					●				●
Clear Skin Face Wash					●				●
Clove	●	●			●			●	
Coriander		●		●					
Cypress	●					●			
Deep Blue						●	●		
DigestZen		●							
Elevation			●	●					
xEO Mega	●	●			●		●		●
Eucalyptus								●	●
Fennel		●		●					
Frankincense			●		●		●		●
Geranium			●						●
Ginger		●					●		
Grapefruit	●								
GX Assist		●			●				
Hand & Body Lotion									●
Helichrysum	●					●			
Lavender	●		●				●		●
Lemon		●			●			●	
Lemongrass					●	●			
Lime		●			●			●	

Product	Cardiovascular System	Digestive System	Emotional Balance	Hormonal System	Immune System	Muscles and Bones	Nervous System	Respiratory System	Skin and Hair
Marjoram	•					•			
Melissa			•						•
Melaleuca					•	•		•	•
Microplex VMz	•	•	•	•	•	•	•	•	•
Myrrh			•		•		•		•
On Guard					•				•
Orange, Wild		•	•		•				•
Oregano					•	•		•	
PastTense						•	•		
Patchouli									•
Peppermint		•				•	•	•	•
Purify	•		•		•				•
Roman Chamomile			•				•		•
Rose			•						•
Rosemary					•		•	•	
Sandalwood			•			•	•		•
SanoBella									•
Serenity			•				•		
Serenity Bath Bar			•				•		•
Slim & Sassy		•	•						
Solace			•	•					•
TerraShield									•
TerraZyme		•							
Thyme					•	•			
Trim Shake		•		•		•			
Vetiver			•	•			•		•
Wintergreen						•			
Whisper			•	•			•		
White Fir								•	
Women's Phytoestrogen			•	•		•			•
Women's Bone Nutrient						•	•		•
Ylang Ylang	•		•	•					
Zendocrine		•		•	•			•	•

Appendix

235

APPENDIX B: SINGLE ESSENTIAL OILS PROPERTY CHART

The following chart presents some of the properties of each of the single oils. An attempt has been made to indicate the effectiveness of the oils for each property, where supporting information existed. However, this information should not be considered conclusive. It is provided to give the beginning aromatherapy student a starting point for personal use and analysis. Also, keep in mind the applicable safety data when applying an oil for its property. For example, cinnamon bark is one of the best known antiseptics, but it is also extremely irritating to the skin. It may work well to sanitize the bathroom with, but it should be used with extreme caution on the skin.

Essential Oil	A-Bac	A-Cat	A-Dep	A-Fun	A-Inf	A-Infl	A-Mic	A-Par	A-Rhe	A-Sep	A-Spa	A-Vir	Analg	Imm
Basil	++	+	+		+	+++				+	+	+		
Bergamot					+	+++		+		+	+		+	
Birch						+			+	+++	+			
Cassia	+		+	+	+	+	++	+		++++	+	+		
Cinnamon	+		+	+	+	+	++	+		++++	+	+		
Clary Sage	+		+		+					+	+			
Clove	+++	+		++	+			++	+	+		+++		
Coriander	++		++		++			+			+		+	
Cypress	+				+			+	+	+	+			
Eucalyptus	++	++			+	+						+++	++	+
Fennel	+	++				+	+	+		+	+			
Frankincense		++	++			+++	+				+			+++
Geranium	+++		++	++	+	+				+				
Ginger		++								++			++	
Grapefruit	++									++				
Helichrysum	++	+++			+		++	++		+	+++			
Lavender			++		+	++	+	+	+	+	++		++	
Lemon	++				+		++		+	+++	+			++
Lemongrass	+		+	+		++	+			+			++	
Lime	++									++		+		
Marjoram	+	+		+	+					++	++	+	++	
Melissa	+		++				+				++	++		
Melaleuca	+++			++++	+	+		+		+		+++		++
Myrrh		+		+	+	+++	++	+		+		+++		
Orange	++		++	+		+				++				
Oregano	+++	+		+++	+++			+++	++	+	+	++	++	++
Patchouli	+		+	+	+	+	+			+		+		
Peppermint	+	+		+	+	++	+			+	+	+	++	
Roman Chamomile	+		+		+	+++				+	+	++		
Rose					+									
Rosemary	+++	+		+++	+	+++							+++	
Sandalwood	+	+++	++	+						++	+			
Thyme	+	+		+++			++	+	++	+	+			++
Vetiver					+					+	+			+
White Fir		+								++			+	
Wintergreen						+++			+	+	+		+	
Ylang Ylang			+		+					+	+			

236

CHART LEGEND

A-Bac (Antibacterial): an agent that prevents the growth of (or destroys) bacteria.

A-Cat (Anticatarrhal): an agent that helps remove excess catarrh from the body. Expectorants help promote the removal of mucus from the respiratory system.

A-Dep (Antidepressant): an agent that helps alleviate depression.

A-Fun (Antifungal): an agent that prevents and combats fungal infection.

A-Inf (Anti-infectious): an agent that prevents and combats the spread of germs.

A-Infl (Anti-inflammatory): an agent that alleviates inflammation.

A-Mic (Antimicrobial): an agent that resists or destroys pathogenic microorganisms.

A-Par (Antiparasitic): an agent that prevents and destroys parasites.

A-Rhe (Antirheumatic): an agent that helps prevent and relieve rheumatism.

A-Sep (Antiseptic): an agent that destroys and prevents the development of microbes.

A-Spa (Antispasmodic): an agent that prevents and eases spasms or convulsions.

A-Vir (Antiviral): a substance that inhibits the growth of a virus.

Analg (Analgesic): a substance that relieves pain.

Imm (Immune-stimulant): an agent that stimulates the natural defense mechanism of the body.

Appendix

APPENDIX C: TAXONOMICAL INFORMATION

The following chart is the taxonomical breakdown of the plant families for each of the essential oils found in this book. Following this division chart, there is further information for each family—including the plants within that family that essential oils are derived from, the body systems affected by these essential oils, the properties of these oils, and general uses for these oils.

Division: Embryophyte Siphonogama (plants with seeds)

Subdivision: Gymnosperm (plants with concentric rings, exposed seeds, and resinous wood)

Class: Coniferae (cone-bearing plants) and Taxaceae (yew-like plants)

Family: Pinaceae (Trees or shrubs with cones and numerous "scales")

Genus: Abies (firs, balsam trees), Cedrus (cedars), Pinus (pines), Picea (spruces), Pseudotsuga (false hemlock), Tsuga (hemlocks)

Family: Cupressaceae

Genus: Callitris (blue cypress), Cupressus (cypresses), Juniperus (junipers), Thuja (Arbor vitae or cedars)

Subdivision: Angiosperm (highly evolved plants with seeds enclosed by fruits)

Class: Monocotyledons (plants with one-leaf embryos)

Family: Gramineae, Zingiberaceae

Class: Dicotyledons (plants with multiple-leaf embryos)

Family: Annonaceae, Betulaceae, Burseraceae, Cistaceae, Compositae, Ericaceae, Geraniaceae, Guttiferae, Labiatae, Lauraceae, Myrtaceae, Oleaceae, Piperaceae, Rosaceae, Rutaceae, Santalaceae, Styracaceae, Umbelliferae

ANNONACEAE

Shrubs, trees, climbers; fragrant flowers; 128 genera, 2000 species; mostly tropical, found in Old World and rain forest.

Body Systems: Cardiovascular System, Nervous System (calming), Hormonal System (aphrodisiac)

Properties: extreme fire and water; nervous sedative, balancing

General Uses: depression, frigidity, impotence, palpitations, skin care

Cananga odorata: two forms exist: var. odorata (var. genuina., *Unona odorantissimum*): ylang-ylang; var. macrophylla: cananga

BETULACEAE

Shrubs, trees; fruit is one-seeded nut, often winged; includes birches, alders, hornbeams, and hazels; 6 genera, 150 species; from northern hemisphere to tropical mountains.

Body Systems: Digestive and Respiratory Systems, Muscles and Bones

Properties: analgesic, draining (lymph), purifying

General Uses: auto intoxication, muscle pain

Betula lenta: sweet birch

BURSERACEAE

Means "dry fire"; resinous tropical timber trees; drupe or capsule fruit; 21 genera, 540 species.

Body Systems: Respiratory System (secretions), Emotional Balance (psychic centers)

Skin Properties: cooling, drying, fortifying

General Uses: anti-inflammatory, expectorant, scar tissue (reducing), ulcers, wounds (healing)

Boswellia frereana: frankincense

Commiphora myrrha: myrrh

COMPOSITAE (ASTERACEAE)

Largest family of flowering plants; inflorescence, small flowers; 1317 genera, 21,000 species; found everywhere, especially around Mediterranean.

Body Systems: Digestive System, Skin

Properties: "perfect balance of etheric and astral forces, promoting realization, reorganization, structure" [Lavabre, Aromatherapy Workbook]; adaptive, calming, regeneration (note: because of the large variety of plants within this family, the therapeutic activity is very diversified; some plants are neurotoxic)

General Uses: infections, inflammation, regeneration

Chamaemelum nobile: Roman chamomile

Helichrysum angustifolium (var. Italicum): helichrysum

CUPRESSACEAE
Conifer cypress family, needle-like leaves and cones; 17 genera, 113 species, most in northern temperate zones.

Body Systems: Hormonal, Respiratory, and Nervous Systems

Properties: appeasing, reviving, tonic, warming

General Uses: antirheumatic, astringent, cellulite (reduces), insomnia, nervous tension (reduces), respiration (when taken through inhalation), stress-related conditions

Cupressus sempervirens: cypress

ERICACEAE
Shrubs and small trees with leathery evergreen leaves, fruit berry, drupe or capsule; 103 genera, 3350 species; cosmopolitan centered in northern hemisphere.

Body Systems: Cardiovascular and Digestive Systems

Properties: detoxifying

General Uses: hypertension, kidney and liver stimulant

Gaultheria procumbens: wintergreen

GERANIACEAE
Herbs or low shrubs, 14 genera, 730 species; temperate and tropical zones.

Body Systems: Hormonal System, Digestive System (kidneys (excretion), liver and pancreas (metabolism)), Nervous System, Emotional Balance

Properties: balancing (nervous system)

General Uses: burns, depression, diabetes, hemorrhaging, nervous tension, skin, sore throat, ulcers, wounds

Pelargonium graveolens: geranium

GRAMINEAE (OR POACEAE)
Nutritious grass family; used for ground covering and food (wheat, rice, corn, barley); large root systems; 737 genera, 7950 species; distributed throughout the world.

Body Systems: Cardiovascular System, Digestive System (stimulant), Respiratory System, Skin

Properties: air purifier, calming, refreshing, sedative

General Uses: air deodorizer, calm digestion, cleanse and balance skin (acne)

Cymbopogon flexuosus: lemongrass

Vetiveria zizanoides: vetiver

LABIATE (LAMIACEAE)
Herbs or low shrubs with quadrangular stems; largest of all essential oil producing plant families; oils are mostly nontoxic and non-hazardous; some antiseptic oils; some oils used for flavoring; most oils helpful for headaches, congestion, muscular problems (analgesic, anti-inflammatory), and stimulate one or more body systems; 224 genera, about 5600 species; main distribution in tropical and warmer temperate regions.

Body Systems: Digestive and Respiratory Systems

Properties: appeases overactive astral body [Lavabre, Aromatherapy Workbook], curative, stimulates, warms

General Uses: anemia, diabetes, digestion (poor), headaches, respiratory problems; "good for people with intense psychic activity to prevent exhaustion and loss of self" [Lavabre, Aromatherapy Workbook]

Lavandula angustifolia: lavender

Mentha piperita: peppermint

Origanum majorana: marjoram

Origanum vulgare: oregano

Rosmarinus officinalis: rosemary; several varieties—var. officinalis: common rosemary; numerous cultivars and forms; chemotypes: CT I: camphor; CT II: cineole; CT III: verbenone

Salvia sclarea: clary sage

Thymus vulgaris: thyme; chemotypes: linalool; thymol (or geraniol)

LAURACEAE

Trees and shrubs with evergreen leaves and aromatic oils; some valued for timber, as ornamentals, or for oils or spices; 45 genera, 200-2500 species; found in tropics and subtropics in Amazona and Southeast Asia.

Body Systems: Cardiovascular System (cardiac stimulant, pulmonary stimulant), Nervous System (regulator), Hormonal System (aphrodisiac), Skin (cellular regenerator)

Properties: antifungal, antiviral, antibacterial, stimulant, tonic (some oils in this family are irritant)

General Uses: depression, headache, hypotension, scars, sexual debility

Cinnamomum cassia: cassia

Cinnamomum zeylanicum: cinnamon bark

Laurus nobilis: laurel (bay)

Ravensara aromatica: ravensara

MYRTACEAE

Mainly tropical and subtropical plants with dotted leaves and oil glands; fruit is woody capsule or berry with one or many seeds; some have ornamental or showy flowers; many produce valuable timber; 121 genera, 3850 species; found in tropical and warm regions, especially Australia.

Body Systems: Respiratory and Immune Systems

Properties: "balances interaction of four elements (earth, air, fire, water)" [Lavabre, Aromatherapy Workbook], antiseptic, stimulant, tonic

General Uses: antiseptic, energy (balances), respiratory (infections), stimulant, tonic

Backhousia citriodora: lemon myrtle

Eucalyptus globulus: eucalyptus

Eucalyptus radiata: eucalyptus radiata

Eugenia caryophyllata: clove bud

Melaleuca alternifolia: melaleuca (tea tree)

OLEACEAE

Trees or shrubs, including olive and ash; used for timber; 24 genera, 900 species; widely distributed, centered on Asia.

Body Systems: Emotional Balance, Hormonal System (aphrodisiac)

Properties: calming, soothing, uplifting

General Uses: anxiety, depression, frigidity, impotence, stress

Jasminum officinale: jasmine

PINACEAE (ABIETACEAE)

Conifers with male and female cones; 9 genera, 194 species; found in northern hemisphere, temperate climates.

Body Systems: Hormonal, Nervous, and Respiratory Systems; signifies air element

Properties: antiseptic, appeasing, reviving, tonic, warming

General Uses: arthritis, congestion (inhaled), oxygen deficiency, respiratory disorders, rheumatism, stress

Abies alba: white fir, silver fir

Picea mariana: spruce, black spruce

Pinus sylvestris: pine, Scotch pine

ROSACEAE

Trees, shrubs, and herbs; some edible fruits; many cultivated for fruits (almond) or flowers (rose); 107 genera, 3100 species; found in temperate climates throughout the world.

Body Systems: Hormonal System (female reproductive); heart chakra

Properties: aphrodisiac, harmonizing, tonic, uplifting

General Uses: emotional shock, frigidity, grief, impotence

Rosa damascena: Bulgarian rose

RUTACEAE

Aromatic trees and shrubs; sometimes thorny; dotted, compound leaves with aromatic glands; includes citrus fruits; 161 genera, about 1650 species; found in tropical and warm temperate regions, especially Australia and South Africa.

Body Systems: Digestive (kidneys, liver) and Nervous Systems, Skin

Properties: cooling, refreshing, secretion (fruits), sedative (flowers)

General Uses: inflammation, oversensitivity, water balance

Citrus aurantifolia: lime

Citrus bergamia: bergamot

Citrus limon: lemon

Citrus nobilis: tangerine

Citrus x paradisi: grapefruit

Citrus reticulate: mandarin

Citrus sinensis: orange

SANTALACEAE
Herbs, shrubs and trees which are semiparasitic on roots and stems of other plants; 36 genera, about 500 species; found in tropical and temperate regions.

Body Systems: Digestive System (excretory balance, genitourinary disinfectant), Nervous System (balances), and Respiratory System (balances)

Properties: balancing, calming, constriction, grounding

General Uses: genitourinary tract infections, impotence, lung congestion, stress-related disorders

Santalum album: East Indian sandalwood, Mysore sandalwood, sandalwood

UMBELLIFERAE (APIACEAE)
Herbs and a few shrubs, flowers borne in umbels (flowers radiating from a central point, like an umbrella); some important as food (carrot, celery), while others are very poisonous; some have medicinal actions; 420 genera, 3100 species; found throughout the world, mainly in northern temperate regions.

Body Systems: Digestive System (balances), Hormonal System (stimulates uterus), Respiratory System, Skin (regenerates)

Properties: air element; accumulation (elimination, excretion), secretion

General Uses: gas, glandular problems, spasms

Carum carvi: caraway

Coriandrum sativum: coriander (from seeds), cilantro (from leaves)

Cuminum cyminum: cumin

Foeniculum vulgare: fennel

Pimpinella anisum: anise

ZINGIBERACEAE
Ginger family comprising rhizomatous herbs; 53 genera, 1200 species; found mostly in rain forests throughout the tropics, but mainly in Indo-Malaysia.

Body Systems: Digestive and Hormonal Systems, Muscles and Bones

Properties: analgesic, fever reducing, scurvy (prevents), stimulant, tonic, warming

General Uses: digestive (stimulant), rheumatism, sexual tonic

Zingiber officinale: ginger

Appendix

RESEARCH REFERENCES

Aalinkeel R et al. (2008 Aug 25). "The dietary bioflavonoid, quercetin, selectively induces apoptosis of prostate cancer cells by down-regulating the expression of heat shock protein 90," Prostate.

Abdel-Sattar E, Zaitoun AA, Farag MA, El Gayed SH, Harraz FM (2009 Feb 25). "Chemical composition, insecticidal and insect repellent activity of Schinus molle L. leaf and fruit essential oils against Trogoderma granarium and Tribolium castaneum," Nat Prod Res. Epub ahead of print: 1-10.

Abedon, B (2008). "Essentra - a patented extract that reduces stress and enhances sleep," (http://www.nutragenesisnutrition.com/images/stories/pdf/ess_stress_wp.pdf):1-4.

Abenavoli L, Capasso R, Milic N, Capasso F (2010 Jun 7). "Milk thistle in liver diseases: past, present, future," Phytother Res. Epub ahead of print.

Adam B, Liebregts T, Best J, Bechmann L, Lackner C, Neumann J, Koehler S, Holtmann G (2006 Feb). "A combination of peppermint oil and caraway oil attenuates the post-inflammatory visceral hyperalgesia in a rat model," Scand J Gastroenterol. 41(2):155-60.

Al-Anati L, Essid E, Reinehr R, Petzinger E (2009 Apr). "Silibinin protects OTA-mediated TNF-alpha release from perfused rat livers and isolated rat Kupffer cells," Mol Nutr Food Res. 53(4):460-6.

Alexandrovich I, Rakovitskaya O, Kolmo E, Sidorova T, Shushunov S (2003 Jul-Aug). "The effect of fennel (Foeniculum Vulgare) seed oil emulsion in infantile colic: a randomized, placebo-controlled study," Altern Ther Health Med. 9(4):58-61.

al-Hader AA, Hasan ZA, Aqel MB (1994 Feb 22). "Hyperglycemic and insulin release inhibitory effects of Rosmarinus officinalis," J Ethnopharmacol. 43(3):217-21.

Almela L, Sánchez-Muñoz B, Fernández-López JA, Roca MJ, Rabe V (2006 Jul). "Liquid chromatograpic-mass spectrometric analysis of phenolics and free radical scavenging activity of rosemary extract from different raw material," J Chromatogr A. 1120(1-2):221-9.

Aloisi AM, Ceccarelli I, Masi F, Scaramuzzino A (2002 Oct 17). "Effects of the essential oil from citrus lemon in male and female rats exposed to a persistent painful stimulation," Behav Brain Res. 136(1):127-35.

Alqareer A, Alyahya A, Andersson L (2006 Nov). "The effect of clove and benzocaine versus placebo as topical anesthetics," J Dent. 34(10):747-50.

al-Zuhair H, el-Sayeh B, Ameen HA, al-Shoora H (1996 Jul-Aug). "Pharmacological studies of cardamom oil in animals," Pharmacol Res. 34(1-2):79-82.

Amano S, Akutsu N, Ogura Y, Nishiyama T (2004 Nov). "Increase of laminin 5 synthesis in human keratinocytes by acute wound fluid, inflammatory cytokines and growth factors, and lysophospholipids," Br J Dermatol. 151(5):961-70.

Amantea D, Fratto V, Maida S, Rotiroti D, Ragusa S, Nappi G, Bagetta G, Corasaniti MT (2009). "Prevention of Glutamate Accumulation and Upregulation of Phospho-Akt may Account for Neuroprotection Afforded by Bergamot Essential Oil against Brain Injury Induced by Focal Cerebral Ischemia in Rat," Int Rev Neurobiol. 85:389-405.

Ambrosone CB, McCann SE, Freudenheim JL, Marshall JR, Zhang Y, Shields PG (2004 May). "Breast cancer risk in premenopausal women is inversely associated with consumption of broccoli, a source of isothiocyanates, but is not modified by GST genotype," J Nutr. 134(5):1134-8.

American Cancer Society (2008). "Cancer Facts and Figures." Downloaded at http://www.cancer.org/downloads/STT/2008CAFFfinalsecured.pdf.

Ammon HP (2002). "Boswellic acids (components of frankincense) as the active principle in treatment of chronic inflammatory diseases," Wien Med Wochenschr. 152(15-16):373-8.

Anderson KJ, Teuber SS, Gobeille A, Cremin P, Waterhouse AL, Steinberg FM (2001 Nov). "Walnut polyphenolics inhibit in vitro human plasma and LDL oxidation," J Nutr. 131(11):2837-42.

Andrews R.E., Parks L.W., Spence K.D. (1980) Some Effects of Douglas Fir Terpenes on Certain Microorganisms. Applied and Environmental Microbiology. 40: 301-304.

Andrian E., Grenier D., Rouabhia M. (2006) Porphyromonas gingivalis-Epithelial Cell Interactions in Periodontitis. Journal of Dental Research. 85: 392-403.

Antimutagenic effects of extracts from sage (Salvia officinalis) in mammalian system in vivo. (2006 Jul 19). "Relaxant effects of Rosa damascena on guinea pig tracheal chains and its possible mechanism(s)," J Ethnopharmacol. 106(3):377-82.

Appendino G, Ottino M, Marquez N, Bianchi F, Giana A, Ballero M, Sterner O, Fiebich BL, Munoz G (2007 Apr). "Arzanol, an anti-inflammatory and anti-HIV-1 phloroglucinol alpha-Pyrone from Helichrysum italicum ssp. microphyllum," J Nat Prod. 70(4):608-12.

Aqel MB (1991 May-Jun). "Relaxant effect of the volatile oil of Rosmarinus officinalis on tracheal smooth muscle," J Ethnopharmacol. 33(1-2):57-62.

Arasada BL, Bommareddy A, Zhang X, Bremmon K, Dwivedi C. (2008 Jan-Feb). "Effects of alpha-santalol on proapoptotic caspases and p53 expression in UVB irradiated mouse skin," Anticancer Res. 28(1A):129-32.

Archana R, Namasivayam A (1999 Jan). "Antistressor effect of Withania somnifera," J Ethnopharmacol. 64(1):91-3.

Asao T, Kuwano H, Ide M, Hirayama I, Nakamura JI, Fujita KI, Horiuti R (2003 Apr). "Spasmolytic effect of peppermint oil in barium during double-contrast barium enema compared with Buscopan," Clin Radiol. 58(4):301-5.

Badia P, Wesensten N, Lammers W, Culpepper J, Harsh J (1990 Jul). "Responsiveness to olfactory stimuli presented in sleep," Physiol Behav. 48(1):87-90.

Bagchi D, Hassoun EA, Bagchi M, Stohs SJ (1993 Aug). "Protective effects of antioxidants against endrin-induced hepatic lipid peroxidation, DNA damage, and excretion of urinary lipid metabolites," Free Radic Biol Med. 15(2):217-22.

Bagchi D, Sen CK, Ray SD, Das DK, Bagchi M, Preuss HG, Vinson JA (2003 Feb-Mar). "Molecular mechanisms of cardioprotection by a novel grape seed proanthocyanidin extract," Mutat Res. 523-24:87-97.

Bagg J, Jackson MS, Petrina Sweeney M, Ramage G, Davies AN (2006 May). "Susceptibility to Melaleuca alternifolia (tea tree) oil of yeasts isolated from the mouths of patients with advanced cancer," Oral Oncol. 42(5):487-92.

Bakirel T, Bakirel U, Keleş OU, Ulgen SG, Yardibi H (2008 Feb 28). "In vivo assessment of antidiabetic and antioxidant activities of rosemary (Rosmarinus officinalis) in alloxan-diabetic rabbits," J Ethnopharmacol. 116(1):64-73.

Balick, MJ, Cox PA. (1996). Plants, People and Culture: The Science of Ethnobotany. Scientific American Library, New York.

Ballard CG, O'Brien JT, Reichelt K, Perry EK (2002 Jul). "Aromatherapy as a safe and effective treatment for the management of agitation in severe dementia: the results of a double-blind, placebo-controlled trial with Melissa," J Clin Psychiatry. 63(7):553-8.

Balazs L, Okolicany J, Ferrebee M, Tolley B, Tigyi G (2001 Feb). "Topical application of the phospholipid growth factor lysophosphatidic acid promotes wound healing in vivo," Am J Physiol Regul Integr Comp Physiol. 280(2):R466-72.

Ballabeni V, Tognolini M, Bertoni S, Bruni R, Guerrini A, Rueda GM, Barocelli E (2007 Jan). "Antiplatelet and antithrombotic activities of essential oil from wild Ocotea quixos (Lam.) Kosterm. (Lauraceae) calices from Amazonian Ecuador," Pharmacol Res. 55(1):23-30.

Ballabeni V, Tognolini M, Giorgio C, Bertoni S, Bruni R, Barocelli E (2009 Oct 13). "Ocotea quixos Lam. essential oil: In vitro and in vivo investigation on its anti-inflammatory properties," Fitoterapia. Epub ahead of print.

Banerjee S, Ecavade A, Rao AR (1993 Feb). "Modulatory influence of sandalwood oil on mouse hepatic glutathione S-transferase activity and acid soluble sulphydryl level," Cancer Lett. 68(2-3):105-9.

Banes-Marshall L, Cawley P, Phillips CA (2001). "In vitro activity of Melaleuca alternifolia (tea tree) oil against bacterial and Candida spp. isolates from clinical specimens," Br J Biomed Sci. 58(3):139-45.

Banno N, Akihisa T, Yasukawa K, Tokuda H, Tabata K, Nakamura Y, Nishimura R, Kimura Y, Suzuki T (2006 Sep 19). "Anti-inflammatory activities of the triterpene acids from the resin of Boswellia carteri," J Ethnopharmacol. 107(2):249-53.

Bao L, Yao XS, Tsi D, Yau CC, Chia CS, Nagai H, Kurihara H (2008 Jan 23). "Protective effects of bilberry (Vaccinium myrtillus L.) extract on KbrO3-induced kidney damage in mice," J Agric Food Chem. 56(2):420-5.

Barthelman M., Chen W., Gensler H.L., Huang C., Dong Z., Bowden G.T. (1998) Inhibitory Effects of Perillyl Alcohol on UVB-induced Murine Skin Cancer and AP-1 Transactivation. Cancer Research. 58: 711-716.

Bassett IB, Pannowitz DL, Barnetson RS (1990 Oct 15). "A comparative study of tea-tree oil versus benzoylperoxide in the treatment of acne," Med J Aust. 153(8):455-8.

Bastiaens M, Hoefnagel J, Westendorp R, Vermeer BJ, Bouwes Bavinck JN (2004 Jun). "Solar lentigines are strongly related to sun exposure in contrast to ephelides," Pigment Cell Res. 17(3).

Bastos J.F.A., Moreira I.J.A., Ribeiro T.P., Medeiros I.A., Antoniolli A.R., De Sousa D.P., Santos M.R.V. (2009) Hypotensive and Vasorelaxant Effects of Citronellol, a Monoterpene Alcohol, in Rats. Basic & Clinical Pharmacology & Toxicology. 106: 331-337.

Basu A, Lucas EA (2007 Aug). "Mechanisms and effects of green tea on cardiovascular health," Nutr Rev. 65(8 Pt 1):361-75.

Behnam S, Farzaneh M, Ahmadzadeh M, Tehrani AS (2006). "Composition and antifungal activity of essential oils of Mentha piperita and Lavendula angustifolia on post-harvest phytopathogens," Commun Agric Appl Biol Sci. 71(3 Pt B):1321-6.

Belardinelli R, Mucaj A, Lacalaprice F, Solenghi M, Principi F, Tiano L, Littarru GP (2005). "Coenzyme Q10 improves contractility of dysfunctional myocardium in chronic heart failure," Biofactors. 25(1-4):137-45.

Benencia F, Courrèges MC (2000 Nov). "In vitro and in vivo activity of eugenol on human herpes virus," Phytother Res. 14(7):495-500.

Bezanilla F. (2006) The action potential: From voltage-gated conductances to molecular structures. Biological Research. 39: 425-435.

Berić T, Nikolić B, Stanojević J, Vuković-Gacić B, Knezević-Vukcević J (2008 Feb). "Protective effect of basil (Ocimum basilicum L.) against oxidative DNA damage and mutagenesis," Food Chem Toxicol. 46(2):724-32.

Bhattacharya SK, Goel RK (1987 Mar). "Anti-stress activity of sitoindosides VII and VIII, new acylsterylglucosides from Withania somnifera," Phytother Res. 1(1):32-7.

Bhushan S, Kumar A, Malik F, Andotra SS, Sethi VK, Kaur IP, Taneja SC, Qazi GN, Singh J (2007 Oct). "A triterpenediol from Boswellia serrata induces apoptosis through both the intrinsic and extrinsic apoptotic pathways in human leukemia HL-60 cells," Apoptosis. 12(10):1911-26.

Bobe G et al. (2008 Mar). "Flavonoid intake and risk of pancreatic cancer in male smokers (Finland)," Cancer Epidemiol Biomarkers Prev. 17(3):553-62.

Bone ME, Wilkinson DJ, Young JR, McNeil J, Charlton S (1990 Aug). "Ginger root--a new antiemetic. The effect of ginger root on postoperative nausea and vomiting after major gynaecological surgery," Anaesthesia. 45(8):669-71.

Boots AW, Wilms LC, Swennen EL, Kleinjans JC, Bast A, Haenen GR (2008 Jul-Aug). "In vitro and ex vivo anti-inflammatory activity of quercetin in healthy volunteers," Nutrition. 24(7-8):703-10.

Bose M, Lambert JD, Ju J, Reuhl KR, Shapses SA, Yang CS (2008 Sep). "The major green tea polyphenol, (-)-epigallocatechin-3-gallate, inhibits obesity, metabolic syndrome, and fatty liver disease in high-fat-fed mice," J Nutr. 138(9):1677-83.

Boudier D, Perez E, Rondeau D, Bordes S, Closs B (2008 Mar). "Innovatory approach fights pigment disturbances," Personal Care.

Appendix and References

Boussetta T, Raad H, Lettéron P, Gougerot-Pocidalo MA, Marie JC, Driss F, El-Benna J (2009 Jul 31). "Punicic acid a conjugated linolenic acid inhibits TNFalpha-induced neutrophil hyperactivation and protects from experimental colon inflammation in rats," PLoS One. 4(7):e6458.

Bouwstra J.A., Gooris G.S., Dubbelaar F.E.R., Weeheim A.M., Ijzerman A.P., Ponec M. (1998) Role of ceramide 1 in the molecular organization of the stratum corneum lipids. Journal of Lipid Research. 39: 186-196.

Bradley BF, Brown SL, Chu S, Lea RW (2009 Jun). "Effects of orally administered lavender essential oil on responses to anxiety-provoking film clips," Hum Psychopharmacol. 24(4):319-30.

Bradley BF, Starkey NJ, Brown SL, Lea RW (2007 May 22). "Anxiolytic effects of Lavandula angustifolia odour on the Mongolian gerbil elevated plus maze," J Ethnopharmacol. 111(3):517-25.

Brady A, Loughlin R, Gilpin D, Kearney P, Tunney M (2006 Oct). "In vitro activity of tea-tree oil against clinical skin isolates of methicillin-resistant and -sensitive Staphylococcus aureus and coagulase-negative staphylococci growing planktonically and as biofilms," J Med Microbiol. 55(Pt 10):1375-80.

Brand C, Ferrante A, Prager RH, Riley TV, Carson CF, Finlay-Jones JJ, Hart PH. (2001 Apr). "The water-soluble components of the essential oil of Melaleuca alternifolia (tea tree oil) suppress the production of superoxide by human monocytes, but not neutrophils, activated in vitro.," Inflamm Res. 50(4):213-9.

Brand C, Grimbaldeston MA, Gamble JR, Drew J, Finlay-Jones JJ, Hart PH (2002 May). "Tea tree oil reduces the swelling associated with the efferent phase of a contact hypersensitivity response," Inflamm Res. 51(5):236-44.

Brand C, Townley SL, Finlay-Jones JJ, Hart PH (2002 Jun). "Tea tree oil reduces histamine-induced oedema in murine ears," Inflamm Res. 51(6):283-9.

Brass EP, Adler S, Sietsema KE, Hiatt WR, Orlando AM, Amato A; CHIEF Investigators (2001 May). "Intravenous L-carnitine increases plasma carnitine, reduces fatigue, and may preserve exercise capacity in hemodialysis patients," Am J Kidney Dis. 37(5):1018-28.

Brien S, Lewith G, Walker A, Hicks SM, Middleton D (2004 Dec). "Bromelain as a Treatment for Osteoarthritis: a Review of Clinical Studies," Evid Based Complement Alternat Med. 1(3):251-257.

Brown AL et al. (2008 Aug). "Effects of dietary supplementation with the green tea polyphenol epigallocatechin-3-gallate on insulin resistance and associated metabolic risk factors: randomized controlled trial," Br J Nutr. 19:1-9.

Brown T.L., LeMay H.E., Bursten B.E. Chemistry: The Central Science. 10th ed. Upper Saddle River: Pearson Prentice Hall, 2006.

Brum LF, Elisabetsky E, Souza D (2001 Aug). "Effects of linalool on [(3)H]MK801 and [(3)H] muscimol binding in mouse cortical membranes," Phytother Res. 15(5):422-5.

Buchbauer G, Jirovetz L, Jäger W, Dietrich H, Plank C (1991 Nov-Dec). "Aromatherapy: evidence for sedative effects of the essential oil of lavender after inhalation," Z Naturforsch C. 46(11-12):1067-72.

Bucher HC, Hengstler P, Schindler C, Meier G (2002 Mar). "N-3 polyunsaturated fatty acids in coronary heart disease: a meta-analysis of randomized controlled trials," Am J Med. 112(4):298-304.

Buck DS, Nidorf DM, Addino JG (1994 Jun). "Comparison of two topical preparations for the treatment of onychomycosis: Melaleuca alternifolia (tea tree) oil and clotrimazole," J Fam Pract. 38(6):601-5.

Bulbring E. (1946) Observations on the Isolated Phrenic Nerve Diaphragm Preparation of the Rat. British Journal of Pharmacology. 1: 38-61.

Burke BE, Baillie JE, Olson RD (2004 May). "Essential oil of Australian lemon myrtle (Backhousia citriodora) in the treatment of molluscum contagiosum in children," Biomed Pharmacother. 58(4):245-7.

Caccioni DR, Guizzardi M, Biondi DM, Renda A, Ruberto G (1998 Aug 18). "Relationship between volatile components of citrus fruit essential oils and antimicrobial action on Penicillium digitatum and penicillium italicum," Int J Food Microbiol. 43(1-2):73-9.

Caldefie-Chézet F, Fusillier C, Jarde T, Laroye H, Damez M, Vasson MP, Guillot J (2006 May). "Potential anti-inflammatory effects of Melaleuca alternifolia essential oil on human peripheral blood leukocytes," Phytother Res. 20(5):364-70.

Caldefie-Chézet F, Guerry M, Chalchat JC, Fusillier C, Vasson MP, Guillot J (2004 Aug). "Anti-inflammatory effects of Melaleuca alternifolia essential oil on human polymorphonuclear neutrophils and monocytes," Free Radic Res. 38(8):805-11.

Candan F, Unlu M, Tepe B, Daferera D, Polissiou M, Sökmen A, Akpulat HA (2003 Aug). "Antioxidant and antimicrobial activity of the essential oil and methanol extracts of Achillea millefolium subsp. millefolium Afan. (Asteraceae)," J Ethnopharmacol. 87(2-3):215-20.

Canyon DV, Speare R (2007 Apr). "A comparison of botanical and synthetic substances commonly used to prevent head lice (Pediculus humanus var. capitis) infestation," Int J Dermatol. 46(4):422-6.

Capasso R, Savino F, Capasso F (2007 Oct). "Effects of the herbal formulation ColiMil on upper gastrointestinal transit in mice in vivo," Phytother Res. 21(10):999-1101.

Cappello G, Spezzaferro M, Grossi L, Manzoli L, Marzio L (2007 Jun). "Peppermint oil (Mintoil) in the treatment of irritable bowel syndrome: a prospective double blind placebo-controlled randomized trial," Dig Liver Dis. 39(6):530-6.

Carnesecchi S., Bradaia A., Fischer B., Coelho D., Scholler-Guinard M., Gosse F., Raul F. (2002) Perturbation by Geraniol of Cell Membrane Permeability and Signal Transduction Pathways in Human Colon Cancer Cells. The Journal of Pharmacology and Experimental Therapeutics. 303: 711-715.

Carnesecchi S., Bras-Goncalves R., Bradaia A., Zeisel M., Gosse F., Poupon M-F., Raul F. (2004) Geraniol, a component of plant essential oils, modulates DNA synthesis and potentiates 5-fluorouracil efficacy on human colon tumor xenografts. Cancer Letters. 215: 53-59.

Carnesecchi S., Langley K., Exinger F., Gosse F., Raul F. (2002) Geraniol, a Component of Plant Essential Oils, Sensitizes Human Colonic Cancer Cells to 5-Flurouracil Treatment. The Journal of Pharmacology and Experimental Therapeutics. 301: 625-630.

Carnesecchi S, Schneider Y, Ceraline J, Duranton B, Gosse F, Seiler N, Raul F (2001 Jul). "Geraniol, a component of plant essential oils, inhibits growth and polyamine biosynthesis in human colon cancer cells," J Pharmacol Exp Ther. 298(1):197-200.

Carson CF, Cookson BD, Farrelly HD, Riley TV (1995 Mar). "Susceptibility of methicillin-resistant Staphylococcus aureus to the essential oil of Melaleuca alternifolia," J Antimicrob Chemother. 35(3):421-4.

Carvalho-Freitas MI, Costa M (2002 Dec). "Anxiolytic and sedative effects of extracts and essential oil from Citrus aurantium L," Biol Pharm Bull. 25(12):1629-33.

Catalán A, Pacheco JG, Martínez A, Mondaca MA (2008 Mar). "In vitro and in vivo activity of Melaleuca alternifolia mixed with tissue conditioner on Candida albicans," Oral Surg Oral Med Oral Pathol Oral Radiol Endod. 105(3):327-32.

Ceccarelli I, Lariviere WR, Fiorenzani P, Sacerdote P, Aloisi AM (2004 Mar 19). "Effects of long-term exposure of lemon essential oil odor on behavioral, hormonal and neuronal parameters in male and female rats," Brain Res. 1001(1-2):78-86.

Centers for Disease Control and Prevention (CDC) (2004 May 7). "Spina bifida and anencephaly before and after folic acid mandate--United States, 1995-1996 and 1999-2000," MMWR Morb Mortal Wkly Rep. 53(17):362-5.

Ceriotti G, Spandrio L, Gazzaniga A (1967 Jul-Aug). "[Demonstration, isolation and physical and chemical characteristics of narciclasine, a new antimitotic of plant origin]," Tumori. 53(4):359-71.

Cermelli C, Fabio A, Fabio G, Quaglio P (2008 Jan). "Effect of eucalyptus essential oil on respiratory bacteria and viruses," Curr Microbiol. 56(1):89-92.

Chaieb K, Zmantar T, Ksouri R, Hajlaoui H, Mahdouani K, Abdelly C, Bakhrouf A (2007 Sep). "Antioxidant properties of the essential oil of Eugenia caryophyllata and its antifungal activity against a large number of clinical Candida species," Mycoses. 50(5):403-6.

Chaiyakunapruk N, Kitikannakorn N, Nathisuwan S, Leeprakobboon K, Leelasettagool C (2006 Jan). "The efficacy of ginger for the prevention of postoperative nausea and vomiting: a meta-analysis," Am J Obstet Gynecol. 194(1):95-9.

Chakraborty PK, Mustafi SB, Raha S (2008 Sep). "Pro-survival effects of repetitive low-grade oxidative stress are inhibited by simultaneous exposure to resveratrol," Phamacol Res. 2.

Chambers H.F. (2001) The Changing Epidemiology of Staphylococcus aureus?. Emerging Infectious Diseases. 7: 178-182.

Chang WC, Yu YM, Chiang SY, Tseng CY (2008 Apr). "Ellagic acid supresses oxidised low-density lipoprotein-induced aortic smooth muscle cell proliferation: studies on the activation of extracellular signal-regulated kinase ½ and proliferating cell nuclear antigen expression," Br J Nutr. 99(4):709-14.

Chapman A.G. (1998) Glutamate receptors in epilepsy. Progress in Brain Research. 116: 371-383.

Chapman A.G. (2000) Glutamate and Epilepsy. The Journal of Nutrition. 130: 1043S-1045S.

Charles CH, Vincent JW, Borycheski L, Amatnieks Y, Sarina M, Qaqish J, Proskin HM (2000 Sep). "Effect of an essential oil-containing dentifrice on dental plaque microbial composition," Am J Dent. 13():26C-30C.

Checker R, Chatterjee S, Sharma D, Gupta S, Variyar P, Sharma A, Poduval TB (2008 May). "Immunomodulatory and radioprotective effects of lignans derived from fresh nutmeg mace (Myristica fragrans) in mammalian splenocytes," Int Immunopharmacol. 8(5):661-9.

Chen YC, Chiu WT, Wu MS (2006 Jul). "Therapeutic effect of topical gamma-linolenic acid on refractory uremic pruritus," Am J Kidney Dis. 48(1):69-76.

Cheung S, Tai J (2007 Jun). "Anti-proliferative and antioxidant properties of rosemary Rosmarinus officinalis," Oncol Rep. 17(6):1525-31.

Chevrier MR, Ryan AE, Lee DY, Zhongze M, Wu-Yan Z, Via CS (2005 May). "Boswellia carterii extract inhibits TH1 cytokines and promotes TH2 cytokines in vitro," Clin Diagn Lab Immunol. 12(5):575-80.

Chinou IB, Roussis V, Perdetzoglou D, Loukis A (1996 Aug). "Chemical and biological studies on two Helichrysum species of Greek origin," Planta Med. 62(4):377-9.

Ciacci C, Peluso G, Iannoni E, Siniscalchi M, Iovino P, Rispo A, Tortora R, Bucci C, Zingone F, Margarucci S, Calvani M (2007 Oct). "L-Carnitine in the treatment of fatigue in adult celiac disease patients: a pilot study," Dig Liver Dis. 39(10):922-8.

Ciftci O., Ozdemir I., Tanyildizl S., Yildiz S., Oguzturk H. (2011) Antioxidative effects of curcumin, β-myrcene and 1,8-cineole against 2,3,7,8-tetracholorodibenzo-p-dioxin - induced oxidative stress in rats liver. Toxicology and Industrial Health. 27: 447-453.

Coderch L., Lopez O., de la Maza A., Parra J.L. (2003) Ceramides and Skin Function. American Journal of Clinical Dermatology. 4: 107-129.

Cooley K, Szczurko O, Perri D, Mills EJ, Bernhardt B, Zhou Q, Seely D (2009 Aug 31). "Naturopathic care for anxiety: a randomized controlled trial ISRCTN78958974," PLoS One. 4(8):e6628.

Couse JF, Lindzey J, Grandien K, Gustafsson JA, Korach KS (1997 Nov). "Tissue distribution and quantitative analysis of estrogen reseptor-alpha (ERalpha) and estrogen receptor-beta (ERbeta) messenger ribonucleic acid in the wild-type and ERalpha-knockout mouse," Endocrinology. 138*11):4613-21.

Cowan M.K., Talaro K.P. Microbiology: A Systems Approach. 2nd ed. New York: McGraw Hill, 2009.

Cox SD, Mann CM, Markham JL, Bell HC, Gustafson JE, Warmington JR, Wyllie SG (2000 Jan). "The mode of antimicrobial action of the essential oil of Melaleuca alternifolia (tea tree oil)," J Appl Microbiol. 88(1):170-5.

Cross SE, Russell M, Southwell I, Roberts MS (2008 May). "Human skin penetration of the major components of Australian tea tree oil applied in its pure form and as a 20% solution in vitro," Eur J Pharm Biopharm. 69(1):214-22.

Crowell P.L., Chang R.R., Ren Z., Elson C.E., Gould M.N. (1991) Selective Inhibition of Isoprenylation of 21-26kDa Proteins by the Anticarcinogen d-Limonene and Its Metabolites. J. Biol. Chem. 266: 17679-17685.

Cui Y et al. (2008 May 15). "Dietary flavonoid intake and lung cancer—a population-based case-control study," Cancer. 112(10):2241-8.

Appendix

Curi R, Alvarez M, Bazotte RB, Botion LM, Godoy JL, Bracht A (1986). "Effect of Stevia rebaudiana on glucose tolerance in normal adult humans," Braz J Med Biol Res. 19(6):771-4.

Curio M, Jacone H, Perrut J, Pinto AC, Filho VF, Silva RC (2009 Aug). "Acute effect of Copaifera reticulata Ducke copaiba oil in rats tested in the elevated plus-maze: an ethological analysis," J Pharm Pharmacol. 61(8):1105-10.

Darmstadt GL, Mao-Qiang M, Chi E, Saha SK, Ziboh VA, Black RE, Santosham M, Elias PM (2002). "Impact of topical oils on the skin barrier: possible implications for neonatal health in developing countries," Acta Paediatr. 91(5):546-54.

Darmstadt GL, Saha SK, Ahmed AS, Chowdhury MA, Law PA, Ahmed S, Alam MA, Black RE, Santosham M (2005 Mar 19-25). "Effect of topical treatment with skin barrier-enhancing emollients on nosocomial infections in preterm infants in Bangladesh: a randomised controlled trial," Lancet. 365(9464):1039-45.

Damiani C.E.N., Rossoni L.V., Vassallo D.V. (2003) Vasorelaxant effects of eugenol on rat thoracic aorta. Vascular Pharmacology. 40: 59-66.

D'Auria FD, Laino L, Strippoli V, Tecca M, Salvatore G, Battinelli L, Mazzanti G (2001 Aug). "In vitro activity of tea tree oil against Candida albicans mycelial conversion and other pathogenic fungi," J Chemother. 13(4):377-83.

D'Auria FD, Tecca M, Strippoli V, Salvatore G, Battinelli L, Mazzanti G (2005 Aug). "Antifungal activity of Lavandula angustifolia essential oil against Candida albicans yeast and mycelial form," Med Mycol. 43(5):391-6.

Davies K (1995). "Oxidative stress: the paradox of aerobic life," Biochem Soc Symp. 61:1–31.

de Almeida R.N., Araujo D.A.M., Goncalvevs J.C.R., Montenegro F.C., de Sousa D.P., Leite J.R., Mattei R., Benedito M.A.C., de Carvalho J.G.B., Cruz J.S., Maia J.G.S. (2009) Rosewood oil induces sedation and inhibits compound action potential in rodents. Journal of Ethanopharmacology. 124: 440-443.

de Almeida R.N., de Sousa D.P., Nobrega F.F.F., Claudino F.S., Araujo D.A.M., Leite J.R., Mattei R. (2008) Anticonvulsant effect of a natural compound α,β-epoxy-carvone and its actioin on the nerve excitability. Neuroscience Letters. 443: 51-55.

Debersac P, Heydel JM, Amiot MJ, Goudonnet H, Artur Y, Suschetet M, Siess MH (2001 Sep). "Induction of cytochrome P450 and/or detoxication enzymes by various extracts of rosemary: description of specific patterns," Food Chem Toxicol. 39(9):907-18.

Deeptha K, Kamaleeswari M, Sengottuvelan M, Nalini N (2006 Nov). "Dose dependent inhibitory effect of dietary caraway on 1,2-dimethylhydrazine induced colonic aberrant crypt foci and bacterial enzyme activity in rats," Invest New Drugs. 24(6):479-88.

DeLeo F.R., Otto M., Kreiswirth B.N., Chambers H.F. (2010) Community-associated meticillin-resistant Staphylococcus aureus. The Lancet. 375: 1557-1568.

Department of Environmental Medicine, Odense University, Denmark (1992 Dec). "Ginger (Zingiber officinale) in rheumatism and musculoskeletal disorders," Med Hypotheses. 39(4):342-8.

De Spirt S, Stahl W, Tronnier H, Sies H, Bejot M, Maurette JM, Heinrich U (2009 Feb). "Intervention with flaxseed and borage oil supplements modulates skin condition in women," Br J Nutr. 101(3):440-5.

de Sousa D.P., Goncalves J.C.R., Quintanas-Junior L., Cruz J.S., Araujo D.A.M., de Almeida R.N. (2006) Study of anticonvulsant effect of citronellol, a monoterpene alcohol, in rodents. Neuroscience Letters. 401: 231-235.

Deters A, Zippel J, Hellenbrand N, Pappai D, Possemeyer C, Hensel A (2010 Jan 8). "Aqueous extracts and polysaccharides from Marshmallow roots (Althea officinalis L.): cellular internalisation and stimulation of cell physiology of human epithelial cells in vitro," J Ethnopharmacol. 127(1):62-9.

Devika PT, Mainzen Prince PS (2008 Jan). "(-) Epigallocatechin gallate (EGCG) prevents isoprenaline-induced cardiac marker enzymes and membrane-bound ATPases," J Pharm Pharmacol. 60(1):125-33.

De Vriendt T, Moreno LA, De Henauw S (2009 Sep). "Chronic stress and obesity in adolescents: scientific evidence and methodological issues for epidemiological research," Nutr Metab Cardiovasc Dis. 19(7):511-9.

Díaz C, Quesada S, Brenes O, Aguilar G, Cicció JF (2008). "Chemical composition of Schinus molle essential oil and its cytotoxic activity on tumour cell lines," Nat Prod Res. 22(17):1521-34.

Diego MA, Jones NA, Field T, Hernandez-Reif M, Schanberg S, Kuhn C, McAdam V, Galamaga R, Galamaga M (1998 Dec). "Aromatherapy positively affects mood, EEG patterns of alertness and math computations," Int J Neurosci. 96(3-4):217-24.

Diggins K.C. (2008) Treatment of mild to moderate dehydration in children with oral rehydration therapy. Journal of the American Academy of Nurse Practitioners. 20: 402-406.

Dikshit A, Naqvi AA, Husain A. (1986 May). "Schinus molle: a new source of natural fungitoxicant," Appl Environ Microbiol. 51(5):1085-8.

Dimas K, Kokkinopoulos D, Demetzos C, Vaos B, Marselos M, Malamas M, Tzavaras T (1999 Mar). "The effect of sclareol on growth and cell cycle progression of human leukemic cell lines," Leuk Res. 23(3):217-34.

Dimpfel W, Pischel I, Lehnfeld R (2004 Sep 29). "Effects of lozenge containing lavender oil, extracts from hops, lemon balm and oat on electrical brain activity of volunteers," Eur J Med Res. 9(9):423-31.

Domitrović R, Jakovac H, Romić Z, Rahelić D, Tadić Z (2010 Aug 9). "Antifibrotic activity of Taraxacum officinale root in carbon tetrachloride-induced liver damage in mice," J Ethnopharmacol. 130(3):569-77.

Doran AL, Morden WE, Dunn K, Edwards-Jones V (2009 Apr). "Vapour-phase activities of essential oils against antibiotic sensitive and resistant bacteria including MRSA," Lett Appl Microbiol. 48(4):387-92.

Drobiova H, Thomson M, Al-Qattan K, Peltonen-Shalaby R, Al-Amin Z, Ali M (2009 Feb 20). "Garlic increases antioxidant levels in diabetic and hypertensive rats determined by a modified peroxidase method," Evid Based Complement Alternat Med. Epub ahead of print.

Duarte MC, Leme EE, Delarmelina C, Soares AA, Figueira GM, Sartoratto A (2007 May 4). "Activity of essential oils from Brazilian medicinal plants on Escherichia coli," J Ethnopharmacol. 111(2):197-201

Dudai N, Weinstein Y, Krup M, Rabinski T, Ofir R (2005 May). "Citral is a new inducer of caspase-3 in tumor cell lines," Planta Med. 71(5):484-8.

Dunn C, Sleep J, Collett D (1995 Jan). "Sensing an improvement: an experimental study to evaluate the use of aromatherapy, massage and periods of rest in an intensive care unit," J Adv Nurs. 21(1):34-40.

Dunstan JA, Mori TA, Barden A, Beilin LJ, Taylor AL, Holt PG, Prescott SL (2003 Dec). "Fish oil supplementation in pregnancy modifies neonatal allergen-specific immune responses and clinical outcomes in infants at high risk of atopy: a randomized, controlled trial," J Allergy Clin Immunol. 112(6):1178-84.

Duwiejua M, Zeitlin IJ, Waterman PG, Chapman J, Mhango GJ, Provan GJ (1993 Feb). "Anti-inflammatory activity of resins from some species of the plant family Burseraceae," Planta Med. 59(1):12-6.

Dwivedi C, Abu-Ghazaleh A (1997 Aug). "Chemopreventive effects of sandalwood oil on skin papillomas in mice," Eur J Cancer Prev. 6(4):399-401.

Dwivedi C, Guan X, Harmsen WL, Voss AL, Goetz-Parten DE, Koopman EM, Johnson KM, Valluri HB, Matthees DP (2003 Feb). "Chemopreventive effects of alpha-santalol on skin tumor development in CD-1 and SENCAR mice," Cancer Epidemiol Biomarkers Prev. 12(2):151-6.

Dwivedi C, Maydew ER, Hora JJ, Ramaeker DM, Guan X. (2005 Oct). "Chemopreventive effects of various concentrations of alpha-santalol on skin cancer development in CD-1 mice," Eur J Cancer Prev. 14(5):473-6.

Dwivedi C, Valluri HB, Guan X, Agarwal R (2006 Sep). "Chemopreventive effects of alpha-santalol on ultraviolet B radiation-induced skin tumor development in SKH-1 hairless mice," Carcinogenesis. 27(9):1917-22.

Ebihara T, Ebihara S, Maruyama M, Kobayashi M, Itou A, Arai H, Sasaki H (2006 Sep). "A randomized trial of olfactory stimulation using black pepper oil in older people with swallowing dysfunction," J Am Geriatr Soc. 54(9):1401-6.

Edwards-Jones V, Buck R, Shawcross SG, Dawson MM, Dunn K (2004 Dec). "The effect of essential oils on methicillin-resistant Staphylococcus aureus using a dressing model," Burns. 30(8):772-7.

Elson CE, Underbakke GL, Hanson P, Shrago E, Wainberg RH, Qureshi AA (1989 Aug). "Impact of lemongrass oil, an essential oil, on serum cholesterol," Lipids. 24(8):677-9.

Elwakeel HA, Moneim HA, Farid M, Gohar AA (2007 Jul). "Clove oil cream: a new effective treatment for chronic anal fissure," Colorectal Dis. 9(6):549-52.

Enan E (2001 Nov). "Insecticidal activity of essential oils: octopaminergic sites of action," Comp Biochem Physiol C Toxicol Pharmacol. 130(3):325-37.

Enshaieh S, Jooya A, Siadat AH, Iraji F (2007 Jan-Feb). "The efficacy of 5% topical tea tree oil gel in mild to moderate acne vulgaris: a randomized, double-blind placebo-controlled study," Indian J Dermatol Venereol Leprol. 73(1):22-5.

Eriksson K., Levin J.O. (1996) Gas chromatographic-mass spectrometric identification of metabolites from □-pinene in human urine after occupational exposure to sawing fumes. J. Chromatrography B. 677: 85-98.

Erkkilä AT, Lichtenstein AH, Mozaffarian D, Herrington DM (2004 Sep). "Fish intake is associated with a reduced progression of coronary artery atherosclerosis in postmenopausal women with coronary artery disease," Am J Clin Nutr. 80(3):626-32.

Erkkilä AT, Schwab US, de Mello VD, Lappalainen T, Mussalo H, Lehto S, Kemi V, Lamberg-Allardt C, Uusitupa MI (2008 Sep). "Effects of fatty and lean fish intake on blood pressure in subjects with coronary heart disease using multiple medications," Eur J Nutr. 47(6):319-28.

Evandri MG, Battinelli L, Daniele C, Mastrangelo S, Bolle P, Mazzanti G (2005 Sep). "The antimutagenic activity of Lavandula angustifolia (lavender) essential oil in the bacterial reverse mutation assay," Food Chem Toxicol. 43(9):1381-7.

Evans J.D., Martin S.A. (2000) Effects of Thymol on Ruminal Microorganisms. Current Microbiology. 41: 336-340.

Fabio A, Cermelli C, Fabio G, Nicoletti P, Quaglio P (2007 Apr). "Screening of the antibacterial effects of a variety of essential oils on microorganisms responsible for respiratory infections," Phytother Res. 21(4):374-7.

Fan AY, Lao L, Zhang RX, Zhou AN, Wang LB, Moudgil KD, Lee DY, Ma ZZ, Zhang WY, Berman BM (2005 Oct 3). "Effects of an acetone extract of Boswellia carterii Birdw. (Burseraceae) gum resin on adjuvant-induced arthritis in lewis rats," J Ethnopharmacol. 101(1-3):104-9.

Feinblatt HM (1960 Jan). "Cajeput-type oil for the treatment of furunculosis," J Natl Med Assoc. 52:32-4.

Ferrini AM, Mannoni V, Aureli P, Salvatore G, Piccirilli E, Ceddia T, Pontieri E, Sessa R, Oliva B (2006 Jul-Sep). "Melaleuca alternifolia essential oil possesses potent anti-staphylococcal activity extended to strains resistant to antibiotics," Int J Immunopathol Pharmacol. 19(3):539-44.

Field T, Diego M, Hernandez-Reif M, Cisneros W, Feijo L, Vera Y, Gil K, Grina D, Claire He Q (2005 Feb). "Lavender fragrance cleansing gel effects on relaxation," Int J Neurosci. 115(2):207-22.

Filoche SK, Soma K, Sissons CH (2005 Aug). "Antimicrobial effects of essential oils in combination with chlorhexidine digluconate," Oral Microbiol Immunol. 20(4):221-5.

Fine DH, Furgang D, Barnett ML, Drew C, Steinberg L, Charles CH, Vincent JW (2000 Mar). "Effect of an essential oil-containing antiseptic mouthrinse on plaque and salivary Streptococcus mutans levels," J Clin Periodontol. 27(3):157-61.

Fitzhugh DJ, Shan S, Dewhirst MW, Hale LP (2008 Jul). "Bromelain treatment decreases neutrophil migration to sites of inflammation," Clin Immunol. 128(1):66-74.

Force M, Sparks WS, Ronzio RA (2000 May). "Inhibition of enteric parasites by emulsified oil of oregano in vivo," Phytother Res. 14(3):213-4.

Fowke JH, Morrow JD, Motley S, Bostick RM, Ness RM (2006 Oct). "Brassica vegetable consumption reduces urinary F2-isoprostane levels independent of micronutrient intake," Carcinogenesis. 27(10):2096-102.

Franek KJ, Zhou Z, Zhang WD, Chen WY (2005 Jan). "In vitro studies of baicalin alone or in combination with Salvia miltiorrhiza extract as a potential anti-cancer agent," Int J Oncol. 26(1):217-24.

Frangou S, Lewis M, McCrone P (2006 Jan). "Efficacy of ethyl-eicosapentaenoic acid in bipolar depression: randomised double-blind placebo-controlled study," Br J Psychiatry. 188:46-50.

Freise J, Köhler S (1999 Mar). "Peppermint oil-caraway oil fixed combination in non-ulcer dyspepsia--comparison of the effects of enteric preparations," Pharmazie. 54(3):210-5.

Freitas F.P., Freitas S.P., Lemos G.C.S., Vieira I.J.C., Gravina G.A., Lemos F.J.A. (2010) Comparative Larvicial Activity of Essential Oils from Three Medicinal Plants against Aedes aeypti L. Chemistry & Biodiversity. 7: 2801-2807.

Fukumoto S, Sawasaki E, Okuyama S, Miyake Y, Yokogoshi H (2006 Feb-Apr). "Flavor components of monoterpenes in citrus essential oils enhance the release of monoamines from rat brain slices," Nutr Neurosci. 9(1-2):73-80.

Furuhjelm C, Warstedt K, Larsson J, Fredriksson M, Böttcher MF, Fälth-Magnusson K, Duchén K (2009 Sep). "Fish oil supplementation in pregnancy and lactation may decrease the risk of infant allergy," Acta Paediatr. 98(9):1461-7.

Gaetani G.F., Ferraris A.M., Rolfo M., Mangerini R., Arena S., Kirkman H.N. (1996) Predominant role of catalase in the disposal of hydrogen peroxide within human erythrocytes. Blood. 87: 1595-1599.

Gaunt L.F., Higgins S.C., Hughes J.F. (2005) Interaction of air ions and bactericidal vapours to control micro-organisms. Journal of Applied Microbiology. 99: 1324-1329.

Gayathri B, Manjula N, Vinaykumar KS, Lakshmi BS, Balakrishnan A (2007 Apr). "Pure compound from Boswellia serrata extract exhibits anti-inflammatory property in human PBMCs and mouse macrophages through inhibition of TNFalpha, IL-1beta, NO and MAP kinases," Int Immunopharmacol. 7(4):473-82.

Ghelardini C, Galeotti N, Di Cesare Mannelli L, Mazzanti G, Bartolini A (2001 May-Jul). "Local anaesthetic activity of beta-caryophyllene," Farmaco. 56(5-7):387-9.

Ghelardini C, Galeotti N, Mazzanti G (2001 Aug). "Local anaesthetic activity of monoterpenes and phenylpropanes of essential oils," Planta Med. 67(6):564-6.

Ghelardini C, Galeotti N, Salvatore G, Mazzanti G (1999 Dec). "Local anaesthetic activity of the essential oil of Lavandula angustifolia," Planta Med. 65(8):700-3.

Ghersetich I, Lotti T, Campanile G, Grappone C, Dini G (1994 Feb). "Hyaluronic acid in cutaneous intrinsic aging," Int J Dermatol. 33(2):119-22.

Göbel H, Schmidt G, Soyka D (1994 Jun). "Effect of peppermint and eucalyptus oil preparations on neurophysiological and experimental algesimetric headache parameters," Cephalalgia. 14(3):228-34.

Goel A, Ahmad FJ, Singh RM, Singh GN (2010 Feb). "3-Acetyl-11-keto-beta-boswellic acid loaded-polymeric nanomicelles for topical anti-inflammatory and anti-arthritic activity," J Pharm Pharmacol. 62(2):273-8.

Golab M, Skwarlo-Sonta K (2007 Mar). "Mechanisms involved in the anti-inflammatory action of inhaled tea tree oil in mice," Exp Biol Med (Maywood). 232(3):420-6.

Gomes NM, Rezende CM, Fontes SP, Matheus ME, Fernandes PD. (2007 Feb 12). "Antinociceptive activity of Amazonian Copaiba oils," J Ethnopharmacol. 109(3):486-92.

Goncalves J.C.R., Alves A.M.H., de Araujo A.E.V., Cruz J.S., Araujo D.A.M. (2010) Distinct effects of carvone analogues on the isolated nerve of rats. European Journal of Pharmacology. 645: 108-112.

Goncalves J.C.R., Oliveira F.S., Benedito R.B., de Sousa D.P., de Almeida R.N., Araujo D.A.M. (2008) Antinociceptive Activity of (-)-Carvone: Evidence of Association with Decreased Peripheral Nerve Excitability. Biological and Parmaceutical Bulletin. 31: 1017-1020.

González-Trujano ME, Peña EI, Martínez AL, Moreno J, Guevara-Fefer P, Déciga-Campos M, López-Muñoz FJ (2007 May 22). "Evaluation of the antinociceptive effect of Rosmarinus officinalis L. using three different experimental models in rodents," J Ethnopharmacol. 111(3):476-82.

Goodwin J.S., Atluru D., Sierakowski S., Lianos E.A. (1986) Mechanism of Action of Glucocorticosteroids: Inhibition of T Cell Proliferation and Interleukin 2 Production by Hydrocortisones Is Reversed by Leukotriene B4. Journal of Clinical Investigation. 77: 1244-1250.

Gorwitz R.J., Kruszon-Moran D., McAllister S.K., McQuillan G., McDougal L.K., Fosheim G.E., Jensen B.J., Killgore G., Tenover F.C., Kuehnert M.J. (2008) Changes in the Prevalence of Nasal Colonization with Staphylococcus aureusin the United States, 2001-2004. Journal of Infectious Diseases. 197: 1226-1234.

Grassmann J, Hippeli S, Dornisch K, Rohnert U, Beuscher N, Elstner EF (2000 Feb). "Antioxidant properties of essential oils. Possible explanations for their anti-inflammatory effects," Arzneimittelforschung. 50(2):135-9.

Grassmann J, Hippeli S, Dornisch K, Rohnert U, Beuscher N, Elstner EF (2000 Feb). "Antioxidant properties of essential oils. Possible explanations for their anti-inflammatory effects," Arzneimittelforschung. 50(2):135-9.

Grassmann J, Schneider D, Weiser D, Elstner EF (2001 Oct). "Antioxidative effects of lemon oil and its components on copper induced oxidation of low density lipoprotein," Arzneimittelforschung. 51(10):799-805.

Grigoleit HG, Grigoleit P (2005 Aug). "Peppermint oil in irritable bowel syndrome," Phytomedicine. 12(8):601-6.

Guillemain J, Rousseau A, Delaveau P (1989). "Neurodepressive effects of the essential oil of Lavandula angustifolia Mill," Ann Pharm Fr. 47(6):337-43.

Gundidza M (1993 Nov). "Antimicrobial activity of essential oil from Schinus molle Linn," Cent Afr J Med. 39(11):231-4.

Guo X., Longnecker M.P., Michalek J.E. (2001) Relation of serum tetrachlorodibenzo-p-dioxin concentration to diet among veterans in the Air Force health study with background-level exposure. Journal of Toxicology and Environmental Health, Part A. 63: 159-172.

Gupta A., Myrdal P.B. (2004) Development of perillyl alcohol topical cream formulation. International Journal of Pharmaceutics. 269: 373-383.

Gurney A.M. (1994) Mechanisms of Drug-induced Vasodilation. Journal of Pharmacy and Pharmacology. 46: 242-251.

Haag J.D., Lindstrom M.J., Gould M.N. (1992) Limonene-induced Regression of Mammary Carcinomas. Cancer Research. 52: 4021-4026.

Hadley SK, Gaarder SM (2005 Dec 15). "Treatment of irritable bowel syndrome," Am Fam Physician. 72(12):2501-6.

Hagen TM, Liu J, Lykkesfeldt J, Wehr CM, Ingersoll RT, Vinarsky V, Bartholomew JC, Ames BN. "Feeding acetyl-L-carnitine and lipoic acid to old rats significantly improves metabolic function while decreasing oxidative stress," Proc Natl Acad Sci U S A. 99(4):1870-5.

Hager K, Kenklies M, McAfoose J, Engel J, Münch G (2007). "Alpha-lipoic acid as a new treatment option for Alzheimer's disease--a 48 months follow-up analysis," J Neural Transm Suppl. (72):189-93.

Hajhashemi V, Abbasi N (2008 Mar). "Hypolipidemic activity of Anethum graveolens in rats," Phytother Res. 22(3):372-5.

Hajhashemi V, Ghannadi A, Sharif B (2003 Nov). "Anti-inflammatory and analgesic properties of the leaf extracts and essential oil of Lavandula angustifolia Mill," J Ethnopharmacol. 89(1):67-71.

Hakim IA, Harris RB, Ritenbaugh C (2000). "Citrus peel use is associated with reduced risk of squamous cell carcinoma of the skin," Nutr Cancer. 37(2):161-8.

Hammer KA, Carson CF, Riley TV (2008 Aug). "Frequencies of resistance to Melaleuca alternifolia (tea tree) oil and rifampicin in Staphylococcus aureus, Staphylococcus epidermidis and Enterococcus faecalis," Int J Antimicrob Agents. 32(2):170-3.

Hammer KA, Carson CF, Riley TV (1996 Jun). "Susceptibility of transient and commensal skin flora to the essential oil of Melaleuca alternifolia (tea tree oil)," J Antimicrob Chemother. 24(3):186-9.

Hammer KA, Carson CF, Riley TV (2004 Jun). "Antifungal effects of Melaleuca alternifolia (tea tree) oil and its components on Candida albicans, Candida glabrata and Saccharomyces cerevisiae," J Antimicrob Chemother. 53(6):1081-5.

Hargreaves IP, Lane A, Sleiman PM (2008 Dec 5). "The coenzyme Q(10) status of the brain regions of Parkinson's disease patients," Neurosci Lett. 447(1):17-9.

Hart PH, Brand C, Carson CF, Riley TV, Prager RH, Finlay-Jones JJ (2000 Nov). "Terpinen-4-ol, the main component of the essential oil of Melaleuca alternifolia (tea tree oil), suppresses inflammatory mediator production by activated human monocytes," Inflamm Res. 49(11):619-26.

Hayes AJ, Markovic B (2002 Apr). "Toxicity of Australian essential oil Backhousia citriodora (Lemon myrtle). Part 1. Antimicrobial activity and in vitro cytotoxicity," Food Chem Toxicol. 40(4):535-43.

Hay IC, Jamieson M, Ormerod AD (1998 Nov). "Randomized trial of aromatherapy. Successful treatment for alopecia areata," Arch Dermatol. 135(5):1349-52.

Hayflick L (1979 Jul). "The cell biology of aging," J Invest Dermatol. 73(1):8-14.

Haze S, Sakai K, Gozu Y (2002 Nov). "Effects of fragrance inhalation on sympathetic activity in normal adults," Jpn J Pharmacol 90(3):247-53.

Hazgui S et al. (2008 Apr). "Epigallocatechin-3-gallate (EGCG) inhibits the migratory behavior of tumor bronchial epithelial cells," Respir Res. 9:33.

Helland IB, Smith L, Saarem K, Saugstad OD, Drevon CA (2003 Jan). "Maternal supplementation with very-long-chain n-3 fatty acids during pregnancy and lactation augments children's IQ at 4 years of age," Pediatrics. 111(1):e39-44.

Hiramatsu N, Xiufen W, Takechi R, Itoh Y, Mamo J, Pal S (2004). "Antimutagenicity of Japanese traditional herbs, gennoshoko, yomogi, senburi and iwa-tobacco," Biofactors. 22(1-4):123-5.

Hitokoto H, Morozumi S, Wauke T, Sakai S, Kurata H (1980 Apr). "Inhibitory effects of spices on growth and toxin production of toxigenic fungi," Appl Environ Microbiol. 39(4):818-22.

Hölzle E (1992 Sep). "Pigmented lesions as a sign of photodamage," Br J Dermatol. 17(Suppl 41):48-50.

Hongratanaworakit T (2009 Feb). "Relaxing effect of rose oil on humans," Nat Prod Commun. 4(2):291-6.

Hongratanaworakit T, Buchbauer G (2004 Jul). "Evaluation of the harmonizing effect of ylang-ylang oil on humans after inhalation," Planta Med. 70(7):632-6.

Hongratanaworakit T, Buchbauer G (2006 Sep). "Relaxing effect of ylang ylang oil on humans after transdermal absorption," Phytother Res. 20(9):758-63.

Hostanska K, Daum G, Saller R (2002 Sep-Oct). "Cytostatic and apoptosis-inducing activity of boswellic acids toward malignant cell lines in vitro," Anticancer Res. 22(5):2853-62.

Howard J., Hyman A.A. (2003) Dynamics and mechanics of the microtubule plus end. Nature. 422: 753-758.

Hoya Y, Matsumura I, Fujita T, Yanaga K. (2008 Nov-Dec). "The use of nonpharmacological interventions to reduce anxiety in patients undergoing gastroscopy in a setting with an optimal soothing environment," Gastroenterol Nurs. 31(6):395-9.

Huang L, Abuhamdah S, Howes MJ, Dixon CL, Elliot MS, Ballard C, Holmes C, Burns A, Perry EK, Francis PT, Lees G, Chazot PL (2008 Nov). "Pharmacological profile of essential oils derived from Lavandula angustifolia and Melissa officinalis with anti-agitation properties: focus on ligand-gated channels," J Pharm Pharmacol. 60(11):1515-22.

Huang MT, Badmaev V, Ding Y, Liu Y, Xie JG, Ho CT (2000). "Anti-tumor and anti-carcinogenic activities of triterpenoid, beta-boswellic acid," Biofactors. 13(1-4):225-30.

Hunan Yi Ke Da Xue Xue Bao (1999). "Experimental study on induction of apoptosis of leukemic cells by Boswellia carterii Birdw extractive," Hunan Yi Ke Da Xue Xue Bao. 24(1):23-5.

Hussein G, Miyashiro H, Nakamura N, Hattori M, Kakiuchi N, Shimotohno K (2000 Nov). "Inhibitory effects of sudanese medicinal plant extracts on hepatitis C virus (HCV) protease," Phytother Res. 14(7):510-6.

Idaomar M, El-Hamss R, Bakkali F, Mezzoug N, Zhiri A, Baudoux D, Muñoz-Serrano A, Liemans V, Alonso-Moraga A (2002 Jan 15). "Genotoxicity and antigenotoxicity of some essential oils evaluated by wing spot test of Drosophila melanogaster," Mutat Res. 13(1-2):61-8.

Imai H, Osawa K, Yasuda H, Hamashima H, Arai T, Sasatsu M (2001). "Inhibition by the essential oils of peppermint and spearmint of the growth of pathogenic bacteria," Microbios. 106(Suppl 1):31-9.

Inouye S, Nishiyama Y, Uchida K, Hasumi Y, Yamaguchi H, Abe S (2006 Dec). "The vapor activity of oregano, perilla, tea tree, lavender, clove, and geranium oils against a Trichophyton mentagrophytes in a closed box," J Infect Chemother. 12(6):349-54.
Inouye S, Takizawa T, Yamaguchi H (2001 May). "Antibacterial activity of essential oils and their major constituents against respiratory tract pathogens by gaseous contact," J Antimicrob Chemother. 47(5):565-73.
Inouye S, Yamaguchi H, Takizawa T (2001 Dec). "Screening of the antibacterial effects of a variety of essential oils on respiratory tract pathogens, using a modified dilution assay method," J Infect Chemother. 7(4):251-4.
Iori A, Grazioli D, Gentile E, Marano G, Salvatore G (2005 Apr 20). "Acaricidal properties of the essential oil of Melaleuca alternifolia Cheel (tea tree oil) against nymphs of Ixodes ricinus," Vet Parasitol. 129(1-2):173-6.
Ishida T, Mizushina Y, Yagi S, Irino Y, Nishiumi S, Miki I, Kondo Y, Mizuno S, Yoshida H, Azuma T, Yoshida M (2012). "Inhibitory effects of glycyrrhetinic Acid on DNA polymerase and inflammatory activities," Evid Based Complement Alternat Med. 2012:650514.
Itai T, Amayasu H, Kuribayashi M, Kawamura N, Okada M, Momose A, Tateyama T, Narumi K, Uematsu W, Kaneko S (2000 Aug). "Psychological effects of aromatherapy on chronic hemodialysis patients," Psychiatry Clin Neurosci. 54(4):393-7.
Itai T, Amayasu H, Kuribayashi M, Kawamura N, Okada M, Momose A, Tateyama T, Narumi K, Uematsu W, Kaneko S (2000 Aug). "Psychological effects of aromatherapy on chronic hemodialysis patients," Psychiatry Clin Neurosci. 54(4):393-7.
Jamal A, Javed K, Aslam M, Jafri MA (2006 Jan 16). "Gastroprotective effect of cardamom, Elettaria cardamomum Maton. fruits in rats," J Ethnopharmacol. 103(2):149-53.
Janahmadi M, Niazi F, Danyali S, Kamalinejad M (2006 Mar 8). "Effects of the fruit essential oil of Cuminum cyminum Linn. (Apiaceae) on pentylenetetrazol-induced epileptiform activity in F1 neurones of Helix aspersa," J Ethnopharmacol. 104(1-2):278-82.
Jang M, Cai L, Udeani GO, Slowing KV, Thomas CF, Beecher CW, Fong HH, Farnsworth NR, Kinghorn AD, Mehta RG, Moon RC, Pezzuto JM (1997 Jan 10). "Cancer chemopreventive activity of resveratrol, a natural product derived from grapes," Science. 275 (5297):218-20.
Jefferies H., Coster J., Khalil A., Bot J., McCauley R.D., Hall J.C. (2003) Glutathione. ANZ Journal of Surgery. 73: 517-522.
Jimenez A, Santos A, Alonso G, Vazquez D (1976 Mar 17). "Inhibitors of protein synthesis in eukarytic cells. Comparative effects of some amaryllidaceae alkaloids," Biochim Biophys Acta. 425(3):342-8.
Jing Y, Nakajo S, Xia L, Nakaya K, Fang Q, Waxman S, Han R (1999 Jan). "Boswellic acid acetate induces differentiation and apoptosis in leukemia cell lines," Leuk Res. 23(1):43-50.
Jing Y, Xia L, Han R (1992 Mar). "Growth inhibition and differentiation of promyelocytic cells (HL-60) induced by BC-4, an active principle from Boswellia carterii Birdw," Chin Med Sci J. 7(1):12-5.
Johny AK, Baskaran SA, Charles AS, Amalaradjou MA, Darre MJ, Khan MI, Hoagland TA, Schreiber DT, Donoghue AM, Donoghue DJ, Venkitarayanan K. (2009 Apr). "Prophylactic supplementation of caprylic acid in feed reduces Salmonella enteritidis colonization in commercial broiler chicks," J. Food Prot. 72(4):722-7.
Juergens UR, Stöber M, Schmidt-Schilling L, Kleuver T, Vetter H (1998 Sep 17). "Anti-inflammatory effects of euclyptol (1.8-cineole) in bronchial asthma: inhibition of arachidonic acid metabolism in human blood monocytes ex vivo," Eur J Med Res. 3(9):407-12.
Juergens UR, Stöber M, Vetter H (1998 Dec 16). "The anti-inflammatory activity of L-menthol compared to mint oil in human monocytes in vitro: a novel perspective for its therapeutic use in inflammatory diseases," Eur J Med Res. 3(12):539-45.
Juergens U.R., Dethlefsen U., Steinkamp G., Gillissen A., Repges R., Vetter H. (2003) Anti-inflammatory activity of 1.8-cineol (eucalyptol) in bronchial asthma: a double-blind placebo-controlled trial. Respiratory Medicine. 97: 250-256.
Juglal S, Govinden R, Odhav B (2002 Apr). "Spice oils for the control of co-occurring mycotoxin-producing fungi," J Food Prot. 65(4):683-7.
Jung SH, Kang KD, Ju D, Fawcen RJ, Safa R, Kamalden TA, Osborne NN (2008 Sep). "The flavanoid baicalin counteracts ischemic and oxidative insults to retinal cells and lipid peroxidation to brain membranes," Neurochem Int.
Kadekaro AL, Kanto H, Kavanagh R, Abdel-Malek ZA (2003 Jun). "Significance of the melanocortin 1 receptor in regulating human melanocyte pigmentation, proliferation, and survival," Ann N Y Acad Sci. 994:359-65.
Kambara T, Zhou Y, Kawashima Y, Kishida N, Mizutani K, Ikeda T, Kamayama K (2003). "A New Dermatological Availability of the Flavonoid Fraction from Licorice Roots—Effect on Acne," J Soc Cosmet Chem Jpn. 37(3)179-85.
Kane FM, Brodie EE, Coull A, Coyne L, Howd A, Milne A, Niven CC, Robbins R (2004 Oct 28-Nov 10). "The analgesic effect of odour and music upon dressing change," Br J Nurs. 13(19):S4-12.
Kanehara S, Ohtani T, Uede K, Furukawa F (2007 Dec). "Clinical effects of undershirts coated with borage oil on children with atopic dermatitis: a double-blind, placebo-controlled clinical trial," J Dermatol. 34(12):811-5.
Katdare M, Singhal H, Newmark H, Osborne MP, Telang NT (1997 Jan 1). "Prevention of mammary preneoplastic transformation by naturally-occurring tumor inhibitors," Cancer Lett. 111(1-2):141-7.
Kato K., Cox A.D., Hisaka M.M., Graham S.M., Buss J.E., Der C.J. (1992) Isoprenoid addition to Ras protein is the critical modification for its membrane association and transforming activity. Proc. Natl. Sci. USA. 89: 6403-6407.
Kato T, Hancock RL, Mohammadpour H, McGregor B, Manalo P, Khaiboullina S, Hall MR, Pardini L, Pardini RS (2002 Dec). "Influence of omega-3 fatty acids on the growth of human colon carcinoma in nude mice," Cancer Lett. 187(1-2):169-77.
Kaur M, Agarwal C, Singh RP, Guan X, Dwivedi C, Agarwal R (2005 Feb). "Skin cancer chemopreventive agent, {alpha}-santalol, induces apoptotic death of human epidermoid carcinoma A431 cells via caspase activation together with dissipation of mitochondrial membrane potential and cytochrome c release," Carcinogenesis. 26(2):369-80.
Kee Y, Lin RC, Hsu SC, Scheller RH (1995 May). "Distinct domains of syntaxin are required for synaptic vesicle fusion complex formation and dissociation," Neuron. 14(5):991-8.
Kéita SM, Vincent C, Schmit J, Arnason JT, Bélanger A (2001 Oct). "Efficacy of essential oil of Ocimum basilicum L. and O. gratissimum L. applied as an insecticidal fumigant and powder to control Callosobruchus maculatus (Fab.)," J Stored Prod Res. 37(4):339-349.
Kennedy DO, Little W, Haskell CF, Scholey AB (2006 Feb). "Anxiolytic effects of a combination of Melissa officinalis and Valeriana officinalis during laboratory induced stress," Phytother Res. 20(2):96-102.
Keogh A, Fenton S, Leslie C, Aboyoun C, Macdonald P, Zhao YC, Bailey M, Rosenfeldt F (2003). "Randomised double-blind, placebo-controlled trial of coenzyme Q_{10} therapy in class II and III systolic heart failure," Heart Lung Circ. 12(3):135-41.
Khan AU, Gilani AH (2009 Dec 10). "Antispasmodic and bronchodilator activities of Artemisia vulgaris are mediated through dual blockade of muscarinic receptors and calcium influx," J Ethnopharmacol. 126(3):480-6.
Khatibi A, Haghparast A, Shams J, Dianati E, Komaki A, Kamalinejad M (2008 Dec 19). "Effects of the fruit essential oil of Cuminum cyminum L. on the acquisition and expression of morphine-induced conditioned place preference in mice," Neurosci Lett. 448(1):94-8.
Kheirkhah A, Casas V, Li W, Raju VK, Tseng SC (2007 May). "Corneal manifestations of ocular demodex infestation," Am J Ophthalmol. 143(5):743-749.
Kiecolt-Glaser JK, Graham JE, Malarkey WB, Porter K, Lemeshow S, Glaser R (2008 Apr). "Olfactory influences on mood and autonomic, endocrine, and immune function," Psychoneuroendocrinology. 33(3):328-39.
Kim HM, Cho SH (1999 Feb). "Lavender oil inhibits immediate-type allergic reaction in mice and rats," J Pharm Pharmacol. 51(2):221-6.
Kim MA, Sakong JK, Kim EJ, Kim EH, Kim EH (2005 Feb). "Effect of aromatherapy massage for the relief of constipation in the elderly," Taehan Kanho Hakhoe Chi. 35(1):56-64.
Kim MJ, Nam ES, Paik SI (2005 Feb). "The effects of aromatherapy on pain, depression, and life satisfaction of arthritis patients," Taehan Kanho Hakhoe Chi. 35(1):186-94.
Kite SM, Maher EJ, Anderson K, Young T, Young J, Wood J, Howells N, Bradburn J (1998 May). "Development of an aromatherapy service at a Cancer Centre," Palliat Med. 12(3):171-80.
Kline RM, Kline JJ, Di Palma J, Barbero GJ (2001 Jan). "Enteric-coated, pH-dependent peppermint oil capsules for the treatment of irritable bowel syndrome in children," J Pediatr. 138(1):125-8.
Klug W.S., Cummings M.R., Spencer C., Palladino M.A. Concepts of Genetics. San Francisco: Pearson Custom Publishing, 2009.
Kobayashi Y, Takahashi R, Ogino F (2005 Oct 3). "Antipruritic effect of the single oral administration of German chamomile flower extract and its combined effect with antiallergic agents in ddY mice," J Ethnopharmacol. 101(1-3):308-12.
Koh KJ, Pearce AL, Marshman G, Finlay-Jones JJ, Hart PH (2002 Dec). "Tea tree oil reduces histamine-induced skin inflammation," Br J Dermatol. 147(6):1212-7.
Komiya M, Takeuchi T, Harada E (2006 Sep 25). "Lemon oil vapor causes an anti-stress effect via modulating the 5-HT and DA activities in mice," Behav Brain Res. 172(2):240-9.
Komori T, Fujiwara R, Tanida M, Nomura J (1995 Dec). "Potential antidepressant effects of lemon odor in rats," Eur Neuropsychopharmacol. 5(4):477-80.
Komori T, Fujiwara R, Tanida M, Nomura J, Yokoyama MM (1995 May-Jun). "Effects of citrus fragrance on immune function and depressive states," Neuroimmunomodulation. 2(3):174-80.
Koo HN, Hong SH, Kim CY, Ahn JW, Lee YG, Kim JJ, Lyu YS, Kim HM (2002 Jun). "Inhibitory effect of apoptosis in human astrocytes CCF-STTG1 cells by lemon oil," Pharmacol Res. 45(6):469-73.
Koo HN, Jeong HJ, Kim CH, Park ST, Lee SJ, Seong KK, Lee SK, Lyu YS, Kim HM (2001 Dec). "Inhibition of heat shock-induced apoptosis by peppermint oil in astrocytes," J Mol Neurosci. 17(3):391-6.
Koo HN, Jeong HJ, Kim CH, Park ST, Lee SJ, Seong KK, Lee SK, Lyu YS, Kim HM (2001 Dec). "Inhibition of heat shock-induced apoptosis by peppermint oil in astrocytes," J Mol Neurosci. 17(3):391-6.
Kooncumchoo P, Sharma S, Porter J, Govitrapong P, Ebadi M (2006). "Coenzyme Q(10) provides neuroprotection in iron-induced apoptosis in dopaminergic neurons," J Mol Neurosci. 28(2):125-41.
Kosalec I, Pepeljnjak S, Kustrak D. (2005 Dec). "Antifungal activity of fluid extract and essential oil from anise fruits (Pimpinella anisum L, Apiaceae)," Acta Pharm. 55(4):377-85.
Krishnakumar A, Abraham PM, Paul J, Paulose CS (2009 Sep 15). "Down-regulation of cerebellar 5-HT(2C) receptors in pilocarpine-induced epilepsy in rats: therapeutic role of Bacopa monnieri extract," J Neurol Sci. 284(1-2):124-8.
Krishnakumar A, Nandhu MS, Paulose CS (2009 Oct). "Upregulation of 5-HT2C receptors in hippocampus of pilocarpine-induced epileptic rats: antagonism by Bacopa monnieri," Epilepsy Behav. 16(2):225-30.
Kuettner A, Pieper A, Koch J, Enzmann F, Schroeder S (2005 Feb 28). "Influence of coenzyme Q(10) and cervistatin on the flow-mediated vasodilation of the brachial artery: results of the ENDOTACT study," Int J Cardiol. 98(3):413-9.
Kumar A, Malik F, Bhushan S, Sethi VK, Shahi AK, Kaur J, Taneja SC, Qazi GN, Singh J (2008 Feb 15). "An essential oil and its major constituent isointermedeol induce apoptosis by increased expression of mitochondrial cytochrome c and apical death receptors in human leukaemia HL-60 cells," Chem Biol Interact. 171(3):332-47.
Kumaran AM, D'Souza P, Agarwal A, Bokkolla RM, Balasubramaniam M (2003 Sep). "Geraniol, the putative anthelmintic principle of Cymbopogon martinii," Phytother Res. 17(8):957.
Kuo YM, Hayflick SJ, Gitschier J (2007 Jun). "Deprivation of pantothenic acid elicits a movement disorder and azoospermia in a mouse model of pantothenate kinase-associated neurodegeneration," J Inherit Metab Dis. 30(3):310-7.

Kwieciński J, Eick S, Wójcik K (2009 Apr). "Effects of tea tree (Melaleuca alternifolia) oil on Staphylococcus aureus in biofilms and stationary growth phase," Int J Antimicrob Agents. 33(4):343-7.

Lagouge M et al. (2006 Dec 15). "Resveratrol improves mitochondrial function and protects against metabolic disease by activating SIRT1 and PGC-1alpha," Cell. 127(6):1109-22.

Lahlou S, Figueiredo AF, Magalhães PJ, Leal-Cardoso JH (2002 Dec). "Cardiovascular effects of 1,8-cineole, a terpenoid oxide present in many plant essential oils, in normotensive rats," Can J Physiol Pharmacol. 80(12):1125-31.

Lahlou S., Interaminense L.F.L., Magalhaes P.J.C., Leal-Cardoso J.H., Duarte G.P. (2004) Cardiovascular Effects of Eugenol, a Phenolic Compound Present in Many Plant Essential Oils, in Normotensive Rats. Journal of Cardiovascular Pharmacology. 43: 250-257.

Lambert R.J.W., Skandamis P.N., Coote P.J., Nychas G-J.E. (2001) A study of the minimun inhibitory concentration and mode of action of oregano essential oil, thymol and carvacrol. Journal of Applied Microbiology. 91: 453-462.

Lampronti I, Saab AM, Gambari R (2006 Oct). "Antiproliferative activity of essential oils derived from plants belonging to the Magnoliophyta division," Int J Oncol. 29(4):989-95.

Lantry LE, Zhang Z, Gao F, Crist KA, Wang Y, Kelloff GJ, Lubet RA, You M (1997). "Chemopreventive effect of perillyl alcohol on 4-(methylnitrosamino)-1-(3-pyridyl)-1-butanone induced tumorigenesis in (C3H/HeJ X A/J)F1 mouse lung," J Cell Biochem Suppl. 27:20-5.

Larder B.A., Kemp S.D., Harrigan P.R. (1995) Potential Mechanism for Sustained Antiretroviral Efficacy of AZT-3TC Combination Therapy. Science. 269: 696-699.

Laurent TC, Laurent UB, Frazer JR (1995 May). "Functions of hyaluronan," Ann Rheum Dis. 54(5):429-32.

Lee HS (2005 Apr 6). "Cuminaldehyde: Aldose Reductase and alpha-Glucosidase Inhibitor Derived from Cuminum cyminum L. Seeds," J Agric Food Chem. 53(7):2446-50.

Lee IS, Lee GJ (2006 Feb). "Effects of lavender aromatherapy on insomnia and depression in women college students," Taehan Kanho Hakhoe Chi. 36(1):136-43.

Lee SK, Zhang W, Sanderson BJ (2008 Aug). "Selective growth inhibition of human leukemia and human lymphoblastoid cells by resveratrol via cell cycle arrest and apoptosis induction," J Agric Food Chem. 56(16):7572-7.

Lee SU, Shim KS, Ryu SY, Min YK, Kim SH (2009 Feb). "Machilin A isolated from Myristica fragrans stimulates osteoblast differentiation," Planta Med. 75(2):152-7.

Legault J, Dahl W, Debiton E, Pichette A, Madelmont JC (2003 May). "Antitumor activity of balsam fir oil: production of reactive oxygen species induced by alpha-humulene as possible mechanism of action," Planta Med. 69(5):402-7.

Legault J, Pichette A (2007 Dec). "Potentiating effect of beta-caryophyllene on anticancer activity of alpha-humulene, isocaryophyllene and paclitaxel," J Pharm Pharmacol. 59(12):1643-7.

Lehrner J, Eckersberger C, Walla P, Pötsch G, Deecke L (2000 Oct 1-15). "Ambient odor of orange in a dental office reduces anxiety and improves mood in female patients," Physiol Behav. 71(1-2):83-6.

Lehrner J, Marwinski G, Lehr S, Johren P, Deecke L. (2005 Sep 15). "Ambient odors of orange and lavender reduce anxiety and improve mood in a dental office," Physiol Behav. 86(1-2):92-5.

Letawe C, Boone M, Piérard GE (1998 Mar). "Digital image analysis of the effect of topically applied linoleic acid on acne microcomedones," Clin Exp Dermatol. 23(2):56-8.

Leung LH (1995 Jun). "Pantothenic acid deficiency as the pathogenesis of acne vulgaris," Med Hypotheses. 44(6):490-2.

Lewith GT, Godfrey AD, Prescott P (2005 Aug). "A single-blinded, randomized pilot study evaluating the aroma of Lavandula augustifolia as a treatment for mild insomnia," J Altern Complement Med. 11(4):631-7.

Liapi C, Anifandis G, Chinou I, Kourounakis AP, Theodosopoulos S, Galanopoulou P (2007 Oct). "Antinociceptive properties of 1,8-Cineole and beta-pinene, from the essential oil of Eucalyptus camaldulensis leaves, in rodents," Planta Med. 73(12):1247-54.

Lima CF, Azevedo MF, Araujo R, Fernandes-Ferreira M, Pereira-Wilson C (2006 Aug). "Metformin-like effect of Salvia officinalis (common sage): is it useful in diabetes prevention?," Br J Nutr. 96(2):326-33.

Lin PW, Chan WC, Ng BF, Lam LC (2007 May). "Efficacy of aromatherapy (Lavandula angustifolia) as an intervention for agitated behaviours in Chinese older persons with dementia: a cross-over randomized trial," Int J Geriatr Psychiatry. 22(5):405-10.

Lin PW, Chan WC, Ng BF, Lam LC (2007 May). "Efficacy of aromatherapy (Lavandula angustifolia) as an intervention for agitated behaviours in Chinese older persons with dementia: a cross-over randomized trial," Int J Geriatr Psychiatry. 22(5):405-10.

Lin SC, Chung TC, Lin CC, Ueng TH, Lin YH, Lin SY, Wang LY (2000). "Hepatoprotective effects of Arctium lappa on carbon tetrachloride- and acetaminophen-induced liver damage," Am J Chin Med. 28(2):163-73.

Linck V.M., da Silva A.L., Figueiro M., Piato A.L., Herrmann A.P., Birck F.D., Moreno P.R.H., Elisabetsky E. (2009) Inhaled linalool-induced sedation in mice. Phytomedicine. 16: 303-307.

Lipovac M, Chedraui P, Gruenhut C, Gocan A, Stammler M, Imhof M (2010 Mar). "Improvement of postmenopausal depressive and anxiety symptoms after treatment with isoflavones derived from red clover extracts," Maturitas. 65(3):258-61.

Lis-Balchin M, Hart S (1999 Sep). "Studies on the mode of action of the essential oil of lavender (Lavandula angustifolia P. Miller)," Phytother Res. 13(6):540-2.

Lis-Balchin M, Hart S, Wan Hang Lo B (2002 Aug). "Jasmine absolute (Jasminum grandiflora L.) and its mode of action on guinea-pig ileum in vitro," Phytother Res. 16(5):437-9.

Liu J, Head E, Gharib AM, Yuan W, Ingersoll RT, Hagen TM, Cotman CW, Ames BN (2002 Feb). "Memory loss in old rats is associated with brain mitochondrial decay and RNA/DNA oxidation: partial reversal by feeding acetyl-L-carnitine and/or R-alpha-lipoic acid," Proc Natl Acad Sci U S A. 99(4):2356-61.

Liu J, Killilea DW, Ames BN (2002 Feb 19). "Age-associated mitochondrial oxidative decay: improvement of carnitine acetyltransferase substrate-binding affinity and activity in brain by feeding old rats acetyl-L- carnitine and/or R-alpha-lipoic acid," Proc Natl Acad Sci U S A. 99(4):1876-81.

Liu JH, Chen GH, Yeh HZ, Huang CK, Poon SK (1997 Dec). "Enteric-coated peppermint-oil capsules in the treatment of irritable bowel syndrome: a prospective, randomized trial," J Gastroenterol. 32(6):765-8.

Liu JJ, Nilsson A, Oredsson S, Badmaev V, Duan RD (2002 Oct). "Keto- and acetyl-keto-boswellic acids inhibit proliferation and induce apoptosis in Hep G2 cells via a caspase-8 dependent pathway," Int J Mol Med. 10(4):501-5.

Liu JJ, Nilsson A, Oredsson S, Badmaev V, Zhao WZ, Duan RD (2002 Dec). "Boswellic acids trigger apoptosis via a pathway dependent on caspase-8 activation but independent on Fas/Fas ligand interaction in colon cancer HT-29 cells," Carcinogenesis. 23(12):2087-93.

Loew O. (1900) A New Enzyme of General Occurrence in Organisms. Science. 11: 701-702.

Lohidasan S, Paradkar AR, Mahadik KR (2009 Nov). "Nootropic activity of lipid-based extract of Bacopa monniera Linn. compared with traditional preparation and extracts," J Pharm Pharmacol. 61(11):1537-44.

Loizzo MR, Tundis R, Menichini F, Saab AM, Statti GA, Menichini F (2007 Sep-Oct). "Cytotoxic activity of essential oils from labiatae and lauraceae families against in vitro human tumor models," Anticancer Res. 27(5A):3293-9.

Long J, Gao F, Tong L, Cotman CW, Ames BN, Liu J (2009 Apr). "Mitochondrial decay in the brains of old rats: ameliorating effect of alpha-lipoic acid and acetyl-L-carnitine," Neurochem Res. 34(4):755-63.

Longley D.B., Harkin D.P., Johnston P.G. (2003) 5-Fluorouracil: Mechanisms of Action and Clinical Strategies. Nature Reviews. 3: 330-338.

Loughlin R, Gilmore BF, McCarron PA, Tunney MM (2008 Apr). "Comparison of the cidal activity of tea tree oil and terpinen-4-ol against clinical bacterial skin isolates and human fibroblast cells.," Lett Appl Microbiol. 46(4):428-33.

Lu LJ, Cree M, Josyula S, Nagamani M, Grady JJ, Anderson KE (2000 Mar 1). "Increased urinary excretion of 2-hydroxyestrone but not 16alpha-hydroxyestrone in premenopausal women during a soya diet containing isoflavones," Cancer Res. 60(5):1299-305.

Lucas M, Asselin G, Mérette C, Poulin MJ, Dodin S (2009 Feb). "Ethyl-eicosapentaenoic acid for the treatment of psychological distress and depressive symptoms in middle-aged women: a double-blind, placebo-controlled, randomized clinical trial," Am J Clin Nutr. 89(2):641-51.

Lu M, Battinelli L, Daniele C, Melchioni C, Salvatore G, Mazzanti G (2002 Mar). "Muscle relaxing activity of Hyssopus officinalis essential oil on isolated intestinal preparations," Planta Med. 68(3):213-6.

Lu M, Xia L, Hua H, Jing Y (2008 Feb 15). "Acetyl-keto-beta-boswellic acid induces apoptosis through a death receptor 5-mediated pathway in prostate cancer cells," Cancer Res. 68(4):1180-6.

Lu XQ, Tang FD, Wang Y, Zhao T, Bian RL (2004 Feb). "Effect of Eucalyptus globulus oil on lipopolysaccharide-induced chronic bronchitis and mucin hypersecretion in rats," Zhongguo Zhong Yao Za Zhi. 29(2):168-71.

Maatta-Riihinen KR, Kahkonen MP, Torronen AR, Heinonen IM (2005 Nov 2). "Catechins and procyanidins in berries of vaccinium species and their antioxidant activity," J Agric Food Chem. 53(22):8485-91.

Mabrok HB, Klopfleisch R, Ghanem KZ, Clavel T, Blaut M, Loh G (2012 Jan). "Lignan transformation by gut bacteria lowers tumor burden in a gnotobiotic rat model of breast cancer," Carcinogenesis. 33(1):203-8.

Maddocks-Jennings W, Wilkinson JM, Cavanagh HM, Shillington D (2009 Apr). "Evaluating the effects of the essential oils Leptospermum scoparium (manuka) and Kunzea ericoides (kanuka) on radiotherapy induced mucositis: a randomized, placebo controlled feasibility study," Eur J Oncol Nurs. 13(2):87-93.

Mahesh A, Jeyachandran R, Cindrella L, Thangadurai D, Veerapur VP, Muralidhara Rao D (2010 Jun). "Hepatocurative potential of sesquiterpene lactones of Taraxacum officinale on carbon tetrachloride induced liver toxicity in mice," Acta Biol Hung. 61(2):175-90.

Malaguarnera M, Cammalleri L, Gargante MP, Vacante M, Colonna V, Motta M (2007 Dec). "L-Carnitine treatment reduces severity of physical and mental fatigue and increases cognitive functions in centenarians: a randomized and controlled clinical trial," Am J Clin Nutr. 86(6):1738-44.

Mandel S, Stoner GD (1990 Jan). "Inhibition of N-nitrosobenzylmethylamine-induced esophageal tumorigenesis in rats by ellagic acid," Carcinogenisis. 11(1):55-61.

Manohar V, Ingram C, Gray J, Talpur NA, Echard BW, Bagchi D, Preuss HG (2001 Dec). "Antifungal activities of origanum oil against Candida albicans," Mol Cell Biochem. 228(1-2):111-7.

Maquart FX, Siméon A, Pasco S, Monboisse JC (1999). "[Regulation of cell activity by the extracellular matrix: the concept of matrikines]," J Soc Biol. 193(4-5):423-8.

Marder M, Viola H, Wasowski C, Fernández S, Medina JH, Paladini AC (2003 Jun). "6-methylapigenin and hesperidin: new valeriana flavonoids with activity on the CNS," Pharmacol Biochem Behav. 75(3):537-45.

Marounek M, Skrivanova E, Rada V, (2003). "Susceptibility of Escherichia coli to C2-C18 fatty acids," Folia Microbiol (Praha). 48(6):731-5.

Maruyama N, Sekimoto Y, Ishibashi H, Inouye S, Oshima H, Yamaguchi H, Abe S (2005 Feb 10). "Suppression of neutrophil accumulation in mice by cutaneous application of geranium essential oil," J Inflamm (Lond). 2(1):1.

Masukawa Y., Narita H., Sato H., Naoe A., Kondo N., Sugai Y., Oba T., Homma R., Ishikawa J., Takagi Y., Kitahara T. (2009) Comprehensive quantification of ceramide species in human stratum corneum. Journal of Lipid Research. 50: 1708-1719.

May B, Kuntz HD, Kieser M, Köhler S (1996 Dec). "Efficacy of a fixed peppermint oil/caraway oil combination in non-ulcer dyspepsia," Arzneimittelforschung. 46(12):1149-53.

McCord J.M., Fridovich I. (1969) Superoxide Dismutase: an enzymic function for erytrocuprein (hemocuprein). The Journal of Biological Chemistry. 244: 6049-6055.

Meier B, Berger D, Hoberg E, Sticher O, Schaffner W, (2000). "Pharmacological Activities of Vitex agnus-castus Extracts in Vitro," Phytomedicine. 7(5):373-81.

Melov S., Ravenscroft J., Malik S., Gill M.S., Walker D.W., Clayton P.E., Wallace D.C., Malfroy B., Doctrow S.R., Lithgow G.J. (2000) Extension of Life-Span with Superoxide Dismutase/Catalase Mimetics. Science. 289: 1567-1569.

Meldrum B.S. (1994) The role of glutamate in epilepsy and other CNS disorders. Neurology. 44: S14-S23.

Meldrum B.S., Akbar M.T., Chapman A.G. (1999) Glutamate receptors and transporters in genetic and acquired models of epilepsy. Epilepsy Research. 36: 189-204.

Mercier B., Prost J., Prost M. (2009) The Essential Oil of Turpentine and Its Major Volatile Fraction (α- and β-Pinenes): A Review. International Journal of Occupational Medicine and Environmental Health. 22: 331-342.

Mills JJ, Chari RS, Boyer IJ, Gould MN, Jirtle RL (1995 Mar 1). "Induction of apoptosis in liver tumors by the monoterpene perillyl alcohol," Cancer Res. 55(5):979-83.

Mimica-Dukić N, Bozin B, Soković M, Mihajlović B, Matavulj M (2003 May). "Antimicrobial and antioxidant activities of three Mentha species essential oils," Planta Med. 69(5):413-9.

Miocinovic R et al. (2005 Jan). "In vivo and in vitro effect of baicalin on human prostate cancer cells," Int J Oncol. 26(1):241-6.

Mkolo MN, Magano SR (2007 Sep). "Repellent effects of the essential oil of Lavendula angustifolia against adults of Hyalomma marginatum rufipes," J S Afr Vet Assoc. 78(3):149-52.

Mohsenzadeh M (2007 Oct 15). "Evaluation of antibacterial activity of selected Iranian essential oils against Staphylococcus aureus and Escherichia coli in nutrient broth medium," Pak J Biol Sci. 10(20):3693-7.

Mondello F, De Bernardis F, Girolamo A, Cassone A, Salvatore G (2006 Nov 3). "In vivo activity of terpinen-4-ol, the main bioactive component of Melaleuca alternifolia Cheel (tea tree) oil against azole-susceptible and -resistant human pathogenic Candida species," BMC Infect Dis. 6:158.

Moon HJ, Park KS, Ku MJ, Lee MS, Jeong SH, Imbs TI, Zvyagintseva TN, Ermakova SP, Lee YH (2009 Oct). "Effect of Costaria costata fucoidan on expression of matrix metalloproteinase-1 promoter, mRNA, and protein," J Nat Prod. 72(10):1731-4.

Moore LE, Brennan P, Karami S, Hung RJ, Hsu C, Boffetta P, Toro J, Zaridze D, Janout V, Bencko V, Navratilova M, Szeszenia-Dabrowska N, Mates D, Mukeria A, Holcatova I, Welch R, Chanock S, Rothman N, Chow WH (2007 Sep). "Glutathione S-transferase polymorphisms, cruciferous vegetable intake and cancer risk in the Central and Eastern European Kidney Cancer Study," Carcinogenesis. 28(9):1960-4.

Moon T, Wilkinson JM, Cavanagh HM (2006 Nov). "Antiparasitic activity of two Lavandula essential oils against Giardia duodenalis, Trichomonas vaginalis and Hexamita inflata," Parasitol Res. 99(6):722-8.

Moreno S, Scheyer T, Romano CS, Vojnov AA (2006 Feb). "Antioxidant and antimicrobial activities of rosemary extracts linked to their polyphenol composition," Free Radic Res. 40(2):223-31.

Moretti MD, Sanna-Passino G, Demontis S, Bazzoni E (2002). "Essential oil formulations useful as a new tool for insect pest control," AAPS PharmSciTech. 3(2):E13.

Morinobu A et al. (2008 Jul). "-Epigallocatechin-3-gallate suppresses osteoclast differentiation and ameliorates experimental arthritis in mice," Arthritis Rheum. 58(7):2012-8.

Mori TA, Bao DQ, Burke V, Puddey IB, Beilin LJ (1999 Aug). "Docosahexaenoic acid but not eicosapentaenoic acid lowers ambulatory blood pressure and heart rate in humans," Hypertension. 34(2):253-60.

Morris MC, Sacks F, Rosner B (1993 Aug). "Does fish oil lower blood pressure? A meta-analysis of controlled trials," Circulation. 88(2):523-33.

Morse M.A., Stoner G.D. (1993) Cancer chemoprevention: principles and prospects. Carcinogenesis. 14: 1737-1746.

Moss M, Cook J, Wesnes K, Duckett P (2003 Jan). "Aromas of rosemary and lavender essential oils differentially affect cognition and mood in healthy adults," Int J Neurosci. 113(1):15-38.

Moss M, Hewitt S, Moss L, Wesnes K (2008 Jan). "Modulation of cognitive performance and mood by aromas of peppermint and ylang-ylang," Int J Neurosci. 118(1):59-77.

Motomura N, Sakurai A, Yotsuya Y (2001 Dec). "Reduction of mental stress with lavender odorant," Percept Mot Skills. 93(3):713-8.

Motomura N, Sakurai A, Yotsuya Y (2001 Dec). "Reduction of mental stress with lavender odorant," Percept Mot Skills. 93(3):713-8.

Moussaieff A, Rimmerman N, Bregman T, Straiker A, Felder CC, Shoham S, Kashman Y, Huang SM, Lee H, Shohami E, Mackie K, Caterina MJ, Walker JM, Fride E, Mechoulam R (2008 Aug). "Incensole acetate, an incense component, elicits psychoactivity by activating TRPV3 channels in the brain," FASEB J. 22(8):3024-34.

Moussaieff A, Shein NA, Tsenter J, Grigoriadis S, Simeonidou C, Alexandrovich AG, Trembovler V, Ben-Neriah Y, Schmitz ML, Fiebich BL, Munoz E, Mechoulam R, Shohami E (2008 Jul). "Incensole acetate: a novel neuroprotective agent isolated from Boswellia carterii," J Cereb Blood Flow Metab. 28(7):1341-52.

Moy KA, Yuan JM, Chung FL, Wang XL, Van Den Berg D, Wang R, Gao YT, Yu MC (2009 Dec 1). "Isothiocyanates, glutathione S-transferase M1 and T1 polymorphisms and gastric cancer risk: a prospective study of men in Shanghai, China," Int J Cancer. 125(11):2652-9.

Muhlbauer R.C., Lozano A., Palacio S., Reinli A., Felix R. (2003) Common herbes, essential oils, and monoterpenes potently modulate bone metabolism. Bone. 32: 372-380.

Mukherjee P.K., Chandra J., Kuhn D.M., Ghannoum M.A. (2003) Mechanism of Fluconazole Resistance in Candida albicansBiofilms: Phase-Specific Role of Efflux Pumps and Membrane Sterols. Infection and Immunity. 71: 4333-4340.

Mumcuoglu KY, Magdassi S, Miller J, Ben-Ishai F, Zentner G, Helbin V, Friger M, Kahana F, Ingber A (2004 Dec). "Repellency of citronella for head lice: double-blind randomized trial of efficacy and safety," Isr Med Assoc J. 6(12):756-9.

Munzel T., Feil R., Mulsch A., Lohmann S.M., Hofmann F., Walter U. (2003) Physiology and Pathophysiology of Vascular Signaling Controlled by Cyclic Guanosine 3',5'–Cyclic Monophospate—Dependent Protein Kinase. Circulation. 108: 2172-2183.

Naguib YM (2000 Apr). "Antioxidant activities of astaxanthin and related carotenoids," J Agric Food Chem. 48(4):1150-4.

Na HJ, Koo HN, Lee GG, Yoo SJ, Park JH, Lyu YS, Kim HM (2001 Dec). "Juniper oil inhibits the heat shock-induced apoptosis via preventing the caspase-3 activation in human astrocytes CCF-STTG1 cells," Clin Chim Acta. 314(1-2):215-20.

Nair B (2001). "Final report on the safety assessment of Mentha Piperita (Peppermint) Oil, Mentha Piperita (Peppermint) Leaf Extract, Mentha Piperita (Peppermint) Leaf, and Mentha Piperita (Peppermint) Leaf Water," Int J Toxicol. 20(Suppl 3):61-73..

Nair MK, Joy J, Vasudevan P, Hinckley L, Hoagland TA, Venkitanarayanan KS (2009 Mar 30). "Antibacterial effect of caprylic acid and monocaprylin on major bacterial mastitis pathogens," Vet Microbiol. 135(3-4):358-62.

Nanthakomon T, Pongrojpaw D (2006 Oct). "The efficacy of ginger in prevention of postoperative nausea and vomiting after major gynecologic surgery," J Med Assoc Thai. 89(4):S130-6.

Narishetty S.T.K., Panchagnula R. (2004) Transdermal delivey of zidovudine: effect of terpenes and their mechanism of action. Journal of Controlled Release. 95: 367-379.

Narishetty S.T.K., Panchagnula R. (2005) Effects of L-menthol and 1,8-cineole on phase behavior and molecular organization of SC lipids and skin permeation of zidovudine. Journal of Controlled Release. 102: 59-70.

Nasel C, Nasel B, Samec P, Schindler E, Buchbauer G (1994 Aug). "Functional imaging of effects of fragrances on the human brain after prolonged inhalation," Chem Senses. 19(4):359-64.

Navarro SL, Chang JL, Peterson S, Chen C, King IB, Schwarz Y, Li SS, Li L, Potter JD, Lampe JW (2009 Nov). "Modulation of human serum glutathione S-transferase A1/2 concentration by cruciferous vegetables in a controlled feeding study is influenced by GSTM1 and GSTT1 genotypes," Cancer Epidemiol Biomarkers Prev. 18(11):2974-8.

Navarro SL, Peterson S, Chen C, Makar KW, Schwarz Y, King IB, Li SS, Li L, Kestin M, Lampe JW. (2009 Apr). "Cruciferous vegetable feeding alters UGT1A1 activity: diet- and genotype-dependent changes in serum bilirubin in a controlled feeding trial," Cancer Prev Res (Phila Pa). 2(4):345-52.

Nielsen FH, Hunt CD, Mullen LM, Hunt JR (1987 Nov). "Effect of dietary boron on mineral, estrogen, and testosterone metabolism in postmenopausal women," FASEB J. 1(5):394-7.

Nikolaevski VV, Kononova NS, Pertsovski AI, Shinkarchuk IF (1990 Sep-Oct). "Effect of essential oils on the course of experimental atherosclerosis," Patol Fiziol Eksp Ter. (5):52-3.

Ninomiya K, Matsuda H, Shimoda H, Nishida N, Kasajima N, Yoshino T, Morikawa T, Yoshikawa M (2004 Apr 19). "Carnosic acid, a new class of lipid absorption inhibitor from sage," Bioorg Med Chem Lett. 14(8):1943-6.

Nishio M, Kawmata H, Fujita K, Ishizaki T, Hayman R, Idemi T (2004). "A new enamel restoring agent for use after PMTC," Journal of Dental Research 83(1920):SpclIssueA.

Nostro A, Bisignano G, Angela Cannatelli M, Crisafi G, Paola Germanò M, Alonzo V (2001 Jun). "Effects of Helichrysum italicum extract on growth and enzymatic activity of Staphylococcus aureus," Int J Antimicrob Agents. 17(6):517-20.

Nostro A, Blanco AR, Cannatelli MA, Enea V, Flamini G, Morelli I, Sudano Roccaro A, Alonzo V (2004 Jan 30). "Susceptibility of methicillin-resistant staphylococci to oregano essential oil, carvacrol and thymol," FEMS Microbiol Lett. 230(2):191-5.

Nostro A, Cannatelli MA, Marino A, Picerno I, Pizzimenti FC, Scoglio ME, Spataro P (2003 Jan). "Evaluation of antiherpesvirus-1 and genotoxic activities of Helichrysum italicum extract," New Microbiol. 26(1):125-8.

Nothlings U, Murphy SP, Wilkens LR, Henderson BE, Kolonel LN (2007 Oct). "Flavonols and pancreatic cancer risk: the multiethnic cohort study," Am J Epidemiol. 166(8):924-31.

Ohno T, Kita M, Yamaoka Y, Imamura S, Yamamoto T, Mitsufuji S, Kodama T, Kashima K, Imanishi J (2003 Jun). "Antimicrobial activity of essential oils against Helicobacter pylori," Helicobacter. 8(3):207-15.

Olajide OA, Ajayi FF, Ekhelar AI, Awe SO, Makinde JM, Alada AR (1999 Jun). "Biological effects of Myristica fragrans (nutmeg) extract," Phytother Res. 13(4):344-5.

Onawunmi GO, Yisak WA, Ogunlana EO (1984 Dec). "Antibacterial constituents in the essential oil of Cymbopogon citratus (DC.) Stapf.," J Ethnopharmacol. 12(3):279-86.

Opalchenova G, Obreshkova D (2003 Jul). "Comparative studies on the activity of basil--an essential oil from Ocimum basilicum L.--against multidrug resistant clinical isolates of the genera Staphylococcus, Enterococcus and Pseudomonas by using different test methods," J Microbiol Methods. 54(1):105-10.

Orafidiya LO, Agbani EO, Abereoje OA, Awe T, Abudu A, Fakoya FA (2003 Oct). "An investigation into the wound-healing properties of essential oil of Ocimum gratissimum linn," J Wound Care. 12(9):331-4.

Osher Y, Bersudsky Y, Belmaker RH (2005 Jun). "Omega-3 eicosapentaenoic acid in bipolar depression: report of a small open-label study," J Clin Psychiatry. 66(6):726-9.

Ostad SN, Soodi M, Shariffzadeh M, Khorshidi N, Marzban H (2001 Aug). "The effect of fennel essential oil on uterine contraction as a model for dysmenorrhea, pharmacology and toxicology study," J Ethnopharmacol. 76(3):299-304.

Paliwal S, J Sundaram and S Mitragotri (2005). "Induction of cancer-specific cytotoxicity towards human prostate and skin cells using quercetin and ultrasound," British Journal of Cancer. 92:499-502.

Palozza P, Krinsky NI (1992 Sep). "Astaxanthin and canthaxanthin are potent antioxidants in a membrane model," Arch Biochem Biophys. 297(2):291-5.

Paoletti P., Neyton J. (2007) NMDA receptor subunits: functions and pharmacology. Current Opinion in Pharmacology. 7: 39-47.

Park SY, Kim HS, Cho EK, Kwon BY, Phark S, Hwang KW, Sul D (2008 Aug). "Curcumin protected PC12 cells against beta-amyloid-induced toxicity through the inhibition of oxidative damage and tau hyperphosphorylation," Food Chem Toxicol. 46(8):2881-7.

Pavela R (2005 Dec). "Insecticidal activity of some essential oils against larvae of Spodoptera littoralis," Fitoterapia. 76(7-8):691-6.

Pavela R (2008 Feb). "Insecticidal properties of several essential oils on the house fly (Musca domestica L.)," Phytother Res. 22(2):274-8.

Peana AT, D'Aquila PS, Panin F, Serra G, Pippia P, Moretti MD (2002 Dec). "Anti-inflammatory activity of linalool and linalyl acetate constituents of essential oils," Phytomedicine. 9(8):721-6.
Peana A.T., D'Aquila P.S., Chessa M. L., Moretti M.D.L., Serra G., Pippia P. (2003) (-)-Linalool produces antinociception in two experimental models of pain. European Journal of Pharmacology. 460: 37-41.
Pearce AL, Finlay-Jones JJ, Hart PH (2005 Jan). "Reduction of nickel-induced contact hypersensitivity reactions by topical tea tree oil in humans," Inflamm Res. 54(1):22-30.
Pemberton E, Turpin PG (2008 Mar-Apr). "The effect of essential oils on work-related stress in intensive care unit nurses," Holist Nurs Pract. 22(2):97-102.
Penalvo JL, Lopez-Romero P (2012 Feb 29). "Urinary enterolignan concentrations are positively associated with serum HDL cholesterol and negatively associated with serum triglycerides in U.S. adults," J Nutr. [Epub ahead of print].
Peng SM, Koo M, Yu ZR (2009 Jan). "Effects of music and essential oil inhalation on cardiac autonomic balance in healthy individuals," J Altern Complement Med. 15(1):53-7.
Perry N, Perry E (2006). "Aromatherapy in the management of psychiatric disorders: clinical and neuropharmacological perspectives," CNS Drugs. 20(4):257-80.
Peters G.J., Backus H.H.J., Freemantle S., van Triest B., Codacci-Pisanelli G., van der Wilt C.L., Smid K., Lunec J., Calvert A.H., Marsh S., McLeod H.L., Bloemena E., Meijer S., Jansen G., van Groeningen C.J., Pinedo H.M. (2002) Induction of thymidylate synthase as a 5-fluorouracil resistance mechanism. Biochimica et Biophysica Acta. 1587: 194-205.
Pevsner J, Hsu SC, Braun JE, Calakos N, Ting AE, Bennett MK, Scheller RH (1994 Aug). "Specificity and regulation of a synaptic vesicle docking complex," Neuron. 13(2):353-61.
Piazza GA, Ritter JL, Baracka CA (1995 Jan). "Lysophosphatidic acid induction of transforming growth factors alpha and beta: modulation of proliferation and differentiation in cultured human keratinocytes and mouse skin," Exp Cell Res. 216(1):51-64.
Pichette A, Larouche PL, Lebrun M, Legault J (2006 May). "Composition and antibacterial activity of Abies balsamea essential oil," Phytother Res. 20(5):371-3.
Pietruck F, Busch S, Virchow S, Brockmeyer N, Siffert W (1997 Jan). "Signalling properties of lysophosphatidic acid in primary human skin fibroblasts: role of pertussis toxin-sensitive GTP-binding proteins," Naunyn Schmiedebergs Arch Pharmacol. 355(1):1-7.
Pina-Vaz C, Gonçalves Rodrigues A, Pinto E, Costa-de-Oliveira S, Tavares C, Salgueiro L, Cavaleiro C, Gonçalves MJ, Martinez-de-Oliveira J (2004 Jan). "Antifungal activity of Thymus oils and their major compounds," J Eur Acad Dermatol Venereol. 18(1):73-8.
Ping H, Zhang G, Ren G (2010 Aug-Sep). "Antidiabetic effects of cinnamon oil in diabetic KK-Ay mice," Food Chem Toxicol. 48(8-9):2344-9.
Pistone G, Marino A, Leotta C, Dell'Arte S, Finocchiaro G, Malaguarnera M (2003). "Levocarnitine administration in elderly subjects with rapid muscle fatigue: effect on body composition, lipid profile and fatigue," Drugs Aging. 20(10):761-7.
Preuss HG, Echard B, Enig M, Brook I, Elliott TB (2005 Apr). "Minimum inhibitory concentrations of herbal essential oils and monolaurin for gram-positive and gram-negative bacteria," Mol Cell Biochem. 272(1-2):29-34.
Preuss HG, Echard B, Enig M, Brook I, Elliott TB (2005 Apr). "Minimum inhibitory concentrations of herbal essential oils and monolaurin for gram-positive and gram-negative bacteria," Mol Cell Biochem. 272(1-2):29-34.
Puatanachokchai R, Kishida H, Denda A, Murata N, Konishi Y, Vinitketkumnuen U, Nakae D (2002 Sep 8). "Inhibitory effects of lemon grass (Cymbopogon citratus, Stapf) extract on the early phase of hepatocarcinogenesis after initiation with diethylnitrosamine in male Fischer 344 rats," Cancer Lett. 183(1):9-15.
Qureshi A.A., Mangels W.R., Din A.A., Elson C.E. (1988) Inhibition of Hepatic Mevalonate Biosynthesis by the Monoterpene, d-Limonene. J. Agric. Food Chem. 36: 1220-1224.
Ragho R., Postlethwaite AE, Keski-Oja J, Moses HL, Kang AH (1987 Apr). "Transforming growth factor-beta increases steady state levels of type I procollagen and fibronectin messenger RNAs posttranscriptionally in cultured human dermal fibroblasts," J Clin Invest. 79(4):1285-8.
Rahman MM, Ichiyanagi T, Komiyama T, Sato S, Konishi T (2008 Aug). "Effects of anthocyanins on psychological stress-induced oxidative stress and neurotransmitter status," J Agric Food Chem. 56(16):7545-50.
Raman A, Weir U, Bloomfield SF (1995 Oct). "Antimicrobial effects of tea-tree oil and its major components on Staphylococcus aureus, Staph. epidermidis and Propionibacterium acnes," Lett Appl Microbiol. 21(4):242-5.
Rao S., Krauss N.E., Heerding J.M., Swindell C.S., Ringel I., Orr G.A., Horwitz S.B. (1994) 3'-(p-Azidobenzamido)taxol Photolabels the N-terminal 31 AminoAcids of β-Tubulin. The Journal of Biological Chemistry. 269: 3132-3134.
Rao S., Orr G.A., Chaudhary A.G., Kingston D.G.I., Horwitz S.B. (1995) Characterization of the Taxol Binding Site on the Microtubule. The Journal of Biological Chemistry. 270: 20235-20238.
Rasooli I, Fakoor MH, Yadegarinia D, Gachkar L, Allameh A, Rezaei MB (2008 Feb 29). "Antimycotoxigenic characteristics of Rosmarinus officinalis and Trachyspermum copticum L. essential oils," Int J Food Microbiol. 122(1-2):135-9.
Rasooli I, Shayegh S, Taghizadeh M, Astaneh SD (2008 Sep). "Phytotherapeutic prevention of dental biofilm formation," Phytother Res. 22(9):1162-7.
Reddy AC, Lokesh BR (1994). "Studies on anti-inflammatory activity of spice principles and dietary n-3 polyunsaturated fatty acids on carrageenan-induced inflammation in rats," Ann Nutr Metab. 38(6):349-58.
Reddy BS, Wang CX, Samaha H, Lubet R, Steele VE, Kelloff GJ, Rao CV (1997 Feb 1). "Chemoprevention of colon carcinogenesis by dietary perillyl alcohol," Cancer Res. 57(3):420-5.
Rees WD, Evans BK, Rhodes J (1979 Oct 6). "Treating irritable bowel syndrome with peppermint oil," Br Med J. 2(6194):835-6.
Reichling J, Fitzi J, Hellmann K, Wegener T, Bucher S, Saller R (2004 Oct). "Topical tea tree oil effective in canine localised pruritic dermatitis--a multi-centre randomised double-blind controlled clinical trial in the veterinary practice," Dtsch Tierarztl Wochenschr. 111(10):408-14.
Reichling J, Koch C, Stahl-Biskup E, Sojka C, Schnitzler P (2005 Dec). "Virucidal activity of a beta-triketone-rich essential oil of Leptospermum scoparium (manuka oil) against HSV-1 and HSV-2 in cell culture," Planta Med. 71(12):1123-7.
Renimel I, Andre P (Inventors) (1995). "Method for treatment of allergic disorders and cosmetic compositions using cucurbitine," USPTO 5714164.
Rhee SG (2006 Jun). "Cell signaling. H2O2, a necessary evil for cell signaling," Science. 312(5782):1882–3.
Rivero-Cruz B, Rojas MA, Rodríguez-Sotres R, Cerda-García-Rojas CM, Mata R (2005 Apr). "Smooth muscle relaxant action of benzyl benzoates and salicylic acid derivatives from Brickellia veronicaefolia on isolated guinea-pig ileum," Planta Med. 71(4):320-5.
Romero-Jiménez M, Campos-Sánchez J, Analla M, Muñoz-Serrano A, Alonso-Moraga A (2005 Aug 1). "Genotoxicity and anti-genotoxicity of some traditional medicinal herbs," Mutat Res. 585(1-2):147-55.
Rosa A, Deiana M, Atzeri A, Corona G, Incani A, Melis MP, Appendino G, Dessì MA (2007 Jan 30). "Evaluation of the antioxidant and cytotoxic activity of arzanol, a prenylated alpha-pyrone-phloroglucinol etherodimer from Helichrysum italicum subsp. microphyllum," Chem Biol Interact. 165(2):117-26.
Rose JE, Behm FM (1994 Feb). "Inhalation of vapor from black pepper extract reduces smoking withdrawal symptoms," Drug Alcohol Depend. 34(3):225-9.
Rowinsky E.K., Donehower R.C. (1995) Paclitaxel (Taxol). The New England Journal of Medicine. 332: 1004-1014.
Roy S, Khanna S, Krishnaraju AV, Subbaraju GV, Yasmin T, Bagchi D, Sen CK (2006 Mar-Apr). "Regulation of vascular responses to inflammation: inducible matrix metalloproteinase-3 expression in human microvascular endothelial cells is sensitive to antiinflammatory Boswellia," Antioxid Redox Signal. 8(3-4):653-60.
Roy S, Khanna S, Shah H, Rink C, Phillips C, Preuss H, Subbaraju GV, Trimurtulu G, Krishnaraju AV, Bagchi M, Bagchi D, Sen CK (2005 Apr). "Human genome screen to identify the genetic basis of the anti-inflammatory effects of Boswellia in microvascular endothelial cells," DNA Cell Biol. 24(4):244-55.
Roy S, Khanna S, Alessio HM, Vider J, Bagchi D, Bagchi M, Sen CK (2002 Sep). "Anti-angiogenic property of edible berries," Free Radic Res. 36(9):1023-31.
Ruthig DJ, Meckling-Gill KA (1999 Oct). "Both (n-3) and (n-6) fatty acids stimulate wound healing in the rat intestinal epithelial cell line, IEC-6," J Nutr. 129(10):1791-8.
Sadraei H, Asghari GR, Hajhashemi V, Kolagar A, Ebrahimi M. (2001 Sep). "Spasmolytic activity of essential oil and various extracts of Ferula gummosa Boiss. on ileum contractions," Phytomedicine. 8(5):370-6.
Saeed SA, Gilani AH (1994 May). "Antithrombotic activity of clove oil," J Pak Med Assoc. 44(5):112-5.
Saeedi M, Morteza, Semnani K, Ghoreishi MR (2003 Sep). "The treatment of atopic dermatitis with licorice gel," J Dermatolog Treat. 14(3):153-7.
Saerens KM, Zhang J, Saey L, Van Bogaert IN, Soetaert W (2011 Apr). "Cloning and functional characterization of the UDP-glucosyltransferase UgtB1 involved in sophorolipid production by Candida bombicola and creation of a glucolipid-producing yeast strain,' Yeast. 28(4):279-92.
Safayhi H, Sabieraj J, Sailer ER, Ammon HP (1994 Oct). "Chamazulene: an antioxidant-type inhibitor of leukotriene B4 formation," Planta Med. 60(5):410-3.
Saha SS, Ghosh M (2009 Jul 18). "Comparative study of antioxidant activity of alpha-eleostearic acid and punicic acid against oxidative stress generated by sodium arsenite," Food Chem Toxicol. [Epub ahead of print].
Said T, Dutot M, Martin C, Beaudeux JL, Boucher C, Enee E, Baudouin C, Warnet JM, Rat P (2007 Mar). "Cytoprotective effect against UV-induced DNA damage and oxidative stress: role of new biological UV filter," Eur J Pharm Sci. 30(3-4):203-10.
Samarth RM (2007 Nov). "Protection against radiation induced hematopoietic damage in bone marrow of Swiss albino mice by Mentha piperita (Linn)," J Radiat Res (Tokyo). 48(6):523-8.
Samarth RM, Goyal PK, Kumar A (2004 Jul). "Protection of swiss albino mice against whole-body gamma irradiation by Mentha piperita (Linn.).," Phytother Res. 18(7):546-50.
Samarth RM, Kumar A (2003 Jun). "Radioprotection of Swiss albino mice by plant extract Mentha piperita (Linn.)," J Radiat Res (Tokyo). 44(2):101-9.
Samarth RM, Panwar M, Kumar M, Kumar A (2006 May). "Radioprotective influence of Mentha piperita (Linn) against gamma irradiation in mice: Antioxidant and radical scavenging activity," Int J Radiat Biol. 82(5):331-7.
Samarth RM, Samarth M (2009 Apr). "Protection against radiation-induced testicular damage in Swiss albino mice by Mentha piperita (Linn.).," Basic Clin Pharmacol Toxicol. 104(4):329-34.
Samman S, Naghii MR, Lyons Wall PM, Verus AP (1998 Winter). "The nutritional and metabolic effects of boron in humans and animals," Biol Trace Elem Res. 66(1-3):227-35.
Santos AO, Ueda-Nakamura T, Dias Filho BP, Veiga Junior VF, Pinto AC, Nakamura CV (2008 May). "Antimicrobial activity of Brazilian copaiba oils obtained from different species of the Copaifera genus," Mem Inst Oswaldo Cruz. 103(3):277-81.
Santos AO, Ueda-Nakamura T, Dias Filho BP, Veiga Junior VF, Pinto AC, Nakamura CV (2008 Nov 20). "Effect of Brazilian copaiba oils on Leishmania amazonensis," J Ethnopharmacol. 120(2):204-8.
Santos FA, Rao VS (2000 Jun). "Anti-inflammatory and antinociceptive effects of 1,8-cineole a terpenoid oxide present in many plant essential oils," Phytother Res. 14(4):240-4.
Satchell AC, Saurajen A, Bell C, Barnetson RS (2002 Aug). "Treatment of interdigital tinea pedis with 25% and 50% tea tree oil solution: a randomized, placebo-controlled, blinded study," Australas J Dermatol. 43(3):175-8.
Savelev SU, Okello EJ, Perry EK (2004 Apr). "Butyryl- and acetyl-cholinesterase inhibitory activities in essential oils of Salvia species and their constituents," Phytother Res. 18(4):315-24.
Savino F, Cresi F, Castagno E, Silvestro L, Oggero R (2005 Apr). "A randomized double-blind placebo-controlled trial of a standardized extract of Matricariae recutita, Foe-

niculum vulgare and Melissa officinalis (ColiMil) in the treatment of breastfed colicky infants," Phytother Res. 19(4):335-40.

Sayyah M, Nadjafnia L, Kamalinejad M (2004 Oct). "Anticonvulsant activity and chemical composition of Artemisia dracunculus L. essential oil," J Ethnopharmacol. 94(2-3):283-7.

Sayyah M, Saroukhani G, Peirovi A, Kamalinejad M (2003 Aug). "Analgesic and anti-inflammatory activity of the leaf essential oil of Laurus nobilis Linn," Phytother Res. 17(7):733-6.

Sayyah M, Valizadeh J, Kamalinejad M (2002 Apr). "Anticonvulsant activity of the leaf essential oil of Laurus nobilis against pentylenetetrazole- and maximal electroshock-induced seizures," Phytomedicine. 9(3):212-6.

Scalbert A, Johnson IT, and Saltmarsh M (2005 Jan). "Polyphenols: antioxidants and beyond," Presented at the 1st International Conference on Polyphenols and Health, Vichy, France. Am J Clin Nut. 81(1):215S-7S.

Schecter A., Birnbaum L., Ryan J.J., Constable J.D. (2006) Dioxins: An overview. Environmental Research. 101: 419-428.

Scheinfeld NS, Mones J (2005 May). "Granular parakeratosis: pathologic and clinical correlation of 18 cases of granular parakeratosis," J Am Acad Dermatol. 52(5):863-7.

Schlachterman A et al. (2008 Mar). "Combined resveratrol, quercetin, and catechin treatment reduces breast tumor growth in a nude mouse model," Transl Oncol. 1(1):19-27.

Schnitzler P, Schön K, Reichling J (2001 Apr). "Antiviral activity of Australian tea tree oil and eucalyptus oil against herpes simplex virus in cell culture," Pharmazie. 56(4):343-7.

Schnitzler P, Schuhmacher A, Astani A, Reichling J (2008 Sep). "Melissa officinalis oil affects infectivity of enveloped herpesviruses," Phytomedicine. 15(9):734-40.

Schroter A., Kessner D., Kiselev M.A., Haub T., Dante S., Neubert R.H.H. (2009) Basic Nanostructure of Stratum Corneum Lipid Matrices Based on Ceramides [EOS] and [AP]: A Neutron Diffraction Study. Biophysical Journal. 97: 1104-1114.

Schuhmacher A, Reichling J, Schnitzler P (2003). "Virucidal effect of peppermint oil on the enveloped viruses herpes simplex virus type 1 and type 2 in vitro," Phytomedicine. 10(6-7):504-10.

Senapati S, Banerjee S, Gangopadhyay DN (2008 Sep-Oct). "Evening primrose oil is effective in atopic dermatitis: a randomized placebo-controlled trial," Indian J Dermatol Venereol Leprol. 74(5):447-52.

Senni K, Gueniche F, Foucault-Bertaud A, Igondjo-Tchen S, Fioretti F, Colliec-Jouault S, Durand P, Guezennec J, Godeau G, Letourneur D (2006 Jan 1). "Fucoidan a sulfated polysaccharide from brown algae is a potent modulator of connective tissue proteolysis," Arch Biochem Biophys. 445(1):56-64.

Shaikh IA, Brown I, Schofield AC, Wahle KW, Heys SD (2008 Nov). "Docosahexaenoic acid enhances the efficacy of docetaxel in prostate cancer cells by modulation of apoptosis: the role of genes associated with the NF-kappaB pathway," Prostate. 68(15):1635-46.

Shankar GM, Li S, Mehta TH, Garcia-Munoz A, Shepardson NE, Smith I, Brett FM, Farrell MA, Rowan MJ, Lemere CA, Regan CM, Walsh DM, Sabatini BL, Selkoe DJ (2008 Jun 22). "Amyloid-protein dimers isolated directly from Alzheimer's brains impair synaptic plasticity and memory," Nat Med. 14(8):837-42.

Shapiro S., Guggenheim B. (1995) The action of thymol on oral bacteria. Oral Microbiology and Immunology. 10: 241-246.

Shao Y, Ho CT, Chin CK, Badmaev V, Ma W, Huang MT (1998 May). "Inhibitory activity of boswellic acids from Boswellia serrata against human leukemia HL-60 cells in culture," Planta Med. 64(4):328-31.

Shapiro S, Meier A, Guggenheim B (1994 Aug). "The antimicrobial activity of essential oils and essential oil components towards oral bacteria," Oral Microbiol Immunol. 9(4):202-8.

Sharma JN, Srivastava KC, Gan EK (1994 Nov). "Suppressive effects of eugenol and ginger oil on arthritic rats," Pharmacology. 49(5):314-8.

Sharma PR, Mondhe DM, Muthiah S, Pal HC, Shahi AK, Saxena AK, Qazi GN (2009 May 15). "Anticancer activity of an essential oil from Cymbopogon flexuosus," Chem Biol Interact. 179(2-3):160-8.

Shayegh S, Rasooli I, Taghizadeh M, Astaneh SD (2008 Mar 20). "Phytotherapeutic inhibition of supragingival dental plaque," Nat Prod Res. 22(5):428-39.

Shankar S, Ganapathy S, Hingorani SR, Srivastava RK (2008 Jan). "EGCG inhibits growth, invasion, angiogenesis and metastasis of pancreatic cancer," Front Biosci. 13:440-52.

Shen J, Niijima A, Tanida M, Horii Y, Maeda K, Nagai K (2005 Jun 3). "Olfactory stimulation with scent of grapefruit oil affects autonomic nerves, lipolysis and appetite in rats," Neurosci Lett. 380(3):289-94.

Shen J, Niijima A, Tanida M, Horii Y, Maeda K, Nagai K (2005 Jul 22-29). "Olfactory stimulation with scent of lavender oil affects autonomic nerves, lipolysis and appetite in rats," Neurosci Lett. 383(1-2):188-93.

Sherry E, Boeck H, Warnke PH (2001). "Percutaneous treatment of chronic MRSA osteomyelitis with a novel plant-derived antiseptic," BMC Surg. 1:1.

Shetty AV, Thirugnanam S, Dakshinamoorthy G, Samykutty A, Zheng G, Chen A, Bosland MC, Kajdacsy-Balla A, Gnanasekar M (2011 Sep). "18α-glycyrrhetinic acid targets prostate cancer cells by down-regulating inflammation-related genes," In J Oncol. 39(3):635-40.

Shibata M., Ohkubo T., Takahashi H., Inoki R. (1989) Modified formalin test: characteristic biphasic pain response. Pain. 38: 347-352.

Shrivastav P, George K, Balasubramaniam N, Jasper MP, Thomas M, Kanagasabhapathy AS (1988 Feb). "Suppression of puerperal lactation using jasmine flowers (Jasminum sambac)," Aust N Z J Obstet Gynaecol. 28(1):68-71.

Shoskes DA, Zeitlin SI, Shahed A, Rajfer J (1999 Dec). "Quercetin in men with category III prostatitis: a preliminary prospective, double-blind, placebo-controlled trial," Urology. 54(6):960-3.

Sies H (1997). "Oxidative stress: oxidants and antioxidants," Exp Physiol. 82(2):291–5.

Sikkema J., de Bont J.A.M., Poolman B. (1995) Mechanisms of Membrane Toxicity of Hydrocarbons. Microbiological Reviews. 59: 201-222.

Silva Brum L.F., Emanuelli T., Souza D.O., Elisabetsky E. (2001) Effects of Linalool on Glutamate Release and Uptake in Mouse Cortical Synaptosomes. Neurochemical Research. 26: 191-194

Silva Brum L.F., Elisabetsky E., Souza D. (2001) Effects of Linalool on [3H] MK801 and [3H] Muscimol Binding in Mouse Cortical Membranes. Phytotherapy Research. 15: 422-425.

Silva J, Abebe W, Sousa SM, Duarte VG, Machado MI, Matos FJ (2003 Dec). "Analgesic and anti-inflammatory effects of essential oils of Eucalyptus," J Ethnopharmacol. 89(2-3):277-83.

Siméon A, Monier F, Emonard H, Gillery P, Birembaut P, Hornebeck W, Maquart FX (1999 Jun). "Expression and activation of matrix metalloproteinases in wounds: modulation by the tripeptide-copper complex glycyl-L-histidyl-L-lysine-Cu2+," J Invest Dermatol. 112(3):957-64.

Singh HB, Srivastava M, Singh AB, Srivastava AK (1995 Dec). "Cinnamon bark oil, a potent fungitoxicant against fungi causing respiratory tract mycoses," Allergy. 50(12):995-9.

Singletary K, MacDonald C, Wallig M (1996 Jun 24). "Inhibition by rosemary and carnosol of 7,12-dimethylbenz[a]anthracene (DMBA)-induced rat mammary tumorigenesis and in vivo DMBA-DNA adduct formation," Cancer Lett. 104(1):43-8.

Siurin SA (1997). "Effects of essential oil on lipid peroxidation and lipid metabolism in patients with chronic bronchitis," Klin Med (Mosk). 75(10):43-5.

Skocibusić M, Bezić N (2004 Dec). "Phytochemical analysis and in vitro antimicrobial activity of two Satureja species essential oils," Phytother Res. 18(12):967-70.

Skrivanova E, Savka OG, Marounek M (2004). "In vitro effect of C2-C18 fatty acids on Salmonellas," Folia Microbiol (Praha). 49(2):199-202.

Skold M, Borje A, Matura M, Karlberg A-T. (2002) Studies on the autoxidation and sensitizing capacity of the fragrance chemical linalool, identifying a linalool hydroperoxide. Contact Dermatitis. 46: 267-272.

Slamenova D, Kuboskova K, Horvathova E, Robichova S. (2002 Mar 28). "Rosemary-stimulated reduction of DNA strand breaks and FPG-sensitive sites in mammalian cells treated with H2O2 or visible light-excited Methylene Blue," Cancer Lett. 177(2):145-53.

Smith DG, Standing L, de Man A (1992 Apr). "Verbal memory elicited by ambient odor," Percept Mot Skills. 74(2):339-43.

Smith-Palmer A, Stewart J, Fyfe L (2004 Oct). "Influence of subinhibitory concentrations of plant essential oils on the production of enterotoxins A and B and alpha-toxin by Staphylococcus aureus," J Med Microbiol. 53(Pt 10):1023-7.

Soares SF, Borges LM, de Sousa Braga R, Ferreira LL, Louly CC, Tresvenzol LM, de Paula JR, Ferri PH (2009 Oct 7). "Repellent activity of plant-derived compounds against Amblyomma cajennense (Acari: Ixodidae) nymphs," Vet Parasitol. Epub ahead of print.

Sorentino S., Landmesser U. (2005) Nonlipid-lowering Effects of Statins. Current Treatment Options to Cardiovascular Medicine. 7: 459-466.

Sriram N, Kalayarasan S, Sudhandiran G (2008 Jul). "Enhancement of antioxidant defense system by epigallocatechin-3-gallate during bleomycin induced experimental Pulmonary Fibrosis," Biol Pharm Bull. 31(7):1306-11.

Stanzl K, Zastrow L, Röding J, Artmann C (1996 Jun). "The effectiveness of molecular oxygen in cosmetic formulations," Int J Cosmet Sci. 18(3):137-50.

Steiner M, Priel I, Giat J, Levy J, Sharoni Y, Danilenko M (2001). "Carnosic acid inhibits proliferation and augments differentiation of human leukemic cells induced by 1,25-dihydroxyvitamin D3 and retinoic acid," Nutr Cancer. 41(1-2):135-44.

Strati A, Papoutsi Z, Lianidou E, Moutsatsou P (2009 Sep). "Effect of ellagic acid on the expression of human telomerase reverse transcriptase (hTERT) alpha+Beta+ transcript in estrogen receptor-positive MCF-7 breast cancer cells," Clin Biochem. 42(13-14):1358-62.

Stratton S.P., Alberts D.S., Einspahr J.G. (2010) A Phase 2a Study of Topical Perillyl Alcohol Cream for Chemoprevention of Skin Cancer. Cancer Prevention Research. 3: 160-169.

Stratton S.P., Saboda K.L., Myrdal P.B., Gupta A., McKenzie N.E., Brooks C., Salasche S.J., Warneke J.A., Ranger-Moore J., Bozzo P.D., Blanchard J., Einspahr J.G. (2008) Phase 1 Study of Topical Perillyl Alcohol Cream for Chemoprevention of Skin Cancer. Nutrition and Cancer. 60: 325-330.

Subash Babu P, Prabuseenivasan S, Ignacimuthu S. (2007 Jan). "Cinnamaldehyde--a potential antidiabetic agent," Phytomedicine. 14(1):15-22.

Südhof TC (1995 Jun 22). "The synaptic vesicle cycle: a cascade of protein-protein interactions," Nature. 375(6533):645-53.

Su KP, Huang SY, Chiu TH, Huang KC, Huang CL, Chang HC, Pariante CM (2008 Apr). "Omega-3 fatty acids for major depressive disorder during pregnancy: results from a randomized, double-blind, placebo-controlled trial," J Clin Psychiatry. 69(4):644-51.

Takaki I, Bersani-Amado LE, Vendruscolo A, Sartoretto SM, Diniz SP, Bersani-Amado CA, Cuman RK (2008 Dec). "Anti-inflammatory and antinociceptive effects of Rosmarinus officinalis L. essential oil in experimental animal models," J Med Food. 11(4):741-6.

Takarada K, Kimizuka R, Takahashi N, Honma K, Okuda K, Kato T (2004 Feb). "A comparison of the antibacterial efficacies of essential oils against oral pathogens," Oral Microbiol Immunol. 19(1):61-4.

Tang J, Wingerchuk DM, Crum BA, Rubin DI, Demaerschalk BM (2007 May). "Alpha-lipoic acid may improve symptomatic diabetic polyneuropathy," Neurologist. 13(3):164-7.

Tanida M, Niijima A, Shen J, Nakamura T, Nagai K (2005 Oct 5). "Olfactory stimulation with scent of essential oil of grapefruit affects autonomic neurotransmission and blood pressure," Brain Res. 1058(1-2):44-55.

Tanida M, Niijima A, Shen J, Nakamura T, Nagai K (2006 May 1). "Olfactory stimulation with scent of lavender oil affects autonomic neurotransmission and blood pressure in rats," Neurosci Lett. 398(1-2):155-60.

Tan P, Zhong W, Cai W (2000 Sep). "Clinical study on treatment of 40 cases of malignant brain tumor by elemene emulsion injection," Zhongguo Zhong Xi Yi Jie He Za Zhi. 20(9):645-8.

Tantaoui-Elaraki A, Beraoud L (1994). "Inhibition of growth and aflatoxin production in Aspergillus parasiticus by essential oils of selected plant materials," J Environ Pathol Toxicol Oncol. 13(1):67-72.
Tao L, Zhou L, Zheng L, Yao M (2006 Jul). "Elemene displays anti-cancer ability on laryngeal cancer cells in vitro and in vivo," Cancer Chemother Pharmacol. 58(1):24-34.
Tare V, Deshpande S, Sharma RN (2004 Oct). "Susceptibility of two different strains of Aedes aegypti (Diptera: Culicidae) to plant oils," J Econ Entomol. 97(5):1734-6.
Tavares AC, Gonçalves MJ, Cavaleiro C, Cruz MT, Lopes MC, Canhoto J, Salgueiro LR (2008 Sep 2). "Essential oil of Daucus carota subsp. halophilus: composition, antifungal activity and cytotoxicity," J Ethnopharmacol. 119(1):129-34.
Terzi V, Morcia C, Faccioli P, Valè G, Tacconi G, Malnati M (2007 Jun). "In vitro antifungal activity of the tea tree (Melaleuca alternifolia) essential oil and its major components against plant pathogens," Lett Appl Microbiol. 44(6):613-8.
Thavara U, Tawatsin A, Bhakdeenuan P, Wongsinkongman P, Boonruad T, Bansiddhi J, Chavalittumrong P, Komalamisra N, Siriyasatien P, Mulla MS (2007 Jul). "Repellent activity of essential oils against cockroaches (Dictyoptera: Blattidae, Blattellidae, and Blaberidae) in Thailand," Southeast Asian J Trop Med Public Health. 38(4):663-73.
Tiano L, Belardinelli R, Carnevali P, Principi F, Seddaiu G, Littarru GP (2007 Sep). "Effect of coenzyme Q10 administration on endothelial function and extracellular superoxide dismutase in patients with ischaemic heart disease: a double-blind, randomized controlled study," Eur Heart J. 28(18):2249-55.
Tildesley NT, Kennedy DO, Perry EK, Ballard CG, Wesnes KA, Scholey AB (2005 Jan 17). "Positive modulation of mood and cognitive performance following administration of acute doses of Salvia lavandulaefolia essential oil to healthy young volunteers," Physiol Behav. 83(5):699-709.
Tipton DA, Hamman NR, Dabbous MKh (2006 Mar). "Effect of myrrh oil on IL-1beta stimulation of NF-kappaB activation and PGE(2) production in human gingival fibroblasts and epithelial cells," Toxicol In Vitro. 20(2):248-55.
Tipton DA, Lyle B, Babich H, Dabbous MKh (2003 Jun). "In vitro cytotoxic and anti-inflammatory effects of myrrh oil on human gingival fibroblasts and epithelial cells," Toxicol In Vitro. 17(3):301-10.
Tognolini M, Ballabeni V, Bertoni S, Bruni R, Impicciatore M, Barocelli E (2007 Sep). "Protective effect of Foeniculum vulgare essential oil and anethole in an experimental model of thrombosis," Pharmacol Res. 56(3):254-60.
Tortora G.J., Funke B.R., Case C.L. Microbiology: An Introduction. 9th ed. San Francisco: Pearson Benjamin Cummings, 2007.
Traka M, Gasper AV, Melchini A, Bacon JR, Needs PW, Frost V, Chantry A, Jones AM, Ortori CA, Barrett DA, Ball RY, Mills RD, Mithen RF (2008 Jul 2). "Broccoli consumption interacts with GSTM1 to perturb oncogenic signalling pathways in the prostate," PLoS One. 3(7):e2568.
Tran KT, Griffith L, Wells A (2004 May-Jun). "palmitoyl-glycyl-histidyl-lysine," Wound Repair Regen. 12(3):262-8.
Trautmann M, Peskar BM, Peskar BA (1991 Aug 16). "Aspirin-like drugs, ethanol-induced rat gastric injury and mucosal eicosanoid release," Eur J Pharmacol. 201(1):53-8.
Trigg JK (1996 Jun). "Evaluation of a eucalyptus-based repellent against Anopheles spp. in Tanzania," J Am Mosq Control Assoc. 12(2 Pt 1):243-6.
Trongtokit Y, Rongsriyam Y, Komalamisra N, Apiwathnasorn C (2005 Apr). "Comparative repellency of 38 essential oils against mosquito bites," Phytother Res. 19(4):303-9.
Truan JS, Chen JM, Thompson LU (2012). "Comparative effects of sesame seed lignan and flaxseed lignan in reducing the growth of human breast tumors (MCF-7) at high levels of circulating estrogen in athymic mice," Nutr Cancer. 64(1):65-71.
Tso MOM, Lam TT (1994 Oct 27). "Method of retarding and ameliorating central nervous system and eye damage," University of Illinois: USPatent #5527533.
Turrens J.F. (2003) Mitochondrial formation of reactive oxygen species. Journal of Physiology.552: 335-344.
Tuzcu M, Sahin N, Karatepe M, Cikim G, Kilinc U, Sahin K (2008 Sep). "Epigallocatechin-3-gallate supplementation can improve antioxidant status in stressed quail," Br Poult Sci. 49(5):643-8.
Ulusoy S, Boşgelmez-Tinaz G, Seçilmiş-Canbay H (2009 Nov). "Tocopherol, carotene, phenolic contents and antibacterial properties of rose essential oil, hydrosol and absolute," Curr Microbiol. 59(5):554-8.
Umezu T (2000 Jun). "Behavioral effects of plant-derived essential oils in the geller type conflict test in mice," Jpn J Pharmacol. 83(2):150-3.
Umezu T (1999 Sep). "Anticonflict effects of plant-derived essential oils," Pharmacol Biochem Behav. 64(1):35-40.
Umezu T, Ito H, Nagano K, Yamakoshi M, Oouchi H, Sakaniwa M, Morita M (2002 Nov 22). "Anticonflict effects of rose oil and identification of its active constituents," Life Sci. 72(1):91-102.
Uribe S., Ramirez J., Pena A. (1985) Effects of ?-Pinene on Yeast Membrane Functions. Journal of Bacteriology. 161: 1195-1200.
van Poppel G, Verhoeven DT, Verhagen H, Goldbohm RA (1999). "Brassica vegetables and cancer prevention. Epidemiology and mechanisms," Adv Exp Med Biol. 472:159-68.
van Tol RW, Swarts HJ, van der Linden A, Visser JH (2007 May). "Repellence of the red bud borer Resseliella oculiperda from grafted apple trees by impregnation of rubber budding strips with essential oils," Pest Manag Sci. 63(5):483-90.
Varga J, Jimenez SA (1986 Jul 31). "Stimulation of normal human fibroblast collagen production and processing by transforming growth factor-beta," Biochem Biophys Res Commun. 138(2):974-80.
Vazquez JA, Arganoza MT, Boikov D, Akins RA, Vaishampayan JK (2000 Jun). "In vitro susceptibilities of Candida and Aspergillus species to Melaleuca alternafolia (tea tree) oil," Rev Iberoam Micol. 17(2):60-3.
Veratti E, Rossi T, Giudice S, Benassi L, Bertazzoni G, Morini D, Azzoni P, Bruni E, Giannnetti A, MaqnoniC. (2011 Jun). "18beta-glycyrrhetinic acid and glabridin prevent oxidative DNA fragmentation in UVB-irradiated human keratinocyte cultures," Anticancer Res. 31(6):2209-15.
Vigo E, Cepeda A, Gualillo O, Perez-Fernandez R (2005 Mar). "In-vitro anti-inflammatory activity of Pinus sylvestris and Plantago lanceolata extracts: effect on inducible NOS, COX-1, COX-2 and their products in J774A.1 murine macrophages," J Pharm Pharmacol. 57(3):383-91.
Vigo E, Cepeda A, Gualillo O, Perez-Fernandez R (2004 Feb). "In-vitro anti-inflammatory effect of Eucalyptus globulus and Thymus vulgaris: nitric oxide inhibition in J774A.1 murine macrophages," J Pharm Pharmacol. 56(2):257-63.
Vigushin DM, Poon GK, Boddy A, English J, Halbert GW, Pagonis C, Jarman M, Coombes RC (1998). "Phase I and pharmacokinetic study of D-limonene in patients with advanced cancer. Cancer Research Campaign Phase I/II Clinical Trials Committee," Cancer Chemother Pharmacol. 42(2):111-7.
Vertuani S, Angusti A, Manfredini S (2004). "The antioxidants and pro-antioxidants network: an overview," Curr Pharm Des. 10(14):1677-94.
Vujosević M, Blagojević J (2004). "Antimutagenic effects of extracts from sage (Salvia officinalis) in mammalian system in vivo," Acta Vet Hung. 52(4):439-43.
Vuković-Gacić B, Nikcević S, Berić-Bjedov T, Knezević-Vukcević J, Simić D (2006 Oct). "Antimutagenic effect of essential oil of sage (Salvia officinalis L.) and its monoterpenes against UV-induced mutations in Escherichia coli and Saccharomyces cerevisiae," Food Chem Toxicol. 44(10):1730-8.
Vutyavanich T, Kraisarin T, Ruangsri R (2001 Apr). "Ginger for nausea and vomiting in pregnancy: randomized, double-masked, placebo-controlled trial," Obstet Gynecol. 97(4):577-82.
Walker AF, Bundy R, Hicks SM, Middleton RW (2002 Dec). "Bromelain reduces mild acute knee pain and improves well-being in a dose-dependent fashion in an open study of otherwise healthy adults," Phytomedicine. 9(8):681-6.
Walker TB, Smith J, Herrera M, Lebegue B, Pinchak A, Fischer J (2010 Oct). "The influence of 8 weeks of whey-protein and leucine supplementation on physical and cognitive performance," Int J Sport Nutr Exerc Metab. 20(5):409-17.
Wallerius S, Rosmond R, Ljung T, Holm G, Björntorp P (2003 Jul). "Rise in morning saliva cortisol is associated with abdominal obesity in men: a preliminary report," J Endocrinol Invest. 26(7):616-9. Walter BM, Bilkei G (2004 Mar 15). "Immunostimulatory effect of dietary oregano etheric oils on lymphocytes from growth-retarded, low-weight growing-finishing pigs and productivity," Tijdschr Diergeneeskd. 129(6):178-81.
Weaver CM, Martin BR, Jackson GS, McCabe GP, Nolan JR, McCabe LD, Barnes S, Reinwald S, Boris ME, Peacock M (2009 Oct). "Antiresorptive effects of phytoestrogen supplements compared with estradiol or risedronate in postmenopausal women using (41)Ca methodology," J Clin Endocrinol Metab. 94(10):3798-805.
Weaver R.F. Molecular Biology. 4th ed. New York: McGraw Hill, 2008.
Wei A, Shibamoto T (2007). "Antioxidant activities of essential oil mixtures toward skin lipid squalene oxidized by UV irradiation," Cutan Ocul Toxicol. 26(3):227-33.
Wilkinson JM, Hipwell M, Ryan T, Cavanagh HM (2003 Jan 1). "Bioactivity of Backhousia citriodora: antibacterial and antifungal activity," J Agric Food Chem. 51(1):76-81.
Wilkinson S, Aldridge J, Salmon I, Cain E, Wilson B (1999 Sep). "An evaluation of aromatherapy massage in palliative care," Palliat Med. 13(5):409-17.
Williamson EM, Priestley CM, Burgess IF (2007 Dec). "An investigation and comparison of the bioactivity of selected essential oils on human lice and house dust mites," Fitoterapia. 78(7-8):521-5.
Winkler-Stuck K, Wiedemann FR, Wallesch CW, Kunz WS (2004 May 15). "Effect of coenzyme Q10 on the mitochondrial function of skin fibroblasts from Parkinson patients," J Neurol Sci. 220(1-2):41-8.
Xia L, Chen D, Han R, Fang Q, Waxman S, Jing Y (2005 Mar). "Boswellic acid acetate induces apoptosis through caspase-mediated pathways in myeloid leukemia cells," Mol Cancer Ther. 4(3):381-8.
Xiao D, Powolny AA, Barbi de Moura M, Kelley EE, Bommareddy A, Kim SH, Hahm ER, Normolle D, Van Houten B, Singh SV (2010 Jun 22). "Phenethyl isothiocyanate inhibits oxidative phosphorylation to trigger reactive oxygen species-mediated death of human prostate cancer cells," J Biol Chem Epub ahead of print. Epub ahead of print.
Xiufen W, Hiramatsu N, Matsubara M (2004). "The antioxidative activity of traditional Japanese herbs," Biofactors. 21(1-4):281-4.
Xu J., Zhou F., Ji B-P., Pei R-S., Xu N. (2008) The antibacterial mechanism of carvacrol and thymol against Escherichia coli. Letters in Applied Microbiology. 47: 174-179.
Xu X, Duncan AM, Merz BE, Kurzer MS (1998 Dec). "Effects of soy isoflavones on estrogen and phytoestrogen metabolism in premenopausal women," Cancer Epidemiol Biomarkers Prev. 7(12):1101-8.
Xu X, Duncan AM, Wangen KE, Kurzer MS (2000 Aug). "Soy consumption alters endogenous estrogen metabolism in postmenopausal women," Cancer Epidemiol biomarkers Prev. 9(8):781-6.
Yang F. et al. (2005 Feb 18). "Curcumin inhibits formation of amyloid beta oligomers and fibrils, binds plaques, and reduces amyloid in vivo," J Biol Chem. 280(7):5892-901.
Yang GY, Wang W (1994 Sep). "Clinical studies on the treatment of coronary heart disease with Valeriana officinalis var latifolia," Zhongguo Zhong Xi Yi Jie He Za Zhi. 14(9):540-2.
Yang SA, Jeon SK, Lee EJ, Im NK, Jhee KH, Lee SP, Lee IS (2009 May). "Radical Scavenging Activity of the Essential Oil of Silver Fir (Abies alba)," J Clin Biochem Nutr. 44(3):253-9.
Yip YB, Tam AC. (2008 Jun). "An experimental study on the effectiveness of massage with aromatic ginger and orange essential oil for moderate-to-severe knee pain among the elderly in Hong Kong," Complement Ther Med. 16(3):131-8.
Youdim KA, Deans SG (1999 Sep 8). "Dietary supplementation of thyme (Thymus vulgaris L.) essential oil during the lifetime of the rat: its effects on the antioxidant status in liver, kidney and heart tissues," Mech Ageing Dev. 109(3):163-75.
Youdim KA, Deans SG (2000 Jan). "Effect of thyme oil and thymol dietary supplementation on the antioxidant status and fatty acid composition of the ageing rat brain," Br J Nutr. 83(1):87-93.

Youn L.J., Yoon J.W., Hovde C.J. (2010) A Brief Overview of Escherichia coli O157:H7 and Its Plasmid O157. Journal of Microbiology and Biotechnology. 20: 1-10.

Younis F, Mirelman D, Rabinkov A, Rosenthal T (2010 Jun). "S-allyl-mercapto-captopril: a novel compound in the treatment of Cohen-Rosenthal diabetic hypertensive rats," J Clin Hypertens (Greenwich) 12(6):451-5.

Yu B.P. (1994) Cellular Defenses Against Damage From Reactive Oxygen Species. Physiological Reviews. 74: 139-162.

Yu YM, Chang WC, Wu CH, Chiang SY (2005 Nov). "Reduction of oxidative stress and apoptosis in hyperlipidemic rabbits by ellagic acid," J Nutr Biochem. 16(11):675-81.

Yuan HQ, Kong F, Wang XL, Young CY, Hu XY, Lou HX (2008 Jun 1). "Inhibitory effect of acetyl-11-keto-beta-boswellic acid on androgen receptor by interference of Sp1 binding activity in prostate cancer cells," Biochem Pharmacol. 75(11):2112-21.

Yuan YV, Walsh NA (2006 Jul). "Antioxidant and antiproliferative activities of extracts from a variety of edible seaweeds," Food Chem Toxicol. 44(7):1144-50.

Zembron-Lacny A, Szyszka K, Szygula Z (2007 Dec). "Effect of cysteine derivatives administration in healthy men exposed to intense resistance exercise by evaluation of pro-antioxidant ratio," J Physiol Sci. 57(6):343-8.

Zha C., Brown G.B., Brouillette W.J. (2004) Synthesis and Structure-Activity Relationship Studies for Hydantoins and Analogues as Voltage-Gasted Sodium Channel Ligands. Journal of Medicinal Chemistry. 47: 6519-6528.

Zhang W, Wang X, Liu Y, Tian H, Flickinger B, Empie MW, Sun SZ (2008 Jun). "Dietary flaxseed lignan extract lowers plasma cholesterol and glucose concentrations in hypercholesterolaemic subjects," Br J Nutr. 99(6):1301-9.

Zhao W, Entschladen F, Liu H, Niggemann B, Fang Q, Zaenker KS, Han R (2003). "Boswellic acid acetate induces differentiation and apoptosis in highly metastatic melanoma and fibrosarcoma cells," Cancer Detect Prev. 27(1):67-75.

Zheng GQ, Kenney PM, Lam LK. (1992 Aug). "Anethofuran, carvone, and limonene: potential cancer chemopreventive agents from dill weed oil and caraway oil," Planta Med. 58(4):338-41.

Zheng GQ, Kenney PM, Zhang J, Lam LK (1993). "Chemoprevention of benzo[a]pyrene-induced forestomach cancer in mice by natural phthalides from celery seed oil," Nutr Cancer. 19(1):77-86.

Zhou BR, Luo D, Wei FD, Chen XE, Gao J (2008 Jul). "Baicalin protects human fibroblasts against ultraviolet B-induced cyclobutane pyrimidine dimers formation," Arch Dermatol Res. 300(6):331-4.

Zhou, J., Tang F., Bian R. (2004) Effect of α-pinene on nuclear translocation of NF-κB in THP-1 cells. Acta Pharmacol Sin. 25: 480-484.

Zhou J, Zhou S, Tang J, Zhang K, Guang L, Huang Y, Xu Y, Ying Y, Zhang L, Li D (2009 Mar 15). "Protective effect of berberine on beta cells in streptozotocin- and high-carbohydrate/high-fat diet-induced diabetic rats," Eur J Pharmacol. 606(1-3):262-8.

Zhu BC, Henderson G, Chen F, Fei H, Laine RA (2001 Aug). "Evaluation of vetiver oil and seven insect-active essential oils against the Formosan subterranean termite," J Chem Ecol. 27(8):1617-25.

Zhu BC, Henderson G, Yu Y, Laine RA (2003 Jul 30). "Toxicity and repellency of patchouli oil and patchouli alcohol against Formosan subterranean termites Coptotermes formosanus Shiraki (Isoptera: Rhinotermitidae)," J Agric Food Chem. 51(16):4585-8

Ziegler D, Ametov A, Barinov A, Dyck PJ, Gurieva I, Low PA, Munzel U, Yakhno N, Raz I, Novosadova M, Maus J, Samigullin R (2006 Nov). "Oral treatment with alpha-lipoic acid improves symptomatic diabetic polyneuropathy: the SYDNEY 2 trial," Diabetes Care. 29(11):2365-70.

Ziegler G, Ploch M, Miettinen-Baumann A, Collet W (2002 Nov 25). "Efficacy and tolerability of valerian extract LI 156 compared with oxazepam in the treatment of non-organic insomnia--a randomized, double-blind, comparative clinical study," Eur J Med Res. 7(11):480-6.

Zore G.B., Thakre A.D., Jadhav S., Karuppayil S.M. (2011) Terpenoids inhibit Candida albicans growth by affecting membrane integrity and arrest of cell cycle. Phytomedicine. doi: 10.1016/j.phymed.2011.03.008.

BIBLIOGRAPHY

Balch, M.D., James, and Phyllis Balch, C.N.C. *Prescription for Nutritional Healing.* Garden City Park, NY: Avery Publishing Group, 1990.

Becker, M.D., Robert O. *The Body Electric.* New York, NY: Wm. Morrow, 1985.

Brown T.L., LeMay H.E., Bursten B.E. *Chemistry: The Central Science. 10th ed.* Upper Saddle River: Pearson Prentice Hall, 2006.

Burroughs, Stanley. *Healing for the Age of Enlightenment.* Auburn, CA: Burroughs Books, 1993.

Burton Goldberg Group, The. *Alternative Medicine: The Definitive Guide.* Fife, WA: Future Medicine Publishing, Inc., 1994.

Cowan M.K., Talaro K.P. *Microbiology: A Systems Approach. 2nd ed.* New York: McGraw Hill, 2009.

Fischer-Rizzi, Suzanne. *Complete Aromatherapy Handbook.* New York, NY: Sterling Publishing, 1990.

Gattefosse, Ph.D., Rene-Maurice. *Gattefosse's Aromatherapy.* Essex, England: The C.W. Daniel Company Ltd., 1937 English translation.

Guyton A.C., Hall J.E. *Textbook of Medical Physiology. 10th ed.* Philadelphia: W.B. Saunders Company, 2000.

Green, Mindy. *Natural Perfumes: Simple Aromatherapy Recipes.* Loveland CO: Interweave Press Inc., 1999.

Integrated Aromatic Medicine. Proceedings from the First International Symposium, Grasse, France. Essential Science Publishing, March 2000.

Lawless, Julia. *The Encyclopaedia of Essential Oils.* Rockport, MA: Element, Inc., 1992.

Maury, Marguerite. *Marguerite Maury's Guide to Aromatherapy.* C.W. Daniel, 1989.

Pènoël, M.D., Daniel and Pierre Franchomme. *L'aromatherapie exactement.* Limoges, France: Jollois, 1990.

Price, Shirley, and Len Price. *Aromatherapy for Health Professionals.* New York, NY: Churchill Livingstone Inc., 1995.

Price, Shirley, and Penny Price Parr. *Aromatherapy for Babies and Children.* San Francisco, CA: Thorsons, 1996.

Rose, Jeanne. *The Aromatherapy Book: Applications and Inhalations.* Berkeley, CA: North Atlantic Books, 1992.

Ryman, Danièle. *Aromatherapy: The Complete Guide to Plant & Flower Essences for Health and Beauty.* New York: Bantam Books, 1993.

Sheppard-Hanger, Sylla. *The Aromatherapy Practitioner Reference Manual.* Tampa, FL: Atlantic Institute of Aromatherapy, Twelfth Printing February 2000.

Tisserand, Maggie. *Aromatherapy for Women: a Practical Guide to Essential Oils for Health and Beauty.* Rochester, VT: Healing Arts Press, 1996.

Tisserand, Robert. *Aromatherapy: to Heal and Tend the Body.* Wilmot, WI: Lotus Press, 1988.

Tisserand, Robert. *The Art of Aromatherapy.* Rochester, VT: Healing Arts Press, 1977.

Tisserand, Robert, and Tony Balacs. *Essential Oil Safety: A Guide for Health Care Professionals.* New York, NY: Churchill Livingstone, 1995.

Tortora G.J., Funke B.R., Case C.L. *Microbiology: An Introduction. 9th ed.* San Francisco: Pearson Benjamin Cummings, 2007.

Valnet, M.D., Jean. *The Practice of Aromatherapy: a Classic Compendium of Plant Medicines and their Healing Properties.* Rochester, VT: Healing Arts Press, 1980.

Watson, Franzesca. *Aromatherapy Blends & Remedies.* San Francisco, CA: Thorsons, 1995.

Weaver R.F. *Molecular Biology. 4th ed.* New York: McGraw Hill, 2008.

Wilson, Roberta. *Aromatherapy for Vibrant Health and Beauty: a practical A-to-Z reference to aromatherapy treatments for health, skin, and hair problems.* Honesdale, PA: Paragon Press, 1995.

Worwood, Valerie Ann. *The Complete Book of Essential Oils & Aromatherapy.* San Rafael, CA: New World Library, 1991.

INDEX

INDEX

Index

Index

Index